MIRRORS OF EMPIRE

MUZAFFAR ALAM *and* SANJAY SUBRAHMANYAM

~ Mirrors of Empire ~
Courtiers, Diplomats, and Intellectuals in Mughal India

SUNY PRESS

First published by Permanent Black, 'Himalayana', Mall Road, Ranikhet Cantt,
Ranikhet 263645, INDIA, for the territory of SOUTH ASIA. perblack@gmail.com
First SUNY Press edition 2026.
Not for sale in South Asia.

Cover credit: "Nur Jahan holding a portrait of Emperor Jahangir, by Bishandas, c.
1627," the Cleveland Museum of Art, Catherine and Ralph Benkaim Collection
2013.325.

Cover design: Anuradha Roy

Published by State University of New York Press, Albany
© 2026 Muzaffar Alam and Sanjay Subrahmanyam
All rights reserved
Printed in the United States of America

EU GPSR Authorised Representative:
Logos Europe, 9 rue Nicolas Poussin, 17000, La Rochelle, France
contact@logoseurope.eu

For information, contact State University of New York Press, Albany, NY
www.sunypress.edu

Library of Congress Cataloging-in-Publication Data
Names: Alam, Muzaffar, author. | Subrahmanyam, Sanjay, author.
Title: Mirrors of empire : courtiers, diplomats, and intellectuals in Mughal India
Description: Albany : [State University of New York Press], [2026] |
    Includes bibliographical references and index.
Identifiers: ISBN 9798855805604 (hardback) | ISBN 9798855805628 (PDF) | ISBN
9798855807073 (epub)
Further information is available at the Library of Congress.

To the memory of

Cornell Fleischer *and* Sunil Kumar

Contents

Maps

Illustrations

A Note on Transliteration
and Calendars

THE PERSIAN AND Indian terms not in common use in the English language have been italicised, and their plurals have been indicated usually by adding the letter *s*. We have in general indicated long vowels. We have also used the *spiritus asper* (‘) and *spiritus lentis* (’) for the *‘ain* and *hamza*, respectively. In order to transliterate words and phrases in Persian, we have employed a simplified version of the system in F. Steingass’ *Comprehensive Persian–English Dictionary*, while avoiding the excessive use of apostrophes and not marking consonants. We have therefore preferred to diverge from the Steingass usage with regard to combined words, as can be seen in forms such as “Nizam-ud-Din” rather than “Nizamu’d-Din”, or “Qutb-ul-Mulk” in place of “Qutbu’l-Mulk”. In regard to Ottoman and Chaghatay Turkish, we have followed standard modern conventions in those languages.

Since many of the texts that are discussed use the lunar Hijri calendar, we have tried to the extent possible to give both the original dates and the equivalents in terms of the Common Era (CE). In the interests of clarity, it may be pointed out that the following broad equivalents apply: 800 H. is 1397–8 CE; 900 H. is 1494–5 CE; 1000 H. is 1591–2 CE; 1100 H. is 1688–9 CE; 1200 H. is 1785–6 CE.

The succession of months is as follows.

1. Muharram	7. Rajab
2. Safar	8. Sha‘ban
3. Rabi‘ I	9. Ramazan
4. Rabi‘ II	10. Shawwal
5. Jumada I	11. Zi al-Qa‘da
6. Jumada II	12. Zi al-Hijja

Abbreviations

BL	British Library, London
BnF	Bibliothèque nationale de France, Paris
IESHR	*Indian Economic and Social History Review*
JESHO	*Journal of the Economic and Social History of the Orient*
PUL	Punjab University Library, Lahore

Preface

THIS BOOK HAS emerged from the languid decantation of nearly four decades of friendship and collaboration that began in New Delhi around the mid 1980s, thanks to the mediation of common friends and kind mentors like Sabyasachi Bhattacharya and Dharma Kumar. Those were different times, when email barely existed and face-to-face communication often required driving long distances in what was already the challenging traffic of India's capital city. They were also turbulent times politically, in the years leading up to and following the destruction of the Babri Masjid in December 1992. But we surely look back at them with a certain fondness too, especially the extended and open-ended conversations we had time and again in Dakshinapuram on the JNU campus, and once in a while in Nizamuddin East, at walking distance from the great medieval Chishti *dargāh*, and the tombs of the emperor Humayun and the grand Mughal *amīr* and literary figure 'Abdur Rahim Khan-i Khanan. These conversations then continued, first in Europe in the late 1990s, and then mostly in the United States in the new century. An intensive period spent at the Wissenschaftskolleg in Berlin in 2000–1 was especially fruitful as it also involved other friends and colleagues, such as Partha Chatterjee, Velcheru Narayana Rao, and David Shulman. Eventually our conversations became a dialogue between Hyde Park in Chicago and Westwood in Los Angeles, with the occasional meeting in Delhi and Paris thrown in for good measure.

All this is to explain that the seeds of this book were planted long ago but they have taken a fair amount of time to germinate. They go back to discussions between the two authors in the late 1980s and early 1990s, which led to the publication of a series of collaborative articles and books on various aspects of the Mughal empire and its culture.

The first of those articles, which emerged from some joint seminar presentations, was published in the French journal *Annales HSS* in 1994. It was followed by others, sometimes written at the request of the editor of a collective volume, sometimes on other occasions. We have also produced three longer works: a reader entitled *The Mughal State* (1998), and two books entitled *Indo-Persian Travels in the Age of Discoveries* (2007) and *Writing the Mughal World* (2012). Of these, the book *Indo-Persian Travels* can be thought of as a close sibling to the present volume. There has been an extended gap between the last of these works and the present book, which can only be explained by the incessant pressures of academic routine and the interruption caused by other individual projects. It finally took an event like the retirement and celebratory conference for Muzaffar Alam, held at Yale University in April 2024 and largely organised by Manan Ahmed Asif, to push us, as it were, over the finishing line.

The list of thanks and acknowledgements for a book like this could potentially be very long. We will limit ourselves to some very essential names of friends and colleagues, who have helped us in important ways over the years. They include Ali Anooshahr, Imre Bangha, Evrim Binbaş, Subah Dayal, Jeevan Deol, the late Simon Digby, Suraiya Faroqhi, Supriya Gandhi, Navina Najat Haidar, Cemal Kafadar, Naveen Kanalu, Shariq Khan, Rajeev Kinra, Sharif Husain Qasemi, the late Waqar Hussain Siddiqui, and Jim and Susie Tharu. Many other colleagues in Ottoman and Safavid studies also helped us widen our horizons, besides the input that obviously has come from both older and younger colleagues in the field of Mughal history. In particular, we are grateful to our research students in Delhi, Paris, Chicago, and Los Angeles. Our families, and in particular our spouses Rizwana and Caroline, have been reliable pillars of support through the years this book was written.

Bill Nelson drew the maps with his customary efficiency, and we thank him as always. Versions of these chapters have been presented as seminars by one or both of us on various occasions, including as part of a lecture series on "ego-histories" at the Collège de France in Paris. Obviously, a key personage in regard to this work, as in much of what we have written in the preceding decades, has been Rukun Advani, our vigilant and patient editor at Permanent Black.

In the past some years, we have lost far too many valuable friends and intellectual companions, in India, Europe, and the United States. This work is dedicated in a way to all their memories. But above all, we remember Sunil Kumar (1956–2021), a single-minded and passionate historian of the Delhi Sultanate, and Cornell Fleischer (1950–2023), a versatile master of early modern Islamic history. Both left us much too soon and have thereby also left the world of scholarship much poorer for their absence.

CHICAGO AND LOS ANGELES
2025

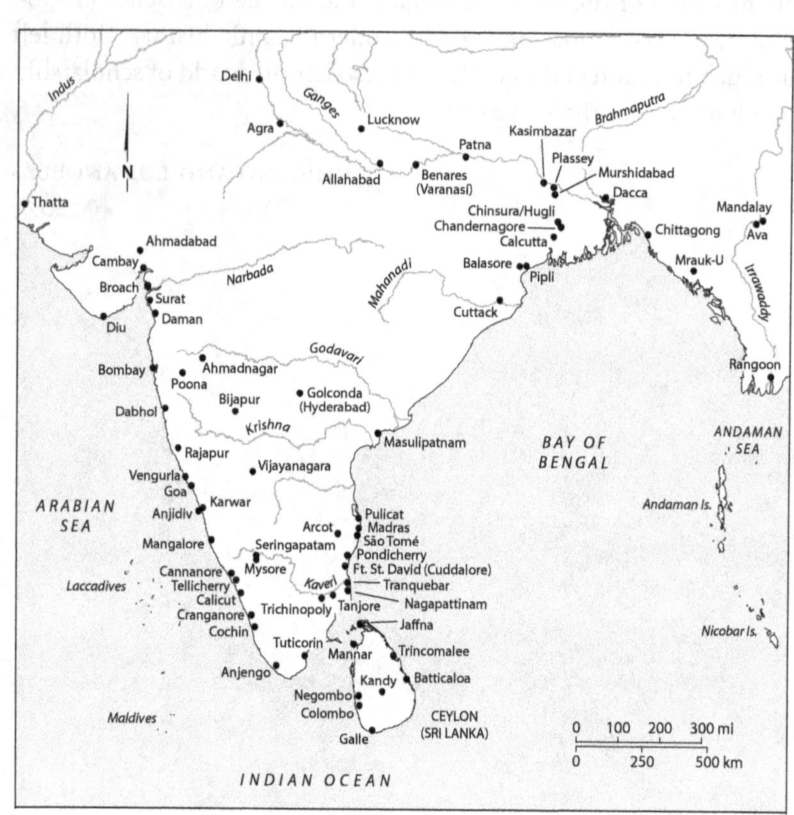

Map 1: India in the Mughal period.

1

Introduction: Self-narratives and Mughal History

> "I, I, I"! What a weird word!
> And so that man there is I? Not another?
> Could even mother love him –
> parchment-faced, greying hair,
> all-knowing as a serpent?
>
> – Vladislav Khodasevich, "Before the Mirror
> (*Pered Zerkalom*)" (1924–5)[1]

Locating Self-narratives

MIRRORS HAVE LONG been found in one form or another in a variety of human societies, much before the invention of glass and its silvered variants. Human ingenuity had far earlier produced versions from polished obsidian and copper, and, even without those, natural reflecting formations such as pools had existed, as the celebrated myth of Narcissus and Echo – recounted by Ovid (in his *Metamorphoses* 3.337) among others – reminds us.[2] This myth, and other like stories, also suggest that self-awareness and self-regard, or even self-worship, are close relatives. This can help us understand why narratives of the self, or ego-narratives, can at times be regarded with suspicion.

Perhaps the most celebrated modern ego-narrative written in South Asia is that of Mohandas Karamchand Gandhi in the 1920s, first set

[1] Zholkovsky, "Quote the Poets Ever More", 111–28.

[2] A very large literature obviously exists on this myth; see, for example, Bergmann, "The Legend of Narcissus".

down in Gujarati and then translated into English. Gandhi begins his text by recounting a conversation with "a God-fearing friend" who, apparently, tried to dissuade him from the project. "'What has set you on this adventure?', he asked. 'Writing an autobiography is a practice peculiar to the West. I know of nobody in the East having written one, except amongst those who have come under Western influence'."[3] This sense of inauthenticity haunts Gandhi's text, including his ambivalence regarding its very title. We thus find another oft-quoted phrase in his preface which reiterates that sentiment: "It is not my purpose to attempt a real autobiography. I simply want to tell the story of my experiments with truth, and as my life consists of nothing but experiments, it is true that the story will take the shape of an autobiography." In other words, what we have here are a set of complex rhetorical manoeuvres intended, with whatever degree of success, to preserve the contrast between Oriental modesty and Occidental self-promotion.

Roughly a decade after Gandhi the anthropologist Marcel Mauss, in his Huxley Memorial Lectures delivered in 1938, addressed what he termed "a category of the human mind," namely the "notion of the person, of the self (*moi*)."[4] As was his wont, Mauss searched far and wide for his examples and did not restrict himself to the textual traditions either. He presented his purpose as writing a brief schematic history of the category, which he saw as "floating, delicate, [and] precious," in order to "substitute a more precise view in place of a naïve view of its history, and its current value." Mixing ethnography and textual study with panache, the anthropologist thus began his exploration with the oral traditions of the Zuñi Pueblo Indians and the Kwakiutl of North America, before moving on to the indigenous populations of Australia, in order to argue that "an immense ensemble of societies have arrived at the notion of the personage, and the role fulfilled by the individual in the context of sacred rituals that play a part in family life." Turning then from the idea of personage to that of person and self, Mauss drew a very rapid sketch of some textual elements from ancient China and India, noting

---

[3] Gandhi, *An Autobiography*, 3–4. The original Gujarati title is: *Satya na prayogo athvā ātmakathā*. For a discussion, see Arnold and Blackburn, eds, *Telling Lives*.

[4] Mauss, "Une catégorie de l'esprit humain", 263–81.

that India "seems to have been the most ancient of the civilizations which had a notion of the individual and his or her 'consciousness', in other words, of the 'self'." Indeed, the preoccupation amongst Buddhist thinkers with annihilation of the self appeared to him, paradoxically, to indicate how significant it was as a category. Mauss then moved on to Western traditions, beginning with ancient Rome, which he saw as a particularly important site in the historical process. However, he stated, "the idea of the person still lacked a stable metaphysical basis . . . which is owed to Christianity." Another rapid survey of key elements in Western Christian thought eventually brought him to a short consideration of Enlightenment thinkers, closing briefly with a reflection on Hume, Kant, and Fichte, "who made of the category of the 'self' a condition for consciousness and for science, and for Pure Reason."[5] The rather astonishing initial gambit of openness to bold and wide comparisons may thus be thought to end in a somewhat disappointing (and, dare one say, even narrowly predictable) endpoint of the trajectory, with a parade of the usual suspects. It should also be remarked that Mauss' well-known interest in classical Indology and Sinology does not extend here as far as the Islamic world, about which he says nothing in relation to any of its many geographical variants.[6]

Mauss' schematic and ambitious account seems to have had relatively few readers among Anglophone historians when they began to reflect in an abstract fashion on what has sometimes been termed "life writing" in the 1970s and 1980s. The influential interventions of James Olney from those years derived their inspiration not from Mauss but rather in large measure from the French philosopher Georges Gusdorf, notably his 1956 essay entitled "Conditions et limites de l'autobiographie".[7] According to Gusdorf, life writings were not only "limited in time and in space," but in fact "the late product of a specific civilization" when the traditional forms of *Gemeinschaft* (community) were

[5] Mauss, "Une catégorie de l'esprit humain", 281.

[6] Also see the discussion in Carrithers, Collins, and Lukes, eds, *The Category of the Person*, which develops the arguments of Mauss. The collection does include essays from a few historians, such as Mark Elvin.

[7] See Olney, *Metaphors of Self*; and also the essays collected in Olney, ed., *Autobiography*, which includes an English translation of Gusdorf's essay.

replaced by the modern structures of *Gesellschaft* (society). In this conception, "throughout most of human history, the individual does not oppose himself to all others; he does not feel himself to exist outside of others, and still less against others."[8] Before the transformation wrought by modernity, "each man thus appears as a possessor of a rôle, already performed by the ancestors and to be performed again by descendants." It is when humans "become more aware of differences than of similarities" that we can witness the emergence of the individuation that helps to produce life writing. Further, it is clear that these are processes that separate the world into distinct spheres: "[I]t would seem that autobiography is not to be found outside of our [Western] cultural area; one would say that it expresses a concern peculiar to Western man, a concern that has been of good use in his systematic conquest of the universe and that he has communicated to men of other cultures." In other words, we are confronted with a schematic conception combining Western exceptionalism with diffusionism, and also wedded to a rather rigid distinction between traditional and modern societies, each with distinct conceptions of space-time.

Gusdorf wrote in this mode despite his likely awareness of a massive project on the history of autobiography that had been under way in Germany since the early twentieth century. This was Georg Misch's *Geschichte der Autobiografie*, of which the fourth volume was only published posthumously in 1969, six decades after the first.[9] Misch — heavily influenced by the German philosopher Wilhelm Dilthey — began his considerations in the ancient Middle East, thus extending his gaze beyond the usual terrain of Greece and Rome. But, as his volumes proceeded chronologically into the later Middle Ages and the early modern period to culminate in the eighteenth and nineteenth centuries, his geographical focus progressively narrowed in a rather inexplicable fashion.[10] Whereas his earlier chronological explorations extend as far as the *qasīda* of the pre-Islamic poet in Arabic, Imru' al-Qais (d. *ca.* 545), over time his interest seemed to be simply "the universal histori-

---

[8] Gusdorf, "Conditions et limites de l'autobiographie", 106.

[9] For a useful summing up of Misch's contribution, see Jung, "Georg Misch's 'Geschichte der Autobiografie'".

[10] See Misch, *Geschichte der Autobiographie*, vol. 3, pt 2, 905–1076, for autobiographical writing in Islam in the Middle Ages.

cal context in which the human intellect manifests itself in Western civilization."[11] The southern shores of the Mediterranean, and the Islamic world more broadly, once again gradually vanish into the mists.

Behind such writings, even of the second half of the twentieth century, on the historical emergence of the autobiography as a form and its links to processes of individuation, one senses an important shadow that has lingered on from the nineteenth century. This is the work of the Swiss historian Jacob Burckhardt, also generally recognised as the intellectual who canonised the notion of the European Renaissance for academic audiences, making of that period the key turning point for the emergence of Western modernity. Burckhardt drew attention to a series of figures from sixteenth-century Italy, who, he argued, entirely transformed autobiographical writing, giving it a new impetus and energy. Key among them was the quarrelsome goldsmith Benvenuto Cellini, whose *Vita* had so impressed Goethe that he translated it into German in the 1790s. Burckhardt argued that the text, though hardly based on profound introspection, "describes the whole man – not always willingly – with marvellous truth and completeness." To be sure, the historian also wanted due consideration to be given to texts written by other sixteenth-century figures, such as Girolamo Cardano and Luigi Cornaro. But it is Cellini for whom he reserves the highest praise:

> It does not spoil the impression when the reader often detects him bragging or lying; the stamp of a mighty, energetic, and thoroughly developed nature remains. By his side our northern autobiographers, though their tendency and moral character may stand much higher, appear incomplete beings. He is a man who can do all and dares do all, and who carries his measure in himself.[12]

The reader is left in no doubt that, in order for such a figure to emerge, a series of attendant political, social, and cultural circumstances are necessary, and that Western Europe alone had been in a position to provide such a context. The birthplace of the autobiographical narrative is thus Renaissance Italy, for it is here that we first find the "keen eye for individuality [that] belongs only to those who have emerged from

---

[11] For Misch's discussion of Imru' al-Qais, see Misch, *Geschichte der Autobiografie*, vol. 2, pt 1.1, 277–96.

[12] Burckhardt, *The Civilisation of the Renaissance*, 334.

the half-conscious life of the race and become themselves individuals."

Subsequent writers did not always show as much enthusiasm as
Burckhardt for Cellini, preferring to centre their accounts of the emergence of autobiography on the late-sixteenth-century essays of Michel
de Montaigne, or even a text as late as the *Confessions* (1782) of Jean-
Jacques Rousseau. But their unwavering focus on Western Europe
nevertheless remained largely in place. However, by the mid 1980s a
number of discordant voices were beginning to be heard. Some of these
emerged in Japan, including from intellectuals who were well aware
of the claims made by Gusdorf, Philippe Lejeune, and others. Lejeune
had gone so far as to arrogate to himself the right to define what an
autobiography was (and was not), based on a narrow sample of modern Western texts: "a retrospective narrative in prose that a real person
produces of his or her own existence, while underlining the individual
life and particularly the history of his or her personality."[13] The scholar
of comparative literature Saeki Shōichi wrote, for example, that

> the autobiography has long been assumed to be an exclusively Western
> intellectual product. Certainly, Western achievements in the genre deserve
> the highest praise, and there is no denying their influence on the non-
> Western world, especially from the second half of the nineteenth century.
> But I would claim that Japan at least has had an equally vigorous tradi-
> tion of autobiographical narrative, and that it bears comparison with its
> Western counterpart.[14]

Saeki traced these writings as far back as the medieval Heian period
(*c.* ninth to twelfth centuries), and the literary activities there of court
women. But he also stressed the significance of the Edo (or Tokugawa)
period in the seventeenth and eighteenth centuries, during which he
brought out the importance of three writers from the samurai class:
Yamago Soko, Arai Hakuseki, and Matsudaira Sadanobu. At much
the same time, Hisayasu Nakagawa produced a more vigorous contes-

[13] Lejeune, *Le pacte autobiographique*, 14: "récit rétrospectif en prose qu'une
personne réelle fait de sa propre existence, lorsqu'elle met l'accent sur sa vie indi-
viduelle, en particulier sur l'histoire de sa personnalité".

[14] Saeki, "The Autobiography in Japan", 357.

tation of Gusdorf's ethnocentric theses, using as his main support the text of Arai Hakuseki, *Oritaku shiba no ki* (Told Round a Brushwood Fire), written in around 1716.[15] Was it not possible, he asked, that in Tokugawa Japan, "in the intervals of the rhythms [of collective existence], which were already irregular and relaxed, new personal rhythms began to be affirmed, organised around the spontaneity of the individual?" Indeed, a further example is provided to us by the satirical writings of Matsudaira Sadanobu, which mocked the very samurai class to which he himself belonged, whereas he had conventionally been portrayed as a "gifted but humourless and didactic proponent of Confucian virtue."[16]

A near-simultaneous challenge to the exceptionalist argument of the European scholars was mounted from a rather different front, namely that of work on the Ottoman empire. In his 1989 essay, "Self and Others", the historian Cemal Kafadar addressed the question of "first-person narratives in Ottoman literature", with the central point of focus being the *Sohbetnāme*, a little-known text written by a seventeenth-century diarist named Seyyid Hasan. However, in order to contextualise this text properly, Kafadar reminded his readers of a far larger corpus of related materials, ranging from other diaries to travel narratives, to captivity narratives, to dream-interpretation texts. He was able to demonstrate the existence of a substantial body of such writings, some hidden in plain sight, but others more obscure. They included the celebrated *Seyāhetnāme* of Evliya Çelebi (1611–82), a massive ten-volume travelogue that playfully mixes fact and fantasy, and which has few if any equals anywhere else in the early modern world. Evliya, who was born in Istanbul by the Golden Horn, travelled for nearly forty years, from 1640 onwards. Robert Dankoff, the leading modern specialist on Evliya's travels, says of him: "Free of marriage ties, but well-placed in court circles; renowned for his wit, his learning, and his fine voice; Evliya had no trouble attaching himself to the retinue of various pashas sent to all parts of the empire as provincial governors, or outside

---

[15] Nakagawa, "Naissance au Japon", 387–403. For a translation, see Arai, *Told Round a Brushwood Fire*.

[16] Iwasaki, "Portrait of a Daimyo", 2.

the empire as emissaries."[17] These included his kinsman Melek Ahmed Pasha, a highly placed official, whom he accompanied on various appointments, especially in the 1650s and early 1660s. The vast majority of his travels took place within the Ottoman domains, and indeed the *Seyāhetnāme* even includes an elaborate account of Evliya's home town Istanbul. Travel thus did not always imply a narrative of the distant or the unfamiliar. At the same time, Evliya visited some regions bordering on the Ottoman domains and even made some rather implausible claims regarding travels in Western Europe, which most historians are inclined to discount.

To a truly exceptional account such as this one, which has long been celebrated in Ottoman and Turkish literary circles, we can in fact add a good sprinkling of others which are far more modest as well as more obscure, with some remaining in manuscript form in various libraries and collections. Amongst these more limited texts we can number some captivity narratives from janissaries and others who had been prisoners in Europe; a dream-log by Asiye Hatun, an early-eighteenth-century woman resident in a Balkan town; as well as the diary of Sidqi Mustafa, a teacher (*mudarris*) from a few decades later.[18] Then, there is the first-person account in verse of the sixteenth-century poet Za'ifi, in which he recounts his "adult life and struggles for a successful career", blaming the Ottoman society of the time for not recognising his talents; and an autobiographical essay – also written in a somewhat embittered tone – by the celebrated historian and bureaucrat Gelibolu Mustafa 'Ali.[19] Concluding his essay, Kafadar says:

> I hope to have shown that there is a wide spectrum of unknown or ignored first-person narratives urging us to reconsider the earlier dismissal of personal writings as a lacuna among Ottoman historical sources. There is every reason to assume that systematic research in manuscript collections will yield many more diaries, dream-logs, autobiographies, memoirs of captivity, or letters, which carry a potential of extending the horizons and traditional boundaries of Ottoman studies, introducing a new personal dimension to Ottoman social and cultural history. At the very least, the

[17] Dankoff, *An Ottoman Mentality*, 2.
[18] See Asiye Hatun, *Rüya Mektuplari*; Zilfi, "The Diary of a Müderris".
[19] Fleischer, *Bureaucrat and Intellectual*.

colourful examples of personal literature might enrich the rather shade-less palette of Ottoman cultural history which so far includes only sharp contrasts.[20]

Roughly a decade after this essay, an important compendium on Arabic autobiographical writing was published, which pursued this challenge and extended its scope. Its editor, Dwight Reynolds, also explicitly contested in his introduction the entrenched prejudices to be found in earlier generations of historiography which had led to what he termed "the fallacy of Western origins".[21] While identifying this fallacy with a particular European teleological mode of thinking which "views literary history as leading inevitably to a predetermined end point – the modern western autobiography", Reynolds also pointed to how European orientalists from the first half of the twentieth century, such as Franz Rosenthal, had examined the body of Arabic texts that might qualify as autobiography and yet found them all wanting: in Rosenthal's words, "none of the [Arabic] autobiographies came into being out of a consciousness of the individual value of the uniquely personal."[22] Rejecting these summary judgments, Reynolds pointed to the reconsideration of the autobiography that had been undertaken in the latter part of the twentieth century by scholars working on Japan, China, and Tibet, including some of those that we have cited above.[23]

As a prominent example from his own corpus, he took the case of the late-fifteenth-century Egyptian scholar Jalal-ud-Din al-Suyuti, who penned a self-narrative entitled *al-Tahadduth bi-niʿmat Allāh* (Speaking of God's Bounty), and began it by noting that his work was in fact part of a centuries-old tradition in which other significant figures had participated. He also showed a clear awareness that the moral purpose underlying such works could vary quite a lot and might

[20] Kafadar, "Self and Others", 149–50. For more recent reflections, following on Kafadar's seminal essay, see the rather mixed collection drawn together in Akyıldız, Kara, and Sagaster, eds, *Autobiographical Themes in Turkish Literature*.

[21] Reynolds, ed., *Interpreting the Self*, 17–32.

[22] Rosenthal, "Die arabische Autobiographie", 40.

[23] But also see Wu, *The Confucian's Progress*; and Gyatso, *Apparitions of the Self*, 101–23.

include pride and even self-aggrandisement. It may be noted that al-Suyuti himself eventually came to be known for his mocking ripostes to his enemies and trenchant personal attacks on other scholars, including one whom he referred to simply as "The Ignoramus" (*al-jāhil*). As the modern editor of his narrative notes, the Egyptian savant was quarrelsome, vain, and constantly craved recognition, besides being generally characterised by "impatience and irascibility".

> The principal traits of al-Suyuti's character, which emerge clearly in his more personal writings, are his self-confidence, his pride, his inflexibility, and his ambition for success. One can infer from incidents in his life that there was a certain brusqueness and a lack of consideration for others in his manner which offended his colleagues, and gave rise to the repeated accusations of arrogance, ingratitude, hard-heartedness, and so on . . . Al-Suyuti himself considered his behaviour to his colleagues was justified, because it was his duty to preserve knowledge in the midst of ignorance. To judge by what he wrote, the inner conviction of a God-given duty, to be carried out at any cost, must have been sincere, even if it was bolstered by a certain amount of self-importance and a human desire never to be in the wrong.[24]

Nevertheless, as Reynolds also points out, al-Suyuti was sufficiently admired by later generations for his literary strategies to be "copied by a number of later Arabic autobiographers." These included at least one significant figure from Mughal India, the Gujarat-based Hadrami shaikh 'Abdul Qadir al-'Aydarus, author of the well-known text *al-Nūr al-Sāfir* (The Travelling Light). Al-'Aydarus was born into a prominent Arabian family in 1570, and even though his mother (as he admitted) was an Indian slave, he was treated well and afforded an excellent education. With the immodesty one encounters in many of these self-narratives, he suggests that his success was foreordained – his father had received omens and signs in his dreams to that effect. Al-'Aydarus portrays himself as unusually studious, and as a voracious reader and collector of books who also made it a point to encounter and cultivate men of learning. Over time he was thus able to produce "a number of well-loved and appreciated books . . . [which] have been greeted with unanimous acclaim, practically the only dissenters being enemies or jealous rivals

---

[24] Sartain, *Jalāl al-Dīn al-Suyūtī*, 116.

of mine." His reputation as a teacher and interpreter of Islamic mystic thought also grew apace, and he was in a position to acquire a number of prominent disciples:

> Then God blessed me with something unexpected – Glory be to the Bounteous, Most Generous, and Giving One, the Bestower of Gifts! My associates spread knowledge of my writings, and scholars far and wide spoke highly of my work. I thus gained the affection and prayers of many a spiritual guide and exemplar. Learned men east and west made much of me. Dignitaries deferred to me, some willingly and others not. Rulers of distant places wrote to me and sent me stupendous gifts and emoluments. Praises reached me from the ends of the earth, including Egypt, remote Yemen, and other distant lands. More than one notable scholar studied with me, and many people learned from me.[25]

Al-'Aydarus tempered his inflated claims with a modicum of humility, recalling that "countless exemplary scholars have preceded me", whereby he was merely a link in a long chain both of the transmission of knowledge and of familial prestige.

How exactly should we define and classify works such as the longer one by al-Suyuti, or its shorter counterpart by al-'Aydarus? As we have seen, some scholars such as Reynolds are prepared to include them simply within the category of "autobiography", while at the same time stating quite bluntly that they partake of "no pattern common to western autobiography." Further, Reynolds proposes that "the diversity of literary form demonstrated by Arabic autobiographies from different time periods obviates the possibility of a single, simple description of the genre in formal terms."[26] Clearly, other terms might equally be used for these texts: the older-fashioned "memoirs", "personal narratives", "first-person narratives" (though all of them may not employ the grammatical first person), and so on.

In the 1990s another candidate emerged for consideration in the spectrum of possibilities: the term "ego-document". The Swiss historian Kaspar von Greyerz has offered a critical account of its emergence,

---

[25] Reynolds, ed., *Interpreting the Self*, 208–15.

[26] Ibid., 5–6. Reynolds' conception has been criticised by Sabri, "Mir Taqi Mir's Ẓikr-i Mīr", 219–22.

spread, and eventual limits in historical analysis, largely confining himself, however, to European examples.[27] In its initial phase, the term seems to have been employed in modern Dutch historiography to deal with twentieth-century materials and contemporary history. However, from the late 1980s its use became more and more common in dealing with writings from the early modern period, such as diaries, family chronicles, and autobiographies, in place of other blanket classifications such as the German terms *Selbstzeugnis* (self-testimony) and *Selbstdarstellung* (self-presentation). By the mid 1990s, however, the term was already being contested by those who found it conceptually imprecise and therefore apt to confuse by its pooling of diverse materials. This led to two distinct outcomes: on the one hand, a firm rejection of "ego-document" by historians who preferred terms such as *Selbstzeugnis* and self-narrative; and on the other, attempts to refine usage of the term by making internal distinctions within the broad category it denoted.

A well-known essay by Winfried Schulze, in particular, explored the latter option by proposing a classification of ego-documents into "voluntary (*freiwilligen*)" and "involuntary (*unfreiwilligen*)", as well as a triage by social class, separating the autobiographies, diaries, dream journals, and personal letters of aristocratic and bourgeois milieus from other texts dealing with the "beliefs and knowledge of simpler folk (*das Glauben und Wissen einfacher Menschen*)."[28] While the latter distinction had the perhaps unintended effect of once more driving a wedge between "elite" and "popular" culture as categories, the former distinction seemed more apt in regard to societies with powerful institutions that enforced social discipline, such as the Inquisition. As is well known, the early modern Inquisitions of Iberia and Italy often produced rather spectacular self-narratives, but these emerged under specific conditions of coercion, raising interesting issues regarding their use by historians. What is certain is that, in the absence of comparable disciplinary institutions, the early modern Islamic empires were not fertile ground for the production of "involuntary" self-narratives.

---

[27] Von Greyerz, "Ego-Documents".
[28] Schulze, "Ego-Dokumente".

To sum up our discussion thus far, much water has flowed under the bridge since the canonical positions regarding autobiography were set down by scholars of Western (largely European) literature in the 1950s and 1960s. Indeed, by the end of the twentieth century even a European historian such as Peter Burke was urging his readers that "we need to free ourselves from the Western, Burckhardtian assumption that self-consciousness arose in a particular place, such as Italy, at a particular time, perhaps the fourteenth century."[29] Rejecting the old diffusionist models of "imitation by Indians, Japanese and others in recent centuries," he went on to argue, "It is better to think in terms of a variety of categories of the person or conceptions of the self (more or less unified, bounded and so on) in different cultures, categories and conceptions which underlie a variety of styles of self-presentation or self-fashioning." Yet, as a survey of the literature of the past two decades shows, such advice has been notoriously easier to give than to take.[30]

Entering the Mughal Domains

Our subject in this book is the period of the Mughal (or Timurid) dynasty which ruled over a good part of South Asia during the sixteenth, seventeenth, and eighteenth centuries. Though these rulers preserved certain crucial elements of cultural and institutional continuity with the various other Muslim dynasties that had ruled over northern India in the three centuries prior to 1500, they also departed from them in some significant respects. The difficulty, as Sunil Kumar has reminded us, is that intellectuals who lived under Mughal rule also manipulated the image of previous dynasties to make them appear as pale predecessors of the Timurids. In particular, their portrayal "framed the intervening fifteenth century of disunity and fragmented regional rule" to justify the need for a strong interventionist hand from the exterior.[31]

[29] Burke, "Representations of the Self", 28.

[30] For two attempts to tackle the issue by accumulating geographically and chronologically very diverse materials, see Siebenhüner and Church, "Introduction: Autobiographical Writings"; and Ruggiu, ed., *The Uses of First-Person Writings*.

[31] Kumar, "The Delhi Sultanate as Empire", 593.

In short, the Mughals and their propagandists marshalled all the evidence that they could to argue for their own originality and distinction. At the same time, we cannot get around the evidence that Mughal rule in India did differ qualitatively from that of earlier dynasties. Its ruling apparatus was more sizeable in both civil and military terms and disposed of greater resources; it also seems to have penetrated deeper into the regulation of both urban and rural society, even if this was done by a combination of negotiation and main force. It is possible to approach Mughal rule through a diversity of materials, ranging from quotidian administrative and legal documents (which unfortunately survive in a very uneven manner), to the reports and narratives of foreign visitors and observers, to the chronicles and other texts produced by the Mughal elite, whether officially sponsored or not.[32]

Between 1200 and 1500 a considerable body of literature in Persian had progressively emerged in India: chronicles, literary compositions in poetry and prose, biographical dictionaries (*tazkiras*) of various sorts, as well as hagiographical works centred on Sufi and other saintly figures. In spite of this proliferation, there are few if any personal texts or self-narratives authored by rulers or their close relatives in the sultanates of northern India. Among the fourteenth- and fifteenth-century books of encomia, and advice for princes and would-be rulers by celebrated authors such as Amir Khusrau and Ziya-ud-Din Barani, no real "do-it-yourself" formulae emerged for conquerors on the make. It seems that there were various competing ways of going about statemaking, of which two stand out. One tried and tested route was secession or rebellion, by which a regional governor or subordinate hived off a piece of an existing structure and made sovereign claims there against an erstwhile superior. This is what had happened in the Delhi Sultanate from the later fourteenth century and had led to the creation of autonomous kingdoms in areas such as Gujarat, Jaunpur, and the Deccan. The same process would recur in the late fifteenth century in the Deccan, with the progressive fission of the Bahmani Sultanate.

The second strategy was capture of the political centre by displacing the former ruler, which is what one sees with the seizure of power by

---

[32] A very wide-ranging listing of sources will be found in Habib, *The Agrarian System*, 467–502.

Bahlul Lodi in the mid fifteenth century after several unsuccessful attempts. In that instance, the previous ruler from the Sayyid dynasty retired to a provincial centre, permitting the Lodis roughly seven decades of rule before they came under challenge. In sum, here the process was not one of fission and relocation but displacement and replacement.[33]

The situation of the later Delhi Sultanate and its offshoots can profitably be contrasted with the neighbouring region of Central Asia, where the Timurids became the dominant force in the first half of the fifteenth century. A new situation emerged in this period, which John Woods has characterised as a "sudden proliferation of narratives" beginning during the rule of Timur himself, in contrast to the relative paucity of such texts earlier in the Chaghatayid tradition. This was acknowledged even by the Damascene chronicler Ibn 'Arabshah, whose writings are in general quite hostile to Timur, whom he often portrays as an illiterate ignoramus, incapable even of understanding elementary Arabic. We gather that, as a consequence, the historical writings that were produced in Timur's milieu tended to favour Persian (and to an extent Turkish) as a language of expression; but, at the same time, Woods notes that these "broke with the orientations and perspectives" of the earlier Ilkhanid Persian historiography represented by prestigious writers such as 'Ata Malik Juwaini and Rashid-ud-Din Hamadani.[34] Timurid texts tended at first to have an overweening, even obsessive, preoccupation with the personality and deeds of the conqueror, a focus that Timur himself undoubtedly encouraged.

Though several such texts have either been lost or come down to us only in fragmentary form, they nevertheless make up an imposing body of writing. In the early generations, they include the writings of historians such as Nizam-ud-Din 'Ali Shami, Hafiz-i Abru, and Mu'in-ud-Din Natanzi, whose lifetimes and careers extended from the late fourteenth century into the reign of Timur's chief successor Mirza Shahrukh. These authors drew upon similar sources and knew one another's work, and there is thus some degree of overlap between them.

---

[33] On the Lodis, see Jackson, *The Delhi Sultanate*, 321–25; also Digby, "The Indo-Persian Historiography".

[34] Woods, "The Rise of Tīmūrid Historiography".

An important, albeit somewhat controversial, figure whose work then consolidated several aspects of Timurid historiography was Sharaf-ud-Din Yazdi, author of the celebrated *Zafarnāma*. This text cast a long shadow and was drawn upon both as a literary and stylistic model and for its actual contents by subsequent generations, though it may in fact have somewhat lacked originality as a historical work. As Evrim Binbaş has noted, in view of the fact that over two hundred manuscript copies of the work can be found, "Yazdi's *Zafarnāma* is certainly one of the most popular Persianate historical works ever written."[35] Binbaş provides us an intricate reconstruction of how this text was produced, including the hesitations and periodic political reorientations of its author between the early 1420s and its eventual completion around 1436. Late in his life Yazdi met important intellectuals of the younger generations, such as 'Ali Shir Nawa'i and 'Abdur Rahman Jami. Yet, having made some problematic political choices in terms of his patrons, in 1454, despite the considerable success of his major work, he died a bitter and disappointed man.

Arguably the most important historiographer of the next generation in the Timurid world was 'Abdur Razzaq Samarqandi, author of the *Matla'-i Sa'dain*, who began his career under Mirza Shahrukh and eventually died in Herat in 1482 under the rule of Sultan Husain Baiqara. Though this work was only completed after around 1470, it seems that its writing involved a process of slow decantation. 'Abdur Razzaq belonged to a family of savants and was trained by them as well as other prominent scholars. His text is in two parts, the first far more derivative than the second. This can be explained in some measure by questions of chronological coverage, since the first part runs from the time of the late Ilkhanids to the death of Timur in 1405, while the second largely overlaps with 'Abdur Razzaq's own lifetime. The latter is remarkable, moreover, for its use of contemporary documentation in relation to diplomatic exchanges with the Mamluks and the Ming dynasty. This part also includes intriguing sections where the author himself becomes an actor in the text – such as in the period of the early 1440s when he was sent by Shahrukh as his emissary to southern

---

[35] Binbaş, *Intellectual Networks*, 218.

India, spending time both in Calicut (Kozhikode) and the inland imperial capital of Vijayanagara.

As the author of a first-person embassy account (or *sifārat nāma*) in Persian, 'Abdur Razzaq had a limited set of predecessors to draw upon, though a larger body of materials in Arabic may have existed from the time of the 'Abbasid Caliphate. The most significant text at his disposal was the *roznāma* (daily account) of the shadowy Ghiyas-ud-Din Naqqash, who was part of an imposing embassy sent by Mirza Shahrukh and other Timurid princes to the Yongle emperor in the years 1419–22.[36] This account was seen as sufficiently important for it to be quickly recovered by Hafiz-i Abru in his writings, and it then became a staple, finding its way into a variety of Timurid accounts through the fifteenth century.

Naqqash provided his readers with handy descriptions of the ritual reception of the embassy, the types of official interlocutors whom he dealt with, the passage through a variety of stages and control points, the character of Chinese urbanism, and the nature of the Ming court itself. His instructions, we are told, were precisely that "from the day they departed the capital Herat until the day they returned, they would record on the pages of their notebooks, without addition or deletion, all they witnessed – events, condition of roads, construction of towns, description of garrisons, situations of buildings, conditions of kings, etc." This explains the relative sobriety of the account, which only lapses into the register of wonders and marvels (*'ajā'ib-o-gharā'ib*) occasionally and is mostly an evaluation of Ming power that must have been useful to its Timurid readers, some of whom would have been aware by then of the Zheng He maritime expeditions into the western Indian Ocean.

Despite certain superficial similarities, the contrast between Naqqash's account and that of 'Abdur Razzaq is quite marked. Where Naqqash keeps a discreet profile throughout, his counterpart frequently thrusts himself into the forefront of the action, thus emphasising the "subjective" rather than the "objective" aspects of the account. In part this is a consequence of the fact that whereas the Ming embassy was

---

[36] Maitra, *Persian Embassy to China*; Thackston, *Century of Princes*, 279–97.

overall a rather orderly and regimented affair, that to India was characterised by its disorderly and improvised character. 'Abdur Razzaq was meant to head a return embassy to Calicut, but he found that port-city and its inhabitants to be well below the standards of Islamicate culture that he expected. It was a stroke of good fortune which took him then to Vijayanagara, an empire that was far more to his taste, but it meant that he had to go well beyond whatever orders and instructions he had been given. Presenting this *terra incognita* to his Timurid audience was the task that he eventually set himself, and he did so by using a set of clever devices which emphasised the prosperity of the kingdom, the ability of its artisans, the affluence of its traders, and the fact that its court met many of the requisites of etiquette (*adab*) in a Persianate world, even if the rulers and their subjects were in a "kingdom of infidels (*mamlikat-i kuffār*)".

We have discussed this account at considerable length elsewhere, and it should be emphasised that the form of emplotment chosen by 'Abdur Razzaq is by no means simple.[37] The initial disappointment at Calicut becomes a positive outcome in Vijayanagara, but even this is not an unalloyed triumph. 'Abdur Razzaq has also to contend with a set of obstacles in the form of the Hurmuzi traders in southern India, who try to undermine him and throw doubt on his credentials. The last audience he has – with the ruler Deva Raya – thus has a somewhat bitter overtone to it.[38] However, he was eventually able to return safe and sound to the Persian Gulf and make his way back from there to Herat in January 1445, where he was apparently received with great honour and was able to speak at length regarding his adventures with Shahrukh himself.

The remaining decades of 'Abdur Razzaq's life were politically tumultuous, especially after Shahrukh's death. Regular warring between rival Timurid princes characterises this period, with short periods of dominance exercised by several figures, amongst whom one must count Abu Sa'id Mirza, direct descendant of Timur's most assertive son Miranshah. The defeat and killing of Abu Sa'id in 1469 eventually cre-

---

[37] Alam and Subrahmanyam, *Indo-Persian Travels in the Age of Discoveries*, 45–87.

[38] For Vijayanagara in this period, see Nagaraju, *Devaraya II*.

ated the conditions for the emergence of a stable regime in Herat, now ruled over by Sultan Husain Baiqara until his death in 1506.[39] Sultan Husain's rule would be celebrated later as a golden age of sorts, even if it was not a period of notable political success or territorial expansion. Rather, diplomatic means were employed to secure the stability of what became in effect a compact regional state in Khorasan, the resources of which were then utilised to build a body of cultural capital whose effects spread into various domains: architecture, literature, and painting.

As was noted by writers like Daulatshah Samarqandi, in his well-known *tazkira* of poets, a number of larger-than-life figures emerged in this context, such as the poet and Sufi 'Abdur Rahman Jami, the historian Mirkhwand, and above all Mir 'Ali Shir Nawa'i, who has been described by a modern historian as "the de facto overseer of the cultural life at the Herat court . . . [who] personally encouraged and financially supported the numerous poets, painters, musicians, calligraphers, architects, and historians who produced a breadth of cultural activity."[40] Nawa'i shaped a number of features of the Herat polity, including its encouragement of Chaghatay (eastern Turkish) as a literary language. But he also appears to have kept a check on certain reforms in terms of political economy, which others deemed necessary. Though the last quarter of the century saw an intensification of agriculture in Khorasan, which sustained vibrant urban centres such as Herat and Balkh, the benefits were often alienated in the hands of *suyūrghāl* holders, a class to which Nawa'i himself belonged. The sultan's attempts at pulling back some of these resources into his own coffers in order to consolidate his position against both external and internal threats eventually proved a signal failure.[41]

The Herat political system cast a long shadow on the early career of the Timurid prince Zahir-ud-Din Muhammad Babur, who was to go on to wrest Delhi and Agra from the Afghan Lodi dynasty in the 1520s. Babur was the grandson of Abu Sa'id Mirza, whose turbulent career

[39] For the circumstances of Abu Sa'id's death, see the discussion in Melvin-Koushki, "The Delicate Art of Aggression".

[40] Subtelny, "'Alī Shīr Navā'ī", 797.

[41] Subtelny, "Centralizing Reform".

and violent death in 1469 we have mentioned above. His drift southward from a boyhood spent in Ferghana and Samarqand was itself the
consequence of complex circumstances, notably the growing power
of a rival Chinggisid clan, led by Muhammad Shibani (or Shaibani)
Khan, which emerged into prominence around 1500. These latter rulers, sometimes designated with the epithet "Uzbek", seized first Bukhara and Samarqand, and then the great centre of Herat after the
death of Husain Baiqara in 1506.[42] The defeat and killing by the Safavid Shah Isma'il of Shibani Khan in 1510 gave some temporary respite
to Babur, but he was eventually and comprehensively expelled southwards by 'Ubaidullah Khan, Shibani Khan's successor. In these years
of wandering or "vagabondage (*qazaliq*)", Babur seems to have conceived the literary project of penning a text, which he himself probably conceived of with the term *Waqā'i'*, but which posterity knows
far better under the title *Bābur Nāma*. Very likely because of the intellectual influence of 'Ali Shir Nawa'i, he chose to write the text in Chaghatay Turkish, his own first language and one in which he also wrote
poetry.[43] Babur's text was to have a long and distinguished career, and
it is thus incumbent upon us to devote some attention to it here.[44]

It is generally recognised now that this text, which remained unfinished at his death, was made up of at least three distinct portions, each
with a somewhat different logic. The first of these concerned Babur's
youth in Central Asia, running to roughly 1503, when around the age
of twenty he was obliged to abandon his home territories. The second largely deals with his Kabul years, beginning in about 1504, but
all the manuscripts of it that have come down to us show two large
chronological gaps, rendering his account of this period particularly
difficult for historians to interpret. Finally, the third section, beginning in about 1525, concerns India and ends abruptly, roughly a year
before Babur's death in December 1530.

Most analysts of the text agree that Babur had taken the time to refine and revise the first two sections, possibly interjecting materials with

---

[42] See Szuppe, *Entre Timourides*.

[43] Ross, "A Collection of Poems".

[44] A helpful discussion of the manuscript tradition and its difficulties may be
found in Mano, "Editorial Choices".

the benefit of hindsight. The third section, on the other hand, is the rawest and represents an early draft that was never polished. This has both advantages and disadvantages from the viewpoint of the historian, inasmuch as it shows, for example, aspects of the emerging conflict between Babur and his son Humayun which later official historians would find embarrassing, but it is also incoherent and unclear at times. The manuscript history of the text is also rather intriguing. Though we are aware that the *Waqā'i'* was read, paraphrased, and commented upon not only by Humayun but other members of the clan in the sixteenth century, the earliest surviving Turkish manuscripts are from the end of the sixteenth century.[45] By this time the court of Babur's grandson, Akbar, had already seized upon the text as crucial to the consolidation of its own dynastic identity, and patronised an official translation into Persian by the great *amīr* and multilingual intellectual 'Abdur Rahim Khan-i Khanan.[46] This version, the so-called *Wāqi'āt-i Bāburī*, was then handed to the imperial painting atelier, where it was lavishly illustrated in several copies, at much the same time that a variety of other dynastic histories were being produced and illustrated.[47] It was in this Persian incarnation, whether illustrated or more frequently not, that the text largely circulated in the Mughal domains in the seventeenth and eighteenth centuries, though some cultivated readers continued to prefer the Turkish original.

Babur's text has over time come to acquire a reputation as an outstanding "self-narrative" in the Indo-Islamic context, perhaps even as a work *sui generis*.[48] But it is arguably both more and less. If the Timurid prince does reveal something of his shifting moods, passions, and humours, he also spends a great deal of time describing places and people

[45] For Humayun and other Timurid family members as readers of Babur, see Beveridge, "Further Notes on the Babar-Nama MSS".

[46] On this figure, see the study by Orthmann, *'Abd or-Rahīm Ḫān-e Ḫānān*.

[47] See Verma, *The Illustrated Baburnama*.

[48] We thus have the opinion of Roy Pascal: "It is beyond my scope to suggest why autobiography does not come into being outside Europe, and the existence of such a work as Babur's memoirs of the sixteenth century, which would occupy a significant place in the history of autobiography had it belonged to Europe, makes one hesitate to generalise." Pascal, *Design and Truth*, 22.

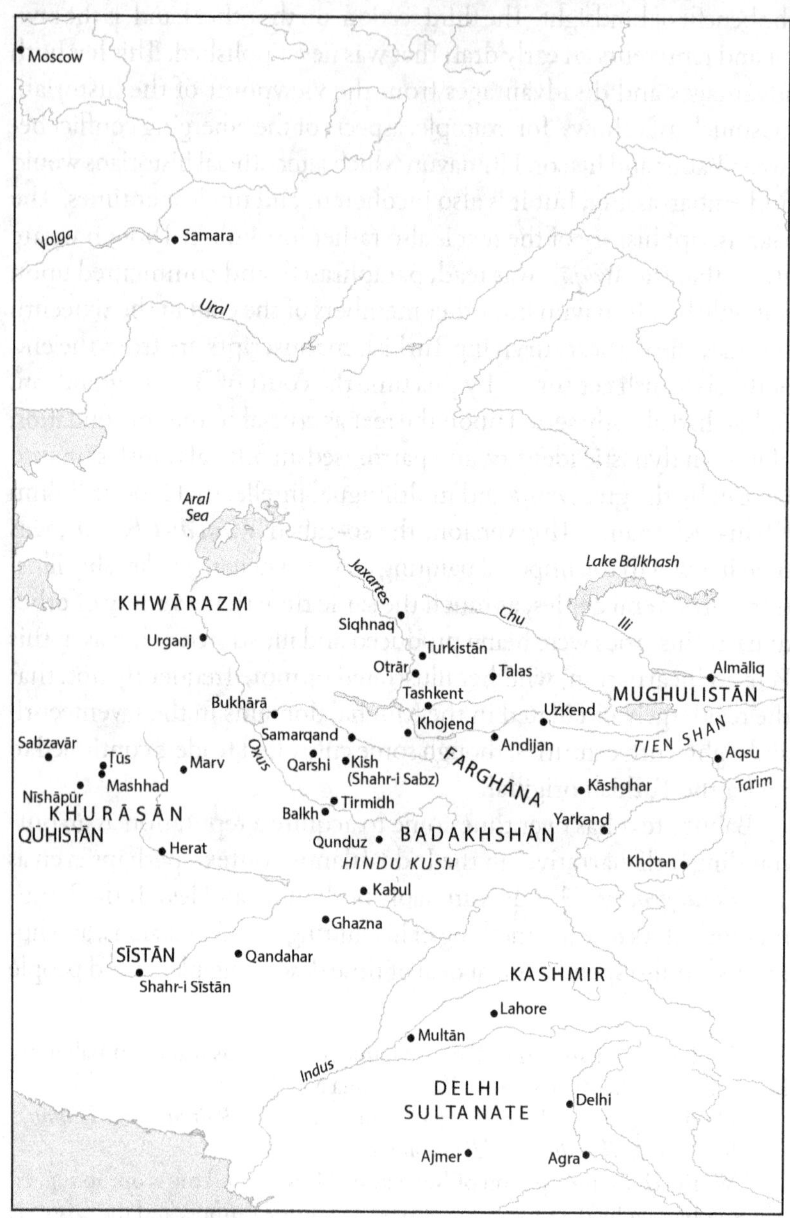

Map 2: The world of Zahir-ud-Din Babur.

in detail, whether in Central Asia or India, thus showing that he had a remarkable eye and capacity for observation. His prose style, which he deliberately kept unadorned (in contrast to that of Mir ʿAli Shir Nawaʾi), can be somewhat deceptive and should not lead us to believe that he was incapable of manipulating a quite sophisticated set of rhetorical tools. It is also worth recalling that Babur, like most well-educated men of his milieu, would have memorised a large corpus of material in poetry and prose, whether in Arabic, Persian, or Turkish, which he could conjure up from memory at will. Some analysts have thus stressed the importance of an intertextual analysis of the *Bābur Nāma*, to take into account his regular re-use of materials from both well-known and more obscure sources.[49]

The central point to be borne in mind, before looking more closely into some matters of detail, is that of the complex narrative arc of the text. When Babur began writing it, he had no means of knowing that it would end with a sort of triumph, namely the successful conquest of Hindustan. Rather, the logic was initially one of a declinist trajectory, heavily flavoured with the sense that the best years of his life were those spent in his youth in Samarqand and its environs. This pervasive sense of nostalgia, both for lost times and places, never leaves the text entirely.

But what paradise had been lost? From Babur's viewpoint the ideal place in the world was Samarqand, which in his view lay "at the edge of the civilized world", with the domain of the steppe beyond. Not only was it termed the "well-protected town (*balda-yi mahfūza*)" since it had rarely been stormed and seized, but it was also in his opinion one of the most pleasant cities in the entire world. Its virtues were many but could broadly be classified as follows. First, the area had been dominated by Muslims from the time of the early Caliphs and was thus a great centre for theologians and the writing of important Islamic texts. Second, despite the harsh winters, its air was generally good and its water sufficient to irrigate orchards of grapes, apples, melons, and other excellent fruit. The city itself was a marvel, its architecture having been greatly improved by the interventions of both Timur and his descen-

---

[49] Anooshahr, *The Ghazi Sultans*, 15–37.

dant Mirza Ulugh Beg in the matter of buildings and gardens. These included a famous observatory from which great texts on astronomy were produced – far superior to those in India, according to Babur. Finally, there was the quality of the artisanal and commercial activity in Samarqand, with "each trade [having] a separate market". In respect of every one of the trades in question, from baking to velvet production to paper-making, Babur sees Samarqand as a city with practically no equal in the world.[50]

But his enthusiasm did not extend equally to every part of Central Asia. The region of Ferghana, with which his text begins, is described (like Samarqand) as being "on the edge of the civilized world" and marked by the plentiful availability of grain and fruit. Its seven major towns are depicted by him as pleasant, somewhat bucolic places, with fat pheasants and game, beautiful tulips and violets, and excellent agricultural products – in particular melons, which were actually something of an obsession with Babur. At the same time, he does not hesitate to call the town of Khojand a "miserable place" on account of its lack of resources and capacity to provide for a man of his stature.[51] In this sense, Samarqand represents an unusual combination: not only was it located in an excellent and sufficiently northerly clime – the fifth – it was also notably urbane and sophisticated, a worthy residence for a man from a courtly lineage. It would remain something of a yardstick against which other cities and centres – particularly those of Hindustan – were compared.

After his expulsion from the Samarqand region, the next phase of Babur's life was spent in Kabul, where he reckons that he grew fully into manhood, since it was in 1504 that "I first put a razor to my face." It was also a phase of rebuilding from the very nadir, since by this time his following had been reduced to a handful of tents and a few hundred men, mostly poorly armed. The nature and causes of the reversal of fortunes remained an enigma, even to Babur himself. As he was well aware, he was caught in a highly competitive space where other Timurid Mirzas (including his younger half-brother Jahangir Mirza), as

<hr>

[50] For the long history of the town, see Grenet, "Maracanda/Samarkand, une métropole pré-mongole".

[51] Babur, *The Baburnama*, trans. Thackston, 72.

well as warlords from other lineages, made pressing claims and demands. The possibilities of betrayal were many, and Babur had to keep his ear to the ground for conspiracies that might be mounted against him. The fact that the young Babur somehow managed to navigate this treacherous space, and persuade the followers of more powerful rival warlords to adhere to his cause, seems to have convinced him that he had indeed been chosen by a divine hand. At a strategic level he was also aided by the weakened state of Husain Baiqara's Herat polity, which appeared increasingly reluctant to confront the aggression of Shibani Khan, and instead remained rather passive. Babur thus quickly made his move, gathering together his now sizeable forces in an attempt to seize Kabul in September 1504. In the event, no great siege or battle ensued: Muqim Beg Arghun, who was in charge of Kabul, appeared so cowed by the show of force that he simply handed the city over to Babur and agreed to become his subordinate.

It soon became apparent that Kabul, described by Babur as "a petty little province, rectangular in shape stretching from east to west", was too small to contain his ambitions. Within a few months he was scouting out the possibilities of further campaigns and initially decided to push on eastwards into Hindustan. But his attention returned for a time to Samarqand, and he made one more ill-fated attempt on that town. However, as he later wrote in the 1520s, "From the year 910 H. [1504–5], when Kabul was conquered, until this date I had craved Hindustan. Sometimes because my *begs* [commanders] had poor opinions, and sometimes because my brothers lacked co-operation, the Hindustan campaign had not been possible and the realm had not been conquered."[52] He also noted that in the late 1510s and early 1520s he had made four unsuccessful campaigns into northern India preceding his final success in 1525–6.

Babur's craving for Hindustan was not matched by his enthusiasm for it, which is to say the northern Indian plains showed him little of appeal. About his he was blunt: a few pages after the passage quoted above he says, "The cities and provinces of Hindustan are all unpleasant. All cities, all locales are alike. The gardens have no walls,

---

[52] Ibid., 329.

and most places are flat as boards." India was in fact "unpleasant and unharmonious . . . there is no beauty in its people, no graceful social intercourse, no poetic talent or understanding, no etiquette, nobility or manners." Its chief attraction, especially to a prince nearly at the end of his tether, was that "it is a large country with lots of gold and money [silver]." Overall there is little doubt that he felt his wanderings had brought him too far south for comfort:

> Hindustan lies in the first, second, and third climes, with none of it in the fourth clime. It is a strange country. Compared to ours, it is another world. Its mountains, rivers, forests, and wildernesses, its villages and provinces, animals and plants, peoples, and languages, even its rain and winds are altogether different. Even if the Kabul dependencies that have warm climates bear a resemblance to Hindustan in some aspects, in others they do not. Once you cross the Indus, the land, water, trees, stones, peoples, tribes, manners, and customs are all of the Hindustani fashion.[53]

This view, and an abiding nostalgia for Central Asia, was not Babur's alone. He notes the case of one of his companions, a certain Khwaja Kalan who, on the eve of his return from Delhi to Ghazna, is reported to have scribbled a rude verse as graffiti on the wall of his quarters: "If I cross the Indus in safety, may my face turn black if I ever see Hindustan again." We cannot know how humbler foot soldiers or cavalrymen from Central Asia felt, though Babur indicates that, as the hot season came upon them in 1526, "many began to sicken and die as though under the influence of a pestilent wind", and murmurings were heard that the chiefs in the army wished to contemplate an early departure. But Babur's argument at the time in council was implacable: "Shall we go back to Kabul and remain poverty stricken?" After all, he notes, many of the men had sent back "gifts for relatives and kinfolk", as well as offerings to the shrines of holy men in areas around Samarqand and Khorasan from which they came. His memoir, with its detailed description of Kabul and its environs, is equally helpful in providing us an understanding of what such men looked back to.

From a political viewpoint, an intriguing question is how Babur managed to transform the failure of the first part of his career into suc-

---

[53] Ibid., 332–3.

cess at the end of it. In an insightful essay, Cornell Fleischer has proposed that the young Babur was overly dependent on the support of the great landed Andijani *begs*, and Mongol aristocrats, as well as the fickle group of Timurid Mirzas with their uncertain loyalties. After several failed attempts at conquest and consolidation, he eventually came to the realisation that the only way out was to develop his household (*ichkilär*) comprising "individuals whose status was conferred by personal service to the prince," a heterogeneous group made up of "people from a variety of backgrounds . . . dispossessed, disenfranchised, or merely junior members of their class."[54] The household had a notional hierarchical structure, from important figures like the major-domo (*eshīk āqāsī*) down to what are termed simple "braves (*yigitlär*)". While the different elements listed above – *begs*, Mirzas, Mongols, and household figures – were all admitted into the war council (*kengäsh*), Babur eventually shifted the balance between them after the capture of Kabul in 1504 and, especially, the subsequent unsuccessful Samarqand campaign. Fleischer writes that "Babur's strategy was to enhance the position of his household officers and thus ensure their supremacy over others; but it was some time before he was able to apply this strategy successfully." By the time he made his serious moves towards Hindustan in 1519, the fangs of the *begs* had been drawn to a large extent. While he remained acutely aware of his Chinggisid and Timurid roots to the end, Babur departed from them to a large extent, beginning the move from confederation to settled empire that his sons would inherit as a conundrum.

A difficult question confronting every reader of the *Bābur Nāma* relates to its author's religiosity and religious outlook. We know that, early in the text, he attempts to define his religious identity in describing his father 'Umar Shaikh Mirza: "He was a Hanafi by sect and orthodox of belief. He never neglected the prayer five times. Throughout his lifetime, he always made up missed prayers and often recited the Qur'an. He was devoted to Khwaja 'Ubaidullah and considered it an honour to participate in his gatherings."[55] But, in a passage not much

---

[54] Fleischer, "Companions to a King Errant".

[55] Babur, *The Baburnama*, trans. Thackston, 9; *The Babur-Nama in English*, trans. Beveridge, vol. 1, 15.

later, he also notes certain of his father's vices, namely excessive drinking, a fondness for *ma'jūn* (an opium-based paste), and a weakness for gambling, none of which would normally be thought of as characteristic of an orthodox Sunni Muslim. Clearly, the Timurid Mirzas as Turco-Mongols had their own habits in the matter, as these forms of consumption, excess, and play find repeated mention in the text in relation to a number of Babur's relatives.

Of particular significance here is the mention of Khwaja 'Ubaidullah Ahrar (d. 1490), a powerful entrepreneurial figure from the Naqshbandi Sufi order who controlled enormous resources of land and other forms of revenue, and who had already been associated with Abu Sa'id Mirza.[56] Khwaja Ahrar and his followers were significant figures in Babur's life: he even claims to have had a vision in which the Sufi saint appeared quite decisively to save his life. Again, in November 1528 when he was suffering from inflammation of the bowels, Babur thought it appropriate to seek the intercession of the spirit of the Sufi by offering him a versified rendering of the Sufi's own treatise, the *Wālidiyya*. Once the task was well advanced, "by the grace of God and the saint's powers . . . [the sickness] began to abate."[57]

At the same time, we are made aware of an anomalous moment in Babur's life in relation to his Sunni and Hanafi identity. Significantly, this concerns an episode that does not feature in the *Bābur Nāma* because it occurred in the early 1510s – the period of one of the gaps in the second part of the text. At this time, the star of the Safavid Shah Isma'il was very much on the rise as he had managed to defeat and kill Babur's arch-enemy Shibani Khan, in the process capturing Babur's older sister, who was one of the Khan's wives. In the aftermath of this victory, Babur accepted the aid of the Safavids to mount an attack on Samarqand and Bukhara. In the face of a joint Timurid–Safavid force, their rivals retreated into the desert, allowing Babur to enter Samarqand without resistance in October 1511. However, it is reported that, on doing so, he had the Shi'i version of the Friday prayer read in

---

[56] On this important figure, see Paul, "Forming a Faction"; and the valuable materials in Gross and Urunbaev, *The Letters of Khwajah 'Ubayd Allah Ahrar*. For the Naqshbandis in Mughal India, also see Alam, "The Mughals, the Sufi Shaikhs".

[57] Babur, *The Baburnama*, trans. Thackston, 420.

the congregational mosques, and allowed himself to be identified as a *qizilbāsh* (red-cap) follower of the heterodox Shah Isma'il. This act caused considerable consternation among the largely Sunni population of the city, and is generally believed to have facilitated Babur's defeat, a few months later, by the forces of 'Ubaidullah Khan, Shibani Khan's nephew and eventual successor. On Babur's later retreat southward after his defeat, a mocking poet thus wrote:

> From Samarqand's gate that pathetic army again
> Fled to Hisar, hidden under a *chādar*.
> Babur, fortunate to have been a Sunni,
> Now through calculation became a friend of heresy.[58]

Over his years in Central Asia and then Kabul, Babur does not seem to have come into much contact with non-Muslims. Entering the northwestern part of the subcontinent, he even shows some mild curiosity regarding some of the older religious sites there, such as Gor Khatri (near Peshawar), famed for its tonsuring ritual. He eventually found it rather disappointing on a visit in March 1519, though the Buddhist monks' ruined cells reminded him of "madrasas and caravanserais". His lasting impression was one of mild disgust: "All around was an unending pile of hair and beard that had been clipped there." Within much the same period, in January 1519, he provides an account of a bloody sectarian dealing with the Afghans of the Bajaur region who resisted his forces and were roundly defeated: "Since the people of Bajaur were rebels, and infidel customs had spread among them, and the religion of Islam had been lost, they were put to massacre and their women and children were taken captive."[59]

Entering northern India some seven years later, Babur's primary enemies were his fellow Muslims, the Lodi Afghans, and as a consequence his rhetoric was not defined in terms of the opposition between Islam and infidelity (*kufr*). To be sure, the context was somewhat exotic in terms of dealing with "an unfamiliar people whose language we did not know and who did not know ours." But

[58] Dale, *Babur: Timurid Prince*, 99.
[59] Babur, *The Baburnama*, trans. Thackston, 265.

Image 1.1: Babur and his warriors visiting the
Hindu temple at Gor Khatri.

the initial opposition was posed also in terms of Sultan Ibrahim's character flaws, since he was immature, inexperienced in battle, and worst of all pusillanimous. The language shifts perceptibly in the text after the defeat of the Lodis, when Babur moves to consolidate his rule. His chief opponent now is the Sisodia Rajpur ruler of Mewar, Rana Sanga, who is incessantly referred to as the "infidel", even if Babur concedes that he "had recently grown so great by his audacity and sword." In the description of the lead-up to the combat with the Rana, the two sides are thus described in religiously marked terms, and Babur's self-presentation as a *ghāzī* warrior is now deliberate and ostentatious. The religious flavour is obvious and all the more marked in the *fath-nāma* (victory bulletin) issued after the Battle of Khanwa, composed by Shaikh Zain-ud-Din Khwafi on 2 March 1527, though one might also see this as fulfilling the generic demands of such a text.[60] No doubt Babur and his entourage were also thinking of a similar text issued by Timur after his conquest of Delhi: in March 1527 the conqueror's army "were ordered to erect a tower of infidel skulls on the top of the mountain", this being an obviously Chinggisid and Timurid act.[61] The bitter combat with Rajput forces carried on into the next year, and once more we are told that, after one of the conquests, "a tower of infidels' skulls was erected on the hill on the northwest side of Chanderi." This victory was also marked by Babur using a significant verse and chronogram:

For a time Chanderi was full of infidels and the realm of war.
I conquered the fortress in battle, the chronogram for which was:
Fath-i dār al-harb [Conquest of the Abode of War].

The violent character of Babur's rhetoric at these moments is not merely a matter of the sensitivity of modern-day observers. As has been pointed out, two generations after the conquest Babur's own descendants evinced some discomfort in relation to it. Thus, Ali Anooshahr notes that in the *Tārīkh-i Alfī*, written in Akbar's reign by Ja'far Beg

---

[60] Ibid., 385–9.
[61] For Timur's *fath-nāma*, see Aubin, "Comment Tamerlan prenait les villes", 90.

and his collaborators, care was taken to eliminate certain "bombastic and provocative passages" while quoting from Babur's text. He adds that

> while not entirely eliminating the rhetorical *Sturm und Drang* of holy war in that particular section of his source the *Bāburnāma*, Ja'far Beg still deleted passages such as: "[these infidels] attached themselves as with chains and bonds to that wicked infidel [Rana Sanga]. These ten infidels, like ten denouncers raising the banner of wretchedness – 'denounce unto them a painful punishment' [Qur'an 3:21] – held many followers, soldiers, and districts broad in extent."[62]

There is also some evidence from these years of Babur's iconoclasm. Thus, on a visit to the great central Indian city of Gwalior in 1528, he begins by noting the existence of Hindu temples there in a somewhat neutral tone: "To the west of the reservoir is a tall temple, next to which Sultan Iltutmish had a congregational mosque built. The temple is extremely tall – the tallest structure in the fortress." However, he then goes on to describe a visit to the important Jaina site of Urvashi, where the Siddhachal caves were noted for their carvings of the Jaina *tīrthankaras*. Here, Babur writes: "The solid rock outcroppings around Urwahi [Urvashi] have been hewn into idols, large and small. On the southern side is a large idol, approximately twenty yards tall. They are shown stark naked with their private parts exposed . . . Urwahi is not a bad place. In fact, it is rather nice. Its one drawback was the idols, so I ordered them destroyed."[63] What took place in the end was defacement rather than the wholesale destruction of edifices or carvings.

Nevertheless, it is worth noting that the deployment of a charged sectarian language when describing instances of violence between different groups of Muslims, or between heterodox and orthodox believers, or between Muslims and non-Muslims is far from exceptional in Babur's text as well as in similar writings of the period featuring victorious Islam. In fact, a disappointing aspect of the third section of Babur's text, when he deals with Hindustan, is the rapid and superficial

<hr>

[62] Anooshahr, "Dialogue and Territoriality", 231.
[63] Babur, *The Baburnama*, trans. Thackston, 415–16.

character of its ethnographic observations, whether in respect of social or religious practices, in contrast with the quite elaborate descriptions of flora and fauna. Whether this was deliberate, or yet again a result of the fact that the text remained incomplete, can only be a matter of speculation. What that hypothetical ethnography might have contained is also unclear; but what is certain is that we can hardly make of Babur a cosmopolitan and tolerant intellectual responding to the criteria of the late-twentieth or early-twenty-first century.

The Successor Texts

Still more complex attitudes can be found amongst the Central Asians of the first few generations after the conquest of 1526. A particularly intriguing case is that of Babur's own first cousin on the maternal side, Mirza Muhammad Haidar Dughlat, a highly successful general and military entrepreneur who is also the author of a somewhat neglected first-person text in Persian entitled the *Tārīkh-i Rashīdī*. Mirza Haidar was born in Tashkent around 1499 in a clan closely related to that of Babur, but which saw itself in many ways as quite distinct in its ambitions.[64] He spent some of the early years of his life in close personal proximity to Babur, for whom he expresses great admiration, but then chose from his mid teens to place himself in the service of another important Timurid clan to the east, that of Sultan Sa'id Khan. Over the next two decades he then fought more or less ceaselessly for this patron in the area between Kashgar and Khorasan, but often extended his operations southwards into the Tibetan plateau as well. This altogether exhausting form of high-altitude campaigning with small forces and high casualty rates took the Mirza across the Pamirs on more than one occasion. In 1531 he invaded Ladakh, Tibet, and western Kashmir on behalf of his patron in what he termed in his text a form of *jihād* against prosperous and powerful infidels. At the same time, he also claimed to have "held discussions with them [the Tibetans] through

---

[64] Haidar Dughlat, *Tārīkh-i Rashīdī*. For an analysis of Mirza Haidar Dughlat that differs somewhat from ours in emphasis, see Anooshahr, "Mughals, Mongols and Mongrels". We return here to themes dealt with in Subrahmanyam, "Early Modern Circulation", 43–68.

a translator" in order to gain some understanding of their religious beliefs. Again, in 1533, he mounted an attack on Lhasa – which, he believed, possessed considerable riches on account of its density of Buddhist monasteries – but was eventually forced back by the poor logistics of his force.[65]

However, when his chief patron Sultan Sa'id died in 1533, in the course of these strenuous mountain campaigns, Mirza Haidar began to anticipate with some trepidation that a powerful warlord like himself would not be treated well by Sultan Sa'id's successors. Rather than test the muddy waters of loyalty, he chose exit as a clearer option. After a complex set of dealings and negotiations he managed in 1536–7 to attain Badakhshan, and then Kabul, from where he sought to revive his far older dealings with the direct descendants of the now-deceased Babur.

His initial contacts were in Lahore, where in 1538 he entered briefly into the service of Mirza Kamran, Babur's younger son and rival of Humayun. Then in 1539 he entered the service of Humayun himself and fought briefly at the latter's side during his disastrous campaign in the Gangetic valley against the Afghan-led armies of Sher Shah Sur. After Humayun's defeat at Kannauj, Mirza Haidar proposed a retreat to the north in the direction of Kashmir, with which he had some earlier familiarity. When the Mughal ruler chose otherwise, Haidar Dughlat himself marched north; in November 1540 he re-entered Kashmir with a force and took it over with very little initial resistance. It may well have been as if he were revisiting the terrain of his distant Mongol ancestors, who had once controlled that region.

Over the next decade, and until his death in battle in 1551, Mirza Haidar's activities in Kashmir remain quite enigmatic. Initially, he seems to have chosen to present himself as a mere "regent" to one of the claimants to the throne in Kashmir, Nadir Shah. Thereafter, from the mid 1540s, he issued coins in the name of Humayun and seems largely to have acted in his name, even though the Mughal ruler was absent in these years, first in distant Iran and then in the Kabul region. In this same period, as discontent with his rule grew, Mirza Haidar was

[65] For these questions, see Elverskog, *Buddhism and Islam*, 175–80.

obliged to defeat various rebellions mounted either by members of the displaced Kashmir dynasty or by other powerful local warlords. One narrative presents him as a ruler whose intolerance grew apace with time and power, and who increasingly revealed himself as an orthodox Sunni Muslim of a Hanafi persuasion, and therefore quite unable to stomach the heterodox Sufi-inflected Islam of the region, as incarnated in particular by the Nurbakhshiya order of mystics who, a modern historian notes, "could not be classified as either Sunni or Shi'i."[66]

It is thus convenient, no doubt, to contrast Babur and Mirza Haidar and their texts from a number of viewpoints, starting with the linguistic one: Babur's text is written in eastern Turkish and that of his cousin in Persian. Further, if the former author appears flexible, pragmatic, and human (and even humanistic, as some of his recent readers have it), to which one can add his metrosexual self-presentation as a further virtue, the latter can easily be presented as the bigoted Sunni from eastern Mughulistan, the failed country-cousin of the cosmopolitan dynast.[67] In the process we may, however, sell Mirza Haidar considerably short. In fact, even if the *Tārīkh-i Rashīdī* borrows extensively from other texts — as its author himself freely admits — the attitudes and perspectives it captures cannot be quite so easily dismissed, nor indeed can the Mirza's wide geographical horizons and connections. These attitudes are, moreover, not simply those of a nostalgia for a Central Asia from which the author found himself in exile. The text of the *Tārīkh-i Rashīdī*, we may recall, was written while Mirza Haidar was in Kashmir in the 1540s, even though he says less about that region than his modern readers might want.

Babur of course saw himself as a Timurid, and also as a Chinggisid; on the other hand, Mirza Haidar saw himself as a Mughul (with a long second ū), and a native of a region he termed Mughulistan, though he also sometimes identified with the Qara-Khitai — an older usage.[68] He

----

[66] See the discussion in Bashir, *Messianic Hopes*, 236–38. For Mirza Haidar's narrative, see *Tārīkh-i Rashīdī*, 262–3.

[67] See the somewhat contrasting views in Dale, "Steppe Humanism", and Anooshahr, *The Ghazi Sultans*, 15–37.

[68] See Biran, *The Empire of the Qara Khitai*.

noted that when he was born in around 905 AH (1499 CE), the towns
in his native region were in poor shape, and that most of his fellow
Mughuls "had never lived in villages; indeed, they had never so much
as seen a settlement, 'A group like beasts of the mountains'."[69] This passage referred then to the easterly groups, in contrast to the more fortunate, prosperous, urbanised, and settled westerly Timurid lineages to
which Babur belonged. But Mirza Haidar's native world was really that
of Kashgar and Yarkand, as we see from the *Tārīkh-i Rashīdī*, where
he regrets having had to abandon that land from the force of circum-
stance.

> Just as it [Kashgar] had advantages, it has disadvantages too. At the be-
> ginning of spring constant dark, black, adverse winds full of dust and grit
> blow. Although Hindustan is famous for this, it happens even more in
> Kashgar and Yarkand. Agriculture is laborious and bears little produce.
> In Kashgar it is impossible to maintain an army on one harvest. In com-
> parison with the Qipchaq steppe and Qalmaq, Kashgar resembles a city;
> but relative to real cities, it is as hell compared to purgatory.[70]

Here, Mirza Haidar rather charmingly quotes a verse from Shaikh
Sa'di's *Gulistān* to telling effect.

> *Hūrān-i bihishtī ra dozakh būd a'rāf,*
> *Az dozakhyān purs ki a'rāf bihisht ast.*

> To the houris of paradise, purgatory seems hell.
> Ask the denizens of hell; to them purgatory is paradise.

Still, in Mirza Haidar's imagination the area around Kashgar and
Yarkand was once prosperous: "in ancient times there were great cities
[in these wastes, but] . . . all have sunk beneath the sands." He even
adds the claim that "some hunters who go to hunt wild camels relate
that occasionally buildings of a city are uncovered, but when they
return after a time there is no trace, and they have sunk back beneath
the sands. There were such cities, but of them neither name nor trace

---

[69] Haidar Dughlat, *Tārīkh-i Rashīdī*, 90; text, 111 (the last phrase is a proverb).
[70] Ibid., 192–3; text, 247.

remains (*nām-o-nishān-i u bāqī nīst*)." Indeed, only Yarkand seems to retain some vestiges of its former glory in his eyes, and he tells us briefly of its impregnably high citadel, with "lofty and charming buildings" and "gardens in which lofty structures have been built, each of which contains a hundred rooms, more or less." Yet despite its excellent water – "the best in the world", and superb fruit and roses that were "better than those of Herat" – it would seem that even Yarkand is a place that by the early sixteenth century was a pale shadow of what it once was.[71]

In sum, Mirza Haidar seems in the final analysis to congratulate himself for his relocation to Kashmir, which he notes "is among well-known countries of the world [and] . . . famous throughout the world for its various delights." Writing in the mid 1540s, a few years before he was killed, he expresses his contentment at "the delightfulness and verdure of its gardens, meadows, mountains, for the pleasantness of its weather throughout the four seasons, and for perfect temperateness, no place like Kashmir has ever been seen or heard of."[72] Not only are the springs, waterfalls, and lakes very much to his taste, but he also appears greatly impressed by some of the architecture attributed to the patronage of the sultans of Kashmir.

An interesting aspect of Mirza Haidar's description of Kashmir is his attitude towards the Hindu temples he encountered there, which he describes as "the first and foremost among the wonders of Kashmir." The fact that they appeared to be made without the use of plaster or mortar strikes him as quite a feat, as well as the fact that many of them repeat versions of the same plan, with pillars, capitals, and dentations, often "made of one piece of stone." The temples are based for the most part on "a square enclosure up to thirty cubits high in some places, and each side is three hundred cubits." He then adds:

The outside coverings are filled with designs and paintings that are beyond description. Some of the paintings are of laughing and crying persons that would astound the onlooker. In the middle is a lofty throne made of

[71] On Mirza Haidar's description of the region, also see Shaw, "A Prince of Kashgar", 277–98.

[72] Haidar Dughlat, *Tārīkh-i Rashīdī*, 258–60; text, 363–5.

hewn stone, and over it is a dome completely of stone. There is no way to describe it. In all the world no such building has been seen or heard of.[73]

In the end, it seems that though Mirza Haidar was notoriously intolerant of heterodox Islam, which he felt should be "treated with nothing but the death penalty", his attitude towards those of other faiths proves to be rather more unexpected, especially when compared to the highly charged rhetoric of some passages in the *Bābur Nāma*, a text that Mirza Haidar appears to have known quite well. In fact, he praises Babur's *Waqā'i'* for its "pure style [which] is chaste and easy to understand" and also for the fact that Babur had led a life full of "amazing things and astonishing battles . . . the likes of which truly have never happened to his peers."[74] It cannot be ruled out, therefore, that his cousin's text may have provided a part of the inspiration for his own, even if its ostensible justification was to keep alive the history of the group of eastern clans to which Mirza Haidar belonged, since "there is not a soul left of this group who remembers these stories."[75]

It remains for us to make some observations on three self-narratives from the Mughal domains that follow chronologically on that of Mirza Haidar Dughlat and belong to the sixteenth century (that is, the second and third generations of Mughal rule in India).[76] The first, and arguably most enigmatic of these, was composed by a certain Mihtar Jauhar Aftabchi and given the title *Tazkirat al-Wāqi'āt* (Memoir of Events) by its own author, who took it upon himself to "write a memorial of conditions and transactions as a sort of record (*ba tarīq-i yāddāsht*) in accordance with my own understanding." It was appar-

---

[73] Ibid., 260–1.

[74] Ibid., 103.

[75] On the relationship between the two texts, see the brief remarks in Mano, "The Babur-nama and the Tarikh-i Rashidi".

[76] These three texts of Jauhar, Bayazid, and Gulbadan have been published as a single volume (in two parts) with text and English translation, by Wheeler M. Thackston as *Three Memoirs of Homayun*. Somewhat confusingly, the pagination is not continuous. Instead, we have the English translations of Gulbadan and Jauhar (respectively 1–67, 69–175), followed by the Persian texts with a distinct pagination; then the text of Bayazid and a general index (1–214), followed by the Persian text.

ently completed in the late 1580s, at which time Jauhar was probably in his late fifties or early sixties, but it largely referred back to the 1540s and early 1550s, and the turbulent reign of the emperor Humayun, in whose service the author found himself.[77] Jauhar belonged to a relatively humble class of body-servants, and his title of *āftābchī*, politely translated as "ewer-bearer", actually referred to someone who carried the water for his master's personal ablutions (of whom there were several in Humayun's retinue). We know little or nothing about his origins or family circumstances, except that he entered Humayun's service in the 1530s, when his narrative begins.[78] He may have either been a slave or a free servant since the term *banda* that he regularly uses for himself could equally be employed in the two contexts. In any event, he had close personal access to Humayun and was able to observe him in a variety of circumstances, including some involving considerable personal and political difficulty. The narrative thus follows the first half of Jauhar's own life, but only as a strange reflection of that of the emperor and his circumstances, and ceases with the death of Humayun in early 1556, not long after he had been reinstalled in his capital, Dinpanah-Delhi. Because of Jauhar's humble status, we are also largely unaware of what became of him between the years 1556 and 1587, when he completed his text, as he does not appear in official chronicles or biographical dictionaries.

Jauhar was known to have, at best, limited literacy, suggesting the intervention of an amanuensis (or more than one) in the production of even the first version of his narrative. This was then further polished and revised (producing some significant misunderstandings and distortions) by Ilahdad Faizi Sirhindi, who presented his own recension, titled *Tārīkh-i Humāyūn*, in court to the emperor Akbar in 1590.[79] This latter version seems to have enjoyed some success and a copy was

---

[77] One of the rare modern studies devoted to this text is Purnaqcheband, *Strategien der Kontingenzbewältigung*, which adopts a broadly narratological approach. But also see the recent work of Anooshahr, *Slavery in the Early Mughal World*.

[78] For a recent speculative interpretation of his origins as lying in the Ottoman empire, see Anooshahr, *Slavery in the Early Mughal World*.

[79] For the relationship between Jauhar's and Faizi Sirhindi's texts, see Ali, "The Use of Sources in Mughal Historiography", 368.

apparently held in a variety of princely and royal collections. On the other hand, the existence of the earlier "raw" copy (of which the first known manuscript dates to 1610) is certainly of greater significance, even if there was already a gap in it between Jauhar's oral expression and what was put down on paper. We may note the defensive tone that is struck from the outset, for Jauhar intended to guard his royal master's reputation from charges that he had been incompetent as both a political figure and a military leader. If the eighteenth-century quip had it that no man was a hero to his valet, Jauhar goes some way to contradicting this aphorism: "My only purpose is that all people may know that, despite so many travails and humiliations, he never compromised his self-respect (*istiqlāl-i khud*), and also that it may not be hidden that, such labours and hardships (*mushaqqat wa shaddat*) notwithstanding, he executed his office to the end."[80]

Jauhar has sometimes been criticised for his faults and deficiencies as a chronicler. Thus, a twentieth-century historian of Humayun's reign, while acknowledging his role as an "eyewitness" and "the most trustworthy authority", goes on to note: "He [Jauhar] is particularly deficient in chronology, he offers few dates and sometimes wrong dates — he commenced the work full thirty years after the death of Humayun. Besides, he cannot distinguish the trivial from the important; he will sometimes describe a petty incident in detail and dismiss an important matter in a few lines."[81] The judgment regarding when the work was commenced must be treated with caution, but the other remarks merit some elaboration. Since we know that Jauhar kept no written record of the events of his life as they occurred, the absence of chronological precision is hardly surprising. His memory for detail is in fact quite remarkable since he was certainly not formally trained in the mnemonic arts. There is, equally, reason to doubt whether the frequent Qur'anic citations, as well as the verses from poets of the Persian canon, came directly from Jauhar or from his amanuensis. Be that as it may, Jauhar was able to produce an extended narrative that went over a period of some two decades — quite a feat in itself.

[80] Jauhar, *Tazkirat*, in Thackston, ed. and trans., *Three Memoirs of Homayun*, 72.

[81] Ray, *Humāyūn in Persia*, 88.

As one follows the narrative from the early 1530s forward, certain tendencies are noticeable. What begins as a political chronicle of Humayun's campaigns against rebels and rivals gradually assumes other dimensions as well, as Jauhar increasingly places himself in the action (at times even using the first person, whether in the singular or the plural), usually as witness but sometimes even as actor. This progressive transformation is particularly visible as one leaves the formal setting of the court and royal camp, and Humayun's extended time of exile and wandering begins in the period following his defeat at the battle of Chausa in June 1539. As Humayun's following dwindled and the difficulties with his younger brother Mirza Kamran grew, one sees him becoming ever more dependent on a small group as he passes with a limited set of supplies and resources from Punjab into Sind. The narrative stresses the miserable condition of the former ruler but also hints broadly at some of his notorious weaknesses in this situation, often by putting critical remarks in the mouths of others – such as Mirza Hindal.

The frequent recourse to reported speech in Jauhar's text is a mark of its birth in orality and suggests that his real talents were those of a raconteur. The complaint regarding his inability to "distinguish the trivial from the important" stems from this very feature, especially as he resorts to reported speech for the most insignificant reasons – as against using it on occasions when it would seem warranted, such as an exhortation to soldiers on the eve of a battle, or a deathbed speech. Here is an example among many that can be found in his work, when news arrived of the birth of Humayun's son, Akbar, in 1542:

> When His Majesty the Padishah finished his prayers, the *amīrs* came to salute him. After that, the emperor said to me, Jauhar Aftabchi,
> "Didn't we entrust something to you for safekeeping?"
> "Yes", I said.
> "What was it?" he asked.
> "There were two things," I replied, "*shāhrukhīs* and a silver glove."
> There was also a musk bag.[82]

---

[82] Jauhar, *Tazkirat*, in Thackston, ed. and trans., *Three Memoirs of Homayun*, 111.

This serves as a prelude to an improvised ceremony for the distribution of gifts to mark the occasion, but the use of reported speech serves no rhetorical purpose other than to bring home Jauhar's proximity to Humayun. This is equally true of some other incidents reported in this part of the text, in one of which Jauhar jumps into a lake when tracking a deer to provide meat for Humayun's table; in another, he evokes the discussions over tactics when the emperor's party is attacked at night by bandits. But the narrative technique can at times be singularly effective, such as in a section towards the end of the text where Jauhar narrates the blinding of Mirza Kamran. The initial small talk between him and the Mirza, the reluctance of the soldiers to lay violent hands on the prince, Humayun's consequent anger and cursing (in Turkish, not Persian), as well as Kamran's courage and refusal to cry out when his eyes are finally pierced – these are all recounted in the simplest and most direct language.

A second narrative, which is also largely located in Humayun's reign – though spilling over into Akbar's – is by a Mughal soldier and official of somewhat higher social status than Jauhar, namely Bayazid Beg. It is considerably longer than that of the *āftābchī*, though not quite twice its length. Bayazid seems to have been from a family of Bukharan origin that had settled in Tabriz, and he joined Mughal service by coming into contact with Humayun during the monarch's phase of exile in Safavid Iran. Over the next four decades and more he played a variety of military and administrative roles in a number of different regions of the empire, rising by the end of his career to the relatively modest *mansab* rank of 300. It was in the late 1580s that he was solicited to write his memoirs, in circumstances that are laid out at the beginning of his text: a royal order had been passed that "any servants of court who had a taste for history should write, indeed that anyone who had any memories of the days of His Majesty Jannat-Ashyani Humayun Padishah's reign should include them." At this time Bayazid was working in the royal kitchens in a supervisory role as *bakāwal beg* (derived from the traditional household post of "taster" or *bökäül*). He thus was supplied with a scribe by the official historian Shaikh Abu'l Fazl ibn Mubarak and dictated his memoirs to him. The scribe insists in this introductory passage both on the weakness of the raconteur's memory because of advancing age, and on the fact that "Bayazid did not know how to read or write and had no rough draft of his work." It would seem that the work was completed in Lahore in 1590–1, by which time he had become quite an urban patron, building and repairing bridges, wells, mosques, and a bath.

Nevertheless, as Simon Digby has rightly pointed out, some of Bayazid's protestations in his *captatio benevolentiae* must be taken with a grain or more of salt: "Bayazid reproduces two date-verses he composed on the deaths of Mughal commanders, manipulations of the numerical value of letters of the *abjad* which imply a considerable degree of literacy", while also mentioning a passage in which he consults the *dīwān* of the poet Hafiz for omens and predictive purposes.[83] Further, if indeed Bayazid's last known official post was of *dārogha* and *amīn* of the royal treasury, as he claims, it would suggest some grasp of letters.

Bayazid's familial circumstances are also worth mentioning in this context. His older brother, who also entered Mughal service at much the same time as him, was a certain Shahberdi Beg who served with success in the north-west of the Mughal empire and was Bayazid's protector to a large extent at the early moments of his integration into the empire. The brother then experienced a radical change of heart and decided to abandon his military-administrative career for that of a dervish and mystic. We thus find him in Delhi in the late 1550s, living on the edges of Dinpanah, having become attached to the Chishti shrines of Nizam-ud-Din Auliya and Qutb-ud-Din Bakhtiyar Kaki. With the *nom de plume* of Bahram Saqqa, he is also known to have composed verse in Persian and Turkish and attracted a considerable popular following for his charitable acts, the existence of his following eventually drawing some hostile attention. Accused by jealous rivals of being an aggressive Shi'i (at much the time that the Shi'i *éminence grise* Bairam Khan had fallen from favour), Saqqa abandoned Delhi and Agra and made his way to western Bengal with the intention of taking a ship to Sarandip (Sri Lanka) on a pilgrimage.[84] He died in

---

[83] Digby, "Bayazid Beg Turkman's Pilgrimage", 177.

[84] See 'Abdul Wali, "The Antiquities of Burdwan"; and 'Abdul Wali, "Notes on

the early 1560s before he could embark, his tomb in Bardhaman becoming a significant site over later decades.

Bayazid Beg's own narrative is a very useful window into the culture of Mughal military and administrative service at a moment when its norms were yet to be stabilised or become routinised. We thus learn of the difficulties of coping with the pulls of loyalty to a variety of patrons from the imperial family downwards. Like Jauhar, Bayazid makes it clear that, even if he was himself of relatively lowly rank, he had had personal dealings with Humayun on numerous occasions. The mere fact of personal acquaintance was guarantee of very little, because he was never properly a part of Humayun's household, even though he had accompanied the emperor early on in visits to Mashhad and Tabriz. Rather, the question for someone of his background and status always remained one of finding suitable patrons who would allow him indirect access to the higher echelons of power, and thereby to fiscal and landed resources in the fledgling empire.

The first significant figure from this point of view for him was Husain Quli Sultan, who held the post of *muhrdār* (seal keeper) and whom he followed for several years until the latter was captured and killed by the forces of Mirza Kamran in 1550. Thereafter, Bayazid entered the service of Khwaja Jalal-ud-Din Mahmud, whom he served as *mīr sāmān* (intendant). However, the nature of such relationships was always tense since they entailed jockeying for small positional gains with rival servants as well as family members of the patrons. In this case, it was the family of the Khwaja which posed a particular problem to upward mobility, and so it was with some relief that Bayazid was able to make the transition some years later to a new patron whose star was on the ascendant, namely Mun'im Beg, later to be titled Mun'im Khan, a powerful Indian-born figure of Turani (Central Asian) origin.[85] This was a relationship that would last nearly two

---

Archaeological Remains in Bengal". The author provides some information on Saqqa's tomb and its inscriptions, as well as passages from his *dīwān*, in the Asiatic Society of Bengal, Kolkata, Oa 57 and Oa 363. Other copies may be found in the Khuda Bakhsh Library, Patna, No. 241, and the British Library, IO. 1822 (Ethé 1436).

[85] For an exploration of his career, see Khan, *Political Biography of a Mughal Noble*.

decades, and, though characterised by several ups and downs, may be termed the defining axis of Bayazid's career in Mughal service.

The first difficulty that had to be weathered was the transition of 1556 caused by the unexpected death of Humayun in an accident in Delhi. Given the fragility of Humayun's newly re-established dispensation, this led to challenges on various fronts, of which the best known is that led by Hemu, a Hindu former commander for the Afghan Sur dynasty, who marched towards Delhi from Bengal and enjoyed some military success against the Mughal forces of the new ruler Akbar. A secondary problem was in the north-west, where Bayazid found himself, and where one of Akbar's Timurid cousins from Badakhshan, Mirza Sulaiman, made a concerted attempt to gain hold of Kabul, the erstwhile stronghold of Mirza Kamran. Hemu was eventually defeated and killed in a rather close-run engagement in November 1556, of which Bayazid offers us a colourful hearsay account:

> Hemu set out to do battle with the emperor, [but] the sultans and khans shot Hemu before he reached the emperor. An arrow came from behind the elephant box in which he was seated and hit the infidel in the eye. He was immediately captured, and the news was taken to the emperor by Shah Quli Mahram, who was then an attendant of Bairam Khan. Later the infidel was placed under the emperor's elephant's foot, and the emperor said, "If you become a Muslim, I will spare your life." The infidel bastard refused to adopt Islam, so in the end the emperor struck him with his sword. From that date on, the emperor's name was written as Jalal-ud-Din Muhammad Akbar Shah Ghazi.[86]

This somewhat unsubtle attempt to make Akbar appear a champion of Islam is not entirely confirmed by other accounts of the battle. We learn moreover that Hemu was decapitated, and his head sent to Kabul, where Bayazid was personally charged with suspending it on the gates.

The next few years were spent in complex negotiations between Mun'im Khan and Akbar's court. The Khan did not fully trust the powerful regent Bairam Khan and preferred to bide his time and consolidate his position in the Kabul region, evading orders to visit the

---

[86] Bayazid, *Tārīkh-i Humāyūn*, in Thackston, ed. and trans., *Three Memoirs of Homayun*, 103.

court. He also acted as guardian for Akbar's half-brother Mirza Muhammad Hakim, who was resident in Kabul with his powerful mother and her family. It was in these years that Bayazid was fully initiated into the business of revenue collection (*tahsīl*), whereas earlier he seems to have been largely engaged in soldierly tasks. It was only in 1560, when Bairam Khan fell from grace, that Mun'im Khan and Bayazid were properly integrated into the Mughal centre, and the former was ceded substantial resources, the key post of *wakīl*, as well as the title of Khan-i Khanan. As an agent on his behalf, Bayazid was given administrative charge of the old Tughluq fortress of Hisar Firoza and its districts, north-west of Delhi, to which he remained attached for some years.

It turned out, however, that Mun'im Khan was not always the most adept either at politics or military management. This was shown in 1563, when he was sent to quell a rebellion by Mirza Hakim and his mother and signally failed to do so. We learn that in these years Bayazid himself received secret offers from Mirza Hakim but thought better of accepting them. This was a time both of Mughal territorial expansion and of periodic rebellions from disgruntled elements in the regime unhappy with some of the new administrative policies and arrangements. Bayazid resisted temptation and played the loyalist card, burnishing his credentials both as a revenue administrator and as a military commander who was able to defend Hisar Firoza.

As a consequence, we find him being placed in charge of what were presumably richer agricultural areas around Banaras (Varanasi) and Jaunpur, still as the agent of Mun'im Khan. However, one gathers that various other servants were all elbowing their way towards the Khan, and thus managed to insinuate that Bayazid was overbearing, disloyal, and corrupt (an accusation that would be repeated several times against him). These servants also managed to turn the powerful Raja Todar Mal, whose influence in Banaras was considerable, against Bayazid, apparently because of his religious bigotry (*ta'assub-i dīnī*). This led to a phase of some years that Bayazid refers to as his time as *durwesh*, when he withdrew from service and retired to his residence in Jaunpur, before being persuaded by Mun'im Khan to re-enter his employ and serve as his agent in court, as well as on a few military campaigns.

By the early 1570s Bayazid's thoughts turned increasingly to a project of making the *hajj*, which he was initially persuaded to postpone. It is clear that by this time, some fifteen years into his relationship with Mun'im Khan, matters had soured considerably between master and servant. Bayazid's criticisms of his master's judgement and actions, already clear on earlier occasions, become more frequent and strident with time. He was also surely aware that Mun'im Khan was progressively being marginalised at the court, and his despatch to the Jaunpur region as governor in 1567 set the seal on the process, as he was now perceived as "too old, too rigid, and too sensitive about his position as the elder Chaghtai noble" to be able to function in a court increasingly dominated by what have been termed "non-Turani upstarts".[87] Mun'im Khan did enjoy a last phase of military success against the Afghans in Bihar and Bengal, managing thereby to salvage some of his reputation both as a general and a diplomat. His death in November 1575 thus opened up the last phase of Bayazid's career and its narrative.

Though we do not know what precisely Bayazid's age was at this point, it is clear that it was too late for him to make a new beginning with a fresh patron. On the other hand, he had three sons whom he wanted to place in the Mughal apparatus, and this was proving difficult. He thus renewed his efforts to obtain permission to make the *hajj* and eventually received imperial permission for it in 1578. The Mughal capture of the port of Surat from the Gujarat sultans a few years earlier had made this project more feasible, it being now possible to board a ship directly from there for the Red Sea. In 1576 a prestigious party of several women from the Mughal royal family, led by Akbar's aunt Gulbadan Begam, had already set out from Surat on two ships, the *Salīmī* and *Ilāhī*.[88] We have dealt at length with Bayazid's pilgrimage account elsewhere and will therefore mention only its highlights.[89]

His departure was hindered, first by Mughal officials who were

---

[87] Khan, *Political Biography of a Mughal Noble*, 95.

[88] For details, see Moosvi, *People, Taxation, and Trade in Mughal India*, 244–6.

[89] Alam and Subrahmanyam, *Indo-Persian Travels in the Age of Discoveries*, 303–12.

suspicious of the liquid resources at his disposal (over Rs 100,000), and then by the Portuguese at Daman who wished to tax the ship. Sailing from Surat in mid March 1580, Bayazid's party made initial landfall at the port of Aden, where they encountered the Mughal royal party mentioned above, which was trying to make its way back to India. They then made their way to Mecca, and Bayazid would spend an extended period (around three years) in the Hijaz. During this time his wife and one of his sons died, and he himself decided in a despondent frame of mind to settle down in Mecca, after instructing his two surviving sons to return. However, news from India caused Bayazid to change this decision, and he then set sail hastily in an unfavourable season. Extended misadventures followed, first in the Hadramaut, and then in Gogha (in Gujarat) from which he was able to extricate himself with the greatest difficulty, returning to the Mughal court only in December 1584.

The last years of his life appear to have been spent in Lahore, after receiving a decent *jāgīr* and revenues. Though now partly an invalid on account of a paralytic stroke, it was in these waning years that Bayazid could dictate his memoirs and receive public acknowledgement in court, not only for the length of his service but his loyalty (*ikhlās*). He states that nine copies were made of the text, of which one was presumably for himself, two for the imperial library, two for the chronicler Shaikh Abu'l Fazl, one for each of the three princes, and one for Gulbadan Begam, whose direct acquaintance he had made in Aden. Even if the text itself would remain obscure thereafter, its contents (and to an extent its perspective) would live on through their partial absorption into the master-narrative of Shaikh Abu'l Fazl's *Akbar Nāma*.

It is Gulbadan who is the author of the last of the self-narratives that concern us here. This is the shortest of the four "successor" texts around Humayun's reign, and less than half the size of Bayazid's account. Nevertheless, its unique perspective has made it the object of several analyses in the decades since it was edited and translated early in the twentieth century. An extended narrative text authored by a prominent female figure is rare enough in the early modern Islamic empires, and this is all the more the case when the figure in question belongs to an important royal house. Despite the significant political role played by women in several of these polities, and notably in many branches of the Timurids in the fifteenth century, this did not translate into direct literary expression by them.[90] At the same time, literacy seems to have been quite common among them, and several even constituted libraries of their own when they settled in prominent centres such as Herat. In the relatively informal setting of military encampments, such as those that Babur was obliged to use for a good part of his "vagabondage", it appears likely that patriarchal norms were less strictly observed than in settled urban environments. It is thus not uncommon to find him referring to the prominent advisory role given to senior women in these spaces: "For tactics and strategy, there were few women like my grandmother Isan Daulat Begam. She was intelligent and a good planner. Most affairs were settled with her counsel."[91] This was Babur's maternal grandmother, but he was well aware from his paternal Timurid ancestors that sometimes things could also go badly wrong. The classic case was that of Gauhar Shad Agha, the junior wife of Mirza Shahrukh, who became extremely powerful on the death of her husband in 1447.[92] In the ensuing decade her power and patronage in Herat grew considerable as she implicated herself in various succession disputes involving her grandchildren and great-grandchildren. Eventually, in 1457, she was executed at the orders of Babur's grandfather Abu Sa'id Mirza, who was afraid of the extent of her influence; her execution proved an act for which he in turn had to pay dearly a decade later.

When Gulbadan, as she states, was "commanded to write" what she knew of the lives of her father Babur, and her half-brother Humayun, her great proximity to them no doubt rendered this task difficult and delicate. Since she had been born in around 1523, shortly before Babur's conquest of Hindustan, her direct knowledge of his earlier life and activities was relatively limited. Consequently, her text commences with a section drawn mostly from the *Bābur Nāma*, to which she obviously had access. It portrays her father in proudly heroic terms, as

---

[90] For a comparative perspective, see Havlioğlu, "On the Margins and Between the Lines".

[91] Babur, *The Baburnama*, trans. Thackston, 29.

[92] See the discussion in Arbabzadah, "Women and Religious Patronage".

someone who had struggled against and finally surmounted incredible odds. The author herself makes an appearance in the first person in March 1527, when she arrives in Hindustan from Kabul, together with her stepmother Maham Begam, and is affectionately received by her father, who "inquired much into my condition and held me in his lap for a long time."[93] Gulbadan then recounts the few remaining years of Babur's life, including a version of the battle of Khanwa and its outcome, and the celebrated anecdote of how he offered up his own life to save that of his ailing son Humayun.

The section that commences with Humayun's accession at the end of December 1530 would pose political problems since it inaugurates a narrative of the long fratricidal struggles between the new emperor and his half-brothers Kamran, 'Askari, and Hindal. Indeed, these struggles are a running thread all the way through to the abrupt end of the text, which terminates with the death of Hindal in an ambush and the subsequent blinding of Kamran. It is of course too much to demand of Gulbadan that she present matters in terms of a contest over Mughal "dynastic theory", but a good deal can be read between the lines of her account.[94] It becomes clear that Humayun and his followers believed he had certain overwhelming claims, not only as the oldest son but as the designated successor of his father. On the other hand, the Mongol tradition of "collegial" rule as well as Timurid precedent in the course of the fifteenth century left matters in far more murky waters.

The reader can discern where Gulbadan's primary loyalties lie in all these instances. Obviously, she cannot criticise Humayun beyond a certain point, so her language towards him is always circumspect, reverential, and formal. At the same time, a number of his prominent weaknesses cannot be avoided, whether his indecision in regard to his brothers, his tendency to sulk and throw tantrums, or his excessive (even obsessive) pursuit of women.[95] On the other hand, her main issue

---

[93] Gulbadan, *Humāyūn Nāma*, in Thackston, ed. and trans., *Three Memoirs of Homayun*, 12.

[94] The reference is to Dickson, "Uzbek Dynastic Theory". For a reflection in the Timurid context, see Markiewicz, *The Crisis of Kingship*, 151–91.

[95] This theme is explored at some length in Anooshahr, "The King Who Would Be Man".

is with Mirza Kamran, which culminates in a wholehearted condemnation of him towards the end of the text – to which we shall return briefly below.[96] A third half-brother, Mirza 'Askari, receives relatively little attention overall. However, it is clear that Gulbadan's greatest loyalty is consistently to her own older (full) brother Mirza Hindal, whose problematic actions she often attempts to pass over discreetly when his interests conflict directly with those of Humayun. An example of this occurs when Hindal orders the killing of the revered figure of Shaikh Bahlul Gwaliyari, whom his brother the emperor had sent to him in 1539 as an emissary, claiming that the Shaikh was secretly conspiring with the Afghans; several other instances of such conflict can be found throughout the text.[97] Her lamentations when Hindal was eventually killed in November 1551 are quite notable and include the extravagant claim that "Mirza Hindal gave his life in devoted service to the emperor." Of the fatal skirmish near Kabul she says: "In that very encounter [Hindal] was martyred. I know not which merciless tyrant put that inoffensive youth (*ān jawān-i kam āzār*) unjustly to the sword. Oh, would that pitiless blade had pierced my own heart and eyes or those of my son Sa'adat Yar or those of Khizr Khwaja Khan!"[98] The blame is laid squarely at the door of Mirza Kamran, described here as a "tyrant and fratricide (*zālim birādar kush*)". The passage may be contrasted with Bayazid's description of the same scene, in which Mun'im Khan, on being told by a weeping Humayun of Hindal's death, dryly responds: "It is one enemy less."[99] Gulbadan's view of the matter is quite different: "From that day on we never heard of anything good happening to Mirza Kamran. On the contrary, day by day he sank into greater and greater oblivion. His affairs became so ruined that luck itself was no longer a friend to

[96] On Mirza Kamran and his career, see the brief but dense study by Khan, *Mirza Kamran*.

[97] On the tomb of the assassinated Shaikh Bahlul (or Shaikh Phul), see Khan, "New Light on the History of Two Early Mughal Monuments". He was the brother of the celebrated Shattari mystic Muhammad Ghaus Gwaliyari.

[98] Gulbadan, *Humāyūn Nāma*, in Thackston, ed. and trans., *Three Memoirs of Homayun*, 65.

[99] Ibid.

Mirza Kamran."[100] She claims that he was eventually obliged to go to the court of the Afghan Surs for help, but that they turned him away with ill-disguised contempt, viewing him as a person without a sense of honour.

Gulbadan's text may be said to move between two modes, one in which the authorial first person (and role as an eyewitness) is more evident, and the other in which she adopts a more standard chronicling style since it concerns events in which she was herself not present. It is the former mode that dominates in the context of the 1530s, when she closely accompanies the activities in Humayun's court. Thereafter, when the emperor moves into exile, Gulbadan – now resident in Kabul – could not have followed his activities as directly, and must therefore have gathered information through hearsay and rumour, or retrospectively. The first-person narrative effectively resumes when Humayun returns from Iran and is able to take Kabul, and she is reunited with him after a gap of about five years. Historians have rightly emphasised the fact that Gulbadan pays attention to aspects of early Mughal court life which other, usually male, chroniclers tend to neglect or pass over rapidly.[101] An example of this is the "talismanic feast (*tūy-i tilism*)" held to mark Humayun's accession in Agra, where Gulbadan provides an elaborate account of the *begams* and *khānams* associated with the Timurids who were present. It is clear that, within a few years of Babur's initial victory, word of it had gone out to his dispersed relatives in Central Asia and Khurasan, for they flocked to Hindustan in substantial numbers, with elite women alone numbering nearly a hundred.[102] In turn, these women had to face considerable hardship as Humayun's star went into decline in the second half of the 1530s, with several of them being killed in the disaster at Chausa, and others having to scatter as the Sur regime came into place.

[100] Ibid., 66.

[101] The extended introduction by Annette Beveridge to her translation of the text (*The History of Humāyūn*, 1–79) was the first important intervention in this direction. More recently, see Lal, "Historicizing the Harem"; Lal, *Domesticity and Power*; and Zaman, "Instructive Memory".

[102] For a discussion, see Balabanlilar, "The Begims of the Mystic Feast", 123–28.

In this context, two groups managed to weather the storm somewhat, one of which remained attached directly to Humayun, and the other (including Gulbadan) taking refuge in Kabul under Mirza Kamran. A careful reading of her account reveals a number of interesting tensions in both contexts. Thus, while recounting Humayun's courtship of Hamida Banu (who was to give birth to his son and heir Akbar), Gulbadan stresses the reluctance of the bride and her family as well as the difficulties the alliance caused between Humayun and Hindal, to whose entourage Hamida Banu was attached. Another set of anecdotes concerns Kabul and its environs in the 1540s, which she portrays as a milieu in which a number of powerful women figures were present, among whom one could eventually count Mah Chuchak Arghun (d. 1564), who would become one of Humayun's wives and give birth to several of his later children.[103]

Taken as a whole, Gulbadan's text is revealing in certain respects but remarkably reticent in others. With the exception of a handful of occasions, notably deaths and reconciliations, the author usually gives away little of her emotions. Of her own married life with Khizr Khwaja Khan – a Chaghatayid second cousin who belonged to the eastern regions of Mughulistan – she says very little beyond the fact that he was more or less unlettered and played some role in the struggles between Humayun and Kamran.[104] One historian has thus written: "The author systematically eludes the reader looking for a record of her selfhood. Though scholars inevitably ransack the text for autobiographical content, the text yields little in this domain. Gulbadan is concerned with lives other than her own, and she narrates them to the exclusion of herself. At one level, she obeys an unwritten rule governing much premodern historiography that a woman should be seen, not heard."[105] This is perhaps an exaggerated judgment, for something of Gulbadan certainly emerges from her work, even if far less than her father in the *Bābur Nāma*. It is nevertheless interesting to return (as Rebecca Gould suggests) to an enigmatic verse that Gulbadan cites

---

[103] See Subrahmanyam, "A Note on the Kabul Kingdom".

[104] Khizr Khwaja Khan was the son of Aiman Khwaja Sultan, and the grandson of the well-known Ahmad Alaq, Babur's maternal uncle.

[105] Gould, "How Gulbadan Remembered", 188.

in the context of the diplomatic exchanges of Humayun and his
Afghan rivals:

> Although the self may be reflected in a mirror,
> the mirror image will not match the self.
> What a miracle to see oneself reflected
> through an other; this miracle is given by God.[106]

In Retrospect

By the end of the sixteenth century a small but not insignificant body
of self-narratives had emerged in the context of a Timurid–Mughal
empire, by that time in the third generation of its existence in India.
This body, which we have rapidly surveyed in this introduction, has
attracted the attention of historians, who have as a consequence been
able to provide a larger context for what could otherwise be seen as a
text that stands in isolation, namely the *Bābur Nāma*. It is also interesting in this context to mention the contrast with neighbouring Safavid Iran, where the sixteenth century yields only one important prose
self-narrative, namely the somewhat controversial *Tazkira-yi Shāh
Tahmāsp*, possibly produced some time in the early 1560s. Thus, while
in their general historiographical production the Safavids and the
Mughals show parallels and at times interconnections, their self-narratives show a divergence.[107]

The question of such self-narratives would, however, take on an
interesting twist in the seventeenth century. In the 1630s, during the
reign of Shahjahan, an individual by the name of Mir Abu Talib Husaini Turbati appeared in the court, claiming that he had, at some earlier
time, gained access while in the Red Sea (Yemen or the Hijaz) to an
autobiographical narrative of Timur himself, written in Turkish. This
was apparently through the Ottoman governor there, Cafer Paşa,
whose administration lasted from 1607 to 1616. Mir Abu Talib had
then translated the work into Persian, and it was presented to the

---

[106] Ibid., 187. Also see Gulbadan, *Humāyūn Nāma*, in Thackston, ed. and
trans., *Three Memoirs of Homayun*, 34.

[107] Quinn, *Persian Historiography Across Empires*.

Mughal court with the title of *Wāqi'āt-i Sāhibqirānī*, or alternatively the *Malfuzāt wa Tuzukāt* of Timur. The Mughal emperor was apparently so impressed by this work that he took to citing it regularly and also had a copy sent to his son Aurangzeb.

Since the language was eventually judged too plain, a more ornate work was then produced by a certain Muhammad Afzal Bukhari, who also "corrected" the text by comparing it with standard Timurid historiography. This improved text enjoyed quite a wide circulation. In the intervening centuries, the authenticity of the tome has been hotly debated. By the end of the nineteenth century it was generally taken to be a late fabrication to flatter the pretensions of Shahjahan who had developed a particular fascination with Timur. In a more recent examination, Irfan Habib has urged the contrary – that the text be treated with greater caution and respect than it has hitherto met. In his view, Mir Abu Talib may indeed have had a Turkish text at his disposal that has since been lost. And, rather than seeing it as a seventeenth-century forgery, Habib suggests that the text "might still have been compiled soon after his [Timur's] death, and many of the documents in it must have been extracted from official records. In such a case, it may indeed represent a very early post-Timur historical tradition."[108]

Further work on the Persian text and its different variants may help shed light on whether this bold hypothesis is sustainable. It is certainly remarkable that no copy of such a Turkish work was found within an extensive inventory of the Ottoman palace library that was made in 1502–4.[109] Did this text then precede the *Bābur Nāma* or come to be written after it? Was it anything else but a part of the very large body of apocrypha on Timur that came to be produced in the seventeenth and eighteenth centuries?[110] Whatever the case, it was not known to the authors of the sixteenth century whom we have considered, and thus had no influence on them.

Our purpose in this chapter has been to provide a launching pad for the discussion that follows, in which each chapter considers either

---

[108] Habib, "Timur in the Political Tradition and Historiography", 308.
[109] Necipoğlu, Kafadar, and Fleischer, eds., *Treasures of Knowledge*.
[110] See Sela, *The Legendary Biographies of Tamerlane*.

a single text or a small group of texts. These narratives will carry us from the late sixteenth century to the middle of the eighteenth century – what we may term the "high Mughal period". Since the works we will be examining are far less known than those of Babur or Gulbadan, we will follow them with some care, laying out their intricacies in some detail. In this respect we will return to the broad methodology laid out in our early book on Indo-Persian travels of reading "with the grain". Obviously, our aim is neither to produce an encyclopaedic work, nor to substitute the labour of critical editions and translations that such works often call for.

2

Faizi's Way

My travelling companions say, "O friend, be watchful,
for caravans are attacked suddenly."
I answer, "I am not careless, but alas!
What help is there against robbers that attack a watchful heart?"

– Abu'l Faiz "Faizi"[1]

Imperial Claim-making

B Y THE LATE sixteenth century, South Asia, once the domain of a set of quite compact regional states, many of which were the offshoots of the old Delhi Sultanate, had increasingly come under the sway of a single, vast, truly imperial polity – that of the Mughals (or Indian Timurids).[2] We know a good deal more about the Mughals than we do about the South Indian state of Vijayanagara, for instance, precisely because they have left us with very rich sources, ranging from their celebrated and elaborate chronicles (*tawārīkh*), to administrative orders and documents (*farmāns*, *sanads*, and the like), to court poetry, an enormous body of paintings, and a set of quite diverse narrative sources that span a significant social spectrum. With the Mughals, as with the earlier sultanates, one can find Sufi collective biographies (*tazkiras*) and the "table-talk" (*malfūzāt*) of saints, but one can also explore materials both in Persian and the vernacular languages that capture

---

[1] Abu'l Fazl, *Ā'īn-i Akbarī*, vol. 1, trans. Blochmann, 555.
[2] The most useful general account of the Mughals remains Richards, *The Mughal Empire*.

the fine grain of individual experience far better than for the earlier centuries. Besides materials in Persian and Turkish, like those referred to in the previous chapter, we have the occasional text in Hindi like the *Ardhakathānaka*, the autobiography in verse of a Jain merchant called Banarasidas.[3] Banarasi, deftly managing to circumvent the generic conventions in which he found himself, succeeded in composing a text that is by turns humorous, ironic, and melancholy, while also conveying the experiences of a middling and not very successful merchant who navigated the reigns of Akbar and Jahangir in North India. We learn of his religious uncertainties and tergiversations, of his dealings with slippery partners, his marriages and his children.

By the time of Banarasi's birth in the mid 1580s, the Mughal empire was a very different affair from the insecure entity it had been at the death of Humayun in 1556. The two most expansive decades were arguably those from 1556 and 1576, beginning with the defeat of the Afghans and their auxiliaries at Panipat and ending with the execution of Da'ud Khan Karrani at Rajmahal. Thereafter, Mughal expansion in Bengal stalled somewhat, to resume only in the 1610s; and after Mughal successes in Kashmir, Odisha, and Sind in the 1580s and 1590s, the plans for a major expansion into the Deccan also failed to materialise in the face of opposition in Ahmadnagar. Nevertheless, the empire of Akbar by 1580 was already the most populous and resource-rich polity in the Islamic world.

In the last months of Humayun's reign, the shipwrecked Ottoman admiral Seydi 'Ali Re'is had appeared at his court and boasted of how the domains of his master, Sultan Süleyman, were far vaster and more diverse than those of the Timurids in India.[4] Some three decades later, such a boast would have sounded rather hollow. The Mughals claimed that they had a revenue capacity (*jama'*) of Rs 90 million in 1580, and even if the actual collections (or *hāsil*) would have been below that figure, this was perhaps as much as eight or

---

[3] Lath, *Ardhakathānaka*. For arguably the best analysis of this work, see Snell, "Confessions of a 17th-Century Jain Merchant"; also Dalmia, *Fiction as History*, 71–81.

[4] See the discussion in Alam and Subrahmanyam, *Indo-Persian Travels in the Age of Discoveries*, 110–14.

nine times the silver value of Ottoman revenues in 1600.[5] Four major provinces (or *subas*) – those of Delhi, Agra, Lahore, and Gujarat – accounted for well over half that amount.

Awash in liquid resources, it was now possible for the Mughals to embark on a series of conspicuous projects, reorganising older cities such as Agra and Lahore but also building new ones such as the chimeric project of Fathpur Sikri in the 1570s. This was also the period when a new institution of numerical ranking (or *mansab*) was reported as a way of organising both the *umarā'* and lesser members of the Mughal military-fiscal system. Initially linked to the control of cavalry resources, the *mansab* would grow more complex and arcane in its actual workings over the decades, but it remained central to the Mughal political system through the seventeenth century and into the first half of the eighteenth century. The Mughals had understood, after their severe defeats by the resurgent Afghans in the 1530s, that the key to military success in India lay in mastering what has been termed the "military labour market".[6] This meant that an elaborate system of intermediaries had to be constructed and maintained between the imperial court and the rural areas from which the common soldiery came. To be sure, the Mughals also had their prestigious forces of heavy cavalry (*tābinān*, and below them *ahadīs*) and artillery, the latter an aspect to which Babur had already devoted precocious attention in the 1520s, and which could prove crucial in siege warfare. But the long and attritional combats against the Afghans in eastern India, which endured through the 1570s and 1580s (and of which Bayazid was something of a veteran), were eventually resolved by the fact that the Mughals proved in the last analysis to be able to recruit more and better soldiers as well as ensure their loyalty. This had not always been the case.[7]

Their weighty military apparatus was thus key to Mughal dominance over much of the Indo-Gangetic plain by 1580. The question remained of how they would manage these conquered territories.

[5] Karaman and Pamuk, "Ottoman State Finances". The authors estimate Ottoman state revenues annually in the period 1600–9 at 122.6 tons of silver, which translates to Rs 10.7 million.

[6] See the fundamental contribution of Kolff, *Naukar, Rajput and Sepoy*.

[7] See Digby, "Dreams and Reminiscences of Dattu Sarvani".

One way forward would have been to maintain a set of dispersed garrisons and negotiate with a variety of local power holders (or zamindars of varying descriptions) for tribute. This appears to have been the manner in which the sultans of Delhi functioned for much of the thirteenth century. But the advisers of Akbar in the 1560s and 1570s were obviously far more ambitious. This may have been partly the consequence of the progressive dilution in these years of the power and influence (if not the actual number) of the Turanis, and the emergence of a diverse group of "new men", including several Khatris who had earlier served the Afghans and understood how Sher Shah's fiscal apparatus had penetrated the countryside.[8]

To rework a celebrated formulation, then, we may say that the Mughals in this phase wished to move from a situation of simple dominance to one of hegemony, from the overt and oppressive violence of the conquest-state to a more subtle conception of the relationship between rulers and ruled. This move involved multiple dimensions, including a widening of the social basis of recruitment into the *umarā*, a political compromise permitting major Rajput lineages to retain their *watan jāgīrs* (or home territories) if they would accept Mughal suzerainty (and at times intermarriage), as well as other ostentatious gestures intended to convey an image of Mughal justice (*'adl*) that would bring them wider acceptance in a settled agrarian society. In turn, such actions created enormous tensions in court society itself, which came to be reflected in the high literary production of the half-century of Akbar's reign. The swings in the ruler's own personal positions on several key questions, such as the imposition of *jizya*, only added to the volatility of the mix.

The Power of the Pen

Despite the instability of his reign, it would appear that Humayun was able to attract a certain number of intellectuals to his court, whether from within India or from lands further west. Perhaps the

---

[8] They included figures such as the celebrated Todar Mal, but also Parmanand (one of his relatives), and Pitar Das, who had begun as a modest military accountant.

most celebrated was the historian Khwandamir (d. *c.* 1534), who had already arrived in India during the last years of Babur's reign, and who went on to write at least one intriguing work dedicated to Humayun. Also of significance, though relatively neglected, is the mystic and prolific poet Hamid bin Fazlullah Jamali (d. 1536), who began a long career under the Lodis that ended during Humayun's rule, making him a valuable figure of continuity between the two regimes.[9] To this one can add at least half a dozen other figures, including Muslih-ud-Din Lari and Muhammad Yusufi Herawi, the former known for his expertise in a number of scientific domains (his career ended among the Ottomans), and the latter a physician who authored an important and widely cited work of *inshā'* – *Badā'i' al-inshā'* – in the 1530s.

To several of these individuals Humayun's attention had been drawn because of his own predilection for mathematics, astronomy, and cosmography. But in the case of Yusufi it would appear that the attraction lay in this scholar having produced a form of political theory that might extricate the figure of the ruler from the tight web of poisonous familial relationships in which the emperor was bound. The forced leave of absence from Hindustan that Humayun was obliged to take from about 1540 meant that the proposals in Yusufi's *Badā'i' al-inshā'* could never be fully discussed, let alone implemented. This text, as Ali Anooshahr has suggested, "was an attempt to raise the position of the emperor above his kinsmen," even as its author was "aware of the potential pitfalls that such a transition would entail" and tried to "assuage the anxiety caused by this rupture through prescribing appropriate responses."[10]

The growing importance and resources of the court of Akbar in the 1560s obviously acted as a magnet among politically oriented intellectuals of various stripes. Though we have a good deal of information on them – whether poets, physicians, theologians, or others broadly classified as *'ulamā'* – it is somewhat surprising that we lack a systematic modern prosopography for them of the kind we

---

[9] For his career, see the useful remarks in Bashir, "India as a Sufi Spacetime".
[10] Anooshahr, "Letter-Writing and Emotional Communities".

have for the military-fiscal elite – or "nobility", as the higher *man-sabdārs* and *umarā'* are often approximately termed.[11] The Delhi Sultanate had not been able to produce anything resembling the Chinese "examination system" that had been consolidated during the Song Dynasty, with its three levels culminating in the *jinshi* classification which opened the way to high office.[12] What this meant was that the Mughal court in the 1560s, like any other re-gional South Asian court of the same period, had inherited an im-provised form of triage in which supplicants were either accepted or set aside. This seems to have functioned on the basis of the twin criteria of competence and compatibility, meaning that one had to have a set of skills but also the capacity to insert oneself into a com-petitive system of patron–client relationships extending all the way up to the emperor and his immediate family. At the same time, it was hardly the ambition of every provincial *'ālim* to join the ranks of the courtly intellectuals, and many were content with their ex-istence as gentry in the *qasba* settlements and small towns of north-ern India.

A complicating factor was the ongoing religious turbulence of the sixteenth century which – it should be recalled – was the tenth cen-tury of the Islamic calendar, inaugurated in 901 AH (1495–6). This was a period when a series of complex and intertwined millenarian movements arose across a wide space in Eurasia, extending from South Asia all the way to the Mediterranean. If some of these have long been recognised, such as the heterodox movement that propelled the Safavid Shah Isma'il to power in Iran in the early sixteenth century, others have attracted the systematic attention of historians only in the last generation or so.

In the case of South Asia, the sixteenth century saw the rise to prominence of the so-called Mahdawiya, a movement that emerged in Gujarat in the 1490s under the impulsion of Sayyid Muham-mad Jaunpuri (1443–1505), a former Chishti Sufi who declared himself to be the messiah of the tenth Islamic century. His followers

---

[11] The historian most responsible for the perpetuation of this terminology was M. Athar Ali. See Ali, *The Mughal Nobility*; Ali, *The Apparatus*.

[12] See Elman, *Civil Examinations and Meritocracy*.

provoked a military conflict with the Gujarat Sultan Muzaffar in the early 1520s in which they were roundly defeated; thereafter they spread both into the Deccan and the Bayana region, not far from the zone where the early Mughals and then the Afghan Surs had their centres of power. This led to a second conflict during the reign of Islam Shah Sur (1545–54), centring around the figures of Shaikh 'Abdullah Niyazi and Shaikh 'Ala'i Bayanwi, both Mahdawi activists who, it is stated, had enjoyed considerable success in drawing prominent merchants (*tujjār*) and landed elites (*dihqānān*) to their cause as well as in challenging orthodox *'ulamā'* to public debates. Both shaikhs were severely punished, and Shaikh 'Ala'i was finally brutally executed.

The echoes of this repression were still very much in the air in the early years of Akbar's reign, when major *'ulamā'* such as Shaikh 'Abdul Nabi and 'Abdullah Sultanpuri (who had been Shaikh al-Islam and was later titled Makhdum ul-Mulk) wished to be vigilant against the recrudescence of forms of heterodoxy among the faithful. A figure who was therefore seen as problematic in this context was Shaikh Mubarak Nagauri, who had migrated to Agra from western India during the reign of Sher Shah and set up a successful madrasa in the city, building a reputation for "his piety, his poverty, [and] his striving in the path of holiness" – as one of his disciples-turned-critics wrote.[13]

Shaikh Mubarak is principally known to posterity not for his own achievements or writings but for those of his oldest sons, Abu'l Faiz (1547–1595) and Abu'l Fazl (1551–1602), both born when Shaikh Mubarak was in his forties. It is the first, better known by his poetic name of Faizi, who is the central figure in this chapter, but it is best to begin with the second, more celebrated, son.

Abu'l Fazl has attracted ample attention from historians for his multiple talents and imposing intellectual profile.[14] His rise to prominence began in the 1570s, when he entered Mughal courtly life

---

[13] 'Abdul Qadir Badayuni, *Muntakhab*, trans, vol. 3, 110; text, vol. 3, 67.

[14] No fully satisfactory modern study exists of Shaikh Abu'l Fazl, but see Rizvi, *Religious and Intellectual History.* Compare this with the excellent study of his contemporary in the Ottoman court by Fleischer, *Bureaucrat and Intellectual.*

and where he remained a central figure for nearly three decades. A stylist with a formidable command of Persian (but also of other languages), he put this to use in producing a very large body of prose: chronicles, encyclopaedic works, letters, translations, and more abstract reflections with a philosophical flavour, couched in an oblique idiom that became his hallmark. Of these writings, two have been particularly prominent. The first is the major chronicle entitled the *Akbar Nāma*, which begins with a long chronological sweep before entering into the history of the conquest of India by the Timurids, and the reigns of Humayun and Akbar. The third part of the text is made up of the *Āʾīn-i Akbarī*, an encyclopaedic work regarding various aspects of Mughal administration, with sections on the geography and ethnography of India, prominent personalities of the time, and so on. Though not entirely unprecedented in the Perso-Islamic tradition, there is no doubt that the *Āʾīn* surpasses any of its predecessors in terms of sheer ambition and coverage.[15]

The second major work of Abu'l Fazl that has consistently retained the attention of readers is his *inshāʾ* – or belles-lettres collection – which shows him at work in a variety of contexts, including a diplomatic one where he produced letters for Akbar's correspondence with important figures both within the Islamic world and outside it (the celebrated letter from the early 1580s to the *dānāyān-i firang*, for example). A tribute to the importance of this work of *inshāʾ* in the Mughal world of letters is the production of apocryphal versions (with falsifications) of it that can be found in some manuscripts.

Towards the end of his *Āʾīn-i Akbarī*, Shaikh Abu'l Fazl penned an intriguing section that was meant to serve as a brief autobiography – *ahwāl-i musannif*, "an account of the author" – which it is clear was intended to move between "life" and "times (*atwār*)".[16] In it he notes that his initial intention had been to produce "a separate volume which should be a source of instruction to the intelligent who look afar," with a combination of family history and "strange incidents" from his

---

[15] For a reconsideration of this work, which also covers much familiar ground, see Speziale and Ogura, eds, "Imperial Historiography".

[16] Abu'l Fazl, *Āʾīn-i Akbarī*, trans. Blochmann and Jarrett, vol. 3, 478–524; text, vol. 2, 258–83.

own life, but that this project had been eventually abandoned. Nevertheless, he briefly recounts his ancestry, beginning with a Shaikh Musa from Yemen who had migrated to Siwistan (in Sind), and then his grandfather Shaikh Khizr who, "impelled with the desire of visiting the saints of India", had settled in the town of Nagaur. This was where Abu'l Fazl's father Shaikh Mubarak was born in 1505.

Mubarak is described as something of a prodigy who by the age of fourteen had mastered the conventional curricula. Thereafter he wished to travel, but, encountering the opposition of his widowed mother, instead became a disciple in Nagaur itself of Shaikh Fayyazi Bukhari, who it is stated was a direct student of the grand Central Asian Naqshbandi Sufi Khwaja 'Ubaidullah Ahrar. According to Abu'l Fazl, his father was very much a Hanafi, but open-minded and well acquainted with the other legal schools as well. After his mother's death, Shaikh Mubarak finally began to travel. In Ahmedabad he was exposed to the work of a number of masters and kept company with Sufis from a number of different orders. Finally, in 1543, he decided to move to the Sur capital of Agra where he came under the protection of the wealthy and influential Mir Rafi'-ud-Din Iji (or Safavi), an Iranian migrant from the Shiraz region. He also contracted an advantageous marriage and began to think of founding a family of his own.

With Shaikh Mubarak's fast-growing fame as a teacher and savant, the Sur rulers Sher Shah and Islam Shah both – so Abu'l Fazl claims – offered him stipends and revenue-free grants which he stoutly refused. However, in the early 1550s he became embroiled in the controversy surrounding the Mahdawi Shaikh 'Ala'i Bayanwi, for whom he obviously had a good deal of sympathy. It would appear that, from this time on, Shaikh Mubarak was regularly at the centre of a number of disputes and controversies and suspected of adhering to a variety of heterodox views. In Abu'l Fazl's portrayal of matters this was nothing but petty jealousy and intrigue on the part of Mubarak's intellectual rivals, who were incapable of comprehending his independence of mind, and unconventional spirit. What he regarded as eclecticism was seen by Mubarak's critics as his opportunism. The return to power of the Mughals, Humayun and then Akbar, in the mid 1550s did not immediately arrange matters for him either.

Abu'l Fazl thus begins his self-narrative with an extended defence of his father in the context of a series of problems that went into the early 1570s. It is interesting that he still regarded this as necessary in the 1590s, when his text was written. The reader is left somewhat perplexed by the long and melodramatic account of Shaikh Mubarak's persecution by his enemies in the 1560s, the more so because it is exceedingly vague on most of the concrete details. The enemies are never named, nor the friends, nor the several duplicitous courtiers who pretended to be friends but turned out enemies. We learn of an episode in which the Shaikh and his two oldest sons fled his house at night on being warned that a great conspiracy was being mounted against him, but this turned out to be a trap since flight was taken by some as an indication of guilt. A period of wandering followed, in which they were obliged to seek refuge with a number of friends and acquaintances, while unpleasant rumours about Mubarak circulated in the court.

The intellectual milieu of Agra at this time is described by Abu'l Fazl in disdainful terms: he writes of being surrounded by "double-faced friends, determined enemies, base and cruel men, and timeservers banded together in pursuit."[17] This time in the wilderness, as it were, seems to have left a profound effect on Abu'l Fazl and stiffened his resolve to become a political actor rather than a victim of machinations. At some point the tide turned in Shaikh Mubarak's favour and he and his oldest son Faizi were reintroduced into the court through the intercession of an unnamed person (whom we know from other sources to have been the powerful *amīr* Mirza 'Aziz Koka). After the elapse of some years, Abu'l Fazl also entered court, which had by now moved from Agra to Fathpur Sikri. As he puts it in his usual style: "I was carried from the hermitage of seclusion to the court of worldly intercourse and the gate of prosperity was opened and I obtained the summit of distinction." This meteoric rise would occupy the latter half of the 1570s, and its circumstances are passed over quite rapidly in his narrative. By the early 1580s the Jesuit Antoni de Montserrat, resident

---

[17] Abu'l Fazl, *Ā'īn- Akbarī*, trans. Blochmann and Jarrett, vol. 3, 504; text, vol. 2, 271.

for a time in the court, painted a vivid if exaggerated portrait of Abu'l Fazl's views and the extent of his influence, terming him "the King's Jonathan".[18]

A few interesting features stand out in this section of Abu'l Fazl's narrative. One is his mention of a visit to the important Chishti *khānqāhs* in Delhi with his father, the only direct mention of the influence of a group of Sufis on his formative years. Two figures, Qutb-ud-Din Bakhtiyar Kaki and Nizam-ud-Din Auliya, even seem to have appeared to Shaikh Mubarak when he was in a liminal state between sleeping and waking. A second point worth remarking, which is carried into the next section of the narrative, is the contrast he draws between himself and his older brother Faizi. Abu'l Fazl suggests that his path into the world of learning was a more tortured one than his brother's, and that after some years of precocity he had fallen into a state of apathy and difficulty. However, he was eventually able to overcome these mental obstacles and hesitations, and with the aid of his prodigious memory emerged by his later teens a somewhat brash young savant willing to challenge even senior figures in public. In contrast, he paints Faizi as immensely talented but politically naïve, and therefore apt to misjudge the tenor of situations, as could be seen during the phase of "internal exile" that the two brothers had had to endure with their father.

In sum, with the exception of these occasional psychological insights, Abu'l Fazl is willing to give away very little of himself in his self-narrative. He does mention one of his earliest memories, when a famine struck Agra in 1556, accompanied by a plague epidemic. Another brief but striking anecdote concerns a public debate with an unnamed senior scholar (possibly Makhdum ul-Mulk) in about 1570, when Abu'l Fazl, who was full of "the conceit of learning and exuberant youth", apparently managed to humiliate his adversary. This capacity as a polemicist would eventually serve him well in court. We learn moreover that he acquired four wives, but do not gather their names or the families to which they belonged: one was a North Indian Muslim, another a Hindu, and one each Persian and Kashmiri. By his twentieth year Abu'l Fazl had had a son named 'Abdur Rah-

---

[18] Monserrate, *The Commentary of Father Monserrate*, 54.

man through the first wife, and at the age of forty he was already a grandfather. We also learn of his extended family, with six brothers and half-brothers besides Faizi, several of whom appear to have entered the courtly milieu in the wake of their older siblings. As he concludes his brief text of self-presentation he notes – with a certain lucidity – that he had both admirers and enemies, with the latter accusing him of worldliness and even "unbelief and apostasy (*kufr wa ilhād*)", and the former seeing him as a paragon of courage, spiritual unity, and understanding.

Introducing Faizi

We now turn to the central figure for the purposes of this chapter, namely Shaikh Mubarak's older son Shaikh Abu'l Faiz "Faizi", to whom several references have already been made.[19] Faizi, or Fayyazi as he later called himself, was like his brother an extremely prolific and versatile author, in particular of poetic works in Persian, and was rewarded for this by being named the third poet laureate (*malik al-shu'rā'*) at the court of Akbar from 1588.[20] Born in Agra in 1547, he – as we have seen – suffered the vicissitudes of his father's up-and-down career and was eventually introduced into the Mughal court around the age of twenty, where he rapidly made a strong impression. He had the misfortune of being asthmatic and died at the relatively young age of forty-eight on 5 October 1595 in Lahore, where his father had passed away two years earlier. It seems he was buried at first in the Ram Bagh at Agra, but perhaps later transferred to another family mausoleum near Sikandra. He only attained the somewhat modest rank of 400 within the ranking of the Mughal *mansabdārī* system but appears to have been, all the same, a man of some means.

Ranked first among the poets of his age by his brother Abu'l Fazl, who stated grandiosely that "the gems of thought in his poetry

---

[19] For biographical details, see Rahman, "Fayzi, Abu'l-Fayz", 457–9, and Ansari, "Faydi", 870–2; and for a more elaborate treatment, Hadi, *Mughalon ke malik*, 81–145.

[20] We have explored some aspects of Faizi's work, focusing in particular on his *masnawī* composition *Nal-Daman* in an earlier essay: Alam and Subrahmanyam, "The Afterlife of a Mughal *Masnavī*", 46–73.

will never be forgotten", Faizi was equally praised for his technical skills by Mulla 'Abdul Qadir Badayuni, otherwise no great admirer of his: "In many separate branches of knowledge, such as poetry, the composition of enigmas, prosody, rhyme, history, philology, medicine and prose composition, Shaikh Faizi had no equal in his time."[21] Badayuni had been a disciple of Shaikh Mubarak and knew Faizi well for some forty years, even before the latter was first presented to Akbar's court.[22] It was an uneasy proximity, as we gather from the other side of Badayuni's judgement of Faizi:

> He was a master of malevolent activity, idle jests, conceit, pride, and malice, and an epitome of hypocrisy, baseness, dissimulation, love of pomp, arrogance, and ostentation. All Jews, Christians, Hindus, and fire-worshippers, not to speak of Nizaris and Sabahis [Isma'ilis], held him in the very highest honour for his heresy, his enmity to the followers of Islam, his reviling of the very fundamental doctrines of our faith, his contemptuous abuse of the noble companions [of the Prophet] and those who came after them, and of holy Shaikhs, both dead and living, and of his unmannerly and contemptuous behaviour towards all learned, pious and excellent men, both in secret and openly, and both by day and by night.[23]

Yet, despite his many enemies, who included the powerful Shaikh 'Abdul Nabi, Faizi came to occupy a number of successive positions of some significance: named tutor to Prince Murad in 1579, he was, two years later in June 1581, appointed *sadr* of the regions of Agra, Kalpi, and Kalinjar. Like his younger brother, Faizi was quite clearly no orthodox Muslim, as emerges not only from Badayuni's bitter denunciation but from his own writings; on the other hand, he was certainly a monotheist, albeit with a rather ambiguous relationship towards the Prophet, whom he scarcely mentions.

Unlike Abu'l Fazl, Faizi did not write a prose account describing his life's trajectory. He did however write a *qasīda* of over two hundred

---

[21] 'Abdul Qadir Badayuni, *Muntakhab al-Tawārīkh*, trans. Haig, vol. 3, 411–12.

[22] Again, in his case, we lack a sophisticated biography; but see Abbas, *Abdul Qadir Badauni*, and especially the reconsideration in Anooshahr, "Mughal Historians".

[23] Badayuni, *Muntakhab al-Tawārīkh*, trans. Haig, vol. 3, 413.

verses in which he says something about himself, albeit in a convoluted vein.[24] This poem, entitled *Nashīd al-safar* (The Song of Travel) opens with a preface encapsulating the chief achievements of Faizi's life, employing the metaphor of a journey, and making use of the term *faiz* (grace) from his name numerous times.

The first part of this text seems to have been composed around the poet's fortieth year, by which time he had already climbed many figurative mountains and braved many jungles. His life had thus been a solitary journey among different sorts of people, some sad and some happy, a trajectory so unique that he could count no competitor except the angel Gabriel. The poet notes that he was born in the month of Sha'ban 954 AH, which was such an extraordinary event that all the constellations of the zodiac had rejoiced, while rain poured down in the Indian spring to greet this new guest on earth. Upon his birth his father spoke the words of faith into his ear. Seven days later Shaikh Mubarak, remarking the graces (*fuyyūz*) of the newborn, decided to name him accordingly as Abu'l Faiz.

Very quickly, the future poet grew up beyond childish play and began to be taught by his father, who was a veritable ocean of knowledge and a true companion of the legendary prophet Khizr. Mubarak's wisdom is spoken of as being such that he could penetrate beyond duality and perceive the Unity of Existence. Faizi's early studies included some knowledge of medicine (*tibb*) which he would consolidate later, but he began very early to compose poetry and songs. He also learnt Qur'anic interpretation, a great deal about the hadith, the rules and regulations of Arabic and Persian grammar, and acquired full knowledge of Hanafi jurisprudence (*fiqh*). Faizi also began quickly to understand the differences between distinct faiths (*adyān* and *mazāhib*) and the sad fact that many people had elevated the idols of falsehood, claiming them to be truth. This led him to a deeper study of *falsafā* – on the inspiration of the ancients in Greece and Rome. Rather than simply accepting what was received wisdom, he studied all this with discernment, including a reflection on the making of

---

[24] For a reproduction of the text, and a discussion, see Grobbel, *Der Dichter Faidī und die Religion Akbars*.

creation in its myriad forms, on earth and in the heavens. In sum, he wishes the reader to understand that, even within his youth, he had become a complete and well-rounded scholar.

Faizi's thirst for knowledge persisted and he wished to venture further. One possibility would have been to espouse the way of the Sufis. To do this, he says, he would have had to bid farewell to his own Self (*widā'-i khud az khud namūdam*), and to move, so to speak, from the earth in the direction of the sun. Eventually, in his quest, he reached the Court of Divine Grace (*taufiq*), where the doorkeeper counselled him, seeing that he had become lost and disoriented. Taking his guidance, Faizi moved on, pursuing his path until he reached the court of Akbar, shaking the chain at the door.

Those who saw him there were astonished at his boldness and his declarations of himself as a manifestation of the Grace of God, a magician born in Hindustan who could challenge even the best singers of Khorasan. Here Faizi lavishes unstinting praise on his own compositions and their effect on the whole world. A divine voice then spoke welcoming him, upon which he declared himself present (*labbaik*). Reaching the ruler's mansion (*aiwān*), he saw a great king (*khadīw*), one truly worthy of praise: wisdom was his minister, and he provided light to the whole world. On reaching this place, Faizi felt fortune smile upon him at last and tell him that this should be his point of rest – which made him believe he should seek a position in this sultan's court.

Several verses follow in praise of Akbar, the ruler of seven kingdoms, the manifestation of wisdom, the master of time and space (*zamān-o-zamīn*). Indeed, if there was one ruler in the world worthy of the term *shāh*, Faizi writes, it was Akbar. Earlier rulers were as faint as stars facing the sun, whereas Akbar represented the perfection of creation itself. He was a protector of the Faith of Mecca, even as he fully respected the tradition of Joseph and other prophets. Such was his power that without him the earth would be bereft of rain and grass.

> Because he has made peace between Unbelief and Faith,
> What is an Unbeliever, a Fire-Worshipper, or a Musalman to him?

Image 2.1: Akbar crosses the Ganges on an elephant,
c. 1590–5.

Az ānjā ki ba kufr-o-dīn sulh dārad
Ba pīshash che kāfir che mugh che musalmān.

In short order, Faizi was fully accepted into this grand court and given a high position. After an unspecified elapse of time the ruler summoned him, instructing him to depart for the Deccan and ensure no one was creating disorder there: he should bring unruly elements to book and was entrusted to do so because he was as much a warrior as a man of the arts.

Faizi reached the Deccan accompanied by a number of people, including several Iranians. There he met many impressive souls while enjoying the landscape and riches of the region. He was able to deal appropriately with the rebels while rewarding those faithful to Akbar. Further, he issued invitations to people of knowledge and wisdom in the Deccan to come to the Mughal court. He instructed into righteousness those tempted by wrongdoing. Faizi concludes by noting that the text of the *Nashīd al-safar* was written as a gift in the year 1000 AH, one of the thousands of verses that he had composed thanks only to his *himmat* (determination) and *taufīq* (divine grace). His work is a versified *curriculum vitae* of sorts, long on elaborate metaphors and allegories and short on concrete details.

Our main concern in the pages that follow is with the letters (or better, reports) written by Faizi when he was sent on his mission to the Deccan. He was entrusted with this task not as a poet but as a trusted lieutenant of Akbar, having been charged to size up the situation in respect of the area of Khandesh (more or less a Mughal protectorate by then), as also more particularly Ahmadnagar, Bijapur, and Golkonda, regions that had a rather more ambiguous political position at this time. For, while the Mughal claim was that these areas fell under their suzerainty, the views of their rulers were quite different. In their titulature and other claims, they obviously saw themselves as independent (if threatened) rulers.[25] It was in this rather delicate situation of contested sovereignties that Faizi found himself

---

[25] See Ahmad, "Adil Shahi Diplomatic Missions", 143–61; texts in Ahmad, "Letters of the Rulers of the Deccan", 280–300. For a general discussion, unsatisfactory in several respects, also see Nayeem, *External Relations*.

embroiled. Added to this was the fact that the ruler of Ahmadnagar, Burhan Nizam Shah II, had spent some years in the Mughal court as an exile, and had returned quite recently to his domains to take charge as Sultan from a situation of having been a mere *mansabdār* in Mughal service.

Faizi's reports are not unknown, but they were rather harshly viewed by British scholars of the colonial period: John Dowson prefaces an extract from them in *The History of India*, for example, with the following cutting statement: "But for the great name of the writer, this little work would scarcely deserve notice. It consists of a series of letters written to the Emperor by Shaikh Faizi, while he was absent on his embassy in the Dakhin, in the thirty-sixth year of the reign." He goes on: "The letters are of a gossiping familiar character and are embellished with plenty of verses; but they contain nothing of importance and throw little light upon the political relations of the time."[26] We beg to differ somewhat.

Faizi's mission finds mention in his brother Abu'l Fazl's chronicle, the *Akbar Nāma*: the pressing need, he writes, was to bring around the "somnolent one [Burhan Nizam Shah] and the other rulers of that quarter. If they listened and apologised, he [Akbar] would withhold his hand from retribution. Otherwise, a victorious army would be appointed, and chastisement would be inflicted."[27] Faizi thus left from Lahore on his travels to the Deccan on 24th August 1591 (in the Hijri month of Shawwal 999) and returned to the court in May 1593, after an absence of over twenty months.[28] His return was a mere four months before the death of his father, Shaikh Mubarak. As noted above, Faizi himself was to die two years later, in October 1595, leaving behind an immense and valuable library of 4600

---

[26] Entry for *Wāki'āt of Shaikh Faizī*, in Elliot and Dowson, *History of India*, vol. 6, 147–9. We have used the text as published in Abu'l Faiz (Faizi), *Inshā'-i Faizī*, ed. Arshad; the letters are to be found in the section entitled *Latā'if-i Faizī*: "Latā'if-i awwal", 75–170.

[27] Shaikh Abu'l Fazl, *Akbar Nāma*, trans. Beveridge, vol. 3, 909.

[28] 'Abdul Qadir Badayuni, *Muntakhab*, vol. 2, trans. Lowe, 389–90, mentions that four envoys were sent out: Faizi to Asir and Burhanpur, Amin-ud-Din to Ahmadnagar, Mir Muhammad Amin to Bijapur, and Mir Munir to Golkonda.

bound volumes that came to be incorporated into the royal collection.

The First Report

We begin with a rather direct look at the opening part of the first report, written some months after Faizi's departure from the court, in which the complexity of the poet's cadences even while writing prose and his ability as an imperial poet-courtier both emerge clearly.[29] Thus, addressing the emperor Akbar himself, we have the following passage, the complex syntax and rhetorical flourishes of which we have deliberately attempted to capture in a translation that may at points seem literal:

> The humbler than humble Faizi, having in the first place turned the face of submission (*niyāz*) and discipleship towards that Qibla of desires whose appearance and inner reality (*zāhir wa bātin*) is the target of the Divine Gaze, I performed the prostration (*sijda*) of sincerity, with that spiritual ablution which makes the spring of purity and truth flow in the heart, cleansing it of deceit and pretence; unlike the ablution of those hypocrites who go to the dark interior of a place of worship, and wash their faces and hands with a few drops of water, and with their hearts still full of thousands of elements of interior darkness and uncleanliness, still call this purity. Secondly, I offer my prayer for the eternal continuation of your life and state (*daulat*), and for the eternal continuity of a lively heart (*dil-i zinda*) and awakened interior (*bātin-i bedār*), which make up *the* real life, and it is with these qualities that the truly pure and divine ones live, and in their case destruction (*fanā*) can find no opening into the high pavilion [which they inhabit]; and when I say *daulat*, I mean that state which is made up from eternal wisdom (*daulat-i dawām-i āgāhī*).
>
> I thank God that you [Akbar] possess both sorts of life, and both forms of state. This, even though prayers from such a humble and unfortunate (*nā-murād*) person as myself may fall well below the expected level of etiquette (*adab*), because a Chosen Person whose noble soul and body have been divinely raised up, and for the fulfilment of whose ends the very sky and stars

---

[29] Abu'l Faiz (Faizi), *Inshā'-i Faizī*, ed. Arshad, 75–97. It is also this report (*'arzdāsht*) from which the excerpts in Elliot and Dowson are drawn.

(*āsamān-o-sitāra*) revolve, in whose lap all wealth and fortune (*daman-i daulat*) have fallen, and upon whose capable shoulders the burden of the whole world and humanity rests, does not need the prayers of this empty-handed earthen lump. However, this slave is helpless, and the duty of a slave is to pray [for his master]; and besides the wise men of every religion press their foreheads to the ground, though God (*parwardigār*) is not in need of their prostration. If slaves were to receive eternal life, and even if they were to spend their whole lives in prayer, they would yet not fulfil their duty to God.[30]

This passage contains a characteristic mix of standard Sufi elements, the usual reflections on the interior life and superficial external reality, and also uses the metaphorical language of slavery to speak of the relationship between subject and sovereign. An elevated tone is established from the outset. Faizi now goes on to cite three couplets of his own, one of which runs as follows:

> When you prostrate yourself,
> if your head be not severed from the body,
> in the Religion of Love (*millat-i wafā*),
> they call it a sin.

"I am ashamed to call what I do *sijda* (prostration)," he writes, "but am hopeful that one day I can sacrifice my head and perform the *sijda-i besar* (headless prostration) in your cause." The slave is willing to sacrifice all, even his own head, for the master. Faizi then continues in a vein that still stresses Sufi themes of separation:

> At any rate, at the time when I became deprived of the fortune of being in the court, I would have been completely lost, overwhelmed and maddened by this sense of sudden deprivation, wandering in the jungle, but for the consolation and admonition from my father and my brother 'Allami [Abu'l Fazl], who are truly wise people, and physicians for the heart's ailments, who prepared a healing paste (*ma'jūnāt-i nasīhat*) to heal my heart and interior.

Voyage here is exile from the master and beloved, a sort of punishment imposed on the poet. This is the trope of *ghurbat* (exile) that

---

[30] Abu'l Faiz (Faizi), *Inshā'-i Faizī*, ed. Arshad, 75–6.

travellers writing in Persian or Ottoman Turkish knew very well. But the royal envoy must continue to represent his master and take care that his master's majesty is acknowledged everywhere. So the text moves quickly to a rather detailed account of the etiquette and ritual surrounding the reception of Faizi and the imperial *farmān* he carried, by the "tributary" ruler of Khandesh, a certain Raji (or Raja) 'Ali Khan Faruqi – an account not without some comic features.[31]

After having travelled a long distance, on the day of Ram, 25th day of the month of Dima, Ilahi [20th December 1591], I arrived at a spot 5 *kos* distant from Burhanpur. The following day, [I went to] the field where tents commensurate with the status and position of your slaves had been erected, which had been divided into two levels: the first one made completely of *zarbaft* (golden brocade), and the second level with a raised platform decorated with golden brocade, covered with canopies (*shāmiyānās*) of velvet and brocade; and on the platform were kept the imperial sword and the special robe of honour (*khil'at*), and the noble *farmān*, and a few well-dressed people stood around the platform with folded hands. The horses for *in'ām* (gifting) were also placed in a visible place, and in a proper fashion. Raji 'Ali Khan came with his people, the representatives of the governors of the Deccan (*wukalā'-i hukkām-i Dakan*), with the full displays of etiquette, in keeping with their loyalty and servility. From a distance, he approached on foot, and at the first level of the tents, he entered and with his own people proceeded ahead; and when he entered the second pavilion, he saw the raised platform from a distance, and he bowed and took off his shoes. When he proceeded a little ahead, he was told where to stand, and was told to bow down three times. He performed this three times with the full etiquette, and then stood there. At that time, I held the *farmān* with both my hands, and called him to advance a little more. I said: "His Highness the Emperor, the Shadow of God (*bandagān Hazrat Zill-i Ilāhī*), out of his great affection and patronage (*banda-nawāzī*) has sent two *farmāns* for you. This is one of them." He held the *farmān* with his two hands, raised it to his head, and performed three *taslīms* (reverences). After that, I told him that this slave himself was the [embodiment of the]

[31] On Khandesh in this period, see Joshi, "Khandesh", 511–15. For *farmāns* and their production and reception, see the valuable essay by Fragner, "Farmān", 282–95.

second *farmān*, upon which he bowed to me again. Then I said: "The emperor has also sent a special *khil'at* for you." He performed the *taslīm*, put it on, and then once more performed the *taslīm*, and in a similar fashion, he performed the *taslīm* for the sword, and every time I mentioned your affection for him, he performed the *taslīm*.[32]

All this elaborate bowing and scraping was of course highly necessary, as anything less would have implied that the ruler of Khandesh was not quite respectful of his Mughal superiors, including the envoy himself. We thus see, in comparison to the rather casual atmosphere that had surrounded the Mughal founder-ruler Babur in the 1520s, how much Mughal court ritual had evolved, even far beyond the reaches of the court itself. Faizi continues:

> Then he [Raji 'Ali] said: "It is years that I have had the desire to sit before you", and he said it in great earnestness. He was then told to be seated, he sat before me with the proper etiquette, and some appropriate words of wisdom were spoken, and I also explained to him the rules and regulations (*ā'īn*) [of the empire], so that he could get guidance from them. This was in order to convey to him the high qualities of your Excellency.

Taking his cue, Raji 'Ali Khan now replied that he was a mere Mughal servant praying for the wealth and state (*daulat*) of the emperor, from whose grace he had benefitted. His desire was to please the emperor and seek his kindness. Faizi now told Raji 'Ali that the emperor's boundless grace was upon him, that Akbar looked upon him both as one of his confidants and special servants. What could be better proof of this than the fact that a person like Faizi had been sent to him? Raji 'Ali for his part performed further *taslīms* and showed signs of great contentment. But the interview had gone on too long. In the meanwhile, twice it had been hinted that he should leave. Yet Raji 'Ali declared himself less than fully satisfied with the brief meeting and expressed a desire to sit on with Faizi till the evening, which he did for four or five watches.[33] In the end, *pān* (betel leaf) and *khushbū* (perfume) were brought. Raji 'Ali requested Faizi to give him the *pān* in person, and with his own hands, so he was given

---

[32] Abu'l Faiz (Faizi), *Inshā'-i Faizī*, ed. Arshad, 77–9.

[33] Four watches (*gharīs*) would have been roughly equal to one and a half hours.

a few folded leaves (*bīdā*), upon which he again paid his respects. Then it was decided to say prayers for the eternal continuity of the life and power of *Bandagān-i Hazrat* (the emperor). Raji 'Ali also joined the prayer, then stood up, went back to the edge of the carpet that had been spread out, and stood in front of the platform (*takht*), where the imperial horses were tethered. He kissed the bridle (*jilau*) and placed it on his neck as a mark of submission, performed *taslīm*, and similarly did so to the horses of Prince Murad, Akbar's son, who was at the time in the Deccan. Faizi's people counted the number of *taslīms* he had performed from start to finish and found it came to a grand total of twenty-five. Raji 'Ali was declared after this remarkably obsequious performance to be very fortunate, pleasant, and full of good qualities.[34]

We may gather from the foregoing that Faizi was travelling in some style, with a quite considerable entourage. But he does not tell us much about the individuals within it and only mentions a certain Amin-ud-Din who had accompanied him throughout, while Mir Muhammad Amin, another Mughal envoy to the Deccan, had been with him as far as the Narbada River before parting ways. Faizi notes that, when he had left the court in Lahore, it was still the rainy season; there had been several showers on the way, and the roads were slushy, forcing him to travel slowly in order constantly to reorganise provisions and repair broken materials. This had also obliged him to stay in the bigger towns for two or three days at a time.

We soon discover that the envoy was also functioning as a sort of surprise inspection party. For, on his way south, Faizi inspected the working of various administrators and revenue collectors (*hukkām* and *'ummāl*) in the "well-protected" Mughal territories in what he terms a "detailed and objective" fashion. Some of his observations he went on to summarise as follows, beginning with the Punjab.

> Baluchi who has been appointed *faujdār*, is stuck [in his job] near the narrow forts between Ludhiana and Sirhind. Bandits (*duzdān*) descend from the mountains, commit thieveries and murders, and go back; a part of their proceeds also come to Baluchi, and they pass freely. As a result, the five

[34] This section of the text, and some others, have been summarised and partly translated in Siddiqui, "*Insha'-i-Faizi*", 198–208.

or six *ijāradārs* (revenue farmers) in Payal have been ruined. In this area, travellers and wayfarers are in difficulties, but Hafiz Rahmat in spite of his old age still makes an effort. In his territory at least, there is some peace. He himself is honest, has made attractive gardens, with plantations of almonds and *chilghauza* (pines). One day he walked with me on foot and said: "I go around on foot so that people know that I am still not so old and infirm that I neglect my duty." The people of Sirhind are happy with him. The peasants are satisfied, and busy praying for you [Akbar].[35]

So the poet's high style comes to be suspended here, being replaced with the rather more businesslike tone of the administrator. A report like this could clearly make or break a career. Obviously, other members of the Mughal administration working on the route taken by Faizi had every interest in keeping this member of the emperor's inner circle happy. The report continues:

Ya'qub Badakhshi, the *karorī* of Thanesar, who is also doing the work of the *faujdārī* and *'amaldārī* of Thanesar and other *parganas* duly, is looking after the safety of the roads besides. He is doing his job competently. The *karorī* of Panipat, Qasim, who is an old clerk (*nawīsinda*), and looks after the work, has the distinction of being truthful, honest and dutiful. It is appropriate that he should get a position at the court, so that he sits in the row of honour and prays for you. The *ra'iyats* (peasants) of this place say that the *deh-'ushr* (tithe of one-tenth) has been ordered. They are hoping that it will be carried out, since this has been promised to them, and they request that this should be done.

Faizi has made his way now to the old heartland of the empire, and is rapidly approaching the royal centres of Delhi, Agra, and Fathpur Sikri, which have earlier served as the principal seats for Akbar in the first three decades of his rule. It is clear that he evinces a certain nostalgia for them, even if he does not criticise the royal decision to move to Lahore taken in the mid 1580s. The report on these cities is a curious mix of the official and the personal, with reflections on the quality of the administration mixed with other unexpected details.

[35] Abu'l Faiz (Faizi), *Inshā'-i Faizī*, ed. Arshad, 82.

Hakim 'Ain-ul-Mulk looks after Delhi, and he performs the service of taking care of the sacred shrines and the places of the *pīrs* of Delhi, and the welfare of the dervishes, and also behaves well with the poor people. The plundering Gujars have been brought to heel and have promised him that they would cease to rob. His son 'Abdullah is a well-conducted young man (*jawān-i rashīd*), always ready to be at your service. Ustad Yusuf who is now aged, lives in Delhi, and his beard has grown white playing the *tambūr* (lute). His lips are whiter now than his beard, and his hands are paler than his fingernails. Nek Muhammad Chaupani is a capable person, efficient and loyal (*namak ra ba-halālī mi khurd*); he deserves your attention.[36]

The text is intended to solicit rewards for some – whether elderly musicians or capable young administrators – and suggest the chastisement of others too distant from the imperial eye. By now, we are close to Agra and Fathpur Sikri. Faizi here writes in a somewhat nostalgic mode as he visits these sites of former glory:

When I reached Fathpur, first I kissed the threshold of the royal palace, and prayed for your safety. What can I write about the city? All the earthen buildings have collapsed, and in their place stone walls have come up. I enjoyed seeing the façades and the insides of some of the houses, some from close quarters, some from a distance. I especially saw the house of Mir Fathullah Shirazi – a man of a kind who is born once in three hundred years (*ba abastan-i sih sad sāl madār-i aiyām ū rā zāda būd*), and who was a divine gift presented to you.[37] I also visited the portico (*pīshkhāna*) and interior of Hakim Abu'l Fath Gilani's house. He too was a distinguished person of his own time. What can I say in his praise? Now we are lucky to have his brother still in our midst. He deserves to be a member of the exalted [inner] group (*majlis*). The residents of the villages and the *parganas* around Fathpur require a person like Shaikh Ibrahim [of the family of Salim Chishti], as administrator. Shaikh Bayazid, son of Shaikh Ahmad [of the same family], is unparalleled in honesty, integrity, good moral conduct, and in many other high human qualities, and deserves this position. He knows everything about this region, and with a small group of people, he can perform great

---

[36] Ibid., 83–4.

[37] On this personage, whose name recurs several times in Faizi's text, see Alvi and Rahman, *Fathullah Shirazi*.

tasks. There is a great difference between him and the others. His relatives also partake in administration and are a factor in the hustle and bustle of this town. He is efficient. I stayed two days in Fathpur but grew tired on account of the unpleasant water (*āb-hā-i sīna kharāsh*).[38]

Fathpur has brought forth memories of an earlier generation of courtiers, men who had served Akbar when Faizi himself was fresh in the imperial service. Still heading south, he is now on the threshold of Agra, to which Faizi feels a special loyalty as the place of his own birth:

> After that, I reached Agra, the city for whose clime a hundred thousand Baghdads and Egypts can be sacrificed. I saw a city full of habitation and wealth, and what can I tell you of the beauty of the noble fort, which protects the high fortune and power of Your Excellency, and astonishes world-travellers? And what can I say of the Jamuna River that passes by, kissing the foot of the fort, and which is the pride of seven climes (*ābrū-i haft iqlīm*)?

Faizi praises the town lavishly and hopes it will once again be graced by the return of the emperor – a hint of sorts, one supposes. For the time being, Shah Quli Khan, who is governor there, attends to the welfare of its citizenry, and Mihtar Khan too is a sincere imperial servant who must be allowed to continue in his post, not least because he takes care of the dervishes and the poor in the city. Both these men are reported to have spoken highly to Faizi of the administrative abilities of Nizam-ud-Din Ahmad (better known to posterity as the writer of the chronicle *Tabaqāt-i Akbarī*), who had chastised the recalcitrant (*mawās*) – those who had refused to pay the revenue (*māl*) and built strong fortresses of their own. There was no doubt that he was one of the real members of the imperial household, the *khānazāds*, having been raised in the city of Agra, and was truly brave and well conducted. He had been dutiful the past thirty years and was now fully informed of all affairs of administration and revenue, never himself discriminating between a high noble and an ordinary soldier

---

[38] Abu'l Faiz (Faizi), *Inshā'-i Faizī*, ed. Arshad, 84–6. On Fathpur Sikri, also see Brand and Lowry, eds, *Fatehpur-Sikri*; and Rezavi, *Fathpur Sikri Revisited*.

(*ahadī*) while performing his duty.[39] Clearly evident in these judgements is the prime importance given to certain virtues: charity (especially to dervishes and the saintly) and justice, but also to the keeping of order and the suppression of actual or potential rebellion.

Faizi's travels now take him to Dholpur, where he sees the large stone *sarā'i* (inn) of Sadiq Khan, and next to it a public bath (*hammām*) with water kept constantly hot, and a lovely garden containing beautiful structures. Sadiq Khan's able son, who was around to take care of the city, was also a public benefactor who had built wells along the streets, another act of charity.

Pursuing his way south, Faizi goes on to the great fort of Gwaliyar before proceeding to Narwar. We now have the sense of a geographical transition since we are entering the territory of Malwa. "How can my pen praise the *wilāyat* of Malwa, full of flowing streams!", Faizi exclaims, and goes on to pen a quatrain in praise of the region's clime and waters. The soil of Malwa was, he noted, cultivable and sound (*sālih*); in some places, sugarcane could be cultivated without artificial irrigation. Groundwater was to be found at five yards' (*gaz*) depth. Prince Murad, Akbar's son, was shortly expected there and he would, of course, bring even more prosperity to the region. The territory was situated, as Faizi notes, in the southern zone (*qutb-i junūbī*), and the prince (*shāhzāda*) likened to a pole of strength (*qutb*) for the empire.

The poet then goes to the town of Sironj, which he says could justly be called a *bandar* (port) on account of its abundant trade, even though it lay far inland. However, the governor of the place, a eunuch called Buland Khan, had left no stone unturned in trying to destroy the town's prosperity. The houses built by the relatives of Shihab Khan, and other *mansabdārs*, had been torn down one after the other, and their wooden beams sold by Buland Khan; the walls and

---

[39] Abu'l Faiz (Faizi), *Inshā'-i Faizī*, ed. Arshad, 88. Nizam-ud-Din Ahmad was a close associate of Faizi, and himself made it a point to note in his *Tabaqāt*: "I have enjoyed intimate friendship with this most learned man [Faizi] of the time from my childhood up. His gentle disposition is equalled by his cheerfulness. His angelic nature imposes an obligation on all his contemporaries"; cited by Wolseley Haig, in 'Abdul Qadir Badayuni, *Muntakhab*, trans. Haig, vol. 3, 413n.

doors of the houses too had been broken. Buland Khan's limbs now trembled with age (and soon the clay of his body too would crumble), yet his heart remained as stony as ever. Here was another imperial servant in need of castigation.

Other administrators were more exemplary. Sujawalpur, the next place on Faizi's itinerary, was held by a certain Khwaja Amin-ud-Din who behaved well with the peasants, regularly gave them *taqawī* loans, attended to everything personally, and had generally made the *pargana* prosperous. Besides, he had built manufactories for textiles (*kārkhāna-i pārcha bāfī*) from which lower garments (*fota*) and turbans were being made for His Excellency, the emperor. Faizi makes a plea: if Sironj, which required close attention, were taken over from the eunuch-governor and handed over to Khwaja Amin-ud-Din, that city too would thrive.

The distribution of bouquets and brickbats continues as Faizi heads closer to the Deccan. A certain Muhibb 'Ali is the main person in control (*ratīq wa fatīq*) not merely of Ujjain but of all of Malwa; he comes in for some praise as a man doing useful work; so does the son of a certain Isma'il Quli Khan, who was also in Ujjain. Another man mentioned is Qazi Baba ("a fine person"), whose sugarcane fields are particularly praiseworthy. Nowhere else in the region is such fine sugarcane to be found, declares Faizi knowledgeably.

He moves on to see the fort at Mandu, which is deserted and lesson-inspiring (*'ibrat afzā*) – in the sense that such deserted spots (like Fathpur Sikri which he visited earlier) point to how all temporal glory is transient. Camels and oxen are to be seen in the vicinity with loads on their backs. Isma'il Quli Khan had kept a certain Nazr Aqa (in the post of *yūz bāshī*) in charge of a part of his *jāgīr* in the region. Earlier, this Nazr Aqa had been in the service of Khan Jahan, Isma'il Quli Khan's brother. Faizi praises him, saying he deserves to be promoted and taken into imperial service. In this area, messengers from Raji 'Ali Khan came regularly with letters for the Mughals stationed there. They were welcomed at every stage with all courtesies.

The sound of the coming of the retinue of Prince Murad had eventually reached the ears of people in the area. Raji 'Ali Khan was ostensibly overjoyed and considered himself and the area fortunate to have the prince's shadow (*sāya*) fall on it. Raji 'Ali Khan insisted on his own loyalty and affection for the prince, and for the Mughal emperor. He broadly hinted too at the rewards he expected in this context. Faizi notes that Raji 'Ali was still arranging the tribute (*peshkash*) for the Mughals; within two or three days, he would send a report (*'arzdāsht*) in connection with the prince's arrival. Besides, he had set aside two girls from his family with their effects (*jahīz*) to send to the court with Faizi; one of them was meant for Prince Salim, the other was destined for Prince Murad – if only Akbar would agree. He requested that an order be sent from Akbar to Murad to facilitate this and avoid unnecessary delay.

Faizi now resumed his Burhanpur narrative. Two days after reaching there he had received an imperial *farmān* instructing him to visit Burhan Nizam-ul-Mulk in Ahmadnagar. Faizi grumbled at this order, for it took him even further from the court. After thirty years of service at the court (this is a slight exaggeration), he feels time and fate had taken their revenge on him. He expresses a desire to return and kiss the threshold of the emperor so that he might attain eternal fortune.

On his way, Faizi notes, he had made it a point to seek out dervishes and religious recluses (*majzūbs*), requesting them to pray for Akbar. Most of them had replied that the emperor needed no prayers since God himself had made him great, to the point that the dervishes needed *his* kind attention (*tawajjuh*). Indeed, Faizi insisted, there was nothing left for Akbar to attain. "May God perpetuate your kind shadow over the world and the people of the world forever."

Faizi now returned to a description of Burhanpur, a small town (*baghāyat tang*), yet full of gardens and greenery (*bustān*).[40] All cultivable land was made good use of: it had figs (*injīr*) of high quality, and Frankish melons (that is, papayas) were to be found hanging in bunches of twenty or thirty on the trunks of trees. There were bananas aplenty, though Indian melons had to be imported into the area. The

---

[40] On Burhanpur and its history, see Gordon, "Burhanpur", 48–65.

wind was a little hot that month; during the day a single layered garment was sufficient; at night a light additional tunic was necessary. As for the water, he found it different from that in the places he had visited earlier. Faizi regrets the approach of Nauroz, being so distant from the court; he consoles himself by returning to praise of Akbar. The far and the near, the rich and the poor, have all benefitted from Akbar's shadow. The occasion for a four-line verse was not lost, and the report ends with it:

> O God, may the emperor be at the vanguard of the triumphant,
> May he be the ruler over the skies of the people,
> So long as shade and sun go together,
> May he shine forever in the sun's shade.[41]

Faizi in Ahmadnagar

Faizi's penchant for poetry and the appropriate imperial rhetoric makes his first report a melange into which plenty of banal administrative detail manages to creep in, the legacy no doubt of Faizi's earlier term in the post of *sadr* (noted earlier). The first report/letter thus has its share of blunt condemnations and recommendations; we do not know to what extent these ideas were implemented at court, whether imperial servants were transferred, promoted, or chastised as a consequence of it.

The second report begins with the same general formula of self-abnegation as the first. Faizi, a mere handful of dust, wandering in the world, pays respects to the all-powerful ruler. Several lines of verse follow, comparing the ruler to Jamshid and Solomon, and other monarchs and viziers of antiquity. The thoughtful and reflective Akbar is one whose qualities are deemed praiseworthy in every way. A hunter of hearts, a killer of lions rapid in his movements, he never leaves his prey once he has it in his grasp. Though called the Wrath of God (*jalāl*), Akbar embodies Divine Grace (*jamāl*).

Faizi's praise now deploys, once again, one of his favourite metaphors centring around the play of light and sun.[42] The beauties of

---

[41] Abu'l Faiz (Faizi), *Inshā'-i Faizī*, ed. Arshad, 97.

[42] Faizi's evocation of the sun draws on an existing tradition but also transforms it. See Beelaert, *A Cure for the Grieving*, 30–120.

the dawn and the rising sun's rays are, he believes, shared equally by
him and Akbar. Faizi and Akbar (like Faizi and God) are joined together by rays of light (*nūr*) in what is a striking and forceful use by the
poet of illuminationist themes. One of his quatrains of the moment
thus runs:

> Every morning, the heart should seek blessings,
> begging for light for the heart of the night.
> O atom! Why are you wandering about carelessly?
> In the presence of His Excellency the sun (*hazrat-i khurshīd*) one
>   should behave correctly.

Posing a rhetorical question, Faizi asks what he can possibly say
about the days and nights that have passed. Regular letters continue
to arrive from his father and brother at the court, with details of the
emperor's welfare. They mention that from the court the world
is being governed in accordance with the laws of perfect rationality
(*qawānīn-i 'aql-i kāmil*) and patterns of justice (*insāf*). News of victories from various parts of the well-protected territories also come
through in these letters. As for the situation in the lands where he himself now is, all depends eventually on the emperor's goodwill. The emperor knows every detail, and his heart is the mirror that reflects the
whole world of reason (*'aql*).

On, therefore, to other things; Faizi moves now to the affairs of
Ahmadnagar.

> Burhan Nizam-ul-Mulk is one of those who has been raised from the dust
> by Your Excellency, and who has been reared on your munificence. It is four
> months that he has entered the *jāgīr* of the 'Adil Khan in a part that is 25 *kos*
> from Ahmadnagar on the bank of the river Nahalwada or Bhima, a big riv-
> er that separates them. And he has built two mud fortresses in the middle
> of the latter's territory. 'Adil Khan is still sitting in the fort of Bijapur and
> has sent his army of 14,000 horsemen. There are skirmishes every day, and
> a large number of people are being slain on both sides.[43]

The uncle of Burhan Nizam-ul-Mulk (never given the royal title
of "Nizam Shah", we note), a certain Baqir who had been living in

---

[43] Abu'l Faiz (Faizi), *Inshā'-i Faizī*, ed. Arshad, 101–2.

poverty in Bijapur, had been now promoted by 'Adil Khan (also not called "Shah") and sent out with an army. The idea was to send him to take over Ahmadnagar, and the latter had been tempted by this. Meanwhile, Raji 'Ali Khan had sent his men to both uncle and nephew, urging them to make peace. It was hence expected that truce would be declared, but for the moment war continued. When Burhan had left Ahmadnagar he had, with great humility, expressed his own sense of vulnerability and declared he was preparing the *peshkash* for the Mughals. While en route, Faizi had tried persuading him to expedite matters, yet he had kept putting things off. Four months had passed thus. Faizi had even met him twice in that connection; now he found himself in Ahmadnagar, a city full of mischief and commotion (*shor-o-sharr*) inhabited by sedition-mongers and ruffians (*fitnasāzān wa aubāshān*), with he himself dependent solely on the emperor's grace for his well-being. As for Burhan, he continued to write regularly to Faizi, beseeching him to intervene and pre-empt Akbar's possible anger. Each time, in his letters, he insisted he would return in a few days. "Since Burhan is your disciple (*tarbiyat karda*), and has grown under your kind eye, I hope he will always remain on the correct path, and that his conduct will be acceptable to Your Excellency, and that it will all end well for him."[44] Akbar, writes Faizi, will come to know everything anyway, for such is the nature of things.

A description of Ahmadnagar follows.[45] The city had been built by the father of Nizam-ul-Mulk Bahri, grandfather of Burhan (himself son of Husain, son of Burhan, son of Ahmad). This Ahmad had built a stone fort at four or five bowshots' distance from the city, and this fort was the seat of the ruler (*hākim*). Around the fort was a *maidān* and open fields. The city was rectangular in shape and had no city walls. At a distance of two *kos* was a lake, and a canal had been excavated to bring water from it to the city for distribution to households. Some houses had tanks while others used well-water of a

<hr>

[44] Ibid., 103.
[45] For a discussion of this site, see Sohoni, *The Architecture of a Deccan Sultanate.*

dubious quality. Faizi quotes an appropriate verse from the poet
Jami:

> Poison kills men,
> but poison is expensive.
> While the water that brings life
> is cheap.

At the time that Murtaza Nizam Shah (naturally "Murtaza Khan"
to Faizi) had become mad, a certain Salabat Khan had built a garden for him with tall cypress trees outside the town. In the middle of
it was a covered tank (*hauz*), though Faizi had not yet seen it. The
air in the area was pleasant. In the days of Cancer (*saratān*), that is, the
month of Tir, a quilt was necessary. Amongst the fruits, good melons
were not to be found; rather, they were sour and lacking in taste.
In fact, they were not really melons, and though the local people
called them so, Faizi refused to accept their claim. The figs were not
bad, the grapes were abundant; other fruits were available in modest
quantities. Pineapples were imported in a big way from nearby and not
bereft of taste. Bananas and apples (*amritphal*) were to be had as well,
and the mangoes met with Faizi's approval. Roses, however, were
not easily found, and those he had seen lacked fragrance. On the
other hand, *champa* and other Indian flowers were prolific. Sandal
trees were visible, as also a plenitude of white pepper plants (*filfil*) —
this last detail seems rather doubtful.

Faizi praises the goldsmiths and finds the weavers unparalleled. He
mentions the fact that, in general, high quality cloth is made in the
Deccan — Patan and Daulatabad are singled out as production centres of excellence. He reports that

> In the last few years, there were massacres (*qatl-i 'āmm*) twice in this city [Ah-
> madnagar], in the course of which not a single person from abroad (*mardūm-
> i wilāyat*) was left alive. The killing spree lasted for three days. Good people
> like the learned men and traders, who had assembled here in this period,
> were all slain, and their houses were destroyed. And at another time, after
> the coming of Burhan Nizam-ul-Mulk, a great plunder and looting was
> carried out with respect to the foreigners (*gharībān*). Whosoever had
> any goods was killed or wounded; the kith and kin of Shaikh Munawwar

were ruined in this process and were wounded. They are so ashamed that they do not dare come out of their houses. He expects favours from you. Lahori Afghan merchants too were plundered in large measure, and some of the servants of Salima Sultan Begam too were looted. How can the things plundered by these ruffians in this commotion be recovered?[46]

These thugs (*aubāshān*) continued roaming the streets unchecked, a sign of matters needing to be taken in hand in Ahmadnagar.

Faizi turns his attention to Ibrahim 'Adil Khan, termed the *hākim* (governor) of Bijapur, and nephew of 'Ali 'Adil Khan, now twenty-two years of age. He is reported to have some good qualities, centrally his devotion to Akbar. Dilawar Khan Habashi, an Abyssinian Sunni, had been his servant, and now had fled to be with Burhan Nizam-ul-Mulk.[47] Muhammad Quli Qutb-ul-Mulk was a Shi'i who had made a new city called Bhagnagar, named after a certain Bhagmati, a hardened whore and his old mistress (*fāhisha-i kuhna wa ma'shuqa-i qadīm*).[48] The territories of the Deccan were divided into the *jāgīrs* of these three men, and also some other rajas who co-existed in a politic fashion (*mubassirāna*). Faizi says he has observed them carefully and promises a fuller report at a later date. "This territory is part of the well-protected [Mughal] territories (*mamālik-i mahrūsa*)", he writes, calling on Akbar to pay them a visit at least once. The mere sound of the emperor's arrival would have a positive effect on them. A long ghazal follows on the possible effects of Akbar's theoretical travel southwards. Given that the ghazal is an emanation from his heart, says Faizi, it is bound to be oracular. After citing Hafiz, he returns to his own compositions extolling the beauty and excellence of the emperor.

On one occasion in Ahmadnagar, he says, the city being deserted — the populace had scurried off for fear of sedition and turmoil (*fitna* and *fasād*) — he had reassured his own friends there by telling them that

---

[46] Abu'l Faiz (Faizi), *Inshā-i Faizī*, ed. Arshad, 106.

[47] For the place of these Abyssinians in the area, see Subrahmanyam, "Between Eastern Africa".

[48] For comments on this legend, and Faizi's recounting of it, see Sherwani, *History of the Qutb Shahi Dynasty*, 339–48.

eternal fortune (*iqbāl*) was on the way. He had recited another ghazal on this occasion, but his friends, failing to comprehend its import, had run away. This had made it incumbent upon Faizi to write another ghazal on the flight of his friends. And various others had followed from his prolific pen, in keeping with the season, his state of mind, and what he was passing through.

Faizi reports that the tomb of Mir Hasan Dehlawi, the celebrated poet, was to be found in Daulatabad. This poet had probably come south with Sultan 'Ala-ud-Din Khalji at the turn of the fourteenth century and died there. It makes Faizi think of writing a ghazal in the dead poet's style. As it turns out, the rhyme in it permits a form of word-play in praise of Prince Murad. Seeing this as an omen (*shugūn*) of the latter's impending victory in the Deccan, Faizi has promptly sent the verses to him.

Having finished citing his own and others' poetry, Faizi returns to mundane details of a commercial and political nature.[49] In that very year, he says, six ships arrived from the Portuguese-controlled Persian Gulf port of Hurmuz. The Iranian Khwaja Mu'ina'i, who was a merchant-prince (*'umdat al-tujjār*), had come in them with his friends as well as 200 'Iraqi horses in three ships that had gone to Goa.[50] It turned out that the Portuguese Franks (*firangīs*) had a rule – that ships with horses were taken first to Goa, where they picked out the ones they wanted for themselves. Thereafter, the ships went on to Chaul, which was in the *jāgīr* of Nizam-ul-Mulk. These people from Iran said their sea voyage had endured twenty-four days. Some traders and some *qizilbāsh* (the Red-Capped Turkmen followers of the Safavid ruler), on account of the turbulence in 'Iraq and Fars, had decided to leave for the well-protected Mughal lands (*mamālik-i mahrūsa*) with the intention of "kissing the threshold" of Akbar. They had now arrived in the asylum of Mughal territories. There was a certain Husain Quli Afshar, a brave youth who in the time of the Safavid ruler Shah Tahmasp (r. 1524–76) had held

---

[49] Abu'l Faiz (Faizi), *Inshā'-i Faizī*, ed. Arshad, 118.

[50] Goa is misread in the edited text as "Kuda", and Chaul as "Jival". The same readings are repeated in Siddiqui's essay, "*Inshā'-i-Faizī*", cited above.

the governorship of some districts around Isfahan. Another important man was Husain Beg, *lashkar-nawīs*, who at the time of the government of Ya'qub Khan had held the post of reporter (*mukhbir*) in Fars and been a friend to Ya'qub. But after the latter's assassination he had been forced to leave. These two men had come with their entourages and were staying in the port of Chaul, pondering their future. They had written to Faizi and he had replied to both in a single letter, of which he sent a copy (together with others) to Akbar.

Also amongst the people on the ship was a certain Hamza Hasan Beg, a relative of the high Mughal noble 'Abdul Rahim Khan-i Khanan, who planned to go to Thatta where his illustrious relative was. Still another person of interest was Haji Ibrahim who had been *rikābdār* (cup-bearer) to Shah Tahmasp. There was also Haji Khusrau, a noted slave of Shah Tahmasp; Ghiyas Beg, and 'Ala'i the goldsmith, both at the Mughal court, knew him and could apparently vouch for him. All these are noted by Faizi as potential recruits to Mughal service. Some of these ship-people from Iran had in fact arrived in Ahmadnagar and given Faizi detailed information concerning the current situation in 'Iraq, Fars, and Rum. What he had learnt was as follows, beginning with the reigning Safavid ruler:

Shah 'Abbas has attained twenty years of age and is aflame with the fire of youth. His horoscope and those of his two brothers, Abu Talib Mirza and Tahmasp Mirza, are hereby enclosed for your [Akbar's] consideration. The court-astrologers will tell you the beginning and the end of the fate of these three. Shah 'Abbas is fond of hunting, *chaugān* (polo), shooting, and javelin-throwing (*neza-bāzī*). He is keen on falconry. Last year, he fell twice from his horse while throwing a javelin, once in Shiraz and the second time in Isfahan. Both times his knee was severely injured.[51] He is a brave man, and proud of himself (*ghairat-mand*), and even if he is prey to the whims and passions of royal youth, he is still sober, and intelligent. He has not so far taken over the reins of governance, and the fiscal and administrative

---

[51] Faizi's information is confirmed here by Safavid sources. Iskandar Beg Monshi, *History of Shah 'Abbas the Great*, trans. Savory, vol. 2, 607: "While the Shah was at Shiraz, he had a riding accident, falling from his horse and severely bruising his leg."

affairs are so far left to the officials. Farhad Khan is his *wakīl-i mutlaq*, and his constant companion, and Hatim Beg Urdubadi, who is very shrewd and economical, is the *wazīr*.[52]

We see, then, the portrait of a monarch who would soon emerge as a formidable rival to the Mughals. Faizi is fully mindful of the danger Shah 'Abbas represents. The time had come, writes Faizi, for the Shah to awake from his stupor and emerge from the intoxica tion of youth. He was now very concerned that most of the lands of Khorasan had been lost to the Shibanid Uzbeks on account of his earlier careless-ness and was making a revanchist effort.[53] Towards this end he had, in the previous year, wanted to attack Khorasan, but when he reached Rayy plague broke out: some of his troops had buboes on their sides, others on their thighs, the size of a gram. Shah 'Abbas had himself fallen ill with fever and been rushed to Qazwin.[54] Thereupon, the Safavid general Farhad Khan had come to Khorasan with some nota-bles, recaptured some of the towns, and arrived in the vicinity of Mash-had, killing several thousand Uzbeks. The son of the Shibanid ruler 'Abdullah Khanhad then made a flanking counterattack from Herat, and Farhad Khan had been obliged to return to Qazwin.[55] The peo-ple of the trading convoy (*kārwān*) had also let slip that 'Abdullah Khan's son had an army of a mere 5000–6000 men, and that had Farhad Khan stood his ground he would have carried the day. The astrologers – who clearly wielded much influence in the Safavid court – had in the previous year prevented the Shah from launching further expeditions into Khorasan. In the present year, however, they had suggested that he himself could lead the army and even predicted that he would emerge victorious. Shah 'Abbas had received a letter with these very contents from Khan Ahmad Gilani, who was an ex-pert astrologer.

[52] Abu'l Faiz (Faizi), *Inshā'-i Faizī*, ed. Arshad, 120.

[53] On the siege and capture of Herat by Shibani or Uzbek forces in 1587–8, see McChesney, "The Conquest of Herat", 69–107.

[54] On the peripatetic life of Shah 'Abbas in this epoch and later, see Melville, "From Qars to Qandahar", 195–224.

[55] Abu'l Faiz (Faizi), *Inshā'-i Faizī*, ed. Arshad, 121–2.

Much other political activity was also afoot in Safavid Iran, all of it of great interest to Faizi. He notes that a certain Daulat Yar Kurd, who had been sent by the Shah to the area between Tabriz and Qazwin with 20,000 people, had rebelled against the ruler. The Shah had at one point sent Husain Khan, the governor (*hākim*) of Qom, with 15,000 men to quell Daulat Yar. But Husain Khan had been defeated, and the thinking had then been that, once the Shah left for Khorasan, Daulat Yar would take advantage of his absence to descend on Qazwin. To pre-empt this, on 10 Ramazan last year the Shah himself had attacked him, and out of their cowardice some of Daulat Yar's brothers had promptly defected to the Shah, wanting Daulat Yar to be captured and handed over.

When the Kurd realised this, he had hung his sword around his neck as a sign of submission and appeared before the Shah. But, instead of showing mercy, the Shah had closed him up in a box or cage (*sandūq*), taken him to Qazwin, and there burnt him alive. This had sent out a stern message concerning Shah 'Abbas' intentions. People said that getting rid of Daulat Yar was no less important than getting rid of the Uzbeks.

In those very days the Shah sent a *qūrchī* (cuirassier) to the elderly notable Khan Ahmad Gilani to register a protest – that while he, the Shah, had been hemmed in by troubles, Gilani had shown no signs of friendship. The aged Khan Ahmad Gilani had pleaded dotage and frailty while protesting his continuing sincerity and loyalty, saying his country (*wilāyat*) and his honour (*nāmūs*) both belonged to the Shah. He had sent a letter, along with his daughter, whom he offered in marriage to Prince Safi, the six-year-old son of the Shah, who had been born in Mashhad. The Shah accepted this offer, sent Hatim Beg to Gilan with a group of *'ulamā'* from Qazwin, and on the night of the festival of Shab-i Bar'at the previous year, the marriage was performed in absentia (*'aqd-i ghaibāna*). For forty days thereafter there were comings and goings of various people, and celebrations. Khan Ahmad had sent gold, silk, high-quality cloth, gold thread, and other gifts worth 10,000 *tomāns* to the Shah, and had also had to extend hospitality to all those who visited. Thus, it seemed that some of the high and mighty notables were coming to heel, while others were feeling the brunt of the Shah's wrath.[56]

Thereafter the Shah had left Qazwin for Isfahan, and en route received a report that in Yazd a group of 150 Uzbeks who had arrived on the pretext of trading (*ba bahāna-i saudāgarī*) appeared to be soldiers. In response, the Shah sent a letter to the *hākim* of Yazd, telling him to keep an eye on the Uzbeks until he himself arrived. When he finally did, he made enquiries about them and decided they were miscreants deserving of punishment. The Uzbeks insisted they were traders and said if they were harmed Iranian merchants would face similar consequences in Uzbek territories.[57] The Shah had relented, let them go, and himself returned to Isfahan. There he sent out messengers (*qūrchīyān*) to all the provinces (*wilāyats*) with a general instruction to the effect that the same year, on the day of Nauroz, the entire army of all quarters should assemble in the vicinity of Tehran. It was agreed that the notables (*umarā'*) and the higher military officials would take their people along with them on the campaign, so that, fearing for the honour of their families, they would not dare turn around. The Safavid court also awaited news from Yadgar Sultan Shamlu, who had gone to the Mughal court in the hope of persuading Akbar to send an army towards Khorasan.[58]

It appeared that if the elites of the distant territories did not go astray and oppose the Shah, Khorasan would be attacked soon after Nauroz. The astrologers of Iraq had said, reports Faizi, that the Shah was under particular danger (*khatr-i 'azīm*) that year, for a hostile force (*taqātu'*) had entered his star. Until it passed, he would face difficulties. The Shah had been told this but, being proud, was seeking the means to fight it. "Let us see what is in his fate (*taqdīr*)",

---

[56] For Shah 'Abbas' slightly later dealings with Khan Ahmad, also see Monshi, *History of Shah 'Abbas*, vol. 2, 621–4.

[57] Compare Alam, "Trade, State Policy and Regional Change", 202–27.

[58] Monshi, *History of Shah 'Abbas*, vol. 2, 606, where he appears as "Yadgar Sultan Rumlu". On this embassy, also see Islam, *A Calendar of Documents*, vol. 1, 108–9. On Safavid–Mughal diplomatic relations in the period, also see Choksy and Hasan, "An Emissary from Akbar to 'Abbas I", 19–29.

concludes Faizi, and goes on to write in far greater detail of Safavid military affairs.[59]

An interesting passage follows concerning the Safavid army being gathered, which Faizi concludes comprises a "great effort" and "must exceed one hundred thousand people." The detailed make-up of this force is as appears in the table below, with the provincial forces, the central (*khāssa*) forces, and the ruler's slaves being quite clearly separated. This is a quite remarkable attempt (even if only a "guesstimate" based on mixed rumours) to provide a concrete sense to the Mughal emperor of the forces at the disposal of a neighbour and rival, and their organisation and divisions. The poet could thus transform himself not only into a diplomat but also into a quite formidable intelligence-gatherer.[60]

Having taken the measure of the Safavid armies, Faizi continues to develop the theme of challenges to the Shah's authority, and potential and actual rebellions brewing. He thus mentions the case of an Arab by the name of Mubarak who, emerging in the districts around Shustar, had fought several times against the Ottoman army (*lashkar-i rūm*) and emerged victorious.[61] He considered himself an ally of the Shah and had sent him valuable gifts. It was now two years since he had gained control of the routes (*rāhguzār*) in Basra and Baghdad. One of his enemies came to the Shah, joined his service as a *qūrchī*, suggested to him that Mubarak was an unreliable hypocrite, and asked that he be tested. Mubarak, he said, had a valuable horse, incomparable as a racing steed, worth 700 *tomān*. He suggested that 'Abbas ask Mubarak for this horse as a test of his sincerity. The Shah did so, claiming that he needed the horse for a journey; he also asked Mubarak for other horses, as well as horsemen. When Mubarak received the request he sent 300 other horses along with his son, and a force of 6000 horsemen to the Safavid court. Once more, this provided affirmation of the Shah's growing power over his satraps and regional power-brokers.

---

[59] For an analysis of the army under Shah 'Abbas, to which these details may be compared, see Haneda, *Le Chāh et les Qizilbāš*.

[60] Abu'l Faiz (Faizi), *Inshā'-i Faizī*, ed. Arshad, 125–6.

[61] Monshi, *History of Shah 'Abbas*, vol. 2, 675–7, concerns later expeditions against the same Mir Mubarak in the area of Khuzistan.

Table 2.1: The Safavid Army, According to Faizi

Zu'lfiqar Khan and his brother Farhad Khan, *hākim* of Ardabil and Damghan	10,000
Farhad Khan, with one of his brothers, and Alwand Sultan	10,000
Husain Khan, the *hākim* of Ganja, and 'Ali Sultan	50,000
Husain Khan Qajar, with a Qajar force	12,000
Shah Quli and Sultan Shamlu, *hākim* of Hamadan	4,000
Chiragh Sultan, *hākim* of Rayy	4,000
Farrukh Khan, brother of Murtaza Khan Turkoman	5,000
Muhammad Quli Sultan, son of Murtaza Khan	2,000
Buniyad Khan, *hākim* of Shiraz, together with its dependencies (*tawābi'*)	10,000
The *hākim* of Yazd together with dependencies	5,000
Amir Hamza Khan and Siyaush Khan, with footmen and cavalry Malik Sultan Muhammad	4,000
Mahdi Quli Sultan Shamlu	8,000
Ahmad Quli Sultan Zu'l-qadr	1,000
Farrukh Husain Khan Shamlu	12,000
The son of 'Ali Khan	5,000
Yadgar 'Ali Sultan, *hākim* of Khwarazm and Simnan, with cavalry	1,000
and foot	2,000
Other cavalry and footsoldiers (*piyāda wa sawār*) from Isfahan	2,000
Footsoldiers (*jama'at-i piyāda*) from other diverse cities	15,000
The Central Force (*lashkar-i khāssa*):	
– That is *qūrchī-yi khāssa* (royal cuirassiers) etc.	8,000
– *Yūzbāshi*, etc., horsemen	15,000
– Footsoldiers (*piyāda*)	8,000
The Shah's slaves:	
– Dalw-i Jamshid of the *hākim* of Qazwin	2,000
– Dalw-i Husain	3,000
– Dalw-i Farrukh Khan	3,000
– Dalw-i Abdal	2,000

It was also reported by Faizi's informants that 10,000 *amīrī* Arabs had gathered in the Khorasan area to await the Shah, stating that they were ready to fight to protect their Shi'i religion and sect (*dīn* and *mazhab*) against the Sunni Uzbeks. Other fresh rumours from Iran noted that, in the previous year, Shah 'Abbas had blinded his own brothers Tahmasp Mirza and Mirza Abu Talib with a hot iron, as also Isma'il Mirza and the son of Hamza Mirza, to pre-empt their royal ambitions. The last of these was so young that he died from the maltreatment. Shah 'Abbas himself had two sons, one Mirza Safi, and the other Mirza Haidar who had been born the previous year. The Shah's own father, Sultan Muhammad, had been totally blinded and lived in the Shah's camp in a separate tent. Arrangements had been made for his food and drink; he occupied himself with various forms of entertainment.[62]

News had also come in of natural disasters that had beset Iran, besides the plague epidemic in Khorasan mentioned above. The year before last, in Ardabil, an epidemic had raged, so that a large number of people had fled the city in different directions; those who remained had all died. Many traders lay dead in various houses and dust gathered on the doors of their deserted residences. However, when the Shah heard of this, he sent a *qūrchī* to look into matters and this man promptly confiscated the property of the dead.

The image that emerges of the Iranian ruler is thus curious and compelling, a mixture of driving ambition, some cruelty (including to his own immediate family members), and an explosive combination of personal courage, political cunning, distrust of others, and intelligence. All this comes together in another incident of the year before the last. Faizi reports that this concerned a certain Yaktash Khan, the *hākim* of Kirman and Yazd, who had had a considerable force at his command and had revolted against the Shah. Ya'qub Khan Zu'l-qadr, the *hākim* of Shiraz, had been sent by the Shah to chastise the rebel; he had killed Yaktash in the fight that followed, and a huge booty in the form of property and goods had fallen into the hands of Zu'l-qadr – which had the effect of rather turning his head. He had begun to claim – somewhat ambiguously – to be a "product of Shah Tahmasp (*man az Shah Tahmāsp hāsil shuda am*)" and even stated he would one day be ruler (*bādshāh*) himself. On returning

---

[62] Abu'l Faiz (Faizi), *Inshā'-i Faizī*, ed. Arshad, 128.

to Shiraz he had openly revolted and built a fort near the tomb of Shaikh Sa'di to this end. The Shah had repeatedly sent for him from Isfahan and asked him to deposit his campaign loot, but the man had refused to appear and resisted sending any of the captured goods. Exasperated, the Shah had finally taken 12,000 men and personally attacked Shiraz, forcing Zu'l-qadr to flee to Istakhar, where he enclosed himself inside the fort with some 400 men. The Shah had besieged him there for four months; during the siege he often said with regret that he had had no better servant than Ya'qub Khan, who had probably been frightened and misled by enemies. Word of this eventually reached Ya'qub Khan, and various emissaries from the Shah reached him too. Finally the Khan, seduced by the soft words (*afsūn wa afsāna*) of the Shah, left the fort and was publicly forgiven by 'Abbas.

But matters did not end there. A certain Khan Beg, who had earlier been Ya'qub Khan's servant, brought rumours to the Shah that Ya'qub Khan secretly wished to kill him, towards which end he had covertly gathered a force. The Shah at first claimed he refused to believe this; but, one day, while he was out on a hunt, he was again warned by Khan Beg that Ya'qub Khan habitually wore a coat of mail, his intention being to rebel at an opportune moment. Pretending affection, the Shah passed his hand over Ya'qub Khan's shoulder and so knew this to be true. Claiming now to have a headache, he abandoned the hunt and returned to the city. The next day he summoned Ya'qub Khan before the audience hall (*dīwānkhāna*) with all his important servants.

It so happened that over those very days a group of ropemakers had requested that they be allowed to demonstrate their skill with rope-play to the Shah. The Shah seated Ya'qub Khan by his side, jokingly took a stick in his hand, and said: "Kingship is coming to Ya'qub Khan. He shall be the king, and we his servant (*Shāhī ba Ya'qūb Khān mīrasad. +Ishān Shāh bāshand wa mā naukar-i ān*)." He then said aloud: "Shah Ya'qub Khan has issued the order that such-and-such a servant should be killed with a rope", and the man was promptly garrotted. Pursuant to this the supporters of Ya'qub

Khan were killed one after another.[63] At last, it was Ya'qub Khan's turn. He was hung by a rope, his body put to the rack (*dar shikanja kardan*), and after the torture his flesh fed in morsels to the dogs (*luqma-i sagān sākhtand*).[64] The Shah then handed over the government of Fars to a certain Buniyad Khan and himself returned to Isfahan. He remained there two months, then went on to Qazwin.[65] Faizi's point is clear: the emerging rule of Shah 'Abbas is that of a formidable and vengeful monarch: he is not one to brook rebellion or resistance to his rule. The Mughal court is enjoined to draw its own lessons.[66]

Faizi here terminates his long description and analysis of the rule of Shah 'Abbas and turns briefly to the affairs of the Ottomans. The news from their domains in Rum was that Sultan Murad was in Istanbul with his epilepsy having worsened: he had fits and seizures, at times in the mornings, and would remain in that state sometimes till midday, at others till midnight.[67] Indeed, he was no longer capable of riding a horse. The regions up to three *kos* to the east of Tabriz were under Ottoman control, and Kotal Shamli marked the border with the Safavids. The Turkoman notable Qara Hasan Ustajlu had been sent over the past year to define the border between

[63] Compare this description with the slightly later suppression, in August 1593, of the Nuqtawis by Shah 'Abbas, described in Babayan, *Mystics, Monarchs and Messiahs*, 3–6.

[64] Faizi's version of this incident differs somewhat from the official Safavid version, reported in Monshi, *History of Shah 'Abbas*, vol. 2, 606–11. For a brief comment on the significance of the death of Ya'qub Khan, also see Quinn, "The Historiography of Safavid Prefaces", 8.

[65] It is of some interest to note that the interest shown by Faizi here in Iran was reciprocated; a recent historian of Iran notes that the Safavid chronicler "Iskandar Beg cites the *Akbar-nama*, and also refers to the author, Shaikh Abu'l-Fazl, on more than one occasion": see, Melville, "Shah 'Abbas and the Pilgrimage to Mashhad", 221. On Iskandar Beg as a chronicler, also see Quinn, *Historical Writing*.

[66] Abu'l Faiz (Faizi), *Inshā'-i Faizī*, ed. Arshad, 129–31.

[67] The reference is to Sultan Murad III (r. 1574–95), on whom some mildly adverse remarks are to be found as well in Abu'l Fazl, *Akbar Nāma*, trans. Beveridge, vol. 3, 1019–20. Faizi's remarks put a rather different connotation on the idea of the "sick man of Europe".

the two states. The *hākim* of Tabriz, an eunuch called Ja'far, was a clever and brave person who had built fortresses in Ganja, Shirwan, Shamakhi, and Qarabagh. It was said that, by comparison with the Uzbeks, the Ottomans were currently happier with the Qizilbash. This was probably because Sultan Murad had written to the Shibanid ruler 'Abdullah Khan to attack the Safavids from the other side, so that the two forces would divide Iran, with the Uzbeks taking the portions to the east of Qazwin. But instead of accepting this offer, 'Abdullah Khan had replied that Qazwin was a part of Khorasan, and that he intended to take it himself. He also wrote to Sultan Murad in a more conciliatory mode, expressing his desire to meet him personally, and to perform the Hajj. But the evasive style of the letter had offended the Rumi Ottomans, who had hence decided actually to aid Shah 'Abbas against the Uzbeks. One of the sons of Safavid prince Mirza Hamza was currently with the Ottomans, who had invited him, claiming that they would advise him. But this was against the custom (*qānūn*) that had governed past relations between the two states, and Faizi hence felt that the Ottomans had been very devious in adopting such tactics.

From Envoy to Talent Scout

Having described the current political and military situation in Safavid Iran, as well as emerging conditions under the direct rule of Shah 'Abbas, Faizi passes to a related problem which interests him a good deal. His view is that it is possible to attract some of the best talent from the Safavid domains to those under Akbar's rule – because Shah 'Abbas' rule was bound to generate discontent. He has thus clearly made extensive enquiries in the Deccan concerning the prospects in the matter. He notes that amongst the scholars (*dānish-mand*) of 'Iraq and Fars there was a certain Mir Taqi-ud-Din Muhammad, famous under the name of Taqiya Nasaba.[68] In that country he was thought unmatched; he was also a disciple of the celebrated

---

[68] It would appear that this savant later migrated to Golkonda; cf. Sherwani, *History of the Qutb Shahi Dynasty*, 404.

Mir Fathullah Shirazi who had already served Akbar. At the time when Mir Fathullah and Maulana Mirza Jan were greatly praised in Shiraz, Taqiya too was already one of the noted teachers of that city. Faizi had heard a lot about his talents, and Mir Fathullah's praise of him on several occasions. Mulla Muhammad Riza'i Hamadani was also a noted scholar from the Shiraz madrasa. Faizi had heard from him that Mir Taqi-ud-Din was keen to come to the Mughal court but lacked means for the voyage – he would else have arrived with the traders that year. Faizi therefore suggests that were Akbar simply to issue a *farmān* granting him the money, it would enable the trip. He was after all the spiritual son, the living memory of Fathullah – this was reason enough to have him in Mughal India. And he in turn would benefit from being in the great centre of this-worldly and other-worldly science that was Akbar's court.

The son of the *qāzī* of Hamadan, a certain Ibrahim, was a great scholar too: he had taught medicine (*shifā*) and written learned commentaries. His fame was growing; at present he was in the camp of the Safavid Shah. Besides, he was a relative of Muhammad Riza'i.

Then there was Shaikh Baha-ud-Din Isfahani, born in Balbaq, who had accompanied his father to Herat when he was seven years old. He was a disciple of his own father and of Mulla 'Abdullah Yazdi. He too was a distinguished scholar of all the sciences living presently in Isfahan. Still another person deserving of a high place in the Mughal court (*majlis-i ashraf*) was Chalpai Beg, who, educated in Shiraz and Qazwin, had in the past twelve years achieved much fame. He was resident in Shiraz and, if accorded Akbar's attention, could be won over to the Mughal cause.[69]

Faizi now turns to the talent available in Ahmadnagar itself. Here, there were two major Iranian poets. The first, Malik Qomi, met people rarely but had a good heart; Faizi cites one each of his quatrains and couplets as proof of this poet's talent. Another notable person was Mulla Zuhuri: his poetry was extremely colourful, and he was, besides, a very good man.[70] Faizi cites two of his couplets and one of

---

[69] On the issue of the migration of Iranian savants to Mughal India, see the details in Golchin-i Ma'ani, *Kārwān-i Hind*.

[70] Both poets are later to be found in Bijapur, as we see from Asad Beg's

his quatrains. All of these men were, in his opinion, perfectly deserving to be called to the Mughal court.

Underlying all this is an image of an Iran characterised by forms of strife of which the poet does not approve. To prove his point, Faizi now returns to anecdotes recounted by those who had come from across the seas (that is, from the Persian Gulf). One of these men had, when recounting the Safavid–Shibanid wars, spoken of an Uzbek who had been captured in whose hand there was always visible a skein of threads. This Uzbek, when asked why he carried the threads, replied that his mother was an old woman who had given them to him saying they should be coloured with the blood of a *rāfizī* (Shi'i); and that when she died her shroud was to be stitched with those very threads.[71] Maulana Zuhuri had told Faizi that, one day in Mecca, when the notables of that place were sitting on the banks of a tank (*hauz*), a man from Transoxania (or Mawarannahr) had arrived and told them that on the Day of Judgment the first four caliphs (*chār yār*) would sit at the four corners of the Hauz-i Kausar and distribute water to the faithful (*mu'minān*). Mahmud Sabbagh Nishapuri, who was seated by the tank, then stood up and said, "O ignoramus! Do you not know that the Hauz-i Kausar is round, and the water shall be distributed by Murtaza 'Ali!" The point of the anecdote seems to be to stress the futility of the strife between Sunnis and Shi'is.[72]

Faizi seizes this occasion to cite a verse from Shaikh Farid-ud-Din 'Attar, to the effect that if one gets involved in debating the relative merits of 'Ali and Abu Bakr, how can one ever attain the Divine? He goes on to note that in the Deccan, for example, there was the cult of a certain Dilawar-ul-Mulk, or Dawar-ul-Mulk, whom people worshipped as a deity (*ma'būd*). According to Faizi, this putative deity was a simple soldier of Gujarat who had been

---

account below (in ch. 3). Cf. Ghani, *A History of Persian Language*, vol. 2, 181–219.

[71] On conflicts across this frontier, also see McChesney, "'Barrier of Heterodoxy'?", 231–67.

[72] Abu'l Faiz (Faizi), *Inshā'-i Faizī*, ed. Arshad, 137.

killed in the Deccan. Yet his grave was to be found in twenty or thirty distinct places. Another "deity" of the Deccan, Faizi writes sarcastically, was Sayyid Muhammad Gesudaraz, whose grave was in Gulbarga in the *jāgīr* of 'Adil Khan, and who had earlier had his *khānqāh* in Delhi. In the year when Hazrat Sahib Qiran (Timur), after a disturbance (*fasād*) in Hindustan, had come to conquer it, this Sayyid had decided to migrate to the Deccan.[73] Faizi mocks the pretensions of this Sufi and his descendants, recounting an anecdote he had heard from Mulla 'Abdul Latif Barbari, who lived in Burhanpur and had drafted letters for Raji 'Ali Khan. He had told Faizi that one of Gesudaraz's descendants, a certain Hazratullah, had come to Burhanpur a year earlier and sent one of his servants (*khādim*) to 'Abdul Latif, to ask where to pitch his camp. 'Abdul Latif, after offering him a cold welcome, had told him to stay in his own house. Some days later, when he met 'Abdul Latif, the incensed Hazratullah asked him whether he knew who he was, for "When the Virgin Mary (Hazrat Maryam) was taken to the heavens, and Gesudaraz was taken there too, she was given to him in marriage. I descend from that union." 'Abdul Latif had sarcastically retorted saying if indeed that were the case, Hazratullah should go to Europe (*firang*) where his brothers presumably were. To which Hazratullah replied that, indeed, Europe was his brother Jesus' territory (*wilāyat*), but that he did not know whether he would receive an appropriate welcome there. "I have heard the name of this brother of 'Isa from Khwaja Nizam-ud-Din Ahmad", writes Faizi, noting that he had then gone off to Gujarat – which was just as well for the inhabitants of the Deccan.[74]

To be set against such pretentious and doubtful personalities were others for whom Faizi felt much respect, such as the celebrated Shah Tahir Husaini, a migrant to the Deccan in the early sixteenth century.[75] He recounts the story of an European (*firangī*) physician called

[73] Interestingly, Faizi's irreverent comments on the much-venerated Chishti Sufi Sayyid Muhammad Gesudaraz confirm at least a part of Badayuni's portrait of his attitudes; cf. 'Abdul Qadir Badayuni, *Muntakhab*, trans. Haig, vol. 3, 413. On Gesudaraz, also see Eaton, *Sufis of Bijapur*, 50–3.

[74] Abu'l Faiz (Faizi), *Inshā'-i Faizī*, ed. Arshad, 139.

[75] Shah Tahir did have relations with the Portuguese in the mid-1540s, most

Bajarz (possibly "Borges") who had been invited to the Ahmadnagar court by Nizam-ul-Mulk Bahri, and was employed by him as a confidant.[76] One day, this doctor (*hakīm*) had asked a certain Khwajagi Shaikh Shirazi (a disciple of Khwaja Jalal-ud-Din Muhammad) in the court of Nizam-ul-Mulk the following question: "If there were a fire at the end of the world, and there was nothing between you and that place, and you were standing on a mountain, you could see the fire . . . Yet you people say that before the sky (*falak*), where the moon is, there is a layer of fire. Why is that not visible?" The Shaikh replied this was on account of distance. To which the *firangī* replied that, were he permitted by Nizam-ul-Mulk, he would start dancing, for such a reply was itself so evasive that it contained hundreds of dances within it. While the debate was on, the celebrated Shah Tahir arrived and asked what was going on. When told, he replied that the shaikh was in fact wrong. When there is a mixture of elements, only then are things visible, as with the usual worldly fires, which had particles of earth in them. But the heavenly canopy of fire was made up of a pure element and was hence invisible. This reply had silenced the *firangī* in a most definitive fashion.[77]

Shah Tahir's was a talent of the past, one no longer available to Faizi's recruiting drive. Still, continuing to speak of other talents in Ahmadnagar, Faizi writes of a Hakim Misri who was very celebrated there for his countless treatments and medicines. Faizi speaks highly of all this doctor's skills – his diagnoses, his ability to cure, his generosity and pleasing personality. There were two other world-famous physicians, one Hakim 'Imad-ud-Din Mahmud who had died in Mashhad long ago, and the second a certain Hakim Kamal-ud-Din Husain who was called from 'Iraq by Khan Ahmad

---

notably with the captain of Chaul, António de Sousa. See the letters of Sousa dated July and August 1546, in Sanceau, ed., *Colecção de São Lourenço*, vol. 3, 233–4, 251, 258.

[76] For relations between Portuguese physicians and the Nizam Shahi court, see the valuable testimony of Orta, *Colóquios dos Simples*, vol. 1, 118–24, *passim*.

[77] On Shah Tahir's career, also see the brief comment in Eaton, *Sufis of Bijapur*, 68–9, as well as the letters summarised in Islam, *A Calendar of Documents*, vol. 2, 119–24.

Gilani to his court, and who had taught him Avicenna's *Qānūn*. Unfortunately, he had died the year before last. At Akbar's court there already was Hakim Abu'l Fath, a disciple of 'Imad-ud-Din, a unique physician of his time, full of merit and excellent qualities. Faizi had seen his horoscope and found some special signs in his star clearly indicative of this. At times when Abu'l Fath fell ill, he consulted his own horoscope and on one occasion found a sign in his star that portended imminent danger. So he told a certain Hindu physician called Gangadhar that, from the movement of his stars, it seemed he would be unable to cure his own disease. He then asked Gangadhar to find a better treatment, which however the latter was unable to do. Expecting that his time had come, Hakim Abu'l Fath now declared that no medicine would work on him, and saying this died. His younger brother Hakim Humam, who had learnt from great masters and looked up to Hakim Abu'l Fath, was also regarded by Faizi as a master (*ustād*). Indeed, all this was proof that capable and wise people from the seven climes wished to come to the court of Akbar.

Faizi was not yet done scouting out physicians. In the court of Nizam-ul-Mulk were two physicians, Hakim Kashi (a man of limited learning, and promoted by Hakim Misri), and the other a certain 'Ali Gilani Wasiti. The latter too was of no great merit, though he had arrived a year before from the great centre of Shiraz. There was also a group of "Hindi" physicians, but of no particular distinction either. Of the prospects, the best seemed to be a certain Hakim 'Ali Gilani, a former disciple of Fathullah Shirazi, who the previous year had been invited to Thatta in Sind from his residence in Shiraz. He was a capable man and, in Faizi's view, Akbar could easily order his general Khan-i Khanan (in Sind at the time) to send him from there to the imperial court. Indeed, the poet notes that the Deccan was not the only – or even the most obvious – route for migration from Safavid Iran to Mughal India. Thatta and Sind were not far from Shiraz, and people were always going and coming between the two places; even Taqiya Nasaba could be invited to travel by that route.[78]

---

[78] Abu'l Faiz (Faizi), *Inshā'-i Faizī*, ed. Arshad, 142–3.

None of the other savants in the Deccan seem to have found particular favour in Faizi's eyes. There was one Muhammad Qasim of whom Faizi had heard mostly bad reports: it was said he had been a disciple of Fathullah Shirazi and Mirza Jan, but hardly a trace of them survived in him. There were also some Arab Shi'is from places such as Jabal-i 'Amil, Najaf, and Karbala, but none of them seemed particularly meritorious. The older Deccanis were for their part either sectarian Sunnis or Shi'is; there were also some descendants of Abyssinians holding positions of authority (*kalān*), but few amongst them were really reliable.

Faizi thus comes to the end of this very extensive second report (*'arzdāsht*) on his travels, probably the most elaborate and comprehensive of all those he sent to the Mughal court in Lahore. As he closes it, he notes that his own men have just arrived from Nizam-ul-Mulk's camp with fresh news that does not augur well. This news is that Baqir, Burhan Nizam Shah's uncle, has with 15,000 horsemen entered the region (*wilāyat*), plundered and set fire to a market town (*qasba*), and reached within 20 *kos* of the city of Ahmadnagar. People are worried and there is commotion all around. Some feared he would enter the city itself, others said he would go to Berar where the ruler, a certain Saif-ul-Mulk, was his ally. This was also the view of Raji 'Ali Khan. Some people also claimed he would head for the camp of the Mughal prince Murad and try to confront him. Nizam-ul-Mulk had sent a large army to pursue him and had himself decided to set off to reach Ahmadnagar soon. Already his army was split in two and he was facing growing difficulties.

Faizi briefly sketches the background to all this. A certain Dilawar Khan Habashi had controlled Bijapur for ten to twelve years, to the point that the young Ibrahim 'Adil Khan dared not even to drink water without his approval and rarely stirred out. His tyranny and misbehaviour had made the people of Bijapur miserable. In the year previous a large number of people had assembled to kill him, with the connivance of 'Adil Khan himself, and Dilawar Khan had then fled to join Nizam-ul-Mulk. After a time 'Adil Khan invited him back and he returned, believing he would be well treated. Instead, when he reached the court his eyes were gouged out and his effects confiscated. His son, Muhammad Khan, was wooed by 'Adil Khan, but when this failed he too was blinded. Now 'Adil Khan had taken to making trouble and fighting a proxy war in Ahmadnagar. The situation was hence rather troubled in the north-western Deccan, as were the inhabitants. Faizi too complains of his own state, confused and completely shaken by all this turmoil that surrounds him. He concludes his report to Akbar on a slightly reproachful note:

> Since I have come here, following your order, when I was leaving you, you had placed your hand on my back. I consider that very auspicious hand of yours as a fortress (*hisār*), protecting my life, and I am sitting here, with full confidence, sincerity and a carefree heart, with my gaze directed at you, remembering my God and my master with perfect attention. May the shadow of your justice and grandeur be over those who are both near and far from you and keep the troubles of this age far from them.

Going Through the Motions

By the end of his second report we sense in Faizi a loss of interest in the whole enterprise of his travels to the Deccan. This is not a mere matter of rhetoric and tropes honed to better express his desire for proximity to the imperial object of his devotion, Akbar. We shall see his protestations grow louder and louder, his poetry beginning to occupy an ever-higher proportion of the reports, and a corresponding decline in the sort of mundane information that characterises the first two reports. The third report thus begins as follows.

> This small particle of the vast field of wonders, Faizi, offers the prostration of sincerity and the salutation (*taslīm*) of discipleship (*irādat*), which is the main pillar of prayer and is in keeping with the law of good fortune [for him]. Remembering the sky-like throne of Your Excellency, the Shadow of God, the master of the earth, time, the world, and the people of the world:

> The emperor whose court
> is higher than the sky's canopy,
> to whose destiny
> victory is eternally wedded.[79]

---

[79] Abu'l Faiz (Faizi), *Inshā'-i Faizī*, ed. Arshad, 145–60.

Over several flowery lines the verses (*qasīda*) continue in praise of Akbar. Having thus paid his respects, Faizi declares his own submission once more before the ruler, and the text moves to Faizi's favourite metaphors using "light" as a representation of Akbar's sovereignty. "Your Excellency's presence is itself a microcosm," he declares, "perfect reason and the divine essence are embodied in you." More follows in this vein: the sun of reality (*āftāb-i haqīqat*) shines on Akbar's personality. The humble report (*'arīza*) that Faizi sends is, naturally, in keeping with his own limitations and personality. However, he swears by the court ("the touchstone of truth, and the kohl on the eyes of truth") that he shall do better and send across ever more information.

At the time of writing this third report Faizi had recently received a letter from his father, Shaikh Mubarak, who was at the court, concerning the important Mughal victory in Kashmir. The poet takes the occasion to ask God to preserve Akbar from the mischief of rebels and the ill intention of enemies. Despite his own humble position, says Faizi, he is elated by this great victory and notes that the people in Ahmadnagar too are greatly impressed by this manifestation of Mughal power. Word has come in, moreover, that the head of Yadgar Kul, a rebel from Kashmir, was hung on the main gate of Lahore as a lesson to others.[80] Faizi recalls the celebrations on the emperor's return to court from Gujarat after his victory there some two decades earlier. On that occasion Mulla Mubarak had declared that even Akbar's exercise of force and severity was, after all, only to ensure peace and stability: Faizi repeats the thought in relation to this new context. For, since the world's continuity depended on justice and the reign of peace, the ill-starred opponent from Kashmir had rightly been shown his place. Faizi had received a letter the next day from his dear brother Shaikh Abu'l Fazl, whose ab-

---

[80] Abu'l Fazl, *Akbar Nāma*, trans. Beveridge, vol. 3, 952–4; the rebellion of Yadgar Kul, nephew of Mirza Yusuf Khan, governor of Kashmir, is noted by Abu'l Fazl, who states that "the head of the brainless one" was brought to court. The rebellion in Kashmir was quelled in September 1592. Also see 'Abdul Qadir Badayuni, *Muntakhab*, trans. Lowe, vol. 2, 394–6, where it is noted that his head "afterwards was exalted to the battlements of the fortress of Lahore".

sence had greatly troubled Faizi. The letter contained further details of the victory, as also the

> miracles of Your Excellency, the high places you have attained, the illumination of your heart, the effectiveness of your fortune, your world-illuminating eye, your eternal destiny and eternal virtue, your ever-increasing power, your high-flown victory, your country-gifting generosity, and stability of character, all of which adorns the state, world-conquering determination, perfect orderliness, the world-capturing majesty (*shikoh-i ʿālamgīr*), and light-impregnated heart.

Indeed, Faizi notes, Shaikh Abu'l Fazl's prose itself was such that it awoke those in deep slumber even as it awoke sobriety among the intoxicated.

Faizi says he presented Abu'l Fazl's letter to Burhan Nizam-ul-Mulk, who considered himself the well-wisher and slave of Akbar, raised from the dust by the good wishes of his court; and Burhan too, overcome with joy on this occasion, had commissioned people to announce this publicly in the bazaar. Cartloads of sweetmeats were distributed, and the man who distributed them cried out aloud: "These sweets are for the victory over Kashmir, from the slaves of the emperor (*ghulāmān-i ʿālampanah*)." Indeed, Faizi notes, it was a regular custom in that region for rulers to thank Allah for their victories by distributing sweets. Thus, all come to know of the victory and enjoy the delicacies. Still another local custom of which Faizi approves is one entailing the lighting of lamps at dusk, and servants appearing before their rulers to bow their heads and praise and pray for them aloud.

Much elaborate praise of Akbar follows, with Faizi turning again to poetic reflections contrasting darkness and light. Faizi hopes that through Akbar's mediation blessings will spread through the whole world, which will thus acquire benefits from his light.[81] Implicit here is a universal claim for Mughal rule, seen as mediating between the sun and all of humankind.

---

[81] Abu'l Faiz (Faizi), *Inshāʾ-i Faizī*, ed. Arshad, 153.

After the administrative details and court etiquette of the first report, and the military reportage and talent scouting of the second, the third report thus finds Faizi in an irrepressibly poetic and philosophical mood. A long passage makes it clear that for every image emerging from behind the curtain of nature, and every song (*naghma*) appearing from fate's instrument, there is a Divine Cause; and in a *qasīda* he asserts that no curtain exists save the Self itself; on tearing it aside, the trance (*wajd*) of Shibli and the enlightenment (*kashf*) of Ghazali will be the listener's.[82]

Returning to prose, Faizi writes of how the whole world is now astonished and wondering at the defeat and destruction of that "base person" (Yadgar Kul, who had rebelled in Kashmir, as noted above). This is a lesson (*nasīhat*) for the sleeping, sent out from the royal court as an admonition. Its import is that those who leave the path of obedience will be treated thus and humiliated, besides being lost in the vast desert of destruction.

It turns out that, some two or three days earlier, Burhan Nizam-ul-Mulk had requested Faizi to write to Akbar asking for an Iranian savant called Mir Jamal-ud-Din Husaini to be sent to his court in the Deccan, since Burhan was starved of adequate literary talent.[83] Faizi agreed to intercede – so long as Jamal-ud-Din was granted an adequate *jāgīr* within that of Nizam-ul-Mulk; but he also took the occasion to give the other a stern reprimand for his general lack of loyalty to the Mughals. Nizam-ul-Mulk's services to the Mughals, he noted, were really not up to the mark, even if this was not wholly intentional. Faizi says both he and his brother Abu'l Fazl have done their best to improve the comportment of Nizam-ul-Mulk, who has promised to behave better, rather like a naughty child. He is said to have replied to Faizi's scolding by thanking God for the poet's presence and expressing the hope that he can make good his past errors.

---

[82] The references are to the mystic Abu Bakr al-Shibli (861–946), and the philosopher Abu Hamid Muhammad al-Ghazali (1058–1111), who might otherwise be considered difficult to reconcile.

[83] This savant appears in a far more prominent way in ch. 3 below.

Faizi's report now notes his imminent departure from Ahmadnagar and return towards the Mughal court, as instructed by Akbar. The poet had hoped to return promptly and make his mission as short as possible, but the return voyage was to take longer than anticipated. An interesting aside follows in the report: Faizi notes that, recently, two relatives of Mulla 'Abdul Qadir Badayuni, a well-known savant in Akbar's court, had come to him weeping and wailing while reporting that the Mulla, being ill, had not been able to attend the court as was required of him. Those at the court had been excessively harsh on him, claimed these relatives, who felt Akbar himself was probably unaware of the fact of the illness. Mulla 'Abdul Qadir has no access to the emperor other than via Faizi, says the poet, explaining why the distraught relatives have pursued him even as far as the Deccan. He protests the full competence of Mulla 'Abdul Qadir and his ability in the usual sciences; besides, he has been the disciple of Mulla Mubarak, Faizi's father. Indeed, Faizi has known him for some thirty-seven years and has no doubts about his scholarship, his poetic capability, his epistolatory craft, and his knowledge of Arabic and Persian. The Mulla, in addition, knows some Indian astrology (*nujūm-i hindū'i*), the music of India (*naghma-i wilāyat-i hindī*), as well as two varieties of chess. He has even learnt to play the *jantar* and *bīn* in his time! Despite all these qualifications he is not greedy and satisfied with little. A man of integrity, Mulla 'Abdul Qadir knows etiquette and has given up many of the rituals of tradition (*taqlīd*); all in all, he is a sincere and loyal (*ikhlās*) man.

Mulla 'Abdul Qadir, the emperor is reminded, had accompanied a force to an expedition in the region of Udaipur (*koh-i malmīr* or Kumbhalmer) and been wounded in the process; Akbar had rewarded him thereafter. He had first come to the court with Jalal Khan Qurchi, who had presented him by saying he had found an *imām* for Akbar. Mir Fathullah had also, to an extent, praised him to Akbar; this was a man equally and personally known to Abu'l Fazl. Since Akbar's court was full of true people, it was a pity for the Mulla's star to have fallen; Faizi wishes to plead his case, for to do otherwise would be to fail in his duty. The letter ends with a call for God's blessing on the court of Akbar, that it might remain true, righteous, and on the right path; and with the hope that the emperor's (benign) shadow will remain on the unfortunate, forgiving their errors and mistakes. "May your fortune, power, greatness, and majesty multiply a thousand times, and remain for ever."[84]

This letter of commendation is curious, for we know – and have noted above – that Mulla 'Abdul Qadir Badayuni was in fact one of Faizi's trenchant critics, one who judged him rather harshly in his own unofficial history, the *Muntakhab al-Tawārikh*. Yet the Mulla's negative judgement had more to do with Faizi's politics and religious proclivities than with his talents as a poet, which he readily admitted were prodigious. In this letter, extracted from Faizi by importuning relatives of the Mulla in the faraway Deccan, one can sense the ties that bound together such men, a sort of *esprit de corps* amongst the Mughal literati that sometimes transcended the obvious differences. The only matter on which Faizi appears to have made a serious error of judgement was in regard to Badayuni's sense of loyalty, which he rather overrated.

A *nazm* composition follows to terminate the relatively brief third report, once more on the subject of dawn, here combined with the theme of separation from the divine, and that of the imminent approach to the emperor's court.

Similar themes are carried over into the fourth *'arzdāsht*, which is very brief , compared in particular to the rather prolix character of the first two.[85] Here, once more, the humbler than humble Faizi proffers prostrations and salutations (*sijda* and *taslīm*). He has been

---

[84] Abu'l Faiz (Faizi), *Inshā'-i Faizī*, ed. Arshad, 157–8. Also see 'Abdul Qadir Badayuni, *Muntakhab*, trans. Haig, vol. 3, 419–20; text: 303–5; this letter in support of Badayuni is dated Ahmadnagar, 23 February 1592 (10 Jumada I, 1000 AH). Badayuni comments on the letter, and his own tortuous relationship with Faizi, in this context, as follows (translation, 421): "If any should ask what rules of humanity and faithfulness I observe in so harshly reviling one who had so much goodwill for me and so much sincere friendship, . . . I reply 'All this is true, but what could I do? The claims of the faith and the safeguarding of one's compact with God are above all other claims'."

[85] Abu'l Faiz (Faizi), *Inshā'-i Faizī*, ed. Arshad, 160–2.

long deprived of being able to present himself before the court and regrets that the end of that state of deprivation still seems far.

The central problem appears to be that Faizi is unable to depart from Ahmadnagar. He lingers on even while pleading that he should return quickly and suggesting that further details on the area could be presented to the emperor far more competently by his brother Abu'l Fazl. But instructions from the court, and a royal *farmān* brought by Mewati messengers, insist that he should delay his departure.

> O emperor, bring the light of hope to my night,
> Bring eternal light to my candle,
> the light that illumines your eye and heart,
> give me a mere particle of it,
> in devotion to the Sun (*ba 'ishq-i khurshīd*).

The Long Way Home

The last two *'arzdāshts*, the fifth and sixth, are also brief, highly literary, almost devoid of political intelligence, and replete with impatience for his return to the court. Were we to analyse them from the purely pragmatic perspective of earlier readers of Faizi, such as the colonial worthies Messrs Elliot and Dowson, we would turn away from them soon enough; but in our opinion they form a whole with the others and must be read as such, both for what they contain and what they leave out.

Once more, the fifth letter begins with Faizi presenting his forehead for prostration before the court that is elevated like the Qibla, the sea of sanctity to those who are pure. A verse praising the court and the emperor follows. Faizi next regrets his separation from Akbar in prose: will he one day have relief from this bitter wine of hopelessness? The affairs of the world now make an appearance: Burhan Nizam-ul-Mulk still considers himself the creature of Akbar, raised by his munificence. He has at last made peace with 'Adil Khan and, returned to Ahmadnagar, is preparing an appropriate *peshkash* payment for Akbar.[86] This is to be sent back with Faizi, who

---

[86] Ibid., 164.

declares himself ashamed of the inordinate delay in the Nizam-ul-Mulk's *jāgīr*.

In the meanwhile, he has read some letters that have arrived from the Hurmuz traders on the west coast to their counterparts in Ahmadnagar. These report that Shah 'Abbas had first gone to Gilan to deal with the recalcitrant Khan Ahmad Gilani (whose tributes and offers have not been deemed sufficient); the latter, unable to withstand him, had escaped on a boat to Shirwan. The Shah deputed his own men there, and then in the month of Sha'ban set out for Khorasan, accompanied by 150,000 horsemen and footsoldiers. There now ensued a great battle (*jang-i 'azīm*); the Shah recaptured Mashhad and Herat from the Uzbeks. The Uzbeks fled the battlefield in the direction of Herat. A certain Kokaltash (an Uzbek commander) attempted to stand his ground, mobilised some persons, and set out for Mashhad. He crossed the Sogawar River with a few men, but one of the Shah's men, Tokhmaq, arrived with a huge army: the Uzbeks suffered a crushing defeat and bolted.[87]

The Uzbeks and the Safavid Qizilbash were thus locked in fierce conflict, with both trying to enter Mashhad. After an extended struggle, Kokaltash with seven horsemen had at last run away, terrified by the rivers of Uzbek blood that were being spilt by the Qizilbash. Thereupon the Shah had entered Mashhad, while Tokhmaq remained in Herat.

Another letter states that the son of 'Abdullah Khan was wounded seriously in all of this but had managed to escape. The great merchant (*saudāgar-i buzurg*) Khwaja Baha-ud-Din had written from Chaul to say that the captain (*nākhudā*) of a ship which was on its way from Hurmuz to Goa had stopped off at his port on some pretext and given him all the latest news. He further stated that once the Shah had taken Khorasan, he had sent sixty 'Iraqi horses, expensive textiles, and a large quantity of goods to Akbar by way of tribute (*peshkash*)! The envoy (*īlchī*) was still in Hurmuz and was about to leave for the Mughal court via Sind. This news had reached Faizi from several sources. Another letter (*khatt-i dīgar*) claims that

87 Ibid., 164–5. For this campaign, also see Monshi, *History of Shah 'Abbas*, vol. 2, 558–61.

a hundred severed heads of Uzbeks and a hundred live Uzbek slaves were being sent to the Mughals by the Safavids.

Faizi portrays Shah 'Abbas here as a mere *mukhlis* (here "devotee") of the Mughals who craved Akbar's attention. He claims that the Safavids admitted freely that their fortune and state (*daulat dar khāndān-i safawī*) was really due to the Mughals (*īn dūdmān-i 'alī*), as was "evident from the pages of history".[88] When wise people reflected, Faizi notes, they would see that the veins and flesh of the people of all the seven climes depend on the munificence of Akbar's well-protected territories (*mamālik-i mahrūsa*).

Finally, the sixth *'arzdāsht* is almost purely ideological in content, with a brilliant and deeply poetic statement combining illuminism, sun-worship, and the mature Akbarian ideology which both Abu'l Fazl and Faizi had striven so hard to articulate from the 1580s onwards.[89] It begins in the usual way with Faizi offering *sijda* and *taslīm* to the emperor, the shadow of God. A *qasīda* follows, after which Faizi presents his last homeward-bound report. When Akbar was on his return from Kashmir to Lahore he had issued a *farmān* to Faizi; on receiving this order, Faizi says he got together a force of a hundred cavalry and a hundred footsoldiers, including archers and gunners, in order to set out for the court. On 25 Bahman, or 9 Jumada I, at dawn, he had reached Burhanpur traversing 52 *kos* in one stretch (*manzil*), a feat that had astonished people in Burhanpur. Faizi declares this merely reflects his determination to return rapidly.

The zamindars of that area were now obedient and sincere; Burhan Nizam-ul-Mulk himself, as one of the slaves of Akbar, had for years kissed the dust of the majestic court; his very veins and flesh being made of the salt of obedience and service, why should he not be permitted to live in peace as an obedient devotee, like other zamindars near the capital? He had sent expensive objects and *peshkash* from his *jāgir*, which would follow in Faizi's train. The slaves of the court had either to pay revenue (*kharāj*) or send tribute (*pesh-*

---

[88] This was, of course, the exact opposite of the real relationship between Babur and Humayun and the Safavid dynasty.

[89] Abu'l Faiz (Faizi), *Inshā'-i Faizī*, ed. Arshad, 166–70.

kash); there was no other way, for this was a court whose servitors had attained the eternal fortune of subjecthood. On the other hand, those who resisted would lose their heads, which would be suspended in a niche of the public gate (*darwāza-i 'ibrat*). Those who really comprehended the chain of order and administration in the world knew that God had chosen Akbar as a standard for the entire universe as a sign of perfection; Akbar's sun-like personality would give light to Reason and help distinguish between good and bad. This brief report terminates then with a set of seven flattering verses.

Conclusion

Faizi's embassy to the Deccan was not considered a particular success from a diplomatic perspective, a fact that even his devoted brother Abu'l Fazl implicitly admits in the *Akbar Nāma*:

> On the 28th [Ardibihisht] the standard of the seekers after knowledge, the *malik al-shu'rā'* Shaikh Faizi, returned from the Deccan, and after an absence of 1 year, 8 months, 14 days, did homage. He was exalted by various favours. He had gone on an embassy. Burhan in his arrogance and self-will had not listened to his counsels. He had not sent fitting presents and had prepared the materials for his own injury. Raji 'Ali Khan had to some extent listened to his commands and had sent his daughter with choice bridal gifts for the wooing of the Prince Royal.[90]

Faizi's own sometime client, the acerbic unofficial chronicler Badayuni, for his part notes that in Muharram 1002 (September–October 1593), four months after Faizi's return, "the other ambassadors arrived from the rulers of the Dakhin having succeeded in their negotiations; and paid their respects. And since Burhan-ul-Mulk had not sent any acceptable present, on the 21st of Muharram, the Emperor appointed the Prince Daniyal to this service, as *wakīl* to the Khan-i Khanan . . . and other *amīrs* with 70,000 specially assigned troops."[91] A snide tone laces this comment: the other ambassadors had "succeeded", so only Faizi had apparently failed.

---

[90] Abu'l Fazl, *Akbar Nāma*, trans. Beveridge, vol. 3, 982.
[91] 'Abdul Qadir Badayuni, *Muntakhab*, vol. 2, 402–3.

This "failure" meant in part that Mughal expansion into the Deccan continued into Ahmadnagar, which was captured by Mughal forces in 1601; on the other hand, the sultanates of Bijapur and Golkonda managed to survive well into the seventeenth century by a combination of diplomatic and other means. But this is surely not what interests us here, not least because it is doubtful whether the course of Mughal expansion hinged crucially on Faizi's abilities as a diplomat. The six reports discussed see the poet in an unaccustomed role, that of reporter and observer, but also in a more usual one – that of "talent-scout" for the Mughal court.

Faizi's window into Iran is thus another example of the sort of mutual reflection that took place across the borders of Mughal India and Safavid Iran, and shows the two political poles in a battle for prestige and talent. This is a battle that would continue into the next decade, as the rich and complex account of Asad Beg's missions into the Deccan amply demonstrate. This further development lies at the heart of the next chapter.

3

Self-promoting Envoys

God takes the boat where he wills, so that
the captain (nākhudā) tears his clothes in despair.
– Asad Beg Qazwini

Introduction

THE PRECEDING chapter took us into the world of an author and traveller who was also — and perhaps above all — a poet rather reluctant to keep his poetical impulses in check. Faizi's narrative, in the form of his six reports of mixed length, occupies a rather particular place in Mughal letters as much due to the literary and ideological nature of his writing as to the prosaic content of the text. Besides appearing in his full *inshā'* collection, the reports also appear in other compendia, notably one that has the apposite title *Tabāshīr al-Subh* (The Break of Dawn), reflecting the constant preoccupation that Faizi shows with light, the sun, dawn, and dusk.[1] If we were to contrast Faizi with other writers of ego-documents, the peculiar character of his writings is immediately apparent. This is a significant point that demonstrates the degree of stylistic flexibility which the writer of such accounts was afforded in the Indo-Persian world.

Faizi did not go quite so far as some other writers who directly

---

[1] This is the manuscript to be found in the Salar Jang Museum and Library, Hyderabad, Adab Farsi, 31, as cited in Sherwani, *History of the Qutb Shahi Kingdom*, 352–3.

adopted the *masnawī*, a rhymed poetical form, as a formal genre for penning an ego-narrative; instead, he preferred to accept the broad constraints of prose writing, made use of certain epistolographical conventions and the idea of successive reports (*'arzdāshts*), and then took advantage of the place that Persian prose affords within it to poetry – whether that quoted from authors of yore or of the writer's own composition.[2] In other words, Faizi took the prose account as far as he could in the direction of poetry without actually breaking the bounds of prose.

As we have seen, this could pose a problem to later readers with a different set of aesthetic conceptions and a far more rigid framework of evaluation. Dowson's late-nineteenth-century dismissal of Faizi thus also carries with it the implicit suggestion that far better writings could be found within the Indo-Persian (and broader Islamic) world. This judgement was based upon the idea that the excellence of the ego-document and travel account was to be measured in terms of its spareness, its prosaic quality, its avowed desire to stick to the point – all qualities in which Faizi was manifestly lacking. From this point of view, the text which we shall address in this chapter is a far "better" account. It comes from the pen of a writer of the same world as Faizi, and perhaps only half a generation younger. But where Faizi is seen in most accounts as a literary giant, in the ocean of whose massive œuvre the reports from the Deccan are a mere drop, Asad Beg Qazwini is a far more obscure figure – though not entirely lacking in literary distinction.[3]

We learn from contemporary literary commentators that Asad Beg was from an accomplished family in Qazwin. His father Khwaja Muhammad Murad was prosperous, well-travelled, and witness to many of the ups and downs of the times. In his early youth Asad Beg left Qazwin for Herat, where he joined the entourage of Khwaja Afzal, the vizier of 'Ali Quli Khan Shamlu, governor of Herat. There, he came

---

[2] See the discussion of a seventeenth-century text in Alam and Subrahmanyam, *Indo-Persian Travels in the Age of Discoveries*, 24–42. Also see Babayan, *The City as Anthology*, 183–95.

[3] For Faizi's works, see Desai, "Life and Works of Faidi", 1–35; and Kirmani, "The Significance of Faidi's Poetry", 26–35. Also the extended reflection in Alam and Subrahmanyam, *Writing the Mughal World*, 204–48.

into contact with various talented and accomplished persons and gained some experience in matters of administration.[4]

One of these other talents was 'Abdul Nabi Qazwini, who writes in his *tazkira* that, after a few years, as was written in Asad Beg's Fate (*ba hasb-i taqdīr*), he left Khorasan and the Safavid domains for the more tempting area of Hindustan, where he quickly joined the service of the great, most pious and virtuous Shaikh Abu'l Fazl who, at the time, was one of the principal nobles of the powerful ruler Jalal-ud-Din Muhammad Akbar. In Abu'l Fazl's service, Asad Beg acquired a reputation for reliability (*kamāl-i i'tibār*), and his devotion to his master was such that he was generally known as Asad Shaikh Abu'l Fazli. After Abu'l Fazl's assassination in August 1602 – an event to which we return below – Asad Beg entered the direct service of the emperor. After a time he was sent by Akbar as envoy (*hājib*) to the Deccan. As he carried out this mission to the emperor's entire satisfaction, he was thereafter well received in court. It is stated that on Akbar's death his son Jahangir took Asad Beg into the group of his own *bandagān* (personal servants) and deployed him in political negotiations (such as with the difficult Mahabat Khan). If 'Abdul Nabi's account was partly based on hearsay, it is also true that he met Asad Beg in Mandu in 1617, when he was able to see the latter's *dīwān* with nearly 8000 verses, including a *masnawī* written in the well-known metre of Khusrau-Shirin, and a *Sāqī-nāma* from which 'Abdul Nabi quotes extensively.

Another contemporary writer named Taqi-ud-Din Auhadi, in his *Tazkira 'arafāt al-'āshiqīn*, also pays some attention to Asad Beg and reproduces a number of his verses.[5] He praises Asad Beg for his sober temperament and understanding, and states he had worked for a time in the household of Mirza Ja'far Asaf Khan, and more recently in the service of Jahangir as a *mansabdār*, where he had been the paymaster (*bakhshī*) in Kabul. In his assessment Asad Beg, known in particular for his eloquence, was able in his dealings with people and always available

---

[4] 'Abdul Nabi Qazwini, *Tazkira-yi Maikhāna*, 248–57. For a summing up of these and other materials, see Mashita, "Asad Beg Qazvīnī".

[5] Taqi-ud-Din Muhammad Auhadi Daqqaqi Balyani, *Tazkira 'arafāt al-'āshiqīn*, vol. 1, 602–4. We have also consulted another edition, by Sayyid Muhsin Naji Nasrabadi (2009), vol. 1, 579–80.

to serve his friends loyally. Auhadi had met him in Agra too and inspected his *dīwān*, which at the time contained 2000 verses of different sorts. He quotes some of these, one sequence of which runs as follows:

> I have made my palate bitter with wine
> On account of my separation from you.
> I have burnt my patience
> With the fire of my restless desire.
>
> Don't spread my blood
> For I fear you'll be ashamed afterwards.
> Just as the cup-bearer feels shame
> After spilling the wine.
>
> Spread my blood if you wish,
> But don't spill my wine.
> For a drop of my wine
> Is worth a hundred of my blood.
>
> I am crying, and people are troubled.
> But I'm happy because they don't know the cause.

The recent rediscovery of what appears to be a copy of Asad Beg's *dīwān* affords us other insights into his place in the Mughal court, especially in the later phase, after the rise of Nur Jahan.[6] The verses contained here suggest a far more turbulent career in Mughal service than what the writers cited above would have us believe. Asad Beg writes in a verse obviously intended to curry favour:

> Nur Jahan, the loving companion of emperor Jahangir,
> Accompanied the ruler with the intention of a lion hunt,
> Four growling lions confronted them in the jungle,
> And the emperor prepared to deal with them.
> Nur Jahan requested the ruler,
> That she would put an end to the lions.
> She brought all four down to earth,
> And the emperor praised her to the skies.

---

[6] British Library, London, Persian Ms., Or. 5437, Asad Beg Qazwini, *Dīwān-i Asad.*

All four were attained by the bullets of her gun,
And the chronogram was: *Chahār adad kam shikār-i shīr*
    (Lit.: "In the lion hunt, four were now fewer.") [1031 H.]
May her fortune, wealth and age ever increase,
So long as the leonine emperor continues to rule over the fourth heaven.
Hold the hand of Asad, and raise him up as well,
So that Asad too might count himself a lion.

There are also clear indications in some of these verses that they were written when Asad Beg needed to re-establish himself in the milieu of the court after a period of disfavour. A verse directly addressed to Jahangir runs:

O merciful benefactor and master,
Even if my offence has crossed the line,
I request you accept my excuses,
For this was a moment of madness.

. . .

The capacity to forgive is God's wonder,
Greater than any other blessing.

Yet another makes this theme of disgrace and rehabilitation even more explicit:

O emperor of the world, do justice to me,
Bring justice to my unfortunate heart.
I have circled your presence for forty years,
And sacrificed myself on the dust of your threshold.
My age has now attained fifty-five years of joy and sorrow,
Now I hope the emperor will fulfil my heart's desire.
Give me a small place in your court,
So that some livelihood may reach my hands.
May I be spared from every misfortune,
And some relief be afforded to me.

Asad Beg's Mirror

Though his corpus of poetry would undoubtedly repay further study, it is not the aspect of Asad Beg that really concerns us. Rather, our central focus is on a text generally termed the *Waqāʾiʿ-i Asad Beg* (Asad Beg's Report), though it is also known by a number of other titles. The late-nineteenth-century compendium of translated texts by Elliot and Dowson contains a significant excerpt from it, since when it has been the object of intermittent but unsystematic attention, mostly from historians of the Deccan. It also survives in a fairly large number of manuscripts, evidence of the fact that it was seen as worthy of attention in the world of Mughal literati in the seventeenth century and beyond.[7]

A marginal note at the start of one of the principal manuscripts states that the text is the *Tārīkh-i Asad Beg Qazwini* (Asad Beg's History), and that its author – who later held the title of Peshrau Khan – was one of the most reliable and sincere friends of none other than Shaikh Abu'l Fazl ibn Shaikh Mubarak Nagauri. It further reports that the text contains a description of the assassination of Abu'l Fazl at the hands of a certain Bir Singh (or Nar Singh) Deo Bundela, with the connivance of Prince Salim, later the emperor Jahangir, near Sironj in 1011 H. (1602 CE), corresponding to the 47th regnal year of the emperor Akbar. Further, the summary continues, the deployment of an army under Mughal nobles for the chastisement of the Bundela chief is described, as is Asad Beg's own appointment to investigate the failure of this expedition. The text continues with his despatch to the Deccan as envoy (*hājib*) to Ibrahim ʿAdil Shah of Bijapur, and his return with tribute (*peshkash*) and gifts, including the daughter of the king of Bijapur to be given in marriage to the Mughal prince Daniyal. We are informed that the account includes other significant events until the death of Akbar in 1014 H. (1605 CE), and the accession of Jahangir in Delhi. There is also some detail of the author's travails, and various other matters. The com-

---

[7] Two recent editions exist: Asad Beg Qazwini, *Waqāʾiʿ-yi Asad Beg Qazwīnī*, ed. Chander Shekhar; and Asad Beg Qazwini, *Risāla-i Tārīkh-i Asad Beg Qazwīnī*, ed. Jamshid Nauruzi. The Chander Shekhar edition uses the oldest extant manuscript, Government Oriental Manuscripts Library and Research Institute, Hyderabad (former Asafiyah Collection), Fann-i Sawānih-i ʿUmrī 41. In our earlier publications, we have also used two manuscripts, primarily British Library, London, Mss Or. 1996. 30 fls (55 numbered pages), which we have collated with the Aligarh manuscript: Maulana Azad Library, AMU, Aligarh, Abdus Salam Collection, No. 270/40 (4). The British Library manuscript, Or. 1996, was copied on Wednesday, 25 Rabiʿ I 1211 H. (28 September 1796) by a certain Kishan Das.

mentator, a certain Ziya-ud-Din Ahmad, notes that it is, all in all, an excellent book, "a dependable treatise, rare even if it is brief." In the colophon there are useful additional biographical details concerning the author which supplement materials by the principal *tazkira* writers. The passage runs:

> Asad Beg Qazwini, the author of this treatise, distinguished for his efficiency, courtesy, and fine sensibility as well as his generosity, was in the service of Shaikh Abu'l Fazl, son of Shaikh Mubarak, for seventeen years. After his death, he gained access to the charmed circle of the confidants of the emperor [Akbar] and performed commendable services and tasks (*kār-o-khidmat*), and thus gained wealth and fame. A few years later, with the death of the ruler, he returned to the court of Jahangir, and though far from favour at first, was able with his constant efforts and excellent service in the last years of that reign to earn the title of Peshrau Khan. He died in the early years of Shahjahan in 1041 H. [1631–2 CE].[8]

We are given a glimpse here of the ups and downs of a career in Mughal service, where close proximity to the court and royal favour in the reign of Akbar is followed by a period of eclipse and subsequent restoration.[9]

Asad Beg's age and year of arrival in India is unclear. If indeed he served Abu'l Fazl for seventeen years, he must have arrived in the Mughal domains from his native Qazwin and Herat as a young man in the late 1570s or early 1580s, at which point he would have been much too insignificant to have been directly "recruited" into Akbar's empire in the manner of the great Iranian intellectuals that Faizi sought out in the Deccan. Whatever stature he did achieve, then, was within the framework of Mughal service, as we see in the pages of his account.

Asad Beg's narrative is a sober and rather modestly written text, set down with clarity and interspersed with the usual verses, of which a few are possibly of the author's composition. It begins:

---

[8] The title Peshrau Khan had earlier been held by a certain Mihtar Sa'adat, a slave who had been gifted by Shah Tahmasp to Humayun, and who died in October 1608, having risen to the head of the carpet department (*farāsh-khāna*). See Jahangir, *The Jahangirnama*, 97.

[9] Compare Metin Kunt, *The Sultan's Servants*.

In the Name of God, who [alone] is the True Knower and who gives and promotes True Strength and Wisdom. The ray of God gives its quality to the greenery in the garden of soul-stirring pleasures. The Eternal Spring of that garden reflects the beauty and eternal youth of God's Garden (*nigāristān*). [Verse]:

Each flower of every garden gains colour from Him.
The nightingale's voice too comes from Him.
If there is a thorn in the garden,
even its freshness is His sign.[10]

Mughal Persian texts of a certain dimension – those that are not enormous encyclopaedic compendia or huge chronicles – usually have an organising conceit, or root metaphor, that defines them from the very start and lends them a structure and direction. Is Asad Beg's organising idea the garden, and the idea of God as Divine Gardener? Two rhymed prose sentences that quickly follow this opening sequence point in a different direction. In these we are told that when an ant seeks its way in the night, its eye too gains sight from God. Further, if traces of the footprints of humble travellers in the lanes of comfort remain, it is from the grace of those in the divine Assembly of Affection. We may rest assured then that the text is going to address the question of movement and travel in a central way, confirmed by the verses that follow.

When an ant travels on a highway,
it is protected by His favour.
The earth is coloured by His waterfall,
even the old leaves remain green in His spring.

To praise God adequately is beyond the power of his languge, declares the "destitute" Asad Beg. For however powerful his speech may be, to describe God's qualities must remain out of his reach.

We then move on in proper sequence to a passage devoted to praise of the Prophet, followed by fulsome praise of his Companions, and prayers to God for them, the leaders of the Faith, and guides on the Path of Belief; from the tone of these passages the author appears to

---

[10] Asad Beg, *Waqāʾiʿ-yi Asad Beg Qazwīnī*, ed. Chander Shekhar, 27.

be either an open-minded Shi'i or a Sunni. He then describes himself as that most insignificant slave of God, by name Asad bin Muhammad Murad Zakani, with no further details adduced. He plunges us directly into the core of his narrative which – as we shall see – does not follow a perfect chronological sequence, but instead moves back and forth, periodically using the structural device of a sort of "flashback".[11]

What then is the heart of the matter? It is of course the tragic and untimely death of Shaikh Abu'l Fazl, that great scholar and "Pearl of His Age", who was assassinated near Sarai Bar in Sironj on 7 Rabi' I 1011 H. (23 August 1602) at the time of the Friday prayer. But the immediate evocation is not of the death itself, and rather of how news of this tragedy reached the Mughal court of Akbar. The text draws us directly into a set of minute details, and assumes that the reader knows of the event and the broad circumstances surrounding it. When news of this terrible but inevitable event reached the emperor, writes Asad Beg, he was filled with sadness and abstained from consumption of his regular intoxicants; nor did he eat as grief made him weep incessantly. In the midst of his lamentations he asked one of his close confidants: "Where is Asad?" Since no one knew Asad Beg's exact whereabouts, this question remained unanswered for a time. In the meanwhile the great noble Mirza Ja'far Asaf Khan reached the court, and seeing the state of the emperor began to weep uncontrollably as well.[12] The emperor asked him too for news of Asad Beg. "Was he with him [Abu'l Fazl] or not?" Asaf Khan replied that he had been with Abu'l Fazl up to Sironj, but that the *faujdār* (military commander) of the new districts – which Abu'l Fazl had received by way

[11] This section of the text appears in a serviceable translation by B.W. Chapman, under the head "Murder of Abu-l Fazl", in Elliot and Dowson, eds, *The History of India*, vol. 6, 154–60.

[12] This Asaf Khan should not be confounded with the celebrated Khwaja Abu'l Hasan, son of I'timad-ud-Daula, who died in 1641. Ja'far Beg, who died in 1612, was also a writer who composed a version of the story of Khusrau and Shirin, entitled the *Nūr-nāma*. Jahangir suspected him of being disloyal with respect to his dealings with Khusrau, but nevertheless did not act against him (cf. the notice of his death in Jahangir, *The Jahangirnama*, 136).

of a *jāgīr* assignment in Malwa – had remained behind with Asad Beg at Sironj at their master's orders. Abu'l Fazl himself had then set out, escorted by a group of armed men raised by a certain Gopal Das Nakta in Malwa, and continued towards the court. The unfortunate Asad had pleaded with his master to allow him to go along till Gwaliyar, but Abu'l Fazl had refused. Thus, Asaf Khan reported his own surmise that Asad Beg was not with his master when he was killed. The emperor now instructed Asaf Khan to write a *farmān* to Asad Beg to return immediately to the court, leaving the rest of Abu'l Fazl's retinue and affairs with Gopal Das. Asaf Khan prepared the order and sent it under seal through a certain Miyan Gada. The Miyan in turn gave it to one of his brothers who was to take it to Sironj and escort Asad Beg back.

This then is our introduction to Asad Beg, through the evocation of what is apparently for him the turning point of his life. His career thus really begins, or at least begins to be interesting, when Abu'l Fazl's life ends. A description now follows of the assassination itself, a key event, but one that must be narrated diplomatically. For behind the assassination was the hand of Jahangir, the reigning monarch at the time that Asad Beg wrote, and this fact was such common knowledge (indeed, Jahangir mentions it clearly in his own memoirs) that there was no sense in denying it. Here then is how Asad Beg approaches the matter.

The assassination was written by Fate, he says, for the Age had turned against Abu'l Fazl; and so it was that the incompetent and poorly equipped men of Gopal Das accompanied Abu'l Fazl, rather than a more competent escort. To take care of his own revenue assignment, the ill-starred Gopal Das had earlier raised a troop levy of about 300 lowly Rajputs (*Rājput-i zabūn*), none of whom had or merited a salary over Rs 20. Rumours were already about that Raja Bir Singh Deo Bundela would attempt to waylay them, but Abu'l Fazl tended not to pay heed to them even when letters to this effect came from his own brother Shaikh Abu'l Khair. Gopal Das, for his part, argued that Abu'l Fazl's own retinue of Mughals was fatigued, and should remain at Sironj to deal with the threat of Indarjit Bundela, another rebellious Central Indian Rajput chief. This view was accepted by Abu'l Fazl, whose death was thus inevitable, in Asad Beg's view, once the poor and incompetent force of Gopal Das was preferred to more experienced cavalry.

[Verse]:

The signal of battle was sounded,
in keeping with the regulations of the ignorant,
and so lives were ruined.[13]

There were still a few great warriors with Shaikh Abu'l Fazl, such as Gada'i Khan Afghan and his son, but they were to lose their lives in the engagement. For the larger force of a hundred men with this Afghan leader had been left behind with Asad Beg, which cost them dear. Gada'i Khan was a brave and experienced man, but what could he do all alone? When they were ambushed, he fell on the Rajput enemy with his son; but the Khan was quickly killed and the son was wounded. Another warrior, Jalal Khan Afghan, was also killed in the engagement, while two other Afghans, Salim Khan and Sher Khan, were surrounded and yet gave up their lives fighting for the Shaikh. A certain Turkoman called Mansur Chatiq (close to Asad Beg), formerly in the service of Khan-i Khanan, was also killed, as was a Mirza Muhammad Qurbegi. The escort was thus decimated rapidly.

When Abu'l Fazl was wounded with a spear and fell, Jabbar Khasakhail, an Abyssinian who always accompanied him, at once killed the Rajput who had delivered the blow. He then came to the side of his master and found him still alive. But before he could carry him off, Bir Singh Deo himself arrived with his men and cut off the great man's head. The others all fled and reached Gwaliyar. A certain Mirza Muhsin, a relative of Qazi Khan Badakhshi, advised him of the incident. But by the time Qazi Khan and his men came back to the spot, taking their own time, it was all over. Whatever comes from Allah goes back to Him, concludes Asad Beg.

This is a rapid summary of the incident, which Asad Beg dilates on at far greater length at various moments later in his text. It is a summary recounted in a defensive mode to make sure he cannot be accused

---

[13] Asad Beg, *Waqāʾiʿ-yi Asad Beg Qazwīnī*, ed. Chander Shekhar, 31; *Nuskha-i Ahwāl-i Asad Beg* (Aligarh Ms), 4.

of negligence. For, he repeats, when Abu'l Fazl ordered Asad Beg to re-main behind in Sironj, the latter had insisted he be allowed to accompany his master as far as Gwaliyar. His request summarily denied, Asad Beg nonetheless got on his horse, being determined to continue, but Abu'l Fazl made him promise not to.

It so happened that Abu'l Fazl's elephant, standards, and other accoutrements had been left behind with Asad Beg, who, using this as a pretext, had asked his own assistant Rustam Khan Turkoman to follow Abu'l Fazl. But he too was sent back by Abu'l Fazl. Asad Beg assures his readers that he was by now thoroughly consumed with anxiety for his master. The question of the standards (*naqqāra-o-'alam*) continued to prey on his mind, and he worried that, in case of an attack, Abu'l Fazl would have to look not only to his own personal safety but also to the standards, since his honour (literally, his "beard") would depend on them. Messages thus went back and forth between master and servant on the issue, but as usual Abu'l Fazl had his way in the end; he kept the standards and sent back word that God was with him, and that he needed only Asad Beg's prayers. Asad Beg quotes a verse from the great poet Sa'di: "Often predictions are made in a playful way (*bāzīcha*),/ But when the stars turn, they become the truth." In this case, states Asad Beg, he had not meant what he said to be a jest: it was his realistic estimate of the situation. For when Abu'l Fazl reached Sarai Bar and camped there, a wandering mendicant (*jogī*) had come to see him and given concrete news that Bir Singh Deo Bundela would attack the party the following day. Instead of taking this information seriously, Abu'l Fazl had simply given the man a few rupees and sent him off; he had not even bothered to keep his own companions informed. This, writes Asad Beg, was Abu'l Fazl's nature, and so it was that he then went to sleep negligently (*dar nihāyat ghaflat*).

The next day, Friday, he bathed and put on white clothes because it was a holy day. Several people from the area came to meet him in his camp, including prebend-holders (*jāgīrdārs*), administrators (*karorīs*), and others. For a chance to meet with the emperor's confidant and boon companion was not to be easily neglected. Among them was the servant of a certain Mirza Rustam with forty or fifty horsemen, while one Shaikh Mustafa, the military commander (*faujdār*) of a place called

Kala Bagh, also brought his own force. Altogether, with these and other forces, there were some 200 more horsemen available to him, but he dismissed them all. Had they but remained with him! exclaims Asad Beg. Yet when Destiny is dictated by the sky, even the intelligent become blind. Instead of protecting himself, Abu'l Fazl ordered his own camp to be disbanded and set out towards the north with Ya'qub Khan, while the drums were sounded to signal his other companions.

His small group had not advanced far when some Bundela foot-soldiers emerged and attacked them. The few soldiers in the Mughal party who were alert advanced against them. A certain Mirza Muhsin Badakhshi went out in advance and looked around from a high vantage point, returning rapidly with an estimate of the enemy force. But when he came back he found that many of those in the Mughal camp were still not ready to fight, or even in their battle dress. A rapid consultation was held on what to do. Should they advance, or take another route? It was decided, presumably as a matter of honour, not to retreat or change route. Mirza Muhsin now advanced rapidly and himself managed to escape the clutches of the Bundelas. But Abu'l Fazl, who was slower to advance, came upon an advance party of Bundelas who – as had been feared by Asad Beg – managed to seize his standard and kettledrum. Abu'l Fazl was now forced to turn back to recover his standard, just as foreseen.

The next Bundela wave of 500 horse, with Bir Singh at its head, now arrived, all clad in chain-mail and armour. Gada'i Khan Afghan attacked them with a few horse and was promptly killed. At this time an unidentified man with Shaikh Abu'l Fazl pointed out that as the enemy had body armour and they did not, refuge at a distance and the use of arrows from there would improve their chances in the fight. He thus took the Shaikh's bridle and led his horse off apace.

But by this time the enemy had reached in numbers and begun to attack them with great vigour. A Rajput pierced the Shaikh from the back with a spear and he slumped to his side. Jabbar Khasakhail, Abu'l Fazl's body-servant, who was immediately behind the Shaikh, at once killed the Rajput and briefly lowered Abu'l Fazl off the horse; he then managed to remount him and lead him away some distance. But being grievously wounded, Abu'l Fazl fell again from his mount. At this point Bir Singh himself arrived in the thick of the action. Thinking quickly, Jabbar hid himself and his wounded master behind a tree, but Bir Singh spotted one of their horses and an elephant. Reaching where they were concealed, he found the helpless Abu'l Fazl practically alone. He promptly dismounted, placed Abu'l Fazl's head on his thigh, and wiped the blood off his cheek with his own scarf (*dupattā*). When Jabbar saw from his nearby concealment that Bir Singh was being kind to Abu'l Fazl, he came out and saluted him. Bir Singh asked who he was, upon which Abu'l Fazl opened his eyes. Bir Singh now saluted him and said to the Shaikh: "Hazrat-i Jahangir has in his grace sent for you," and showed him a *farmān* bearing the seal of the prince.[14] When he saw the document, Abu'l Fazl made a wry face, but Bir Singh still swore he had come to take him to meet the prince in all safety. The enraged Shaikh now began to curse him and utter vile insults (*dushnām-o-fahsh*). Some of Bir Singh's other men who had now arrived said he was gravely wounded and could not be saved, suggesting that there was really no point in helping him further. Sensing the inevitable, Jabbar now pulled out his sword and felled two or three of these Rajputs, and then advanced towards Bir Singh. Bir Singh stood up to defend himself, Jabbar was killed by others, and the men with the Bundela chief decapitated Abu'l Fazl. The action having ended, no one else in the Mughal party put up further resistance.[15]

It is unclear what Asad Beg's sources for this account really were. Jabbar obviously, having been killed according to this narrative, could not have been the direct informant. Perhaps another member of the Mughal party (such as a certain Niyaz, mentioned below) was also concealed nearby. In any event, the lessons Asad Beg draws from the episode are somewhat unexpected. His major point is that all of this hap-

[14] Jahangir was fully implicated in the death of Abu'l Fazl, as he himself admitted; cf. Jahangir, *The Jahangirnama*, 32–3. He defends his act, stating that "although this [the death] caused distress to His Majesty Arsh-Ashyani [Akbar], in the end it resulted in my being able to proceed to kiss the threshold of my exalted father's court without fear."

[15] Asad Beg, *Waqāʾiʿ-yi Asad Beg Qazwīnī*, ed. Chander Shekhar, 36; *Nuskha-i Ahwāl-i Asad Beg* (London), 5; Aligarh Ms, 11. This is the close of the extract published by Elliot and Dowson.

pened because Abu'l Fazl, out of a sense of arrogance, overconfidence, and a false estimation of his own strength had proceeded with an insufficient force. There is also a suggestion that Bir Singh had not really intended to kill him but was provoked by Abu'l Fazl's "vile insults".

The account now turns to Asad Beg himself who – ignorant of all that had transpired – was preparing the next day to depart from Sironj. His departure was somewhat delayed on account of a faulty kettledrum, seen by him as an ill omen. While this was being sorted out, a messenger arrived with news that he whispered to one of Asad Beg's companions, a certain Muhammad Nasir, whose face altered visibly on hearing it. But he said nothing to Asad Beg. A certain Sher 'Ali Aqa, one of Asad Beg's other servants, had been sent out ahead on the road to Sarai Bar, and he too returned at this time, desperately spurring his tired horse. Asad Beg recognised him from a distance and sent men out to meet him. But before he arrived at the camp Muhammad Nasir said: "This is the news. The Nawwab [Abu'l Fazl] has been in a battle. Sher 'Ali is bringing the news of his death." Asad Beg does not tell us of his emotions of the moment: on hearing this, he merely says he retreated at once into Sironj and began to improve its fortifications, fearing a further Bundela attack. A few days later an official order came from Asaf Khan at the court with news of Abu'l Fazl's death, and an imperial order to calm the soldiers and leave them behind with Gopal Das. Asad Beg himself was required to return to the court without delay. He left at once, and on reaching the way station of Sarai Kala Bagh encountered two of his master's other servants, Rai Chand Bakhshi and Parmanand, who had taken shelter there. They said Abu'l Fazl had left many of his effects with them before moving northwards, saying they themselves could take their time. However, before they could leave, news had come of Abu'l Fazl's death, so they had decided to stay put. Asad Beg directed a few encouraging words at them, loaded up some camels, elephants, and horses with Abu'l Fazl's goods – worth some Rs 400,000–Rs 500,000 – and advanced through the area of Vandira, and on to Nanhala, with the intention of making for the court at Agra.

It so happened that a small box full of excellent jewels (*jawāhir-i nafīs*), which Abu'l Fazl was bringing back as a *peshkash* tribute for

Akbar, had been handed to a servant called Niyaz, son of Ayaz. When Abu'l Fazl was killed the box was on an elephant with this servant, who had jumped off and hidden in the jungle. Once the Bundelas had left, Niyaz had managed to come back to Sarai Kala Bagh, to seek the company of a Mughal party and reach safety. Hearing of this, Asad Beg promptly took it upon himself to recover the box for the emperor. Abu'l Fazl was dead, nothing could be done about it; but Asad Beg, by recovering as much of the goods and tribute as he could, still intended to put the best face on it when he arrived in court, fearing as he did the wrath of a grieving emperor.

Asad Beg at Court

A new chapter of the account opens with Asad Beg's arrival in Akbarabad-Agra accompanied by a party of some 200 horse. He notes that he had left Rai Chand and the others in the party some distance behind with the baggage, so that he first appeared at the court with only his own small retinue and the box of jewels, accompanied too by a certain Sarbaragh Khan who had carried the imperial *farmān* to him. Asad Beg now describes his own entry into court. It was afternoon, and the emperor was seated in the viewing balcony of the audience-hall (*jharoka-i-khāss-o-'āmm*).[16] Leaving his other men near the gate to the inner enclosure, Asad Beg came to the *jharoka* with five or six others; Sarbaragh Khan had already preceded him to inform the officials (*bakhshīs*). Shaikh Farid, the official who ultimately controlled access to the emperor, now called him inside the first set of railings alone, and announced his name aloud. When the emperor heard his name, and his glance fell on him, tears began to flow from his eyes and he started to wail aloud. Abruptly leaving the balcony and audience, he went into his quarters. All were astonished, the emperor's reaction being so at variance with established etiquette. It seemed as if the deep mourning since news of the calamity had resumed in full force. The court was abuzz with speculation when the emperor asked his

---

[16] For aspects of Mughal court ritual, see Khan, *The Court of the Great Mughuls*, 29–45.

confidant Raja Ramdas to summon Asad Beg to his quarters.[17] The rumour was that he was intent on chopping Asad Beg to pieces with his own hands.

A nervous Ramdas led him to a corner from where a visible number of high nobles – such as Khan-i A'zam Mirza 'Aziz Koka, Asaf Khan, and Shaikh Farid – attempted desperately to distract and placate the emperor, who told Ramdas to ask Asad Beg: "In spite of boasting of the bravery and sincerity with which you served Abu'l Fazl, in which hell were you [concealed] that you proved to be of no help to him in his extremity? Now you've come running to me! I will not leave you alive. I'll kill you in such a way that the whole world will remember it." From where he stood Asad Beg heard the livid emperor; his head began to swim and he lost his composure. "How can I reply?" he eventually asked Ramdas, requesting him to intervene while resigning himself to his fate. It was well known that Akbar was just: he killed no one on a whim. So, if really he wanted to kill Asad Beg, it would be for some alleviation of his grief, and therefore justified. All the same, Asad Beg wanted to assert his own innocence and the truth of the matter to reach the emperor's ears.

Returning to Akbar, Ramdas explained all this and served as intermediary. Akbar sent word to ask why Asad Beg had abandoned Abu'l Fazl to the jaws of death. Asad Beg explained thus: On the first part of the journey, from Sarra to Sironj, Asad Beg with Mahdi 'Ali Kashmiri and 1000 horse (both Mughal and Afghan) had accompanied Abu'l Fazl. But at Sironj Gopal Das had reminded Abu'l Fazl that he had no *jāgīr* assignment in the Mughal heartland of Hindustan. The men who had come back with him from the Deccan were not only tired but would bother him en route for their emoluments, which Abu'l Fazl would be hard pressed to pay since his own financial resources were in Central India. So, it would be best to leave them there with Asad Beg, and they would be used later to take revenge for the death of Fannu Kamboh, who had been killed earlier by rebel Bundelas. In their place, Gopal Das would send fresh soldiers with his own brother. Abu'l

---

[17] On Raja Ramdas Kacchwaha (d. 1613), see Shahnawaz Khan, *Ma'āsir ul-Umarā*, trans. Beveridge and Prashad, vol. 2, 587–9.

Fazl found this offer reasonable and summoned Asad Beg, telling him that he had received the area of Chanderi recently as a *jāgīr*, and that it was rebellious terrain on account of the Bundelas; hence it was prudent to leave a force behind to chastise the Bundelas and push on himself. Asad Beg demurred, insisting he would first go with him to court, then return to complete this work. To this Abu'l Fazl replied that as God was with him there was no need to accompany him. Asad Beg declared at court that the emperor knew Abu'l Fazl's stubborn character all too well: he could not be resisted once he had decided on a course. In sum, then, Abu'l Fazl had brought it all upon himself.

All this was conveyed by Ramdas to Akbar. The other high Mughal nobles too were unanimous in their opinion that Asad was entirely faultless in the matter: "He was a servant, and a servant cannot control things beyond a point," they said. Indeed, Asad Beg had gone far beyond the call of duty in his insistence that he would stay.

On hearing all this, and the pleas of Khan-i A'zam in particular, the emperor relented, his anger was calmed, and Asad Beg was allowed to go to his own house and meet his children, which he had not done thus far. Akbar also instructed Shaikh Farid to allow no servant of Abu'l Fazl other than Asad Beg direct access to him. Presently, Ramdas informed Asad Beg – to his very great relief – that things had turned out quite well for him. It was a moment to give thanks to God. But Asad Beg also took the opportunity to tell Ramdas that he had so far been unable to do his formal prostration (*sijda*) to the ruler. Could he be allowed this? The request was conveyed and at the end of the day the emperor instructed Ramdas to bring Asad Beg to a particular part of his inner apartments, to the so-called *chaukandī*.

We now receive a close glimpse of inner court ritual, in a version mixing formality and informality which is far more credible than that presented by European observers such as Sir Thomas Roe.[18] The emperor had finished his prayers (*tasbīh*) by the time Asad Beg was taken to him by Ramdas. Asad Beg ceremonially presented the standing ruler with a single gold *muhr* and nine rupees (as *nazr*, tribute) and

---

[18] Richards, "The Formulation of Imperial Authority"; also, more recently, Subrahmanyam, *Explorations in Connected History*, 143–72.

performed two forms of prostration (*kūrnish* and *sijda*). The emperor asked Shaikh Farid to bring Asad Beg closer, to allow him reverentially to kiss his feet. Akbar then placed his hand on Asad Beg's back twice by way of benediction, and the latter saw to his relief that the emperor's visage was now full of serenity (*bahjat*). The emperor asked about his origins in terms of both place and community (*az kujā ast wa az che mardūm ast*). Asad Beg hardly dared reply directly yet; instead, a certain Iranian noble called Naqib Khan replied that Asad Beg was of good origins, from Qazwin in Iran, which was also his own city. The emperor now gave him a particular look of attention. Asad Beg glanced towards Asaf Khan to indicate indirectly that he knew him well too. Asaf Khan now moved closer to Akbar and stated: "Asad Beg is a close relative of mine. His father was known as Murad Beg Aqa Mulla, and was amongst the best-known people of Qazwin." The emperor expressed surprise that Asad Beg was a relative of Asaf Khan — he had not known this. Screwing up courage, Asad Beg said that as merely a humble servant of the emperor he had no need of any other lineage (*nisbat*). The emperor replied that, in truth, accomplished people had no need of a *nisbat*. He then asked Asad Beg how long he had been in the service of Abu'l Fazl, and Asad Beg said for about seventeen years. The emperor commented on the length of the service and his good fortune therefrom. The others present added words of support and praise, confirming Asad Beg as perfectly trustworthy. At this the emperor said he had in fact long had his eye on Asad Beg; he had even desired to wean him from Abu'l Fazl's service, but the latter had not wanted it. Asad Beg replied that he too had long wanted to enter the direct service of the emperor but had lacked the opportunity.[19]

The fact that the conversation had gone on for so long emboldened Asad Beg: he seized the occasion to cite a verse in a Turkish dialect (which he terms *zabān-i rāmandi*).[20] When the emperor heard it he was surprised and asked after its language and meaning. Naqib Khan said it was in the Ramandi language and meant:

[19] Asad Beg, *Waqā'i'-yi Asad Beg Qazwīnī*, ed. Chander Shekhar, 44; *Nuskha-i Ahwāl-i Asad Beg* (London), 9; Aligarh Ms, 20.

[20] Asad Beg, *Waqā'i'-yi Asad Beg Qazwīnī*, ed. Chander Shekhar, 45. This may imply that Asad Beg originally hailed from the area of Ramandi, west of Baghdad.

I have the desire to see you,
but since I cannot,
I must seek a place to see
those who gaze upon you.

The emperor, greatly appreciating this flattering verse, promptly told Khwaja Amin-ud-Din to get a honorific robe (*khil'at*) ready for Asad Beg. The Khwaja went off to fetch the box in which such things were stored. A certain "head-to-foot" robe (*sar-o-pā*), of particularly high value – greater than that normally given to those of Asad's station – was picked out by the emperor himself and given to Shaikh Farid.[21] The Shaikh and the Khwaja then took Asad Beg behind a curtain, placed the cloth on him, and brought him back to perform *sijda* once more.

Further remarks were exchanged, and Asad Beg assures his reader that, in general, his replies pleased the emperor. Indeed, Asad Beg claims he was the main subject of conversation in court that evening, from which many of his friends gathered he would soon get a significant position. Before the end of the evening the emperor once more made special mention of Asad Beg to Ramdas and told him to take care of him – as well as to remind him from time to time of such an excellent servant. Ramdas bowed, Asad Beg prostrated himself, and then taking leave of Ramdas departed the court with Asaf Khan.

From the brink of disaster, the situation had been quickly turned around. While leaving the court, Asaf Khan assured Asad Beg he was now in favour and warned him never to commit an error in the emperor's service. Also, he told him to try being present at the viewing ceremony for Akbar (*jharoka darshan*) from the next day. This conversation continued till Asaf Khan mounted his horse, at which point he spoke further words of encouragement and an appropriate prayer for Asad Beg's well-being.

The greater part of a day had passed since Asad Beg had entered Agra, but it was only now that he was able to return home, and thanks to God, see his own children after a gap of six years. He assures the reader that, on account of the royal interview, he was in an emotional and euphoric state all night, weeping and praying.

[21] On these robes, see Gordon, ed., *Robes of Honour*.

The next day, as advised, he went to the *jharoka darshan*, and thereafter to see Khwaja Amin-ud-Din. At this later time of the day, the emperor came out once more to the *jharoka-i 'āmm-o-khāss*. On this occasion Asad Beg produced and presented Akbar the jewel-box of Abu'l
Fazl, which he had on his person. The emperor asked him what it was;
he replied that it contained all the jewels and gold *muhrs* that Abu'l
Fazl had gathered in the Deccan for Akbar. On the day of his death,
it had been taken by his servant Niyaz, who had hidden in the jungle.
Rai Chand and Parmanand in Kala Bagh had then got hold of it, from
where it had passed to Asad Beg. It was thus offered to the emperor
now as a tribute (*nazr*). Moved, the emperor protested that he could not
bear to have things associated with Abu'l Fazl near him: Asad Beg
should give it to Shaikh 'Abdul Rahman, the son of the deceased
savant. To this Asad Beg responded that all his master's goods had been
given over to the charge of the *tahwīldārs* (custodians of goods) before
being transmitted to Abu'l Fazl's son. But this box was an exception –
Abu'l Fazl had particularly wanted it to be given to the emperor.
When he insisted a thousand times in this fashion, the emperor had
it sent to the inner quarters (*mahal*); sadly, all traces of it had been lost
ever since.

By now Asad Beg had begun wandering about the palace with a certain sense of familiarity. He thus went to one of the offices (the *katehra*)
to enquire after the evaluation of his own *mansab* rank in the Mughal
hierarchy. Thereafter, he was taken once more by Ramdas to the *ghusl-
khāna* and *chaukandī* in the inner part of the palace. Various procedures
and negotiations involving much going back and forth continued the
next five or six days, after which the emperor told Shaikh Farid to decide
Asad Beg's position in consultation with Asaf Khan. Both then asked
Khwaja Amin-ud-Din for his opinion, and designated him to ascer-
tain what Asad Beg's position had been before. The Khwaja took Asad
Beg aside, behind a curtain, and asked him confidentially what his previous *mansab* rank really was. To this Asad replied saying when in
Sironj he had had a salary of Rs 1000, and also under his command a
good-sized body of troopers whose expenses were amply taken care of.
Asad Beg thus adroitly avoided a direct answer to the question and the
Khwaja reported his response to the others. Asaf Khan now expressed

surprise at having no clear *mansab* – as all of them had usually had at the start of their service. After extended discussions, they went and told the emperor that Asad Beg was probably exaggerating his rank somewhat. The emperor then intervened directly and said he should be given a rank of 100 *zāt*/20 *sawār*. The paymasters (*bakhshīs*) were informed of this, and Asad Beg went to offer his reverence (*taslīm*) to the emperor in gratitude for what he had been granted. He then thought to say something in his own favour, but was told peremptorily by Asaf Khan to remain silent; a good servant should be confident of the emperor's benefaction. Taking the path of discretion, Asad Beg decided to remain quiet and left matters at that.

Murtaza Khan now went in to the emperor and stated that Asad Beg had accepted the position; Asad Beg did his *taslīm* of acceptance and the emperor showed his pleasure. The strategy of silence paid off, to an extent, for when the paymasters were finalising matters the emperor intervened once more and said that, for Abu'l Fazl's sake, the *mansab* could be increased slightly to 100/25. However, though Asad Beg received this rank he was never able to stand at court with those of 100 and 200 rank, as was customary in Mughal ritual. This was because, within a few days of this assignation, he received another assignment, to which his narrative presently turns.

Potential disgrace had thus been transformed into a decent position in direct imperial service. Asad Beg now began to be drawn into court intrigues. It turned out that Khwaja Qasim (titled Diyanat Khan), and Mirza Mukhtar Beg (uncle of Asaf Khan) jointly looked after the office of *ihtimām* ("supervision" or "superintendence"). Mukhtar Beg being also the tutor (*atālīq*) of Prince Parvez, he was unable to take care of his *ihtimām* duties full-time, so he and Khwaja Qasim (who was more devoted to the job) were always quarrelling. As a result, one day a report reached the emperor of this, with a particular complaint against Mukhtar Beg. Asaf Khan defended his uncle by saying he was overburdened with the care of Prince Parvez. So it was decided to put someone else in his place, and Asaf Khan hinted strongly that the post could go to Asad Beg. The emperor was glad of this suggestion and called Asad Beg to give him this position formally. Again, this involved a particular court ceremony – which in Asad Beg's view was in accordance with the Chaghatay custom (*tūra-i chaghatāy*) – entailing the emperor taking an object in his hand, placing his hand on Asad Beg's shoulder, and declaring he was allowed into the circle of the *ahl-i yatāq*, equivalent to the status of paymaster (*bakhshīgirī*).[22] This gave him a joint position with Khwaja Qasim, who always reminded him thereafter that it was on his account (or at any rate on account of his complaints against Mukhtar Beg) that Asad Beg had ascended to the post of *bakhshī*.

Soon after this, the emperor pointed out to Asaf Khan that nothing had been done about Asad Beg's *mansab*, and that he had not been given a proper *jāgīr* assignment. Despite the fact that Asaf Khan was very busy, he found the time to assign some villages in *sarkār* Narnaul west of Delhi, which had earlier been in the *jāgīr* of the late Shah 'Ali Khan. This was a quite lucrative assignment, for in the first year Asad Beg got Rs 17,000 from it, in the second year Rs 20,000, and in the third year as much as Rs 23,000.

A New Assignment

Two or three months went quickly by with Asad Beg deeply immersed in the affairs of court.[23] Then, news arrived in Agra that the army sent out under the command of the great Mughal noble Rai Rayan against Bir Singh (it included high nobles such as Ziya-ul-Mulk Kashi, its *bakhshī*) had roundly defeated the Bundela chief and forced him to take refuge in the fort of Iraj with some 400 Rajputs.[24] The fort having been besieged by the imperial army, it was decided that the very next

---

[22] Asad Beg, *Waqā'i'-yi Asad Beg Qazwīnī*, ed. Chander Shekhar, 49; *Nuskha-i Ahwāl-i Asad Beg* (London), 10; Aligarh Ms, 23.

[23] A new section begins here, entitled "The appointment of Asad Beg to investigate into the failure of the army of Rai Rayan": Asad Beg, *Waqā'i'-yi Asad Beg Qazwīnī*, ed. Chander Shekhar, 49; *Nuskha-i Ahwāl-i Asad Beg* (London), 10. Extracts from this section appear in Elliot and Dowson, *History of India*, vol. 6, 160–2.

[24] The title of Rai Rayan had been given by Akbar to a certain Pitr Das, who was later to hold the title of Raja Bikramjit. See Jahangir, *The Jahangirnama*, 31, where Jahangir describes him "as of the Khattri caste", and notes further that "during my

day the redoubt would be taken by storm. Now, Iraj had a wide and deep river on one side, and on the other three sides it was open. Rai Rayan paid little attention to the side with the river but sealed off the three other sides. Unluckily for him, after nightfall when everyone slept the Rajputs broke open the walls on the side of the river, crossing it where it became fordable – and in fact after walking through Rai Rayan's elephant stables. By the time the other *amīrs* were roused with this information, the Rajputs had vanished. When this news was read out Akbar, thirsting for Bir Singh's blood, flew into a great rage. He told Shaikh Farid to enquire and apportion fault. Shaikh Farid suggested they send Shaikh Abu'l Khair, Abu'l Fazl's brother, to make the required enquiries. But the emperor did not approve this suggestion and sent for Asad Beg instead, who was in the quarters of Aqa Mulla, where he heard the voice of the pages (*naqībs*) crying out: "Asad should reach the pavilion (*burj*) at once." Flustered, Asad ran all the way and saluted in front of the emperor, who was still seething. Yet when he saw Asad Beg he smiled and proferred him all the reports that had come in. Asad Beg read the report (*ʿarzdāsht*) of Rai Rayan, and had just begun to read a second report when the emperor asked him if he had understood what had transpired. To this, Asad replied cautiously: "To a certain extent." The emperor told him that things had turned out very badly and that Asad Beg needed to reach the army and identify the sources of error.

This was an onerous responsibility, but Asad Beg accepted it and guaranteed with his own life that he would do all that was necessary. The emperor now ordered some five *farmāns* to be brought by Shaikh Farid, which were given to Asad Beg: one was for Rai Rayan, one for Rai Raj Singh, one for Rai Raja Bhadoria, one for Ziya-ul-Mulk Bakhshi, and the fifth was directed to all the other *amīrs* and *mansabdārs* enjoining them to tell Asad Beg all they knew. The emperor personally handed him the *farmāns*, took a shawl from his own waist, and tied it as a turban on Asad Beg's head in another gesture of personal favour. He was told to hasten the same night and expedite the enquiry.

------

father's reign he was promoted from overseer of the elephant stables to divan and the rank of amir," adding that "he is not devoid of understanding soldiering and strategy and tactics."

Asad Beg returned to Aqa Mulla's, ate a little something, and went back home. He then got together his servants, and with Sher 'Ali Aqa and another companion took his horses, a camel, and a mule; and having got together two or three sets of clothes, some books, pens, an inkstand, and paper, he set out at once towards Gwaliyar.

The affairs of the late Shaikh Abu'l Fazl were hence by no means settled, as adequate imperial revenge for his assassination had still not been taken. By the third day Asad Beg had reached Gwaliyar and gone on to Chaharsu, where he set up camp. Here he met Keshav Maru, son-in-law of the Gwaliyar raja, and set out with the protection of his 500 horsemen to guard himself against the rebel Bundelas.

This Keshav Maru was considered one of the best swordsmen amongst the Rajputs. Nevertheless, he was afraid of the Bundelas, whereas Asad Beg declares that he himself, protected by the emperor's fortunate star, was not. In view of the fear that the Bundelas inspired, they travelled for safety by night. On the third day they reached Rai Rayan's camp and Asad Beg sent Sher 'Ali Aqa ahead to Ziya-ul-Mulk to carry the news they had come.

Somewhat like Faizi's in the Deccan, Asad Beg's status was now far greater than his formal *mansab* rank, for he came directly as an envoy from the emperor. Various nobles came to see him, including Rai Rayan, Raj Singh, and Raja Bhadoria. A separate elaborate tent (with a curtain, *sarā-parda*, rigged up for privacy) was quickly made ready for Asad Beg to conduct his interviews. But he decided to go and visit Ziya-ul-Mulk during the day, using his special tent only at night. When he returned from the paymaster's camp, he found that the tent prepared for his use was half full of sacks of money. Sher 'Ali said five sacks had been delivered by the agents of Raja Raj Singh, and he had not been able to refuse them. Another Rs 5000 came from Rai Rayan. As they were talking, an agent of the *bakhshī* too arrived with Rs 3000. All in all, by morning the *umarā'* and *mansabdārs* had sent in Rs 18,000 to sweeten the disposition of the imperial envoy, and the next day Rai Rayan's men came and offered further hospitality. But Asad Beg refused, saying he had orders to the contrary. Instead, he had all the *umarā'* and *mansabdārs* called in. On the way, while in Gwaliyar, he had already gained much information, so he was far from naïve. Presently, Rai Rayan came to the camp and declared he wanted to talk to him alone: "I am of 5000/1000 rank. I hope with your grace to remain in this position. I am always at your service, and offer you this fine elephant. Rest assured that I shall never make a mistake." Asad Beg replied that this was strange talk. Having already made a major mistake in the emperor's service, the great noble was now trying to keep his *mansab* and even gain a promotion. Rai Rayan replied that with Asad Beg's aid the mistake could be excused. To this Asad Beg responded diplomatically, saying Rai Rayan should rest confident in him. His own uprightness and personality would be confirmed to Rai Rayan by the latter's sons and servants in the court. But he would not take a single *dīnār*, either from Rai Rayan or from anyone else; for, after all, this was his first job as the emperor's emissary and he did not wish it polluted by bribes. Rai Rayan was tactful: this was not a matter of money, for what he was offering was a mere gift of thanks (*shuk-rāna*) as Asad Beg's arrival had cleared the cloud over him. His fear of the emperor's wrath (which he felt was as powerful in its way as Divine Wrath) had now been allayed. Such auspiciousness (*shugūn*) required gifts ensuring a fruitful conclusion towards which Rai Rayan and his sons were in a position to assist. Little by little, he drew Asad Beg into his own quarters and gathered together all the *umarā'* and *mansabdārs*; a good number of famous Gwaliyari singers with pleas-ing voices (*kalāwantān-i khwush sarod wa āwāz-i Gwāliyār*) were brought to entertain them.

But Raja Raj Singh was not present, since he and Rai Rayan blam-ed each other for the Bundela "escapade". Asad Beg commented on this and said to his agents that his absence was not appropriate. He made it a point to send his own slave Musahib to the Raja, conveying to him that as the enquiry proceedings were on the emperor's orders, they were best conducted with everyone present. A high noble like Raj Singh needed to be present for his own good and for other servants of the emperor. The dispute between Raj Singh and Rai Rayan also needed to end.

When Musahib reached Raj Singh, he called for Kishna, his min-ister (*madār-i daulat*), to whom Asad Beg had already sent a separate message insisting on the need to reconcile his master and Rai Rayan, and threatening dire consequences if he did not co-operate. Raj Singh did not initially wish to comply, but Kishna told him that recalcitrance would result in problems both for himself and others such as his loyal minister – everything, including the earlier failure of the army, would be blamed on him as adviser: "You'll be saved, and I will be killed." So, little by little, he brought the Raja round and led him to the meeting. Meanwhile, Keshav Maru had arrived with his own Rajput warriors. When Raj Singh and his party reached the *sarā-parda*, Rai Rayan went forward to greet them, and only after seating them took his own place. A congenial conversation followed and the bitterness between the two melted away. Asad Beg claims this as a triumph of his own tact and powers of persuasion.

The crucial matter to be resolved was how Bir Singh had managed to escape. For this Asad Beg had an ingenious solution. A cloth (*chādar*) several yards long – made large by pieces stitched together – was brought and a sketch (*shakl*) of Iraj fort drawn on it showing the river on one side, and the walls and doors on the three other sides. The encampments (*morchal*) on all sides were indicated, and Ziya-ul-Mulk, the *bakhshī*, was told to write the names of the commanders at the correct locations, each being certified by the commanders affixing their seal to indicate assent to this drawing and its account. The place from which Bir Singh had escaped was also shown, as was the point where he had crossed the river. The nobles having placed their seals (*muhr*) on the drawing (*naqsha*), Asad Beg told them this was the self-explanatory report he would send to the emperor. They then all ate together and chewed betel-leaf (*pān*), so that the evening ended on a cordial note.

The son of Muhammad Khan Niyazi, who was a friend of Asad Beg, was deputed with 1000 horse to accompany the imperial emissary, who decided to leave that very night. When he reached his tent, he found that Rai Rayan had sent him an 'Iraqi horse with a saddle, two Turkish horses, and some high-quality cloths as a gift. Since they had already had a discussion on the subject of gifts, Asad Beg thought it was within the bounds of propriety to accept them. Rai Rayan had also written to his son Mohan Das that en route Asad Beg should be given an elephant: this gift Asad Beg refused as excessive. When Raja Raj Singh went back to his tent, he too sent (besides the Rs 5000 that he had already given) one good unspecified horse, another 'Iraqi one, and some good-quality cloth. Besides, twenty maunds of high-quality Gwaliyar rice and two maunds of jasmine oil (*fulel*) were to be sent by camel to Agra with him. Kishna delivered the message (*rasd*) with these, and also slipped in some Rs 2000–Rs 3000 of his own. All in all, Asad Beg, who had not even finished three days of his assignment, had already collected Rs 18,000, twenty-one horses, and a good camel (from Ziya-ul-Mulk). Clearly, being an imperial emissary had its advantages. He thus set out for Gwaliyar, where he picked up the other goods, apart from some gifts of his own for his friends. In this redistributive economy it behoved receivers of gifts to give in due manner to others.

Fifteen days after his departure from Agra, in the second watch, when the emperor was still in the *jharoka-i 'āmm-o-khāss*, Asad Beg arrived at court. He sent the gift items to his own house, then reached the *darbār* with Musahib. Since he had notified no one in advance of his return, he first informed Ramdas, and through him was duly presented to the emperor, before whom he bowed and gave the customary one *muhr* and nine rupees as *nazr*. Wasting no time, the emperor at once asked whose fault the whole fiasco with Bir Singh had been. Asad Beg held back, saying he would give him the details, but the emperor insisted on an answer at once. When he insisted several times, Asad Beg said that in his understanding no one had made an error (*taqsīr*) deliberately, and that at worst there had been negligence (*ghaflat*) implicating all. Hearing this, Shaikh Farid said negligence too was an error. But Asad Beg demurred: an error implied mistaken intent whereas negligence was unintended. Shaikh Farid was about to reply when the emperor stood up and said with relief on his face: "Asad is right."

Later, Asad Beg came to know that the emperor had greatly liked his distinction between the notions of *ghaflat* and *taqsīr*. Asaf Khan told him he deserved to be congratulated a hundred thousand times for having been so deft in saving various people from the emperor's wrath. I'timad-ud-Daula too said he had wondered what Asad Beg would do under the emperor's incessant pressure, before offering him a thousand felicitations on his wit and understanding. At the end of the day, no finger had been pointed at anyone in particular. All those who were in court, such as Rai Rayan's son, the agents of Raj Singh, the brothers of other nobles, etc., were content on learning of the report he had given. They then sent back reports to their principals to the effect that they had all been saved from the emperor's wrath, and the relatives of the soldiers who were on the campaign were also content – to the point that many of them gave offerings (*nazraha wa tasadduqāt*) in happiness.

Later that evening the emperor appeared in the *chaukandī*. Asad Beg showed his ingenious *chādar* plan of the escape to Ramdas, who in turn displayed it to the emperor. We may note in passing that since Akbar could not read, an explanation in the form of a drawing probably appealed particularly to him. Ramdas pointed out that, even in the course of a day's stay, Asad Beg had performed marvels that others would not have over several days. The emperor replied, "This is why Asad is Asad [a lion]." He then inspected the map and had Asad explain things to Ramdas. The affair was now treated as closed.

This, Asad Beg writes, was his first real service to the emperor (*khidmat-i awwal*), and it passed off so well that he had to give particular thanks to God; he had moreover gained considerable wealth thereby. He was thus able to return to his post of *ihtimām* and work efficiently; soon, the emperor was pleased enough to appoint him to the post of receiver (*tahwīldār*) of the tribute (*peshkash*). This post he retained for some six or seven months and was able to keep up close contacts with the *darbār*. Then, at last, one day, a second opportunity came his way – he was deputed as emissary (*hājib*) to the Deccan.

The Deccan Frontier

A good deal of water had flowed under the bridge since the time of Faizi's mission of the early 1590s to the Deccan. The Mughal prince Murad had led a major campaign there and had more or less brought the Ahmadnagar kingdom under the Mughal sway, when he died mysteriously in 1599.[25] After a short interruption, Mughal expansion then resumed, with Akbar himself taking direct charge of it for a time,

[25] For more on this subject, see Subrahmanyam, *Explorations in Connected History*, 71–103.

capturing the fort of Ahmadnagar in August 1600, and the major stronghold of Asirgarh in January 1601. With the death of the Ahmadnagar queen Chand Bibi, resistance to the Mughals largely came to be centred on a certain Miyan Raju Dakhni, and a group of Abyssinian warlords of whom an early example was a certain Abhang Khan Zangi. It seemed now that the Bijapur Sultanate might be the next target of Mughal expansionism.

When the emperor was temporarily resident in Burhanpur, he sent an emissary called Mir Jamal-ud-Din Husain Inju Shirazi – a well-born Iranian Sayyid and noted savant and lexicographer – to Ibrahim 'Adil Shah (whom Asad Beg terms 'Adil Khan Sawa'i) of Bijapur, ostensibly to improve relations with him.[26] The Mughals continued episodically to show their displeasure at the behaviour of this Deccan ruler, but thought it fit to allow him some space for manoeuvre and negotiation. Asad Beg notes for example that since 'Adil Khan claimed to be nothing less than a disciple (*murīd*) of the emperor, it was thought appropriate to raise his rank by way of a marriage between his family and that of the emperor. His daughter was hence to be married to Prince Daniyal. But instead of accomplishing this mission, the Sayyid from Shiraz remained at 'Adil Khan's court for a long while, and the emperor grew restive. Also, reports came in meanwhile from the Mughal general 'Abdul Rahim Khan-i Khanan in the Deccan, and from Mir Jamal-ud-Din, in which the latter gave far-fetched reasons for his failure to return. At length the emperor grew angry and decided to set him straight by sending a troubleshooter; Akbar's eye once more fell on Asad Beg ("the humblest of his slaves"). He told his *bakhshīs* of his intent to send Asad Beg to the Deccan and haul Mir Jamal-ud-Din back without so much as allowing him a sip of water. He then addressed Asad Beg in court and told him he would be going as emissary to the Deccan both for Mir Jamal-ud-Din and to bring back some treasure and goods (*zar-o-māl*). Asad Beg at once began to bow

---

[26] The section is entitled "My appointment to go to the Deccan to bring Mir Jamal-ud-Din Husain": Asad Beg, *Waqā'i'-yi Asad Beg Qazwīnī*, ed. Chander Shekhar, 58; *Nuskha-i Ahwāl-i Asad Beg* (London), 10a/14. Brief extracts appear again in Elliot and Dowson, *History of India*, vol. 6, 162–3. With reference to Mir Jamal-ud-Din Shirazi (d. 1626), also see Jamal-ud-Din Shirazi, *Farhang-i Jahāngīrī*, 3 vols.

and make his salutations, as did his ever-present ally Asaf Khan. The emperor then gave Mir Jamal-ud-Din's last report to Asaf Khan and explained his own intentions. Asaf Khan declared his contentment on behalf of Asad Beg, and having read the report bluntly told the emperor it was full of lame excuses. The emperor agreed and told Shaikh Farid to procure a list of important people in the Deccan, in order to make up a series of *farmāns* and gifts to be taken along. Mirza Ghiyas Beg I'timad-ud-Daula was told to give Asad Beg Rs 20,000 for his expenses on the way.

The necessary preparations including the *farmāns* were rapidly made. The *farmān* in the name of 'Adil Khan Bijapuri stated: "Since it seems you wish to take Qasba Kwaliyar, as we see from Mir Jamal-ud-Din's report, declare your intentions to Asad, our loyal slave. We shall then have Kwaliyar handed over to you, so that you can send your governor (*shiqdār*) there." Mir Jamal-ud-Din's *farmān* stated menacingly that if he did not return with Asad to the Mughal *darbār*, the consequences for his person and children would be dire. Besides, Asad Beg asked for a *farmān* for the emerging Abyssinian warlord Malik 'Ambar, which turned out useful later.[27] At an auspicious time the emperor took his leave of the envoy, giving him a horse and a special *khil'at*. He also instructed Asad Beg to, in particular, bring back an elephant called Atish Para belonging to 'Adil Khan, which he had so far not given to Mir Jamal-ud-Din Husain. Besides, writes Asad Beg, the emperor did him a thousand other kindnesses which his pen simply does not have the power to relate.

Another *farmān* was issued in the name of the great Timurid noble Mirza Shahrukh, governor (*hākim*) of Ujjain, in which he was sternly instructed to discontinue the discriminatory tax (*zakāt*) he had reimposed in spite of an earlier imperial order to the contrary; he was also told specifically to rule with justice in his province.[28] Akbar equally

---

[27] On Malik 'Ambar, also see Shyam, *Life and Times of Malik Ambar*, and Tamaskar, *Life and Work of Malik Ambar*. For an earlier account of dealings between Asad Beg and Malik 'Ambar, see Saksena, "A Few Unnoticed Facts", 601–3.

[28] On Mirza Shahrukh (d. 1607), grandson of Mirza Sulaiman, the Timurid ruler of Badakhshan, see Jahangir, *The Jahangirnama*, 33, where he is described rather patronisingly as "a real simpleton Turk by nature." Elsewhere, in his obituary

asked Asad Beg to convey an oral message to the Mirza, stating that he had declared the *zakāt* tax unlawful (*harām*). The paymasters had arranged some troopers to accompany the envoy, but the emperor eventually decided against sending them. We are given the impression throughout that Akbar took a close personal interest in the preparations of the mission, himself looking into every detail.

Asad Beg's first major halt was Ujjain, where he was met by Mirza Shahrukh, who welcomed him with great kindness, sending a force two leagues (*kos*) out from the city to meet him. He accompanied him to a house designated as his residence; he gave Asad a horse with a saddle, 5000 *muzaffarīs*, and some valuable pieces of cloth. He also told his relative Mirza Badi-al-Zaman to take particular care of the envoy. Asad Beg then went on to Mirza Shahrukh's own house, where musicians and singers from Ujjain were brought together for a soirée. At the end of the day, a horse and more excellent cloth were given to Asad. From Ujjain he proceeded to Mandu, a city that was in his words "the envy of Paradise". Here he paid homage to a certain Maulana Ghausi, a Sufi and sage of the time from whose wisdom he profited.

Asad Beg's account here is rapid and perfunctory. He does not spend much time describing the way stations or the landscape through which he passes. Very much the political actor, his main concern is with people and places of courtly and political significance, and it is thus that he quickly passes on to the town that had emerged at this time as the great centre of Mughal activity in the region, namely Burhanpur.[29] Here, his initial encounters are with Prince Daniyal and the generalissimo Khan-i Khanan (to whom he was charged to deliver imperial *farmāns* and robes of honour), but Asad Beg also took the time to seek out a number of his own previous acquaintances and "matchless friends", who included cultured savants (*ahl-i dānish wa bīnash*) such as Maulana Shikani, Maulana Naziri, Nom Quli Beg A'ini, Mir Muhammad Qasim Asir, Maulana Nau'i, and Mir Husain Kufri. Most

---

notice (p. 82), Jahangir also adds that "he never did anything that would trouble the royal mind and always served in loyalty." The account of Asad Beg suggests a more complex view.

[29] On Burhanpur, also see ch. 2 above; and Gordon, "Burhanpur".

of them were Iranians, and all had apparently found a place in the sub-imperial court that had emerged around the Khan-i Khanan. Asad Beg notes that he had wished his quarters close to those of the Khan-i Khanan, but he was instead put in a particularly delectable spot. However, he could not tarry long and in the space of a few days began to make preparations for his departure towards Bijapur. The Khan-i Khanan and the other Mughal nobles stationed in the area (*sūba* Berar) helped him on his mission by getting together the sum of Rs 100,000, fifty 'Iraqi and Turkish horses, and ten camels (both male and female).

While he was leaving the Khan-i Khanan asked Asad Beg whether he was ready to undertake an important task, stressing that he himself would be very grateful if he were. It seemed there was a quarrel between the great Abyssinian warlord Malik 'Ambar and a certain Hasan 'Ali Beg. The Khan-i Khanan wanted Asad Beg to try reconciling the two, a responsibility that the Mughal envoy accepted gladly. A suitable escort was now made up for him, and at an auspicious time he set out, leaving behind his own brother Ibrahim Beg and servant Nasir – who so far had accompanied him – with the Khan-i Khanan so that they might send him news from the Mughal court periodically. Another companion, a certain Khwaja Murshid Beg Qabadoz, was given money and left behind at Burhanpur in preparation for his journey to 'Iraq. Asad Beg's party on the second leg was thus reduced to a far smaller number than those who had initially accompanied him from Agra.

This initial meeting with the Khan-i Khanan seems therefore to have passed off rather pleasantly, in distinct contrast with the somewhat poor relations that were to obtain between them later. The next major way station for Asad Beg was Bir, where he met Mirza Hasan 'Ali Beg, one of the two parties in the quarrel mentioned above that Asad Beg had promised to resolve. The following diplomatic solution was found. On receipt of a note from Asad Beg, Hasan 'Ali Beg was to organise a celebration (*majlis*) in a place called Karbar, near Narpur, and Asad Beg was to bring Malik 'Ambar there on his own, to effect a reconciliation. In order to do this, Asad Beg had to set out westwards towards the region of Balaghat. A messenger of Hasan 'Ali Beg was sent out in advance with word that an envoy (*ilchī*) of the Mughal emperor was going towards Bijapur; and that he also had a *farmān* for Malik 'Ambar, who should hence meet him and receive the imperial order. Now, the Abyssinian warlord clearly had an efficient intelligence network in the area, and his spies quickly brought him news that Asad Beg was on the road, so that he at once advanced with his own army and elephants to receive the *farmān*. When he saw that the envoy was Asad Beg, he was astonished, since the two apparently already knew each other. He received the *farmān* with ceremony, the two embraced and fell to exchanging old memories. Indeed, declares Asad Beg, Malik 'Ambar was so content that it was beyond description. He treated the Mughal envoy very well, had him stay near his own camp, and handled him with every sign of warmth and friendliness.

The next day there were festivities (*jashn*), in which several nobles of Ahmadnagar and learned persons and turbaned scholars as well as Sayyids were present. Asad Beg goes so far as to declare that in this meeting alone there were so many scholars (*hāfiz*) of the Qur'an, learned and saintly people, that not even a fraction of such could have been espied over a single meeting anywhere in Hindustan. The deep discussions held on the Qur'an and hadith were only perhaps comparable to those in Mashhad, exclaims Asad Beg. Special things to eat, called *kandūrī* in the language of the Deccan (*istilāh-i Dakhan*), were made for the occasion.[30] An encampment set up in a large field had chintz from the Golkonda port of Macchlibandar (Masulipatnam) decorating it. Dishes of copper and silver were placed to a man's height on all sides, marvellously spiced and tasty. The cooking was truly perfect: the sweetmeats, dry fruits, preserves (*āchār*), and breads (*nān-hā wa kamāj-hā*) were so superior that Asad Beg declares himself at a loss for words. This is an aspect of Asad Beg, namely the irrepressible *bon vivant*, that we shall encounter time and again.

When this part of the festivity was over, Asad Beg raised the delicate question of Mirza Hasan 'Ali Beg. Malik 'Ambar, after brief hesitation, replied that he was so well disposed to Asad Beg that he could refuse him nothing, and would hence attend the meeting with

---

[30] Asad Beg, *Waqā'i'-yi Asad Beg Qazwīnī*, ed. Chander Shekhar, 65.

his enemy. Asad Beg at once sent off a message to Hasan 'Ali Beg. The very next evening a reply arrived with the following verse, obliquely confirming that everything was in order for the meeting:

The bird of good omen (*humā*) has fallen into our net.
If you happen to pass, come visit our house (*maqām*).[31]

The next day, as planned, Asad Beg went to the meeting spot with Malik 'Ambar and an escort of 500 horse. From the other side Hasan 'Ali Beg, Bahadur-ul-Mulk, Shamshir Khan, Rustam Khan, and Sa'id Khan came forward to meet them. They all sat together and then Hasan 'Ali Beg and Malik 'Ambar talked alone for a while. Once the unstated misunderstandings had been cleared up, pledges of renewed friendship were made, and after that food was partaken of together. An elephant and a fine horse were given to Malik 'Ambar by Hasan 'Ali Beg, who returned from there to his own encampment. Asad Beg for his part went back with Malik 'Ambar to his camp and sent a report from there with all these details to the Khan-i Khanan.

He also sent a submissive report ('*arzdāsht*) from Malik 'Ambar himself to the Khan-i Khanan, to be sent on to the court in Agra. In this document he declared his allegiance, and fervent desire to serve the emperor. For some ten or twelve days Asad Beg stayed on with Malik 'Ambar; on each day he found himself well treated and given much wonderful food. On the twelfth day he was given a small and sturdy elephant and three good Arab horses with decorated saddles, Rs 10,000 in cash, as well as some trays of cloth and a decorated and rare palankeen. Two of the elephants he received at this time were eventually passed on to the emperor on Asad Beg's return to Agra; Akbar, it is noted, declared that he liked them very much, particularly the tough little elephant.

Asad Beg takes the occasion to dilate somewhat on Malik 'Ambar and his own past dealings with him. It turned out that, at the time when Abu'l Fazl was in the Deccan, Malik 'Ambar was in distress and searching service. He wished to join Abu'l Fazl; but a certain Raja Harbans, who was in charge of the Deccan and disliked 'Ambar, did

[31] Ibid., 65; verse on *Nuskha-i Ahwāl-i Asad Beg* (London), 16; Aligarh Ms, 38.

not take to the idea and strongly advised Abu'l Fazl against it.[32] So Malik 'Ambar did not get a proper hearing or employment and departed disappointed. But God eventually answered his prayers and enabled him to use his talents. On those previous occasions Asad Beg and he had had several pleasant meetings, and this was manifestly the reason why he Malik 'Ambar treated him well over this later encounter.

Asad Beg is here fulsome in his praise for Malik 'Ambar, claiming that if he were to recount the qualities of this "bravest of the men of the time", a chapter – nay, a whole book – would be needed. Nor was he simply brave, rather he was exemplary in his piety too. In 'Ambar's camp, on every Friday evening, 12,000 recitations of the Qur'an were carried out. When he read the *namāz* in an assembly, no less than 20,000 people were present. Besides, he was in the habit of giving countless alms. Here then is a portrayal of Malik 'Ambar that sits askew of the image that emerges of him later in the 1610s and early 1620s, when he was treated by Jahangir's court as an arch-villain, sedition monger, and impediment to Mughal ambitions in the Deccan.[33]

It was with some reluctance that, after some days, Asad Beg eventually left 'Ambar's camp, courteously accompanied by 'Ambar himself on his horse for a league (*kos*) or so. 'Ambar's own young nephew with 1000 horsemen then went with him as far as the frontier of Bijapur (*tā sarhad-i Bījāpūr*), a clear sign in the text both that the Mughals did recognise Bijapur's sovereignty in some form, and that "frontiers" were far from alien to them as a concept.

Now, when Asad Beg entered the country of 'Adil Khan, he was still two way stations (*manzils*) short of Mangalbedha, where Mir Jamal-ud-Din and Mustafa Khan, the head of the army (*sar-i lashkar*) of 'Adil Khan were stationed. Yet, already at this spot, he received a missive from Mir Jamal-ud-Din in response to an earlier letter that Asad Beg had sent him. This contained declarations of joy at Asad Beg's coming and stated that the next day Mustafa Khan's son would meet him with a force. The day after that, he would be welcomed by Haibat

---

[32] Asad Beg, *Waqā'i'-yi Asad Beg Qazwīnī*, ed. Chander Shekhar, 67; *Nuskha-i Ahwāl-i Asad Beg* (London), 18; Aligarh Ms, 43.

[33] See Jahangir, *The Jahangirnama*, 135, 165, 187.

Khan, and thereafter by Mustafa Khan himself with the nobles of Bijapur and men on elephants. Orders also arrived from ʿAdil Khan on the nature of the reception to be given to Asad Beg.

This was more or less how matters transpired. First, the sons of Mustafa Khan and Haibat Khan came together to meet the Mughal envoy; then, at a distance of one *kos* from Mangalbedha, Sayyid Jamal-ud-Din and his entourage came and saluted Asad Beg. He was given the imperial *farmān*, which he received with due ceremonies and honours. Mustafa Khan, one of the greatest nobles of the court of ʿAdil Khan, Haibat Khan, and Rumi Khan, then all came to meet Asad Beg with signs of the greatest attention. In the late afternoon they reached Mangalbedha, where arrangements had been made for Asad Beg's stay. After a while the Sayyid (for Asad Beg is insistent on Jamal-ud-Din's status, in a somewhat sarcastic vein) arrived once more and the two Mughal envoys again had a pleasant meeting. Asad Beg expressed gratitude for being so well treated even in such a strange land (*begāna dayār*). But his remarks were full of ambiguity, as we see when he told Sayyid Jamal-ud-Din: "As is well known, unless you enter into a transaction or go on a journey (*muʿāmala-o-safar-i rū-i nā dehad*) with someone, you do not know the truth about each other (*haqīqat-i yak dīgar*)." The Sayyid may have realised that he was being put to the test, but matters remained cordial and over the next few days the two spent a good time together in Mangalbedha.

It is clear that Ibrahim ʿAdil Shah had decided to assess the extent to which Asad Beg was proof against the blandishments with which he, ʿAdil Shah, had been so successful earlier with Sayyid Jamal-ud-Din.[34] Hence, a few days later, on his instructions, festivities were held in Mangalbedha in honour of his daughter, to which Mir Jamal-ud-Din and Asad Beg were invited. This encounter lasted all day, and during it high-quality food and drink and all sorts of other things were made available; when the festivities ended Asad Beg was given a fine large elephant and two Arab horses with gilded saddles, as well as silver accoutrements. Further, he received nine trays of diverse

---

[34] We lack a good biography of Ibrahim ʿAdil Shah. However, see Eaton, *Sufis of Bijapur*, 89–105; and especially Overton, "Book Culture", 91–154.

cloths, and rare chintz from the Karnatak, together with a rare golden tray with all sorts of jewels, rings, etc., including a special necklace (*dhukdhukī*).[35] A golden betel-leaf holder (*pān-dān*) thrown in for good measure had room for nine rolls (*bīrās*).

In the days that followed, this lavishness continued; Asad Beg was invited by one after another of the great Khans of the Bijapur court, and each took care of him after his fashion. From every one of them he received Arab horses and high-quality Deccani gifts: none were in the least parsimonious. But the stay in the border town could not be stretched out forever, and presently it was decided to prepare for the departure to the city of Bijapur. Asad Beg declared to his hosts that he would return immediately on having met 'Adil Khan: he had no intention of staying on. However, it was reported to him that when 'Adil Khan learnt this, he declared it was an insult and wholly contrary to their custom. So, writes Asad Beg, 'Adil Khan got together his clever Brahmins (*barhamanān-i dānā*) and had a letter written to Mir Jamal-ud-Din asking him to change Asad Beg's mind. But when the matter was broached, Asad Beg demurred, stating he was not there as resident envoy (*hājib*), but rather to take back Mir Jamal-ud-Din. His only task, besides, was to deliver a Mughal *farmān* to 'Adil Khan, so he had no reason to stay beyond its delivery.

Now moves began in earnest to suborn him. Asad Beg reports that 'Adil Khan's agents tried to tempt him with an offer of 200,000 *hūns* (the prevalent gold coin in the Deccan, worth about Rs 3), if he would defer leaving Bijapur until 'Adil Khan wished it. But Asad Beg refused virtuously, though he held a mere 200 *mansab* rank in Mughal service, while the bribe amounted to Rs 600,000. Mir Jamal-ud-Din, the devious Sayyid from Shiraz, was astonished when he learnt this and said to Asad Beg: "You are getting so much money, and [the offer of] happy times, why then are you refusing them?" Asad Beg reports that he replied with a half hemistich:

Our hand is empty,
but our eyes are full.

[35] Asad Beg, *Waqā'i'-yi Asad Beg Qazwīnī*, ed. Chander Shekhar, 69–70; *Nuskha-i Ahwāl-i Asad Beg* (London), 19; Aligarh Ms, 46.

But this pointed hint had no effect on the Sayyid. Asad Beg now told him if reports reached the emperor that he had been bribed to stay on, his honour (*'izzat*) would be tainted. God knows what would happen to him when he returned to the court. He quoted a line of poetry once again: "Fortunate the man who looks to the result."

But it eventually became quite clear that Mir Jamal-ud-Din inhabited a rather different world of values from his fellow Iranian. Consequently, Asad Beg was obliged to tell him rather peremptorily to get himself ready, for he had no intention of leaving without him. But the Sayyid's heart was impervious to orders: he declared he really had no desire to leave the Deccan. This was because each year he received 300,000–400,0000 *hūns* from Bijapur and Golkonda, and, through the money he remitted them, his children were making as much as the holder of a *jāgīr* of 5000 rank.

Asad Beg now becomes blunt in his accusations, declaring that Mir Jamal-ud-Din was not the only one involved in duplicity. Besides him, the Khan-i Khanan too was receiving like sums of money, and there was an agreement between the two that until the Khan-i Khanan's man Mirza Iraj did not reach Mangalbedha with 5000 horse, 'Adil Khan would not send his daughter's palankeen beyond that spot into Mughal territory. They had the following compact in mind: 'Adil Khan could claim that since Mirza Iraj had not reached his lands, he would do nothing; while Mirza Iraj would claim he could not go there out of fear of Malik 'Ambar. The Khan-i Khanan also claimed, besides, that he could not detach a larger force from his own army without putting himself in danger. Thus, between them, they put off the task of moving 'Adil Khan's daughter, and the marriage plans of Prince Daniyal remained at a standstill.

The Visit to Bijapur

Asad Beg begins a new section of his account now, a description of his eventual arrival in Bijapur and meeting with the recalcitrant and slippery 'Adil Khan.[36] He wants the reader to understand that he was

---

[36] Joshi, "Asad Beg's Mission to Bijapur", 184–96; also Joshi, "Asad Beg's Return from Bijapur", 136–55.

no dupe, for he had a clear sense of the various conspiracies (*kangāsh*) that were afoot. His strategy however was different from what it had been with the Rai Rayan and the others: where Asad Beg had been happy to receive gifts and then present a solution that saved face for everyone, here in Bijapur matters were rather different. For Sayyid Jamal-ud-Din – whom he refers to sarcastically at times as the "refuge of the Sayyids" (*siyādat panāh*), and at others as the "unfortunate Mir" (*mir-i nāmurād*) – had to be dragged out of the "whirlpool of his greed" (*gharqāb-i hirs wa sargardanī*) by Asad Beg. The agents of the Bijapur ruler, seeing Asad Beg impervious to all their ploys, sent their master a report making this clear and he agreed reluctantly to receive Asad Beg in Bijapur. Since he had only a "dry *farmān*" for 'Adil Khan, Asad Beg thought it best to arrange a present to accompany it, drawing on his own resources. He thus got together some horses, camels, imported cloth, and Kashmiri shawls, and showed them to the Sayyid, who then added some things of his own, making the gift worth about Rs 20,000–Rs 25,000. Accompanied by a slave, Asad Beg then set out for the Bijapur court.

But matters were not to be so simple. When the Mughal envoy was still one way station (*manzil*) short of Bijapur, it was decided by 'Adil Khan that the meeting could only be held after the lamps of Shab-i Bar'at – a predominantly Shi'i festival – had been lit. It was still only the second day of the month of Sha'ban (we are in the year 1012 H., so this would have been early January 1604 CE). This meant Asad Beg had to wait another thirteen days – on each of which there were all sorts of food, drinks, and fresh fruits to gladden the *bon vivant* Asad Beg, and additionally fodder for his animals. The custom was for the food to be brought in copper dishes (*degh*) and chinaware (*chīnī*) which served as gifts not taken back. Asad Beg thus came to accumulate a number of vessels and utensils inconveniently difficult to store. Besides, 'Adil Khan had ordered that, every day, two men from amongst his principal courtiers (*az majlisiyān-i khāssa*) would converse with Asad Beg to keep him entertained. They included Maulana Malik Qomi, Maulana Zuhuri, Bichitr Khan, Mirak Mu'in-ud-Din, and others mentioned, interestingly enough, in Faizi's report concern-

ing men of talent who could be recruited in the Deccan. In return for the
gifts that they brought, Asad Beg sent back horses, objects, etc., and
this went on till 14 Sha'ban.

Now it turned out that in Bijapur, Shab-i Bar'at was celebrated
in some style. Lamps were lit and fireworks set off in great number.
Sweetmeats, fruit, and dried fruits were made ready, and many things
were brought expressly for Asad Beg from Bijapur. They included two
mock "fortresses" (*qil'a*) made of fireworks that were set off by intelligent and efficient fireworkers (*ātishbāzān*) sent to entertain the
Mughal party. Those in Asad Beg's entourage lit lamps "in the 'Iraqi
fashion", and a pleasant musical evening, redolent of perfume and
punctuated with the consumption of betel-leaf, ensued, in which
many excellent singers performed.

The only blot on the festivities occurred when, halfway through the
night, the two firework castles (made at an expense of 2000 *hūn*) were
set off side by side. The nature of the artifice was such that, when set
alight, it seemed they were firing arms and cannon (*top-o-tufang*) at
each other. It was all so noisy and frightening that the horses, camels,
and elephants in the camp panicked, except for the sturdy elephant of
Malik 'Ambar which, astonished by the two forts, charged repeatedly
at one and then the other. The mahouts tried to control this elephant,
but to little avail: by the time they brought it under control the animal
had managed to push over one of the two fortresses. Until dawn,
reports Asad Beg, the two forts continued to "fight" with each other
and the elephant continued to maraud between them. This bravura
display so impressed the envoy that, disregarding the elephant's lack
of restraint, he decided to forward the beast to the Mughal emperor,
who subsequently had it placed within his special stable.[37]

Eventually, on 17 Sha'ban, Asad Beg set out at last to meet 'Adil
Khan, first to a house that had been kept ready at the edge of the tank
(*tāl*) of Bijapur. Within two or three hours of his arrival excellent carpets had been laid inside his residence. After the hour of midday
prayer, 'Adil Khan arrived with his entourage. It was apparently the

---

[37] Asad Beg, *Waqā'i'-yi Asad Beg Qazwīnī*, ed. Chander Shekhar, 75.

established custom there that, when a Mughal *farmān* arrived, the envoy who brought it awaited in his house the ruler and his close courtiers who came to receive it. But Asad Beg decided to change the custom: he instructed the others that only 'Adil Khan would be let in, his courtiers would remain outside. This made it clear that until 'Adil Khan performed the appropriate rituals associated with the *farmān*, none of his nobles would be allowed entry. 'Adil Khan initially agreed to this, but when he dismounted from his elephant and entered the house, two of his courtiers – Antu Pandit and Kafshdar Khan – rudely forced their way in and stood behind him. The ceremony to receive the *farmān* now began. First Nasir Khan, Asad Beg's servant, greeted 'Adil Khan, took the order from Asad Beg's hand, kissed it, and put it to his eyes and head. Asad Beg then took the *farmān* from his hand and placed it on the turban of 'Adil Khan, saying: "Perform the prostration (*sijda*) to it." Asad Beg also instructed the Brahmin courtier Antu Pandit to step out and bring in the other close courtiers. In the interval when Antu and the others had stepped out, 'Adil Khan was asked to prostrate himself in the direction of the emperor (*ba jānib-i hazrat*). When he had finished, others such as 'Ambar Khan and Shahnawaz Khan entered. At this point in the rather elaborate proceedings, 'Adil Khan took the *farmān* off from his head and gave it to Shahnawaz Khan, who bowed to it and wanted at once to open its seal.

But Asad Beg was not finished with instructing the Bijapur courtiers. He now ordered Antu Pandit to perform *nisār*, that is, to offer some money. The Brahmin ran out and brought back a tray of *hūns* and a plate of pearls (*marwārīd*); as the *farmān* was opened, the contents of the two plates were scattered and allowed to remain on the ground. After everyone had gone, reports Asad Beg, the sweepers (*farrāsh*) who gathered it up found 300 *hūn* and 500 pearls which they were allowed to keep.

Shahnawaz Khan now began to read the *farmān* out aloud. When he reached the part that said: "If it is true that you want Kwaliyar, I will give you the management of the town," 'Adil Khan became visibly angry and said in the Marathi tongue (*ba zabān-i Marhāta*) to Antu Pandit: "So the Mir spoke an untruth when he said Asad Beg was bringing a *farmān* for Kwaliyar, whereas now it says 'if you want

Kwaliyar'. I see that I am being toyed with here."[38] When Asad Beg saw that he was getting angry, he said it was in fact a *farmān* for the grant of Kwaliyar. The Mir had written to the emperor of how 'Adil Khan desired the place, and this document was to state that he had only to ask in clear terms to receive it. Indeed, if 'Adil Khan wanted it, Asad Beg could send an *'arzdāsht* to the court right away, and before he left Bijapur the Mughal *farmān* would have arrived. We can thus see that the Bijapuri side were not quite as subservient as, say, the Faruqi ruler of Khandesh had been with Faizi.

The meeting entered a phase of some awkwardness; the closing section of the *farmān* was read out, which said in effect that, whatever was discussed verbally would be the basis of further dealings, for the emperor saw him, 'Adil Khan, as a true disciple (*murīd*), as he did Asad Beg. The two were hence enjoined not to keep secrets from each other. On the other hand, on one matter the Mughal side was firm: there should be no delay in sending Mir Jamal-ud-Din Husain back. 'Adil Khan now put the *farmān* away. Asad Beg, addressing Antu Pandit, told him and the others to step out once more, for he needed to talk to 'Adil Khan in private. When they had left, Asad Beg had a screen brought down. 'Adil Khan declared he wanted to continue the discussion standing – he would be uncomfortable sitting down. Anticipating this, Asad Beg had prepared a comfortable velvety cushion (*toshak*) with brocade, stuffed full of feathers, which he now offered, and 'Adil Khan accepted it together with a cylindrical cushion (*gautakiya*) to lean on. He then asked Asad Beg to sit near him and they began to discuss matters.

Asad Beg's main purpose was to offer a gloss on what the emperor had really wanted to convey in the document. But the conversation was awkward, and Asad Beg notes: "He understood Persian well, but he could not answer in that language, and spoke in a broken (*shikasta*) way." When the conversation finished the two stood up and began their leave-taking. 'Adil Khan now declared that Asad Beg could not leave the same day as this was against their tradition (*rasm*). To this Asad Beg replied that he was not the resident ambassador (*hājib*), while the

---

[38] Ibid., 77.

real one, Mir Jamal-ud-Din, had been the guest of Bijapur for far too many years. He himself was a mere servant sent to deliver a message, and to find out why the Mir had stayed so long. Now that he had met 'Adil Khan in person, he would carry his reply back to Akbar. As for the Mir, he would do with him whatever 'Adil Khan said. But, he added, he would also declare a few truths to 'Adil Khan. The latter remained sitting and asked him to go on.

Asad Beg then said: "You claim to be a disciple (*murīd*) of the emperor. It is not correct for you to have concealed intentions against him." The other replied: "God forbid. I don't even do him a hair's worth of harm." Asad Beg retorted: "How do you say that? What could be greater opposition than keeping the Mir with you all this time, rather than letting him go with [your daughter's] palankeen?" 'Adil Khan responded: "In truth, whatever I could give with my daughter, I have sent to the frontier of my territory (*wilāyat*). If she does not go on from there, what can I do?" Asad Beg writes that he pursued his line of attack, stating bluntly: "That is not so. In reality you have not given her away. Else Mustafa Khan would not have accompanied her with such an army. He is there to protect her, and sees to it that she does not leave." At this 'Adil Khan swore energetically it was not so. Mustafa Khan had simply been sent as escort, and Mir Jamal-ud-Din was not leaving Bijapur on account of his own greed – he was taking much money every year. What could he do? He could not drive away an aged, important man like the Sayyid with blows!

Asad Beg now asked his assurance that he spoke the truth. When 'Adil Khan insisted it was so, the envoy declared he would have the factotum Antu Pandit summoned. A *farmān* from the Bijapur ruler could then be drafted in the name of Mustafa Khan, Haibat Khan, and Rumi Khan, in which they were to be told that, as soon as the Khan-i Khanan sent an escort to his side of the frontier, the palankeen should be sent on with the elephants and other luggage. No further orders from the Bijapur court should be awaited. Asad Beg also insisted he would carry the *farmān* himself, and promised to escort the princess and her party safe to Ahmadnagar. 'Adil Khan would thus be saved his yearly expense of bribing the Sayyid, and his good name would be established in the process.

Antu Pandit was duly summoned; he prepared three *farmāns* that were sealed and handed over to Asad Beg. A letter with similar contents was also sent to Mir Jamal-ud-Din. Asad Beg took these *farmāns* and said: "*Bismillāh*. I now have replies to the *farmāns* that I brought, to the verbal messages I brought, and to the question of Kwaliyar. I shall take leave from you and depart tomorrow. Tell me whatever else you have to say." At this time he was apparently confident he had cut the Gordian knot, and that his blunt diplomacy had brought a speedy end to a difficult task. But 'Adil Khan protested. Calling in 'Ambar Khan and Shahnawaz Khan, he declared that his *gurūbhā'i* – his "brother" with whom he shared a common guru, namely Akbar – was leaving summarily. How could he let him depart empty-handed? At this moment, Asad Beg remembered the other task with which he had been charged by Akbar. So he replied that the only other thing he wanted was the celebrated Atish Para elephant. On hearing this 'Adil Khan swore that this particular elephant had been rendered useless (*bar taraf shudā*) two years before. In its place was another female elephant called Chanchal, whose superior qualities were known to everyone. Faced with this, Asad Beg declared he would accept Chanchal. But this only brought forth loud protests from Shahnawaz Khan and 'Ambar Khan, who stated it had never been the custom to send such elephants from the Deccan to Hindustan. Asad Beg replied that no ruler of the Deccan (*bādshāh-i Dakhan*) had to that day become the disciple (*murīd*) of the Delhi ruler (*bādshāh-i Dillī*). Now that the ruler of Bijapur had in his magnanimity decided to become the disciple of the Delhi ruler, what harm was there in sending an elephant from the disciple (*murīd*) to the master (*pīr*)? 'Adil Khan intervened in the discussion and declared: "Gurubhai speaks the truth. What is Chanchal when I am prepared to give up my very life [for Akbar]? But I request that you wait a few days, so that we may prepare some jewelled trappings for her. When they are ready, then you may go." Asad Beg immediately agreed, but on condition that he be allowed to take care of preparing the trappings himself, and as quickly as possible. The Bijapur ruler acquiesced, stating that some ten maunds of gold would be spent on the trappings. Asad Beg was told that he should go into the city of Bijapur and reside in a house specially prepared for him.

The meeting was now drawing to a close. Asad Beg notes that he had carefully arranged outside his house the gifts he had brought; now he took 'Adil Khan, who, seeing the gifts, asked once more in Marathi: "Were these sent by the emperor for me?" Antu Pandit replied that they were the tribute (*peshkash*) brought by Asad Beg; 'Adil Khan inspected and accepted them. The elephants and camels with trappings, as well as Arab and Turki horses, all pleased him. He then instructed 'Ambar Khan to take Asad Beg to the house in the city that had been prepared for him and departed.

Instead of setting out immediately, however, the Mughal envoy and the Bijapur courtier stayed on together a while and shared a meal in the first house, which had carpets from Kirman and Joshkan, and red silken stuffs as decorations. Asad Beg identifies 'Ambar Khan as a capable Abyssinian youth (*jawān-i habshī*). In his company the Mughal envoy then set out to his new mansion (which he notes is locally called a *chhajja*), amongst the best in the town, where he quickly settled in. He immediately asked 'Ambar Khan to send for goldsmiths to make the elephant trappings as soon as possible, and was told they would be there the next day. He also thought to look into what else he could

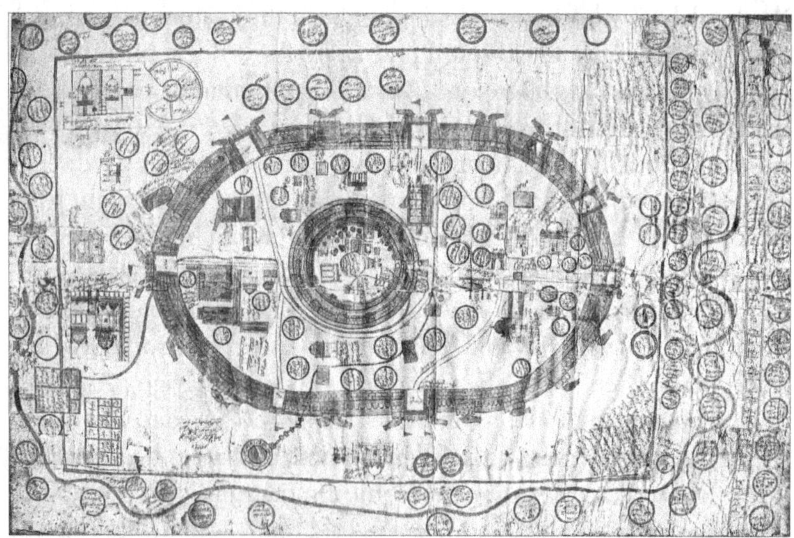

Image 3.1: Bijapur Map (late seventeenth century).

take back to Agra by way of gifts. The Bijapur courtiers assured Asad
Beg, however, that 'Adil Khan would not send him back with only the
elephant, he would be given other presents too. Reassured, Asad Beg
decided to spend the evening in festivities, with a sense of having largely
accomplished his mission.

This is the first moment in the narrative of the embassy when Asad
Beg takes time to describe his surroundings with some care. Clearly,
he believes his readers will be curious to know what life in the great
and celebrated Deccan city of Bijapur was like, and these passages bear
some resemblance to the description of the city of Vijayanagara a century and a half earlier by 'Abdur Razzaq Samarqandi.[39]

The section begins with a description of the type of mansion in
which Asad Beg resides. The house and his own apartment within it
both had balconies, with two levels of doors (*dū-āsitāna*). The main gate
led into a large building with several apartments and buildings, and
the whole structure was airy and spacious despite being located in
the middle of the town. The northern gallery led towards the bazaar,
which was very large, 30 yards (*gaz*) wide and 2 leagues (*kos*) in length.
Each shop in this market street had a tree or plants in front, and all were
kept very neat and clean, full of high-quality articles hardly to be seen
or heard of in any other town. There were shops for cloth, jewellers'
shops, weapons shops, wine shops, bread and fish shops, and shops
with prepared food. One could guess at the extent of the bazaar from
all this, writes Asad Beg. The jewellers' establishments had a variety of
gems, and objects studded with stones such as daggers and mirrors,
as well as necklaces; there were also images of birds – such as parrots,
pigeons, and peacocks – made with gold and silver and studded with
stones. All sorts of bread (*nān*) could be found in other shops, ranged
in steps. In the cloth shops could be found all sorts of choice textiles,
and next to them stitched clothes. In other shops there was chinaware
and glass flasks and jars with sherbets (*'arq*), and twice-distilled liq-
uids. And this commercial paradise extended further still:

> If one advanced somewhat further, there were fruit shops with pistachios –
> dry and fresh – almonds and similar things. Just beyond was a wine-shop

[39] Alam and Subrahmanyam, *Indo-Persian Travels*, 69–74.

(*sharāb-farosh*), and another where musicians and pleasant-voiced singers
(*ahl-i sarod wa kalāwant-i khwush-āwāz*) and beautiful as well as made-
up girls (*zanān-i khwush sūrat ba 'anwa'-i zīb-o-zīnat*) could be found. In
short, the entire bazaar was full of wine, beauty, song, perfumes, jewels,
and a variety of high-quality cloth and food. On one side were thousands
of places where people stood with cups in their hands, full of love, pleasure, and song; everyone was content with his own place and troubled
no one else. No greater wonder is likely ever to have been seen in all the
world by any traveller.[40]

Here is a vision then that may be sharply contrasted to the description of Bijapur by a Jesuit author in the 1560s who found the town full
of hovels scarcely fit for human habitation.[41] Asad Beg's evocation of
the marvels of Bijapur also contrasts interestingly with Faizi's description of Ahmadnagar which – as we have seen in the preceding chapter – mixes a few elements of praise with a large number of negative
comments. This is characteristic of Asad Beg's descriptions and continues into later sections of his text. If there is a wonderful city in the
world, it must be Bijapur!

The following day, Asad Beg says 'Ambar Khan came to visit him
in his mansion (*haweli*) with ten maunds of gold and a hundred goldsmiths. Asad Beg's own servants Aqa Raza and Nasir Khan were to su-
pervise them in their tasks. Time passed quickly, and in ten days everything was ready, so that 'Ambar Khan went to tell his master 'Adil
Khan that the trappings (*yarāq*) for the famed Chanchal were now
ready. The Mughal envoy wanted to leave quickly, the Bijapur ruler
was told. But 'Adil Khan declared he was not happy to give him just
one elephant in gift. He decided to offer him a rare Arab horse called
Chini which he had bought in Bijapur for 3000 *hūn* (the equivalent
of Rs 9000). This horse was black and thought to be of the rarest. The
Bijapur sultan also declared he needed more time to ponder over what

[40] Asad Beg, *Waqā'i'-yi Asad Beg Qazwīnī*, ed. Chander Shekhar, 83; *Nuskha-i
Ahwāl-i Asad Beg* (London), 15a/24; Aligarh Ms, 59 *et seq*. Another translation
appears in Elliot and Dowson, *History*, vol. 6, 164.

[41] For a discussion of this account, see Subrahmanyam, "Palavras do Idalcão",
513–24.

else he could add to the gift, and then, on 27 Sha'ban, he officially invited Asad Beg to a high-level farewell ceremony.

Gathering together the best men in his group, Asad Beg went first to see 'Ambar Khan, who lived at a distance of 1 *kos* from his mansion. In order to reach his house he had to go through the bazaar he had just described, and from there they went towards the fort of Bijapur where 'Adil Khan resided. When they reached the door of the fort they found its portal lofty, with two large domes. A number of elephants stood by the door. When the Mughal party passed through and had gone some distance, they came across a moat (*khandaq*), and then to an interior area. After passing through a second multi-domed door, with chained elephants by it, they traversed another equal distance that took them across a second moat, and beyond it to a third door. Here too excellent elephants could be seen, a particular trademark, it seemed, of this kingdom.

It was thus made known to Asad Beg that Bijapur, the seat of 'Adil Khan, had powerful triple concentric fortifications and could not easily be seized. Beyond each wide moat full of water was a double wall, and between each level of fortification were two lines of trees and much greenery. Beyond the third door were two lines of gunners, archers, and swordsmen. When at last they reached the interior palace (*daulat-khāna*), they passed through another gate. Up to this point Asad Beg and his men had been on horseback with 'Ambar Khan. After they passed into the palace, at a second interior gate they dismounted in the midst of armed men. Some 300 men in the visiting Mughal party advanced towards an open area, with balconies (*aiwān*) which Asad Beg compared to the similar *chauki-khānas* of Hindustan. He and his men now passed on foot through a third interior gate, the real gate to the building (*khwān-i asl*) where the ruler himself was to be found. 'Ambar Khan now indicated to them that the soldiers in the party should go off in the direction of a certain gallery (*aiwān*) where carpets were spread and vases positioned. Only Asad Beg and ten of his close attendants accompanied 'Ambar Khan into the interior. In the first courtyard they found themselves in an open area of some expanses (*jarīb*) of land, clean and sparkling, with decorated galleries and covered vestibules (*dālān*) set out in parallel. The main gallery was at two yards height, and some sixty hands in width, but with no columns (*sutūn*). This gallery had three walls with ten niches (*tāq*) each, three yards high and ten yards wide. Each had a royal chinaware jar (*martabān*) with a decorated silk cover.[42] These were as high as the niches themselves, and the walls behind them were well decorated with trappings and mural paintings. Asad Beg declares his astonishment at this display.

The nobles and commanders of 'Adil Khan were seated all around. Other galleries were perfectly arranged and in their midst was a tank (*hauz*) forty yards by forty yards, with a fountain in it. On three sides of the tank were lamp-holders placed next to one another, and the light of their lamps was reflected in the water. Asad Beg's pen picture thus takes pains to evoke the space accurately, no doubt with the mental image of various Mughal imperial courtly spaces – Agra, Lahore, or Fatehpur Sikri – in mind.

In the lower vestibule were five standing men: Antu Pandit, Shahnawaz Khan, Kafshdar Khan, Lakhu (or Lanku) Pandit, and a fifth whose name is not mentioned. In this particular gallery was a golden throne studded with jewels, on which was a seat (*masnad*) with a number of reclining cushions, and single and double lamp-stands of gold and silver, some twenty in all. Small pieces of velvet and brocade had been spread around, and between every two lamp-stands and incense-burners were trellis-works of gold or silver.

Asad Beg now went and sat at the *masnad* by the throne. After a brief wait a door opened at the other side of the palace, and Ibrahim ' Adil Khan in all his splendour, accompanied by three or four persons, entered. Asad Beg stood up to greet him. Ibrahim first advanced towards the envoy, but then stood by a very large double lamp-stand that was between the throne and the *masnad*. The three or four people with him, heavily perfumed from neck to waist, stood by in attendance. Asad Beg notes that, as a backdrop to this scene, music flowed continuously through the door from which the ruler had emerged, and 'Adil Khan's attention still seemed distracted by that music. But since Asad Beg was his guest he began with an effort to make conversation

---

[42] Asad Beg, *Waqā'i'-yi Asad Beg Qazwīnī*, ed. Chander Shekhar, 85.

Image 3.2 : Portrait of Ibrahim ʿAdil Shah II of Bijapur
(*c.* 1590).

with him. Parallel to this gallery were three niches, one very high, and two somewhat smaller. In the largest was the elephant Chanchal, and in the other two were a pair of female elephants. All three were offered by 'Adil Khan to Asad Beg – to take back with him. While he and the ruler conversed, the courtiers stood around, erect like walls, as unmoving as the shade of a tree. They neither talked to each other nor made any signs to each other, a measure of the power and discipline the ruler exercised over them. This went on until two watches of the night, and then Asad Beg took leave. By the time he reached home, he writes, it was almost dawn.

The account of the conversation itself is curious and, as noted, Asad Beg has a liking for reporting conversation as direct speech. He notes that at the outset of the conversation 'Adil Khan asked him: "Does your ruler listen to music all the time?" Asad Beg replied, "Sometimes." Ibrahim then asked: "Does Miyan Tansen, his master musician (*ustād-i sarod*), sing sitting or standing?"[43] Asad said since the emperor himself was often standing in the assembly, his musicians too had to remain standing. But on some nights, when he was seated in the pavilion (*burj*), Miyan Tansen with his sons would sit and sing for him. Further, on occasions of festivity and Nauroz, the Miyan sang with his sons and other singers while seated, and the emperor with his close courtiers listened attentively to the music. 'Adil Khan was affected by this response and said: "Music is a thing that should be listened to at all times and in every manner. Musicians should be kept happy." Asad Beg replied saying two things produced elation (*inti'āsh*) in men: one was music and the other was perfume, and one could never have enough of these. No matter what state a man was in, these two things always brought relief. When 'Adil Khan heard this sentiment, he declared he was happy to have it spoken. Asad Beg insists in his account that his intention was not to flatter, it was just a coincidence that 'Adil Khan was at the time doused in perfume (*'itr*) from waist to neck. Ibrahim now asked what Akbar liked most of all, and Asad replied – in

---

[43] Ibid., 87. On Tansen , see Jahangir, *The Jahangirnama*, 239, where he is mentioned as "Tan Sen Kalawant, who was in my father's service and without equal in his own time – or any other for that matter." For a more general discussion, see Delvoye, "The Image of Akbar", 194–201.

what was a broad hint indeed – that he liked precious stones and high-quality elephants. The other stated he had heard this from other sources too. He showed Asad a necklace of pearls around his neck, one of several he had on his person, in Asad's opinion each better than the next. 'Adil Khan said since he knew the emperor liked jewels, he had already picked and sent him one of great value; now, yet again, he was sending his best elephant with Asad Beg. Chanchal was not only unparalleled in his own stables, but in the entire Deccan; in the Mughal stables, too, he believed there would be few of her quality.

But Asad Beg's intention was clearly to extract as much as he could even at the very moment of his departure. So he responded saying that as 'Adil Khan had called him his brother, and given him his best possession for the Mughal court, he should also send some of his best jewels to Akbar with him: the jewels sent earlier to the Mughals were after all of no consequence, being matters of the past.[44] Under this somewhat unsubtle pressure 'Adil Khan now swore to Asad Beg, once more calling him "Gurubhai", that he had no more worthwhile jewels, either uncut or worked. All that he had, he had already given with his daughter to Mir Jamal-ud-Din, so he now found himself bereft. What he still had were some old worn-out jewels to wear, such as those on his person. To this Asad Beg uttered a pious wish: that God keep the Bijapur ruler wealthy.

He then returned to the offensive. Surely Ibrahim could give something nevertheless? It was well known that all the best precious stones of the world were his, 'Adil Khan's. The honourable gift of a first-rate elephant apart, he might care to proffer some jewels of comparable quality to enhance his prestige in the Mughal court, and so that all that he reported about 'Adil Khan was more easily accepted. Pressed thus, 'Adil Khan fell into a reverie, called Antu Pandit, and said something to him *sotto voce*. But Antu Pandit seemed to refuse what he had been asked. However, seeing Asad Beg's eye on him, Antu Pandit appeared to say something which seemed to satisfy 'Adil Khan; he then turned to the envoy and said: "Gurubhai, I've found something good for you to

---

[44] Asad Beg, *Waqā'i'-yi Asad Beg Qazwīnī*, ed. Chander Shekhar, 87–8; *Nuskha-i Ahwāl-i Asad Beg* (London), 16a/ 26.

take back. My mother on my accession gave me a vase-holder (*kūza-dān*) which she had made. It is very delicate and has exquisite jewels and stones in it. Perhaps the emperor would be glad to have it. Since you are my Gurubhai, how can I refuse it to you? If not you, who would I give it to? It's just as well that an elephant like Chanchal, a horse like Chini, and a *kūza-dān* like this can be given to you, so that you do not return empty-handed." Asad Beg thanked him very warmly and uttered prayers for him.

But a major diplomatic fracas was about to break out. For at this time 'Adil Khan espied the emblem of imperial discipleship (*shast-i murīdī-i hazrat*) on Asad Beg's turban, which indicated that the envoy belonged to the circle of Akbar's direct disciples in the context of the imperial sect (*tauhīd-i Ilāhī*) created some years before. He asked him: "Gurubhai, what is that?" To which Asad Beg said it was the emblem (*shast-i murīdī*) which the emperor chiselled with his own hands and gave to his disciples (*murīds*). 'Adil Khan then took it out of Asad Beg's turban, examined it closely, and without further ado tied it on the bejewelled crown of his own turban, saying he too was now a disciple (*murīd*) of the Mughal emperor. He refused bluntly to give it back to Asad Beg, telling him he could in return take anything else that he was wearing on his person. Annoyed, Asad Beg told 'Adil Khan he was not even willing to exchange the *shast* against the rulership (*bādshāhī*) of Bijapur, so precious was it to him. But 'Adil Khan was insistent, repeating that he too was a disciple of Akbar, and refused absolutely to give it back. He wished Asad Beg a safe return journey and suggested that he get a replacement from the emperor upon his return: he could even tell Akbar, if he so wished, that it had been taken from him by Ibrahim. This in his view would be the best solution for all concerned; Asad Beg would get a new *shast* and 'Adil Khan would be grateful to him for having given him his own. Asad Beg refused to countenance this. To placate the ruler he promised he would, on his return to the Mughal court, get a *shast* for him and send it. To this Ibrahim replied: "When you send a new one to me, I will return this one to you with a hundred other gifts."

So, despite Asad Beg's repeated remonstrances, he was unable to make further headway in the argument. The night now far advanced, an exhausted Asad Beg returned to his house escorted by 'Ambar Khan. He was still sleeping the next day when the agents of 'Adil Khan brought Chanchal, Chini the horse, and the *kūza-dān*. As Asad Beg was inspecting them, Lanku Pandit arrived at his residence with another elephant with tusks, three rare horses with gold and silver saddles, and 100,000 silver *lārīs* on a camel – all personal gifts for Asad Beg. The Pandit handed him a list of these things written on a piece of paper, and conveyed a message from 'Adil Khan to the effect that, though he had tried to persuade Asad Beg to stay on a few days so that he might serve him better, Asad Beg had refused; so, in view of his early departure, he was giving him this small gift. He also expressed the hope that Asad Beg and he, having established a firm acquaintance (*āshnā'ī*), would remain mutual well-wishers. To this Asad Beg replied (speaking to the Pandit) that, thanks to the grace of the Sahib-i Qibla – meaning either God or the emperor – he lacked for nothing. He himself cared little for worldly possessions, and so had refused what had been offered him on the first day. He asked the Brahmin to take back what he had brought, but insisted that he render him back the *shast* in exchange. As a further sign of his firmness, he ordered his own men not to accept what had been brought for him, only taking the horse, the elephant Chanchal, and the *kūza-dān* because they had come as tribute (*peshkash*) for the emperor. Declaring his disappointment at this attitude, the Pandit had to return, abandoning in the vestibule (*dālān*) of the envoy's mansion the goods he had brought – those refused by Asad Beg.

It then came to Asad Beg's knowledge that the Pandit would not gain an audience with 'Adil Khan that day, and so the goods would remain where they lay. The next day, however, both Lanku Pandit and Antu Pandit met 'Adil Khan and apprised him of what had happened. They had not brought the goods back out of fear of his wrath, they said, but Asad Beg too had refused them. What should they now do?

On hearing this, 'Adil Khan sent a small chest of European make (*sandūqcha-i firangī*) filled with jewels for Asad Beg, stating in his message that this was in exchange for the gifts (*saughāt*) that Asad had brought. He apologised for having nothing really worthy to offer, but expressed the hope that the things in the chest would help Asad Beg or his children in times of need. His message also expressed the hope that on returning from his kingdom (*dar mulk-o-wilāyat-i mā*) to the Mughal *darbār*, Asad Beg would not forget him.

The bearer of the message and gifts, Lanku Pandit, who in Asad Beg's estimation was a capable and understanding man, pleaded with the Mughal envoy to accept the gifts. But Asad Beg remained adamant: he would accept nothing until he got his *shast* back. This message was repeated to 'Adil Khan, who at last relented and returned the emblem with a final message: "May God have mercy on you and your sincerity. I wanted to test you. If anyone is a disciple in this world, let him be like you. I hope that my Gurubhai will procure a *shast-i murīdī* from the emperor and remember to send it to me." The month of Ramazan 1012 H. was about to begin, and Asad Beg could now depart from the capital of the 'Adil Shahi kingdom. He left Bijapur for Mangalbedha the very next day.

In the time he had spent in Bijapur, awaiting Chanchal's jewels and trappings, Asad Beg had kept a lookout for other jewels and jewel-studded objects in the bazaar for his friends in the court and for the emperor.

He had also asked Aqa Raza and Mansur Khan to act on his behalf, and they had spent two or three busy days making purchases. The objects they procured were quite astonishing to the Mughal envoy. However, when he showed these things to some of the merchants of Bijapur whom he had come to know, they told him that a certain Ramji Mal Jauhri, the head (*muqaddam*) of the jewellers there, should be contacted as he was the best in the business. He could also give Asad Beg advice and arrange other transactions for him. So Asad Beg sent for Ramji Mal, who inspected what he had purchased to that point, and bluntly told him they were pretty much to be rejected (*radd*). How much money could he really spend, he asked Asad Beg. As it happened, Asad Beg did not have much money at the time, nor knew how much 'Adil Khan would give him. So, somewhat evasively, he said for the emperor he needed diamonds, pearls, and rubies of as high a quality as possible. Ramji went off, returning the next day with a fine diamond worth Rs 30,000, a fine ruby pendant (*dhukdhukī*) surrounded by old emeralds for which he asked Rs 25,000, and a special

Image 3.3 : Sultan Ibrahim 'Adil Shah in procession.

pearl. Asad Beg himself also purchased other things from the bazaar, such as emeralds, sapphires, cat's eyes, and carved animals, though some of these were disapproved by Ramji Mal. Asad Beg agreed to pay Rs 55,000 to Ramji Mal for the diamond and the ruby on condition that he would show them in Mangalbedha to Mir Jamal-ud-Din, and pay up only if the latter approved of them. But Ramji demurred, saying he must first receive the money; if Mir Jamal-ud-Din turned down the goods, he could return them and be refunded. Asad Beg agreed, feeling he had made quite a killing on the jewellery market.

The Return from Bijapur

It was 2 Ramazan when Asad Beg set out from Bijapur. When Mir Jamal-ud-Din heard this, he met Asad Beg one way-station (*manzil*) short of Mangalbedha, together with Mustafa Khan and some others, taking Asad Beg to a special residence prepared for him. The others left, and Mir Jamal-ud-Din was now alone with Asad Beg, who said to him: "I have prepared matters with 'Adil Khan for your departure from here. You should start getting ready. We should not delay further." Since all this had been done without the Sayyid's knowing, he thought it was all in jest and paid no attention to it. The rest of that day was spent in pleasant conversation, and Asad Beg left him with his illusions. The next day, early in the morning, he showed Mir Jamal-ud-Din the *farmān* of 'Adil Khan and recounted his discussions with Ibrahim. Mir Jamal-ud-Din was shaken by the turn that events had taken and said: "*Bismillah*. Tell me what has to be done." Asad Beg now asked him to write a letter to the Khan-i Khanan. At this, Mir Jamal-ud-Din began to twist and turn but could see no way out. Asad Beg pressed him to write the letter and prepare to leave quickly. In the letter to the Khan-i Khanan he was to say their arrival was imminent.

The great Sayyid (*sayyid-i buzurgawār:* here, Asad Beg is sarcastic) then did the needful. The Khan-i Khanan was apprised that 'Adil Khan had given permission for the Sayyid to leave, and had sent orders to Mustafa Khan and the others to this effect. The moment a Mughal party arrived on the other side of the frontier, the Bijapur royal party could leave without any further reference to 'Adil Khan or the capital. He was also sent a copy of the orders, together with two *'arzdāsht* reports, one from the Mir and one from Asad Beg.

When he received these documents, writes Asad Beg, the Khan-i Khanan saw that things had taken a complexion different from what he had anticipated. In the well-supplied jewel-bazaar of excuses he employed, no sparkle remained. So he got together a good force with Mirza Iraj and Mirza Rustam and sent them on to the Bijapur border. He also sent a letter to Asad Beg and Mir Jamal-ud-Din that he had done the needful, and that he himself was on his way too, through Patan. The Khan-i Khanan also said he had sent word to Prince Daniyal of their good work, and told him to return quickly to Ahmadnagar via Nasik-Trimbak. He equally sent instructions to Asad Beg to make preparations for the departure of Mir Jamal-ud-Din and the Bijapur princess' palankeen, and to come to Ahmadnagar. This letter arrived in Mangalbedha in seven days.

Asad Beg now sounded the drums (*naqqāra*) of departure, but the Sayyid continued trying to hold out for a few more days. However, word was out that the party was on the point of departing, and Mangalbedha was in tumult. The next day they moved to the edge of the river in preparation for crossing into Mughal territory. It was Nauroz, and Mustafa Khan and others came to congratulate Asad Beg on the occasion. Asad Beg reports the Bijapur noble saying to him: "I have been here for a long time, and now it seems it is over. The Mir and the bridal party are ready to leave. But until I receive word from 'Adil Khan, how can I leave?" At this, Asad Beg produced the *farmān* that he had till then kept concealed from the others. Everybody fell silent at this, seeing there now remained no way out.

That evening Lanku Pandit, who was to accompany them, joined the party. Since it was Nauroz, 'Adil Khan had sent Asad Beg (by way of an auspicious gift, *shugūn*) a further 9000 *hūns* and nine bales of cloth through the Pandit. As the party began to cross the river, Mustafa Khan and the other Bijapur nobles (*umarā*) tried to delay one last time, saying that as their soldiers had not been told in advance, they were in a panic. They demanded two days' respite. Since Asad Beg trusted Mustafa Khan and felt he had human qualities (*mard-i ādmī būd*), he accepted his request.

Three days after Nauroz, it was the festival of 'Id-i Qurban. It was found that 'Adil Khan in Bijapur had learnt they had still not crossed the river, and so sent Mirak Mu'in, one of his trusted courtiers, to greet them on 'Id. With him he also sent some things for Mir Jamal-ud-Din, and farewell robes (*khil'at-hā-i rukhsat*) for those of his nobles accompanying the party. For three days there were further pleasant festivities with Mirak Mu'in, though at last, as the party crossed the river, he returned to Bijapur.

But things continued to proceed at a snail's pace. The Bijapuri nobles now said that this was their frontier (*sarhad*), and that they would not advance further until a Mughal force with one of Khan-i Khanan's sons had arrived to accompany them. They refused to move any further than the riverbank, which they claimed they had crossed solely on Asad Beg's account – who accepted their view and decided once more to play the waiting game. Later in the day there was a great dust storm (*jhakkar*) which uprooted one or two tents, making it seem like the end of the world. In the midst of all this someone shouted out that Malik 'Ambar had come to attack them. When the Bijapuri soldiers heard his name they began fleeing. Rumi Khan, who was in charge of the princess, crossed the river with her and went back in the direction of Bijapur, his army in indescribable panic, showing up his ill-fortune and cowardice (*nā-mardī*). It was once more up to Asad Beg to take a firm stand, so he sent a man to Mir Jamal-ud-Din to ask whether Malik 'Ambar was really on his way. He also instructed him not to retreat, but to join forces with him, Asad Beg. He warned that if the Sayyid fled, it would be considered a dereliction (*khatā*) for which he would pay. As for 'Ambar, Asad Beg declared he himself was afraid neither of him nor his army. This message turned out timely. For when Asad Beg's man reached the Mir's camp, he – ever the poltroon in Asad Beg's description – was already mounted and ready to abandon the princess. On reading the message he dismounted and decided to stay put.

In the third watch of the day, Asad Beg writes, the storm settled somewhat, and it became clear there was no threat from an enemy force. At this point, by chance, a certain Khwajgi 'Inayatullah Kitabdar, who had been sent from Ahmadnagar to 'Adil Khan's court, arrived in their camp. He reported that Mirza Iraj and Mirza Rustam were now only some four *kos* distant from them. This news transformed the mood in the camp, and on hearing it Mir Jamal-ud-Din too came to see Asad Beg. The next day, early in the morning, Mir Jamal-ud-Din and Khwajgi 'Inayatullah went after the party of the princess, and after much persuasion got them to return. Rumi Khan and the palankeen were brought back in shame to the camp, where the Mughal force had already arrived under Mirza Iraj and Mirza Rustam.

The next day the whole group set out to the north. Leading the way were Mirza Rustam and Miyan Fahim with an advance guard (*harāwal*) of Rajputs. Then followed the Deccani party with the palankeen and Mir Jamal-ud-Din. The rear (*chandāwal*) was brought up by Mirza Iraj, with Asad Beg in his party. The convoy made its way rapidly to Ahmadnagar, where they met the Khan-i Khanan. Here, things had been made ready for their stay. In the Ahmadnagar fort, the Sona Mahal had been kept aside for Prince Daniyal, with everything there ready and decorated. The newly arrived princess was also to stay in the Sona Mahal, while a good house was made ready for Rumi Khan inside the fort. Mustafa Khan, Haibat Khan, and the other commanders from the Deccan were asked to stay outside the fort, while Asad Beg and Mir Jamal-ud-Din stayed in the town. Three days later the prince himself arrived with his party, and there was such a crowd in Ahmadnagar of Mughals and others that it was difficult to walk the streets. In those days, writes Asad Beg, there were wine parties aplenty and much pleasure was partaken of. The prince gave away high-quality *khil'ats* and 'Iraqi horses with decorated saddles, as well as swords with bejewelled scabbards, to the Bijapuri party. Asad Beg's good services were brought to his attention, in particular the fact that he had managed to persuade the devious Mir Jamal-ud-Din to return – with the daughter of 'Adil Khan and the elephants and *peshkash* to boot. Hearing all this, the benevolent prince treated him very well.

Despite his general disapproval of the Khan-i Khanan, Asad Beg finds some kind words to say about him at this moment. After spending the next few days drinking wine, he presented himself before the Mughal generalissimo, to seek his permission to depart for the court, and this was agreed to – though Asad Beg stresses that the prince was reluctant to see him go. The next day there was a royal party (*jashn-i bādshāhāna*) in a special garden, the Farh Bakhsh Bagh. Mughal and Bijapuri nobles attended, and on this happy occasion, "when people's faces were flushed crimson with wine", Asad was given a special lace-and-brocade *khil'at*, a gilded sword, a bejewelled dagger, an 'Iraqi horse with a gilded saddle, and leave to depart. As the paymasters (*bakhshīs*) were leading him to the prince, the latter took a pearl neck-lace from his own neck and placed it around Asad Beg's. He then completed the farewell ritual with the royal cup in his hand. Asad Beg writes at some length of the prince's benevolence to him:

> May God protect that prince endowed with high fortune, and keep him under his protection. Were I to write of his good qualities, it would make another book. I kissed his feet and had begun to leave when he asked the Khan-i Khanan, "What did Asad receive when he reached here, from us, from you, and the other nobles?"
>
> "Perhaps Rs 50,000," replied the Khan-i Khanan. The World-Enlight-ening Prince then said, "Such a sum might well have been spent just on this service." The Mir [Jamal-ud-Din] who was seated nearby then said, "He also received very little from 'Adil Khan because he took his leave of him on the very day he arrived. 'Adil Khan did not like this, and so gave him very little – it was not even equal to what Asad Beg had given him." The Khan-i Khanan then said, "Without doubt, Asad Beg has performed this service very well. He has shown courage and generosity in this matter. I have learnt he was offered two lakh *hūns* in order to stay on [in Bijapur]. But he turned them down. This shows his great courage and generosity." When the prince heard this, he said, "Give him Rs 10,000 as was done when he came here the first time. Bring the money on twenty trays imme-diately." He also told the Khan-i Khanan, "The money that was given to him by the *umarā'* the last time is in your care. Make sure he gets it." The nawwab sent instructions to the agents (*muhassils*) of the *umarā'* to get the sum together.[45]

Asad Beg notes that the Khan-i Khanan had given him Rs 10,000 the first time round, and to this he added a promissory note (*nawī-shtan*) for 2000 *muzaffarīs*, to be collected from his agents in Bur-hanpur. This was a particularly great favour for, at the time, their establishments were groaning under great expenses. Asad Beg left the prince's *darbār* and said his farewell to the Khan-i Khanan, from whom he equally received some excellent books (*kitāb-i nafīs*), superi-or in value to all the other gifts, and also took from him a sealed report ('*arzdāsht*) written in the Khan-i Khanan's own hand, enumerating

---

[45] Asad Beg, *Waqā'i'-yi Asad Beg Qazwīnī*, ed. Chander Shekhar, 100–1; *Nuskha-i Ahwāl-i Asad Beg* (London), 19a/32.

Asad Beg's services to the emperor. He now made his way at last to see Mir Jamal-ud-Din, who was waiting for him. Here, Asad Beg notes that, whatever his other bad or good qualities, the Sayyid was after all a good travelling companion (*hamrāhī*) who had always treated him well. At the farewell Mir Jamal-ud-Din gave him an elephant and a certain piebald horse which Asad Beg had long had his eye on. He then returned home in the middle of the night laden with these gifts.

The Departure from Ahmadnagar

Early next morning Asad Beg set out once more from Ahmadnagar, this time headed north for Agra. He first prepared the elephant Chanchal – of which the prince had become very fond – which was temporarily lodged in the prince's stables, and then made for the intermediate station of Burhanpur. At this time the *kotwāl* of Burhanpur, the brave and well-born Sayyid Mir Hashim (*sayyidzāda mardāna*), who was a good friend of Asad Beg's, expedited matters when he was on his way through. The prince had not wanted Asad Beg to take away Chanchal, suggesting that he merely carry a portrait of the elephant to his father, with the animal itself following. But Asad Beg was afraid that if he allowed this to happen, the credit would accrue to Mir Jamal-ud-Din when he arrived later at court with the elephant. Meanwhile Asad was receiving letters from Ramdas and others in the *darbār* saying he should return as soon as possible with Chanchal in tow so as not to be tricked out of getting full credit for the animal. Chanchal's fame had spread far and no other elephant was believed even worth looking at. The devious Mir had tried to influence matters by sending reports to the court of Asad Beg neglecting everything but the elephant. There were rumours that he had even managed to get a *farmān* from the court ordering that Asad Beg should stay in Burhanpur until he was joined by Mir Jamal-ud-Din and the other elephants. Asad's friend Mir Hashim, who got wind of this, told him to leave Burhanpur as quickly as possible so as to cross the Narmada river, for then Mir Jamal-ud-Din would not be able to catch up with him, whereas if he stayed on this side of the river he might be ordered to come back.

Asad Beg reports leaving Burhanpur post-haste, but he fell ill with fever that very night. Early next morning a mediocre Khorasani physician (*tabīb*) called Mulla Sana'i gave him a drink mixed with some powder. This was a grave error, for it was a laxative (*mulaiyan*) ill suited to Asad Beg's high fever. His condition thus grew far worse, and it seemed to him he would die in his palankeen while on the road. His party struggled to the village of Kargaon, by which time he was in the very jaws of death. Here he found another physician, a Hindu *vaid* (*baid-i hindū'ī*), whose ministrations helped, but only a little. It seemed all was over, and his brother Ibrahim Beg (who appears episodically, and who was with him on this leg) had given up hope for his life. It began to appear to Asad Beg as if his last breath was leaving his body, and he began to contemplate the Divine, saying: "Ya Murtaza 'Ali! Help this humble slave to this extent. I have accomplished my task and am now returning, and am so very close to my destination. At least give me the time to go back to court and recount my services and render my accounts to my master. I ask nothing else."

At this very time, in his state of stupor, he had a vision of the emperor (*hazrat*).[46] The emperor said to Asad Beg (rather prosaically): "Why don't you eat some watermelon?" Some time later, when he felt he had died, Asad Beg opened his eyes and saw his brother, who had torn open his shirt in sorrow and was standing there beside him. Asad Beg indicated his need for watermelon but the brother was in such distress that he did not understand the request. His servant Musahib, standing next to him, understood and ran to fetch the fruit. By the time he returned, Asad Beg was again unconscious; the watermelon was cut and a piece put to Asad Beg's lips. Opening his eyes, he managed to take in a little bit, and the juice had only reached his throat when he felt he had drunk the Elixir of Life. Swallowing some more, his stupor ended. He asked for more in a cup, ate some soft pieces of fruit with watermelon juice, and sat up. Having eaten a second cup of watermelon he felt the call of nature. The materials that then emerged from his body, says Asad Beg, lay beyond all description.

[46] Compare the dream of Mirza Nathan, in which Jahangir appeared to him while he was in a fever in Bengal; Nathan, *Bahāristān-i-Ghaybī*, trans. Borah, vol. 1, 74. Also see the discussion of the passage in Richards, "The Formulation of Imperial Authority", 310–11.

In sum, by the grace of God and the attention (*tawajjuh*) of the emperor, he recovered to the point that on that very day he could digest a little broth (*shorbā*). The night passed peacefully; the next day he was able to eat a rice-and-lentil preparation (*shula-i biranj*). He then set out and crossed the river. From there he wrote a letter to Mir Hashim with news of his illness and recovery, and sent it back with some of his men. He went on to Mandu the next day, where once more he met Mulla Ghausi, his acquaintance, and one of the best-respected people of that place. Through him, in gratitude for his recovery from his extreme illness, Asad Beg gave the sum of 1000 *muzaffarīs* to the poor of the town of Mandu in the name of the Commander of the Faithful, Hazrat 'Ali.[47]

From Mandu Asad Beg departed for Akbarabad-Agra, passing through Ujjain, where he stayed for a day with the lordly Timurid noble Mirza Shahrukh, whom he had met on his southward journey and who again treated the envoy very well. On the way out of Ujjain it rained heavily, so Asad Beg decided to take the route via Ranthambore. When the party had gone beyond Qasim Kheda, the rain was so heavy that he was obliged to camp at an elevation. Here he remained for seven days while it rained continuously and nothing was visible at all.

Fortunately, Asad Beg and his party were fully equipped, and so in general they lacked for nothing. But Chanchal, the elephant, which was used to a daily ration of two Akbari *man* of wine (*sharāb*), began to create a problem. Where were they to obtain the wine to placate the irascible she-elephant? Eventually two casks (*sandūq*) of high-quality Portuguese wine (*sharāb-i nafīs-i purtagālī*), which Asad Beg had acquired in Bijapur as a gift for the emperor, had to be broached. The waste of this wine evokes an apposite verse:

> Were a drop of this wine to fall on the snow,
> Red tulips would spring forth there at once.

However, when Chanchal drank the wine she became normal and her blood began flowing more calmly. Then, on the seventh day of the

---

[47] Asad Beg, *Waqā'i'-yi Asad Beg Qazwīnī*, ed. Chander Shekhar, 105; *Nuskha-i Ahwāl-i Asad Beg* (London), 19b/33, bottom.

deluge the weather improved. But they waited another two days, and only on the tenth day after their arrival at the spot set out with their animals loaded up with luggage.

But the ground was so soft and slushy that Chanchal was in danger of getting mired. Still, by the grace of God they managed to reach Fatehpur with the horse Chini and the elephant. Asad then left these animals and some other goods with his brother Ibrahim Beg, with instructions to follow him at greater leisure, while he himself went rapidly with the studded vase-holder (*kūza-dān-i murassaʿ*) to the court. He also wrote a quick letter explaining all that had happened to him and how he had left his brother at Fatehpur, and sent the missive on ahead to Raja Ramdas at the court. This letter reached in good time, and Ramdas took it to the emperor, who was all appreciation for Asad Beg's efficiency. The following day, at the time of the *darshan* of the second watch (*do-pahari*), Asad Beg reached court and through the intercession of Raja Ramdas bowed down before the sacred threshold (*āstān-i muqaddas*) and "washed his dust-laden face with the water of the heaven-like court."

This was Asad Beg's crowning moment, and he does not conceal his sense of exultation at returning to the court and presenting his *nazr*: a high-quality container (*khwāncha*) containing a special set of coins (*sikka*) from Bijapur, including a *nauras-hūn* (on which more below), and nine other diverse *hūns*, as well as nine *ibrāhīmīs*, nine coconuts, and nine *lārīs*. The emperor was delighted with these and asked briefly about each. But when he saw the *nauras-hūn*, he manifested a particular curiosity. Asad Beg explained to him that ʿAdil Khan had recently issued a new *hūn* equal in value to nine normal *hūn* of the Deccan, with the following mixed verse inscribed on it:

Za nauras-i muhr-i ʿĀdilshāhī
Jagat gurū dād-i ilāhī.

On hearing this, Akbar's countenance lit up. Asad Beg writes: "How can I, Qazwini, lacking an agile tongue, describe the extent of the kindness of the emperor to me?", and cites a verse:

I need a mouth as wide as the sky,
to describe the kindness of that angel.

What then were the specific kindnesses showered on him? First, as soon as Asad Beg arrived in court, the ruler remarked that Asad's beard had grown from neglect during his sojourn in the Deccan and sent his favourite barber (*hajjām*) to shave him in a corner of the court, thus relieving him of the burden of his beard. On account of the recent death of his mother Maryam Makani, the emperor himself (like his close courtiers) had shaved his moustache and the hair on his head. Asad Beg too thought he had best shave his head, moustache, and beard. When the emperor saw him thus, he was very happy at the gesture and gave him a special *khil'at*. He also told him presently to go home after his long journey, meet his children and spend time with them, then return in the evening to the ramparts (*burj*) where they would discuss matters further. Before taking his leave, Asad Beg told Akbar that the horse and the elephant would be presented before him two days later, but that he also had a *kūza-dān* for him. This he produced immediately, and Akbar appreciated it greatly after a brief look. Khwaja Muqim, the intendant of the household (*khān-i sāmān*), was instructed to take charge of it so that Akbar could look at it at leisure later, in the *burj*. Asad Beg was now given leave to depart, which he did after also saying goodbye to Ramdas. Thus, after a long gap, Asad was once more able to meet his children and friends, an occasion of considerable joy.

Until sunset, when the lamps were lit, he remained in conversation with his family and friends. But at dusk, in accordance with the emperor's orders, he sat in a palankeen and made his way towards the *burj-i khāss*. Again, his access to this privileged spot was managed through the intercession of Ramdas, who went with him as far as the inner apartments (*nashīman*, literally "nest"). At the time, records Asad Beg, the emperor had the habit of retiring into his apartments for some time after the dusk prayer (*tasbīh*). He would appear later and meet people, and meanwhile his dispersed servants and attendants would return.

That day, it so happened that Akbar, in order to have news from the Deccan, came out to the *burj* (pavilion) earlier than usual. He saw no one there, but nearing the throne and the *masnad-i Saltanat* spotted a torch-bearer leaning somewhat disrespectfully on the *masnad*, fast asleep. The emperor was so enraged that he ordered the man to be picked up and thrown off the pavilion to his death below. At this time, the unfortunate Khwaja Amin-ud-Din, whose turn it was to serve as page, came into Akbar's line of vision. The emperor, still in a rage, began to curse him and pushed him physically out of the pavilion, telling him to go off and attend on Prince Daniyal in the Deccan. Daulat Khan, who was equally meant to serve that evening as attendant, was also told off roundly. As for Ramdas, though Akbar looked at him in a hostile manner, he said nothing to him overtly. Only after all this had happened did Akbar sit down.

Asad Beg, with thousands of fears in his heart, now came in and saluted him from a distance. When the emperor saw him, he ordered that Asad Beg be given the place of Khwaja Amin-ud-Din. Raja Ramdas was given instructions to this effect, and Akbar praised Asad Beg, for he was sure the latter would perform the task very well. Asad was ordered closer and asked to perform *taslīm*. He approached with Ramdas and performed *sijda* and *taslīm*; he had just stood up straight after this when the emperor took the shawl off his waist and asked a certain Yazdani that it be tied around Asad's head. He was now sent out to write down the list of those who sought an audience. Asad Beg went out and looked at the nobles from the Deccan (*umarā'-i Dakhan*) outside; he went back and reported their names, and Akbar ordered them in. Thus, even while the unfortunate torch-bearer had met his death, Asad Beg's star continued to rise, and he writes of how conscious he was of the particular favour shown to him through this privileged appointment.[48]

The next day, in the interior space of the *ghusl-khāna*, the semi-disgraced Khwaja Amin-ud-Din, through the intervention of Ramdas and Asad Beg, was allowed briefly to see the emperor. He then left for the Deccan, having received a special shawl to be conveyed to the prince. At this time Asad Beg was also put in charge of the *pesh-khāna*, which had earlier been the responsibility of the Khwaja. The latter personally handed over charge of this to Asad, and gave over to him the carpets, brocades, and other materials that were in this divi-

---

[48] Asad Beg, *Waqā'i'-yi Asad Beg Qazwīnī*, ed. Chander Shekhar, 110; *Nuskha-i Ahwāl-i Asad Beg*, 35; Aligarh Ms, 88. For a translation of this passage, also see Elliot and Dowson, *History*, vol. 6, 164–5.

sion. The day after, the emperor did him further favours, to the point that Asad Beg began to feel overwhelmed. His brother Ibrahim Beg arrived meanwhile in the court from Fatehpur, and Asad went with Ramdas to see the emperor, to inform him that the elephant Chanchal and the horse Chini (as well as Lanku Pandit, with the *peshkash* tribute from Bijapur) had arrived. They awaited the emperor's orders in order to proceed further.[49] The emperor then ordered the intendant (*bakhshī*) to send for the horse and the elephant. The elephant was brought forward, and then Ibrahim Beg and Lanku Pandit came forward with *nazr*. Ibrahim gave one *muhr* and nine rupees, and the Pandit gave one *nauras hūn* of the sort described earlier. When the emperor saw this coin once again, he asked him about the *nauras sikka*; and a short discussion followed in a light vein. The emperor now told Ramdas to take care of the Pandit, and bestowed some favours on Ibrahim Beg, asking Asad Beg about his services.[50] The latter – careful not to make too much of the occasion – made it clear that Ibrahim Beg had not gone further than Burhanpur, but that he had been left there as a precaution. The next day, again in the *ghusl-khāna*, Asad Beg presented the emperor with further varieties of *peshkash* from the Deccan which were much admired. They included the elephant from Malik 'Ambar, of good pedigree and excellent in appearance, later lodged in the first category of the royal stables. Six other elephants were also inspected and accepted. Of the royal elephants, one was given as reward to Asad Beg for those he had brought.

Now, tobacco was quite common by this time in Bijapur, but Asad Beg had never seen it in Hindustan. He had hence had a golden pipe (*chilam*) procured in Mangalbedha, studded with precious stones. The pipe, of a beautiful colour and three yards long, was originally from Aceh (in northern Sumatra). It was decorated at both ends, and the

---

[49] Asad Beg, *Waqā'i'-yi Asad Beg Qazwīnī*, ed. Chander Shekhar, 111; *Nuskha-i Ahwāl-i Asad Beg* (London), 21a/36.

[50] Lanku seems to have remained in the Mughal court until early 1610. Thus in Jahangir, *The Jahangirnama*, 105, we learn that "Lanku Pandit, who had come with offerings from the 'Adil Khan during Arsh-Ashyani's reign [received] permission to accompany Khan Jahan."

mouthpiece was fitted with a good-quality Yemeni ruby. He also had a gilded torch-stand typical of the Deccan with him, and a golden box given to Asad Beg by 'Adil Khan, originally filled with betel-leaves. Into this Asad Beg filled good-quality tobacco and presented it at court. The high-quality tobacco was such, writes Asad Beg, that when a single leaf of it was lit the rest caught immediately. The whole gift was put in a silver container, itself covered with velvet, together with the pipe. The emperor initially appreciated the presentation greatly and remarked on how Asad Beg had gathered together so much in so short a time in the Deccan.

The tobacco and its accoutrements appearing now before him, Akbar asked what it was and what it was meant for, especially the pipe. The high noble Mirza 'Aziz Koka Khan-i A'zam, who was present, said it was called tobacco (*tambākū*), and that it was already in use in Mecca and Medina. He also said that, earlier, the physician Hakim Dawa'i had brought it to court, but that Akbar had paid it no attention. On this occasion, the emperor asked the pipe to be prepared so that he could smoke it. But the Hakim came forward immediately and advised against it. Still, since the emperor wished to show Asad Beg favour, he said he would imbibe a little, if only for his sake. He placed the pipe in his mouth and drew on it two or three times. However, in order not to displease the Hakim too much, he then passed it on to the Khan-i A'zam, who also pulled on it apace. Hakim Dawa'i was now summoned to explain its properties. He said it had been recently discovered and so there was no mention of it in the books of past knowledge (*hikmat*). As for the pipes, they came to the ports (*banādir*) of India from Aceh. European physicians (*hukamā'-i firang*) had, however, attributed many properties to it. Another physician at the court, Hakim 'Ali, added that it was as yet an untried medicine. The ancients had written nothing about it, so he could not recommend it further for lack of knowledge – he felt it was not really worthy of the emperor's attention.

At this Asad Beg – who had after all brought the tobacco from the Deccan – intervened to defend himself. He declared to Hakim 'Ali that the Franks were not so naïve as never themselves to have reflected on this: they too had wise men in their midst who rarely assessed such matters erroneously. Without having experimented with it and ascertained its properties, essence, and true character they could not have recommended it as they had done – for their own doctors and kings, or for people high and low. No doubt tobacco had both good and bad effects, but it could not be termed a vice. To this Hakim 'Ali averred it was not necessary that they follow the Franks in such matters; in matters where their own tradition said nothing, they were surely not obliged to blindly accept the Franks' word.

Asad Beg now responded saying this was a strange reflection. After all, new things were constantly being found out in the world. Since the time of Adam, things had been discovered step by step. If something new were put out by some nation (*qaum*), it was bound to spread out into the world at large, the task of philosophers and wise men being to discover its benefits and ill effects. Everyone was not likely to immediately know the benefits of a new discovery, as was the case with Chinese radix (*chūb-i chīnī*), which was not much used in ancient times but had been recently found useful in curing several diseases.[51]

When the emperor had heard Asad Beg's arguments he was pleased and said: "God bless you." He then added to the Khan-i A'zam that what Asad Beg had said was indeed very reasonable, for in actuality (*fi'l wāqi'*) something not being mentioned in the ancient books was not sufficient reason to stop it. Instead, what had become current in the world needed observation. However, the Hakim was adamant and asked the emperor to prohibit tobacco. The emperor now sent for one of the Jesuit priests in the court, who came forward and explained the benefits of tobacco. But Hakim 'Ali – who Asad Beg admits was a great physician – remained unconvinced and unmoved. For all this, the new product had great success at court. Asad Beg had brought back many pipes and much tobacco, which he distributed among several people; others asked him expressly for it. Soon enough, almost everyone expressed a desire for tobacco, to the point that traders imported it and began to sell it at whatever price they wished. Its

[51] Asad Beg, *Waqā'i'-yi Asad Beg Qazwīnī*, ed. Chander Shekhar, 113–14; *Nuskha-i Ahwāl-i Asad Beg*, Aligarh Ms, 90–2; for a discussion also see Qaisar, *The Indian Response to European Technology*, 118–20.

popularity came to be widespread, though ironically the emperor himself never took it again.

The gifts from the Deccan were not yet at an end. The very next day, Asad Beg presented the European casket to the emperor. Though Mir Jamal-ud-Din had described this casket (*sandūqcha*) in more than one missive, the emperor feigned ignorance and asked Asad Beg what it was. The latter replied that 'Adil Khan had at first sent presents that were not up to the mark. Then, discovering them abandoned outside Asad Beg's home, he had sent Lanku Pandit with this more worthy gift in exchange for what had been given to him as a present (*saughāt*). 'Adil Khan had declared that the contents of the casket were for Asad Beg's children. For this Asad had complimented him and wished him prosperity, but said he needed nothing from 'Adil Khan as he was content with his master (*murshīd*), who was his Qibla and Ka'aba.

The emperor now asked for details of the presents exchanged. Asad Beg replied that, on his arrival in Bijapur, he had taken the royal *farmān*, and also some 'Iraqi horses, male and female camels, Kashmiri shawls, and rare and high-quality cloths, all of which were worth some Rs 30,000. These he had gifted to 'Adil Khan on Mir Jamal-ud-Din's advice. The emperor declared this a considerable gift indeed, but asked what he had received in exchange. Asad Beg replied that, had he stayed on in Bijapur in keeping with 'Adil Khan's wishes, he would have received much more. But since he had decided that the emperor's best interests were served by not staying too long, he had rejected direct and indirect entreaties to tarry and returned quickly. This Mir Jamal-ud-Din could confirm as a witness. And when 'Adil Khan saw this he had sent another elephant, three Arab horses with their saddles, and 100,000 *lārīs* on camels, with seven bales of cloth. All these Asad Beg said he had refused, and only then had he sent the casket. The suggestion made by Asad is of a game played for ever higher stakes in which he, Asad Beg, had outmanoeuvred his adversary.

Akbar asked what one lakh *lārīs* were worth, and, on being told it was approximately Rs 35,000, exclaimed that Asad Beg had played his cards very well indeed.[52] Not many people would have had the

---

[52] Asad Beg, *Waqā'i'-yi Asad Beg Qazwīnī*, ed. Chander Shekhar, 116; *Nuskha-i Ahwāl-i Asad Beg* (London), 22a/38.

gumption to refuse a gift of Rs 30,000–Rs 40,000. He asked what was inside the casket – had Asad Beg opened it to see what it contained? Asad Beg strenuously denied having looked inside it, and its key was sent for. But Asad Beg denied even having seen its key and said he had brought it exactly as received.

The emperor now sent for an artisan locksmith (a certain Saliba-han), and asked him to open the casket. He did so and diverse contents emerged. The first item was a green bag sealed with 'Adil Khan's seal (which showed that Asad Beg had in fact not tampered with it), at which the emperor whispered loudly to Khwaja Muhammad Muqim: "Look at the large-heartedness of Asad. Do you know what his *mansab* is, and what he has received so far? Yet see his generosity and content-ment with what he has." The jewellers at the court were asked to assess the contents. It turned out that there were nine objects inside, all of the highest order, and the jewellers estimated their value at a lakh of ru-pees. The emperor wrapped them back in the bag and it was handed to Asad Beg. But Asad Beg pleaded that the gift was for the emperor, not for him. He had done well out of the voyage and explained that on the way up and down he had received gifts from the prince and other nobles. This casket was for the emperor (*lāyaq-i sarkār*), not for the likes of him. But the emperor insisted and said he could not take away what 'Adil Khan had in fact given Asad Beg.

This discussion went on until Asaf Khan made it clear to Asad that he should insist no further. So he performed the *sijda* and said polite-ly that the emperor should at least take one of the items from the casket. At this the emperor reopened the casket and took a European ruby-ring worth Rs 14,000. To please Asad he accepted this directly from him – and when the emperor pushed his finger through the ring it fitted perfectly: a strange coincidence indeed! All in all, this incident caused some jealousy among the other courtiers.

Thus, each day Asad Beg writes that he was given some special treatment (*tarbiyat*), growing in favour until the day when he was ap-pointed Mughal representative to the four provinces of the Deccan (*ilchīgirī-i chahār sūba-i Dakhan*), as he recounts later in the text. His *mansab*, which had earlier been 100/25, was raised on the day after the incident of the casket to 200/50, with a payment (*tankhwāh*) from the same *mahal* of Shah Quli Khan, which rendered Rs 17,000 annually.

Asad Beg comments nostalgically: *"Subhān Allāh!* What a blessed time that was!" In that very period, he had been appointed to the post of page to the pavilion (*burj*) and inner quarters (*ghusl khāna*) in place of Khwaja Amin-ud-Din. This post he held jointly with Khwaja Muhammad Taqi', but with a difference between them, namely that, when it was Asad Beg's turn, even Muhammad Taqi' could not enter the *burj* without being announced, whereas when Taqi' was the page Asad Beg had free access. Another difference was that when requests were carried in by Asad Beg, the emperor would inevitably ask the person in. In fact, at times, Khwaja Taqi' did not dare to carry in certain requests and had Asad Beg carry them instead, since he was more likely to get a good reception. Before Asad Beg's time, this work was done jointly by Amin-ud-Din and Taqi', and at this time things normally passed through Raja Ramdas and Khwaja Daulat, the *nāzir*. But when Asad Beg took over the page's function, this particular regulation (*zābita*) was suppressed by the emperor, who left matters to Asad Beg's discretion. With the passage of time, even Raja Ramdas and Khwaja Daulat could not get access to the *burj* without Asad Beg, so powerful had he grown.

A New Voyage South

Asad Beg assures us that, after his return from the Deccan, for about a year he had a substantial amount of independent power and influence in the court, despite his low official rank. But matters changed with news of the sudden death of Prince Daniyal in the Deccan (perhaps from an accident related to his excessive drinking). When this devastating news reached the emperor his state was such, writes Asad Beg, that it is hard to describe. Had the emperor not been endowed by God with special wisdom, had he not been so pious and such a believer, he and all those around him would have been devastated by sadness. But his enormous courage, and his knowledge of Reality (*haqīqat*), enabled him to drain this bitter cup with patience. He showed no external sign of his heavy burden, setting an example to all those around him, and even to great and pious men of faith (*arbāb-i yaqīn*). On Daniyal's death the emperor wept within himself and mourned by composing a lament (*marsīya*) in the manner of the great poet Jami.

Image 3.4 : A Mughal prince, perhaps Daniyal, holding a sprig of flowers, *c.* 1580–90.

But where Jami wrote in Persian, Asad Beg tells us Akbar's verse was in the language of India (*surūd-i hind*). The verse he quotes is a literary curiosity, and also a sign that, after two decades in Mughal India, this native of Qazwin had come to grasp at least some aspects of the northern Indian vernaculars:

Chashmān-i man chū sāwan-o-bhadon shud ze ashk
Ke nām-i Gang mī kunam-o-gāh Narbadā.

My eyes became the year's rainy months with tears,
that I may call them Ganga or even Narbada.[53]

Still, one night, after the period of mourning was over, a musical evening was held at the *burj*. On this occasion Asad Beg whispered to Raja Ramdas, saying one night in Bijapur 'Adil Khan had asked him whether the musician Tansen (who had been dead some years by then) sang standing up or sitting down. The emperor overheard this despite being absorbed in music and asked why 'Adil Khan's name had come up. Ramdas recounted what had been whispered to him. On hearing this the emperor smiled and understood its significance. He said to Ramdas that Asad Beg should return to the Deccan, implying that he seemed to miss his time in Bijapur. To this Asad Beg replied that the rains would have made the roads difficult, and it was better to make the journey after the rains. The emperor nevertheless ordered preparations to be made and the necessary horses purchased from the exchequer. Raja Kishan Das was told to get 'Iraqi and Turkish horses for Asad Beg: this was counted a great favour, the sort never given to envoys earlier in the reign. Asad wishes to stress once more his privileged personal relationship with Akbar.

Within a month, 180 'Iraqi and Turkish horses had been bought. Over this time, in the evenings, the emperor gave him detailed instructions and advice on his mission while at the *burj*. This included the writing of royal *farmāns* for the four "governors" of the Deccan (*hukkām-i arbāb-i Dakhan*), namely of Bijapur, Golkonda, Bidar, and Karnatak (meaning the Vijayanagara rump state of the Aravidu

<hr>

[53] Asad Beg, *Waqāʾiʿ-yi Asad Beg Qazwīnī*, ed. Chander Shekhar, 120; *Nuskha-i Ahwāl-i Asad Beg* (London), 22b/39.

dynasty). He also told Asad Beg that his last visit had been on account of the problems caused by Mir Jamal-ud-Din, the daughter of 'Adil Khan, and the *peshkash*. But now he had full authority over the four provinces (*sūbas*) of the Deccan, and wherever he went he had to meet specific commercial objectives. Good elephants and high-quality jewels were to be sought out, which were to be found in all four. Some were to be sent ahead to the court, and some paid for and brought back by Asad Beg. Other than elephants and jewels, there was no need to bring anything unless there was something strikingly novel about it (*tāzgī*). Any other goods or money that he collected and brought back, he could keep. He should be so comprehensive in his purchases that not even a single good elephant or jewel should be left in the Deccan. These then were his instructions, and two months were spent in making the arrangements.

Asad Beg, who was now given a fresh *mansab* of 200/300, gathered together a considerable force of 'Iraqis, Khurasanis, and Turkomans, giving each an advance of three to four months' pay. Besides, each trooper was given a good horse, and all in all he managed to amass a thousand or two thousand men, with Shah 'Ali Isfahani, a very capable scribe (*nawīsinda*) as paymaster (*bakhshī*). The force included a hundred musketeers (*bandūqchīs*) and a hundred archers on foot, worthy of the escort of a proper Mughal envoy.

In those very days, tribute (*peshkash*) and a supplication (*'arz-dāsht*) arrived from the ruler of Bidar with the returning Mughal envoy (*wakīl*), Amin-ul-Mulk. In this he requested that he be given a fort in Berar so that he might move there with his family and enter Mughal service; in exchange he offered his own fort and town to the emperor. Amin-ul-Mulk was now given to the charge of Asad Beg, with a *farmān* for the Malik of Bidar stating that he should hand over his fort directly to Asad, and that any fort he wanted in Berar be given to him. Asad was then to put an agent in charge of Bidar and continue on his mission.

Asad Beg also asked for a *farmān* for Malik 'Ambar (as he had done on his previous trip) and was told to draft it himself. In a measure of the influence he enjoyed, an imperial order was issued that Asad Beg be given several plain papers with a royal insignia (*tughrā*) and a *muhr-i auzak* (the main seal), which he could fill whenever required. This, writes Asad Beg, was an extraordinary favour of a sort conceded to relatively few people by the emperor. To emphasise this point, his text now returns to an account of the frequent evenings he spent in the pavilion (*burj*) with the emperor, just before his departure for the Deccan.

One night, he reports, the emperor, while getting up from his throne and entering his inner apartments, told Asad he had given him a *mansab* rank of 1000 but that he would be confirmed in it only on his return from his voyage. Asad made his bows (the usual *taslīm* and *sijda*), as was appropriate. He was also given a special horse from the royal stables, and a brocade *khil'at* on another day; on still another occasion he received a royal shawl from Akbar's waist – with his own hands the emperor tied this on Asad's head. On the occasion of his eventual southward departure an honourable farewell ceremony was organised, but Asad was also told to wait a few days in the vicinity of the city of Agra for possible last-minute instructions.

The envoy-designate eventually remained camped outside the capital city for fifteen days, and on each day one or the other royal servant (such as Rup Khawass, Miyan Salibahan, or the sons of Miyan Janu) would come to the camp with messages from court. On the fifteenth night, Khwaja Muhammad Taqi' came with word from the emperor that he could leave. Asad Beg notes that, in the fifteen days that he was camped outside Agra, every evening groups of friends, naturally loath to let him go, would gather for festivities (*suhbat*). At last, "drinking their liver's blood" (a metaphor for swallowing their chagrin), they declared their willingness to let him depart towards the Deccan. A close friend of Asad Beg's, Mirza Aqa Shah, a man of "angelic disposition", now brought two Iranians youths from Tabrez with him, who were amongst his close acquaintances (and who turn out later in the account to be merchants). He assured Asad Beg that the two – whose names were Muhammad Sharif and Muhammad Qasim – were full of good grace and understanding. The latter had brought along a young boy called Umul, handsome and with a "salty" (*namakīn*) countenance, of a sort particularly pleasing to middle-aged *bon vivants* such as Asad Beg. All of them were hence admitted into the envoy's group, and he had ribald parties with them along the way.

This went on until the time when they arrived in the territory of a certain Raja Bhoj, whose people controlled the area of Chanda Ghati.[54] His people demanded octroi (*rāh-dārī*) from the traders (*saudāgarān*) of the party, which did not please Asad Beg. Nevertheless, the party paid up for safe passage through the mountains of the area. Asad was told by the same Raja Bhoj's men that there were hostile groups such as Bhils and Girasis in the area, against whom they could not offer much protection. But they would all the same get them through the territories under their own control. Consequently, Asad Beg's party grew alert. Some twenty horsemen with fifty musketeers and fifty archers were sent with Ibrahim Beg, Nasir Khan, and Shah 'Ali in the vanguard (*harāwal*) of the group.[55] Asad Beg himself with Mahdi 'Ali Sultan, Aqa Raza, and the others remained in the middle, along with the elephant and camel trains and the goods, while Amin-ul-Mulk with the Deccani people and their 300 horse brought up the rear. Thus, cautiously, they marched through this hostile terrain, not unlike that through which Asad had marched with his master Shaikh Abu'l Fazl less than three years earlier.

When a part of this dangerous route had been covered, there came a moment when the Rajputs of Raja Bhoj under the command of the Raja's nephew (who had come to escort them, but whom Asad Beg did not entirely trust) were attached to the Deccanis. Asad Beg had warned the Deccanis not to mix with the Rajputs. Suddenly, at a narrow gorge, one of the obstinate camels of the Baluchi transporters with the soldiers' goods on it decided to lie down on its side. It was unable to rise: its bags had been slit on one side with a knife. Some people began to loot it, and there was commotion. Amin-ul-Mulk arrived quickly and the Rajputs too converged. The result was a clash between the Rajputs and the Baluchis. Amin-ul-Mulk himself was unarmed and defenceless, an arrow struck him below the navel and he fell to the ground. Others trampled on his body in the confusion. When word of all this reached Asad Beg, he instructed Mahdi 'Ali to stay on the spot and

---

[54] Jahangir visited this region in November 1618, and refers to Raja Bhoj (or Rai Bhoj Hada) on this occasion. Cf. Jahangir, *The Jahangirnama*, 287–8.

[55] Asad Beg, *Waqā'i'-yi Asad Beg Qazwīnī*, ed. Chander Shekhar, 125; *Nuskha-i Ahwāl-i Asad Beg* (London), 41; Aligarh Ms, 103.

himself turned back with a force. On arriving he found that the nephew of Raja Bhoj had been killed, as had some other Rajputs. The camels were in confusion and the caravan in disarray. Asad Beg and Aqa Raza managed to impose some order, the Rajput party withdrew to some distance, Asad Beg raised up the wounded Amin-ul-Mulk and placed him on a palankeen. Asad Beg then decided to stay with him and sent a message to his brother Ibrahim Beg to advance slowly with the caravan. Ibrahim was to maintain his place, not turn back lest he be looted by the rebellious Kolis and Girasiyas. The caravan was rearranged with the aid of Mahdi 'Ali and a camp was pitched. By this time Amin-ul-Mulk was half-dead; fortunately he was accompanied by his family (including a newborn infant son). This son's birth, observes Asad Beg, proved inauspicious, for on that very night Amin-ul-Mulk died; he was buried the next morning.

At the same time, news came that some three thousand hostile Rajputs attached to Raja Bhoj (angered perhaps at the death of his nephew) were approaching, ready for battle. This news, on top of the bad omens, spread panic in Asad Beg's camp.[56] It was decided to send Nasir Khan ahead with fifty horsemen, and for the others including the Deccanis to start moving gradually from the camp. Some way along, the caravan came to be divided into two parts. The Deccanis on foot were sent on with Shah 'Ali. They continued to travel even by night in their anxiety to get through hostile Rajput territory. Thus, they arrived at Qasim Kheda in the Ujjain region and camped near the fortress. Amin-ul-Mulk's wife and child were lodged inside the fort, and their entourage now felt confident against the Rajputs. However, at the end of the day, when the Rajputs found no trace of the Mughal party on the route, they sent a message to the older son of Raja Bhoj asking for instructions and, fortunately, he ordered them to turn back rather than persist in the confrontation. A few days later the party reached Ujjain proper, where Asad again met his old acquaintance Mirza Shahrukh. A camp was pitched outside the town, and for a time the party rested, oblivious to worldly cares. The last phase of the journey had after all been

---

[56] Asad Beg, *Waqāʾiʿ-yi Asad Beg Qazwīnī*, ed. Chander Shekhar, 127; *Nuskha-i Ahwāl-i Asad Beg* (London), 23b/41.

rather tiring and stressful. On the fourth day they thought of moving on. At this time, Nawwab Mirza 'Ali Beg Akbarshahi, who was on his way back to the Mughal court from the Deccan, stopped near Asad Beg's camp. Since Asad claimed him as a good friend, he decided to stay an extra day. They met for extended and pleasant conversations.

In the midst of this happiness, quite suddenly, a letter arrived from some Hindus in the court (perhaps Raja Ramdas is meant), with news that the emperor Akbar was seriously ill. At this, everyone fell into confusion and the party's further plans were called into question. They decided to stay on near Ujjain another day and await further news. The following night letters came from the *wakīls* of Mirza Shahrukh and the "Hindus" with heartbreaking news of the emperor's death (which implies we are in late October or early November 1605). The entire world, declares Asad Beg, fell into confusion.[57] A verse is cited:

> In a moment, in an hour, in a breath,
> the affairs of the world may be wholly altered.

Asad Beg felt this most personally as a black day for himself. He cites a few apposite verses of the courtier Asaf Khan:

> Autumn has aged the leaves of every garden,
> I am not the only one who was uprooted.
> Flowers in every garden have wilted.
> My garden too has been laid to waste.

Another verse uses the metaphor of a ship in a storm, in which fire has broken out to add to its misfortunes:

> The captain (*nākhudā*) was frightened by the storm,
> The wind was so fierce that fire entered the ship.

But things were to become even worse. On the day that the sad news of the emperor's death arrived, the "accursed Baluchis" who were in charge of the camels (fifty of Asad Beg's own and another hundred

[57] Asad Beg, *Waqā'i'-yi Asad Beg Qazwīnī*, ed. Chander Shekhar, 128; *Nuskha-i Ahwāl-i Asad Beg* (London), 42; Aligarh Ms, 106.

with the merchants' goods) took their animals with them and fled in a panic. Besides, it was feared that the Badakhshis of Ujjain, unruly Central Asian soldiers who were not much in awe of their commander Mirza Shahrukh, might now do something untoward. Mirza 'Ali Beg had meanwhile left in haste for the court, telling Asad Beg that he too should do the same. But Asad declares he could not turn back without his caravan, especially as he had some merchants (including the two great Tabrezi traders) in his charge. One way or another, this caravan (*qāfila*) had to be taken as far as Burhanpur.

To add to the predicament, men began to desert from within Asad Beg's own party. First among them was the royal musician Baiju (*Baijū-i kalāwant bādshāhī*), with his brethren (*birādarān*), despite the fact that Asad Beg had been most attentive and considerate to them. In fact, he had given each of them excellent horses as well as money in advance. Yet they proved to be disloyal (*mardūm-i bīwafā*). One wonders whether the reference is to a musician later to be mythologised under the name of "Baiju Bawra".[58]

The panic was now widespread, and the very next day the *bakhshī*, Shah 'Ali, who was in charge of the news and accounts, ran away with some horsemen and troopers. Faced with this veritable débacle, Asad Beg regrouped his caravan with 150 additional camels and went to meet Mirza Shahrukh. The latter lent him his own *wakīl* Mir Kalan with 500 horse to accompany the caravan as far as the Narbada river.

Thus, on the fourth day after the bad news of the emperor's death had arrived, the envoy's party managed at last to leave Ujjain.[59] But the unfortunate turn to events had not ended. More shocking still was the fact that the greater part of the troopers, who were Turkomans under the command of Asad Beg's long-time companion Nasir Khan ("the black-faced"), now hatched a conspiracy against Asad Beg. Nasir Khan

---

[58] On Baiju, another reference may be found in in Baha'-ud-Din Chishti Barnawi's *Chishtīya-i bihishtīya*, for which see Sherani, "Makhdum Shaikh Bahā'-ud-Dīn Barnawī", 72–99. In the twentieth century, perhaps based on earlier oral legend, he has been presented as the untutored rival of Tansen; cf. the film by Vijay Bhatt, *Baiju Bavra* (1952).

[59] Asad Beg, *Waqā'i'-yi Asad Beg Qazwīnī*, ed. Chander Shekhar, 129; *Nuskha-i Ahwāl-i Asad Beg* (London), 24a/42.

himself had long been Asad Beg's deputy (*wakīl*), with practically unlimited powers. Fortunately, Ya'qub Aqa and Sher 'Ali Aqa, though they were a sworn part of the conspiracy, revealed it to Asad Beg, who declares his own consternation at this disloyalty of his own closest servants. Who could he turn to now for help? Fortunately, God protected him, not allowing the conspirators a chance to implement their plans. For the time being he was protected by the troopers detached by Mirza Shahrukh. But when they reached the banks of the Narbada, the Mirza's troops thought to go back. However, at this stage Asad Beg went to Mir Kalan's tent and explained the ingratitude and betrayal (*harām khorī*) by his own men, requesting him to remain for two or three more stages of the journey to protect him. The Mir accepted, and Asad Beg did not reveal to the conspirators that he knew what they were up to. However, once the river had been crossed and they took the road to Burhanpur, the conspirators guessed he knew and feared for themselves. At Karkun, Asad Beg assigned the Turkomans to the vanguard, keeping the Deccanis and Mirza Shahrukh's men with him. However, on reaching hilly country he found all the would-be conspirators in a row, their hands folded. The "black-faced" Nasir Khan and Khalifa Sultan now dismounted and fell at Asad Beg's feet, pleading with him to release them so that they would not have to go with him to Burhanpur, saying they preferred to go back north to Khwaja Beg Mirza. They also asked him not to be vindictive with their other associates.

Asad Beg decided there was no point in insisting and decided to let them go, calling (no doubt sarcastically) for God's blessings on them. Thus, granting them some supplies, and the horses on which they were mounted, the ungrateful Nasir Khan and others went off to Khwaja Beg Mirza Safavi. But there were other conspirators too who also represented a danger, in that they might attack Asad Beg's party from the rear. Against them suitable precautions were now taken. Asad Beg notes that most of the men who had decided to desert on this occasion were killed in one or the other fashion within a year, thus paying a price for their ingratitude. He cites a verse:

Let Time take care of your ill-wishers,
for Time is the best judge, and you can divest yourself.

Thus, shattered and exhausted by these travails, Asad Beg at long last reached Burhanpur and camped at the house of Akhund Mulla Hayati. He thanked Mirza Shahrukh's men and sent back a letter to the Mirza through them, praising Mir Kalan in particular for his help. In compensation, Asad Beg now gave Mir Kalan a high-quality 'Iraqi horse and excused himself verbally for having given him such trouble. The following day Asad Beg met Nawwab Khwaja Abu'l Hasan, the governor (*hākim*) of Burhanpur. He was very gracious and throughout their stay in Burhanpur treated the party very well, organising several sumptuous banquets in Asad's honour, raising his morale. Asad's old acquaintance, the generalissimo Khan-i Khanan, and Mirza Rustam had gone towards the fortress of Daulatabad to combat the forces of Raju Dakhni. After Asad had rested a few days at Burhanpur he took leave from Khwaja Abu'l Hasan and went on to meet the Khan-i Khanan. His brother Ibrahim Beg was left behind at Burhanpur with his baggage and horses, while Mahdi Quli Sultan accompanied him on his way.

There was now no real danger on the road, but since Asad Beg went accompanied with his men (who had been proven untrustworthy), Khwaja Abu'l Hasan had made ready a force to accompany him. However, Asad decided to leave on his own, not taking this other force. So, when he was two stages outside Burhanpur, the Khwaja praised Asad for his courage in a letter to the Khan-i Khanan, while explaining the awkward situation with the escort. He told the generalissimo, however, that if anything happened to Asad Beg it would not be his (the Khwaja's) fault, but simply the consequence of Asad Beg's foolhardiness (*bī-parwāhī*). This letter reached the Khan-i Khanan before Asad Beg could arrive, and the former became somewhat alarmed. A certain Quli Beg A'ini was hence sent out with 1000 horse to meet him en route. The two parties eventually met up in the jungle near Thana, and the other saw that Asad Beg was escorted by only a hundred horse and fifty musketeers, a matter of some surprise. The next day Asad Beg, now rather better escorted, advanced to within two *kos* of the Mughal army.[60] Quli Beg A'ini took the imperial *farmāns* in the name

---

[60] Asad Beg, *Waqā'i'-yi Asad Beg Qazwīnī*, ed. Chander Shekhar, 132; *Nuskha-i Ahwāl-i Asad Beg* (London), 25a/43.

of the Khan-i Khanan, Mirza Rustam, and Mirza Iraj and went on in advance.

The Khan-i Khanan, with Mirza Rustam, approached to receive the *farmāns* of the deceased emperor and prostrated themselves before them. With tears in his eyes, and a heart full of warmth, he made enquiries from Asad Beg about his well-being. Asad expressed his gratitude for all the kindness shown by the Khan-i Khanan – who, he declared, was not only old but also full of wisdom. They reached the principal camp, and Khan-i Khanan instructed Mirza Rustam to take special care of Asad Beg. The latter accompanied him to the Khan-i Khanan's court, where food, fruit, and drinks (*ashraba*) were consumed in quantities. Asad then departed and went back with Mirza Rustam to his camp at the end of the day, in the Mirza's own palankeen.

Some happy days followed over which Asad Beg was particularly gladdened by the services offered him by a certain Mirza Murad, a reflection of his newly expressed (if not newly found) interest in handsome young men. There were truly joyous soirées (*asbāb-i 'aish-o-kāmrānī*) full of circulating glasses of wine (*jāmhā-i rāh-i rehānī*) that brought fresh life (*raunaq-i tāzā*) back to a world all too full of gloom and death. Even Asad Beg, whose palate had been made bitter with the poison of repeated failure, was able to gain a little pleasure in these circumstances, though his heart was heavy – for reasons that will presently become clear. He, of course, insisted that all this should not be done in his honour, and it was only upon realising Mirza Rustam would be saddened by his refusal that he agreed. Having drunk a few glasses, Asad declared that Mahdi Quli Sultan, who had accompanied him on his way, should also be invited to the meeting (*mahfil*). The Mirza was happy to hear this and at once dispatched a messenger to fetch Mahdi Quli. After some hesitation, and a certain number of polite demurrals, Mahdi Quli arrived. After a few glasses, he too warmed up. At this Asad Beg sent his servant (*musāhib*) to fetch a stringed instrument (*chahār tār*). The Mirza asked who played the instrument, and it was explained that Mahdi Quli Sultan was the master of this lute and had even taught it to Musahib. The Mirza was even happier to hear this, and a discussion began on technical musical matters (*tarz-i sāz wa tarh muqaddamāt-i ishtibāt*). Mahdi Quli presently grew excited in the course of this discussion; he took up his instrument and began a song (*naghmā*). He played in such a manner, declares Asad Beg, that in the sky Zohra (Venus) herself began to look out from behind the veil of Nilofar (the sapphire veil of the sky), full of desire to join this happy meeting. Mirza Rustam, who was himself an aficionado of music, was greatly content at all this.

That night, writes Asad Beg, for the first time after a long period of travails, he spent a happy time listening to music and verses. Only the cock's crowing at dawn brought an end to it. Asad Beg and Mahdi Quli now returned home, and had slept but a few hours when Asad Beg's new favourite Mirza Murad – compared here to the sun, and the very centre of the world in terms of his talent, indeed no less than any royal prince in these terms – arrived once more in their quarters. He brought with him Maulana Nau'i, and a certain Mir Husain Kufri. Again a discussion began, and several glasses of wine were consumed, whether really or metaphorically is somewhat unclear. Between the music and discussions of the night, and those of the day, Asad Beg assures us he can hardly describe the happiness of this time. He cites verses that evoke his duration in the company of the handsome Mir Murad:

> *Bū-yi pairāhan-i Yūsuf ba juz az bād-i sabā,*
> *ke rasānad ba mashāmi ki mu'attar gardad.*

> Who besides the breeze is spreading the fragrance of Joseph's coat,
> that it is here to perfume our nostrils?

After some days spent in this manner, Asad Beg went to meet the Khan-i Khanan once more and was invited to a repast with him: over this time he was privy to great favours from that man of eminence. While with the Khan-i Khanan, a certain Mirza Hasan 'Ali Beg (a friend of Asad Beg) arrived. He and the Khan-i Khanan had a whispered consultation, and the general indicated that Asad Beg be informed of the matter. Later, when Asad and he were returning home, Hasan 'Ali Beg told him that the Khan-i Khanan had long had his eye on him, since the time Asad Beg had been in Abu'l Fazl's service. But there had been no occasion to approach him. Now the time was ripe, and the Khan-i Khanan had been expecting him. It was known that he had been appointed on a mission to Bijapur and Golkonda, amongst other things to return 'Adil Khan's widowed daughter – earlier married to Prince Daniyal – to him (this is the first time this part of the mission is mentioned). The Khan-i Khanan's *bakhshī*, Khwaja Abu'l Hasan, has meanwhile left for Iran, and he has appointed Khwaja Nizam-ud-Din's son to that post for the time being. In view of the changing circumstances, the Khan-i Khanan wished to offer Asad Beg a high *mansab* rank and suggested that he stay on in all comfort. The hint was that he might well be made *bakhshī* one day, particularly in view of his intellectual and personal qualities (*suhbat*). On hearing all this, Asad Beg declares himself truly happy; he will give the offer due consideration and respond properly.

Asad Beg now returned to his quarters where he found Mirza Rustam awaiting him. Mirza Rustam had meanwhile asked Asad Beg's slave to show him the horses they had brought along so that he could select a few. Though most of the horses were in Burhanpur, he managed to find four, and then an additional three. Such transactions were clearly a device for Asad Beg to ingratiate himself with significant figures in the Khan-i Khanan's circle. Asad now reported his conversation with Hasan 'Ali Beg, which Mirza Rustam declared was very good news indeed.

Though some hours were still left in the day, another drinking party was organised.[61] The musician Mahdi Quli Sultan joined them, and that night was once more spent joyfully. The next morning, the Khan-i Khanan asked Hasan 'Ali Beg what had transpired in the discussion with Asad Beg, and then sent for his *dīwān*, Mirza 'Abdul Malik Arghandi (also an old friend of Asad's), as well as Hasan 'Ali Beg, Miyan Fahim (who held the post of *wakīl-i mu'tabar*), and Mulla Hayati. The four were instructed to go and talk to Asad Beg in his quarters, to seek an auspicious time to confirm the arrangement that had been proposed. When the four arrived, Asad was at home with Mahdi Quli Sultan. A few introductory polite remarks were made and they were offered dried fruits and sweetmeats. They then broached the

---

[61] Asad Beg, *Waqā'i'-yi Asad Beg Qazwīnī*, ed. Chander Shekhar, 137–8; *Nuskha-i Ahwāl-i Asad Beg* (London), 26a.

matter at hand, with Mirza 'Abdul Malik taking the lead after having washed his hands. Asad Beg grew a little uneasy, thinking the others might think him arrogant if he were to hesitate. Mulla Hayati, his special friend, now pressed him for an answer. Asad presently replied, stating that he could hardly refuse the offer, especially in view of his own relatively inferior status compared to that of the Khan-i Khanan. Nevertheless, he expressed anxiety: the deceased emperor had given him an important charge, and Prince Salim, now the emperor Jahangir, too had very kindly shown concern at his departure in the interval that he was camped outside Agra, awaiting his final dispatch. However, on the day of his departure, despite the prince's concern for him, he had not taken proper leave of the prince. Now that the prince had become emperor, Asad Beg was sleepless with anxiety at the possibility that the prince had not forgiven the discourtesy. Besides, all that had happened from the time that Asad Beg had been Shaikh Abu'l Fazl's servant was no doubt still on Jahangir's mind. This too was weighing heavily on his, Asad Beg's, mind. He was thus in the Deccan, waiting either for an imperial *farmān* or for a messenger to invite him back to the new emperor's service. He could not go back on his own initiative. Asad Beg's account finds an appropriate verse here:

> No one knows my troubles like I do,
> for I alone have been with myself all the while.

Asad requested the four messengers to return and report all this to the Khan-i Khanan for him to make the final decision. Miyan Fahim, who was an understanding man, took pity on him and complimented him on his lucid vision of his circumstances. He also stated that only the Khan-i Khanan's intercession could resolve his problems with the court. They took leave with the usual exchanges of betel-leaf (*pān*) and perfume (*khwushbū*), and Asad Beg presented them with four saddled horses as they were departing. Miyan Fahim's polite demurrals at this generosity were soon overcome.

When the tenor of these negotiations was reported to the Khan-i Khanan, he became silent and went off to reflect. Mulla Hayati then returned to see Asad Beg, and they pursued the discussion. While these talks were going on, Mirza Murad, Mulla Nau'i, and Kufri showed up in Asad Beg's quarters once more, and festivities began, as was the custom. On hearing they had all gathered, Mirza Rustam too arrived, accompanied by Hasan 'Arshi, Aqa Raza, and several musicians (*sāzanda*); at the end of the revelries each member of the group, suitably intoxicated with wine and music, returned to his respective home.

The next day Asad Beg awoke late, dressed, and went to see the Khan-i Khanan. He saluted him and saw that the general was accompanied only by Miyan Fahim. The Khan-i Khanan now instructed Fahim to keep others away from the chief audience-hall (*dīwānkhwāna-i khāss*), for he wished to talk things over alone with Asad Beg — who took the occasion to repeat what he had said earlier to the intermediaries. The Khan became quiet and thoughtful, and at last asked what he intended to do with regard to the court. Asad Beg replied that his only thought was to put himself at the disposal of the Khan-i Khanan because he could see he was not in control (*ikhtiyār*) of anything, and insisted once more on his low status. To this the Khan replied:

> You should not allow any of your troubles even a hair's space. What fortune the future holds for you is something that neither you nor anyone else may imagine. May God be thanked that you are here at this time; and I am content with you. Let us see what the unseen world of the future has in store. My home is yours, and so do not even be weighed down to the extent of a hair. Live as I do; indeed, it is a matter of pride for me to have met you. This is a great occasion for me — that you were able to come here. Come and go as you want.

The Khan-i Khanan told Miyan Fahim that he had been considering Asad Beg as one of the important notables and *mansabdārs*, but after these latest transactions he felt an even closer relationship to him. Miyan Fahim declared that he, for his part, already knew, as an old servant of Khan-i Khanan, that the general and Asad Beg had a special relationship. Meanwhile, a number of people had gathered outside to see the Khan-i Khanan and they sent in requests (*du'ā*) to see him; they were asked in, and Asad was meanwhile asked to sit next to the Khan-i Khanan, leaning on a special cushion.[62] He thus gained precedence

---

[62] Asad Beg, *Waqā'i'-yi Asad Beg Qazwīnī*, ed. Chander Shekhar, 140–1; *Nuskha-i Ahwāl-i Asad Beg* (London), 27a.

over everyone else, and this special treatment continued over the following days.

In the period that followed there were diverse festivities, feasts, and music in the camp every day. Asad managed in the process to accumulate a number of gifts – books, saddle-cloths, some horses, and elephants – all through the kindness of the Khan-i Khanan. One of those nights was the festival of Diwali, when a particularly lively party was held; Asad Beg – as was the custom at such occasions – played dice (*nard*) with Mirza Rustam and the other notables. On this occasion he received the sum of 500 gold *muhr*, which the Mirza seems to have lost to him deliberately, and which he accepted after some initial hesitation praising God, the fount of all wealth, whose grace was clearly upon him at that moment. But a sense of unease continued to haunt him, for Asad Beg knew that he was living, as it were, on borrowed time. Sooner or later the emperor would recall him and he would have to answer for his past actions.

The Return to Agra

This is precisely what eventually transpired, as we learn in the next section of the account, entitled "The arrival of a cold and indifferent *farmān* of summons from Jahangir". When a good number of days had thus passed in the Khan-i Khanan's camp, writes Asad Beg, one day a certain Ya'qub Aqa, Asad Beg's agent (*wakīl*) at court, arrived with an imperial *farmān* and some letters from his friends at Agra. This *farmān* was not given to Asad Beg but instead taken and delivered, sealed, to the Khan-i Khanan. When opened an order was discovered to the effect that Asad, who had been sent in embassy (*hijābat*) to the Deccan, should return to the court, no matter where he was. When the Khan-i Khanan saw this, he knew what Asad Beg feared had come to pass. He asked Ya'qub Aqa to clarify why this *farmān* had been issued, and in what circumstances. He was told that the man responsible was none other than a person called Baiju, one of the musicians (*kalāwants*) whom the deceased emperor had sent to 'Adil Khan in order to learn some of the latter's compositions (*tasnīfāt*). That ill-starred character, upon hearing of the emperor's death while in Ujjain, had run away and turned back to Agra. One day, he was espied by Jahangir at court and recognised as a musician who had gone with Asad Beg. He was asked where he had left the envoy, and the latter replied they had parted company in Ujjain. Baiju had further claimed that, when he heard of Jahangir's succession, he and the others in the party had decided to come back, but that Asad had obstinately gone onwards to Burhanpur.

Jahangir was visibly angered to hear this, and so decided to order the envoy back at once. However, the chief vizier (*wazīr ul-mulk*), who was a friend of Asad Beg's, had pleaded that he had been sent from the court on a mission and that he would surely return when the mission was accomplished. Further, Mirza 'Ali Beg, whom Asad Beg had met in the Deccan, also returned to the court and told Jahangir that he had seen Asad Beg there. When news of Akbar's death had reached, he reported, Asad Beg had been abandoned by many of his company. He had in fact wanted to return to the court, but since he had a large caravan with him, and some people from the Deccan, he had to take care of them. Had he returned, abandoning the caravan, it might well have been destroyed. These were the reasons, he pleaded, that Asad Beg had not returned at once.

But why had he not returned after carrying the convoy (*qāfila*) to Burhanpur, demanded the emperor. Perhaps he was delayed, said the Mirza, still making excuses for his friend. Besides, he added, the Deccan was far away. At this, Jahangir said in a tone of indifference: "God knows here he has gone now." A third character, a certain Mirza Jan Beg, who felt warmly about Asad, now intervened. Why did Jahangir not send a *farmān* at once with Asad's *wakīl*, he suggested; and so it was that a *farmān* was drafted at once and given to Ya'qub Aqa. Asad Beg was also sent an informal message by his own friends to return as soon as possible to court, to try and get back into the good books of Jahangir. This informal letter did not reach in time, and the *farmān*'s arrival – incidentally, the first *farmān* from the new emperor to reach the Deccan – closed off Asad Beg's options.

Asad notes that once the seals had been opened and the contents perused, he himself went forward to meet the *farmān*, performed prostrations (*sijda*) to it, and took it in his hands. He then read it entirely, while the Khan-i Khanan expressed concern about its consequences. There was consternation all around. When a few days had passed, writes Asad Beg, it seemed no other solution was possible than to "tie the turban of pilgrimage" and return to the court. He now describes how he took leave of the Khan-i Khanan, and with particular regret of Mirza Rustam and his other friends. He then returned to Burhanpur, where he found his horses and other baggage with his brother Ibrahim Beg, and added to them some other accumulated stuff from Daulatabad for safekeeping. However, some giftable items (*ke li-yāqat-i peshkash-o-saughāt dāsht*) were hastily put together, namely Karnatak chintz cloth and some small diamonds (*sang reza*), to take back. Accompanied now by 150 of his old troopers (*sawār*), Asad Beg made his way rapidly to the court. An appropriate hemistich is cited:

> When the beast is hunted,
> it makes straight for the hunter.

Asad Beg says he was now fully prepared for death, and his foot seemed so firmly caught in a trap that his friends and foes, both, were moved to pity. But he felt there was really nothing to be done except face matters directly. Thus, just before arriving in Agra, he first deposited his goods outside the town with Ya'qub Aqa and Sher 'Ali (with instructions that they should be carried to his house), and then himself made straight for the *darbār*. Here he found Khwaja Amin-ud-Din in charge once more, and the latter greeted him with joy. He had spent a fair deal of time (some two or three *gharīs*) there, when the ceremonial music (*naqqāra*) sounded and the emperor emerged. The Khwaja approached him to enquire about the placement of the usual *nazr* and *peshkash*; Asad Beg sent nine *muhrs* and nine rupees through him with a message on a piece of paper. He was quickly taken into the *katehra*, in fact to the level of the special enclosed balustrade (*katehra-i narda*). Khwaja Amin-ud-Din advanced together with the chief vizier and announced: "Asad has arrived from the Deccan. He makes his salutations." When Jahangir's eyes fell on him, Asad Beg at once performed all forms of prostration and salutation (*taslīm, kūrnish,* and *sijda*). The vizier presented the *nazr*, which Jahangir took with a show of reluctance and said contemptuously: "Where was this little

man (*mardak*) till now, and how has he come here at this moment?"
Asad Beg had gone to the Deccan as envoy, and he has now returned,
was the reply. At this time Asad saw that the Amir ul-Umara (Sharif
Khan) had arrived and was performing his own *sijda* under the balcony (*jharoka*).[63] As he stood up, Jahangir said, pointing to him: "This
is Asad. He has come from the Deccan." The Amir welcomed him formally. "You've never met him before?", asked Jahangir. No, it was the
first time, said the Amir. It was then that Jahangir realised that Asad
Beg had arrived in the *darbār* straight from his voyage, not stopping
to meet anyone else at court.

But this did not really improve the tone of the exchange. Instead,
Jahangir began to list his complaints against him. "Asad deserves to
be killed," he concluded bluntly. The Amir ul-Umara replied: "How
many people deserving death have you killed so far, that you want to
kill Asad? He is merely your unfortunate servant." Jahangir then said:
"When I wanted him here, he was not present. Now he has come
running. I don't have the heart to even look at him. Let him go where
he wants." In short, writes Asad Beg, all that he had done and all the
hopes he had accumulated, while also accumulating blisters on his
feet in imperial service, had come to naught. What did Fate (*fāl*) have
in store for him now?

Rather than answer this question, however, he proceeds on a digression concerning the death of Akbar and the nature of the succession struggle. The digression begins with a verse from "the best of the
later poets", Anwari.[64]

If everything in the fate of beings were not predetermined,
How then does Man's state go against his own will?
Truly, for better or worse, Destiny has every man's reins in its hands,
for no matter what one does, one still finds that things end in error.
The age makes myriad images,
but the image in one's mind's eye remains unmade.

---

[63] On Muhammad Sharif, titled Sharif Khan, Amir ul-Umara (d. 1612), sometime governor of Bihar, see Jahangir, *The Jahangirnama*, 9, 13, 140, *passim*.
[64] Asad Beg, *Waqāʾiʿ-yi Asad Beg Qazwīnī*, ed. Chander Shekhar, 146; *Nuskha-i
Ahwāl-i Asad Beg* (London), 50; Aligarh Ms, 126.

He then goes on to note that when the "poor, unfortunate Asad" had left for Bijapur, Golkonda, Bidar, and the Karnatak for the second time, matters in the court had begun to deteriorate. At this time the emperor was much concerned with a projected fight between the elephant Chanchal (the animal Asad Beg had brought back from Bijapur) and another called Giranbar belonging to Jahangir. The emperor had even suggested that Asad Beg delay his departure to see this fight, but this turned out to be impossible. If only this fight had never happened, exclaims Asad Beg. For he had heard that the elephant fight had led to Akbar's violent seizure. When the news had reached him in Ujjain, Asad Beg had been with Mirza Shahrukh. This, he recapitulates, had led the Baluchis to flee with the camels, and also had led Mirza 'Ali Beg to leave for Agra. Asad had at that time refused to go with him, and even cited a verse on the occasion.

> May God preserve everyone from my state.
> as he preserves the flower from blooming, and the bird from crying.

The text now goes over the conversation at Ujjain. At the time, Asad Beg had told Mirza 'Ali of his close relations with Abu'l Fazl, his death at the behest of Jahangir, and his own subsequent closeness to Akbar. He had also recounted briefly his having been sent to the Deccan, his successful return, and his second journey there. In all this, Asad Beg noted, he had never been able to serve Jahangir, so he was convinced Jahangir nursed a grudge against him deep in his heart.[65] Mirza 'Ali Beg, who was an understanding man, had told him that since he still had wealth and a position he should enter directly into Jahangir's service with no waste of time. But Asad had ignored his advice since Fate was not on his side. In fact, in face of this attitude Mirza 'Ali Beg had left him with some annoyance. At the same time, staying at Ujjain had eventually done Asad Beg no good. The Baluchis had not returned and the *qāfila* was in imminent danger. He had hence been obliged to appeal to Mirza Shahrukh for help. The latter had helped him through his *wakīl*, and appointed a certain Shah 'Imad as an

---

[65] Asad Beg, *Waqā'i'-yi Asad Beg Qazwīnī*, ed. Chander Shekhar, 148; *Nuskha-i Ahwāl-i Asad Beg* (London), 28b.

escort with five hundred horse. He had thus managed to make it to Burhanpur, and then some days later the *farmān* from Jahangir had arrived. Asad Beg now insists, in stark contrast to his own earlier account of drunken festivities and interminable musical soirées in Daulatabad, that he had arrived as soon as possible at court.

Still, he notes, at the time he had left Agra the emperor's health (*takassur*) had declined only a little. What had made it far worse was the elephant fight.[66] For in the midst of this fight a quarrel had broken out between the followers of Prince Salim and those of Salim's son Prince Khusrau. When news of these incidents was brought to the emperor, he had become enraged and had had a seizure. The physician Hakim 'Ali was now brought in and declared he could do nothing. The great noble Khan-i A'zam, who saw the signs of imminent death, had called in the pre-eminent Rajput noble Raja Man Singh and suggested that Sultan Khusrau be raised to the throne.[67] The two, Khan-i A'zam and Man Singh, were powerful men, writes Asad Beg, and though their idea was quite improper they managed to have it gain ground. It was decided that when the heir-apparent Salim appeared before the emperor for his daily *kūrnish*, he would be seized. But they had not realised, writes Asad Beg in a flattering tone, that one cannot diminish the sun's light by throwing up handfuls of dust. What Fate's pen has drawn cannot be wiped out by mere trickery. He cites a verse:

The lamp that is lit by God,
If anyone blows on it, his beard will catch fire.

Thus, God's selected one (that is, Jahangir, here further flattered by Asad Beg), had left his quarters and, getting on a boat with some

[66] For a parallel account of an elephant fight between Giranbar and Khusrau's elephant Aprup, see Jahangir, *The Jahangirnama*, 15–17, Preface by Muhammad Hadi. It is unclear whether either Muhammad Hadi or Asad Beg in fact confused these two fights.

[67] See Muhammad Hadi's "Preface", in Jahangir, *The Jahangirnama*, 17–18. Mirza 'Aziz Koka eventually died in 1625, and Jahangir's obituary for him appears in *The Jahangirnama*, 431, where it is noted that "in the fields of biography and history he was perfectly knowledgeable, and he was without peer in writing and composition." It is also pointed out that he was an excellent calligrapher, a brilliant raconteur, and a fair poet.

attendants, reached a certain part of the fort called Batta Burj. When Jahangir had wished to descend from the boat, a distressed Mir Ziya-ul-Mulk Qazwini had come running up and brought news of the emperor's death. He had also informed Jahangir of the conspiracy. The prince now turned back the boat, and with eyes full of tears and a heavy heart returned to his quarters, so that the arrow of the rebels was unable to attain its target. Another appropriate verse is found:

> God takes the boat where he wills, so that
> the captain (*nākhudā*) tears his clothes in despair.

While the emperor still had some life left in him, the Khan-i A'zam and Raja Man Singh had gathered some notables and told them that Prince Salim's past rebellious behaviour being known to all, and the emperor's will being evident – he had never wanted to give the Sultanate over to Prince Salim – the latter's son Sultan Khusrau was the appropriate successor. (It may be noted that Man Singh was Prince Khusrau's maternal uncle, and the Khan-i A'zam was his father-in-law.[68]) When this declaration was made, a certain Sa'id Khan, a great noble and related to the emperor by clan, a Turk and Mughal of clear heart, objected vehemently. How could one place Salim's son on the throne while Salim was still alive? This was against the laws and customs of the Chaghatays (*shi'ār-o-tūra-i chaghatāy*) and could never happen. Qilij Khan Andijani, another great noble, supported him and they both then left the gathering. The Khan-i A'zam, who in Asad Beg's view was at the root of this sedition (*fitnā*), held his tongue and the meeting ended in confusion.[69]

Sensing the potential for conflict, Asad Beg's old acquaintance Raja Ramdas Kacchwaha now came forward with a group and took control of the treasury (*khazāna*), in order to protect it. The Sayyid noble from North India, Murtaza Khan, had also left the fort, but returned

---

[68] On Raja Man Singh Kachhwaha (d. 1614), ruler of Amber, see Jahangir, *The Jahangirnama*, 160–1, where nothing is made of this act of disloyalty. For a different image of Man Singh, see Busch, "Portrait of a Raja", 287–328.

[69] For an earlier discussion, see Qaisar, "Jahangir's Accession", 251–2.

to his quarters and got together his people from Barha. Mirza Sharif Mu'tamad Khan had come to see him and ask his advice; he had replied that there was nothing to do except see Prince Salim. The two had hence decided to go to the prince's quarters, with Mu'tamad Khan taking the lead and the other following with his Barha clansmen.

By the time he reached the prince's quarters, the latter had turned back from his boat trip to the fort on account of Mir Ziya-ul-Mulk's warning. He had already been surrounded by some panicky and short-sighted people who had spread rumours of Sultan Khusrau having been placed on the throne, and of cannon put into position to blow away Shah Burj. The prince had more or less accepted these rumours, and had apparently even begun to prepare special boats in order to flee, thinking his was a lost cause. However, one of his close allies, a certain Shaikh Rukn-ud-Din Rohila, had arrived and with his large military contingent reassured the prince, asking him to wait for another two watches.

While this was going on, Mu'tamad Khan arrived with news that the conspiracy had fallen through and that Murtaza Khan had walked out of it. The prince was happy to learn this and those around him too were greatly relieved. Murtaza Khan and Qara Beg also turned up with the Barha Sayyids and saluted the new ruler. Ceremonial music (*naqqāra-i shādiyāna*) was now sounded, but the prince asked the courtiers to desist as his father had just died.[70]

Prince Salim now began to take charge of matters. One of his first acts was to give the loyal Murtaza Khan a special robe of honour (*khil'at-i khāssa*) and a bejewelled sword. Now, other courtiers arrived pell-mell and fell over each other to salute the new ruler. That very evening the Khan-i A'zam too arrived and shamefacedly made his salutations. The prince did not reveal his true feelings and treated him well. When Raja Man Singh saw how things had turned out, he took Prince

---

[70] For another contemporary account of the succession, see the letters in British Library, London, Additional Manuscript 9854, "Jesuit Missions in India, 1582–1693", fls 38–52, in Rego, ed., *Documentação*, vol. 3, 62–91. We have commented on these accounts at some length in Alam and Subrahmanyam, *Writing the Mughal World*, 123–64.

Khusrau with him and secretly prepared boats to leave for Bengal the next day.

Now that matters were secure, Prince Salim decided to go to his father's side accompanied by some of the chief nobles. It turned out that Akbar was still just barely alive – it was as if he were awaiting his son. When Jahangir (Salim) reached the side of his bed, he touched his face to Akbar's foot and the emperor opened his eyes. He signalled that a *sar-o-pā* and a turban, which had already been made ready, be brought out. Salim put these on, tied his sword, and did another *tas-līm*. As if on cue, Akbar died and lamentations broke out on all sides. A verse appears in the text:

> When Akbar Shah took leave of this world,
> a lament broke out from the sky above.

Asad Beg himself composes further verses to the effect that in this world the axle of life is so fragile that no one is destined to last. Once the boat of life begins to move, its end is sure; some vessels are destroyed by storms, some are drawn into a whirlpool. Once Jahangir had succeeded, he writes, he wanted the last rites for his father to be performed according to the *sharī'a*, and the emperor's close attendants were instructed to do the necessary. Akbar's body was prepared and taken out in a huge procession. The new emperor helped carry the bier on his shoulders, from the side of the feet of the corpse, taking it from the room where the body was prepared to the edge of the *dau-latkhāna-i khāss-o-'āmm*. From there it was taken by the nobles to the gates of the fort, and the new emperor accompanied them on foot. Various learned men – Sufis, nobles, and others, barefoot and bareheaded – accompanied the body with innumerable horses and elephants. The procession went from Akbarabad fort to Bihishtabad (Sikandra), with people chanting "Allah-o-Akbar" on the way, and with coins being thrown into the crowds en route. Food, sweets, and drinks were distributed to one and all.

Asad Beg's account here is drawn entirely from hearsay, but he seems to feel it incumbent to describe the transition in the fullest possible way. When this work for the funeral ceremony had been completed, he thus writes, the new emperor handed over charge of the fort and treasury to Raja Ramdas.[71] At this time it came to be learnt that Raja Man Singh, accompanied by his nephew Prince Khusrau and a force, had left for Bengal. Jahangir was grieved to learn this, but since Man Singh's brother Madho Singh was still at the court, he instructed him to reason with his brother and get him to return. Madho Singh followed his brother and remonstrated with him, but Man Singh's reply indicated helplessness: Prince Khusrau was still young, and he feared the boy might be killed by his father, which was the reason Man Singh had been obliged to take such an extreme step. He asked Madho Singh to tell the emperor that if he were willing to guarantee Khusrau's safety with a document (*qaul*), he would return. Madho Singh returned to report this, and Jahangir, being a kind and conciliatory person, gave the required assurance. Raja Man Singh hence returned to the *darbār* with the prince; Jahangir embraced his son publicly and kissed his face, then sent him back to his quarters. The mourning for the dead emperor Akbar now continued for some more days, and money and gifts were distributed to the poor. Only after an interval did Jahangir's formal coronation take place.

Asad Beg now concludes the digression with a section entitled "the accession of Nur-ud-Din Muhammad Jahangir Badshah to the throne of his ancestors".[72] On the day of the accession the *darbār* was much bedecked and Jahangir left his residence (*daulatkhāna*) in a boat for the fort, under the Sukh Pul Bridge, accompanied by a large number of people. Then, scattering silver and gold coins, he entered the Agra Fort. All around were notables and viziers who accompanied him until he formally sat on the throne with the title of Jahangir. His immediate task, writes Asad, was to conquer the hearts of the people and ensure that with his administration the affairs of the world would be settled. Fresh *mansab* ranks and titles were bestowed on many nobles, including the highly placed *umarā'* and viziers. Besides, in order to "console the hearts of the populace in general, both high and low (*khāss-o-'āmm*)," the new ruler had a gilded chain of justice installed,

---

[71] Jahangir however continued to see Raja Ramdas as one of his father's loyalists, and referred to him as someone "who had been patronized by my father"; cf. Jahangir, *The Jahangirnama*, 31.

[72] Asad Beg, *Waqā'i'-yi Asad Beg Qazwīnī*, ed. Chander Shekhar, 158.

in order to "remove the rust" from the hearts of his subjects. A verse appears in this context:

> On the first day, the emperor Jahangir made a chain for justice,
> with one end tied inside the palace, and the other dangling out
> of the window.
> Whoever was oppressed could ring on it to complain,
> and without a word said, justice would be rendered.

A few days after the accession Mahabat Khan, Sharif Khan, and others reached the court. Mahabat Khan was made generalissimo (*sipāh-sālār*) and Sharif Khan given the title of Amir ul-Umara. Within a few days of this an official announcement was made that certain cesses and poll taxes levied on Hindu subjects (*zakāt* and *jizyā-yi hunūd*) were once again to be abolished within the empire. As a consequence, writes Asad Beg, Jahangir's fame came to spread all across Hindustan. This is the occasion for a set of somewhat mediocre verses praising the new emperor's justice, fine administration, and consideration for his subjects.[73] Having praised the wrathful sovereign – who had greeted him contemptuously on his return to the court as no more than a "little man" (*mardak*) – Asad Beg concludes his account without resolving what became of him in the years after 1606. In some manuscripts his pedestrian verses of flattery are succeeded with these rather laconic lines:

> These are a few lines of the history, and a small part of the news that shows the high status and the glories of the Glorious Timurid Sultans (*salātīn-i 'azīm al-shān-i Tīmūriyya*) in Hindustan. What the position and status was in those times of this humble servant will have become evident from these lines. Finished.

Asad Beg's Text in Context

Asad Beg's extended ego-document lies in the space between a courtly memoir and a travel account. As a memoir it is somewhat curiously conceived, for it covers a relatively brief period rather than extending back into the moment of its chief protagonist's arrival in India

---

[73] Ibid., 159; *Waqā'i'-i Asad Beg*, Aligarh Ms, 139.

in the 1580s or earlier. Nor does it relate the long period over which he continued in Mughal service after the accession of Jahangir. Rather, it affords us a specific window into those moments in Asad Beg's life when his actions seem to him to have been most interesting and most fraught. Consequently the text does not have a purely linear logic to it; its broadly linear sequence, beginning with the death of Shaikh Abu'l Fazl in the second half of 1602 and ending with the author's eventual return to Agra in 1605–6, shows a tendency to loop backwards periodically into sequences in which an episode that has been treated briefly is treated again in far greater detail.

The principal set pieces of the narration are clear enough: first, the circumstances of the death of Abu'l Fazl; second, the enquiry by Asad Beg into the Rai Rayan's doings; third, the embassy to Bijapur (in some sense the meatiest part of the narrative); fourth, the second and abortive embassy to Bijapur; and fifth, the hearsay account of the succession problems at the death of Akbar. But underlying all these are extensive and very valuable accounts of the functioning of the court itself, as narrated not by an official chronicler but by a close participant who rose from a peripheral position to one where he enjoyed considerable access to the most exalted members of the court. Mughal court ritual, as seen and narrated by Asad Beg, is a curious mix of highly stylised formality and anomalous moments when everything seems to dissolve into a welter of informal actions as well as fits of bad temper. To be sure, this narrative concerns only the very last phase of Akbar's reign, after his return from Lahore to Agra, but it is a particularly valuable narrative for this very reason, since it is also of a phase narrated neither by Badayuni nor Abu'l Fazl.

Asad Beg's account is comparable to others such as the one by 'Abdul Latif (see the next chapter). Another significant text that comes to mind, also written by an Iranian migrant to India, is the *Bahāristān-i Ghaybī* of Mirza Nathan (or 'Ala-ud-Din Isfahani), which is largely concerned with the reign of Jahangir. Mirza Nathan's text is far more a classic memoir and its chronological coverage is correspondingly far more extensive. While courtly life plays a role in the text, it is more an account of campaigns and military actions than Asad Beg's. The two share some preoccupations, notably their authors' positions as "disciples" of the Mughal emperor, a fact that has attracted the attention of a certain number of historians in the case of Mirza Nathan. But what sets them apart is Mirza Nathan's particular view on the Mughal empire not in terms of the court, or the framing of the diplomatic mission, but as an active participant on the frontier of expansion. In this respect the *Bahāristān* is linked to several others that follow in the seventeenth century, some dealing largely with the eastern frontier of the Mughals, others with their campaigns in the Deccan in the latter half of the seventeenth century. Amongst these we should certainly number the work of Bhimsen Saksena, but also Shihab-ud-Din Talish's *Fathīyya-i 'Ibrīyya*, which is concerned amongst other matters with the Mughal campaigns in Chittagong and the frontier with the Arakan kingdom.[74]

Asad Beg, on the other hand, occupies a very particular place in Mughal writings. His is a classic work of self-promotion, where the reader comes to learn that, far from being a mere cog in the wheel, as his lowly rank might suggest, the author was in fact a master of diplomacy and manipulation, capable of managing most situations with tact and guile – with the possible exception of that which confronted him at the death of Akbar. It is even a boastful text, but still one that manages to seduce, by presenting its author as both actor and victim. Circulation here is a means to advancement and success in a career, as well as a crucial means for the accumulation of wealth. It is a way of seeing marvels while barely leaving the borders of Hindustan; Asad Beg presents himself as dazzled by the wealth of possibilities that lay even in the nearby Deccan. This is to the point that he suggests Akbar decided to send him back to the Deccan precisely because he understood that he, Asad Beg, had an almost obsessive fascination with the place, for he chattered on about it incessantly even after his return to the Mughal court. Thus, Asad Beg manages to present himself as something of an innocent, while equally being a guileful diplomat who gets the better of Ibrahim 'Adil Shah.

Another running theme in the text is wealth and money, whether in the context of gift-giving and receiving, or in the rather complex

---

[74] Shihab-ud-Din Talish, *Fathīyya-i 'Ibrīyya*, Bibliothèque nationale de France, Paris, Supplément persan 321; Bodleian Library, Oxford, Bodl. Or. 589 (Sachau-Ethé 240).

relations that various Mughal actors seem to have with "corruption".
Now, while the word itself does not appear anywhere, it is apparent
that the problem of legitimate reward as opposed to bribery is everywhere present in the Mughal world of Asad Beg. We see this already
in the episode of his visit to the Rai Rayan's camp, where a fine line
is drawn between a "gift of thanks" (*shukrāna*) and a bribe. Later,
in the context of Bijapur it is made clear than both Mir Jamal-ud-
Din and other Mughal officials were in fact being suborned by 'Adil
Shah in such a way that they were acting contrary to the interest of the
Mughals. The problem does not seem to be simply one of accepting
money or gifts, for Asad Beg too does so on almost any occasion he
can. Rather, it is one of suggesting that these gifts in cash or kind do
not interfere with one's primary loyalty to the emperor. Accepting
such money in the correct performance of one's task is thus not seen
as a bribe; it is when the gift changes the nature of one's actions that it
appears to enter that category. Further, ideas of correct action themselves can be stretched, and Asad Beg's defence of the Rai Rayan and
others by playing on the distinction between error (*taqsīr*) and negligence (*ghaflat*) is a case in point. His implicit suggestion is that while
he defended the Mughal generals in the matter partly because they
had rewarded him well in advance, nevertheless his defence of them
was not wholly specious and also helped avoid unnecessary conflict
between the emperor and powerful Rajput nobles.

What is eminently clear from various episodes in the text is the
crucial role that a cash economy and the accumulation of personal
wealth played already by the early seventeenth century in the Mughal court. The emperor himself was well aware of this, and Akbar
seems to have motivated envoys such as Asad Beg in their missions by
suggesting that these would be occasions for them to advance themselves financially. The language of honour (*'izzat*) is certainly prevalent, as is a form of etiquette that requires the initial refusal of a gift
offering before its ultimate acceptance; but there is no mistaking the
powerful commercial impulses that motivated middling officials such
as Asad Beg.

For what emerges clearly is that, although their worlds intersect,
Asad Beg's station leads him to look at matters far differently from
high nobles such as 'Abdul Rahim Khan-i Khanan or the Khan-i

A'zam Mirza 'Aziz Koka. Unfortunately, we do not possess memoirs or autobiographies from either of those great individuals, but texts about them, such as 'Abdul Baqi Nihawandi's *Ma'āsir-i Rahīmī*, certainly suggest that the relationship between wealth and power was both perceived and articulated rather differently in the rarefied world of 'Abdul Rahim than in the down-to-earth one of Asad Beg.[75] The great noble had to insist above all on his role as a patron, and as one who supported the arts and letters; in brief, as one whose social role had to be primarily one of giving rather than receiving (even if to give, one had usually first to receive). Asad Beg's imaginary reader on the other hand seems to be a middling sort of official who is being told that even in a somewhat uncertain political world (where irate monarchs can throw their lowly servants down from the ramparts to their death), it is still possible to survive and prosper.[76] Its didactic function – for it seeks not simply to entertain with its anecdotes but also to edify – lies precisely in its insistent suggestion that the shrewd official can prosper, and even become quite wealthy, without ever transgressing the limits set by a court where one must serve the emperor while preserving one's own sense of honour and rectitude.

75 'Abdul Baqi Nihawandi, *The Ma'āsir-i-Rahīmī*; also the account in Orthmann, *'Abd or-Rahīm*.

76 Also compare O'Hanlon, "Manliness and Imperial Service", 47–93.

4

Of Visible Frontiers and Concealed Gardens

Even if the King shows his unlimited favour,
The slave must know his limit.

— From a *farmān* of Jahangir[1]

Introduction

I F THE SIXTEENTH century saw the full-fledged emergence of the Mughal chronicle in Persian as a formal genre, as expressed in the contrasting works of Shaikh Abu'l Fazl, Khwaja Nizam-ud-Din Ahmad, and Mulla 'Abdul Qadir Badayuni, the seventeenth century was the great moment of the less formal ego-document, or "memoir" as historians of an older generation termed it.[2] The texts we have examined in the preceding chapters certainly prefigured it, with the work of Asad Beg serving as an important opening statement with the coming of the seventeenth century (eleventh century Hijri). These were both less ambitious texts than the chronicles in terms of their chronological and spatial coverage, and a more ambitious intellectual enterprise in other respects, precisely because they were more personal and flexible as forms of expression. Further, they emerged at a moment when subtle changes were taking place in the role of Persian in India,

---

[1] Nathan, *Bahāristān*, trans. Borah, vol. I, 213.

[2] On the Mughal Persian chronicling tradition in a wider context, see the useful consideration by Quinn, *Persian Historiography*.

as an administrative and literary language.[3] These changes were partly the consequence of the progressive retreat of eastern Turkish (or Chaghatay) as a language of literary expression in the Mughal court, and the increasing access to Persian across a larger group of both elites and the more middling classes that engaged with the Mughal state. To be sure, we can distinguish between many different levels of Persian, both at the level of comprehension and literary use. The upper Mughal elite, even in the later seventeenth century, could gently mock those Rajputs who spoke a broken Persian with a syntax derived from Hindi. Even among the upper echelons of Muslim notables, the knowledge of the literary canon of Persian prose and poetry, as well as associated skills such as *inshā'* (belles-lettres), accountancy (*siyāq*), and calligraphy, would have varied considerably. The matter is rendered all the more intricate when one bears in mind that, over the course of the seventeenth century, the use of the Persian language and its associated cultural norms and habits also spread into a part of the non-Muslim population that dealt willy-nilly with Mughal institutions.

The analysis of this question requires us to re-investigate aspects of Mughal social history that have been somewhat neglected or set aside in the past few decades. The *locus classicus* in the matter is a well-known essay from 1969 by Irfan Habib, which appeared as part of a general consideration regarding whether any form of capitalistic change was feasible in the non-European world prior to about 1800.[4] Habib's answer was emphatically negative and rested on his stylised description of the Mughal social structure, which consisted in his view of a small and highly extractive fiscal elite of *mansabdārs*, a great mass of impoverished peasants and artisans, and a largely impotent and numerically limited group of urban merchants (*tujjār*). In his judgement, this situation was "largely parasitical, depending upon a system of direct agrarian exploitation by a small ruling class." He admitted, to be sure, that some internal distinctions in terms of wealth and access to resources existed among the peasants, especially because of the presence across the width of the countryside of rural magnates and power-

---

[3] See Alam, "The Pursuit of Persian", 317–49.

[4] Habib, "Potentialities of Capitalistic Development", 32–78; Habib's analysis can be fruitfully contrasted to that of İnalcık, "Capital Formation", 91–140.

brokers termed zamindars. Nevertheless, in this view, which bears more than a superficial resemblance to Marx's Asiatic Mode of Production (and before that, to the Oriental Despotism of Enlightenment authors), the Mughal state was no less than an "insatiable Leviathan" with an "unlimited appetite for resources" which were then squandered in unproductive and luxury-oriented consumption in the mansions of the miniscule elite.[5] This view then gave rise to long-term historical analyses in which the "class structure" of Mughal India was seen as radically polarised, far beyond what might be seen in contemporary Europe or China, with significant consequences for the developmental trajectory of South Asia.[6]

A few years after Habib's essay, a cautiously sceptical note was sounded by his close colleague Iqtidar Alam Khan. Khan saw in the Mughal empire "a peculiar form of feudalism" in which the principal tension was between two opposed classes around the control of landed resources.[7] However, he argued that a somewhat heterogeneous third group could also be found, which he termed a "middle stratum" or "middle class", whose wealth and income were not directly tied to land. Drawing on sources distinct from the usual imperial chronicles, he provided examples of such figures who, especially in the seventeenth and early eighteenth centuries, were men of substance outside the familiar categories of *mansabdārs* and zamindars. Even members of the lower echelons of the revenue bureaucracy could apparently become somewhat prosperous, though Khan suspected that this was largely through means that he characterised as "embezzlement" and "defalcation". Besides, there was a substantial and somewhat vaguely defined group that he referred to as the "urban intelligentsia". And finally, an important role was attached by him to one particular social category, namely physicians (*tabībs*) – in cluding both respectable practitioners and "quacks" – who had amassed reasonable wealth.

To build this picture in rapid brushstrokes, Khan used the accounts of lower-level revenue bureaucrats, men such as Surat Singh in the

---

[5] Raychaudhuri, "The State and the Economy", 173. The views set out by Raychaudhuri in this chapter closely reflect those of his collaborator and co-editor Habib.

[6] Maddison, *Class Structure and Economic Growth*, 15–34.

[7] Khan, "The Middle Classes in the Mughal Empire", 28–49.

seventeenth century in Punjab and I'timad 'Ali Khan in the early eigh-teenth century in Surat, as well as a versified ego-document in Hindi of the Jain merchant Banarasidas (to which we have referred earlier).[8] He closed with an undeveloped suggestion that the origins of the modern "middle class" in South Asia might in part be found within this group.

Significantly, besides some casual references to European history, Khan did not look further afield in the Islamic world for comparative inspiration. This was all the more curious because by the 1970s, and es-pecially the 1980s, Ottoman historians had made considerable strides in the matter of a nuanced social history that went beyond simple binary class oppositions. This was in part because the stranglehold of a certain style of Marxist history was less evident there; but it was also because of the availability of rich source materials such as *kadı*-court registers that permitted urban social histories of great detail. It was thus possible for Suraiya Faroqhi to discuss the "men of modest substance" who inhabited significant but secondary urban nodes such as Ankara and Kayseri in the seventeenth century, and for others to look into the social fabric of centres such as Damascus, Cairo, and Jerusalem.[9] In turn, these studies could be combined productively with the study of imperial ideological formations, and art and architectural history – to take just a few avenues. A particularly significant intervention, to which we have referred in our introduction, was by Cemal Kafadar in an essay today recognised as a classic.[10] Kafadar stated his intention to revive a "sociologically informed *Kulturgeschichte*" for the Ottomans, a call that influenced not only his colleagues in Ottoman history but also the two of us when we commenced a few years later to write a series of essays on Mughal *safar nāmas* (travel narratives).[11] These essays even-tually led us ineluctably in the next decade to our own book on *Indo-*

---

[8] Surat Singh, *Tazkira-yi Pīr Hassū Telī*; Rezavi, "I'timād 'Ali Khān", 79–90.

[9] Faroqhi, *Men of Modest Substance*; Raymond, *Arab Cities*. For a comparative view of Mughal and Ottoman social history literature, see Faroqhi, *The Ottoman and Mughal Empires*.

[10] Kafadar, "Self and Others", 121–50. The essay is brought together with other related ones by the same author in Kafadar, *Kim var imiş*.

[11] Alam and Subrahmanyam, "From an Ocean of Wonders", 161–89; idem, "Dis-covering the Familiar", 131–54.

Persian Travels in the Age of Discoveries, in which we dealt with Ottoman, Iranian, and Central Asian travellers to the Mughal domains, as well as the voyages of Mughal writers and intellectuals to their northern and western neighbours.[12] While for its sheer size and exuberance we may have failed to find a text to match Kafadar's favourite example, namely Evliya Çelebi's *Seyāhatnāme*, we did manage to locate, list, and discuss a not inconsiderable number of travel texts and other first-person narratives, some rather well known, others quite obscure or even fragmentary.[13]

In this chapter we return to Kafadar's themes from that classic work, using texts from the Mughal empire in the seventeenth century, and reflect on the dilemmas of their authors as imperial subjects. Chief amongst these is the ego-document of 'Abdul Latif 'Abdullah 'Abbasi Gujarati (d. *c.* 1638–9), a reasonably well-known Mughal diplomat and administrator, but who is probably best recognised for his deep philological work around the *masnawī* of Rumi. Our recent rediscovery of his misplaced travel text – which will be somewhat the equivalent for us of Seyyid Hasan's little-known *Sohbetnāme* for Kafadar – allows us to look into how a Mughal official perceived the empire and its frontiers, as well as his own place in their construction. This can permit a wider comparison with better-known authors of the period such as 'Ala-ud-Din Isfahani (or Mirza Nathan) and Bhimsen Saksena, which we will touch on more briefly here.[14] Another obvious point of comparison could undoubtedly be with the writings from the second half of the seventeenth century of the young Mughal *munshī* Nek Rai, to which we have devoted another essay; Nek Rai was brought up in Mughal Hindustan, in cities like the newly emergent capital of Shahjahanabad-Delhi, but eventually accompanied the empire's armies in their victorious advance into the Deccan in the 1680s.[15] As we have

<hr>

[12] Alam and Subrahmanyam, *Indo-Persian Travels*.

[13] For a comparison with the vast corpus of first-person accounts from early modern Western Europe, see Amelang, *The Flight of Icarus*.

[14] On Bhimsen, see Richards, "Norms of Comportment", 255–89 (esp. pp. 270–89). This can be read with other useful and relevant essays by the same author in Richards, *Power, Administration*.

[15] Alam and Subrahmanyam, "The Making of a Munshi", 61–72, reproduced (with some revisions) in idem, *Writing the Mughal World*, 311–38.

pointed out, he represents the widening reach of the Persianised sphere in the Mughal domains, as it included an increasing number of "Hindus" – largely belonging to the Kayastha, Khatri, and scribal Brahmin castes – into the bureaucracy and administration. This was a phenomenon that had no precise parallel in the Ottoman domains and was certainly quite distinct from the *devşirme* levy that brought non-Muslims into the Ottoman administration, since *devşirme* involved a process of forcible conversion and deep acculturation as well as what some have called "natal alienation".

By the seventeenth century, and the reigns of emperors Jahangir and Shahjahan, the Mughal military-fiscal, bureaucratic, and scribal classes – like those of the Ottoman Empire but perhaps even more so – were a highly diverse group made up of a mix of elements drawn from a variety of ethnic backgrounds. The most elevated of these men were termed the *umarā*, just as they were in the Ottoman case.[16] Those who belonged to this category in India had to attain a certain rank (or *mansab*), a practice that the Mughals derived from Central Asian practice but which the Ottomans did not follow. From the mid seventeenth century onwards the Mughals periodically produced biographical dictionaries (or *tazkirats*) of this class, of which one of the earliest examples was Shaikh Farid Bhakkari's *Zakhīrat al-Khawānīn* (c. 1650), the source in turn for some later and more celebrated compilations of the same sort, such as the eighteenth-century works *Tazkirat al-Umarā* by Kewal Ram, and *Ma'āsir al-Umarā* by Shahnawaz Khan.[17] The Ottomans too produced numerous biographical dictionaries of poets and literati as well as scholars, and even a certain number of the "judicial elite".[18] But they seem never to have chosen the *umarā* class as the distinct object of one of these exercises. As Baki Tezcan has noted, moreover, while the judicial elites emerged as an important focus of Otto-

---

¹⁶ Kunt, *The Sultan's Servants*.

¹⁷ Farid Bhakkari, *Zakhīrat al-Khawānīn*; idem, *The Dhakhīratul-Khawānīn*; Kewal Ram, *Tazkiratul-umara of Kewal Ram*; Shahnawaz Khan, *Ma'āsir al-Umarā*. These works were partly the basis for the construction of a modern biographical dictionary (unfortunately shorn of much of the rich narrative information); see Ali, *The Apparatus of Empire*.

¹⁸ For analysis of the scholarly milieu based on these and other materials, see Atçil, *Scholars and Sultans*.

man writers in the sixteenth and seventeenth centuries, as the dynasty somewhat lost its lustre they too lost ground by the eighteenth century. Tezcan thus contrasts the highly successful work of Atayi in the first half of the seventeenth century with that of Şeyhi (d. 1731) a century later, "the last representative of the genre,"[19] until its revival at the very end of the dynasty. Such biographical dictionaries from the Mughal world can give us a socio-historical context for figures such as 'Abdul Latif, besides what we know about them from their own writings.

The Question of 'Abdul Latif

Who then was 'Abdul Latif Gujarati? Born in the provincial capital of Ahmedabad in western India in the late sixteenth century, we know that his family had a history of both literary learning and service with the Mughals. Amongst his teachers in his city of birth was the migrant Iranian scholar Muhammad Sufi Mazandarani, author of the well-known anthology of verse entitled *But-khāna* (dated to 1601). It would appear that 'Abdul Latif aided his master in this work of compilation, which then launched him on his own literary career. Not long after, he entered Mughal service and worked with the great Iranian Mughal *amīr* Mu'taqad Khan (later titled Asaf Khan), with whom he served in eastern India (Orissa and Bengal).[20] Subsequently, he also worked closely with another important *amīr* named Lashkar Khan Mashhadi, governor of Kabul in the late 1610s and early 1620s. By the early years of the reign of Shahjahan (r. 1628–58), 'Abdul Latif had begun to play a quite prominent role in the court: he was awarded an important *mansab* rank, as well as the title of 'Aqidat Khan and the post of *dīwān-i tan*.[21] His competence as a secretary, draftsman, and financial specialist was widely recognised by now, and in 1633 he was

[19] Tezcan, "The Politics of Early Modern Ottoman Historiography", 191–2.

[20] It is a matter of some surprise that there is no careful study of the career of Asaf Khan (1569–1641), on which there are considerable textual, visual, and archival materials. But see Kumar, *Asaf Khan and His Times*, for a sketch. His early title appears as both Mu'taqad Khan (in this text), and I'tiqad Khan.

[21] For a summing up of his career (with some inaccuracies), see Tirmizi, "Scholar-Diplomatist from Gujarat", 85–98. For details of his rank, see Ali, *Apparatus of*

even appointed to a crucial diplomatic mission in the sultanate of Golkonda in the Deccan. Although he was unable to complete this particular mission on account of illness, he appears to have lived on for some years, dying in around 1639. It is reported that he was for a time appointed to write an official chronicle of the reign of Shahjahan, but he does not seem to have advanced in that task, nor is any part of such a work extant.

It is above all as a literary scholar and commentator that 'Abdul Latif gained recognition. He continued to work on emendations and addenda to the work of his master Mazandarani, *But-khāna*, including a set of biographical notices on the poets included in the anthology entitled *Khulāsa-i ahwāl al-shu'arā* (Brief Account of Poets). He also devoted a good part of his literary life to reflecting on the *masnawī* of Rumi, preparing a sort of critical edition of it as well as a lexicon of difficult words, and a commentary (*sharh*) on the text, in addition to which he wrote extensively on the works of another important poet who had preceded and influenced Rumi, namely Sana'i (d. 1131). We have discussed 'Abdul Latif's work as a philologist elsewhere, so will leave that aside here.[22] Besides these works of literary scholarship and criticism, we also have a text of his in the tradition of *inshā*': the *Ruq'āt-i 'Abdul Latīf*, which includes letters exchanged with important officials and *mansabdārs* of the time of Jahangir, such as 'Abdur Rahim Khan-i Khanan, Asaf Khan, and Mahabat Khan, as well as an intriguing (albeit brief) account by 'Abdul Latif of a ceremonial visit paid to Akbar's tomb in Sikandra in the company of some visiting diplomats from Safavid Iran.[23]

The Scholar-Official as Traveller

In the midst of all this scholarly activity, and at times linked to it – because 'Abdul Latif was an inveterate manuscript-hound – the Gujarati

---

Empire, S810, S1193, S1753, S1946, S1986 and S2411, where his highest *mansab* is given as 900/200.

[22] Alam, "Mughal Philology", 178–200.

[23] Asiatic Society of Bengal, Kolkata, Ms. Ivanow 364, *Ruq'āt-i 'Abdul Latīf*, 82 folios. No other manuscript copy of this valuable work is currently known to

scholar also found the time to pen a travel text entitled *Risāla-i sair-i manāzil wa bilād wa amsār* (Treatise on a Journey Through [Various] Places, Cities and Countries). The text was first noticed and commented on by the Bengali historian Jadunath Sarkar (1870–1958), who also translated some excerpts from it, especially those relating to eastern India, in a couple of brief essays written in the 1910s and 1920s.[24] In the first of these Sarkar was rather laconic as regards the manuscript itself, only noting that "through the help of a friend at Delhi I secured access to what is probably the only copy extant of Abdul Latif's travels"; in the second he says even less, merely noting that "only one manuscript of this Persian work is known to exist." Roughly a half century later, in the 1960s and 1970s, the Punjabi scholar N.D. Ahuja wrote two further essays on the text, one a brief account of 'Abdul Latif's travels in the Punjab, and the other a longer and more general or biographical essay focusing on the author, his works, and varied activities.[25] In these essays he located the manuscript of the travel account used in the Hardinge (later Hardayal) Municipal Public Library in the old city of Delhi. However, after the mid 1970s this manuscript entirely disappeared from view. When we began our own attempt at a conspectus of such texts from the Mughal era in the early 1990s, it was nowhere to be found, and enquiries with our senior colleagues, such as the late Ziyauddin Desai (who had some interest of his own in 'Abdul Latif), provided no clues. It was therefore with a sense of surprise that, a few years ago, we found a microfilm of the text hidden in plain sight in the National Archives of India (New Delhi).[26] The text bears the stamp of ownership of the Lal Chand Research Library, DAV College, Lahore. Though the manuscript collection of this college was allegedly

---

exist. For the Sikandra visit, see the translation in Desai, "A Foreign Dignitary's Ceremonial Visit", 188–97.

[24] Sarkar, "Travels in Bihar", 597–603; Sarkar, "A Description of North Bengal", 143–6.

[25] Ahuja, "'Abd-al-Latif al 'Abbasi", 93–8; Ahuja, "An Indian Memoirist", 147–72.

[26] National Archives of India, New Delhi, Microfilm: Acc. No. 5915, *Risāla-i sair-i manāzil wa bilād wa amsār*, 51 pp.

transferred at the time of Partition to DAV College, Chandigarh, the latter institution has no trace today of 'Abdul Latif's text. What we are left with therefore is not even a single manuscript, but the microfilm of a ghostly manuscript. It is apparently not the same as that consulted by Sarkar and Ahuja, as we see from certain sections that do not overlap. Our copy, which (like theirs) ends rather abruptly, seems to be from the late eighteenth or the nineteenth century, though there is no name of a copyist or place of transcription.

Sarkar, in his brief essays on 'Abdul Latif's travels, was fairly complimentary about him as a writer, which was not often the case when he evaluated Mughal-period authors.[27] He stated that the work was "of unique value as giving us the topography of Bihar early in the seventeenth century," which he argued was the result of the fact that 'Abdul Latif "took accurate notes of what he saw during his travels." So even if the *Risāla-i sair-i manāzil* was written (or so Sarkar felt) "in the reign of Shah Jahan" (that is, in the early 1630s), it did not suffer overly from the fact that much time had elapsed between the travels and

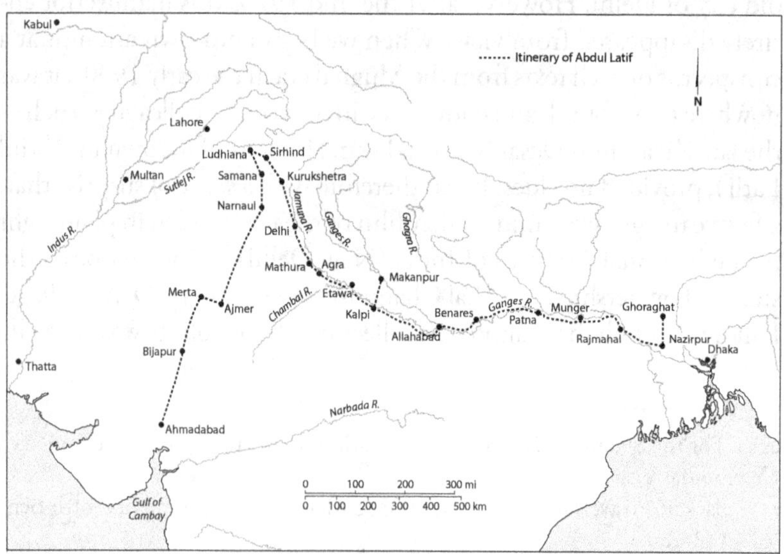

Map 3: The Itinerary of 'Abdul Latif Gujarati.

[27] See his dispersed essays in Sarkar, *Studies in Mughal India.*

the writing. As Sarkar presents it, the account is simple and unadorned, packed with a wealth of information regarding geography, natural history, and so on. His brief annotations to the translations mostly consist of comparisons to details he found in colonial-period gazetteers, or in James Rennell's *Bengal Atlas* (1781). Excluding points where he found his manuscript copy corrupt – i.e. showing copyist's errors – Sarkar considered the text well suited to the form of positivist, descriptive history that he held up as an ideal (even if he only practised it intermittently himself).[28] In what follows we will use the writings of both Sarkar and Ahuja where needed, but also attempt our own global reading of 'Abdul Latif's text from a perspective which departs somewhat from that of our predecessors.

We should note to begin with that the *Risāla-i sair-i manāzil* commences with a brief preface which runs more or less as follows:

Since the true purpose and natural reason for the Creation of Man is that the products and wonders in this Divine Workshop might be discovered, and the strange and wonderful (*'ajā'ib-o-gharā'ib*) vestiges and traces (*āsār wa alāmāt*) of past rulers and great saints, which may be found in every city and country, might be observed with the eyes of wisdom, taking lessons therefrom in order to be able to recognise God; and that what is good and bad in this workshop could be properly distinguished. It is for this reason that in accordance with the Qur'anic verse: "Travel on this earth, for God's earth is very wide (*sīrū fī al-ard inna ard Allāh wāsi'ah*)," many prophets, saints and pious people have resorted to travel (*siyāhat*). Verily:

> Travel is the patron of Man, and the master of skill
> *Safar murabbī-yi mard ast, wa ustād-i hunar.*

Travel becomes a reason for experience and maturity. When man travels up to heaven, he discovers those matters of faith and the world, and they are revealed to him, although he had earlier been oblivious. Even with a little travel in the unseen world (*'ālam-i ghaib*), he comes to know different patterns of behaviour, etiquette, in speech and action, amongst

[28] On Sarkar as a historian, see the recent reinterpretation in Chakrabarty, *The Calling of History*. Unfortunately, neither Chakrabarty nor many of those who have discussed his work are well grounded in Mughal history or its sources. In our view, it would eventually be interesting to contrast Sarkar's approach to that of his near-exact contemporary Fuat Köprülü (1890–1966).

different people of the world. Travel thus becomes the cause of perfect talent, and of stable understanding, in every man.

This succinct and quite conventional preface is intended merely to establish the fact that travel produces wisdom in humans, and that the observation of places is important for lessons from the past and to comprehend the actions of both saints and rulers. Man's existence itself is justified because he is meant to be a witness to God's creative powers and capacities. The idea that every physical landscape is marked by "traces (*āsār*)" from the past is also deployed, and so is the concept of travel as a necessary form of *Bildung*, corresponding no doubt to the fact that 'Abdul Latif was still a relatively young man when he undertook these journeys, rather than someone with a great deal of experience outside his home region of Gujarat.

It is now time for the author of this ego-document to appear on the page. 'Abdul Latif notes that he had travelled long back in the past to the neighbouring regions of Khandesh and Berar. He, the most humble slave, 'Abdul Latif son of 'Abdullah 'Abbasi, a resident of the region of Gujarat – may it be protected by God from untoward accidents! – had since stayed put in his homeland. Though now apparently seized with the desire to see cities and distant regions, it was only natural, he writes, for any sensible person to be drawn to the idea of staying permanently in the fine city of Ahmedabad, which was properly comparable in quality to holy Mecca itself – yet it seemed he was destined to go elsewhere. In 'Abdul Latif's proud and patriotic view Ahmedabad and its inhabitants, as well as its air and water (*āb-o-hawā*) and soil were all very superior. Some people said Ahmedabad was the Yazd of India; in fact it was the other way around, for Ahmedabad set the standard and Yazd followed.[29] People who came from the lands of 'Arab and 'Ajam to Hind in fact quickly forgot their original land (*autān-i qadīm*), despite the fact that this went against every man's natural love of his homeland. Those returning home felt strangers there until returning to India once again. Whoever sets foot in India even once, 'Abdul Latif declares, is determined to stay on. Therefore, he states his own intention – on his return to Ahmedabad after his imminent travels – to write a history of that city and its surrounding

---

[29] 'Abdul Latif, *Risāla-i sair-i manāzil*, 2.

region. Since the region of Gujarat was at the edge of the sea, sometimes this had discouraged its natives from travelling. But he had decided to undertake his travels while accompanying none other than Khwaja Abu'l Hasan, and this was to be his good fortune.[30] For this great *amīr*, also known as Mu'taqad Khan (later Asaf Khan), would eventually be recognised as one of the greatest of the *wazīrs* (suggesting the account was written or revised in Shahjahan's time, when Asaf Khan had emerged as a major figure). It turns out that Khwaja Abu'l Hasan had arrived in Gujarat some time earlier and become his patron, so that in the course of just one year in his service our author had been able to obtain a great deal by way of benefits. This was to the point that, despite his attachment to Ahmedabad and his people, he decided to accompany the Khwaja from there. For sometimes man must embrace his destiny and leave one's own land (*watan-i khwud*) and travel, if only in order to gain respect. This is even justified in reference to the hadith which says: "In movement, there is benefit (*fī al-harkat barakat*)." A verse follows:

> A man, no matter how great, is not valued in his own town,
> Just as a diamond has no value when it lies inside the mine.[31]

'Abdul Latif also cites a verse — later used by the well-known Iranian intellectual Muhammad Mufid as well — regarding how a tree, if only it knew how to move, would not be cut down by an axe.[32] So, in the interests of his own employment, he decided the time had come to travel, and on 1st Ramazan 1016 H. (late December 1607), corresponding to the month of Bahman in the 2nd regnal year of the Mughal emperor Jahangir, he set out from the auspicious town of Ahmedabad.

---

[30] Since the text follows Khwaja Abu'l Hasan's travels and career between late 1607 and 1609, it corrects the rather distorted image of some historians, who have claimed he had "no meritorious accomplishment" before 1611; see Findly, *Nur Jahan*, 44–5. For his later career, see numerous references in Jahangir, *The Jahangirnama*, 126, 157, 163, 167, 169, 189–90, etc.; also see Shahnawaz Khan, *Ma'āsir al-Umarā'*, trans. Beveridge and Prashad, vol. 1, 151–60, for his biographical notice.

[31] 'Abdul Latif, *Risāla-i sair-i manāzil*, 4.

[32] Alam and Subrahmanyam, *Indo-Persian Travels*, 1.

Thanks to the grace of his patron the Nawwab, he then travelled from Gujarat (known as the door to Mecca), and went all the way to the frontier of Bengal, from which access to Cathay and Aqsa-i Chin and Khotan was feasible. Wherever he went, he wrote down a memoir (*yāddāsht*) for the benefit of his friends regarding the towns and countries he visited. The implication is that notes are being made by him in a notebook (*sahīfa*) along the way, to be revised in good time. In a later phase he was transforming it into a travel journal (*roznāmcha-i safar*), and, realising it contained failings and shortcomings, asks the reader in advance for forgiveness.[33]

After this preliminary throat-clearing, the travels begin in earnest, with their first destination being the Mughal court to which Khwaja Abu'l Hasan has apparently been recalled. After leaving Gujarat, the party headed north into Rajput territory and after a few weeks, on 20th Ramazan, reached the town of Bijapur (today in Pali District) in Marwar, a well-known place situated at the edge of mountains. This had once been in the hands of infidel kings (*rājhā-i kāfir*), but the old sultans of Gujarat and the *ahl-i Islām* had then taken charge of it. It was given over hereditarily into the hands of a certain Khan Jiu Bijapuri, father of 'Izzat Khan, and now it was still in the *jāgīr* of 'Izzat (or perhaps Ghairat, the text being unclear) Khan, with whose behaviour the subjects were very pleased. The place was well-populated and had excellent religious buildings with high minarets. There was a hilltop fortress near there called Sungar, which was marvellous to look at.

On the 28th of the month they moved on and reached Merta, which was an old settlement with seven or eight Hindu temples (*ma'bad-i hunūd*), on which a huge amount of money had been spent by devotees. From here the desert was only a half *kos* away, close to a powerful fort which the sultan (of Gujarat perhaps) had once captured, but now the town had been largely abandoned. The Mughal emperor had granted it to Raja Suraj Singh, the son of Mota Raja (the nickname of Uday Singh, d. 1595), ruler of Jodhpur.

The party did not remain here long, and the next day left for the incomparable town of Ajmer. Here, by the grace of the great Sufi Khwaja

---

[33] 'Abdul Latif, *Risāla-i sair-i manāzil*, 5.

Mu'in-ud-Din Chishti, a large number of important graves had accumulated. There was a fort here too (the reference being to Taragarh), and again the settlement was located at the edge of the hills. 'Abdul Latif reports that in earlier times the Muslims (*ahl-i Islām*) had conducted a *jihād* here against the accursed infidels (*kuffār nābkār*). As a consequence there were graves in the hills of several Muslim martyrs such as Sayyid Husain Khing Sawar. Latif found this celebrated city to be of importance but nevertheless decided not to describe it in detail, perhaps because other descriptions could be found.[34] He noted a small detail, namely that just outside Ajmer there was a tank called Ana Sagar which looked artificially made, when in fact it was a natural construction, its water particularly good and sweet.

These preliminary passages give us a first flavour of 'Abdul Latif's style of description. The focus is very much on urban centres, fortifications, and religious sites. The recent political history of each region is sketched, even if only briefly. Occasionally, he interrupts this flow for a more general reflection. For instance, while his party is at Ajmer he makes some general comments on the nature of Mughal rule. He writes that the emperor Akbar, who was particularly caring of the people, had invested in *sulh-i kull* – or "universal peace" – with all groups of men, so that no contemporary ruler in the world could be compared with him. Indeed, he had also surpassed every other past ruler of India and had managed to capture lands hitherto only possessed by separate kings. These territories ran all the way from Qandahar to the Deccan and from Kabul to the end of Orissa. God had indeed bestowed the key to victory on him! When Akbar had begun his rule he was greatly devoted to Khwaja Mu'in-ud-Din, and every year he would walk the distance of 120 *kos* from Fatehpur Sikri to the tomb in Ajmer in order to circumambulate it. He therefore built wayhouses at each station en route, and in Ajmer itself he constructed a sizeable building which was still a source of wonder to onlookers.[35]

<hr>

34 Ibid., 6. For a useful discussion of the Khing Sawar tomb, see Asher, *Architecture of Mughal India*, 79–80.

35 For the larger context of these relations, see Alam, "The Mughals, the Sufi Shaikhs", 135–74.

After a few days in Ajmer, on 3ʳᵈ Shawwal 'Abdul Latif and his party went to Sambhar, which had a salt mine in its neighbourhood. Then, on the 6ᵗʰ of the same month, they reached Narnaul, a large and populated city in the province of Agra. The traveller reports that a certain Shah Quli Khan, a pious and virtuous man who had been close to the late emperor, had been governor there for quite some time, and had constructed a bath, a bridge, a bazaar, and a number of other buildings.[36] Besides, outside the town he had excavated a tank comparable to the Hauz-i Kausar in Paradise, with a lovely building in its middle. But Shah Quli had had a troubled life. Some people had levelled false accusations against him for womanising. Deeply insulted, he had responded in defence of his virtue by cutting off his own instrument of masculinity (*ālat-i rujūliyat*), remained celibate for the rest of his life, and therefore had had no sons. His buildings and works were thus his only offspring. Because of the tank, animals had a tendency to gather in this place, but Shah Quli had appointed a group of people to ensure it was kept clean. On the days of the full moon, usually, a feast was held there, and Shah Quli's tomb – completed by his brother Islam Quli Khan – was a prominent monument.[37] Even after his death, many of his relatives continued to live in the town and treated it as their home territory (*watan*). 'Abdul Latif also notes that the place had some significance for Afghans, and that the tomb of Sher Shah's father was to be found there.[38]

From Narnaul the party went to some of the *qasbas* of the sarkar of Hisar, such as Jind, and Kaithal, and also to the area of Sirhind. Concerning these, Latif decides again not to proffer a detailed description, considering them unworthy. The travelling party then made its way to Samana, which in 'Abdul Latif's view could legitimately be compared to Khambayat in terms of its people and buildings, as well as for its famous textiles. There was also a considerable diversity in the population and much pleasant greenery (*sabz-o-khurram*). On

---

[36] 'Abdul Latif, *Risāla-i sair-i manāzil*, 7.

[37] See Yazdani, "Narnaul", 581–6, 639–44; also see the brief but useful discussion in Asher, *Architecture of Mughal India*, 82–5.

[38] In reality, this appears to be the tomb of his grandfather, Ibrahim Khan Sur. See Yazdani, "Narnaul", 584–6.

28th Shawwal they reached the river of Ludhiana, known in the Indian language (*zabān-i Hindi*) as Sutlej. This marked the beginning of the country of Punjab (*ibtidā'-i mulk-i Panjāb*) and was their point of departure for Sarai Phillaur, some five way-stations before their destination, Lahore. But at this point, rather unexpectedly, the imperial army arrived at the spot. Unable to advance further, Latif and his group could not properly visit Lahore (a source of unstated disappointment). Instead, they spent their time around the banks of the Sutlej, near the substantial *qasba* of Ludhiana, where the emperor Jahangir had built a major caravanserai.

Nevertheless, this was an opportunity for Latif to see the imperial camp and court at close quarters, probably for the first time, and he was much impressed. The text changes its tone – high-flown phrases and adjectives laud the ruler Nur-ud-Din Jahangir Badshah. There are some remarks on the court, its ceremonies and rituals. Just before the second watch of the day the emperor, in keeping with the tradition (*sunnat*) of his father and predecessor, was in the habit of saying a litany (*tasbīh*) with the names of the sun.[39] This ceremony would end when the second watch was sounded. After this the emperor would from inside the palace blow a horn (*būq*), which was called a *bādur-sīng* in the Hindi language. People desirous of his *darshan* (or vision) who had gathered outside – and who would not eat or drink until they beheld his visage – would then raise their voices in a chant following the voice of their master. As the sound of the horn diminished, the emperor would emerge like the sun and spread his light over the world. Some said that, rather than the names of the sun, the emperor actually took the thousand and one names of Allah, but only God knew what the truth really was! 'Abdul Latif himself was witness to the prostration (*sijda*) of the people, with an impressive roar reaching up to the very skies. Everyone took up their place below the *jharoka*-window in keeping with their ranks, and elephants and horses were taken out in a procession. These ceremonies went on for an hour and a half at the beginning of the day.

---

[39] 'Abdul Latif, *Risāla-i sair-i manāzil*, 9.

Image 4.1: The Great Mughal Jahangir's *darbār*
(*c.* 1620).

The emperor would then emerge on horseback and proceed town-wards to allow the throngs there to see him.[40] Eventually, he would return to his throne (*takht-i khilāfat*), receive people, and render them justice until the evening. He would then retreat to his private apartments (*khalwat-kada*), and after the evening prayers drink his usual quota of around six cups of wine (*shurb-i rām-rangī*) with his intimates. This would go on into one watch of the night, after which he would disappear into the interior quarters of the *harāmgāh*.

Jahangir is amply praised here by 'Abdul Latif for various acts and innovations. These include the installation of a chain of justice (*zan-jīr-i 'adl*) thirty yards long and six fingers wide, weighing four maunds. In Agra, one end was on the Shahburj and the other at the banks of the river Jamuna, wrapped around a stone. If a Mughal administrator happened to seem indifferent to the needs of the people, this chain when pulled was the ruler's way of finding out. The emperor himself, we are assured, regularly spent huge amounts of money on the people. Each zamindar had been told to take good care of traders (*ahl-i tijārat*) and travellers; no one dared prey on the populace because several revenue officials (*karorīs* and *'ummāl*) had been punished for misbehaving. At the time of the previous emperor, Akbar, when some of the *amīrs* had accumulated a great deal, their goods had been confiscated (*zabt mi shud*) into the imperial *khālisa* at their deaths, though their children were then taken care of and partly compensated. But Jahangir had stopped this practice of confiscation altogether, and even those who had left behind lakhs of rupees would not be deprived of their goods. Instances of this were *umarā'* such as Sa'id Khan, Qutb-ud-Din Khan, and Hakim Jalal-ud-Din Muzaffar. Properties were not even absorbed into the *khālisa* of those who died childless, but used to build tanks, wells, bridges, caravanserais, mosques, and so on.[41] According to 'Abdul Latif, this was why Jahangir's rule was marked by such stability, and all the *amīrs* were ready to lay down their lives for him. Such was the degree of their loyalty that when Jahangir noticed some of them spending excessively on the annual Nauroz festival – to the extent

---

[40] Ibid., 11.
[41] Compare the account in Jahangir, *The Jahangirnama*, 24–6.

that they felt deprived of their fortunes – he decided to give them generous grants to compensate their profligacy.

Further examples are added of the emperor's justice and generosity. From Agra to Lahore he had ordered trees to be planted on both sides of the road for a distance of some 300 *kos*. Proper caravanserais had been made and deep tanks dug for access to water. The graves of dead rulers (*salātīn-i māziya*) had been properly restored and *waqfs* instituted for their maintenance, with appropriate servants (*khādim*) appointed to this end. It would appear, claims 'Abdul Latif, that Jahangir had even exceeded the legendary Naushirwan in his justice.

But still, all was not quite well in the kingdom. Sultan Khusrau, the oldest son of the ruler, had made some serious political mistakes, even opposing his own father at the instigation of some of Jahangir's enemies when Akbar died.[42] But Jahangir had continued to be kind to him and forgiven him. He had even thought, despite it all, that as Khusrau was to be his eventual successor, he could be sent as governor to a considerable province such as the Deccan, Bengal, or Gujarat, each of which had been a substantial kingdom in past times. But it seemed Khusrau's star was already doomed: he listened to bad advice and, instead of being of service to his father, decided to rebel. He turned his back on his fortune, for as the Arabic saying went: when Death is nigh, man becomes blind. So, on 7th Zi-Hijja 1014 H. (April 1606), after five watches of the night, he had fled the city of Agra for Lahore. When the emperor found out, he sent a certain Shaikh Farid Bukhari, titled Murtaza Khan, with a force to chase him down.[43] When Khusrau reached Lahore, the emperor's supporters would not let the prince into the fort, so he had to besiege the city. But on learning he was pursued by an imperial force, he turned around. While still in the neighbourhood of Lahore, Khusrau with his 15,000 men clashed with the imperial army of Shaikh Farid, who, despite commanding a small force of only 3000–4000 men, prevailed in the battle. Shunning detail, Latif outlines Khusrau's fated end: Khusrau went on to a place called Gujrat (in the Punjab) and tried to cross the Chenab river. But the imperial army pursued him there, and after desperate attempts to

---

[42] For a discussion of the question, see Alam and Subrahmanyam, "Witnessing Transition", 104–40. Also Lefèvre, *Pouvoir impérial*.

[43] 'Abdul Latif, *Risāla-i sair-i manāzil*, 14.

flee he was captured. On 3 Muharram 1016 H. (late April 1607) he was brought back to Agra with Hasan Beg and his other followers, while some 300 of his men who had been captured were executed on 8 Muharram; their bodies were displayed on the wayside from Mirza Kamran's garden to the gate of Lahore. Thus was the world freed from this unruly rebellion (*fitna-o-fasād*).[44]

In spite of all this, Khusrau was not physically punished: the emperor simply ordered him imprisoned and forbade him going out hunting or pursuing other leisure activities. Indeed, the emperor even wanted to free him, but in Kabul there was now a fresh rebellion in Khusrau's support. It was clear that Khusrau was mulishly recalcitrant, so he was ordered to be blinded. Latif suggests this was done most reluctantly and only after other reasonable means had been exhausted. He then cites a verse:

> If you want to be a son, be a follower
> For if you are unfaithful, destruction will follow.

As for the emperor, he returned to Agra from Lahore and ordered festivities on the scale of Nauroz to be celebrated, involving very substantial expenditures. Though 'Latif was not himself present at these events – being still in Gujarat – he learnt that the celebrations lasted as long as ninety days and involving all sorts of musicians, poets, and beautiful women performers. Clearly, the end of Khusrau's rebellion was remembered as marking a major event early in the new reign.

Closing this parenthesis on the rebellious prince and his affairs, 'Abdul Latif returns to his own travels from the Punjab.[45] After all the excitement of encountering the emperor's camp, he found himself with the returning imperial army in Sirhind, which he describes as a fine city where large buildings and gardens had been made, with all kinds of fruit trees. (He seems to refer in particular to the Bagh-i Hafiz Rakhna.[46]) Our author is particularly impressed by the elaborate irrigation system, which involved such a complex arrangement of wells and

[44] See the account in Jahangir, *The Jahangirnama*, 48–50, 56–7.

[45] On the economic and political geography of Punjab in the period, see Singh, *Region and Empire*.

[46] 'Abdul Latif, *Risāla-i sair-i manāzil*, 18.

tanks that nothing comparable to it was allegedly to be found in all of Hindustan (*dar mamlikat-i Hind nīst*). In contrast, he quite disliked Thanesar, which seemed charmless; even the people could not be compared to those of the good old days of Shaikh Jalal Thanesari (d. 1582) a generation ago. Latif did visit a great tank outside Kurukshetra which the infidels (*kuffār*) believed holy, as a consequence of which people came from faraway places to bathe in it. All kinds of absurd stories (*dāstānhā-i wāhī*) were recounted about this tank, he notes sceptically. Nevertheless, the emperor had ordered a building to be made there to facilitate pilgrims.

From Kurukshetra, the party made its way quickly through the small town of Panipat before coming to Dar al-Islam Delhi, the capital of India (*pāya-i takht-i Hind*), the fame of whose beauty had by then spread all over the world. So wonderful was its climate, location, and water that it could justly be considered a paradise on earth. 'Abdul Latif recounts his good fortune in visiting the shrine of the great saint Nizam-ud-Din Auliya, refuge of both kings and beggars. The grave of the veritable king of speech, Amir Khusrau, was naturally high on his list of places to be visited, and on finding himself there he felt the fatigue of his travels fall away. But he equally recalls that, since he was still in the train of the imperial army, he was not the master of his own time. So unfortunately he could not visit the shrines of the Chishti saints Khwaja Qutb-ud-Din and Khwaja Nasir-ud-Din Chiragh-i Dehli, or the sultans buried in Old Delhi (*Dehli-i qadīm*) some 4–5 *kos* from the *shahr-i jadīd* (probably meaning the erstwhile Dinpanah of Humayun). He notes besides that Humayun himself was buried in the vicinity, and his tomb – on the banks of the river Jamuna – impressed our traveller a great deal. The tomb of Prince Murad and many other past *amīrs* could be found there too, and the great Khan-i Khanan had built an excellent tomb for his wife in the very same area. 'Abdul Latif also mentions Tughlaqabad nearby, said to comprise seven forts and fifty-two gates; however, it had been abandoned: only Jats and pastoralist Gujars inhabited its environs. Still, its location remained so prominent that it could be seen from a distance of one *kos*.

Another excellent place near Delhi that he considers worthy of mention was called Salimgarh, a fortress made by Salim Khan, son of Sher Shah Afghan, during the period of his rule, by the Jamuna. Shaikh Farid Bukhari, called Nawwab Murtaza Khan, had been *mīr bakhshī* and *pīshkār* in the time of Akbar, and was considered one of the prominent men of his generation. This included his role in suppressing the rebellion of Khusrau. As a result of these actions he had been given a *mansab* rank of 5000, made governor of Gujarat and tutor (*atālīq*) to Prince Shahryar. Shaikh Farid had settled in Salimgarh and constructed several buildings in Delhi, besides his own gardens and structures. Men like the late Shihab-ud-Din Ahmad Khan had made bath-houses and imposing buildings in the city. In short, Latif gives us an early-seventeenth-century Delhi which, though no longer used by Jahangir as a capital, remained an important religious and administrative site, and also because of memories of its past glories.[47]

From Delhi our traveller eventually made his way southwards to Brindavan and Mathura, which he noted were "established temples of the Hindus (*ma'bad-i muqarrara-yi Hunūd ast*)." As a result one could find great praise of these places in the *dhrupads* and *bishnupads* (sung texts), and the "misguided books (*kutub-i zalālat*)" of these people. There were no comparable temples anywhere else in India, and this was why people called themselves Mathra Das and Bindraban Das, which 'Abdul Latif translates as being akin to 'Abd al-Mathra or 'Abd al-Bindraban. It was claimed that this used to be the residence of Sri Krishna Jiu, and there have long been many idol-houses (*but-khānas*) of decent standing here. He also notes that the suffix *-ban* means a jungle, which explains why here large numbers of monkeys abound and greet the Hindus in a tame and friendly way, even going so far as to eat grain from people's hands. Recently, the important *mansabdār* Raja Man Singh had built a rather large stone temple, the like of which was not to be seen anywhere else, at an expense of Rs 500,000. Latif is wonderstruck by the skill of the architect who constructed such a building, but he also shows some ambiguity – between the notion that all this is misguided in its purpose, and praise at the wonders and skills deployed. "If only such beautiful buildings had been made for Muslims (*ahl-i Islām*) to worship in, and such a match-

---

[47] Compare Koch, "The Delhi of the Mughals", 163–82.

less place had been the mosque of the people of the Qibla," he re-marks.

> Sometimes when God's grace blows a breeze
> The idol-house becomes a mosque.
> And, at times, when the hot wind of his wrath blows,
> The mosque becomes an idol-house.[48]

The considerable tolerance shown to the Hindus (*hunūd*) and their institutions in the Mughal domains clearly troubled 'Abdul Latif somewhat, especially when he found himself in sites such as Kuruk-shetra, Brindavan, or Mathura. Mathura itself, he noted, was a size-able *qasba* on the banks of the Jamuna, where the ascetics among the unbelievers (*zuhhād-i kuffār*) gathered in great numbers in the hope of rewards for the hereafter. Of this he disapproves via a Qur'anic verse (*khasir al-dunyā wa al-ākhirah*) to the effect that such people have lost both the world and their faith. Nor is he happy to learn that in those very days the villainous Raja Nar Singh (or Bir Singh) Deo Bundela had obtained permission from the emperor to build another high tem-ple in Mathura, parallel to the one in Brindavan.

From these holy sites of the Vaishnavas, Latif made his way to Sikandra, called Najibabad at the time, located some three *kos* from Agra. This place had a wonderful garden around the seven-storeyed tomb of the emperor Akbar, which elicits several passages of praise. The emperor had ordered a continuous set of gardens and buildings from Sikandra to the city, and this plan has been largely carried out. On 4th Zi-Hijja (or 2 Farwardin, according to the Iranian calendar he some-times employs), Latif's group entered the great city of Agra along with the imperial party. The old city as he describes it was to be found on the two sides of the Jamuna river.[49] On the near side, which was the great-er part, the extent of the settlement was 7 *kos*, that is, 2 *kos* length and 1 *kos* width; while on the other side the extent was 2 ½ *kos*, of which the length was less than 1 *kos*, and the width ½ *kos*. He notes that the city was considered to be in the second clime. To the east of it was Qannauj, to its due west was Nagaur, and to the due north Sambhal.

---

[48] 'Abdul Latif, *Risāla-i sair-i manāzil*, 21.
[49] Ibid., 22.

The greatness of this city, its population and affluence, were beyond description. Its fortifications had been strong for a long time, so that even the great Mas'ud Sa'd Salman (d. 1121) had praised it. 'Abdul Latif cites a section of Salman's *qasīda*, also mentioned by Jahangir in his own memoirs.[50]

> The fort of Agra emerged from the midst of the dust,
> Like a mountain, littered with rocks like a range of hills,
> In strength it had attained the ultimate,
> so that even the Ungrateful Age could not terminate it.

In the very same text, Latif notes, a certain Sultan Muhammad, grandson of the famous Sultan Mahmud of Ghazna, had uttered words in praise of Agra, which he describes as a virgin fort, beyond the grasp of any conqueror. Akbar had rebuilt the fort recently and improved the buildings there at an expense of Rs 18 lakh, with the reconstruction taking eighteen years. (Here, as elsewhere, 'Abdul Latif gives equivalents between rupees and *tūmāns*, suggesting that some of his intended readers were located in the Iranian world.) The stone had come from nearby Fatehpur Sikri, and the whole task was undertaken with such skill that the whole fort appears made from a single stone. In sum, the fort was a wonder unrivalled.

As has happened once earlier, while describing the imperial camp, there is a perceptible shift in the tone of the text; some extremely flowery passages, replete with a series of elaborate metaphorical constructions, follow. At the principal gate of Agra are two stone elephants so well made that they appear alive, causing 'Abdul Latif to recall the story of Abraha the Abyssinian, the Aksumite governor of Yemen who had attacked Mecca with his army of elephants before the birth of the Prophet. On the other hand, before the fort of Agra, he declares, even Alexander's fabled wall would seem a mere spider's web.

Eastward Bound

'Abdul Latif stayed on in Agra for all of a month, just as the hot season was about to begin. But Bengal was written in his fate: his Nawwab,

---

[50] Jahangir, *The Jahangirnama*, 23.

Khwaja Abu'l Hasan, had in the past been the paymaster (*bakh-shī*) there, and was now made its finance minister (*diwān*).[51] It is noted that Abu'l Hasan had been the past intimate of princes and had gained considerable experience in various administrative and responsible capacities in the Deccan, Gujarat, and elsewhere; but it is equally implied that he was somehow not happy with this new appointment, even seeking out a Sufi master to console him in his time of sorrow. Still, there was no getting around an imperial order, and so it was that on 2nd Muharram 1017 H. (April 1608) the party set out eastwards by boat on the Jamuna river. (In parenthesis, 'Abdul Latif states that, according to the Hindus, the Jamuna comes from the Kalindi Mountains, but since that upper area is very cold, it is more or less inaccessible.) He begins by noting that he quite enjoyed this river journey, which was after all on sweet water, and bore no comparison to a sea voyage on salt water. The boat had a roof, and they could stop at various places that were protected, and wander around. Accompanied by his friends on the trip, he was able to enjoy exchanges of poetry (*suhbat-i shi'r wa sukhan*), as well as the joys of music and entertainment. This section thus contains verses in praise of pleasant breezes and birdsong.[52]

But the river journey also had its less pleasing side; it was very long and brought out in him a sense of nostalgia for his homeland (*watan*) of Ahmedabad, despite the quality of the company and the relative comfort of the trip. At the first stage they reached the town of Chandwar, where the Hindi tongue (*zabān-i hindī*) was spoken in a simple and flowing manner. After a further three days they reached the larger *qasba* of Etawah, 15 *kos* distant from the Chambal river which emerged from the hills of Mandu far to the south and merged with the Jamuna.[53] On Saturday, 10th Muharram, they crossed the Chambal confluence, and then another river 3 *kos* away called Panjnad, meaning the joining of five streams. Two days later they reached the ancient

---

[51] 'Abdul Latif, *Risāla-i sair-i manāzil*, 24.

[52] Ibid., 25.

[53] For the relationship between Agra and its hinterland in the period, see Trivedi, "The Emergence of Agra", 147–70.

town of Kalpi on the banks of the Jamuna, which had regrettably seen better days. Travelling more or less in the heartland of the Mughal domains, Latif seems to have maintained a quite accurate idea of both terrain and hydrography, and indeed of local variants in language. In Kalpi, as they did periodically, the party descended briefly and spoke with people; the traveller noted that the candied sugar (*nabāt*) here was justly famed, a fact noted by other Mughal writers as well.[54]

Latif's fondness for visiting the shrines of Sufis, especially those of the Chishti order, is now again evident, though his tastes could be rather more heterodox as well. From Kalpi the party made its way due north over land to Makanpur, where the tomb of the celebrated Shah Madar was to be found at some 8 *kos* distance.[55] Since there was a *takiya* of his followers, the Madaris, at Kalpi, where the Shah had carried out a penance (*chillā*), there were also pilgrimages (*ziyārat*) between the two towns, and Latif seems to have accompanied one of these pilgrim groups.[56] He notes that although Shah Madar had no children, buildings dedicated to him were to be found in many places, and these were in many respects his true successors, for this was how God had compensated him for not having children. At a further 12 *kos* from there was a small stream called Chhapparkhat Mua, and a few *kos* beyond was the Gomti river which flowed below the Kalinjar fort and joined the Jamuna. This was the celebrated fort where Sher Shah had been killed. There was also an area called Shadipur near Kalinjar, in which some of the inhabitants had the bizarre habit of selling off their beautiful daughters (*dukhtarān-i jamīla*) to anyone, whether Hindu or Muslim, for a suitable price. 'Abdul Latif had heard this tale before and found it unbelievable and absurd, but people he now spoke to confirmed it. He declares that he finds this custom so shameful that he would prefer to think it false, even though the Qur'an tolerantly states that every group has its own customs.

The detour to Makanpur having been accomplished, the river

---

[54] Kalpi was long famed for its sugar-candy, which is referred to in a number of texts of the period.

[55] On the complex figure of Shah Madar (d. 840 H./1436), see Coslovi, "Aspetti 'indiani' della figura",187–203; also Alam, *The Mughals and the Sufis*, 128–63.

[56] 'Abdul Latif, *Risāla-i sair-i manāzil*, 26.

voyage was resumed. Some three weeks after setting out from Agra, on Thursday 22nd Muharram, the party reached the celebrated centre of Ilahabad (Allahabad), which Latif notes was once better known as Payag. The three districts (*mahāls*) that lay side by side were Payag, Jori/Jhusi, and Arail, with Jhusi being on the other side of the Ganges.[57] When visiting this place, Akbar had decided to give the names Ilahabad to Payag, and Jalalabad to Arail. The Ganges and Jamuna rivers met at the base of the fort here, and, though one could see only two rivers, the Hindus (*hunūd*) called it Triveni – the place where three rivers met. This was on account of their claim that a river called Saraswati from the hidden world was part of the confluence, though it could not be seen. The source of all these rivers was Svarg, or Paradise, in their view. 'Abdul Latif adds that, according to this misguided community (*jama'at-i zalālat*), any man who comes and bathes here will go straight to their Svarg, where all his sins will be deleted from the Register of His Acts (*jarīda-i 'amal*). What a false set of beliefs, what a mistaken set of thoughts! But the result is that everyone who had any resources was willing to come from afar, spending 5 or 10 lakhs and joining a *sangh* or pious caravan, just as Muslims go on the *hajj*. They then stayed on here for a time, believing they had attained some perfect honour (*sharaf-i tamām*) or release. Latif also adds a slightly enigmatic phrase to the effect that, in olden times, the place of confluence of the rivers had a huge *karwat* (saw-blade) erected on the spot (suggesting, but not stating, that this was an instrument of ritual suicide).[58] In sum, even though it was a reasonable place in which to live, relatively few noble Hindus and Muslims chose to reside there. To emphasise the gap between its holy character and lack of secular importance, he notes that earlier, before Akbar elevated it to a provincial (*sūba*) headquarters, it was just the chief place of a *pargana*, that is to say, of local administration. He adds:

> Since this is on the way to Bihar and Bengal, and because it is a significant place of worship of the Hindus, and also because so long as unbelief (*kufr*)

---

[57] Ibid., 28.

[58] On the question of ritual suicide in Prayag, see Chattopadhyaya, "Religious Suicide at Prayag", 65–79. For a comparison with Benares (and the Kashi Karvat temple), see Justice, *Dying the Good Death*, 43–5. Also compare the account of Mahmud Wali Balkhi, in Alam and Subrahmanyam, *Indo-Persian Travels*, 139–40.

remains alive in the world, it will be the visiting-place of these infidels, and will ever be mentioned, on account of these factors the king [Akbar] built a huge fort, and stone buildings which leave men in a state of astonishment. I have already given you an account of the fort of Agra, and the beauty of its red sandstone; but the mansions and buildings here are better by several degrees than the buildings in Agra, Lahore or Fatehpur.[59]

There were apparently twelve great buildings, with the names of the twelve solar months, and besides them a royal dome overlooking the river that stood on fifty pillars. There was also a two-layered garden with a wonderful breeze through it that stirred the soul. Again, high-flown phrases compare the earth here to the purity of the Virgin Mary, and the river pebbles to pearls.[60] Some Rs 30 lakh, or 100,000 *tūmāns*, were spent by the Mughals on this construction. A long set of verses – possibly 'Abdul Latif's own compositions – follow, implying that mere prose can hardly do justice to this city. It would appear from his description that Akbar's mother Maryam Makani, the Khan-i Khanan, Raja Todar Mal, and several other *umarā* – knowing that Akbar had built major palaces there and perhaps intended to make it the capital of his empire (*mī khwāstand pāya-i takht kunand*) – made substantial buildings of their own. But, he adds, it was a matter of great pity that, despite such edifices here, Akbar was not able to shift his capital or even revisit the place. Rather, the flag of the Mughals had moved west to Agra. But for this city it was a matter of great pride that the current emperor Jahangir had spent considerable time there as a prince.[61] Here, after all, was the tomb of his wife Badshah Begam, the mother of Prince Khusrau and the sister of Raja Man Singh.[62] Unfortunately, says Latif, when our emperor was still a prince this lady committed a crime on her own person by taking an excess of opium and left this world for the Garden of Paradise.[63] Around her tomb (*maqbara*) Jahangir had recently built a fine garden. Since the waters of the Ganges rose high in the rainy season and had a tendency to enter the town,

---

[59] 'Abdul Latif, *Risāla-i sair-i manāzil*, 29.
[60] Ibid., 30.
[61] In reality, these were above all Jahangir's years in rebellion against his father!
[62] 'Abdul Latif, *Risāla-i sair-i manāzil*, 32.
[63] For Jahangir's account of her death, see Jahangir, *The Jahangirnama*, 50–1.

the emperor had also ordered the building of a substantial stone wall (*band-i sangīn*). Rs 6 lakh were spent on it, and more may yet be spent to fill some incomplete sections. The city thus remained in some respects a missed opportunity, the possible centre of a Mughal empire squarely centred on the Gangetic valley rather than on the dusty western fringes where the riverine plain met the desert.

'Abdul Latif and his party remained in Allahabad for only three or four days and left again to make their way east to Chunar, where they arrived on 26th Muharram. This was the chief place of a sarkar, at a distance of 15 *kos* from Jaunpur. The governor here lived in an imposing fort near excellent buildings on a hilltop overlooking the river. When the rains came, water filled up all around and it was quite picturesque. The great *amīr* Bayazid Sultan Turkoman had apparently been in charge of the place for quite a while, and had built a caravanserai on the other side of the river for pilgrims, as well as a proper place of residence for the governor. He had left many imprints on the area, and Chunar was really one of the better forts in India.[64]

By this stage, the party having moved east, the Ganges had absorbed all its tributaries. The group was to enter Benares the following day, which Latif calls *Dār al-kufr qadīm* (Ancient Abode of Infidelity) and *Bait al-shirk 'azīm* (Huge House of Idolatry). Located on the banks of the Ganges, this was a highly populated town, but lacking in any real light because of its association with unbelief (*kufr*). The city ran along the riverbank, and Hindus of high status and wealthy men were to be found here in good numbers:

> The city's external appearance is [attractive] like the interior of Muslims, but on the inside, they are like slaves of the idols. The breeze of Islam has never even blown through here, and the voice of faith has never attained their ears. It is like a Holy Book in the house of a heretic. Here, Raja Man Singh has constructed a lofty idol-house (*but-kadah*). One can rarely find Muslims who think of this as their homeland. But many Hindus have built idol-houses here in keeping with their capacities. Infidels of all regions, in particular the Deccan and Gujarat, having given up their own homelands, reside here because of the nobility of this place and with the objective of

---

[64] 'Abdul Latif, *Risāla-i sair-i manāzil*, 33.

acquiring a reward in the life hereafter. They have a baseless belief (*i'tiqād-i bībuniyād*) that whatever living being, whether human or animal, including even dogs and cats, if they die here go directly to Paradise, and do not return to the world of rebirth. They thus remain for all time in Heaven. One of the signs of such a death is that the left ear of such a person becomes higher than the other one. Though it is evident that this is completely false, our emperor has written in the *Jahāngīr Nāma* that when some illiterate groups said this with great exaggeration, he sent some trustworthy people from his court to investigate the matter. It was shown to be totally false.[65]

Srihari, the father of Pratapaditya, the present zamindar of Jessore (in Bengal), had built a huge temple here, which was even grander than the temple of Raja Man Singh. Jahangir, when he was a prince, had ordered this temple to be destroyed, but under the influence of Raja Man Singh had rescinded his order. The inhabitants of the town were not lacking in beauty, but the darkness of their infidelity acted as a curtain over the light of their beauty. 'Abdul Latif continued to hope that this veil would be removed by the mediation of Islam (*ba wasīla-i Islām*).[66]

Our author moves on from Benares to a consideration of Zamaniya, a good-sized *qasba* also located on the river. In earlier times one of its important nobles was Khan-i Zaman, who had played a major role in the Mughal conquest of Bihar but then turned rebel. He and his brother Bahadur Khan were captured by loyalists and killed, but before his death the name Zamaniya was given to the place by him, and he had built a fort, a bath, a mosque, and mansions there. The place had been a great centre for the Afghans, even if it had suffered some recent decline.

This takes Latif to a short reflection on the transitory nature of power in the world, since owls and nocturnal creatures have made their home in the mosque and the *hammām* of Khan-i Zaman. So it is everywhere: the owl enters the home of the peacock; the wolf and fox have built houses where men lived; and vultures have constructed

[65] Ibid., 34.

[66] For Benares and its architecture under Mughal rule, see Desai, *Banaras Reconstructed*, 30–56.

their nests there too. Where once cups of wine flowed, and the flute and drum sounded, now one finds gravestones and cawing crows.

After this sobering lesson on worldly transitions and the effects of futile rebellion, the party reached Ghazipur, which was the head of another sarkar in the Allahabad province. Here too there was a proper fort on the banks of the city, and it was a decent-enough town. In its vicinity Latif again saw troubling traces of the glories of the ancient past (*māziya wa guzār*), but despite his best efforts was unable to get a proper account of the place from its inhabitants.[67]

Into the Mughal East

We now enter the eastern Mughal provinces of Bihar and Bengal, and it was in fact these sections of the text that really interested Jadu-nath Sarkar writing a century ago. From Ghazipur the party travelled downriver to Chausa, which Latif clearly notes marked the transition into Bihar (*ibtidā'-yi mulk-i Bihār az ān jā ast*). It was well known that key battles had taken place here between the Mughals and the Afghans, and here too Humayun had fought Sher Khan Afghan and suffered an unfortunate defeat. The party stopped and took stock of the fact that it had once been a considerable place. However, more recently there had been certain disturbances and consequent depopulation. The rivulet Karmanasha entered the Ganges nearby, and the Hindus of olden times wrongly believed that if one placed one's feet in its water it would destroy the record (*hisāb*) of your past deeds. Therefore it was called *karam-nāshā*, that is, "the destruction of karma". But in reality its water had neither taste nor appearance and was enough to make your bile turn cold.[68]

The party arrived presently in Sahsaram, which had the tomb of Sher Khan Afghan at a distance of some 16 *kos* from Chausa. The nearby fort of Rohtas, the greatness and size of which was famous, had a circumference of 14 *kos*. It was very high and several thousand *bīghās* of land around it was cultivated, with flourishing gardens and tanks. It was at a distance of two *manzils* from Sahsaram. By this time

[67] This may be a reference to the Bhitari ruins of the Gupta period.
[68] 'Abdul Latif, *Risāla-i sair-i manāzil*, 36.

it was the end of the month of Muharram and the beginning of the month of Safar. On 3rd Safar the party crossed the broad and deep Diwa river, which came all the way from Bahraich (spelt Bharuch in the text) and Awadh and entered the Ganges. Latif notices a change in the hydrography here, as large rivers such as the Are, Gangi, Son, and Gandak all entered the Ganges from 15 *kos* above Patna down to that city. Thereafter, some small rivulets whose names were not worthy of mention also joined the Ganges. The result of this was that the width of the river at Patna was as much as 3 *kos*, giving it almost the appearance of a sea (*muhīt*).

On 4th Safar (10th May) the Mughal party reached Hajipur-Patna, the capital of Bihar. Patna was situated on the right bank of the river and Hajipur on the left, above Patna. At a distance of 16 *kos* lay the ancient city of Bihar, which used to be the capital, as Latif was informed by reliable informants, who also told him that many old saints were buried in it.[69] Certain eminent people were still around, such as a certain ascetic (*majzūb*) called Shaikh Humayun. This man's miracles (*khāriq-i ʿādāt*) were apparently many, but Latif discreetly refrains from offering details.

Moving on to the village of Hilsa he sees the grave-shrine of a certain Jumman Chishti (an error for what should be Madari); on top of its imposing dome was a pitcher (*taʿbīyah*, which miraculously turned by itself once at every watch, as reported by some reliable witnesses.[70] Over time the population had shifted across the river to Patna, which was now the capital of Bihar and where the governor resided. The river protected the city on one side, and there were mud (*khām*) fortifications on the other three sides. In the time of Akbar's rule, after a long siege, the city had been wrested from the Afghans. Munʿim Khan Khan-i Khanan had besieged Daʾud Khan – who had been the ruler (*wālī*) of Bihar and Bengal for a long time – until Akbar himself had taken charge of the operation, whereupon the city surrendered. It was considered a very fine and noble city (*bighāyat latīf wa maqām-i sharīf*), its climate always seeming like spring. Its water was very sweet

---

[69] Ibid., 37.
[70] See Askari, "The Mausoleum of a Saint", 40–52.

and invigorating, and as a result the inhabitants were healthy and robust. The city calls for the highest compliments in Latif's vocabulary: the expanse and order of it were such that it seemed like Ahmedabad, "the best of the cities". This was also because daily needs such as food and clothing were cheap and abundant, so that a large number of traders and wealthy men had chosen it as their home. He concludes this section by noting: "In no other city of India can be seen so many men of 'Iraq and Khurasan, as have taken up their residence here."

It turns out that by the end of the sixteenth and early seventeenth centuries many of the Mughal *umarā'* had begun to invest heavily in the public spaces of Patna. One of these was a certain Jahangir Quli Khan (well known as Lala Beg), who had been one of the great *amīrs*; he had died in Bengal in the early seventeenth century. During his time as governor in Patna he had cleared a space and made a large bazaar, and though he himself was known for being haughty and ill-mannered, the city had gained in grace and currency. Further, Mirza Yusuf Khan when he was governor had made an excellent bath-house with several rooms; its effect was both hot and refreshing (*shādāb*), qualities which it apparently shared with the human soul. The late Sadiq Khan had also left a mosque there in his own memory, and Mirza Shams-ud-Din Husain, son of A'zam Khan, had laid out an excellent garden outside the city. And, most importantly, we learn that 'Abdul Latif's patron Khwaja Abu'l Hasan (Asaf Khan) had lately built an edifice inside the fort where the governor lived overlooking the river, and a garden outside the city. Verses therefore follow in praise of the great Asaf Khan, who is compared to the very sun in the sky.[71]

After a week or so, on Monday, 11th Safar, 'Abdul Latif and his party left Patna and arrived in *qasba* Munger, where there was a strong fort. This place was halfway between Bihar and Ghati, the doorway to Bengal. The externalities of this town appeared better than its interior, and there had been some diminution in the settlement of late. The emperor Akbar, in the early years of his rule, had stayed here for quite some time with the intention of capturing Bengal, and a number of notable engagements had occurred between the imperial forces and

---

[71] 'Abdul Latif, *Risāla-i sair-i manāzil*, 39.

the Afghans. At 2 *kos* distance was a place called Sitakund, situated at two or three arrows' flight from the river. It was noted for two remarkable ponds (*chashma*), one hot and the other cold, indeed so cold that it made one's teeth icy. As for the heat, it was such as to reduce hell's bile (*zohra-yi dozakh*) to water. Munger did not detain them long, and the very next day the party arrived in the *qasba* of Mashan, still in Bihar. This was a half *kos* from the river, but the air continued good; in fact moonlit nights here were quite soul-stirring. In the rainy season the storms that flooded the Ganges made the earth and ambience green and pleasant here. At an attractive small hill someone had built a lovely mosque, the residence of a dervish there who for the past thirty years had been immobile in ascetic prayer (*mu'takif*), abiding only in a small room which provided him water, his courage drawn from his devotion to Allah. Seeing this man seemed to put Latif in a reflective mood about his own life, leading him to pen some verses on the subject of asceticism and celibacy (*tajrīd*).[72] How much better, he exclaims, to live this life of ascetic poverty than to have the books of the poets 'Unsuri and Anwari, or even the throne of Alexander!

Latif and his party seem to have spent quite a few days – perhaps even a couple of weeks – in this area. Their voyage on the river was coming to an end as they made their way to the town of Akbarnagar (Rajmahal), the capital of Mughal Bengal, to which he and his patron Khwaja Abu'l Hasan were posted. By the grace of God, he writes, the river journey had been broadly peaceful and pleasant and nothing untoward had happened: "May all travellers on land and sea in the world reach their destination and objective with as much safety and comfort (*ba khair-o-khūbī*)."

However, the text itself has not quite come to an end: Latif now begins a description of the "customs and wonders of this kingdom (*auzā' wa 'ajā'ib wa ghar'āib-i īn mulk*)" of Bengal, beginning with its capital Akbarnagar. Until the time of Akbar, he writes, the place was no more than a decent-sized village, and was called Ag-Mahal. The old kings of Bengal had maintained their capital in Gaur, where the traces and vestiges of ancient rulers could be found in abundance, reflecting the

---

[72] Ibid., 41.

wisdom in the Qur'anic verse to that effect. These rulers would regularly come towards Bihar, and on their way stop at this spot: so "Ag-Mahal"
meant the advance post in front, while on the other side was a village
called Tanda, which was called "Pach-Mahal", on the way to Orissa or
Bhati. However, there was also an implicit pun, because the houses were
made of thatch and frequently caught fire, and so the common people
described it using the word *āg* (fire).

At the beginning of the period of Akbar's rule the imperial army under Mun'im Khan and Khan Jahan Turkoman (known as Hasan Quli
Khan) had often fought in this area with Da'ud Khan, the erstwhile ruler (*wālī*) of Bengal and Bihar. When at last Da'ud Khan fled from Bihar, he was killed in this very area by the swords of the imperial *ghāzīs*.
The imperial army often camped here, and, because it was at the foot
of the hills, Raja Man Singh found it safe, especially in the rainy season
when his enemies made use of their boats to launch attacks. The climate here was also good, and hence he built a fort and mansions and
called the complex Rajmahal.[73] Officially, it came to be called Akbarnagar in honour of the emperor. During the rainy season the whole
area was regularly flooded, so a sizeable embankment had been constructed against the waters. The town was however not particularly
distinguished and had only a few areas that were notable, such as
Shahpur and Shaikhpur, settled respectively by the prince Shah Murad
and Shaikh Abu'l Fazl. Among the other Mughal *umarā* associated with
the place was Rana Sagar, uncle of Rana Pratap, Rajput ruler of Chittor.[74] To him was owed the quarter called Sagarpura, built on a hill-
ock. In the same area was the much-frequented tomb of a certain Mir
Murshid Ahmad Bukhari, for whom the Rajput Rana Sagar had great
reverence, to the extent of having built a dome over his grave after a
dream.

Latif notes that, after the time of Raja Man Singh and Rana Sagar,

[73] Unfortunately, pages 43–4 are missing in the microfilm copy available to us. We
have therefore used the summary and translation in Sarkar, "Travels in Bihar".
For a discussion of Rajmahal, and Man Singh's intervention there, see Asher, *Architecture of Mughal India*, 72–4.

[74] For the politics of this family in regard to the Mughals, see Sharma, "Some Aspects of the Mewar Polity", 261–5.

this place had become linked to the *dīwān*'s office, and all subsequent holders of the office had chosen to reside there.[75] It was a fine but strange place, with an excellent climate, rare indeed among most kingdoms of the world. There was greenery all around, and during the rains the waters of the Ganges mixed with those of nearby rivulets. In his time of residence, Rana Sagar had made buildings here in the Hindu taste (*hindū pasand*). Then, when Wazir Khan got there, he made other bungalows (*bangala*) and imposed greater order on the place. Even so, it was still not quite worthy of people of high stature. Now it was a well-known fact that the author's own patron Mu'taqad Khan (Asaf Khan) had always made his mark wherever he went.

He was aware that in this world only two things gave one eternal life: the praise of poets and the making of buildings. In Burhanpur in Khandesh, for example, Mu'taqad Khan had made an excellent bazaar, bath-house, buildings, and a bridge (*tripuliyā*). It was on his behest that even in Gujarat a caravanserai was made and named after Murtaza Khan, better known as Shaikh Farid Bukhari. So, the result was that as long as Ahmedabad remained, his name would too. In the case of Rajmahal, when Mu'taqad Khan had been there a mere ten days, he had already decided to make some buildings, partly with the idea of providing employment to people (*ba wasīla-yi mazdūrī wa gilkārī*). He began work on a treasury (*toshakhāna*) in the Sagarpur quarter, with two treasure-houses (*makhzan*), and two verandahs (*aiwān*) to the north and south. To avoid making a triangle he ordered another construction with a raised platform. These were now appropriate buildings for people of elevated status. The difficulties that people from northern India faced when reaching the bad climate of Bengal were mitigated by the good fortune of living in these structures (*kulfat wa āzurdagī-yi kasāfat-i āb-o-hawā-yi Bangāla mī gardad*). 'Abdul Latif concludes: "Every man who had hitherto seen himself as unfortunate saw matters differently now, as if he had a friendly face before him. Others also built new buildings there according to their capacities."

Soon after this work had begun, on 9th Ramazan 1017 H. (December 1608), Latif left Akbarnagar along with Islam Khan, better known

---

[75] 'Abdul Latif, *Risāla-i sair-i manāzil*, 45.

Image 4.2: Portait of Asaf Khan.

as Shaikh ʿAla-ud-Din Chishti, who was the grandson and direct successor of the great saint Shaikh Salim. On the death of Jahangir Quli Khan, this grandee had been named governor of Bengal, and he was leaving for Bhati, which was the part of the Bengal kingdom below the waters (*zīr-i āb*).[76] Latif therefore begins a section here on their travel further eastwards. But before commencing he feels the need to briefly tell the story of Akbar's dealings with Shaikh Salim Chishti.

Akbar, he recalls, had had no son for a long time, and of course the importance of a successor was crucial.[77] He imagines verses that Akbar may have recited in prayer asking for his problem to be solved, and made Fatehpur Sikri his capital. Here he built many impressive buildings, and after a time, due to the saint's grace, a child was born who was now emperor and the envy of the very heavens. Akbar took him and placed him on Shaikh Salim's lap, asking for his blessing. This is why he was given the name of Sultan Salim, and Akbar called him "Baba Shaikhu". Nowadays, on account of that close bond, Shaikh ʿAla-ud-Din, his grandson had been given an elevated *mansab* of 4000, standards and drums (*naqqāra*), and the title of Islam Khan. He was made governor of the great kingdom of Bengal. Here the brief parenthesis closes.

The party now embarked southwards in a fleet of boats (*nawāra*) from Akbarnagar towards Goash, a *pargana* headquarters in sarkar Naurangabad, while enjoying pleasant sights on the banks of the river. They passed the towns of Gaur, Tanda, Malda, and Pandua (albeit not in that order), in the last of which Shaikh Qutb-i ʿAlam, the notional disciple of Nizam-ud-Din Auliya, was buried.[78] All these places were on the left-hand side as they sailed downriver (the river's course has since shifted somewhat).[79]

---

[76] On Islam Khan in Bengal, see Eaton, *The Rise of Islam*, 151–8.

[77] ʿAbdul Latif, *Risāla-i sair-i manāzil*, 47.

[78] Shaikh Nur Qutb-i ʿAlam died in 1459, after having lived through turbulent times; see Eaton, *Rise of Islam*, 89–91.

[79] The geographical details of ʿAbdul Latif's account are somewhat disordered here. We have thus been guided by the account in Bhattacharya, "Conquest of Islam Khan", 247–70.

On the 5th Shawwal, the *wakīl* of a certain warlord called 'Usman Aghan came in the company of Mirza 'Ali, who was the representative of Islam Khan, and they had a meeting with the governor. These men brought along a letter saying that 'Usman had decided to accept the service of the Mughals, and that he would send his younger brother with gifts and tribute to the imperial capital. It was agreed that the party would cross the Ganges at the ferry-crossing (*ghāt*) of Goash, where they would hold a consultation and head either for Bhati or for Ghoraghat, which was the seat of 'Usman Afghan. When they crossed the Ganges, the brother of the well-known Raja Shatrajit, also known as Shahzada Rai, and who was the zamindar of Bhusna in sarkar Mahmudabad, was there to welcome them with some elephants. There was also word from the Raja of Jessore (Jashore), Raja Pratapaditya, the greatest of the rulers of Bengal, who possessed 700 armed boats, 20,000 infantry (*pāyak*), and revenues of Rs 15 lakh; his son had already been in Akbarnagar with gifts and a few elephants. The son had been sent back with due formalities and now he said he was returning to meet the Mughal party post-haste. A certain Muhammad Yar, envoy of Mukund Narain, Raja of Kuch, came with three elephants and eight *tānkan* horses. 'Abdul Latif explains that these were wild horses native to Bengal, sturdy and hard-working, with the dark colour of buffaloes (*gāv-mesh*) and reputedly as strong.

Clearly the arrival of Islam Khan, the new governor, made quite a stir among the zamindars of Bengal. One or two months were spent in all these dealings, and while waiting for the messages to go back and forth with them. The Mughal party was quartered for a time in 'Ala'ipur on the river, a place that 'Abdul Latif does not really consider worth describing.[80] But he does mention two nearby villages called Malik and Bagha, where one of the residents, a wise man about a hundred years old, was called Hawadha Miyan. There was also an excellent tank, called *phokara* in the local tongue, with superior drinking water. The descendants of that aged sage had made several quadrangular residences (*chaukandīs*) around the tank, and there was also a mosque dating to 930 H. made by Sultan 'Ala-ud-Din, better known

---

[80] 'Abdul Latif, *Risāla-i sair-i manāzil*, 49.

as Husain Shah, a former ruler of Bengal. In the house of the wise man, Hawadha, there was a sort of madrasa and many of his followers were able to get tutoring and an education there. The whole place was sustained by mango and jackfruit orchards, all held as a revenue-free grant (*madad-i ma'āsh*).[81] Here at last Latif felt he had found the perfume of Islam (*bū-yi Islām*) in an exotic land. No other village seemed to have this particular character in the area, and he could only felicitate the people of this wilderness (*bīsha*).

The whole riverine landscape in the Rajshahi and Pabna areas seems to have left Latif rather nonplussed. For four or five months a year, he reports, most of the country was covered in water. Travel, fighting, and hunting, everything was done through fleets (*nawāra*), and one got to see all sorts of strange boats and vessels as a result. Among these were the "Kosa Prazi" which have 40 boatmen (*mallāh*), 10 artillerymen (*topchīs*), 4 bowmen, 2 other gunners (*gola-andāz*), miscellaneous armed men, and a drummer. But there were also other boats of differing dimensions, some used for fishing, others for other purposes.[82]

Eventually, on 5th Zi-Hijja (early March 1609), the party moved on from 'Ala'ipur towards Nazirpur, and then to Fatehpur (both today in the vicinity of Pabna), where they celebrated the 'Id-i Qurban and Nauroz. Here, Raja Shatrajit of Bhusna arrived in person and was given an audience by Islam Khan; he brought eighteen male and female elephants as a tribute and gift. They remained about a month in Fatehpur, until on 4th Muharram 1018 H. they went on to Mauza Rana-Tandapur. Here, Salim Khan, the zamindar of Hijli in Orissa, and the brother of Raja Indra Narayan, ruler of Pachet (a mountainous region to the south), as well as Brahim [sic: for Bir Hambir], the Raja of sarkar Mandaran, accompanied by a certain Shaikh Kamal (a reliable confidant of Islam Khan), came bringing with them 109 more elephants. On 1st Safar, Raja Pratapaditya himself arrived and met the imperial party in Bajrapur. He too brought six small and large

---

[81] The reference appears to be the great Bagha Masjid in Rajshahi, with an inscription dating to 930 H./1523–4. See Siddiq, *Epigraphy and Islamic Culture*, 24.

[82] 'Abdul Latif, *Risāla-i sair-i manāzil*, 50.

elephants, fine textiles, camphor, and incense, as well as Rs 50,000 in cash, and stayed for several days. In short, as he penetrated deeper into the province, the Mughal governor made sure his presence was registered, and also systematically accumulated tributary wealth in cash, goods, and above all elephants. On 5th Safar (late April), the party moved on to Shahpur and stayed there for a time. They set up camp on the banks of the Jamuna (or Jamuneshwari) river, where the water was of good quality, and Islam Khan left his army with a smaller party in order to hunt out elephants in the vicinity of Nazirpur with a few chosen companions; after nine days and nights in the jungles, he returned with 32 male and female elephants. On his return he quickly set about making a bridge on the Jamuna, so that the army could cross over to Ghoraghat, and on 9th Rabi I 1019 H. (2nd June 1609) they finally reached that destination. By now the monsoon rains had begun in earnest but Ghoraghat – an old *qasba* in Bengal, located at a slight elevation – was apparently considered better than most other towns of the province because it was spared somewhat from flooding. Further, it was the headquarters of Kuch, territory of their new tributary 'Usman Afghan, and considered excellent for the trade in wild horses, *dupattās*, and fine textiles from that region.

Islam Khan and his party remained in Ghoraghat for all of four and a half months, and only set out on 26 Rajab (15th October) for Bhati. In the time that he was in Ghoraghat the governor apparently had a mosque built, improved the bazaar, and shored up the fortifications. It turns out that Mu'taqad Khan too had earlier founded gardens in this town. This time of enforced leisure in Ghoraghat on account of the monsoon and its aftermath turned Latif's attention somewhat away from his usual preoccupations – cities, buildings, past conquests, and Sufi shrines – to a brief consideration of the wonders of nature. He treats us to a small digression on the mynah-bird, which was like a small crow and very intelligent. If you taught these birds, they could speak any tongue and any style (*rawish*) that you liked – and impressively so. They could actually repeat what they had learned in an eloquent language and after a while they could copy any words spoken in their presence, and even imitate the sounds of a horse or a cockerel. The mynah could also copy the sound of every musical instrument and thus arouse laughter such as the pen could not describe. As for its upkeep, the mynah ate milk and rice but was extremely delicate, and if you took it out of its usual habitat it would die. It was apparently brought to Ghoraghat by traders and often offered by them as gifts.

Latif also notes that in Bengal, but particularly in the vicinity of Ghoraghat, there were plenty of places for hunting and that a hunter could in a single day kill ten or fifteen cheetahs, and other animals such as stags (*gawazn*), and hare (*kotāh-pā*). Wild buffaloes too could be found here, some of them comparable to fourteen elephants in strength with tusks of five or six yards. A horse was simply no match for this animal, Latif exclaims; eight *tufang*-bullets and sword blows and arrows later he still would not yield, but instead would attack you like an elephant. However strange it might seem, in proportion to the buffalo's strength was the cowardice and fearfulness of the tigers of the region. When the two encountered one another, the buffalo always had the upper hand. There were also a lot of rhinoceros (*kargadan*), and these too could in principle be hunted with a gun (*tufang*), even if their hide was so tough that it resisted guns and arrows. The rhinoceros, he notes, had a single horn in the middle of its head, and was carried to far distant parts as a gift. Besides, at Ghoraghat, one could find pineapples (*anānās*) which were fine, sweet, and abundant. They had thorns, and leaves like the flowering lily (*sūsan*) but were as large as a melon. In these jungles one could often find jackfruit trees, as well as bananas, mangoes, betel-nut, etc. So fertile was the land that on a single jackfruit tree one could obtain as many 300 or 400 fruit, each fruit being as big as a liquor jar (*sabū*). The mango here was equally special in comparison to that of other countries. When the fruit began to appear, an insect grew inside it along with the fruit; it was popularly said this was on account of the curse of the great saint Nur Qutb-i ʿAlam on a countryman.

There was also another fruit of the size of the orange, called the *komala*, that was so juicy and enjoyable that it was better than the orange in many ways.[83] The emperor had taken a particular liking to this fruit and often had it along with his wine (*shurb-i rām-rangī*), so that

---

[83] The reference here is to the sweet lime, or *Citrus limetta*.

people coming to the court from Bengal often brought it along as a gift. Another excellent fruit here was the so-called Martaban banana (*kela martabānī*), to be preferred even to the bananas from his native Gujarat. Concluding his brief digression on the local fauna and flora, Latif notes a type of *champā* flower in Bengal that he had never seen elsewhere called *āsākhānī*, and with a special and rather disagreeable odour.

The text of the *Risāla-i sair-i manāzil* ends rather abruptly, with 'Abdul Latif still in Ghoraghat or its vicinity. Both copies of the manuscript seem to end in the same place, namely with a short mention of a migrant soldier and saint of Sayyid origin called Shah Isma'il Ghazi, whose hospice (*āstāna*) was to be found outside Ghoraghat. Shah Isma'il had apparently entered the region at the time of the Bengal sultans in the second half of the fifteenth century. We are left to wonder whether 'Abdul Latif simply did not have time to complete his text, which (as we may gather) was probably revised a couple of decades after his travels; or whether a more complete redaction was indeed produced but has not survived. We know that he did return from Bengal, and that he had a rather successful career for another three decades after his time listening to the mynah-birds of Ghoraghat.

The text of 'Abdul Latif Gujarati occupies a modest but interesting place among first-person narratives from seventeenth-century Mughal India. Traversing the width of the empire from west to east – from his origins in the province of Gujarat to the eastern frontier of Mughal expansion in Bengal – he provides us an original view of the Mughal territories as they were constituted after the second phase of massive expansion under Akbar. This was the world of Hindustan proper, which is to say the Indo-Gangetic plain, preserving a certain cultural and linguistic unity despite a marked degree of ecological and social diversity. To be sure, other significant first-person accounts exist in Persian from the period, notably that of Mirza Nathan (d. 1641–2), whose *Bahāristān-i Ghaybī* was another text uncovered and studied by Jadunath Sarkar.[84] Mirza Nathan was present in Bengal at the same time as 'Abdul Latif, and equally gives a view of Islam Khan's

---

[84] For the unique manuscript, see Bibliothèque Nationale de France, Paris,

forays into northern Bengal in the early years of Jahangir's reign. Still other important and somewhat similar texts come to us later in the same century, such as Shihab-ud-Din Talish's *Fathiyya-i 'Ibriyya*, largely focused on the Mughal eastern frontier in the 1660s during the government of great *amīrs* such as Mu'azzam Khan and Shayista Khan.[85] However, when one reads the latter two texts, it is clear that the organising principle behind them is one of recounting battles, campaigns, and expeditions, in reference both to the careers of their authors and chief patrons. A variation is presented to us by the text of Bhimsen to which we will presently turn, where we find a mix of such accounts of campaigns (largely in the Deccan), and the narrative of the twinned careers of the author and his patron Dalpat Rao Bundela.[86]

No eccentric or outlier, 'Abdul Latif presents us instead with the steady view of the Mughal functionary, with pride in the empire and its accomplishments, notably in triumphing over the threat represented by the ever-present Afghans (they punctuate the text at various locations). This is an empire, moreover, which is squarely constructed on the axis of the river Ganges, to the point that one senses that the notion of centring it on Allahabad rather than Lahore or Agra much tickles the author's fancy.

At the same time, there is an interesting tension between Latif's own religious views and those propagated by the stated imperial ideology of *sulh-i kull*.[87] From the very outset of his travels, while at Ajmer, he makes it clear that he has considerable devotion and respect for the Chishti Sufis, who had emerged in the ascendant during the reign of Akbar, and this is a theme that recurs elsewhere, whether at Thanesar, Delhi, or

---

Blochet Suppl. Pers. 252, 328 folios. For a serviceable translation, see Nathan, *Bahāristān-i-Ghaybī*, trans. Borah, 2 vols.

[85] For a selective translation, Shihab-ud-Din Talish, *Tarikh-i Asham*, trans. Pavie. For an extensive discussion, with translated excerpts, Sarkar, *Studies in Mughal India*, 118–67.

[86] British Library, London, Ms IO. 94 (Ethé 445), 104 folios: Bhimsen ibn Raghunandandas, *Nuskha-i Dilkushā dar ahwāl-i rājahā-i Bundelkhand*.

[87] Kinra, "Handling Diversity", 251–95.

further east. Nor is he averse to somewhat more heterodox forms of Islam, such as that presented by the Madariyya in their various sites. But it seems he has a real issue with the extent of liberty of worship and religious expression afforded to the Hindus (*hunūd* or *kuffār*), whether in Mathura and Brindavan, or Benares. While suggesting that this may be a necessary political compromise to ensure the loyalties of indigenous rulers such as Man Singh Kacchwaha or Bir Singh Deo, or even the rulers on the Bengal frontier, it is clear that Latif would have much preferred an imperial culture in which the perfume of Islam (*bū-yi Islām*) could spread further and penetrate deeper. His discomfort with the "composite culture" of the Mughals thus parallels tensions one finds in the Ottoman case, in regard to the treatment of minorities such as the Christians and Jews.[88] It has been argued elsewhere that the Mughal regime had a complex relationship to this question, one that combined its Mongol heritage, Nasirean reflections on political ethics (*akhlāq*), and the pragmatic business of ruling in a stable manner over a vast population that could simply not be converted to Islam. But we are also aware that – just as in the Ottoman case – there was simply no unanimity on the proper policies to be followed, even among the administrative elites of the empire. 'Abdul Latif provides us further food for thought when we ponder on the question of the management of religious diversity in this early modern imperial context.

Intermezzo: The Case of Mirza Nathan

A contemporary of 'Abdul Latif and Asad Beg who also spent a good deal of time on the eastern frontier of Mughal expansion was 'Ala-ud-Din Isfahani, best known as Mirza Nathan. He also held other titles at various points of his career in Mughal service, as well as using the pen-name "Ghaibi". Unlike 'Abdul Latif, Mirza Nathan was a *khāna-zād*, a hereditary servant of the Mughals, whose father Malik 'Ali, titled Ihtimam Khan, had occupied several positions, including as *kotwāl* of Lahore in 1605–6 before moving on to the Bengal frontier as an

---

[88] For a survey of positions, see Veinstein, *Les Ottomans*, which seems overly influenced by the tendentious analysis in Moačanin, "Some Remarks", 209–15.

important military commander, the *mīr bahr*.[89] As we are well aware, over the course of Akbar's reign the presence of Iranians at the Mughal court, and more generally among the ranks of the *mansabdārs*, had grown apace from modest beginnings at the time of Humayun's return from the Safavid court of Shah Tahmasp. It has been estimated that between 1575 and 1595 roughly a quarter of those who held a rank of 500 or above were classed as Iranis, slightly below the number of Turanis who had constituted the initial base for the elite of the Mughal conquest state.[90] Mirza Nathan came to hold a number of middling posts in Mughal Bengal as *thānedār* of Pandua, and later *faujdār* of Dakhinkul. He was eventually also given the title of Shitab Khan.[91]

The *Bahāristān-i Ghaybī* follows a chronological sequence and is divided into four parts, corresponding to four administrative terms in the Bengal province. It has come down to us in a single manuscript, and on the fly-leaf one finds details of the manuscript's history. It had been lost and was found in Agra during the author's lifetime, and was then gifted by Shitab Khan himself to Nawwab Asalat Khan on 1 Rabi I 1051 H., shortly before his own death. Asalat Khan then gifted it immediately to a certain Aqa Muhammad Baqir (son of 'Ali Raza Tirmizi), who in turn gave it away a few days later to his slave Zirak. The manuscript thus changed hands very rapidly, with one of the later purchasers – a certain Amirullah – possibly adding marginal notes. In the 1770s it was acquired by the French mercenary and collector Jean-Baptiste Gentil, possibly in the region of Faizabad, and sent back to France along with a valuable collection of other manuscripts and paintings.[92]

The text itself seems to have followed a complex evolution while being composed. We may infer that the first two books were written

---

[89] We learn, on the occasion of Ihtimam Khan's death, that he had a "palace situated near Sirhind" which he considered his real home; Nathan, *Bahāristān*, trans. Borah, vol. I, 204.

[90] Husain, "Growth of Irani Element", 166–79. Also Husain, *The Nobility Under Akbar*.

[91] See Athar Ali, *Apparatus of Empire*, J333, J694, J800, J825, J828, J1011, J1020; S1882, S2850. For a reference to Ihtimam Khan, see A918.

[92] Richard, "Jean-Baptiste Gentil", 91–110.

in the reign of Jahangir and destined for the emperor's consumption; the author goes so far as to propose that "with the grace of Divine Favour . . . it would not be strange if this deep piece of eloquence is incorporated into the perfection of understanding (*balīgh al-maʿanī*) which is the *Jahangir-nāma* (*dākhil-i Jahāngīr-nāma numāyand*)," meaning that he submits his work as a possible contribution to the official record of the reign. On the other hand it seems likely that the last two books were completed in Shahjahan's time (probably in 1041 H., or 1632) as a way for the author to re-establish himself because Mirza Nathan had encountered serious difficulties in the transition from Jahangir to Shahjahan, as we shall see below.

The *Bahāristān* can be considered at one level to be a sort of extended campaign memoir dealing with the attempted pacification of Bengal and areas further to the north-east by the Mughals. This was a process that endured almost a century and was considered somewhat complete only much after Jahangir's reign, under the governorship of Shayista Khan in the 1660s.[93] But the period of Mirza Nathan's residence in the region, which corresponded to the administrations of the governors Islam Khan, Qasim Khan, and Ibrahim Khan, did see penetration deeper into the east, the defeat of a number of significant oppositional figures, and the emergence of Jahangirnagar-Dhaka as the centre of Mughal administration.

The main foci of resistance were various zamindars of differing dimensions, including both Hindu rajas and Afghans, the latter having transformed themselves into powerful figures in the countryside over the course of the sixteenth century. In the eastern Bhati region they included Musa Khan (titled *masnad-i aʿlā*) and Khwaja ʿUsman, while further west we encounter the formidable figure of Raja Pratapaditya of Jessore (mentioned by ʿAbdul Latif). Beyond the limits of Bengal, there were formidable challenges posed by the so-called Magh rulers of Arakan in Burma (Min Razagyi and Min Khamaung), as well as a number of north-eastern kingdoms and principalities. A final complication took the form of the Portuguese *firangīs*, who allied themselves opportunistically both with some of the eastern zamindars and the

---

[93] Eaton, *The Rise of Islam*, 236–8.

Arakan rulers to mount a lucrative maritime operation of raiding and slave-trade from their maritime bases in Chattogram and Sandwip.[94]

In the face of this intricate landscape, with a formidable cast of major and minor characters, Mirza Nathan provides a lively narrative, full of dramatic anecdotes and scenes of battle and intrigue. His sprawling text (in which he refers to himself usually in the grammatical third person) lends itself, in the first instance, to a politico-military account of how the Mughals managed in the early seventeenth century to consolidate their position in the difficult terrain of riverine Bengal, deploying boats and elephants. As has been concluded from his account, "the Mughal campaign in Bengal was entirely different from other Mughal operations. Instead of pace and mobility, it was the slow but sustained movement, as well as the concentrated employment of the Mughal army, that one by one rounded up the divided and spread-out forces of the Bengal *zamindars*."[95] But the Mirza is meticulous enough as a recorder of events for his text to be also profitably read somewhat against the grain, to provide a "subalternist" view of the rebellions and uprisings against the empire's expansion on the frontier.[96] A third point worth noting is that this is the account of a man in a very unfamiliar environment coming to terms with a climate and set of diseases with which he (and many of the other Mughal officials) were apt to struggle. However, Mirza Nathan's is also a tale of acclimatisation and acculturation, and the effective use of local knowledge. Fairly early in the text is an episode in which the author's father Ihtimam Khan fell seriously ill while in Ghoraghat. He was then moved to Kalabari, where Mirza Nathan was resident, but his condition grew steadily worse, accompanied by periodic bouts of unconsciousness. Physicians were sought from all around, and messages sent as far as Benares, sparing no expense. Eventually, a solution was found in the form of a Hindu *kabirāj* from Alapsingh (in the Mymensingh region), described as "a skilful and expert physician [who] also possessed a knowledge of astrology." Having made a cautiously optimistic astrological prognosis,

---

94 Flores, *Nas Margens do Hindustão*, 307–14.
95 Gommans, *Mughal Warfare*, 170–9.
96 Bhadra, "Two Frontier Uprisings", 43–59.

the physician asked that matters be entirely left up to him. The account continues:

> Mirza Nathan and all others agreed to allow him to begin the treatment. Then that enlightened, wise, and experienced man dissolved three red [doses of] deadly poison in a quantity of lemon and ginger water and put it in the mouth of Ihtimam Khan; after a moment it went down the throat. Before the administration of the medicine, he said, "If the most Merciful God grants him relief then, after four astronomical hours he will ask for water; if he does not ask for water, then the case is hopeless." Therefore, every man, small or great, was in great suspense and was unconscious of himself, when suddenly the Khan asked for water in a loud voice. The aforesaid Kabiraj and Mirza Nathan paid their prostrations of thanks to the Almighty and showed signs of relief. After a short time a little quantity of water was given to Ihtimam Khan. In this way, for three days consecutively he was given poison-pills, each day reduced by one. Thus the Khan gradually recovered and regained his health.[97]

In view of this remarkable success, the *kabirāj* was taken first into Ihtimam Khan's entourage, and after his death was inherited by Mirza Nathan, who showed considerable faith in the man's skills both as astrologer and physician. A subsequent episode is related from some years later, when Mirza Nathan, finding himself at death's door, dispatched one of his eunuchs to fetch the same *kabirāj* from Alapsingh. After rapidly traversing a large swathe of country, the physician quickly set to work, using his habitual and counterintuitive Ayurvedic technique of "a deadly poisonous drug [mixed] with the juice of ginger and lemon." Despite the scepticism shown by those present, "that wise man of the age who was an ornament to the science [he practised], applied the necessary remedies and began to treat with the aid of God in such a way that after twelve days from his arrival, he made the Mirza take a bath, and perfect health was restored to him from the invisible house of cure."

A significant preoccupation in the text of the *Bahāristān*, which arguably grows more significant as one proceeds, are the twinned ideas of loyalty (*ikhlās* or *ʿaqīdat*) and honour (*ābrū*). Mirza Nathan suggests

---

[97] Nathan, *Bahāristān*, trans. Borah, vol. I, 38–9.

that Mughal service was often fraught with tensions in this regard, as not all superiors commanded – or indeed deserved to command – the loyalty of their subordinates. The first section of the text is replete with issues centring on the figure of the governor Islam Khan Chishti, whose treatment of both Mirza Nathan and his father Ihtimam Khan is seen as mean-spirited and arrogant. This is to the point that on one occasion the Mirza threatens to take his loyal men and turn them into dervishes and *qalandars*, forcing the governor to take a step back. Honour also appears to imply the proper behaviour of troops that might otherwise be inclined to oppress the subjects who have placed themselves under Mughal protection. In one instance Mirza Nathan found that his troops had attacked a group of peasants and "brought away as captives more than four thousand of their women, old and young," stripping them of their belongings and even their clothes. Growing indignant at this injustice, he responded by ordering the peasants to be set free and even compensated. However, there were other moments when pride and ideas of honour came into conflict, as in this episode from Jessore.

> One day envoys of Kumar Udayaditya came to see Mirza Nathan. The Mirza told them in anger, "You are giving Mirza Makki [son of Iftikhar Khan] bags full of gold and gold coins and other valuable articles of dress because he plunders your territory. You never remember me even with fruits like mango and jackfruit; my kind disposition and humanity are my faults. Alright, tomorrow is my turn and you will see what is meant by looting of a territory." He said to the leaders of the fleet and the land force, "We shall start at midnight." In short, at midnight they rode out on horses and started without paying any attention to the entreaties of the envoys; and such a plunder was made on that day the like of which had not been seen since the day of the first attack upon Jessore.[98]

Nathan even boasts that such actions made him "an object of great terror to the people of the country," oblivious to the fact that this was gratuitous violence visited on a community that had been conquered simply out of jealousy between two Mughal officials. Indeed, the text is full of instances of backbiting and petty manoeuvring that set one

[98] Ibid., 142.

mansabdār against another, often over the division of spoils. The high-flown rhetoric of conquest, and the recourse to citations from epic-style poetry, does not really conceal this brute reality from readers.

The question of loyalty grows more acute in the latter half of the text. This was because of the crisis caused by the rebellion of Prince Khurram (or Shahjahan), who appeared in Bengal and Orissa in the early 1620s, forcing Mughal officials to choose between loyalty to him and his father.[99] The episode is dealt with at some length by Mirza Nathan, who makes it evident that the choice was a bitter one for most. Among those who chose to remain loyal to the emperor Jahangir was the Bengal governor Ibrahim Khan, who was killed in the process but still treated with honour. The governor of Patna, Mukhlis Khan, chose not to resist Shahjahan but, seeing himself in grave risk of losing his honour and reputation, eventually committed suicide by poison. As for Mirza Nathan himself, he informs us that he decided to take the prince's party and even made exaggerated displays of devotion to him. This included spending extended periods of time with the prince in Rajmahal, reinforcing the relations he seems to have enjoyed with him since his childhood. However, after a time it became clear that he had chosen the losing party in the struggle, as Shahjahan prepared to flee Bengal for the Deccan. At this stage the Mirza abandoned the prince's camp and fled by crossing the river Ganges to a Sufi shrine. It is with this act that the text closes in a rather abrupt fashion.

These questions of loyalty and betrayal may well be the reason why the third book of the *Bahāristān* has an additional preface written by a certain Shaikh 'Abdul Rasul Sufi Jaunpuri, Mirza Nathan's spiritual guide or *pīr*; we may note that it was to the shrine of his son Miyan Sayyid Nizam-ud-Din that the Mirza fled at the end of his narrative. This is how the Mirza justifies the inclusion of this preface:

> My heart's desire has daily remained to be in the service of virtuous people. In this quest, I came to Chausa to see Shaikh 'Abdul Rasul Jaunpuri, an excellent master of gnosis, who is amongst the spiritual leaders of the time in that area. The purpose of these lines is to give a brief account of this

---

[99] For a careful analysis of these aspects, see Anooshahr, "No Man Can Serve", 54–63.

meeting. He then returned to Jaunpur from Chausa via *pargana* Chainpur alias Chaund. It so happened that on our first meeting, he had read the second *daftar* written by this humble person. In spite of the poor pebbles I had accumulated, because of his noble nature, he praised the work. Since I had also drafted the *dibācha* [preface] of the third *daftar* of the *Bahāristān*, I presented it to him as well so that he could correct its errors. He said, "It is not my intention to write a *dibācha* to this." I then said it was nevertheless my desire to see the miraculous writing (*kalām-i mu'jiz-bayān*) of that master grace this third part of the work as a blessing and sign of auspiciousness. In the process, my own *dibācha* was also corrected by him, and he too wrote one of his own which I place here on the reverse of my own. I have written these words so that the intelligent reader of today and tomorrow may know of the purpose of these two prefaces. This has emerged from the heart on to the tongue, and from the tongue to the pen on the 7th Zi al-Qa'da of the Year [10]41 Hijri, the 5th regnal year of the Sahib-Qiran.[100]

This is then followed by 'Abdul Rasul's very flowery text, which is extremely elevated and abstract in nature and for the most part an exercise in style. He insists that the Mirza's is a work full of lessons (*'ibrat*) regarding the world, and those who have attained eminence in it. As usual, even this brief text is organised in terms of the praise of God and the Prophet and included are some of the Sufi's own verses. He mentions how he went to Chausa and met the author of the work there, whom he refers to with a long string of extremely high-sounding and complimentary titles. He suggests that it is really Mirza Nathan who is doing him a favour by allowing him to write this prefatory text, and requests human errors, if any, be forgiven and corrected. This layering of *captatio benevolentiae* clearly is meant to protect Mirza Nathan in view of his slippery behaviour and shifting loyalties at the time of Shahjahan's rebellion.

Mirza Nathan's text has, since the time of Jadunath Sarkar, justifiably attracted the attention of historians of political events and processes in early-seventeenth-century Bengal. It has also been read as an insight into how someone in a relatively modest position on

---

[100] Bibliothèque Nationale de France, Paris, Suppl. Pers. 252, f. 205b. The passage is omitted in Borah's translation.

the *mansab* hierarchy lived out his life inside the Mughal system in relation to the demands of imperial authority. It can be argued, however,
that the *Bahāristān* in fact does more than that. It shows how different sources of social power interacted in a particular space, that of a
frontier. The first of these was Timurid dynastic power, based on a
combination of lineage and charisma, which was in itself a somewhat
unstable and fissiparous form, as we see from the recurrence of struggles between emperors and princes. A second significant source of power was less top-down and more rooted in territory, as we gather with the
powerful zamindars of Bengal, who were themselves a mix of Muslim
and Hindu lineages with their own internal pecking order. In the
1610s and 1620s the Mughals defeated and killed a certain number
of these figures, especially the troublesome Afghans such as Khwaja
'Usman, but they also came to terms with many others. Moreover, as
is well known, they were unable to penetrate deep into the Bengal countryside at this time with their cadastral apparatus of systematic land
measurement (or *zabt*), as they had in many other provinces, depending instead on an improvised combination of tribute and reve-
nue-farming.

However, a third and intriguing source of power is revealed to us by
the case of Islam Khan Chishti, which largely occupies the first *daftar*
of Mirza Nathan's narrative. Here was a figure who, as the grandson of
the celebrated Shaikh Salim Chishti, disposed of substantial cultural
and symbolic capital, and enjoyed personal proximity to the emperor,
besides having a sizeable personal following and entourage. Jahangir's
decision to send him as governor of Bengal with a high *mansab* rank
was apparently based on his view that the status quo in the province
needed to be shifted. This decision did prove effective, though it was
eminently fraught with risk. Accompanied by a fresh injection of
military power, Islam Khan managed in the years from 1608 to 1613
to break the back in particular of the significant Afghan warlords of
the region. But in the process it is suggested that he accumulated excessive powers and even began to infringe on imperial privileges, such
as the use of the *jharoka* and demands for specific forms of ritual
obeisance. The biographical notice on him in the eighteenth-century
Ma'āsir al-Umarā' paints him in decidedly lurid terms, as surrounded

in Bengal by dancing-girls and men "holding trays of jewels and silken stuffs," adding that "he carried the customs of high office (*tūzuk-i amā-rat*) to such a pitch that he [made use of] . . . things fitting only for kings."[101] This is in curious contrast to Jahangir's own obituary notice in his memoirs: "None of the *khānazāds* or protégés had ever exhibited the competence he [Islam Khan] had. He governed Bengal autonomously and brought into the jurisdiction of the province areas held by *jāgīrdārs* that had not previously been under imperial control. If he hadn't met his end, he would have performed superior services."[102] This was perhaps a tactful manner of dealing with the memory of an obstreperous figure who had been on the receiving end of at least a few reproachful *farmāns*.

Bhimsen in the Deccan

The third figure to occupy our attention in this chapter comes from a couple of generations after Asad Beg and Mirza Nathan. This is Bhimsen, the son of Raghunandandas, born as he tells it into a Saksena Kayastha family in the Central Indian town of Burhanpur in 1705 Vikram Samvat, which he also translates as 1059 Hijri (and we render as 1649 CE). The bulk of his career in Mughal service coincided with the long reign of the emperor Aurangzeb-ʿAlamgir, from 1658 to 1707.[103] The use of the Vikram Samvat calendar when he refers to himself is quite deliberate and consistent, and we gather from early on that Bhimsen was a Vaishnava (who incidentally did not greatly appreciate Saivite ascetics). Though his text was known to early British colonial scholar-officials such as Jonathan Scott, it became the focus

[101] Shahnawaz Khan, *Maʾāsir al-Umarā*, trans. Beveridge and Prashad, vol. 1, 692–3; text, ed. ʿAbdur Rahim and Ashraf ʿAli, vol. 1, 118–20.

[102] Jahangir, *The Jahangirnama*, 155.

[103] British Library, IO. 94 (Ethé 445): Bhimsen, *Nuskha-i Dilkushā dar ahwāl-i rājahā-i Bundelkhand*. A second more complete manuscript dated to 1740, from *sarkār* Iraj (Agra), and belonging to Jonathan Scott, is to be found as British Library, Or. 23 (Rieu, I, p. 271), copyist Mitrasen, son of Muralidhar Kayasth Bhatnagar; and a third in the Bibliothèque nationale de France, Supplément Persan 259 (Polier 14, undated but obviously from the eighteenth century).

of renewed study in the twentieth century, once again through Jadunath Sarkar, in the course of his work on Aurangzeb.[104] Sarkar was
well aware that from the time of Akbar various Kayasthas, Khatris, and
Brahmins had entered Mughal service in a diversity of bureaucratic
functions. In the texts we have dealt with in the preceding chapters,
we encounter them time and again, both in the context of the imperial household and in those of Mughal functionaries such as Ihtimam
Khan and Mirza Nathan. This is in addition to the presence of well-
placed men from warrior castes like the Rajputs, who obviously played
a significant role in the Mughal command structure, and could –
in some cases like the Kacchwaha Rajputs – even intermarry with the
royal family, and go so far as to attempt to meddle in its succession
politics.

When Mughal writers of the mid seventeenth century looked back
to these earlier times, a certain number of personalities undoubtedly
stood out. One of these was the Khatri notable of modest origins Raja
Todar Mal (d. 1589), whose name came to be closely associated with
a number of important reforms of the revenue administration, though
he also had an appreciable number of detractors who accused him of
religious intolerance and lack of ecumenical spirit. At much the same
time we also find other Khatri figures, such as Rai Pitar Das, who had
initially been a humble official in the elephant stables but rose to prominence as *mīr ātish* and in other capacities. There seems to be a significant growth in the numbers of such Kayasthas and Khatris, as well
as scribal Brahmins, in the Mughal administration in the early decades of the seventeenth century, though a proper census of them has
not been conducted, to our knowledge. These included Harkaran
Das Kamboh, a Khatri from Multan who came to exemplify a certain
level of excellence in belles-lettres. Harkaran's father Mathura Das had
already achieved a fair degree of literary notoriety and other members of the family too had entered Mughal service by the time of Jahangir's reign, so that it seems appropriate to speak of familial rather than
individual strategies in this regard. Harkaran himself was attached

---

[104] See the free translation in Scott, *Ferishta's History*, vol. 2, 3–123, "Aurungzebe's Operations in Dekkan".

to the *amīr* I'tibar Khan and was never directly in the service of the imperial court. His influence over subsequent generations was exercised through his production of an important and widely read *inshā'* text called *Irshād al-Ṭālibīn*, in which he set out examples of different types of correspondence, royal orders, and other documents. Rajeev Kinra's meticulous study of Chandar Bhan "Brahman" (d. 1663) sheds much light not only on these individual figures and their careers, but the manner in which they constructed a collective past for themselves as a bureaucratic community.[105] Given his own life trajectory, it was self-evident that Chandar Bhan should lay particular emphasis on the decades when Shahjahan ruled as Mughal emperor. Two figures who stood out from this time were Kayasthas, namely Rai Raghunath and Diyanat Rai, the latter a close associate of the vizier Afzal Khan Shirazi. As they rose in the Mughal hierarchy, it was only natural that rivalries should develop between them and with others like a certain Sabha Chand, an influential *munshī* from the Lahore province.

As noted, Bhimsen's text attracted the attention of Jadunath Sarkar, who produced an abridged translation (though not an edition of it) which was published posthumously.[106] He also devoted an essay to him, terming him a "great Hindu memoir-writer," and paralleling another essay he devoted to Ishwardas Nagar, author of the *Futūhāt-i 'Ālamgīrī*.[107] The Bengali historian, often grudging in his evaluations, is fulsome in his praise of Bhimsen:

> The character of Bhimsen as a man is unfolded in his *Memoirs* without any disguise. We see his weakness, but we also see his strong fidelity to friend and master, his devotion to his kith and kin, his love of children and his devout faith in Hinduism. Bhimsen was a charming character, tender, unpretentious, frank and serene, loving social gaiety but also deeply touched by sorrow. If it be true that "the style is the man", then we must highly

---

[105] Kinra, *Writing Self*, 28–9, 76–7.

[106] Bhimsen, *Tarikh-i-dilkasha*, trans. Sarkar, rev. Khobrekar. The translation uses British Library, IO. 94 (Ethé 445), fls 1–104 for the first part, and British Library, Or. 23, fls 95–158, for the second part. In our citations of this translation, we have corrected its faulty syntax and usages, which seem more due to Khobrekar than Sarkar.

[107] Ishwardas Nagar, *Futūhāt-i 'Ālamgīrī*.

praise this master of a simple business-like prose, in which there are no useless flowers of rhetoric, no profuse wordiness, no round-about expression, yet plenty of accurate observation and concise but clear statement of all essential points.[108]

In the preface to the work, Bhimsen writes of his desire to renounce the world of the Mughal state and instead write this text as a sort of retiree, though he had apparently begun it while still active in around 1700. There are several gestures in the direction of mysticism, and he seems to indicate that the work is the result of a long struggle with his own self. Nevertheless, he has decided that it is time to tell the truth, even if it is costly to him in a Kaliyuga "when firmness of heart, consolidation of the inner self, purity of deeds and improvements in general conditions, are not to be found." The preface ends with a somewhat enigmatic verse, implying that the reader may expect the unvarnished truth from the text.

> Though I'm all twisted [by my past]
> with shame and embarrassment,
> the work of the sharp-edged sword
> is, after all, to drink blood.

The author now says something to introduce himself to the reader, which includes some mention of the most illustrious member of his family, his paternal uncle Diyanat Rai (or Bhagwandas). He also feels the need to evoke the most important patron he has had, namely the Bundela Rajput chieftain and *mansabdār* Rao Dalpat, who was killed in 1707 in the succession wars after the death of Aurangzeb. This was in fact the occasion for Bhimsen to retire from active service as a bureaucrat, and the details of his last years remain unknown.

> I, Bhimsen, son of Raghunandandas, the nephew of Bhagwandas, who at the time of 'Alamgir Padshah Ghazi received the title of Diyanat Rai and attained the *dīwānī*, have from my childhood been a friend [of the Bundelas]. I became his [Dalpat's] companion and shall describe his generos-

---

ity in its proper place. Since I was not particularly constrained by worldly matters, and did not have much work, I thought to put down matters of my own experience (*sarguzasht-i khwud*), including what I had seen and heard (*wa dīda-o-shunīda*) from the time I gained consciousness, with neither understatement nor exaggeration. By these means, I kept myself busy.

> My own experience
> Neither more nor less
> Has appeared through pen and ink
> On the face of the paper.
> When it is read
> the heart's opening will be manifest.
> So, from the all-knowing scribe above
> This work of mine received
> its title of *Dilkushā*, "Heart-opening [Narrative]".

Based on his analysis of the text, Sarkar put forward a reconstruction of Bhimsen's extended clan, beginning with his grandfather Jivmal, whose origins were apparently in the town of Etawah. Bhagwandas was the oldest of his six sons, and Raghunandan was the fourth; the others were Shyamdas, Gokuldas, Haridas, and Dharamdas. Of the brothers, Bhagwandas or Diyanat Rai (d. 1664) obviously had the most illustrious career and the others seem in some measure to have depended on his prestige and connections.[109] Haridas, for example, held a financial position in Khandesh, while Gokuldas and Raghunandan were based in Aurangabad. Diyanat Rai's sons Jogram (or Jograj) and Sukhraj also came to hold reasonable posts, the former in the elephant stables and the latter in the matter of supplying water and betel-leaves at the court. Raghunandan had three sons, of whom Bhimsen was the oldest, followed by Sitaldas and Hamirsen. When we consider this whole network over three and even four generations, including cousins and nephews, we see how a Saksena Kayastha family could effectively penetrate and to an extent take over a section of the lower Mughal bureaucracy.

[109] Khan, "A Kayastha Family", 386–94, suggests alternative versions of some of these names.

Bhimsen's account of his life and career occupies about six decades, even if not everything appears in a chronological sequence in the text. There is a first part, up to the age of roughly twenty-one, when he was a child in Burhanpur, received his education in Persian in Aurangabad with his father, and then became his assistant while Raghunandan served as *mushrif* of the arsenal (*top-khāna*). A moment of transition is then marked when it became clear that his father was unable to cope and that Bhimsen would have to seek out his own career. Over the next phase of nearly two decades he thus enlisted in the imperial service through a variety of patrons such as Da'ud Khan Quraishi, Maharaja Jaswant Singh, and Bahadur Khan. But these were also difficult years marked by some setbacks, when the rival Kayastha clan of Rai Raghunath sometimes impeded his bureaucratic advancement. One post he appears to have held over some years was that of the *mushrif* of the muster and branding of horses. Finally, a third phase was inaugurated after the Mughal conquest of Bijapur and Golkonda in the late 1680s when Bhimsen decided to enter the personal service of Rao Dalpat, whom he then served more or less loyally until the latter's death, accompanying him into situations of siege and combat and even riding atop the same elephant. We gather that by the end of his career in 1707 he had attained a modest but respectable *mansab* rank of 500. The killing of the Bundela prince effectively appears to have concluded his career as he was unable thereafter to find other amenable patrons.

In his account of Aurangzeb's eleventh regnal year (1668–9) Bhimsen unexpectedly interjects a passage in which he speaks of his early years:

Now, a brief account of my own self (*mujmal-i az ahwāl-i khwud*). When I was two years old, I used to speak about the circumstances of my death (*hālat maran*) in my previous life (*'umr-i sālif*). Some concrete signs of it were really present. When I was three years old, I rapidly forgot about those things. My father (*walī-yi ni'mat*) equally tried hard to get me to forget those words. I spent seven years of my childhood in Burhanpur and another seven years in the city of auspicious foundation [Aurangabad], where I learnt to read and write, and gained knowledge of a proper conduct in the company of older people (*buzurgān*).

This enigmatic passage seems to refer to a widely held folk belief in northern India that someone who dies prematurely in an abrupt or violent fashion retains some memories of that life into their next incarnation. Eventually, as the individual grows into adolescence or even before (as was the case with Bhimsen) such memories fade away. The same passage continues:

> Mir ʿAbdul Maʿbud, who held a rank of 500, and was the *dārogha* of the arsenal (*top-khāna*) worked together with my honoured father, and had a close brotherly relationship with him. He cared for me even more than for his own children. In the matters of my education, archery, and the use of matchlocks (*barkandāzī*), he meticulously supervised me. Thanks to the grace of that man, I received an enormous benefit. When the Mirza Raja [Jai Singh] became the governor of the Deccan, my honourable father decided to move towards retirement. At that time, he decided to make me his deputy. As an assistant, this unworthy person had the good fortune to look after different departments and the wealth my father had accumulated from the *jāgīrs* in Burhanpur. But I did not understand the value of that wealth, and I began to squander it.
>
>> The fact is that my heart was really not in it.
>> Don't ask for this world,
>> For silver and gold are nothing.
>> From the viewpoint of the wise,
>> Pearls and rubies have no value.
>> In whatever you see,
>> God is really manifest.
>> That is: except for God,
>> Nothing else exists.[110]

This flight of ascetic mysticism seems appropriate from the viewpoint of a man who has retired from active life in Mughal and Mughal-related service. But it is also through such passages that Bhimsen departs from the fairly orderly and sequential narration of politico-military events that comprise the bulk of his narrative. It is naturally the latter aspect of his text which has usually been prized by historians, especially bearing in mind the relative lack of chronicles for

---

[110] British Library, Or. 23, *Nuskha-i Dilkushā*, fl. 38b; compare the translation of these passages in Bhimsen, *Tarikh-i-dilkasha*, trans. Sarkar, 63–6.

Aurangzeb's reign, and the directness of Bhimsen's approach to matters. The Marxist historian Irfan Habib, to mention one prominent example, repeatedly cites his account to evoke conditions in the Deccan in the mid to late seventeenth century, and notes that "as a contemporary appraisal of the causes of Maratha success Bhimsen's statements are invaluable." Bhimsen is also called upon as a witness to "the oppression of the peasants in the imperial territories," which in Habib's controversial view was the principal cause of Mughal decline.[111] In contrast, the historian Athar Ali drew on the same text for interesting details of the war of succession of the 1650s, in which Bhimsen's family was ranged with the Bundelas (and Aurangzeb), and thus against Dara Shikoh. Here, he also informs the reader regarding the shifting loyalty of Raja Jaswant Singh, for example.[112] Yet, even in these political matters, the memoirist's judgement can be somewhat unexpected. His discussion of Malik 'Ambar, or Ambar Habashi, for example, is extremely positive, both regarding his military prowess and his patronage of buildings and public works. 'Ambar is described as "an experienced man [who] knew the art of war very well. He had no match as far as his mastery of administration and the love for justice and peace were concerned." Two chronograms cited for his death are fulsome in their praise of his righteousness and opposition to tyranny (*zulm*), and one includes the witty phrase: "'Ambar left and his fragrance (*khushbū*) remains."[113]

Equally interesting is his view of the Maratha leader Shivaji, who unlike 'Ambar was a contemporary of Bhimsen and figures regularly and at frequent intervals in his text. His death is reported with slight inaccuracy as part of the events of the twenty-first year of Aurangzeb's reign (1678–9), not long after that of Maharaja Jaswant Singh of Jodhpur. Bhimsen suggests that his death was caused by the curse of a Muslim holy man, Sayyid Jan Muhammad of Jalna, whose *dargāh* Shivaji had previously attacked.[114] Nevertheless, Bhimsen also stresses the Maratha

---

[111] Habib, *Agrarian System of Mughal India*, 400–1.

[112] Ali, *Mughal India*, 245–52; also Ali, "Karnatik at the end of the 17th Century", 236–44.

[113] Bhimsen, *Tarikh-i-dilkasha*, trans. Sarkar, 8–9.

[114] For Jan Muhammad or Jan Allah Shah Qibla (d. 1682), see Green, "Auspicious Foundations", 88–9.

ruler's positive qualities, including the tight organisation of his cavalry, which reputedly numbered 40,000 horse. The Machiavellian side
of Shivaji had already been noted by him in his narrative of the celebrated encounter with the Bijapur general Afzal Khan in 1659, in which
he embraced him and at the same time savagely disembowelled him.
He also provides a fairly elaborate account of Shivaji's failed attempt
at reconciliation with the Mughals in 1666 and his subsequent escape
from Agra. His closing judgement is worth citing in full:

> He was a straight-forward man and a matchless soldier and knew the
> administrative side of kingship well. He enjoyed the full confidence of
> his soldiers and he would seek the advice of all and [each] one before
> going on an expedition. Whatever he found reasonable and within the
> limit of his deliberations and efforts, he would execute. And he would
> never expose his plans unless and until they were actually brought into
> reality. Everywhere he laid the foundations of firm buildings and forts.
> The procurement of wealth and having a treasury was like a God-given
> gift to him. He had also mastered the art of cunning and shrewdness. His
> men would go everywhere to cause chaos and to plunder.[115]

The contrast is marked with Shivaji's son, who "always remained
busy in luxuries and enjoyments and in drinking. He did not have
any capacity too and adopted a way of life so that the servants of [his]
father's time were disturbed." Profligate and irresponsible, Sambhaji
apparently lent his ear to ill-intentioned advisers and rapidly acquired
a bad reputation. It is almost with an air of indifference that Bhimsen
notes a decade later, in 1689, that Sambhaji had been captured by
the Mughals, brought before Aurangzeb, blinded and "his shoulders . . . were lightened of the load of his head." Nor does he show
much esteem for Sambhaji's brother Rajaram, who succeeded him and
eventually died (apparently of smallpox) in 1700. Far greater regard
is manifested by him for Rajaram's wife Tarabai, who Bhimsen claims
then "became all-in-all and regulated things so well that not a single
Maratha leader acted without her order," and it was clear in the following years that she was "a stronger ruler than her husband."[116]

[115] Bhimsen, *Tarikh-i-dilkasha*, trans. Sarkar, 127: compare the description in
Apte, *et al.*, *English Records on Shivaji*, vol. I, 73.
[116] Bhimsen, *Tarikh-i-dilkasha*, trans. Sarkar, 232, 256.

A Narrative of Decline

As noted above, the chronology of Bhimsen's text is largely congruent with the reign of Aurangzeb, even if it contains occasional remarks on the preceding period. The bulk of the events dealt with have to do with the Deccan and southern India, with episodic mentions of Hindustan. As we have noted, the overall chronology can be divided into three sections, each of roughly two decades. The problem then remains of determining whether there is some further logic to the narrative arc. We would argue that it is indeed possible to discern an underlying declinist organisation to the work. There is a first moment when cities such as Burhanpur and Aurangabad come under Mughal rule and are built up gloriously, and this is undoubtedly the high point, corresponding to the reigns of Akbar, Jahangir, and Shahjahan. Bhimsen goes so far as to imply that at this time the conquest of the Deccan could actually have been completed by the Mughals, were it not for the underhand complicity between 'Abdur Rahim Khan-i Khanan and the Deccan rulers. This high point coincides with Bhimsen's own upbringing in these very cities in the latter years of Shahjahan's reign and the early years of Aurangzeb's rule. He recalls an idyllic time around 1660 when Shayista Khan was able to "bring about a state of peace and prosperity . . . with complete satisfaction." Even modest Mughal officials lived comfortably within their regular emoluments and "hated to accept bribes"; Bhimsen's own father, with a rather modest *mansab*, "led a very decent life with all the suitable luxuries and prosperity." Wheat, pulses, and barley were available at very low prices, and the cost of fodder was so reasonable that cavalrymen could maintain their expensive Arab horses and still provide amply for their families. New buildings and gardens sprang up and people could "spend lavishly on the marriage ceremonies . . . and [they] threw parties and feasts for their friends."[117]

Economic historians who have read these claims too literally have been disappointed to find that official reports of prices in Aurangabad were far higher (in fact, well over double) what he claims, and have therefore concluded sadly that "either his [Bhimsen's] memory was

[117] Ibid., 31; British Library, Or. 23, *Nuskha-i Dilkushā*, 20b.

playing him false or the low prices did not prevail for long."[118] In reality the baseline of such a Golden Age of a land of milk and honey was necessary for his rhetorical structure. The decline then begins for him as the Mughals push further and further into the Deccan in the 1670s and 1680s, and, paradoxically, it accelerates after their decisive victories and the fall of Bijapur and Hyderabad. This inaugurates a situation in which a Mughal–Maratha dyarchy or implicit condominium takes firm hold. It is understood that the death of Aurangzeb in 1707 will mark a further point of inflection in the slippery slope of decline.

Historians of the empire have often preferred to ignore the fact of the overall declinist emplotment of the narrative, preferring to simply treat Bhimsen as an "objective" reporter of his circumstances rather than someone who, as an Ottoman historian of similar materials puts it, employed "rhetorical devices that served more to express dissatisfaction with the present than to portray a historical reality."[119] An example of this is an essay by John Richards, where he states:

> During the first three decades of his imperial service (circa AD 1658–89), Bhimsen held a succession of respectable posts as a lower- and middle-ranking imperial *mansabdār*. For this period, he gives an account of a generally prosperous imperial structure. The empire confidently expanded into the Deccan at the expense of the two remaining Muslim sultanates of Bijapur and Golconda and successfully absorbed the rural aristocracy of western India, the Marathas, into its service. For the latter two decades (*circa* 1689–1707), Bhimsen, after a brief retirement, accepted an appointment as a secretary and deputy of Dalpat Rao Bundela, the Raja of Datia. The latter was an extremely capable Rajput field commander who followed his family's tradition by becoming a high-ranking Mughal noble in the emperor's service. From this vantage point, Bhimsen's account becomes much more sober. He describes the steady demoralization, the general devastation, and the disarray of the imperial territories in the south as the endless wars against the rebellious Marathas dragged on.[120]

---

[118] Habib, *Agrarian System of Mughal India*, 100.
[119] Fleischer, *Bureaucrat and Intellectual*, 268.
[120] Richards, "Norms of Comportment", 270–1.

The point to be made is that Bhimsen is very much a moralist, and even if he does not care to place his text directly under the sign of "advice literature (*nasīhat*)", we are constantly made aware that this is also a family and community history written for the benefit of the extended clan of Kayasthas in Bundela service.

The moralising can sometimes take improbable forms, such as in an anecdote which marks the death of Shahjahan in 1666. This emperor, we are assured, was generally known for his praiseworthy acts and moral conduct, even if this was expressed in an unusual manner (*ba tarīq-i nudrat*). It thus happened that a *mansabdār* of 500 rank called Rustam had a beautiful aunt; the emperor's roving eye fell on her and she was taken by him into his pleasure quarters. When Rustam came to know of this, he felt his honour was violated and he killed her, because of which he was then taken into custody for appropriate punishment. The emperor, who was angry and frustrated at the death of this lovely woman, summoned him to his presence. Commands were then issued for his summary execution but the other courtiers, who recognised Rustam's manliness and soldierly qualities, dragged their feet on the matter. However, rather than getting angry, Shahjahan reflected and decided eventually that Rustam should be given an additional 200 *zāt* in his *mansab* rank, as well as a saddled horse, a robe of honour, and some jewels. When the prince Dara Shikoh queried the decision, Shahjahan apparently replied: "My anger, which is intense at this time, is inclined to destroy all opposition to me. But forbearance too is a part of the generosity of rulers. So, I vanquished my anger. And in thanks for this great victory, I gave a concession to this person." Bhimsen thus carries away a lesson about this act of imperial lust disguised as virtue enigmatically expressed in this hemistich:

> In this vast wilderness,
> There is a mystery
> That is revealed
> only to the intoxicated.[121]

When one turns to the imperial decline that Bhimsen sees as characteristic of the closing decades of the seventeenth century, it is interest-

---

[121] Also see the translation in Bhimsen, *Tarikh-i-dilkasha*, trans. Sarkar, 42–3.

ing to analyse the varied structure of his explanations. One approach he takes is generic and cyclical, for empires and states did rise and fall at regular intervals, and even the power of great heroes of the past (such as Jamshid) proved ephemeral. Bhimsen also reflects briefly on the occasion of the fall of Hyderabad to the Mughals, on the earlier defeat of Vijayanagara in 1565 when Ramraj Karnataki, a glorious ruler who had been endowed with a throne and crown (*rāja-i 'azīm al-shān sāhib-i takht-o-tāj*), and who possessed incalculable wealth and a huge army, received his comeuppance on account of his arrogance and carelessness.[122] But moving beyond this, it is striking where he, as a bureaucrat and *jāgīrdār*, finally seeks to locate the blame. Everything is laid at the door of the rapacious *jāgīrdār*, the tyrannical zamindar, and the fearful and insecure revenue collector (*'āmil*), all breathing down the necks of peasants. Significantly, the emperor Aurangzeb himself is presented in all of this as the very paragon of virtue, somewhat innocent of the chaos around him. Bhimsen's admiration and even adoration of the emperor becomes very clear at the time of his death in 1707:

> After a few days, the emperor adorned the throne of the other sacred world (*'ālam-i quds*), and there was a great commotion on earth and in that time. This happened on the Friday, 28th Zi al-Qa'da of 1118 H., fifty years and two months after the accession of 'Alamgir. Within three hours, I began to compose a chronogram. The second hemistich came to my mind as: *Aurangzeb Ghāzī rū dar zamīn nihuft*. The other line was: *Bidār gasht fitnā insāf-o-'adl khuft*.
>
> The *ghāzī* Aurangzeb has hidden his face in the ground.
> Sedition awoke, and justice went to sleep.

It is thus clear that from Bhimsen's point of view this death – even if long anticipated – was a major disaster, representing the end of a long period of just rule and the beginning of an epoch of chaos. He praises the emperor: "Whatever qualities were needed for rulership, they were present in his high-statured personality. From one morning to another, besides prayer and the pursuit of truth (*haqq parastī*), he had

---

122 British Library, Or. 23, *Nuskha-i Dilkushā*, 94b–95a; the passage is omitted in Bhimsen, *Tarikh-i-dilkasha*, trans. Sarkar. It appears from the details that Bhimsen drew here on the chronicle of Firishta, in its section on Ahmadnagar.

no other activity. Even when he became old and weak, he did not grow negligent. His hand was ever oriented to work, and his heart to the Friend [God], with ethics ever present in his mind."[123]

Bhimsen reproduces a set of anecdotes about Aurangzeb, all intended to demonstrate various aspects of his personality, ranging from humour, self-deprecation, and sarcasm, to piety, bravery, and devotion to justice. Clearly, over the emperor's long reign and even longer life such materials had accumulated and circulated both in court circles and even beyond. One such anecdote runs:

> A certain man appealed for justice on a number of occasions, and each time the emperor would give an order [in his favour]. Still he was not satisfied that he had received justice. One day, when the emperor was riding, he addressed him in complaining terms. The emperor lowered his head into his chest in thought. Then he said: "If you are unable to obtain justice, pray to God for another emperor."

A somewhat different anecdote is intended to demonstrate that the emperor's prayers for good things were usually acceptable to God. When the town of Islampuri, which was known as Brahmapuri, on the banks of the Bhima, came to be flooded on account of excessive rains, causing great damage, it was reported that the emperor simply wrote a prayer (*dū'ā*) on a piece of paper and ordered it to be cast into the river. At once the waters began to recede and the panic of people, both great and small, was assuaged. Bhimsen maintains that Aurangzeb always reposed faith in God (*tawakkul*), and that he conformed to the highest standards of etiquette (*ādāb shi'ār*). Here is his summing up of this monarch, virtuous to the point of being thaumaturgical:

> In terms of determination and effort, he was so strong that he fought a *jihād* in the Deccan for thirty years. In terms of his faith (*dīn wa ā'īn*), he was very steadfast. In matters of justice, he was so strict that he would not even forgive himself. Twice or thrice a day, he would sit on the throne to deal with matters of justice. He possessed fortitude (*hilm*), forgiveness, and good conduct as well as generosity. He was always attentive to giving time for the people. He dealt with excellent dervishes and divines

---

[123] British Library, Or. 23, *Nuskha-i Dilkushā*, 158b–159a.

(*durweshān wa sāhib-i hāl*) with humility, and was respectful even to their
rags. He always kept his word, and lived up to his promises, ever ready to
meet the needs of the indigent. Everything in matters of the treasury and
justice always took place according to his written orders. He kept a check
on himself even when he was enraged. Besides being brave, he was also
far-sighted. He combined political acumen (*siyāsat*) with incisiveness and
intelligence (*farāsat*). He was also of an ascetic temperament. He always
kept in mind the rights (*huqqūq*) of other people. He would insist on the
proper training of servants (*khadam*) and men of the army, to remove
their vices. It is a general rule that man's temperament is made up of four
elements – earth, water, fire and wind – but no other rulers of the near or
distant past can compare to this one in this matter.[124]

As Bhimsen sees it, Aurangzeb's qualities had been visible even
when he was a mere child in the court of his grandfather Jahangir, and
he illustrates this with a story (which in fact took place during Shahjahan's reign) of how two maddened elephants were fighting and could
not be separated. The emperor ordered the princes Shuja‘ and Aurangzeb to deal with the elephants but Shuja‘'s horse was terrified and
would not advance. Aurangzeb's horse on the other hand reached the
trunk of one elephant which then charged at him. But Aurangzeb hit
the elephant's forehead with such force with his lance that the animal
turned back in fear; impressed, his grandfather praised him and gave
him the title of Aurangzeb Bahadur. Later, during Shahjahan's reign, he
was apparently victorious in the campaigns against Qandahar, Balkh,
and the Rana of Chittor, and as *sūbadār* of the Deccan he captured the
fort of Daulatabad and founded the city of Aurangabad. Nevertheless,
against the wishes of the other brothers, Dara Shikoh was given superior status (*karār-i rāj-i ‘ālī*). In Bhimsen's version, Aurangzeb attempted amicably to end the quarrel (*qat‘-i khusūmat*), but despite his efforts
he was not successful and constrained to enter into conflict. He thus
fought four battles in a year, the first against Maharaja Jaswant Singh,
the second against Dara Shikoh in Samugarh, the third against Shuja‘
at Khajwa, and the fourth a repeat engagement against Dara Shikoh
in the neighbourhood of Ajmer. In each battle he was victorious, and

---

[124] Ibid., 160a.

finally he was able to enter Shahjahanabad with all dignity and sit upon the throne.[125]

Once enthroned, Bhimsen's Aurangzeb proved an ideal monarch. He engaged in hunting and pleasure, ensured justice, populated the country, worshipped God, and pursued the truth, all of which were a part of his innate disposition. In the twenty-fifth regnal year he was able to take Bijapur and Hyderabad through force of the sword, making both their rulers prisoner. That sedition-monger, the hellish Sambhaji – son of Shivaji – was beheaded, and the land of the Deccan to the shores of the sea known as Rameswaram was brought under his control. These additional lands were given over to the salary (*tankhwā*) of the emperor's servants or held in the *khālisa*. In Bhimsen's view, though splendid jewels had been accumulated in the treasury since the time of Akbar, the additional rare jewels seized from the sultans of Bijapur and Hyderabad were such that their value could only be estimated by God.

In addition to all his public and official qualities, Bhimsen points out that Aurangzeb knew several languages (*ba aksar zabān āshnā*), and for his time was unique in his conversational witticisms and pleasantries (*latīfa gū'ī*). Despite all these accomplishments, some days before his death he made a will to the effect that his coffin should be prepared like that of a dervish, and not decorated like that of an emperor. He asked to be buried in a corner of the precincts of the shrine of Zain al-Haqq, adjacent to the tomb of Burhan-ud-Din Awliya, 2 *kos* distant from Daulatabad. He also asked that his grave should have no building over it (*qabr-i pukhta*), and in view of his piety everything was carried out according to his will.

But the will (*wasīyyat*) itself created a set of issues. In it the following division was laid out: the prince Shah 'Alam was to inherit the territory from Kabul to the vicinity of Akbarabad-Agra; Muhammad A'zam was to get the area from Akbarabad to the river Bhima; and Kam Bakhsh was to receive Bijapur (and presumably Hyderabad as well).[126] The most prominent *umarā'* who had been trained in Aurangzeb's

<hr>

[125] Ibid., 160b.
[126] Ibid., 160b–161a.

Image 4.3: The emperor Aurangzeb-'Alamgir
with a minister.

court were to be retained by one or the other. This return to Ching-gisid tradition was hardly to everyone's taste, and the emperor's death led each prince to make his moves. Muhammad A'zam, who was on his way to take over the governorship of Malwa, hastened back, came and paid his respects to the body, and consoled his sister Zinat al-Nisa as well as his father's wife Udaipuri Mahal, the mother of Kam Bakhsh. According to the emperor's will, he then sent the bier off for burial. Since it was the custom that the former emperors all had a posthumous title – Babur as Firdaus Makani, Humayun as Jannat Makani, Akbar as 'Arsh Ashiyani, Jahangir as Jannat Ashiyani, Shahjahan as Firdaus Ashiyani – 'Alamgir was given the name 'Illiyin Makani (which was eventually not retained). Hamid-ud-Din Khan, son of Sardar Khan, who was a close servant and knew the emperor well, accompanied the bier bare-headed and barefoot. For his part Kam Bakhsh, who had been sent to the governorship of Bijapur, held his ground and consolidated his position there.

Bhimsen notes, rather flatly and with little commentary for the implications, that on 10th Zi al-Hijja, Tuesday, the day of 'Id al-Zuha, Muhammad A'zam ascended the throne in an effective rejection of the idea of division. His various sons had their *mansabs* increased and were ordered to appear in Hyderabad. The Amir-ul-Umara Asad Khan was also given a higher rank but he did not appear in court to pay obeisance, and instead made many fine excuses. The new king also sought out some of the other crucial *umarā* and offered them rewards and promotions that are listed in some detail. More to Bhimsen's own direct interest, Zu'lfiqar Khan Bahadur Nusrat Jang made his way near Hyderabad and appeared in the royal presence, accompanied by Rao Dalpat Bundela, who was now of 5000 rank, Ram Singh Hada of 4000 rank, Sujan Singh Rathor, and Chattrasal Rathor. For this immediate show of loyalty, all these latter men also had their ranks increased and received new titles of Khan and Raja, as well as standards and kettledrums. In the process Bhimsen was also able to attain a *mansab* rank of 500, the high point of his career.

Preparations were now made to face the main challenge, in the form of the senior prince Shah 'Alam, based in Hindustan. As Bhimsen notes, most of the *umarā* were not enthusiastic about accompanying

Muhammad A'zam, believing that he was not properly informed about the situation in the north, but they were still seduced by his sweet words and went along. Further, some close servants of the ruler had their heads turned by the fact that he had now formally ascended the throne. In their unnecessary haste some of the smaller and larger cannon as well as many gun-carriages and other supplies were left behind in Ahmadnagar and Hyderabad, and they thus set out for Hindustan with an incompletely supplied baggage and train (*bhīr-o-bangah*). Muhammad A'zam apparently had his own notions of chivalric warfare and declared: "Warfare with cannon is child's play. Besides swords, nothing else is worth experimenting with." It gradually became clear that relations between him and the late emperor's nobles were turning sour, as they also did not appreciate the disparaging words he habitually employed about his brothers. Some of the Deccani *umarā'* deserted for the service of Kam Bakhsh, while several senior figures dragged their feet, claiming ill health. All in all, there was a certain inevitability to the dénouement.

Bhimsen is a significant eyewitness for the eventual battle that took place at Jaju, south of Agra, in early June 1707, as well as the preceding march there from the Deccan in late April and May.[127] All along the way, logistical and tactical errors were committed, leading to a large number of deaths in the army and among the camp followers. We gather that when the battle was finally engaged, many of those who were wearing heavy armour and chain-mail suffered greatly in the blazing summer heat, exacerbated by insufficient water. The early skirmishes seemed to favour Muhammad A'zam and his son Bidar Bakht, but the tide began to turn. In the midst of the engagement a crucial attack was mounted by Baz Khan Afghan, who was in the service of Prince 'Azim al-Shan, against the contingent of Zu'lfiqar Khan Nusrat Jang. In the process two of his chief lieutenants, Ram Singh Hada of Bundi and Rao Dalpat Bundela, were killed – in the case of Rao Dalpat a ball from a swivel-piece (*gola-yi zambūrak*) entered through his chin and came out through his back, lodging in the arm of Bhimsen

---

[127] Various narrative sources for this battle and campaign, including Bhimsen's account, are discussed in Irvine, *Later Mughals*, ed. Sarkar, 11–35. The name is spelt "Jajau" by Irvine.

who was seated behind him on his elephant. Nevertheless, the attack
was repulsed and things might have turned out differently save for the
fact that Zu'lfiqar Khan dismounted from his elephant, retired from
the battle, and eventually fled on horseback to Gwaliyar. As Bhimsen
remarks with some bitterness: "If Nusrat Jang, as required by his apparent loyalty, had joined actively with the other leaders in the attack,
and had even for a little while held his own in the battle, all the difficulties that fell upon A'zam Shah would never have happened."[128] In
reality, Zu'lfiqar Khan had never been too enthusiastic about the combat and was quick to seize his opportunity. The Bundela and Hada
contingents now pulled away, carrying the bodies of Rao Dalpat
and Ram Singh.

The closing pages of Bhimsen's account are thus somewhat morose, as he continues to recount the manoeuvres of the *umarā* in and
around the court in the aftermath of the battle.[129] Though wounded
himself, he accompanied Rao Dalpat's corpse (along with the Bundela
chieftain's younger son) for its cremation at Dhamsi, south of Agra,
and then made his way to Orchha and Datiya. Finding little to en-
courage him there because of internecine familial disputes among the
Bundelas, he then retreated to Gwaliyar and eventually returned to
try and find favour at the court of the new emperor Bahadur Shah.[130]
Though unable to do so for himself, it appears that both Bhimsen's
son and his adopted son obtained minor positions with the prince
Jahan Shah, one of the emperor's younger sons. His narrative ends then
with a chronogram inserted in a verse for the year of completion of
1120 H. (1708–9), assuring the reader that he has truthfully recounted what took place in its time, balancing the good and bad of every
person he has encountered in order to keep these events fresh in the
world. However, as Sarkar noted, "we know nothing of his death, nor
of the after-history of his family."

[128] British Library, Or. 23, *Nuskha-i Dilkushā*, 166a; Irvine, *Later Mughals*, 30.
[129] This included Raja Jai Singh Kachhwaha, who had accompanied Muhammad A'zam from the Deccan, but then switched sides.
[130] For the disputes between Rao Dalpat's sons, Ramchand, Bihari Chand, and
Prithi Singh, see Shahnawaz Khan, *Ma'āsir ul-Umarā*, text, ed. 'Abdur Rahim
and Ashraf 'Ali, vol. 2, 317–23; trans. Beveridge and Prashad, vol. 1, 442–6.

Anomalies and Excursions

As we have remarked, while Bhimsen's text may chiefly follow the political events of his time from the perspective of a participant-observer, other aspects of it also merit attention. The text includes descriptions of towns and other sites that strike him as interesting, including for religious reasons. Bhimsen equally evinces a great interest in genealogies, especially of Rajput and other Hindu rulers, including the Marathas, and his genealogical trees easily stretch back seven or eight generations. He rarely cites other texts, though he does mention the *Akbar Nāma*, and refers in vague terms to some "Indian books (*kutūb-i Hindī*)" at one or two places. We can be certain, nevertheless, that he had received the education of the mid-seventeenth-century Mughal *munshī* in its broad contours and was able to quote the Persian classical poets. He was equally capable of showing his Indic knowledge, such as when he refers for the first time to "the river Narmada, which is one of the seven famous rivers like the Ganga, Jamuna, Godavari, Sarasvati, Narmada, Sindhu and Kaveri of India, just as there are seven immortals like Aswatthama, Bali, Vyas, Hanuman, Bibhishan, Kripacharya and Parashuram."[131] As we shall see below, his knowledge of the religious sites he visits can at times be shaky, but it is all the more interesting for being based on oral information from local interlocutors rather than mechanical textual transmission.

Early in his account Bhimsen gives us a view of his visit as a child of around ten to the site of Trimbak along with his father Raghunandan. The site was considered auspicious as the Gangadwar, or the origin of the river Godavari. Raghunandan was apparently keen on visiting the place in order to be a patron to charitable acts of public feeding, as well as to perform the ceremony of *parikrama* (circumambulation). He went accompanied by a large entourage and was given a suitable welcome by the *qil'adār* of the Mughal fort, whom he knew fairly well. As Bhimsen tells it, the spot was a gathering place for mendicants,

---

Ramchand's relations with Rao Dalpat were poor and he had intrigued against him earlier.

131 Bhimsen, *Tarikh-i-dilkasha*, trans. Sarkar, 18.

mystics, and *sanyāsīs*, some of whom came from as far afield as Hardwar, especially for the *simhastha* festival which took place every twelve years. But as could happen on such occasions, there were also violent disputes between different groups of armed ascetics in which a "huge number of people" could be killed, a matter of some chagrin for Bhimsen. Other disasters also occurred periodically, such as when a large cave full of water collapsed, leading to the destruction of a number of Brahmin houses located nearby. Nevertheless, Raghunandan was apparently seduced by Trimbak and Gangadwar to the point that, after this visit, he "got pleasure only in mixing with mystics and saints and developed utter hatred for this world and the things connected with it." He also profited from the occasion to take his young son along for a visit to the Ellora caves, which left a deep impact on Bhimsen's impressionable mind. He thus recounts an oral tradition according to which a prosperous ruler (called Raja "Abal") was cured of a disease to his skin through a miracle and decided to make a sizeable temple to Mahadev, with "many halls within halls and sculptures of every size, big and small . . . carved on their ceilings and walls."[132] The extent of the site was such that Bhimsen felt such a task could not have been accomplished without divine intervention.

We learn from his account that, until nearly the age of fifty, Bhimsen had not visited Hindustan, or even crossed the river Narmada. The first time he did so was in 1698, when he was sent by Rao Dalpat to clear the latter of false accusations made against him at the imperial court. While visiting Mathura, Bhimsen made it a point to make a detour to Brindavan. Of this place he writes, very much in the mode of a devout Vaishnava:

> I went to Brindavan, three *kos* off, a wonderful place to behold, which leaves "no sense in the body" [quotation]. Love and devotion increase in the heart on seeing the place. A very charming spot but, alas, I visited it when my mind was distracted. Why should a place, where Sri Bhagawan played his *rasa-krīda*, that is merriment and sport, not be delightful in the eyes

---

[132] See Sharma, "Narratives of a Place Named Ellora", 73–111, which recounts a legend of a king suffering from leprosy; also see Ernst, "Admiring the Works of the Ancients", 98–120.

of those who seek Him? O protector of the poor! Give us heart that your seekers may not neglect to remember and recite your name, and by remembering you may live happily. Have mercy on this sinful slave, so that he may attain emancipation and escape from distraction![133]

Bhimsen's fascination with temples, and Vaishnava temples in particular, increases considerably in the 1690s. This was the phase after the fall of Bijapur and Hyderabad, when he wound up spending considerable time in the Karnatak, and more particularly in the Telugu and Tamil country. In a reflective passage on the matter he wrote: "The temples in the Bijapuri and Hyderabadi Karnatak are beyond numbering, and each temple is like the fort of Parinda and Sholapur. In the whole world, nowhere else are there so many temples. The cause of the building of these temples is that the country is very wealth-producing, every year it yields four crops, and a large revenue is raised, the amount of which is known only to the Recording Angel."[134] Among these temples was the Tirumala-Tirupati complex, which Bhimsen had occasion to visit once, probably in the late 1690s, at around the time of the marriage of his young son Shambhunath in Hyderabad. He found it enormously impressive as an achievement, especially the monumental gateways on which "they have spent not less than three or four lakhs of rupees, [and] on most others thirty or forty thousand rupees." It was a rapid visit, and Bhimsen's impressions on some matters are rather confused. For instance, while he notes the existence of the important Kodanda Rama temple, he states repeatedly that the principal shrine on top of the hill is devoted not to Venkateshwara but to Lakshmana (or "Lachman"). He says: "They have made an image of Lachman of black stone, and put on it costly clothes and ornaments. This idol cannot be moved; round it they place some other idols. Every night they bring out of the temple one of the images, mounted sometimes on the figure of a lion, sometimes of a *garuda* or peacock (*sic*: for eagle), made of copper and wood, with wheels like carts. There is

---

[133] Bhimsen, *Tarikh-i-dilkasha*, trans. Sarkar, 213; British Library, Or. 23, *Nuskha-i Dilkushā*, 127a.

[134] Bhimsen, *Tarikh-i-dilkasha*, trans. Sarkar, 193; British Library, Or. 23, *Nuskha-i Dilkushā*, 112b–113a.

a great display of pomp amidst a large gathering of sight-seers." He also mentions certain special occasions such as Dasahra and Diwali, as well as festivals when there is a chariot (or *rath*) taken out in procession. The public distribution of food, "cooked daily at great expense," is another aspect that strikes him, and the fact that this supports a great number of mendicants and ascetics, including people who "come from thousands of *kos* off out of devotion." Such a place attracts its share of wonders, including a pair of white birds which appear regularly to be fed rice and milk; and "two large tigers [which] come outside the gate when five or six *gharīs* of the night still remain, sweep the ground with their tails, and go away."

In 1694 Bhimsen and Rao Dalpat were also part of the Mughal force that was sent out to gather *peshkash* from the rulers (referred to as zamindars) of Tanjavur and Tiruchirappalli-Madurai.[135] Here, he remarks:

> In Tiruchirappalli the supreme authority in administration is in the hands of a woman, the mother of the Raja of the place and the Raja is a child. The rule and the control of this lady are such that none disobeys her. A lofty temple named after Rangaswami with splendid decorations has been built by the Raja of the place on the banks of the rivers Kaveri and Kollidam. The local people have much piety, the pious works, alms, and *sadābarta* [distribution of food] are beyond limit. The Queen Mother often comes with full pomp for visiting the temple [as] she has a great liking for shows of all kinds.[136]

The reference here is to the celebrated Mangammal (d. 1708) of the Madurai Nayaka dynasty, and that dynasty's close relationship with the Srirangam temple.[137] On other occasions Bhimsen mentions visiting holy sites such as Tirukkoyilur and Tiruvannamalai, but his longest description is reserved for Kanchipuram, which he visited with Rao Dalpat's army in late 1691. He notes that it was one of seven great holy sites which "exceed all other places in spiritual dignity," and

---

[135] Nayeem, "Mughal Documents", 425–32.

[136] Bhimsen, *Tarikh-i-dilkasha*, trans. Sarkar, 195; British Library, Or. 23, *Nuskha-i Dilkushā*, 114a–14b.

[137] See Branfoot, "Mangammal of Madurai", 369–77.

was dominated by lofty temples. Waxing lyrical, he writes: "The two temples [Siva Kanchi and Vishnu Kanchi] together are not less in extent than the fort of Bijapur. Such buildings and four successive walls within it they have constructed, that reason is confounded in estimating the cost. Where are such stone buildings in Bijapur?" Thus, even though the width of the city was quite limited, it was immensely impressive, teeming with shops and houses, many of which were inhabited by Veda-reciting Brahmins, "grocers [and] traders of the country." There were also many reservoirs for water with stone steps, on which "large sums have been spent," that were used for ritual bathing. Interestingly, Bhimsen reckons that the recent comings and goings of the Mughal armies have had a deleterious effect on the place – they had "brought hardship to the inhabitants"; but he believes nevertheless that it still yielded a sizeable revenue which was assigned to the resident Mughal *faujdār* for his expenses.[138]

Despite this praise heaped on the monumental temples of the Karnatak, and the religiosity and charity there, Bhimsen's enthusiasm for the region is in fact rather limited. He expresses a fair degree of contempt for the "naked inhabitants of the country" who eat little more than coarse rice and gruel (*kanjī*), spiced up with a little tamarind. Lacking wheat and pulses in their diet, they remain weak and emaciated. Even their clothing is less than respectable: "the males wear a coarse kerchief around the head, a small cloth round the loins and a cotton sheet suffices for years. The higher people among them tie a thin kerchief [around the head]. The women wear a piece of cloth three or four cubits long for covering their shame, in the manner of a *lungī*, leaving their heads and breasts bare." The Deccan-based Kayastha's contempt for his southern neighbours can in fact be quite marked: "They are dark of complexion, ill-shaped and ugly of form. If a man who has not seen them before, encounters them in the dark night, he will most likely die of fright. Not to speak of white skin in this community and country, even the wheaten complexion is not to be found."[139] This is a reference to the ordinary peasants of the Telugu

---

[138] Bhimsen, *Tarikh-i-dilkasha*, trans. Sarkar, 180; British Library, Or. 23, *Nuskha-i Dilkushā*, 104a–04b.

[139] Bhimsen, *Tarikh-i-dilkasha*, trans. Sarkar, 193–4; British Library, Or. 23,

and Tamil country encountered while on the march or in the Mughal camps. Occasionally, Bhimsen pauses to mention the existence of some more exotic people still. Thus we have his description of the aboriginal Chenchu people encountered in the hilly country:

On the way between Karnul and Nandyala, the high road skirting the hills, we saw *ban-mānush* or savage men; they do not know the tongue of men who live at the foot of the hills and the villagers do not understand their speech. Their food is honey, the seeds of plants and game meat. They are very dark with hair all over their bodies. They tie leaves on their heads. They all hold in their hands arrows without feathers and barbs, and a bow (*kamān*) for hunting. They have no quarrel with [other] men. They live in the midst of the hills and pits, under shady trees, and thus escape the violence of rain and sun. The men of the [plains] villages cannot go up into these hills. If one tries, he does not find a path, as there is a dense jungle . . . They have no word for gold and silver, and showed no sign of joy at receiving *muhrs* and rupees.[140]

Where Bhimsen's direct experience ceases, he resorts to hearsay, adding exotic touches and at times lapsing directly into the vocabulary of the wondrous (*'ajā'ib-o-gharā'ib*). Malabar, for instance, is described as spacious and fertile, with the best elephants in the world. He claims to have heard that "women have authority over the country and all affairs [and] therefore it is called *strī-rāj*." Whether or not for this reason, the kingdoms only fought mock battles between them, firing their muskets into the air so that "nobody is wounded or put to any loss." Bhimsen adds that every man in that region had ten or eleven wives, and every woman had an equal number of husbands. Drawing a contrast to his earlier remarks, he asserts that "the women of that country [Malabar] are beautiful, and spend comparatively more than the people of Karnatak on apparel and food." It was a pity therefore that the Mughals rarely had contact with them.

Nuskha-i Dilkushā, 113a. Also see the discussion in Ali, "Karnatik at the End of the 17th Century", 236–44.

[140] Bhimsen, *Tarikh-i-dilkasha*, trans. Sarkar, 179; British Library, Or. 23, *Nuskha-i Dilkushā*, fls 103a–03b.

When we turn to Ceylon, the threshold of fantasy is clearly crossed. For here is an island that is mostly wilderness, and full of ferocious beasts as well as "creatures with bodies like men and faces like horses, bears, swine, and donkeys." At the same time, the possibilities of trade are considerable, especially in rubies and other gems, and the ruler is favourably disposed to merchants. Bhimsen then adds an enigmatic phrase to complete the picture: "The people of Ceylon are mostly magicians." We are reminded of a far earlier passage (referring to the 1660s), in which Bhimsen lapses entirely into the mode of "wonders and marvels".

> News arrived from the Land of the Franks that a supernatural being (*dev*) had appeared, with the head and face of a horse, and the body of a human being. The Franks had cleverly captured it alive. But in a few days, it died. But its portrayal (*taswīr*) was sent by them to the emperor. In the auspicious city [of Aurangabad], a child was born in the house of a poor man. A single eye without a head was dangling from its belly. The child's hands, feet, stomach and back were otherwise of normal appearance, but he could not move them. That single eye did not have a corresponding head. When the child needed to urinate or defecate, it used to be evident even from that [third] eye. He lived as a wonder for ten or twelve years and then died.

In passages such as these Bhimsen can appear naïve and credulous. But his is also a critical spirit, and one that can turn precisely such a gaze on institutions, communities, and even himself. He makes it clear on more than one occasion that Mughal rule was not necessarily a blessing; referring to the coastal Karnatak, for example, he writes that "during the sovereignty of Bijapur, Hyderabad and Telang, the country was extensively cultivated. Many places have been turned into waste on account of the passage of the imperial troops, which has caused hardships and oppression to the people."[141]

Among those in Mughal service, he frequently criticises not only the Afghans but also the Rajputs, even those of relatively high status. For example, in the context of the early 1680s, we learn of Kishan

---

[141] Bhimsen, *Tarikh-i-dilkasha*, trans. Sarkar, 194–5; British Library, Or. 23, *Nuskha-i Dilkushā*, 114a.

Singh, grandson of Mirza Raja Jai Singh, who had "combined in himself both the Rajput style and the ways of the Mirzas (*tarīqa-i mirzā'i*) [and] given himself over to drinking." For Bhimsen, "the barbarity of the Rajput, of which they are all proud, was manifest in his character [and] dissoluteness had become his profession." It therefore came as no surprise when one day he was killed in a brawl by an Afghan over a "woman of easy virtue (*zan-i fahshā*)." In a similar vein he criticises a certain "Jagat Singh, son of Mukund Singh [Hada], of 2000 rank," who according to Bhimsen "was always drinking wine, to the point that he was an utter drunkard (*makhmūr*)," incapable of exercising control over himself.[142] Even his master Rao Dalpat, to whom Bhimsen is generally faithful, occasionally becomes the target of his barbs, such as when he foolishly refuses an increase in his *mansab* rank because he is "seized by Rajput pride."

It would appear from some coy allusions that in his younger days Bhimsen was something of a man-about-town. An example of this is an event from roughly his twentieth year, while at Aurangabad:

> At that time, a strange event also occurred. One night, a beautiful woman (*jamīla*) appeared to me in a dream. When I awoke, I felt that wakefulness was poorer than sleep. What I had seen, and the reflection of that beauty, remained in my eyes.
>
>> It's not just that I have inscribed
>> your name on the gemstone of my heart;
>> rather, from pent-up desire,
>> I have made every teardrop into a gemstone.
>
> My heart's concern was certainly not oblivious to that attraction. One day, while walking in a lane, I spied her on a terrace. A familiarity was immediately established in her eyes. I met her, and learnt that she too had seen me in a dream. I thus spent seven years in enjoying this spectacle, but also in the service of great people.[143]

Over a decade later, however, when Bhimsen had entered his thirties, he informs us that his inner life took a different turn.

[142] Bhimsen, *Tarikh-i-dilkasha*, trans. Sarkar, 134.
[143] Bhimsen, *Tarikh-i-dilkasha*, trans. Sarkar, 63–6; British Library, Or. 23, *Nuskha-i Dilkushā*, 38b.

Until now, as is the well-known custom of my community (*mā mardūm*), and on account of my own arrogance, I had not practiced prayers (*shābdat-hā*). Through the mediation of Mayaram, son of Shitalram, of the Kayastha Gaud community, who is matchless in matters of friendship, I received the attention of an elderly and wise man – may my life and heart be sacrificed to him! From him I learnt the rules of worship (*qawānīn-i bandagī*), and by regularly following them, I transformed them into the source of my comfort.[144]

This refuge in the conventional religiosity of his community seems then to have been an anchor for Bhimsen in the second half of his career, as much as his loyalty to the dynasty that he served directly and indirectly. It is obvious, nevertheless, that he continued to frequent people across the social spectrum of those who served the Mughals, and was even able to express his admiration for the city of Hyderabad as he found it in the mid 1680s, before its conquest by the Mughals. The palaces, gardens, and lakes there, as well as structures such as the Charminar, all were the objects of his admiring and occasionally critical gaze, in contrast to the rather dilapidated state in which he found Bijapur, the capital of the competing sultanate. He seems in particular to have quite enjoyed the company of the epicurean Abu'l Hasan Qutb Shah, who he reports stayed awake most of the night "for the sake of luxuries," and had the curious habit of eating five times a day.[145]

Bhimsen's self-presentation remains that of a man who cared little for wealth, though a number of remarks suggest that this was largely a posture. He complains more than once of his lack of advancement, or that luck did not favour him. In his memoirs for 1700 he writes:

At this time, owing to certain causes and desolation, little money came from my *jāgīrs* and I suffered from a lack of resources. But I did not feel downcast, because formerly too I had no love for money, and now too I did not care for it. Men do not look at money, but at their name and honour. He who looks at his name is a man, and whoever does not have the

---

[144] Bhimsen, *Tarikh-i-dilkasha*, trans. Sarkar, 134.
[145] Ibid., 151–2.

courage (*himmat*) is not a man. So far as I have seen and experienced, courage looks all the more beautiful in the midst of poverty.[146]

Bhimsen's view thus seems to be of an idealised imperial moral economy in which the *mansabdār* both received and gave, without an eye on accumulation. This is a theme that he has already rehearsed in an earlier passage in his text, on the sad occasion of the death of his nephew (once removed) Dayaldas, grandson of the celebrated Diyanat Rai. There, he writes of how the deceased had spent his life from his early youth "in ease and comfort which very few men have attained," but also "spent large sums in expenditure and conferred favours on friends and acquaintances." As a consequence he had not accumulated a large fortune and been somewhat indifferent to gold and wealth. As for his acts, good and bad, he leaves that judgement to the Almighty, who may "give me recompense for my good deeds and shut your eyes to my bad deeds and forgive them."[147]

Concluding Remarks

The three seventeenth-century personalities and narratives that have occupied us in this chapter offer an interesting study in contrast. All belong to the lower or middling ranks of the Mughal *mansabdār* hierarchy, but they reflect the experiences of men with differing profiles. Intellectually, 'Abdul Latif was clearly the most accomplished of the three, and his capacities as a philologist and literary scholar stand out; his activities as a bureaucrat and minor diplomat are arguably secondary. In his case what is of interest is the presence of a certain tension in his narrative regarding prominent aspects of Mughal ideology, especially the relations between Muslims and non-Muslims. Without openly criticising *sulh-i kull*, as laid down by Shaikh Abu'l Fazl and his followers, one gathers that men like Latif would have preferred it if Muslims (*ahl-i Islām*) were given rather more weight and importance

---

[146] Bhimsen, *Tarikh-i-dilkasha*, trans. Sarkar, 223; British Library, Or. 23, *Nuskha-i Dilkushā*, 133b–34a.

[147] Bhimsen, *Tarikh-i-dilkasha*, trans. Sarkar, 172; British Library, Or. 23, *Nuskha-i Dilkushā*, 99a.

in the empire's make-up. At the same time, loyalty to the imperial institution, to the ruling dynasty, and to one's direct patron (in his case, Asaf Khan) were of paramount importance. The individual's honour and pride were intimately tied up with an ethic of service that may have come out of older medieval precedents, but was in the process of being modified in the sixteenth and seventeenth centuries.

These issues, and in particular themes of loyalty within a profoundly hierarchical structure, remain at the heart of Mirza Nathan's text. In his case we are dealing with a service career that centred above all on military activity, and to a lesser extent administration, in the unstable environment of a frontier of territorial expansion. Throughout his text the Mirza makes it clear that making a career was a matter of playing off one hierarchical superior against another, while relentlessly pursuing the logic of family- and clan-based solidarities within the imperial framework. With the help of such networks of solidarity, even a modestly ranked individual could publicly defy and resist a powerful figure like the Bengal governor Islam Khan Chishti. However, as we have seen, when competing demands of loyalty came from within the Mughal royal household itself, the price to be paid could be quite heavy.

By the second half of the seventeenth century, when Bhimsen Saksena was making his career in the Deccan and Karnatak, matters had evolved. Rather than Indian-born Muslims, or Iranian migrants, a significant proportion of these middling *mansabdārs* and *munshīs* now belonged to Hindu castes such as the Kayasthas, Khatris, and Brahmins. They could serve a variety of masters, whether directly or indirectly, and these might include those of Iranian or Afghan ascent, as well as a spectrum of Rajputs with different status claims and pretensions. Interestingly, after a career under figures such as Maharaja Jaswant Singh and Da'ud Khan Quraishi, Bhimsen settled for a long and loyal period with Rao Dalpat, from the lesser clan of the Bundela Rajputs. This was despite the fact that the Bundelas were a notoriously quarrelsome lot, given both to internecine disputes and recurrent problems with the Mughals. Bhimsen seems to have survived all these difficulties, again thanks to his extended clan of brothers, uncles, cousins, and nephews lodged in different niches of Mughal service. His ambitions remained relatively modest, even though he did participate in warfare, along with his principal role as a *munshī*. And like his older contemporary Chandar Bhan "Brahman", he claimed to meet up to the ethical standards of Mughal service: "to avoid greed, to work hard, to cultivate one's moral self, and to make the most of life."[148] Yet the cultivation of such modesty did not prevent him from occasionally criticising the empire as a whole, even in the person of the emperor: "I have found the men of the world very greedy, so that an emperor like 'Alamgir, who is not wanting in anything, has been seized with such a longing and passion for taking forts that he personally runs about panting for some heaps of stone."[149] A wiser emperor might have held back, then, consolidating what he had rather than pursuing territorial expansion to its bitter end in the far south of the peninsula, where Rao Dalpat threw his men at the recalcitrant fortress of Palaiyamkottai and sustained severe losses. By the time Bhimsen ended his text, a few years after the emperor's death, he might have felt justified in his judgement that less could have been more.

---

[148] Kinra, *Writing Self,* 199.

[149] Bhimsen, *Tarikh-i-dilkasha,* trans. Sarkar, 223; British Library, Or. 23, *Nuskha-i Dilkushā,* 134a.

5

On Discovering the Familiar

Wāqa'i' ki safar mihakk-i tajriba-yi ādam ast.
In truth, travel is the touchstone for Man's experience.

– Anand Ram "Mukhlis"

The World of the Capital

THE PRECEDING CHAPTERS have regularly taken us to the frontiers of the Mughal empire, whether to the east or the south, where imperial servants wrote of their lives and experiences. However, the heartland of the empire in which the capital cities were located was obviously where the great weight of the imperial apparatus was to be found. The Mughals experimented with a number of urban centres as their capitals: Agra, Delhi, Fatehpur Sikri, and Lahore being the most important. These were all sites for important building projects into which large amounts of money and materials were poured. Of these, the case of Delhi was arguably the most curious, because it witnessed two distinct projects: Humayun's building up of the site of Dinpanah in the 1530s, to which he returned briefly in the 1550s; and, more importantly, the founding and consolidation of the city of Shahjahanabad.[1] According to official Mughal chronicles, the latter project was officially begun in April 1639, and Shahjahan first took up his residence there in April 1648, implying a rapid rate of construction which appears to have diverted resources from various parts of the

---

[1] Koch, *The Planetary King*, 239–47.

empire. The same chronicling tradition focused above all on the grandeur of the "mighty defensive fort" itself, devoting rather less attention to the larger urban environment in which it was located.[2]

The location for the city was presumably chosen with some care.
The Mughals had some familiarity with this particular area because of
the presence there of the Afghan river-fort of Salimgarh, constructed
by the Surs in the 1540s and periodically used by later rulers on their
visits to the Delhi region. Further south along the western bank of the
Yamuna river were other locations that had a prestigious history, beginning with the fourteenth-century Tughluq citadel of Firuz Shah,
after which one came to Shergarh-Dinpanah, the urban complex begun by Humayun and completed by Sher Shah in the first half of the
sixteenth century on an earlier site of the Lodi dynasty. At the southern
fringes of this zone was located the celebrated *dargāh* of the Chishti
Sufi Nizam-ud-Din Auliya, in the vicinity of which the Mughals chose
to build the impressive tomb-complex for Humayun on the banks
of the river. Still further south were found other Khalji and Tughluq royal
sites and fortifications, culminating in the zone of Mehrauli, housing
the shrine of another prestigious Chishti Sufi, Qutb-ud-Din Bakhtiyar Kaki. By the 1640s, when Shahjahanabad was being completed,
none of these places had been wholly abandoned, but it is obvious that
the new capital would initially have acted as a magnet to draw some
of the population away from the surrounding areas.

One of the earliest descriptions of the cityscape of Shahjahan's
Delhi in the Persian literary tradition comes to us from the pen of Chandar Bhan "Brahman", who presumably took up residence there soon
after the court moved from Agra. In his work *Chahār Chaman*, Chandar Bhan provides an extensive and lyrical description of the city in
the 1650s, going well beyond an account of the fort and palace. He
stresses the cosmopolitan character of the urban setting, and also the
fact of its bustling commerce, an aspect that is at times obscured in descriptions which portray Shahjahanabad primarily as a political centre. Chandar Bhan writes:

---

[2] Rezavi, "'The Mighty Defensive Fort'", 1108–21. For official accounting of
the expenses involved, see Moosvi, *People, Taxation*, 199–212.

Within this impregnable fort complex (*hisn-i hasīn*), on one side a grand, impressively long, covered bazaar has been arranged, containing shops, coffeehouses (*qahwa-khāna-hā*), porticoes (*tāq-hā*), and canopied galleries (*riwāq-hā*). Here merchants (*tājirān*), traders (*saudāgarān*), impresarios (*mutamauwilān*), and goldsmiths (*sunār*) from every city and region ply their stocks of all manner of colourful merchandise for a comfortable livelihood.

> 'Iraqis and Khurasanis beyond limit
> spread their fortunes out before them;
> *Firangīs* hailing from Europe
> do likewise with choice rarities from the seaports;
> Indeed, when a king is attentive to the needs of his realm
> a path from East to West is cleared.[3]

The reference to the Europeans was not entirely fanciful, since the first embassy of the Dutch Company led by Joan Tack had already arrived in Shahjahanabad in 1648, followed two years later by the English Company's envoy Richard Davidge, who received a significant *farmān* from Shahjahan in August 1650.[4] Chandar Bhan thus claimed that the city's commercial establishments "burst with capital, jewels, commodities, silks, and choice rarities from every region," and that the bazaars were "enriched and adorned by the bustle of people coming and going." The Mughal empire's capital was apparently capable of putting other great cities of the Islamic world like Isfahan or Cairo to shame: "On every patch of open space there is some entertainer or performer, and there are *ghazal* singers, melody makers, storytellers, and expert musicians and revellers sitting and standing all over the place."[5]

---

[3] Kinra, *Writing Self*, 139. We have occasionally made slight modifications to Kinra's translations.

[4] For Tack's embassy, see Siebertz, "How to Obtain a *Farmān*", 144–65; for Davidge's letters from Delhi in 1650–1, see British Library, London, East India Company Records, IOR, E/3/22, documents OC. 2187, OC. 2196, OC. 2203, and OC. 2212. For the text and a translation of Shahjahan's *farmān*, see Hasan, "Mughal Records", 37–9.

[5] Kinra, *Writing Self*, 139.

A more prosaic account comes to us from the French physician
François Bernier, who resided in Delhi in the late 1650s and early
1660s:

> Dehli, then, is an entirely new city, situated in a flat country (*une rase cam-
> pagne*), on the banks of the Gemna [Jamuna], a river which may be com-
> pared to the Loire, and built on one bank only in such a manner that it ter-
> minates in this place very much in the form of a crescent, having but one
> bridge of boats to cross to the country. Excepting the side where it is de-
> fended by the river, the city is encompassed by walls of brick. The fortifica-
> tions, however, are very incomplete, as there are neither ditches (*fossés*) nor
> any other kind of additional defence, if we except flanking towers of an-
> tique shape, at intervals of about one hundred paces, and a bank of earth
> forming a platform behind the walls, four or five feet in thickness. Al-
> though these works encompass not only the city but the citadel, yet their
> extent is less than is generally supposed. I have accomplished the circuit
> with ease in the space of three hours, and notwithstanding I rode on horse-
> back, I do not think my progress exceeded a league per hour. In this com-
> putation I do not however include the suburbs, which are considerable,
> comprising a very long suburb in the direction of Lahor, the extensive re-
> mains of the old city of Dehli, and three or four smaller suburbs (*moindres
> faubourgs*). By these additions the extent of the city is so much increased
> that a straight line may be traced in it of more than a league and a half; and
> though I cannot undertake to define exactly the circumference, because
> these suburbs are interspersed with extensive gardens and open spaces, yet
> you must see that it is very great (*d'une prodigieuse grandeur*).[6]

The western suburbs beyond the Lahori Gate included the 'Idgah
and its environs, and areas such as Teliwaran and Mughalpura. As for
Bernier's "old city", it would have comprised the old site of Firuz Shah
Tughluq's fort, but above all the complex further south, which Chandar Bhan also refers to as *Dehlī-yi kuhna* where "many gnostics and
other holy men (*'ārifān wa darweshān*) have their final resting place . . .
such as that wise knower of truth, Khwaja Qutb-ud-Din, the essence
of eminent saints, as well as Shaikh Nizam-ud-Din Auliya, Shaikh

---

[6] Bernier, *Travels in the Mogul Empire*, 241–2; Bernier, *Un Libertin dans l'Inde
Moghole*, 237. We have sometimes modified the English translation against the
original French text.

Nasir-ud-Din 'the Lamp of Delhi' (*chirāgh-i Dehlī*), and Shaikh Hamid-ud-Din Nagauri."[7]

Bernier's vision of the city, despite his avowed cosmopolitanism, had little place for Sufi saints and their shrines. Rather, he constantly measured Delhi up against his template, namely the French capital of Paris: "[I]n regard to the comparative population of Paris and Dehli . . . I conclude, that if the number of souls be not as large in the latter city as in our own capital, it cannot be greatly less." This has led demographers to propose that the population of Delhi in 1663 must have been around 500,000, a remarkable fact considering that the court had moved there a bare fifteen years earlier. Like Chandar Bhan, Bernier underlines "its vast extent and its numberless shops," but equally he lays a great deal of emphasis on the influence on the city of the great households of *umarā'* and military personnel; in his account "the city never contains less than thirty-five thousand troopers, nearly all of whom have wives, children, and a great number of servants, who, as well as their masters, reside in separate houses; that there is no house, by whomsoever inhabited, which does not swarm with women and children."[8]

Stephen Blake's modern study of Shahjahanabad between its foundation and 1739 proposes that "the mansions of princes and great *amīrs* were grouped in three areas: along the river near the palace-fortress, about the Jami' Masjid, and on the periphery of the walled city near the main gates."[9] In the city's first phase, during Shahjahan's reign, they included the *hawelīs* of figures such as Dara Shikoh, 'Ali Mardan Khan, and Shayista Khan, as well as the vizier Sa'dullah Khan and Sidi Miftah or Habashi Khan. Dara's large mansion which apparently was constructed at a cost of Rs 400,000 was located north of the palace along the river and was adjacent to that of 'Ali Mardan Khan, near the Kashmiri Gate. After Dara's death and Shahjahan's deposition in 1658, several of these mansions changed hands, with Aurangzeb's son Prince Mu'azzam taking over Dara's establishment.

---

[7] Kinra, *Writing Self*, 142.

[8] Bernier, *Travels in the Mogul Empire*, 282; Bernier, *Un Libertin dans l'Inde Moghole*, 278.

[9] Blake, *Shahjahanabad*, 50.

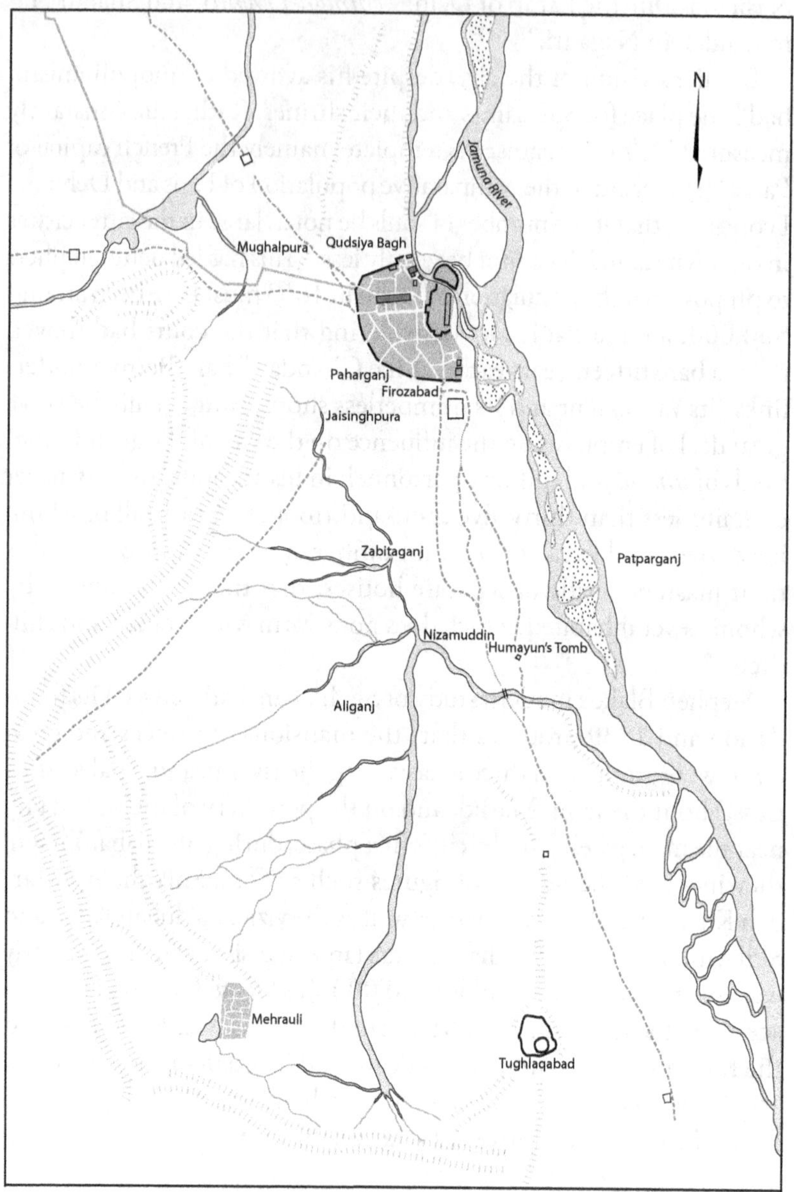

Map 4: Delhi and its environs in the
eighteenth century.

Such *hawelīs* implied a sizeable number of employees and clients, from scribes to carpet-beaters, engaged in all manner of activities; they also had stables for horses and elephants, and could even have artisanal workshops (*kārkhānas*) as appendages. The largest of them were compared by European visitors, no doubt with some element of exaggeration, to small towns in themselves. We are also aware that some important *amīrs* preferred to live outside the limits of the city, creating subsidiary settlements known generically as *purājāt*, which involved some negotiation with the empire's fiscal and legal apparatus. A prominent example of this was Jaisinghpura, founded by the Rajput aristocrat Mirza Raja Jai Singh Kacchwaha (d. 1667), to the south-west of the city. These external quarters (or *faubourgs*, in Bernier's terms) could also possess a distinctly sectarian character, such as the strongly Shi'i area around 'Aliganj and the Shah-i Mardan shrine, where the eighteenth-century power-broker Safdar Jang (d. 1754) was eventually buried.

But they could equally perform other functions, such as the settlements around wholesale grain and produce markets (*ganjs*), which in the second half of the seventeenth century were typically located to the west of the walled city. Basing himself largely on the seventeenth-century text of Muhammad Salih Kamboh, Stephen Blake has suggested that within the city walls, "although some well-to-do Hindu or Armenian merchants may have lived in houses as tall as six or seven stories, their homes were on average more modest than those of the nobles. They were not elaborately carved and decorated and didn't boast large gardens. Ordinary merchants often lived in quarters behind their shops."[10] The question of religious diversity within the city has been addressed more systematically by the architectural historian Catherine Asher:

> Before the nineteenth century we have no figures for the breakdown of Delhi's population in terms of Muslims and non-Muslims. In 1845, however, it was about equal, suggesting that the Hindu population since the inception of Shahjahanabad in 1639 was always sizeable. Even in Shah

---

[10] Ibid., 44. For his descriptions of Shahjahanabad, Blake draws heavily throughout on Salih Kamboh, *'Amal-i Sālih*, vol. 3, 29–46.

Jahan's time, highly desirable plots in the Chandni Chowk vicinity had been allocated to Hindu and Jain bankers and merchants. Wealthy Khatri Hindu merchants and Jains, including one branch of the Jagat Seth family, played a role in the city's economic well-being. So it is not surprising that between 1639 and 1850 Hindus and Jains built over a hundred temples that still survive; others must have been destroyed, for example, in the massive rebuilding of Faiz Bazaar [i.e. Daryaganj].[11]

According to Asher's tentative reconstruction, most of the temples would have been dedicated to Shiva, and only a small number to Krishna; typically, they would have been inconspicuous, and without prominent towers (*shikharas*) on the urban skyline. Still, she argues for a certain density of such establishments as well as small Jaina temples in areas such as Naya Bans (near the Fatehpuri mosque), Katra Nil, and Balli Maran, all with a strong presence of trading and artisanal communities.

It is conventionally argued that Shahjahanabad initially enjoyed a flourishing period for roughly three decades, from 1648 to 1679, followed by another period of roughly the same duration when the absence of the emperor and court shrank both population and economic vitality. We can gather a sense of the city as it still was in the late 1670s and early 1680s from the autobiographical narrative of an obscure *munshī* called Nek Rai, who spent some time there in his early youth. In his text entitled *Tazkirat al-Safar wa Tuhfat al-Zafar* (Account of Travels and the Gift of Success), he begins with his birth in the city of Allahabad in the thirteenth regnal year of Aurangzeb, or 14 Zi al-Hijja 1080 H. (2 May 1670).[12] It turns out that his grandfather Har Rai and father Lal Bihari were Saksena Kayasthas in the service of a well-known *amīr*, Ilahwardi Khan Ja'far, the former as his *dīwān* and the latter as *bakhshī*; and after his death both continued for a time with his son Amanullah Khan.[13] Ilahwardi Khan had apparently been in the

---

[11] Asher, "Mapping Hindu–Muslim Identities", 126.

[12] Alam and Subrahmanyam, "The Making of a Munshi", 61–72. The essay uses the unique manuscript of Nek Rai's text known to date: Salar Jang Museum and Library, Hyderabad, Ms. 648/07.

[13] Lal Bihari (Bhojpuri) was also the author of a significant legal text entitled *Ahkām-i awāmir wa nawāhī-yi mazhab-i hunūd* (The legal rulings on command-

administration of Shahjahanabad for a period, and Nek Rai's grand-father had used the occasion to build a fine house (*imārat-i 'ālī*) in that city, besides other residences in Mathura and Agra as well as Benares and Gorakhpur. The death of the patriarch Har Rai led to a short period of unemployment for Nek Rai's father, Lal Bihari, in the mid 1670s. The young boy then began his formal education at the beginning of his sixth year, in keeping with tradition (*az rū-i rasm-o-'adat*) with the first letters on a tablet. These years were spent first in Agra, with some relatives, and then with his father in Shahjahanabad.

It was thus in the Mughal capital, at the age of seven, that Nek Rai was married off to the daughter of a certain Daya Ram, son of Bhagwan Das Shuja'i. After a brief interlude of some months in Gorakhpur, accompanying his father's new master Tahir Khan – a journey which allowed Nek Rai to visit the famed Sufi shrine at Kichauccha Sharif – the family returned to Delhi. The city of Shahjahanabad now merits proper mention in Nek Rai's text as a wonderful place with excellent buildings and beautiful women. It seems there is an early coming of age, for Nek Rai – though barely eight or nine years old at this time – begins to speak of the sensual pleasures of the town. Shahjahanabad is a place, he writes, where hundreds of handsome Yusufs pursue their Zulaikhas; where the air is like the breath of Jesus, bringing the dead back to life. The reader is provided with many allusions and comparisons, and Nek Rai shows his mastery amongst other things of Old Testament and ancient Iranian metaphors. Thus, the *dabīrs* of the town wield their pens like the staff of Moses; the trees on the bank of the river Jamuna are like pearls in the beard of the Pharaoh; and the canal made in the time of Shahjahan by the great Iranian noble 'Ali Mardan Khan has waters that are so sweet (*shīrīn*) as to be the envy of Farhad himself.[14] Besides the incomparable fort constructed by the second Sahib-Qiran (that is, Shahjahan), Nek Rai also mentions older forts in the area such as Tughlaqabad which touch the very sky, but suggests nonetheless that life under the Timurids is far better than it ever

---

ing right and forbidding wrong of the *mazhab* of the Hindus), which has been discussed at some length in Gandhi, "*Dharmaśāstra* in Aurangzeb's India", 33–56.

14 Nek Rai, *Tazkirat al-Safar* (Hyderabad Ms.), 13b.

was under the older Delhi sultans. In fact, he concludes that if the great Amir Khusrau, emperor of the domain of speech, were alive in the 1670s he would have taken his mastery of the word even higher. Not for nothing was Mughal Delhi called "Little Mecca" (Khwurd Makka) by people in this time.

Like many of their Kayastha brethren in Mughal service, Lal Bihari and Nek Rai seem to have had a marked fondness for Chishti Sufis and their shrines. Noting the considerable devotion to the Mehrauli *dargāh* of Khwaja Qutb-ud-Din Bakhtiyar Kaki, Nek Rai cites a number of verses in his praise taken from Amir Khusrau and other authors.[15] He also recounts a well-known incident involving the other saint Nizam-ud-Din Auliya and a verse of the poet Amir Khusrau, the recitation of which occasioned the death of a certain Mulla Ahmad Mimar. Nek Rai also sheds light on the intellectual milieu of the city, and the names of teachers who were available to instruct the younger generation. In his own case, this included a certain Shaikh Khairullah, nephew of Durvesh Muhammad, who had earlier been his teacher, and with whom he studied the *Gulistān* and *Būstān* of Sa'di, the *Tūtī-nāma*, and the *Sikandar Nāma* of Nizami. After the Shaikh left Delhi for a post in the Lucknow area, Nek Rai began to study with Sayyid 'Abdul Qadir Lahauri who, he declares, was one of the best-educated men of his time.

Nek Rai and his family left Delhi not long after Aurangzeb turned his back on the city, but they lingered on far longer in Hindustan, in towns like Mathura, Agra, Gwaliyar, Jalesar, and Gorakhpur. It was only in the late 1680s, after the fall of the last Deccan sultanates and the death of Lal Bihari, that they thought to follow the emperor on his southward move. This move is one we have followed through our reading of Bhimsen in the preceding chapter, and it is a decision that still poses issues for historians of the Mughals. In his magisterial synthesis of Mughal history, John Richards proposes that Aurangzeb's move out of Delhi was at first a tactical move, meant to crush a series of rebellions, most notably that of his son Muhammad Akbar who became allied to the Marathas. What is puzzling is why he did not

---

[15] On the cult of this saint, see Kumar, *The Present in Delhi's Pasts*, 43–5.

return a decade later, once Bijapur and Golkonda had been conquered, and the Maratha leader Sambhaji had been killed. As Richards sees it, in the view of most contemporaries it was understood that

> after a brief period of overseeing initial arrangements, the emperor would lead his grand encampment and central army triumphantly north back to Shahjahanabad. As they had dozens of times in the past cadres of imperial administrators could assume those powers exercised by their defeated counterparts in each of the three kingdoms . . . Instead, the reverse occurred. Aurangzeb remained in the Deccan, year after year, fighting an endless war and hoping to reverse a descending spiral of public order and imperial power in that region.[16]

The Reinvention of Delhi

The period from 1679 to 1712 is thus an intriguing one of an imperial power vacuum of sorts in Delhi; it is followed by another period of considerable dynastic turbulence that settled somewhat only with the accession of Muhammad Shah, grandson of the emperor Bahadur Shah, in September 1719. In an analysis of this period in Delhi's history, Satish Chandra has nevertheless suggested that it would not be wise to paint it purely in gloomy colours.[17] This is for at least two sets of reasons. Firstly, though Aurangzeb and his court were no longer present in the city, it was not as if all other members of the royal family or upper state apparatus and *umarā'* had abandoned the place. To a fair extent, emperor or no emperor, it was still business as usual in the running of city and province. Those who maintained a presence were several royal women including Aurangzeb's daughter Zeb-un-Nisa, who – despite being under a form of confinement for her critical political views – continued an important patron with a salon in her residence. A crucial figure who maintained close relations with her was 'Aqil Khan "Razi", deputed by Aurangzeb to hold charge of the city in 1680, which he did until his death in 1696. 'Aqil Khan had been associated with the emperor since the latter's time as a prince in the Deccan, and was himself both a patron of the arts and a literary figure.

---

[16] Richards, *The Mughal Empire*, 225.
[17] Chandra, "Cultural and Political Role of Delhi", 106–16.

As a disciple of Shah Burhan-ud-Din Raz-i Ilahi (d. 1673), a charismatic Shattari Sufi from Burhanpur, he also had some claims to esoteric knowledge and appears to have encouraged some important Sufis to settle in Delhi in the 1680s and 1690s. Perhaps the most important such figure was the mystic and poet Mirza 'Abdul Qadir "Bedil" (1644–1721), who also counted amongst his patrons the family of Shukrullah Khan, the *faujdār* for an extended period of the Mewat region near Delhi. The same period also saw the affirmation in status of Chishti Sufis such as Khwaja Shah Kalimullah, a descendant of an established Delhi family, who had enjoyed the patronage of the princess Jahanara and others.

Secondly, as noted by Satish Chandra, the social and political dynamism of Delhi was not only the consequence of elite political impulses: "Delhi remained an important centre for trade, commerce, and manufactures" through this period, with "one of the biggest money markets of the country." Together with Agra, it was one of the two major nodes through which commodities from Bengal and eastern India passed by way of the Gangetic riverine traffic, before crossing into the Punjab, and from there to the markets of the north-west. Delhi was also strongly connected via the towns of Rajasthan to the prosperous regional economy of Gujarat, which in turn opened the doors to the trade of the western Indian Ocean. This view is a corrective to a mistaken conception propagated by authors such as K.N. Chaudhuri, who had stated that the Mughal empire had six "primate cities" in Lahore, Delhi, Agra, Patna, Burhanpur, and Ahmedabad, but then affirmed that "with the exception of Delhi, which was in a special class, all the others were important centres of trade, banking, industrial handicrafts, and agricultural processing."[18] In his sweeping overview of urban–rural relations in Mughal India, based largely on European travel accounts, the same author had equally skirted the question of the relationship between cycles of political change and urban expansion and contraction.

In this context, it may be useful to return briefly to the classic distinction made by the Austrian political economist Bert Hoselitz between what he terms "parasitic" and "generative" forms of urban-

---

[18] Chaudhuri, "Some Reflections on the Town", 86–7.

ism. Though presented in terms of modernisation theory, Hoselitz's analysis drew very widely for its historical examples, both in time and space, and concluded that the widespread prejudice which saw cities as fundamentally "parasitic" of the larger societies in which they were located had little real basis. Rather, they could in many cases be both economically and culturally generative, the more so if they were (again, in his old-fashioned vocabulary) "heterogenetic" in character.[19] For our purposes, a few aspects of his analysis are particularly worth retaining with regard to a city such as Mughal Shahjahanabad. First, even if it was founded by imperial decree, the city quickly became far more than the fragile imperial camp writ large, which observers like Bernier tended to see.[20] By the 1670s and 1680s many other social groups and cultural institutions formed the urban fabric than simply the palace and its offshoots. Second, an emphasis on the "generative" aspects of the city takes us beyond the familiar opposition between fiscal oppressors and oppressed that has long been the leitmotif of Mughal historiography. It therefore allows us a more nuanced conception of the social structure and dynamics of the city and the empire more generally.

These reflections serve as a preamble for the central personage who occupies us in this chapter, Anand Ram (1699–1751), known by the pen-name of "Mukhlis" (the "sincere"), the wealthy member of a Khatri family from Delhi but originally from Sodhara, near Wazirabad, in the Punjab.[21] A prolific author, Anand Ram is generally recognised as one of the foremost stylists of Indo-Persian letters in the eighteenth century together with Mirza 'Abdul Qadir Bedil, Ghulam 'Ali Azad Bilgrami, and Siraj-ud-Din 'Ali Khan "Arzu". He was also the personal friend of a number of scholars, most notably Khan-i Arzu, the well-known critic, poet, and lexicographer who was born around 1688 or 1689 and died in 1756.[22] Anand Ram wrote extensively and has left

[19] Hoselitz, "Generative and Parasitic Cities", 278–94.

[20] For some useful comparative remarks, see Raymond, "Islamic City, Arab City", 3–18.

[21] For a biographical study, albeit unsatisfactory in many respects, see James, *Anand Ram "Mukhlis"*.

[22] On Arzu, see Keshavmurthy, *Persian Authorship*; and Dudney, *India in the Persian World*, 25–7 (for Arzu and Anand Ram).

behind a large number of works on epistolography, on farriery, a manual for scriveners and officials, collections of anecdotes, poems and *masnawīs* in both Persian and the northern Indian vernacular, as well as a major work of lexicography, the *Mir'āt ul-Istilāh*.[23] He was also the author of some 10,000 verses and penned two *dīwāns*, one of *ghazals* and the other of quatrains (*rubā'ī*).[24] Less well known than some of these other works is a *tazkira* (biographical dictionary) containing entries on over four hundred poets with samples of their poetry. They include contemporaries such as Bedil and Arzu, as well as prestigious older figures like Faizi, 'Urfi Shirazi, and Sa'ib Tabrizi; there are also a number of poets whose works do not figure in any other collection.[25] The work that concerns us above all however is his *Badā'i' Waqā'i'-yi Muhammad Shāhī*, a well-known memoir which first came to the attention of historians because of its account of Nadir Shah's invasion of Delhi in 1739.[26]

[23] There are two editions of this text: Anand Ram Mukhlis, *Mir'āt ul-Istilāh*, eds Chandar Shekhar, Qilichkhani, and Yusufdihi; and Anand Ram Mukhlis, *Mir'āt ul-Istilāh*, ed. Sharif Husain Qasemi. For a very rapid overview of his works, see Marshall, *Mughals in India*, 75–6; and Storey, *Persian Literature*, vol. I: 1, 612–14.

[24] See Rana Begum, "A Critical Edition of Diwan-e-Anand". On Mukhlis as a translator into Persian, also see Phukan, "'Through Throats'", 33–58.

[25] Anand Ram Mukhlis, *Tazkira-yi shu'arā*, 77–8 (Arzu), 95–7 (Bedil), 97–100 (Payam). Special praise is reserved for Bedil, described as the greatest poet born on the soil of Hindustan since Amir Khusrau. Anand Ram states, incidentally, that Bedil was buried in the courtyard of the *hawelī* of a certain Betwant.

[26] Several manuscripts of the text can be found: in the Maulana Azad Library, Aligarh Muslim University, Abdus Salam Collection, 344/114; Rampur Raza Library, Loharu Collection L 22 (Accession No. BE5); National Museum of Pakistan, Karachi, Ms. 1957, 982/13, etc. According to Riazul Islam (*Calendar of Documents*, vol. 2, 67–8), the Karachi version is "the author's manuscript copy". The identification by Storey of Bibliothèque nationale de France, Paris, Supplément persan 310, as a version of the same is problematic. The part of Anand Ram's narrative concerning Nadir Shah's invasion of Delhi is extensively paraphrased by Jadunath Sarkar in his revisions and additions to Irvine, *Later Mughals*, vol. 2 (based apparently on the Aligarh manuscript). For our part, we have depended on the relatively complete and reliable manuscript in the Punjab University Library, Lahore (henceforth PUL), Persian Manuscript Pi XI/89, Accession No. 2140, though it contains some copyist's errors.

Anand Ram's family was closely associated with the Mughal court at the time of the emperor Muhammad Shah (d. 1748), and his grandfather Gajpat Rai was already an influential man who had reputedly arranged the marriage of the *amīr* Khan-i Dauran Samsam-ud-Daula. His son, Anand Ram's father Lala Hriday Ram, was in the service of *wazīr* I'timad-ud-daula Muhammad Amin Khan Chin Bahadur, father of Qamar-ud-Din Khan. We are thus particularly fortunate in his case to be able to trace details of his family and circle of friends, and to place him squarely in the context of literary and political life in mid-eighteenth-century Shahjahanabad-Delhi. This is also because a number of the major *tazkiras* of poets of the eighteenth century have notices on Anand Ram, and all of them clearly identify him as belonging to the community of the Khatris (or "Chhatris"). One of these writers, Aqa Husain 'Ali Khan, known as 'Ishq 'Azimabadi, wrote in his contemporary work *Nashtar-i 'Ishq* that, of the "Hindus of the time," he was the best litterateur, adding, "Mukhlis Anand Ram, son of Raja Hriday Ram, belongs to the brave community of the Chhatris, who have since the beginning shared in the rulership of Hindustan. He is a native of Sodhara, which is in the vicinity of Lahore."[27] A slightly later author, Ghulam 'Ali Azad Bilgrami, in his *Khazāna-i 'Āmīra*, added in a similar vein, "Mukhlis, Anand Ram, belongs to the community (*qaum*) of the Chhatris, to whom the rulership over the people of India pertains since ancient times." These writers also make it clear that Mukhlis was first trained in poetry by Bedil, and became a disciple of Khan-i Arzu after Bedil's death.

The same biographical dictionaries provide us some more indiscreet personal details on Mukhlis' life and lifestyle. Thus, Ahmad 'Ali Sandilawi states in his *Makhzan al-Gharā'ib*: "On account of his corpulence, he [Mukhlis] was excused from daily attendance on the emperor, and another person was sent in his place. He used to enjoy life, with leisure and music (*'aish-o-tarab*). In his house in Shahjahanabad, poets and the learned used to gather regularly."[28] It is reported

---

[27] 'Ishq 'Azimabadi, *Tazkira-yi Nashtar-i 'ishq*, as cited in Anand Ram Mukhlis, *Muraqqa-e-Mukhlis*, Introduction, 8–10.

[28] Sandilawi, *Tazkira-yi makhzan al-gharā'ib*, as cited in Anand Ram Mukhlis, *Muraqqa-e-Mukhlis*, Introduction, 8–9.

that he died eventually of breathing problems (*nafs al-dam*), perhaps on account of his corpulence.

We also learn of Anand Ram that, in the Mughal court-politics of the time he was reckoned closer to the Turani nobles and had for a time been the *wakīl* of Anwar-ud-Din Khan of Gopamau, later Nawwab of Arcot. It also emerges that Mukhlis progressed into a quite staid middle age from a rather dissolute youth. Thus, when young Mukhlis was a compulsive gambler (he played *ganjafa*), and his father greatly disapproved of this. The family was a rather wealthy and influential one already in the early decades of the eighteenth century. Besides the fact that his grandfather had arranged the marriage of Samsam-ud-Daula (as noted above), Lala Hriday Ram had pulled strings in order for the same noble to be made governor of Ahmedabad, and had advanced Rs 50,000 as surety on the occasion.[29]

Further details emerge from a rather curious manuscript in the British Library entitled *Muraqqaʿ-i Mukhlis* (The Mukhlis Album), made up of examples of his writing.[30] This manuscript contains autograph documents that were apparently put together for that very reason, as calligraphic exemplars rather than for their literary quality. Thus, one of the letters documents the sending of *mewa* (fruits) by Mukhlis to his master, the *wazīr* Qamar-ud-Din Khan; another documents the sending through his son Kripa Ram of *harīra* (chutney) and *achār* (pickles), made with Deccani *masāla*, to the same noble; a third is a note to Qamar-ud-Din Khan's wife (Begam Sahiba) concerning the receipt of baskets of mangoes. Occasionally, the letters detail financial transactions such as the arrival of a bill of exchange (*hundī*) of Rs 40,000 that had been demanded by the *wazīr*, or the affair of a slave-trader (*burda-farosh*) who had kidnapped the son of a certain barber. But the letters, with their incessant references to mangoes, fruit, and cooked food, certainly buttress the image of Mukhlis as an inveterate *bon viveur*. This is an aspect that we shall have occasion to remark time and again in his writings.

---

[29] Anand Ram Mukhlis, *Muraqqa-e-Mukhlis*, Introduction, 15.

[30] Anand Ram Mukhlis, *Muraqqa-e-Mukhlis*. Other collections of his correspondence include the miscellany in Khuda Bakhsh Library, Patna, Ms HL 882, *Mansūrāt-i Ānand Rām*. For a careful edition with commentary of one of his letters as *munshī*, see ʿAbdur Rashid, "Muhammad Shah's Letter", 91–110.

Mukhlis and His Memoir

Our main focus in this chapter is on Anand Ram and his account, *Badā'i' Waqā'i'* or *Badā'i' Waqā'i'-yi Muhammad Shāhī*.[31] Complete manuscripts of this text, which is divided into three parts, are somewhat rare; but they make it clear that the account runs from the month of Rajab 1145 H. to 11 Jumada II 1161 H. (December 1732 to June 1748). Mukhlis himself died in 1164 H. (1751 CE), and it would appear that he worked on this text intermittently from at least the Hijri years 1152 to 1161. At the outset of the work, he informs the reader that, one day in spring while seated all alone, it suddenly occurred to him that in the past the masters who had laid the foundations of the science of history wrote about the lives of others and incidents relating to them. But it was a matter of regret that they wrote little about themselves. So Anand Ram thought:

> If I describe my own condition, it will not be devoid of pleasure (*lutf*). Rather, it would enhance the hearts' delight of poets and impeccable men of sentiment, who are themselves intoxicated with joy (*arbāb-i wajd-o-hāl ki sar khushān-i nasha-yi kamāl and*). For this reason, my quill which spreads fragrance like a violet (*banafsha*) was employed to write some stray fragments. When it was completed, this *faqīr* gave it the title *Badā'i' Waqā'i'* (Unique Events).[32]

The work thus contains a somewhat kaleidoscopic account of events during the reign of Muhammad Shah, but deliberately remains rather personal, including a short account of a journey (*sair*) to Brindaban, the "abode of love" (*dār al-'ishq*), as well as accounts of travel to Garhmuktesar and Bangarh.

The opening passage is an occasion to present the following quatrain:

> O young man with a feeling heart,
> If you see only thorns around you,
> Don't turn away from these fragmented pages,
> For it is the story of Mukhlis the Madman.

[31] See Shafi', "Iqtibās az Badā'i' Waqā'i'", 89–124.

[32] We cannot be certain if Anand Ram was aware of the Timurid text with a variant title: see Zain-ud-Din Mahmud Wasifi, *Badā'i' al-Waqā'i'*; and for a discussion, Dunbar, "Zayn al-Dīn Maḥmūd Vāṣifī".

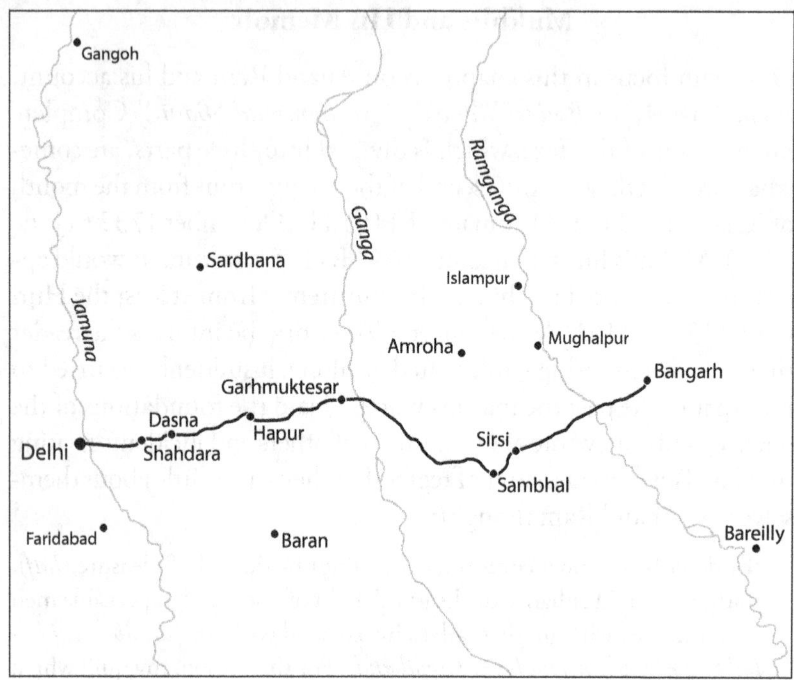

Map 5: Anand Ram Mukhlis' itinerary to Bangarh.

The particular tone of the work is announced from the very outset.
Anand Ram begins the text proper with events from the first ten days
of Rajab 1145 (December 1732), when, as he tells it, Muhammad
Shah Badshah Ghazi was ruling in the excellent city of Shahjahana-
bad, and his vizier was none other than the exalted Qamar-ud-Din
Khan, Mukhlis' own patron.

But we hear nothing of grand events at the court. Rather, Mukhlis
tells us, it was decided at this time to go on a hunt towards Mas'udabad, to the south-west, which was in the prebend (*tuyūl*) of the vizier,
and the humble *faqīr* Anand Ram had the good fortune to accompany
him.[33] Since this was the harshest season in Delhi, a fairly cold wind
was blowing, bringing various thoughts to Mukhlis' mind on the

---

[33] Mas'udabad lay to the south-west of Delhi and was in the vicinity where
Najafgarh would be founded later in the eighteenth century.

Image 5.1: Posthumous portrait of the Mughal emperor
Muhammad Shah (r. 1719–48) holding a falcon.

subject of winter. Nevertheless, the whole group, described as one of "intoxicated (*sarkhushān*) people", were undeterred by this. The life and soul of the party was apparently a certain Muhammad Jan Diwana, who had been Mukhlis' friend of twenty years, and was well regarded by one and all.

Once they had gone beyond Mas'udabad, Mukhlis and Muhammad Jan decided to wander off in the fields to inspect the wonders of nature. They were in the midst of mustard fields in flower, which appeared like a golden sea as far as the eye could reach, as if the treasure of Korah had emerged from the bowels of the earth. Indeed, Anand Ram remarks, this was a sight only comparable to the famed saffron fields of Kashmir at the time of the harvest. On this occasion, Mukhlis apparently said to Muhammad Jan: "O my friend, what reverie are you lost in that you cannot appreciate what is around you? Awake, open your eyes, and take it in. Let us spend some time in conversation and appreciate these wonders." To this Diwana replied: "You are right, I am ready and my heart is open to this. Let us take in another grain of opium and enjoy this." Since Mukhlis was not a great enthusiast in the matter of intoxicants, for which Diwana had a particular weakness, he called for his water-pipe and some coffee while the other was busy consuming his opiated wine. Mukhlis then wrote some verses in praise of the mustard fields, as did Muhammad Jan. These exchanged verses are reproduced extensively when they are by Mukhlis, less so when by Muhammad Jan. The text then turns to a later part of the same day, and Mukhlis's desultory search for some food (*shīr wa khurma*) when he had rejoined the main party. This exercise turned out to be rather difficult, as supplies were short in the area. Eventually, he was able to have some *khichrī* and *do-pyāza* made, and mentions in passing that his sons Rai Kripa Ram and Fateh Singh joined him. Some small pleasantries on domestic matters are recounted, including a minor episode in which some milk spills on their quilt.[34]

On 26 Rajab, a few days later, the party decided to make a trip to the water in order to profit from the weather, which had improved. They rented a boat on the splendid and clean waters of the river Sahibi, known for its variety of birds that could be hunted. Though

---

[34] Anand Ram Mukhlis, *Badā'i' Waqā'i'* (PUL manuscript), fl. 5b.

the weather seemed propitious, threatening clouds suddenly appeared during the hunt, followed by a sharp shower. Here again was a poetic sight very much to Mukhlis' taste. Verses addressed to Muhammad Jan follow on the rain, one of them being:

> Just as the Indian worshippers of Nanak,
> Who have invented this new faith (*tāza-mazhabī*),
> in place of the sacred thread,
> wear a golden chain,
> the silvery raindrops were tightly joined,
> and hung like a silver-gold embroidery,
> under a velvet black canopy.

When it began to pelt, panic spread in the camp and the horses were controlled with difficulty. They all passively awaited an order from Qamar-ud-Din Khan in order to return to Delhi. Mukhlis initially observed all this with some irony and humour. But it began to appear less amusing when the central support of a large tent collapsed and he had to intervene. The others in the camp then screwed up courage and it was decided to return to Delhi, some 25 *kos* away. Fortunately, the weather improved, the skies cleared, and after a whole day's travel Mukhlis was able to return to his mansion.

This opening section may appear somewhat puzzling if what that reader expects is a chronicle of courtly life and experience. These passages establish two facts. One is the importance given to Mukhlis' own subjective life experiences, even those that seem trivial. Second, they show the reader that he is both master of a certain elevated style of prose and also a perfectly competent poet. The reader expecting a political chronicle will not find much about Muhammad Shah's court in these pages as they intend to introduce the personage of Mukhlis as an author and a stylist. They also suggest that the work will tend in the direction of a sort of auto-ethnography, which the following section makes increasingly clear.

The text now turns to his sons Kripa Ram and Fateh Singh, and Anand Ram's own family life.[35] The central issue concerns the marriage of his son Lala Fateh Singh which had apparently been planned

---

[35] Ibid., fl. 8b.

now for four months. The preparations began with the making of white candied sugar sweets, and next a determination of the right time and date had to be made with the astrologers. By the Indian reckoning, 23ʳᵈ Phalgun (or 15 Ramazan 1145 H., equivalent to 12 Isfandiyar) in the evening was thought to be the properly auspicious date. According to the custom, on 2nd Sha'ban, as spring was about to commence, a group of Brahmins were fed in a *brahma-bhoj*. The next day another ritual ceremony termed *lagan* was held in which Mukhlis' close friends sent their presents, involving gold, pearls, and brocades, and in exchange they were all lavishly entertained in his mansion. These included some friends who had by now become old, toothless, and incapable of enjoying such occasions. The festivities lasted for some four days, with Mukhlis also giving away sums of money as a present to his invitees. It turned out that the marriage itself was to take place not in Delhi but in Batala, a well-known and prosperous *qasba* in the Punjab. The groom was sent out first, with elaborate preparations being made for this purpose; 200 horses and 500 *bandūqchīs* were to accompany him and the contingent. The entire wedding party that followed was made up of another 700 men and women. The groom Fateh Singh was then sent to take leave from Qamar-ud-Din Khan and received an excellent robe of honour and turban from him, as well as Rs 1001 as recompense for Mukhlis' status as a servitor of the dynasty (or *khānazād*). To make a point of it, the vizier even sent an additional 100 horsemen and the same number of footmen (*piyāda*) to join the existing escort.

On Monday, 16th Sha'ban, at the auspicious hour the party then left for Batala, with the groom all decked up with the customary flowers. The procession threw out coins into the attending crowd as it advanced, and joyful music was played by singers and instrumentalists. The first station was Sarai Badli on the way northwards, where they made a two-day stop, and further celebrations, including the taking of intoxicants and much music and laughter. Anand Ram's particular friends Sukh Ram, Sewak Ram, Chainsukh, and Jaspat Rai were among those who engaged in extravagant celebrations. But not everything was fun and games, because a certain Pir Muhammad, who had been sent along by the vizier, was troubled by vicious bedbugs (*khatmal*) in his quilt, which some malicious people found very amusing. Station by station the party then advanced towards Batala, with the sons in the advance party and Mukhlis following. In order to help them out the vizier had sent particular instructions to the *faujdārs* and *'ummāl* on the way to take care of them. 'Usman Yar Khan, who was the governor of Sirhind, added fifty horsemen and another fifty footmen to the escort, as well as offering them gifts of cash and sweetmeats.

On 2nd Ramazan they eventually reached Phillaur and remained there for a day, using the occasion to carry out ceremonies involving the renewal of their sacred threads (*zunnār*). The party then made their way to Fatehbad where they received a *parwāna* from Zakariya Khan, the governor of the Punjab province, asking them to come and meet him before going on to Batala.[36] Though time was short and the request awkward, Anand Ram decided to send his two sons with an escort to see the governor, some 40 *kos* away. When they had reached Patti Haibatpur, the *mutasaddī* of the area, Rai Bhawani Das, came to receive them and asked them to stay on since it was the festival of Holi. This was celebrated very happily and only then did they move on to the governor's residence. The *dīwān*, Raja Sangat Singh (or perhaps Jagat Singh), received them, as did a certain Kifayat Khan. When they eventually reached Zakariya Khan, they kissed his feet, and he embraced them, assuring them he counted them among his true well-wishers; the sons then retired to the sleeping quarters where the governor joined them. Later, singers and dancers were summoned and festivities were held for several hours. The sons requested that they be allowed to stay on for an additional day and the governor said he was pleased to allow it, while his servants treated Mukhlis' sons with great generosity. The older son was given a robe of honour, an additional turban, an elephant with its accoutrements in silver, as well as a supplementary escort.[37] Further presents in cash and kind were given by other Mughal officials such as Adina Beg, the *nā'ib faujdār* of Jammu. Mukhlis stresses that throughout the journey, and all the way to the wedding ceremonies in Batala, extensive amounts of money were spent,

---

[36] Zakariya Khan was the son of the powerful 'Abdus Samad Khan, a protégé of Zu'lfiqar Khan; see Alam, *Crisis of Empire*, 80–9.

[37] Anand Ram Mukhlis, *Badā'i' Waqā'i'* (PUL manuscript), fl. 15a.

largely by the bride's party but also by other Mughal officials with their generous gifts.

The narrative of the wedding now continues at greater length.[38] On 15th Ramazan, Rai Kripa Ram was sent out to make the needed arrangements for fireworks and decorations, with Mukhlis' uncle Lala Gaur Sahai also helping out in this matter, since he was a well-connected man. The expenses on this alone seem to have amounted to Rs 4000. Lala Dakhni Rai and Khan Bahadur Abu Turab Khan were also amongst those who lent a hand. The groom was mounted royal style and sent out in the afternoon, which Mukhlis states must have been an unprecedented sight for even the older people of Batala.[39] A thousand workmen were employed in these festivities; the horses in the procession were flanked by elephants, and people threw silver and gold coins, as well as flowers made of these precious metals. Through the town they proceeded until they paused at the tank of Shamsher Khan on the outskirts of the settlement (*qasba*), where there was a lovely garden. On behalf of the in-laws (*samdhāna*) a certain Raizada Kalyan Mal came out to meet them, rosewater with saffron was sprinkled everywhere according to the custom of the time, and Rs 501 gifted. The groom now changed his clothes and tied his head-dress anew with pearls, as well as his decorated crown (*mukat*).

This was the time for setting off a series of magnificent fireworks which are considered sufficiently important for Mukhlis to devote a whole section to it, punctuated by significant verses, some his own and others quoted from known poets.[40] The decorations for the occasion are compared to a flower-seller's shop in its display, the jewels to the lips of idols, and the textiles to those so greatly appreciated by the Franks. The fireworks themselves are compared to a flock of pigeons in full flight, and their golden flames apparently lit up the whole *qasba*. All in all, Mukhlis clearly wishes to insist that this was no ordinary wedding, but rather one of the most notable of the time.

These festivities went on well into the night until they reached the houses of the in-laws. The groom then dismounted and went on foot

[38] Ibid., fls 15b–16a.

[39] On Batala in the later Mughal period, see Grewal, *In the By-lanes of History*.

[40] Anand Ram Mukhlis, *Badā'i' Waqā'i'* (PUL manuscript), fl. 17a.

into the *harām-sara*, or women's quarters, while his companions remained in the reception hall (*janwāsa*). As dawn approached, the groom was seated on a throne (*singhāsan-i arūsī*), surrounded by Brahmins versed in the Vedas and Shastras, who began chanting until the first full signs of daylight became visible. The formal marriage ritual followed, with Mukhlis using a series of metaphors to describe the union of groom and bride. Women began to sing beautiful songs of love and union, again following the custom of the time. In many of these songs some insults (*dushnām*) were proffered, obviously in jest.[41] In these pages Mukhlis thus offers his readers a glimpse into the customs and practices of his community, the Khatris of the Punjab. The assumption is that the average reader in Mughal India, lacking exposure to these, will find them charming and exotic. This is a characteristic example of Anand Ram's strategy of auto-ethnography, to which he takes recourse time and again.

The next section now shifts radically in tone, and for some pages becomes more of a political and military chronicle rather than a first-person account. Mukhlis initially recounts the return of his sons to Shahjahanabad and their presentation at the court. Meanwhile, news had come that the emperor had decided to pay a visit to Akbarabad-Agra. Some 50,000 Maratha horsemen (*ghanīm-i Dakanī*) had reached the frontier of Malwa and Gujarat and begun to create chaos there. Maharaja Jai Singh of Amber was appointed to take charge of this region, but he realised that he was not in a position to handle the Marathas alone and was obliged to ask the emperor for help. As a result Muhammad Shah himself set out on the advice of high-placed courtiers in the direction of Sonepat, in the transparent guise of a hunting expedition. First, he reached Shalimar Bagh and then Talkatora Bagh, where some courtly ceremonies were held; the next stage was Khizrabad, which was on the banks of the Jamuna. Crossing the river, news kept arriving of the misdeeds of the Marathas in Bundelkhand and Bhadawar. On hearing this the emperor firmed up his resolve to confront them. Mukhlis mentions the fact of ongoing divisions among the nobles, such as Qamar-ud-Din Khan and Burhan ul-Mulk, so that the

---

[41] Ibid., fl. 18a.

emperor attempted to reconcile them, as well as appealed to the Amir ul-Umara Khan-i Dauran. This was necessary because rumours were rife by now about these differences in the Mughal ranks, which was all to the enemy's advantage.[42] The Amir ul-Umara then made his way towards Akbarabad after seeking the advice of Qamar-ud-Din Khan. It was decided that they should collectively think back to the good old days of Aurangzeb as their guide, with a proper combination of diplomacy (*tadbīr*) and force (*shamshīr*), in the firm belief that if they did so the Marathas could quickly be reduced to ashes.

Khan-i Dauran therefore forded the Jamuna and set up camp on the other shore, while Delhi was left in charge of the young prince Ahmad Shah, with Khan Zaman installed as his deputy; ceremonies were held in which the prince was moved from a mansion of Ja'far Khan in the city to the fort proper. The emperor meanwhile had plans to move via Sikandra to Agra, and instructions were given to the army to move discreetly in order not to frighten the wild animals in the vicinity. Eventually, they reached a place called Phukel, where the weather was starting to heat up (by now, we are in early Shawwal). As for Mukhlis, he was torn between his attention to the court to which he had returned post-haste and his concern for his own sons, whom he had left behind. The world of service (*naukarī*) at times does not permit one to follow one's own sentiments, he writes regretfully.

But since his thoughts remain with his offspring, a new section begins on the return of his sons after the wedding in Batala.[43] It appears that right till 18th Ramazan, the festivities had continued in Batala. The party then accumulated various goods for their travel, including robes and textiles, vessels, and other supplies. Muhammad Hanif Khan, Anand Ram's son's tutor, was placed in charge of most of these arrangements. Many other items from the dowry (*jahez*) were also brought together along with these supplies, so many in fact that they could not properly be accounted for. The Brahmins who had gathered there for the ceremony also had to be paid off, with the expenses for them accounting for Rs 4500. It was therefore only on 23rd Ramazan that the party was able to set off for the capital, reaching Fatehbad on

---

[42] Ibid., fl. 19b.
[43] Ibid., fl. 21b.

the 26th, crossing the Beas and Sutlej rivers on boat near Ludhiana, and making a halt at the Sarai-yi Lashkar Khan on 1st Shawwal. The next important stop was Sirhind, where some extensive purchases worth Rs 2000 were made, especially of *phulkārī* textiles. In this important centre the party was well taken care of by 'Usman Yar Khan, who had long been a friend of Mukhlis. After a week's further travel they reached Narela in the vicinity of the capital. By now Mukhlis was so anxious to see his sons that he sought special permission from the vizier on 11th Shawwal to meet them outside the city. The next day he was able to welcome them, end the pangs of separation (*hijrat*), and offer many thanks. The return to Delhi took place accompanied again by fireworks and the public distribution of coins, closing the narrative cycle concerning the wedding.

Mukhlis can now return to his parallel narrative of political affairs and the court.[44] It appears that in the middle of Ramazan the vizier Qamar-ud-Din Khan had set off for Chaitpur and managed to catch up the next day with the emperor. He conveyed that there had been further unpleasant news from Malwa and Gujarat. A southward campaign was indicated, which might even take them as far as Satara, the centre of the Maratha ruler Sahu. The emperor was inclined to let Qamar-ud-Din go forward and he began to make the necessary arrangements with the *dārogha* of the *tosha-khāna*, Jawahir Khan. The Khan also protested that he did not need that much help and could largely manage with his own resources. He solicited just one auspicious gift from the emperor, and the latter then tied on his turban with his own hands. Reading the *fātiha*, he bade him adieu and added 15,000 more troops to the 40,000 men he already had at his disposal, as well as Rs 5 lakh in cash for expenses. Further, 150 field-cannon (*rahkala*) were attached to the force, as were 2 large pieces and 20 travelling cannon (*zarb-i rahrau*), 500 maunds of gunpowder, 12 elephants, and other military supplies. A certain Hatim Khan Ikhlaskhani was appointed the superintendent of this force, while Raja Aniruddha Singh of Bhadawar, Durjan Singh of Koda, and Rao Ramchand Bundela of Datiya, as well as Raja Chhatar Singh, were ordered to accompany it and follow Qamar-ud-Din Khan's orders. A further

---

[44] Ibid., fl. 23b.

list is given of prominent Mughal warriors who were awarded special swords, including several close associates of Qamar-ud-Din; his own son Mir Badr-ud-Din Muhammad Khan was appointed the deputy and the *bakhshī* of the army. On 21st Ramazan the force set up camp near Sikri, where they remained for several days. Following the river's course, they then approached Mathura and proceeded south on the main route. Mukhlis writes apologetically that he had had every intention of accompanying the vizier, but he had also had to represent Saif ud-Daula and Zakariya Khan, the governors of Multan and Punjab, in the court. The vizier therefore told him to stay on for the time in Delhi, and so he returned north via Faridabad, entering Delhi on 27th Ramazan, well in time to meet his sons.

Just as the previous transition has been from family affairs to those of the court, here we begin a new section of the narrative which appears to refer to Mukhlis' love-life and how much he has suffered in the past, like a moth drawn to a flame.[45] He wishes to tell the reader this tale, he declares, because not to do so would be dishonest. When he returned to Delhi in late Ramazan, he was feeling despondent and detached from the world. At this very time he espied a marvellous Beloved (*ma'shuqa-yi laylī-yi jamāl*) whose glances penetrated him like arrows. Mukhlis thus felt that in his old age he had been attained once again by a maddening love. He began to contemplate and produce verses of love during the day like a nightingale, while at night he was like the proverbial moth. He would wander at times in gardens and gaze at the cypress tree, comparing it to his Beloved. He abandoned his usual bookish pastimes and turned to something else instead. Since he composed some ghazals at this time, he offers us some examples.[46]

> There must be a true purpose for the open grace,
> that you are showing me.
> I am an old lover by profession,
> And I can understand your real intention.
> How many times might one

---

[45] Ibid., fl. 26a.
[46] Ibid., fls 27a–27b.

have fallen into the trap of the company of beauties?
But that free Mukhlis has now
become slave to your beauty alone.

In another he invokes the love of the legendary Joseph of the Old Testament, comparing himself to the breeze of Egypt. The fact of his having been ensnared has attained very wide fame, he declares, but he still feels like a flower in bloom. A series of other allusive verses mention celebrated lovers of the literary past.

Selections from extensive verses follow, some reproachful, others exalted in tone. The whole section concludes after several pages, with very little in the matter of concrete details, but much by way of poetic and metaphorical display.[47]

And then, just as quickly, we are back again to politics. The next section turns to the rebellion of a certain "accursed" Bhagwant Rai, and Qamar-ud-Din Khan's moves to crush him. This is a typical move in this text, with its rapid shifts between sub-genres. In the world of service (*'ālam-i bandagī*) in which Mukhlis lives, one must always be prepared to turn away from one's private affairs to those of politics. For his part, the emperor had left Qamar-ud-Din Khan and turned back towards the city and the court was now back in full pomp. Meanwhile, Qamar-ud-Din and his men advanced along the Jamuna and reached Shirgarh, a fort built by Sher Shah Afghan. He then made a trip on the river to meet the former governor of Malwa, Muhammad Khan Ghazanfar Jang. In order to do this he left Agra, crossed the Chambal, and reached Gwaliyar on the 20th of Zi al-Qa'da. Here he was joined by Ghazanfar Jang with 5000 horses. Once again, extensive gifts were exchanged between the two, a ritual whose endless subtleties seem to engage Mukhlis. They also visited the important shrines of Sufis in the area and only then began to think seriously of engaging the Marathas.

After going through a pass in the region, an advance party was sent out to reconnoitre the situation. A new *farmān* also arrived at this stage from Delhi, which hardly helped clarify the situation. On the way to Sironj was a place called Shivpuri where they learnt that the

[47] Ibid., fl. 31a.

Image 5.2: Anand Ram Mukhlis, *Kārnāma-yi ʿishq*:
Prince Gauhar and his companion Khiradmand surviving the storm,
by Govardhan II, 1734–9.

Marathas were now gathered on the other side of the Narbada. But the Mughals had no orders to cross the river, so they halted, until on 2nd Zi al-Hijja they decided to proceed via Bundelkhand, the territory of Chhatrasal Bundela, since his children had begun to make trouble again. Another notorious troublemaker in the area was Bhagwant Rai, a Khichi Rajput who had become boastful and arrogant after organising the killing of Jan Nisar Khan. The Mughal army proceeded cautiously via Iraj and Bhander, periodically receiving news from Delhi. For example, they were informed of the death of the mother of the emperor, and her burial in the precincts of Nizam-ud-Din's *dargāh*.

Anand Ram's narrative also makes it clear that the Mughal force was inflexible and slow-moving, and accompanied by many women and children. For instance, in a nearby place called Kotla Sa'adat the wife of Muhammad Ghazi Khan gave birth, a sign of the constant presence of families in these entourages. A few days later they reached Kalpi, famed for its sweets, and from there, on 2nd Muharram, departed for Koda, where they arrived fairly rapidly in preparation for the expedition against Bhagwant Rai.

They camped half a *kos* from the enemy's fort and met several of those whom he had persecuted. Bhagwant himself had anticipated the arrival of the Mughal force and sent his goods and treasure to diverse places, fortifying himself inside Ghazipur. The Mughal force had clear orders to besiege and destroy the fort, and so they began to build siegeworks. After some final parleys an attack was planned. On 9th Muharram, shouting "Ya Fattah", the Mughals advanced and tried to force the doors of the fortress. But the fort was strong and resisted for a while; Bhagwant took advantage of the stalemate to flee and could not be found. A certain Mir Badr-ud-Din was deputed to tally and check the booty that had been taken and send it on to Delhi. Mukhlis here copies an *'arzdāsht* that he himself drafted on this occasion.[48] The expeditionary party then raised camp and left for Makanpur before returning to Delhi.

The alternation between politico-military chronicling, even of relatively trivial expeditions, and passages with a more personal tone

---

[48] Ibid., fls 35a–35b.

remain a feature of the *Badāʾiʿ Waqāʾiʿ*. An example of the latter is the section entitled: "The saddling up of the caravan of speech with the intention of setting down details of the journey to Bindraban [Brindavan], the Abode of Love".[49] In its introduction Mukhlis notes that he was usually very tied up with matters of court and attending on the vizier. But at the time that Qamar-ud-Din Khan was sent southwards to chastise the Marathas, it had been decided that Mukhlis would not accompany him on the campaign. Instead, he only accompanied the expeditionary force as far as Mathura and made his own plans from there. But as usual Anand Ram did not travel alone and was accompanied by Lala Sewak Ram, as well as the eloquent Mir Sharaf-ud-Din ʿAli (known by his pen-name "Payam"), his close friend Muhammad Jan Diwana (mentioned above), Mirza Muhammad Quli, and Sayyid Lutfullah. The members of the group would often get together for seances where verses and songs would be exchanged. However, there was one notable absence, which was of Khan-i Arzu. Even though Mukhlis had known him well for twenty years, and it was a particular matter of regret that he did not come along, he did not wish to reproach Arzu for this either. Indeed, he remarks, their relations were so close that they were like two grapes from the same bunch.

The expedition put Mukhlis in mind of an incident that had happened some years ago in the mid 1720s, or 7th regnal year, when he and his friends had been out on a hunting trip in the same vicinity. A major disaster had almost happened because of a fire, and they all managed to escape. Rai Kripa Ram, his young son, who had been on an elephant had also managed to save himself, even though he did not run away. They were all so contented at having escaped that they then distributed some alms to the poor and made their way with difficulty to Hasanpur. The moral of the story was that those who panicked in times of difficulty would only face more problems, while those who kept a level head would be far better off.

To return to the main narrative, Mukhlis recounts that when he and his friends were at their camp on the riverbank near Khizrabad, there was an untoward incident. Most of them had retired, but he was still

---

[49] Ibid., fls 55b–63b.

awake and busy with his books, when he spied a thief scuttling about the camp. The man was initially chased by the guards, but he got to Sayyid Lutfullah's tent and slashed it open with a knife. He had begun to gather up things but the Sayyid's major-domo awoke and in the ensuing fracas thief and servant came to blows. Finally, other people came along and the thief fled; the Mewati guards were unable to catch him even after a pursuit. After this the party felt it safer to move on to Shirgarh on the banks of the Jamuna where there was a fort with four doors, and a bazaar with various prosperous shops. Mukhlis and his friends had an enjoyable stay and partook of a good meal. It turned out that their eventual destination, Bindraban, was still 9 *kos* distant.

Towards dusk Mukhlis and his friends got on their horses and moved on, preferring to initiate travel after dark. As the sun went down, they enjoyed the sights and the somewhat cooler breeze.[50] Various wonderful birds, especially peacocks, were a sight to behold. Mukhlis' vocabulary now shifts to a particular Vaishnava mode, speaking of Krishna and his own devotion to him; he also refers to the local women who were singing pleasing songs in Hindi. By the next evening, they thus reached Brindaban at an easy pace and passed through the town, glancing at the gardens on the way, before descending at a ghat by the Jamuna river. It was a moonlit night as they raised their tents and chose a proper spot to retire. Meanwhile, they remained fully aware that about 3 *kos* away the vizier and his sizeable army were encamped. It had begun to drizzle a little by this time. Mukhlis cites an appropriate verse of Mirza Sa'ib Tabrezi – one of his favourite poets. But not everything had gone smoothly: Lala Sewak Ram's effects had not reached, and he was thus obliged to move into the tent of Kripa Ram, while the other bedding and supplies had to be redistributed amongst those whose servants had lost their way. It had grown quite chilly by this time, so Mukhlis sent his servants off to the bazaar with some money to buy additional supplies. Happily, it was possible to prepare some hot *khichrī*, a consolation in view of the unpleasant cold they were having to deal with.

<hr>

[50] Ibid., fl. 60b.

Those among the party who fancied their talents as musicians, the budding Tansens of the day, were now encouraged to provide music. A circle was formed and some people began to sing *bishnūpads*. The local food was reputed to be delectable, so they procured it: some oil, pickles (*āchār*), and *chaghrat*, the specialities of Braj. Anand Ram remarks that this vegetarian food was in fact so delicious that it was better than any meat preparation, whether a *korma*, *do-pyāza*, or *pilāf*. Eventually, those members of the party who had lost their way also joined them and a proper camp could be set up. At Mukhlis' request some horsemen under Amin Yar Beg Khan were detached to protect them from an eventual sally by the Marathas. They thus remained camped there for some days, exchanging stories, pleasantries, and gossip.

Now, Brindaban was known as a place where *faqīrs* retired from the travails of normal life. They speculated on how many were there; one well-informed man told them there were between five and six thousand. Mukhlis thought it beneficial to render some service to these renouncers (*fuqara-yi gosha gazīn*) – a way of garnering virtue for this life and the hereafter. He therefore instructed his brother Lala Hargopal to set out and give four annas to each *faqīr*, and, though the Lala dragged his feet a bit, he eventually went along with the idea. They thus went to each *ganj* and *takiya* and gave alms to each *faqīr* that they found. Finally, on 14th Rajab they left Brindaban and returned to Shahjahanabad on the 21st of the month.

The episode discussed above shows Anand Ram in a particular light, that is, as a devout Vaishnava, even though he does not tell us which particular temples he visited or how he gave vent to his devotion. On the other hand there are sections of the text which suggest that his religiosity was more eclectic, as we see from late August 1738, the 21st regnal year of the emperor Muhammad Shah. It was now quite cool because of monsoon showers.[51] Along with Arzu, Lala Sewak Ram, Mirza Muhammad Quli, and his sons Kripa Ram and Fateh Singh, as well as the usual Muhammad Jan Diwana, Anand Ram decided to visit the celebrated *dargāh* located 7 *kos* from Shahjaha-

---

[51] Ibid., fl. 72b, *et seq.*

nabad of Khwaja Qutb-ud-Din Bakhtiyar Kaki (referred to by him reverentially as "Qutb al-Haqq wa'l-Din"). The rain had produced greenery everywhere and it was overcast; flowering creepers of gourds (*kaddu* and *tori*) were to be seen all along the way. In the late afternoon they left Shahjahanabad and after stopping in one or two places reached their destination early in the night. Some members then went off to other sites in the area, but Mukhlis was hungry and wanted something to eat. Supplies had to be quickly procured by Lala Bijay Ram and an improvised meal was made involving the usual *khichrī*, some Kabuli peppers (*mirch*), and so on. After a brief smoke of his water-pipe, Anand Ram went to bed.

On the next day, some Hindu mourning rituals of *dūj shrāddh* were performed after bathing, as this was the astrologically appropriate time (*ayyām-i ganākat*). It turned out that Mukhlis had his own garden there in Mehrauli with mangoes and red flowering trees. There were both women and men in this party, and despite some of the usual literary exchanges the occasion seems to have been a sombre one. This was nevertheless a time for Mukhlis to compose several ghazals which are reproduced in the text. One is in Hindi, and seems to be addressed to a dancer (probably male):

Zulf ki khol jab tūn bāl wālī,
Mere dil ki kal janjāl dālī,
Makhan Jiu nāch majlis is gat,
Chaman mem mor jium kripāl dālī.

When you open out your tresses, long-haired one,
With your net, you ensnare my heart.
Makhan Jiu, dance before the gathering,
Like a merciful peacock in the garden.

The next day the servants were eager to return to Shahjahanabad as they anticipated a storm. But Mukhlis was in no hurry and dragged his feet. He visited Qutb-ud-Din's shrine, bowed down before him, touched his forehead to the ground, hoped his sinful acts would be pardoned, and felt blessed. It now turned out that Mukhlis' grandson Musahib Singh had been ill in the month of Jumada al-Awwal of the previous year. As a result Mukhlis also had begun to suffer from a liver ailment (*harārat-i jigar*). Various medicines were tried but nothing seemed to work, and for two months he felt excessive heat in his body all the time. Mir Isma'il Baqa Khan, an important royal physician, the vizier's own doctor Hakim Ibrahim, and Mirza Muhammad Hasan (Mukhlis' close friend who was also a doctor), tried their solutions: three times purging (*mushil*) and two episodes of bloodletting. For his part, Mukhlis thought that if he left the confines of the city, he might get better. In Ramazan he went out of town via the *khānqāh* of 'Inayatullah Khan. Though the weather was chilly, his body still felt overheated. Mukhlis was by now feeling so unwell that he decided to give up all intoxicants, reaching the state of despondency when death approaches. He therefore remained for over two weeks at the shrine of Qutb-ud-Din, only taking some minimal medicines recommended by Mirza Muhammad Hasan. Miraculously, he reports, at the end of seventeen or eighteen days he was cured. Devotion to the greatest of Delhi's Chishti saints had had its desired effects and ensured that he returned there time and again.[52]

Anand Ram and Nadir Shah

This brings us to the best-known section of the text, namely that dealing with Nadir Shah's invasion of northern India and seizure of Delhi in the late 1730s.[53] Partial translations and paraphrases of passages from this part have existed since the nineteenth century and continue to attract the attention of scholars.[54] To rapidly summarise the historical context, the Mughals and the Safavids had long had an uneasy relationship on their frontier, characterised by the contest over Qandahar, which changed hands several times after the Mughals took it over in 1595. In 1649 the Safavids retook the city and fortress and

[52] Ibid., fl. 78b.

[53] This section begins on fl. 114b.

[54] See the "Tazkira of Anand Ram Mukhlis", in Elliot and Dowson, *History of India*, vol. 8, 76–98 (the translation is attributed to Lt Perkins); for the more complete translation from which these published excerpts are taken, see British Library, London, Addn. Mss. 30,780, fls 162a–184a. For a recent use, Tucker, "1739".

held off several Mughal sieges. However, they did not make further incursions into the Mughal territories and the frontier remained more or less stable during the long reign of Aurangzeb. The decline of Safavid power in the late seventeenth and early eighteenth centuries seems also to have lulled the Delhi court into a false sense of security. It was therefore with something of a shock that they awoke to the threat posed in the 1730s by a new figure, Tahmasp Quli Khan Afshar, to be known as Nadir Shah. From about 1730 diplomatic exchanges had begun between Nadir Shah and Muhammad Shah, with the sending of 'Ali Mardan Khan Shamlu to Delhi. A series of other embassies followed, with the main question being the presence in the Mughal domains of Afghans who had fled Nadir Shah's expansionary campaigns, a fact to which the Iranian ruler strenuously objected. The Mughals attempted flattery as well as some chicanery, but the tone of relations began to deteriorate over the years.

In 1737 Nadir Shah began a long siege of Qandahar with the aim of seizing it from the Ghilzai Afghans who controlled it at the time. When the fortress yielded in 1738, he consolidated his position in the area and the pressure began to mount on the Mughal governor of Kabul, Nasir Khan, who appealed for help to the court in Delhi.[55] Anand Ram was obviously quite well informed about these goings-on, and even seems to have acted as a *munshī* to draft one of the letters in this long set of diplomatic exchanges. Like other chroniclers of the time, he was also perfectly aware that the Mughal court was riven by internal dissensions, which had a significant impact on the manner in which external threats were dealt with.

Largely on account of these disputes, the garrisons of the northwest had been starved of resources for some time, first by Raushan-ud-Daula and then by the powerful Indian-born noble Samsam-ud-Daula Khan-i Dauran, who held the important financial position of Mir Bakhshi. As the threat from Nadir Shah became ever more obvious, Anand Ram suggests that those in the Kabul garrison grew nervous and appealed to the *sūbadār* to at least pay his soldiers their arrears and secure their loyalty.

---

[55] Anand Ram Mukhlis, *Badā'i' Waqā'i'* (PUL manuscript), fls 118a–18b.

Nasir Khan used to reassure them by saying: "Friends! Why this anxiety? I have written to the Emperor and also to my agent (*wakīl*) at Court, and the money is sure to come tomorrow if not today." When his agent presented the application to Khan-i Dauran, the Amir-ul-Umara', and in fear and trembling described the alarming situation in Afghanistan, that noble replied in derision, "Do you think that I am a petty simpleton that I shall be impressed by such a tale as yours? Our houses are built on the plain: we do not fear anything except what we can see with our own eyes. Your house stands on the Bhochla Hill, and therefore you have probably sighted Mongol and Qizilbash armies from the roof of your house! Reply to your master that we are writing for money to the governor of Bengal: and when the Bengal revenue arrives after the rainy season, the money due will be quickly sent to Kabul."[56]

The cost of such procrastination presently became evident, and Anand Ram noted: "If the Afghans had been set to guard the frontier with their whole hearts and customary bravery, they could have stopped the advance of the Persian army long enough to enable reinforcements to reach them from Delhi, and then India would not have been sacked."[57]

There was a certain inexorable character to what followed given the nature and quality of the Iranian military machine in comparison to that of the Mughals. In mid June 1738, Kabul was attacked and fell to Nadir Shah after a short siege on the 23rd of the month. Thereafter the Iranian ruler sent a peremptory letter to Muhammad Shah accusing him and his court of dishonourable behaviour and of not keeping his word. After several months of further preparation the march on India was resumed in early November, but this respite was not enough for the Mughals to summon up any real resistance in the Punjab. Nasir Khan was defeated handily, and Nadir Shah entered Peshawar on 18th November. In early January 1739 his army crossed the Chenab river and headed for Lahore, the main Mughal centre in the region. Here the governor, Zakariya Khan – with whom Anand Ram (as we have

[56] See Malik, *The Reign of Muhammad Shah*, 162; Anand Ram Mukhlis, *Badāʾiʿ Waqāʾiʿ* (PUL manuscript), fl. 119a (where the wording is slightly different).

[57] Irvine, *Later Mughals*, vol. 2, 324–5; Anand Ram Mukhlis, *Badāʾiʿ Waqāʾiʿ* (PUL manuscript), fl. 119b.

noted) had relations – made an initial effort at resistance but, lacking support and reinforcements, surrendered on 23rd January, offering a handsome tribute and saving his own city from plunder. Anand Ram notes that, had he been better supported from Delhi, he could well have advanced as far as the Jhelum or Chenab, defended the river crossings and resisted Nadir Shah in pitched battle rather than trying to fall back and defend Lahore. At any rate, other centres in the Punjab were not quite as lucky as the provincial capital: according to Anand Ram, "cities like Wazirabad, Yaminabad, Gujarat, et cetera and big villages (each like half a city) were reduced to black ashes. All over the land, property was plundered and women outraged."[58]

The Mughal grand strategy was ostensibly to draw the invader in and meet him on the plains to the north of Delhi, in a place where water was plentifully available and defensive positions could be defined with relative care. To the forces that were available already at the Mughal centre, largely meant to be marshalled by Khan-i Dauran, were added contingents from the Deccan under the wily Nizam-ul-Mulk Asaf Jah, and those that arrived belatedly from Awadh under Sa'adat Khan Burhan-ul-Mulk. These three groups were somewhat at cross-purposes, and the desperate ploy by Khan-i Dauran of calling for support on the reluctant Rajputs and even the Marathas may have added even further to the confusion. The Mughals had assembled then near Panipat by mid January 1739 (Shawwal 1151 H.), albeit in a rather passive mode and without a clear battle plan. Anand Ram writes:

> When news came that Nadir Shah had reached the banks of the Atak river [Indus], the commanders urged upon the emperor the necessity of his joining them in person, and with one accord they moved forward in the early days of Shawwal. The author himself, Anand Ram, accompanied by his beloved sons Rai Kripa Ram and Fateh Singh, left the capital on the 11th of the month, in the service of Nawwab Sahib Wazir-ul-Mamalik Bahadur [Qamar-ud-Din Khan]. When the army reached Panipat, the author obtained leave to revisit his home, where some private affairs required his presence.[59]

[58] Irvine, *Later Mughals*, vol. 2, 333; Anand Ram Mukhlis, *Badā'i' Waqā'i'* (PUL manuscript), fls 122b–123a.

[59] Anand Ram Mukhlis, *Badā'i' Waqā'i'* (PUL manuscript), fls 124a–124b.

He thus rushed back to Shahjahanabad, and made his way there rapidly in about three days.

Though Anand Ram does not say it in so many words, it is clear that he had sensed somehow that the Mughals were about to taste defeat. Perhaps this was because of the relatively effortless manner in which Nadir Shah had sliced a path from Kabul through the Punjab, brushing aside every effort to resist him. Or perhaps the manifest chaos and dissension in the ranks of the Mughal commanders made him take precautions. He thus writes:

> The author has already related how he obtained leave to visit Shahjahanabad, and left the army for this purpose when it had reached Panipat. The emperor had taken his departure from the town the day before the writer reached it. Strange to relate, numbers of people of every degree followed the royal standards. Some thought thus to enjoy a pleasant excursion through the Punjab, while others were of opinion that a battle would be fought and won in the neighbourhood of the town, and that their absence would only be of short duration. The writer sought in vain for a house within the walls in which to place his wife and family; he could find no suitable one. Under these circumstances, he resolved to leave his family in their usual residence outside the town. The security of the entrances to the lane was looked to, and armed servants above the ordinary number were entertained. The author now prepared to return to the army, and sent on his advanced tents.[60]

As it turned out, Anand Ram had dallied much too long in Delhi. The emperor Muhammad Shah had left the capital on 29th January 1739 and reached Panipat some nine days later, at a quite leisurely pace. The battle with the Iranians was joined some days later at Karnal, north of Panipat, on 24th February (15th Zi al-Qa‘da). It was a short and decisive affair, and by the time Anand Ram could leave Delhi to join the imperial camp news had already trickled in of the disastrous defeat. The Mughals had been both outmanoeuvred and shown up in their obsolete manner of conducting war by a far smaller army. A lack of co-ordination had led to an impulsive sortie by Burhan-ul-Mulk,

---

[60] "Tazkira of Anand Ram Mukhlis", in Elliot and Dowson, *History of India*, vol. 8, 85–6; Anand Ram, *Badā'i‘ Waqā'i‘* (PUL manuscript), fls 129b–230a.

whose conduct is roundly criticised by Anand Ram: "[W]ith a head-long impetuosity (*bī-parwāhī*) misplaced in a commander, [he] flew to the scene of action accompanied by only the few horsemen who were with him, without collecting his artillery or waiting to form his men in any kind of order." These forces were caught in the withering fire of Nadir Shah's musketeers and swivel-guns, and Burhan-ul-Mulk was surrounded. Khan-i Dauran then moved his troops up in support on the emperor's orders, only to fall into a version of the same trap, and was eventually mortally wounded, in some versions by a musket shot. The remaining Mughal forces, including those from the Deccan, had failed to engage substantively. In the course of a single afternoon's engagement, the Mughals were decisively humiliated and obliged to sue for terms.

The inhabitants of Delhi, Anand Ram included, now had to prepare for the worst eventuality. As panic spread, there was also the fear that civic order would totally break down because of sedition-minded city residents (*fitna-ārāyān-i shahr*). Here, Mukhlis singles out for praise Haji Faulad Khan, the *kotwāl* of the city, who was "no ordinary man, [and] was at his post day and night; his exertions were unceasing, and, wherever there was an appearance of sedition, he seized and punished the guilty parties. The roads were infested with malefactors, and there was safety for none." As word came in that the Mughal imperial camp was totally encircled, and had been rendered inaccessible, Anand Ram abandoned any fleeting plans he might have had of returning to Panipat and Karnal, and instead began to think of defending his own quarter (*mohalla*) of Wakilpura, a near suburb located outside the city walls. Improvised patrols were organised, sentries employed, and munitions were gathered and distributed.

As it turned out, Nadir Shah only entered Delhi on 20th March, even though he was preceded by his chief agent Tahmasp Khan Jala'ir, accompanied by Burhan-ul-Mulk, to whom the Delhi governor Lutfullah Khan handed over the keys of the fortress and treasuries. The reason for this long delay was that elaborate negotiations had to be carried on between the Mughals and Iranians before arriving at a first version of a formal agreement (or *'ahd-nāma*), that would later be ratified, including the payment of a large indemnity (*khasārat-i jang*) to Nadir Shah. Anand Ram carries on his account of these dealings which, like his description of the preceding battle, was obviously based on hearsay, though it corresponds in both its broad outlines and many details with the other contemporary sources. He notes that on entering Shahjahanabad Nadir Shah took up residence in the main imperial quarters of the fort, while Muhammad Shah was relegated to a mansion near the Asad Burj. The Iranian army was quartered in various parts of the city and went about making demands on the population. The *khutba* was read in the Iranian ruler's name, and fresh silver coins issued from the mint to mark the occasion. Not long thereafter, tensions in the city, which had been simmering for some weeks, exploded in the open. The proximate cause appears to have been a violent altercation between Nadir Shah's collectors and merchants in the important grain-market of Pahar Ganj, just south-west of the city. Thereafter, rumours spread that Nadir Shah himself had been assassinated, leading to many attacks on his soldiers, apparently spearheaded by men from the Awadh contingent of the Mughal army. At first, Nadir Shah seems to have believed that this was no more than a minor affray and took no action. However, on realising overnight that the situation might be grave, he rode out from the fort in the morning to the nearby mosque of Raushan-ud-Daula and from there gave an order for a general massacre (*qatl-i 'āmm*) in the city. Anand Ram writes:

In the morning, on 11th Zi al-Hijja, from the seat of royal dignity (*jalāl-i shāhī*) the order was given for a general massacre, which was like the Day of Judgment (*qiyāmat*) for the city. It seemed that in a moment the whole city would be destroyed. The whole of Chandni Chawk, the fruit market, the Dariba bazaar, and the area around the Masjid-i Jami' were set on fire and reduced to dust. Orders were given to destroy everyone by the sword. What can I say about this Day of Judgment! In many places people [women] committed *jauhar* [immolation] according to the Indian custom. Many people also committed suicide and took their lives [by other means]. A large part of the *qizilbāsh* force took control of the city and opened the doors wide to bloodshed. Many expensive cloths, jewels, pearls, and gold and silver vessels were looted by them for their benefit. The writer of these lines was with his dear friends in the Betwant *hawelī* in the Wakilpura *mohalla* outside the city walls. They included my dear friend Mirza

Sahib Muhammad Quli Khan, who had been appointed *mutasaddī* of Batala. I witnessed this chaotic scene, but I had drawn my lessons and decided that if, God forbid, these evil people entered the area, there would first be *jauhar*, and if God so willed, we would then sacrifice our lives. Praise be to God that the blood-letting did not come this way and was limited to the area of the Jami' Masjid. In 794 Hijri [*sic*: for 801 H.] Hazrat Sahib-Qiran Amir Timur, after subjugating Delhi, had given an order for a general massacre. Since then to this day, 1151 Hijri, three hundred and forty eight years have passed and this city has been safe from such a disaster, but now every lane and quarter which was once fragrant and lovely like the beloved's tresses, and in which the nightingale's sweet voice was heard everywhere, has been wounded and had its eyes blinded by topsy-turvy Fate. Much time will be needed before this Abode of Love (*Dār-ul-'ishq*) can return to its original state.[61]

By way of elaboration Anand Ram offers us some Hindavi verses of his friend "Payam"; and by way of comparison some references to Sharaf-ud-Din Yazdi's classic account in his *Zafar Nāma* of Timur's destruction in Delhi. After several hours of this unremitting slaughter of civilians and destruction, an order was given to cease, which seems to have largely been implemented. Some thousands of people had already been killed, and their bodies remained on the streets as a gruesome reminder of Nadir Shah's vengeful wrath, until they were eventually collected for mass cremations or to be thrown in the river.

In the aftermath of this orgy of urban violence, Nadir Shah's army set about the business of extorting money from the inhabitants of Delhi. This was in addition to the money, gold, and jewels that they demanded from the Mughal court, which was already an enormous sum. As Anand Ram tells it, charge of the overall operation was given to the redoubtable Tahmasp Khan Jala'ir, who went about creating a rapid urban census, listing the names and residences of the wealthy citizens and their estimated resources. Both Iranian *nasaqchīs* and the Mughal *kotwāl's* administration were drawn into this process, and certain members of the city's elite took the occasion to settle scores with their own neighbours by informing on them. An estimate of some two *karors*

[61] Anand Ram Mukhlis, *Badā'i' Waqā'i'* (PUL manuscript), fls 132b–133a. The translation in "Tazkira of Anand Ram Mukhlis", 88, omits some parts.

(twenty million) rupees was arrived at, and Nadir Shah then divided the city and its suburbs up into five sections, given over respectively to Nizam-ul-Mulk Asaf Jah, the vizier Qamar-ud-Din Khan, 'Azimullah Khan, Sarbuland Khan (titled Mubariz-ul-Mulk), and Murtaza Khan to collect the indemnity. Anand Ram's own *mohalla* of Wakilpura came under the charge of Sarbuland Khan, a quarrelsome and somewhat profligate former governor of Gujarat who was by now in the twilight years of his career.[62] As he puts it: "In the two *mohallas* where the collection was entrusted to Nizam-ul-Mulk and the vizier, the people were treated humanely, as the vizier [even] paid a great part of the money from his own chests. But in the other three *mohallas*, especially in that assigned to Mubariz-ul-Mulk, the sufferings of the people knew no bounds . . . Whole families were ruined. Many took poison and others stabbed themselves to death."[63] This ill-treatment extended to the vizier himself and his *dīwān* Majlis Rai, who after suffering public humiliation and torture apparently committed suicide.

The initial demand on Anand Ram and his household amounted after some bargaining to Rs 137,000, which he was able to pay from his household reserves and by liquidating stocks of brocades and *pashmīna*. However, the voracious Sarbuland Khan then revised his demand upwards, accompanying this with some further threats of force. Mukhlis was forced to scramble, pawning jewels, and taking loans at exorbitant rates from Delhi financiers. He even went so far as to contact one of Nadir Shah's generals, who agreed to tide him over, against a payment to be made a few months later.[64] By these means Anand Ram managed to extricate himself, but we may gather by implication that not everyone, even amongst Delhi's elite, was so fortunate or so well-connected.

Once the matter of extraction, both from Delhi's elite and the Mughal treasury, had been taken care of in its broad outlines, Nadir Shah still had some unfinished business. At the same time, he may have

---

[62] On Sarbuland Khan, see Shahnawaz Khan, *Ma'āsir al-Umarā'* (text), vol. 3, 801–6; (trans.), vol. 2, 704–8.

[63] Irvine, *Later Mughals*, vol. 2, 372–3; Anand Ram Mukhlis, *Badā'i' Waqā'i'* (PUL manuscript), fl. 136b.

[64] See Kaicker, *The King and the People*, 50.

Table 5.1

Indemnities Paid by Prominent Delhi Citizens, 1739[65]

Name	Amount
Sita Ram (1), attached to Qamar-ud-Din Khan	Rs 600,000
Majlis Rai	Rs 400,000
Nagar Mal	Rs 350,000
Khushhal Chand	Rs 275,000
Rai Naunidh (for the group of *khālisa* accountants)	Rs 275,000
Jugal Kishor	Rs 250,000
Shaikh Sa'dullah	Rs 250,000
Sita Ram (2), from the royal treasury	Rs 250,000
Rai Naunidh s/o Bhog Chand	Rs 200,000
Sujan Rai	Rs 150,000
Rai Naunidh, in the salary office	Rs 150,000
Mu'in-ud-Din Khan	Rs 50,000

been anxious not to delay his departure too long for fear of the scorching heat of the northern Indian summer. In late March he sent a *farmān* back to Iran, declaring that with the financial cushion provided by the proceeds of the Indian campaign he could decree a tax holiday in his home territories.[66] Negotiations were then completed for the marriage of his son Nasrullah to a Mughal princess, daughter of the prince Yazdan Bakht, and the wedding itself held with much pomp in early April.

Between that time and Nadir Shah's eventual departure from Delhi on 16th May 1739, further details of the agreement (*'ahd-nāma*) between the two parties were worked out. This document, probably completed around 1st May (or 3rd Safar 1152 H.), was obviously largely

[65] Bodleian Library, Oxford, Ms. Ouseley 387 (Sachau-Ethé, I/263), fls 109–20, *Muhāraba-yi Muhammad Shāh wa Nādir Shāh*, summarised in Khan, "The Middle Classes", 46; also see Kaicker, *The King and the People*, 83. Additionally, very large sums were allegedly taken from the grandees Safdar Jang, Nizam-ul-Mulk Asaf Jah, and Qamar-ud-Din Khan; see Malik, *The Reign of Muhammad Shah*, 180.

[66] See Islam, *A Calendar of Documents*, vol. 2, doc. Post-Ab. 278.1, 77–8. In some versions, the taxes were remitted for three years.

dictated by Nadir Shah's ministers; Anand Ram notes that "the situation demanded that whatever the Persians said should be forthwith accepted." The text begins with an admission that the Mughal ministers and advisers had misbehaved in their diplomacy leading to a "war of the kings (*jang-i sultānī*)" at Karnal, in which they were defeated. Thereafter, Nadir Shah had behaved with great kindness, bearing in mind the fact that both rulers were Turkmans, with the Mughals described as belonging to the *gurkāniya* (Timurid) family. When the two rulers had entered Delhi in the aftermath of the battle, the Mughals had generously offered the Shah all their treasures, jewels, and valuables, and he in his munificence had accepted only some of these. There was also the matter of the indemnity (specified only in some versions of the *'ahd-nāma*), and the fact that all the former Mughal territories west of the Indus were henceforth to be made an adjunct of Nadir Shah's domains (*Daulat-i Nādira*). The Mughals agreed that their officials would have no further authority there, nor would their revenue collectors enter them.[67] These territories are specified in some detail. In a great *darbār* held on 12th May, Muhammad Shah was then reinstated formally as ruler, and Nadir Shah enjoined the Mughal *umarā* and subordinate rulers to henceforth obey him faithfully. However, as Lockhart has noted: "Muhammad Shah was thus once more a sovereign, but his kingdom had shrunk, and his commander-in-chief [Khan-i Dauran] and many thousands of his soldiers and subjects had been slain. Further, his jewels were gone, his treasuries were empty, and his prestige, which his own indolence and pusillanimity had done so much to injure, had been still further impaired."[68]

Anand Ram now goes over some of the details of Nadir Shah's return westward to his home territories. Not only did the Iranian ruler carry away pack-loads and carts of treasure, but he also obliged a fair number of Delhi's skilled artisans to return with him, many of whom were subsequently released or escaped. En route he also made further demands on Zakariya Khan in Lahore, who agreed to pay him an additional indemnity of Rs 10,000,000 (one *karor*), and to curry

---

[67] For a full discussion, ibid.
[68] Lockhart, *Nadir Shah*, 153.

favour accompanied him as far as the Chenab river. But all did not go smoothly on this return trip. The departure had been delayed too long and a good many men perished in the blazing heat of the Punjab plains from exhaustion and thirst, besides those stragglers from the main body who were apparently picked off by groups of Jats and Sikhs. By the time the Chenab was reached on 5th June, morale was already running low. But worse was to follow, as the main bridge over the Chenab collapsed, allegedly killing some two thousand of Nadir Shah's men. Anand Ram, like other Mughal chroniclers of the time, can hardly conceal his *Schadenfreude* at this turn of events. It then took nearly a month and a half to reconstruct a bridge, hampered as they were now by the arrival of heavy monsoonal rains. Making their way to Hasan Abdal in October, the Shah's returning force was able to enter Kabul only in the beginning of December.

However, as Anand Ram makes clear, Nadir Shah continued to maintain contact with both Zakariya Khan and the court in Delhi in the subsequent months and years. These dealings initially had to do with the transition in the territories west of the Indus that had been ceded to him, and how their administration should be managed. Anand Ram, on account of his contacts in Lahore, obviously had access to this correspondence and reproduces a good number of these letters in his text.[69] Later, some other matters came up, notably the dispatch by Nadir Shah of two collectors (*muhassils*) named Muhammad Salih Beg and Muhammad Karim Beg in March 1740, in order to look into the vexed matter of *qizilbāsh* from the Iranian army who had deserted and preferred to settle down in India. They had chosen to do so in the foothills, changing their clothing and appearance to appear less conspicuous, and Nadir Shah was furious at this. Zakariya Khan was thus instructed to help in hunting down such men and sending them back to Iran in chains.

The two *muhassils* arrived in Delhi, causing some panic, as people feared that Nadir Shah himself might return. It turned out however that

---

[69] Islam, *A Calendar of Documents*, vol. 2, 84–91. For an analysis and full translation of one of these letters, based on the original *farmān* (with a seal and *tughra*) dated Jumada II 1152 H., see Hasan, "A Letter from Nadir Shah".

they were largely there to make further monetary demands, to the tune of Rs 2,500,000. Since the Mughal imperial treasury could not produce ready cash at short notice, it was obliged to turn to Hindu bankers in the city. The money was sent back with the two collectors, who were accompanied by the son of Qamar-ud-Din Khan as far as Lahore. In a show of courtesy, Nadir Shah apparently "reciprocated" by sending the Mughal emperor a gift (*dāli-yi mewa*) of camel-loads of melons, grapes, and pears, which, considering the monetary value of the gift, seems like the rubbing of a lot of salt in an already gaping wound.[70]

The Bangarh Expedition

In mid 1739, on Nadir Shah's departure, Delhi and its court were left in a turbulent state. Fortunately a good monsoon and a successful *kharif* harvest brought grain prices under control later that year. Competing readings quickly emerged of the debacle in February, and historical texts and literary works in the following decades continued to debate the matter beyond the mere military facts of what had transpired at Karnal, and in the lead-up to the battle. Khan-i Dauran, who certainly bore some responsibility both for the lack of preparation and the diplomatic miscalculations, emerged in the eyes of some as a martyred figure who had sacrificed himself at the altar of imperial loyalty.[71] Initially, a good amount of popular hostility was directed at the Turanis, whose *chef de file* Nizam-ul-Mulk Asaf Jah was suspected in many quarters of having entertained secret negotiations with Nadir Shah in order to undermine his rivals at the court.[72] In the aftermath of Karnal it is certainly true that he moved to consolidate his position, in the absence of key rivals, and remained in Delhi and its environs until July 1740 before withdrawing once more to the Deccan. His admirers claimed that, far from being disruptive, he had urged

[70] Islam, *A Calendar of Documents*, vol. 2, 92–103.

[71] For an account highly sympathetic to him, see Muhammad Muhsin Siddiqi, *Jauhar-i Samsām*, British Library, London, Or. 1898.

[72] This was also Anand Ram Mukhlis' view, since he states that Nadir Shah invaded at the behest (*ba-mūjib-i talab*) of Nizam-ul-Mulk and Sa'adat Khan.

Muhammad Shah to take matters in hand, revive the army, travel more frequently to the provinces, and show greater interest in overseeing administration at the *dīwān-i khāss*.[73]

But Muhammad Shah was no Aurangzeb in terms of either his ambitions or horizons, and his principal interest was in adjudicating the interests of different groups at his court. He thus permitted the temporary ascension of Amir Khan 'Umdat-ul-Mulk, an ambitious Iranian who was allied to Safdar Jang in Awadh, to the detriment of the position of the vizier Qamar-ud-Din Khan, Anand Ram's master. Over the next months, however, Nizam-ul-Mulk managed to outfox Amir Khan, ejecting him from the inner circles of the court, and reasserting the position of the vizier Qamar-ud-Din. This tussle between Iranians and Turanis would continue to play itself out over the next years, until the end of the reign of Muhammad Shah and even beyond.

Our examination of Anand Ram's narrative resumes in these very years, after the dust had settled somewhat on Nadir Shah's invasion. The focus is on an imperial expedition in 1745 against 'Ali Muhammad Khan Rohila (d. 1749), the founder of the eighteenth-century Indo-Afghan regional state based in Rampur. Anand Ram's narrative begins in the first month (Muharram) of the year 1158 H. (February 1745), and ends some four months later, at the close of the month of Jumada I of the same year; the account itself was finished on the 12 Ramazan 1158 (8th October 1745). At least one version of this section of Anand Ram's text can be found in an autograph copy (in the Rampur Raza Library) and his title for it is *Ahwāl-i Safar-i Bangarh* (Account of a Journey to Bangarh). The *Ahwāl* is on the face of it a very matter-of-fact, day-to-day description, of this long and rather slow-moving expedition where nothing of terribly great political consequence actually took place. It is notable for its relatively simple and direct style, and we can sense that Anand Ram did not wish to deploy all the literary skills and devices that we know from elsewhere he had at his disposal. In comparison to the previous section on Nadir

---

[73] Abu'l Faiz Ma'ani, *Tārīkh-i Futūhāt-i Āsafīya* (Hyderabad Ms.), cited in Malik, *The Reign of Muhammad Shah*, 184–5.

Shah's invasion, it is at times a more personal text, not only in the sense
of reflecting its author's emotions or moods, but rather in its accumulation of petty personal details, including how much Anand Ram
spent for a number of trivial transactions. Now, quite unlike travellers
from Iran or Central Asia (to say nothing of Europe) in the Mughal
domains, Anand Ram was travelling in an area that was for him culturally familiar, and which he may have even travelled in before. Thus,
there is much less of exotic colour in this view of the upper Gangetic
valley than local detail, much more pointillism than impressionism.

Let us briefly recall the politico-historical context of the Mughal
polity as it stood after the humiliating defeat by Nadir Shah. In the
face of a Mughal centre that appeared weak and uncertain, other challenges had begun to arise from locally anchored chieftains in northern
India, amongst them from the Indo-Afghans (Rohilas) of the region
east of Delhi. There were thus two factions in the Mughal court with
respect to this campaign.[74] That of Qamar-ud-Din Khan, the *wazīr*
(with whom Anand Ram had been intimately associated as his *wakīl*
since 1729–30), on the one hand, and that of Safdar Jang, best known
as the governor of Awadh, on the other, had opposing views concerning the Rohila threat.[75] Qamar-ud-Din was content to let the Rohilas be, whereas Safdar Jang, who was directly threatened in Awadh
by their growing military power, was keen on a strong stand against 'Ali
Muhammad Khan. The undercurrents of this quarrel come through in
this account and can be profitably read with attention to detail by afi-
cionados of Mughal court-politics.[76] The names of many minor officials in the court also come to light in the process.

Anand Ram comes through once more in this part of the text as
someone who was fond of the good things of life, notably food and
creature comforts. As before, he also notices matters of religious interest
and provides valuable testimony on the socio-religious attitudes of
those who were brought up in Indo-Persian culture in northern India

[74] On court factions leading up to this period, see Chandra, *Parties and Politics*.

[75] For Mughal politics in this period in the context of Awadh, see the earlier
discussion in Alam, *The Crisis of Empire*, 263–70, *passim*.

[76] Cf. Gommans, *The Rise of the Indo-Afghan Empire*, 120–4, for a discussion
of the campaign against Bangarh.

in the early eighteenth century. The *Ahwāl* thus begins with the heading: "The setting out (*mutawajjih shudan*) of the Hazrat Zill-Allah Muhammad Shah Badshah Ghazi to Garh Muktesar in the manner (*ba tarīq*) of a pleasure-trip (*sair*), and for hunting. The presence of the writer of these words, the *faqīr* Mukhlis, in this auspicious company, on account of the favour of the times." It then continues:

> On 23rd Muharram 1158 H. [25th February 1745], the 27th regnal year, an imperial order was issued to Sa'ad-ud-Din Khan, *khān-i sāmān*, and Hadi Yar Khan, *mushrif* of the *farāshkhāna* to take the royal tents, and going across the river Jamuna, pitch them at a garden near the town of Loni. The next day, the 24th, the emperor intended to travel in his gilded palanquin and leave the palace of Dar-ul-Khilafat Shahjahanabad with the intention of a hunt in Garh Muktesar, and in that context also chastise 'Ali Muhammad Khan Rohila, who had become arrogant and was claiming a sort of autonomy. It was decided that the *wazīr* I'timad-ud-Daula Chin Bahadur Nusrat Jang, 'Umdat-ul-Mulk Amir Khan Bahadur, Abu'l Mansur Khan Bahadur, the *mīr ātish*, and the other great notables (*umarā-i 'izām*) would accompany the royal retinue.[77]

On the 29th of the month, the account continues, the vizier joined the camp and exchanged presents with the emperor. Anand Ram mentions a robe of honour (*khil'at*) which was given on this occasion to his own son Rai Kripa Ram, and also notes that an earlier misunderstanding between Abu'l Mansur Khan and the vizier was sorted out by the exchange of gifts and mutual invitations to dine. The whole court agreed, temporarily at least, on the need for the campaign. It was decided to send out an advance party under the vizier, and Rai Bhagwant Singh, the imperial *waqā'i'-nigār* (newsletter writer) was also charged with going ahead to prepare the details of the route ahead, with maps (*naqsh*). By now they were already in the next month of Safar, and on the 12th the emperor entered a camp that had been prepared near the Hindan river. But the camp did not suit his taste on account of a lack of water there. Thus, on the 15th they moved closer to

---

[77] Anand Ram Mukhlis, *Safar Nāma*, 1–3. The published text of the *Safar Nāma*, based on the Rampur manuscript, corresponds to Anand Ram Mukhlis, *Badā'i' Waqā'i'* (PUL manuscript), fls 193a–228a.

the water's edge, and here the festival of Nauroz was celebrated according to the advice of the court astrologers. Once more, gifts were exchanged among the notables and the courtiers all dressed in festive green for the occasion; then on the 19th the party reached Dasna *pargana*. It was decided here that the official in charge of riverine affairs (*mīr bahr*) should be sent ahead to build a bridge on the Ganga, and two days later they reached the village of Dhappa. Here, Sa'adat Khan Bahadur Zu'lfiqar Jang was appointed governor of Shahjahanabad-Delhi, and sent back. Obviously, important political negotiations were a part of this voyage, and notables were jockeying for position at the emperor's side as well as for posts elsewhere.[78]

The account now takes a more personal tone, whereas earlier it has been largely restricted to official events. Anand Ram writes that his own initial intention had been to stay behind in Delhi and send his sons with the imperial party. Yet, after the preliminary description of the imperial departure he pauses to speak of how he came to make his own trip and adds somewhat wryly: "I leave this account at this point, to set down an account of myself (*mājarā-i khwud*), which is the [real] reason for recording these lines." He notes that if it were a matter of merely going as far as Garh Muktesar, this was something that he and other people in Delhi did anyway every year in the month of Kartik (we note that there is a switch in the calendrical system of reference to an Indic one). His account then continues, with a fresh caption: "A description by the writer of these letters, engaged in writing about wonders (*ahwāl-i rāqim-i hurūf, ba badā'i'-i nawīsī masrūf*)".

> At first, I had thought it reasonable to stay back in the city, and that Rai Kripa Ram and Rai Fateh Singh [his sons], who with the grace of God, are adequately familiar with the affairs of the *darbār-i mu'allā*, should go along with the auspicious retinue (*rikāb-i sa'ādat*). For, this journey, if it is to end in Garh Muktesar, was not to be more than a pleasure trip and for hunting. Every year, most of the people of Delhi in the month of Kartik travel In order to have a bath in the Ganga, and there they arrange happy feasts. But it so happened that when preparations were being made, it occurred to me that it was not advisable for me to remain in the city. In the first

---

[78] Anand Ram Mukhlis, *Safar Nāma*, 8.

place, I would have to bear the suffering (*alam*) of separation from my sons who had never been apart from me. Secondly, I had never been separated from the retinue of the Master (*khudāwand-i ni'mat*). At this time, when there is the possibility of a fight, were I to remain behind, people might accuse me of selfishness (*khwud-dārī*). Therefore, I too decided to set out on the voyage and started preparing things (*yasāq*) for the trip.

We notice the characteristic nervousness that he might be taken for a coward, a theme that Mukhlis pursues later in the text as well. Hence, he too decided to go on the voyage and purchased three camels for Rs 330, a pair of Gujarati oxen for his cart for Rs 450, and a two-humped camel (*ushtur*) for Rs 240, the last in order to transport the boxes of his library. Thus, in three or four days, having spent Rs 2020, he was adequately prepared for the voyage.

When Anand Ram was more or less ready to leave, on that very day a letter arrived from Zakariya Khan, the governor of Lahore, to the effect that Nadir Shah Afshar had once more reached Atak (or Attock) to chastise the Yusufza'i Afghans, and then planned to go on into Kashmir. Anand Ram thought it was incumbent on him to be the first to inform the emperor of this, and hence decided to send his son Fateh Singh post-haste to Dhappa. On the 21st Safar his son, with some other members of Anand Ram's party, namely Bhag Mal, Mirza Momin Beg, and Manmohan Singh, left their *hawelī* in Shahjahanabad-Delhi and very rapidly reached the imperial camp with the news. Anand Ram gave his son Rs 21, on the occasion of his departure – to ward off the evil eye. He states that despite the fact that he himself was to leave a mere two days later, he still missed his son in the course of their brief separation.

The next section details Anand Ram's setting off from Delhi under the head: "Departure of the writer of these lines from Shahjahanabad for Garh Muktesar, and his arrival in the high army laden with marks of victory".[79] The mood is a rather mixed one, as we see from the section's introductory set of phrases itself, which describe how on Monday, 24th Safar, he set out once five watches (*gharī*) of the day had elapsed. But a rueful verse immediately intervenes: "Voyaging does

---

[79] Ibid., 12.

not suit me,/I'm a flower plucked from the branch." Nevertheless, the decision once taken could not be so easily reversed. Anand Ram hence gave money – 11 *ashrafīs* and Rs 100 – to his retainers and slave-girls (*farzandān wa kanīzān*) by way of ensuring auspiciousness (*shu-gūn*), and also broke some coconuts to the same end. He bade fare-well to the female apartments (*darūn*) of his house, and, accompani-ed by his other son Rai Kripa Ram, who was injured in his left hand from having fallen of a horse, at last departed Delhi. He tells us that the prospect left him saddened; at the moment of leaving, Anand Ram had tears in his eyes, and his heart ached out of separation from friends. However, he seems far from bereft of other friends: "Thus, with my dear brother Mir Najm-ud-Din, son of the late Mir Sharf-ud-Din 'Ali, who had as pen name 'Payam', and Ratan Singh, and others, and some twenty horsemen, I left the city, crossing the river Jamuna by pontoon-bridge (*pul-i kashtī*), and reached Ghazi Nagar."

Arriving at this spot, the party stopped to eat, and then made for Sarai Lal Khan, two *kos* before Dasna. Here they camped before a mango orchard and idly watched goats graze. Anand Ram bought one of them belonging to the *mīr ātish* for half a rupee, had it slaughtered, sent half of it ahead to the Khwaja Badshah (a particular friend of Anand Ram in the imperial camp). The rest of the goat served for ke-babs and mutton *do-pyāza* (mutton with onions), but only in a rough and ready way as they could not get spices or even turmeric (*zard-chūb*) in that benighted spot. *Khichrī*, the usual preparation with rice and lentils, was also made, and giving thanks to God for what they had, the party managed with bland food. It turned out that Sarai Lal Khan was more or less abandoned, and populated only in name. Who this Lal Khan was, however, remained unknown. Perhaps, Anand Ram jokes, it was made by Lal Bujhakkar, a legendary figure in northern India, who was supposedly so wise that he answered all sorts of riddles and problems.[80]

---

[80] The editor Azhar 'Ali notes that in his *Mir'āt-ul-Istilāh*, Anand Ram Mukhlis has an explanation on Lal Bujhakkar, where he notes: "It is said that in Hindustan too, there were Miyan Lal Bujhakkar and Shaikh Chilli, who understood every-thing": *Safar Nāma*, 14, fn. 1.

The night was cold and a little windy. But since spring had begun, Anand Ram was unprepared for the chill and was without a quilt (*razā'i*). Nevertheless, he made do with some shawls. On the 25th Safar, having bathed, they left Sarai Lal Khan and reached Dhappa, where the imperial party had been somewhat earlier. Since their provisions were scattered, and nothing to eat was ready to hand, some of the party collected fresh ears of wheat from the local fields and roasted them, and, sprinkling some sugar over the whole, washed it down with a few fresh cups of coffee (*qahwa*).[81] Then they moved quickly on as they heard that the emperor had rerouted his travels because of tough jungle, and was camped at Kali Nadi, two *kos* before Hapur – which was where the party of Anand Ram now directed itself. The location of the imperial camp prompts another joke from Anand Ram: "If Kali Ganga is not attainable, we might as well hold on to Kali Nadi" – Kali Ganga being a celebrated courtesan in the Delhi of those days.

The morose mood at the moment of departure from Delhi has clearly passed, and Mukhlis is now in far better humour. We can see this from his account of a meeting with another courtier, Khwaja-i Badshah, at the edge of a well. Anand Ram notes that the Khwaja had said to him in a bantering vein: "We should not neglect this well, even as we should not neglect the cleft in the chin. For its water has such qualities, as the cleft enhances the beauty of a women's face." To this Anand Ram replied: "Is the water cool?", and the Khwaja responded: "It's even better than the water of the Gulabi Kuia." The reference is to a small well by Mukhlis' house where he kept his drinking water cool by storing it inside. The well was known as the Gulabi Kuia (rose-flavoured well), prompting Mukhlis to recall one of his own verses in the mixed idiom of *rekhta*:

Khalq kon tishnagī dīdar tujh gul kī hubābī hai
'arq seten tere chāh-i-zaqan goyā gulābī hai.

---

[81] On the introduction of coffee into the Mughal domains, see Hakala, "A Sultan in the Realm of Passion". For comparative materials, see Hattox, *Coffee and Coffeehouses.*

Thirst bubbles up in people
to see your flower-like face
Even the sweat that collects in the cleft
of your chin is rose-flavoured.[82]

After this exchange of pleasantries and poetry they went on together to Hapur in some haste, so as to be able to join Rai Fateh Singh,
Anand Ram's son, whom he had sent ahead. But Fateh Singh turned
back and rejoined them halfway, leading to some more poetic expres-
sions of fatherly love by Anand Ram. Finally, arriving at the imperial
camp, Anand Ram pitched his tents (*misl*) some distance from those of
the vizier. The next day, after bathing, he wrote a few letters to Lahore
and Shahjahanabad, ate, and rested in the afternoon after watering down
the dust in his tent. In the evening he got together with his friends
Lala Sukhpat Ram, Lala Basant Ram, Lala Dalip Singh, and others,
and a pleasant time was spent in conversation and snacking within
a warm ambience (*suhbat-i nuql wa gap garm mānd*).

On the 27th Safar (31st March 1745), which was *ākhirī chahār-
shamba*, the Muslim festival on the last Wednesday of Safar, he met
his very close friend the celebrated poet Siraj-ud-Din 'Ali Khan Arzu,
who was in the camp of another notable, Ishaq Khan. On the next
day, the imperial camp moved on to Baksar village, 5 *kos* before Garh
Muktesar. Here it was found that water was short, so the camp was
moved still further ahead, and Anand Ram himself decided to go on
directly as far as the banks of the Ganga to find a good spot while his
two sons went off hunting. Later his sons joined him, and at night
the inevitable *khichrī* and *sāg methī* (a form of fenugreek spinach) was
made. Since he was hungry, and the food this time was well cooked,
he enjoyed his meal. There was also the satisfaction of being able to
return to the river after an absence of two years, which he expresses
in a quatrain.[83]

O Mukhlis, I left the city for the jungle.
I bore the sufferings of the journey.

[82] Anand Ram Mukhlis, *Safar Nāma*, 16.
[83] We turn to the later travel account by Mukhlis with a description of his journey to Garhmuktesar, begun on 5th Zi al-Qa'da 1160 H., in the following sections.

In the year 1158, hundreds of thanks,
that I could again bathe in the Ganga.

The next day, the rest of the imperial camp arrived. Anand Ram
now bathed in the river, performed the rituals to which he was habitu-
ated, and took a vow that so long as he was by the banks of the Ganga,
he would think no more of meat. This nicely captures Anand Ram's
Khatri culture, caught between his fondness for mutton *do-pyāza* and
his temporary vegetarianism. The next day he went through a round
of meetings with the vizier, other notables, and even the emperor, with
whom he reports a minor conversation:

I presented two *ashrafis* to him, and since by the Grace of God, he had a
pleasant temperament, he said, "I am seeing you after a long gap. I was
eagerly looking forward to seeing you. Are you well?" I responded: "It is
true that on account of some work, I could not have the privilege of an
audience with you. But, thanks be to God, I was never oblivious to the
requirements of service. Though it is said: (Verse)

Keep the slave who has grown old happy,
by granting him liberty,

still I am in your service. In spite of my absence [from your side], I was
all the time in your glorious retinue. Now that I have some more time, I
thought that I should come here instead of resting". The emperor replied,
"It was solely on account of your sincerity (*ikhlās*) that your heart could
not allow you to remain in the city, so eager were you to be in my company. This even though you did not accompany me initially". I made my
salutations and returned home.

There is word-play here on the terms "sincerity" (*ikhlās*) and "sincere" (*mukhlis*) on the part of the emperor, and a sense of comfort and
intimacy that makes the journey seem more worthwhile; all seems to
be proceeding well and uneventfully. In the afternoon Mukhlis met
a certain Muhammad Quli Khan and they conversed pleasantly, and
that evening saw the new moon with a red glow, which made him recall
a poem of Asifi, a contemporary of Sultan Husain Baiqara of Herat,
playing on the idea of moonlight that is white, and the contrast with the
red glow, like the whiteness of age tempered by the redness of wine. It
was now the beginning of the month of Rabi' I. The sense of comfort

was further enhanced when Khan-i Arzu came to see him again. Though he remains for a short time, there is some conversation and the exchange of verses. The following day a magic entertainment was provided by the so-called Bhanumati group, which included covering a mango-seed with a sheet, making it sprout, flower, and give fruit, but after a while making the whole disappear. This prompts Anand Ram to reflect on the expression *sabz bāgh* (literally "verdant garden"), which means promising the earth but delivering nothing; perhaps the conjurer's trick was an illustration of that.

Meetings with other courtiers and friends continue. One of these is a certain Lala Chainsukh, who is in the emperor's camp, and who comes to meet Anand Ram. Most of his family was in the jewellery trade. He came and declared: "I consider you to be a dear friend." Anand Ram replied, "Why not?", citing a hemistich to him: "The goldsmith knows the true value of gold,/and the jeweller that of jewels." He then asked him where he was coming from, the emperor's camp or elsewhere. Lala Chainsukh complained of the long and hot voyage that he had undertaken. Since the vizier too had come to meet the emperor the same day, Anand Ram replied: "Master, the travails that you are complaining about, the vizier too has undergone them." To which the other said, "How am I inferior to the vizier?" Mukhlis responded, somewhat ironically no doubt, "Oh, you are the very emperor of this age." Gossip followed. Chainsukh said he had heard that the emperor was going, bow in hand, in the direction of the Rohilas' settlement, and that on pulling its string had declared: "*Mārā hai* (I've killed him)." 'Umdat-ul-Mulk Amir Khan had sarcastically replied, "*Mūe kon mārā hai*. (You've killed what is dead)." Anand Ram responded in a more conciliatory vein that Amir Khan must in fact have said, "*Mūe kā kyā mārna hai?* (What good is it to kill the dead?)."[84]

On the 4th of the month, a Mughal war party returned to the imperial camp from Amber, whose ruler it had gone to aid, and on the 5th the vizier crossed the river Ganga by a pontoon bridge, as did Anand Ram himself with his children. However, the cart (*chhakrā-yi*

---

[84] Anand Ram, *Safar Nāma*, 32.

modīkhāna) with supplies was delayed, and so food that evening was very ordinary. Mention is incidentally made of a tragic incident, namely the death of the Faridnagar zamindar's handsome twenty-year-old son by drowning in the Ganga, and how his daughter-in-law became a sati as a consequence.

Courtly news and gossip continued. On 12th Rabi' I, the emperor got on a boat to go fishing on the river. He reached the tent of Amir Khan and formally visited him; Amir Khan presented him 1100 *ashrafīs*, and the emperor remained there for four watches, and even shared a meal. On 16th Rabi' I, Kishan Chand, the *wakīl* of Qa'im Khan, received a *khil'at*, and requested leave to go back to his master. On 17th Rabi' I, baskets of provisions arrived from Shahjahanabad, brought by Hriday Ahir and Jhanda.

Enough has been said to give the reader a flavour of the style and nature of the first part of this travel account, as well as the type of information it contains. We can now proceed to highlight some of the passages that appear to us of greater interest. Anand Ram's preoccupations have so far largely been with the imperial camp, and with his own household; he scarcely deigns to look around him at either natural or man-made sights. This may also be the result of his total familiarity with the route as far as Garh Muktesar, where he has told us he was in the habit of travelling practically every year. Once past this spot, his awareness of the outside world seems to increase.

Thus, crossing the river, his sons went on a hunt and brought back birds, such as partridges (*durrāj*) and larks (*charz*). The cooks busied themselves in making a special preparation (*dam-pukht*) with the birds, and Anand Ram remarked the abundance of larks in the region. Then, in Shahbazpur, he commented on the mango orchard where he stayed, the quality of the surroundings, the beauty of the night, and the swings (*jhūlā*) in the gardens. Interspersed with the usual political matters (the arrival of letters from 'Ali Muhammad Khan, etc.), the outside world begins to intrude more and more into the account. It turned out there were lions in the jungle nearby and a cart-puller had been attacked by one of them. Conviviality now began to extend to local zamindars, and as delicacies arrived for Anand Ram from Delhi he took over a sort of grain silo in a nearby village, had it converted into a clay oven (*tanūr*), and made unleavened bread (*nān-i tanūrī*). Other supplies arrived from Bareilly and meals were held on a more extended scale, with a large number of guests.

Others in the camp, not so well-off, had taken to raiding the nearby villages for cattle and using elephants to carry off food supplies. The *qizilbāsh* (the Turkoman "Red-Top" soldiers, left behind from Nadir Shah's invasion) were particularly implicated and given a stern warning. One such incident (*sāniha*) is reported:

> Some of the people, in particular the Qizilbash who were the servants of Safdar Jang, under the pretext of bringing fodder for the animals, had gone inside the villages around, and plundered the villages and their cattle. This was brought to the notice of the emperor by the vizier. The emperor deputed some of the people of the army to protect the villages and the cultivated fields. An order was issued that whoever committed the crime of plunder would be chastised. Those who were deputed for protection brought about thirty Qizilbash with some forty elephants, laden with bushels of wheat. They were all punished, and Safdar Jang also had them thrashed to such an extent that two of them died in the process.[85]

The next major stop after Shahbazpur was meant to be Bangarh, with the intention of chastising the rebellious 'Ali Muhammad Khan. The imperial party passed through Hasanpur town, the army was made ready, and entertainments provided at night by puppeteers and others. Anand Ram noted that these puppeteers were in their style different from those of Delhi. Hasanpur too is described, the first town that actually attracts Anand Ram's attention. A place dominated by Afghans, it had large gardens with "tanks full of clean water" (comparable in quality to those in Shahjahanabad), impressive buildings in a row "like lines of poetry," broad streets, and markets full of diverse goods. Roaming the streets and lanes at night, the middle-aged (but in his own eyes, ageing) Anand Ram noticed beautiful women peering out of their houses, which he gallantly declares gave the whole trip a different flavour. "One or two women showed their heads from the

[85] Ibid., 34.

windows. May God be praised (*al-hamdul-illāh*), that this made all the wandering through the lanes worthwhile."

Anand Ram's usual gastronomic preoccupations continue to dominate. Finding aubergines in a nearby field, he orders a special dish (*bhurtā*) made from them, mixed with tender mangoes for a sour taste. By this time they had arrived at the Sot river, where they ate *qaliya* (meat cooked with vegetables) and *khushka* (rice). The next day, the 21st of the month, fish were caught in large numbers at a spot indicated to them by local inhabitants; some were sent to friends such as Bhaiya Bhag Mal, others cooked and eaten there and then. Mukhlis' friend Rai Sukhpat Ram, another *bon vivant*, had a form of stuffed bread (*sālan-i kulchā-i maida*) made, while Anand Ram's son made a *sālan-i gūlar* with his own hand. All this cooking was done in a small, pole-less tent (*khaima-i bīchūba*).

Once more, troubles arose on account of the indiscipline of the army, which had raided nearby wheatfields. Anand Ram was obliged to intervene and have some of the culprits brought to book. Other untoward incidents (*sāniha*) followed. There was a fight between the attendant of Mir Najm-ud-Din 'Ali Khan and a Baksariya over water. The attendant struck the other with a spear, but he was not too seriously wounded. Since the incident was deemed obstreperous, the servant was punished. One of the looters in the army was seen carrying off a wooden cot. Anand Ram thought to buy it for his grandson, but the man refused to sell it, relenting only when threatened and selling it for a small sum. This reminded Anand Ram of a story. A man had stolen a horse and then went to sell it in the bazaar. The owner was there and recognised it; he then took it from him and returned home. When the thief went back to his own home he was asked how much he had sold it for. He replied that he sold it at exactly the price for which he had bought it.

On the 23rd and 24th they remained in the same spot, and it was here that the emperor Muhammad Shah's forty-fifth birthday was celebrated. A certain Muhammad Hasan Khan, whose pen name was Sami', came to meet Anand Ram and the latter recited a number of verses, of which some are reproduced in the text. They are mostly from the classical poets, Maulana Rum, Mirza Ibrahim Adham, and Sultan

Abu Sa'id Abu'l Khair.[86] Then, he mentions a certain Muhammad Rafi', who had come to see him. This was once more a moment of encounters and exchanges in the camp, but not all of them were happy ones. For example, a certain 'Aziz Khan, who had received a fairly high *mansab* of 4000 in the aftermath of Nadir Shah's invasion, paid Anand Ram a visit. This man had the habit of talking incessantly without making much sense, and the encounter did not please Anand Ram. In the case of Rafi', it turned out that he was previously a servant in the establishment of the late 'Azimullah Khan (cousin and brother-in-law of Qamar-ud-Din Khan). He had a son who was nine years old, and was the pupil of a master (*mu'allim*) in the camp. One day, the cruel master, in the process of teaching him, stabbed him with a knife not once but twice, so that he died. Thereafter the assassin stabbed himself too. God alone knew the reason for this strange incident, writes Mukhlis, whom the story clearly troubles a good deal.

The party now arrived at Sambhal at the month's end. The town, he noted, was at some distance from the main highway, but he thought nevertheless to take the trouble to visit it. The whole area was full of huge mango trees, and in that season the fruit was available in plenty. The town's main gate was very high, with a peculiar feature – a huge iron ring with a circular millstone fixed in it. The story had it that a strong acrobat (*bāzīgar*) of the past had in one leap fixed the ring in the doorframe, and with a second the stone in the ring. The challenge was thus open to all comers to try and equal this feat from the past, or to bring the stone down. Only those who could meet the challenge could pass through the door, and if not they should pass elsewhere. As a result, no other *bāzīgar* had since tried to pass through the door.

A large part of the town, considered one of the older in the region, was in ruins by the 1740s. The people of the town were as cultured as those of Delhi, and Amin-ud-Daula, a well-known notable (of 7000 *mansab* rank) from the time of Bahadur Shah, had originally been from there.[87] He had his own *hawelī* made up of several buildings,

---

[86] Ibid., 42–3.

[87] This is presumably the same noble who appears as Amin-ud-Din Sambhali in Chandra, *Parties and Politics*, 182.

besides having constructed a number of gardens and market-places; in fact, even his tomb was situated there. Amin-ud-Daula's mansion had a large bath (*hammām*) and an *ā'ina khāna* – a sort of glass-house (*shīsh mahal*).

This brings Anand Ram to one of the most particular features of the place. On the town's other side was a high dome, that was at one time a temple called Har Mandal. Of this it used to be said, recounts Anand Ram:

> *Bhāg bare Sambhal ke*
> *ke Harjī har mandal āvenge*

> Great is the fortune of Sambhal
> where Harji will come to the Harmandal.[88]

The reference is an interesting one, for it comes from one of the refrains of the Nihkalanki Avtar section of the *Dasam Granth*, which has been described as a "compendium of theological, mythological and narrative works attributed to Guru Gobind Singh," the tenth guru of the Sikhs.[89] Here, the idea carries strong millenarian overtones of the returning figure of Kalki, who usually appears as a somewhat sinister horseman in a Vaishnava context (though perhaps recovered from an earlier Buddhist theme). Clearly, as a Punjabi, Anand Ram's wide reading extended into the Sikh scriptures.

To return to his narrative: when Babur took Hindustan, writes Anand Ram, he gave Sambhal as a *jāgīr* to his son Humayun Mirza, and converted this ancient building into a mosque, so that it was now the *jāmi' masjid* of the town. "Earlier too it was a place of worship (*'ibādat*

---

[88] For an earlier brief mention of the Har Mandal, see the late-sixteenth-century account by the Mughal chronicler and courtier Abu'l Fazl, *Ā'in-i Akbarī*, trans. Jarrett, rev. Sarkar, vol. 2, 285, where he states: "the tenth avatār will appear in this spot". For details of the mosque, also see Asher, *Architecture of Mughal India*, 28–9. Asher follows Jarrett in reading "Har" (in the text) as "Hari" (Vishnu).

[89] We owe this identification to Jeevan Deol, who discusses the matter briefly in Deol, "Eighteenth Century Khalsa Identity", 31 (and note 16). Deol gives the original Dasam Granth refrain as: *Bhalu bhāg bhaya iha Sambhal ke/Harjī har mandal avāhinge*.

kadah), and even now it is a place of worship," concludes Anand Ram calmly, as if this were the most natural of things, noting that the high dome (*gumbad*) of the mosque was similar to that of the temple. He even cites the chronogram inscribed on one of its arches, noting that it was constructed on Babur's orders by a certain Hindu Beg. The inscription ran as follows:

> He who collects in himself all buildings of virtue and excellence,
> who raises high the flags of kingdoms and communities,
> who spreads the carpets of peace and safety,
> who builds the edifices of knowledge and good acts,
> that king of high stature Muhammad Babur,
> may God keep him safe, and raise him high.
> When the candle of his power was lit in Hind,
> Sambhal was illumined by its rays.
> In order to build this mosque,
> so that it would be protected from harm,
> he issued an order to this humble slave,
> who was one of the important supports of the state.
> When the wise and understanding Mir Hindu Beg,
> who was exemplary in his moral conduct,
> in keeping with the *farmān* of the emperor of the age,
> completed the work with God's grace,
> the year, month and day was such:
> *Yakum az shahr-i Rabī'-ul-awwal.*[90]

Further, Anand Ram notes the existence of a tank, now in poor condition, but still thought to be holy, where people came and bathed. Brahmans and flower-sellers still visited in numbers to sell flowers and recite *shlokas* there. The tank was almost dry, but people bathed in it still, using the sludge from it. The traveller also saw the ruins of the fort at Sambhal, largely lying in the dust. He praised the quarters of different communities and professions, and noted in particular that tobacco was a local speciality. Once dried in the sun, it was mixed with other fragrant products and smoked. Anand Ram too had an urge to smoke, and when he tried it he found the tobacco to be of really good quality.

---

[90] Anand Ram Mukhlis, *Safar Nāma*, 48. For a discussion of the mosque, see Crane, "The Patronage of the Zahir-ud-din Babur", 101–2.

But with the onset of summer the journey was proving too long and tedious. Tempers began to run short, as the following incident suggests. Anand Ram had asked a mason (*beldār*) to make a platform (*chabūtra*) inside the tent so that he could spread a carpet over it and rest. The latter replied to him in a rather impolite manner. Anand Ram noted that he himself was on that day in a bad temper on account of the hot weather and the dust. So he caught hold of the *beldār* and beat him up. Later, though, he repented and felt disgusted with himself: "Damn this world and worldly affairs, which lead to this sort of unpleasant actions. If you do not act, it creates arrogance in others, and if you do, it takes away from your humanity, for all human beings are made equal."[91]

Battles and Negotiations

By now we are in the month of Rabi' II 1158 H. (which had begun on 3 May 1745). Since Anand Ram was obliged to continue his life in the open, he decided to appreciate what the environment had to offer, waxing eloquent on the red rays of the setting sun — the town-dweller appreciating his communion with nature. Qa'im Khan, an Afghan potentate of Farrukhabad (and son of the founder of the Farrukhabad state) arrived with his vast brood of brothers and was received by the emperor with honours, although some of the other nobles, notably Safdar Jang, appear to have had reservations about his loyalty in the upcoming campaign. Preparations were now firmly afoot for military action, but the storms of summer had made their appearance. One of these occurred while they were near the Sot river and was so violent that it made some of the tents fly in the air and fall down flat like carpets. Anand Ram cites his own quatrain, in which one can suspect at least a small dose of sarcasm:

> The year when Muhammad Shah, the Auspicious Khaqan,
> went with his army to the eastern country,
> one day, on account of the wind
> people's tents flew in the sky like paper-kites (*kāghaz-i bād*).[92]

---

91 Ibid., 50.
92 Ibid., 53–4.

The verse also carried a nostalgic reference to the Delhi summer custom of flying kites, in which Anand Ram apparently took part. But not everything was gloomy. Mukhlis continued his culinary pursuits. Some venison was sent to him by Hatim 'Ali Khan and made into *kabābs*. The party continued to eat well while keeping an eye on political developments around.

Nine days into the month the agents of 'Ali Muhammad Khan arrived at last to negotiate, but the emperor demanded an enormous tribute (*peshkash*) of a crore (ten million) of rupees and imposed further conditions which the other's agents seemed reluctant to accept: "The emperor then said that considering that the blood of Muslims should not be shed, it was necessary to initiate negotiations." However, battle seemed inevitable, and the signs of nature too were inauspicious: the preparations were accompanied by another violent summer storm. Anand Ram meanwhile took time out to eat his *pūrīs* and *khichrī*, noting that now that it had really come time to fight many of the notables – making one or the other excuse – had begun to return to Delhi. He reflects ironically on this situation, and especially the role therein of his own community (the Khatris) and of the Kayasthas. "O friends, now that matters have come to arrows and swords (*shamsher-o-tīr*), why should we stay here, for we are not soldiers? We are Multawi Mal and Pakodi Das [Postponement Mal and Cutlet Das]; why should we then not leave for the city to do business there?"[93]

Among those who left was Anand Ram's friend Bhaiya Bhag Mal, who had been in charge of some of the imperial camp's arrangements. Anand Ram himself stayed on despite being indisposed with a fever (*tap*) cured in the end through the intervention of Hakim 'Abdul Shafi Khan. Others in his party fell ill too; his son Fateh Singh was taken ill with fever (*harārat*). Anand Ram continued to report minor discussions with his friends, some of which have a characteristic mid-eighteenth-century flavour about them, in the sense of containing playful remarks deflating the claims of the Mughal sovereign himself, of a type that would have been frowned on a half-century earlier. But pursuits other than gossip have to be found in order to keep time from

---

[93] The text (p. 58) has *byohār*, which should probably be read *byopār* (business).

hanging too heavy. "One of the mahouts (*mahāwat*) found a long bamboo from the village of Basi, which was in the *jāgīr* of Dondi Khan, who was the *jama'dār* of 'Ali Muhammad Khan, when the Mughal armies were plundering the village. When I saw it, I thought it could be planted in the courtyard of my tent and a lamp hung from it at night. This was greatly appreciated in the camp. In Hindi, such a lamp is called *ākāsh diyā*."[94]

By the middle of the month, the imperial camp had finally advanced as far as Bangarh, where the emperor now sought to reconcile the jealousies of Qa'im Khan and Safdar Jang in his entourage. Anand Ram Mukhlis continued to think of matters of the stomach, even mocking himself for it on the occasion of a visit to a mango grove. "Quite a lot of mangoes were taken from the trees, and some were set aside for making pickles while some others were kept apart for ripening. How crazy I am, that in the midst of an army camp, I am concerned not just with ripening mangoes, but even with making pickles in this commotion of looting and raiding (*hangāmā-i gīr-o-dār*)!" Further, these arrangements were rather spoiled by the weather, for with the onset of the proverbial eastern winds associated with the pre-monsoon (*bād-i sharqī*) things became cooler, whereas more heat was needed for the mangoes to ripen properly.

Skirmishes began now with 'Ali Muhammad Khan's forces on the banks of the local river (*daryā-i sot*, or Sot Nadi). Anand Ram noticed that, in the process, some local villages came temporarily to be deserted, though with all the inhabitants' goods and effects left behind in them. None of this seems to have ruffled his equanimity, for he continued his old habit of after-lunch siestas (*qailūlā*), usually taken under a mango tree near an abandoned well, even though he abstained from eating much on account of his recent indisposition. He notes that his sons made quite succulent meals, including local varieties of greens and spinach (*sāg khurfa* with *chaulāi*).

On the 22nd the forces of the two sides were finally prepared to fight, and on the 24th the Rohilas mounted a night attack (*shab-khūn*)

---

[94] Anand Ram Mukhlis, *Safar Nāma*, 61. The *ākāsh diyā* is shown in the drawing facing page 27 of the manuscript, which we reproduce here.

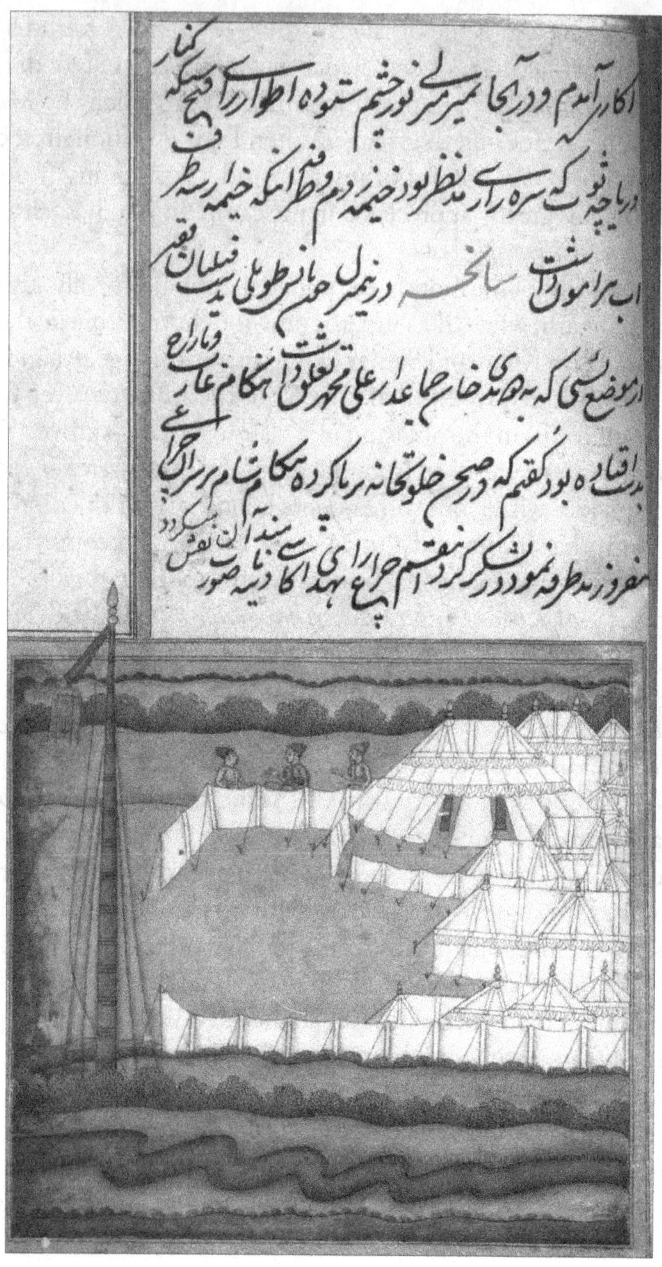

Image 5.3: Anand Ram Mukhlis, *Safar Nāma*.

on the imperial army. Annoyed, the emperor now made a resolution to capture and destroy Bangarh, even if it were to prove as difficult as the proverbial stronghold of Qandahar – or so he said. Perhaps hearing of this new-found determination, 'Ali Muhammad Khan sent a message to the emperor and asked for terms, even though skirmishes continued. Some factions amongst the Mughals were for making peace, but the powerful Safdar Jang was opposed to it (for reasons set out earlier). Anand Ram comments on these divisions, noting that it was on account of them that the *qizilbāsh* – that is, Nadir Shah and his men – had earlier imposed themselves on the Mughal court; as for 'Ali Muhammad Khan, who was a mere *ta'alluqa-dār* over a few villages, Anand Ram says it was wholly inappropriate for the Mughal emperor himself to have come out on an expedition against him. What a state Mughal sovereignty has been reduced to, when 'Ali Muhammad Khan hasn't the courtesy either to submit or flee! As for the nobles, they keep changing their minds, while the emperor has no opinions to express.

On the 28th of the month there was another great storm and everything was covered in mud and dust. Anand Ram repeats his critique of Mughal politics on this occasion, noting how ridiculous it is that the emperor (*farmānrawā*) of Hindustan has set out with 100,000 horse, and cannon enough to reduce Bangarh to dust with a single salvo, and yet nothing concrete has been achieved. At this point, Muhammad Shah has a painting of the imperial encampment (*khaima-gāh*) made by the painter Mir Kalan (and a copy of it, by one Govardhan, was in fact appended to Anand Ram's manuscript).

At last, in the month of Jumada I, 'Ali Muhammad Khan arrived in the Mughal camp through the intervention of Qa'im Khan, and symbolically submitted to the emperor as if he were a Mughal captive. But before doing so he had taken certain precautions. As he approached the royal camp from Bangarh, a village which was next to his fort was set on fire by his orders. It was also reported that he had ruefully inspected his warehouses and their contents in case of negotiations. Anand Ram now cites a Hindi couplet, ironically reflecting on the departure of this "king" from his camp: "*Rājā chhore nagari, jo chāhe so le* (The King is leaving town, let anyone take it over)." Indeed, overcome by a bout of sarcasm, he adds to this another verse in Persian of Naziri:

> Naziri burnt both city and jungle
> with his sigh of separation.
> He departs in a like manner
> to wisdom leaving the world.[95]

'Ali Muhammad Khan's appearance in the Mughal camp is now described. His hands were tied with a kerchief, which the emperor ordered opened, thus symbolically freeing and forgiving him. 'Ali Muhammad Khan, a fair, forty-year-old man of medium stature, is described down to the details of his style of tying his turban; the Rohilas' encampment is also briefly described, in particular the fact that almost all there were rather well armed: "Each Rohila horseman and foot-soldier had a gun, and each commander of ten and one hundred foot-soldiers would carry a different small banner (*nishān-i kūchak*) of a different colour. They all were going along in an orderly procession with the Rohila chief. It appeared as if he were accompanied by a flowering garden."

The campaign thus seemed to draw to a gentle and anticlimactic close. It was now time to return to Delhi, preparations being made in a leisurely way. Since the imperial army had remained camped for so long by the Sot rivulet, the emperor honoured the stream with a title: "The Loyal Friend and Brave Companion (*yār-i wafādār wa hamdil-i tehtamān*)". On 4th Jumada I proclamations were issued that the camp would return to Shahjahanabad. 'Ali Muhammad Khan's revenue assignment was given over to someone else, and a thousand masons and construction workers were sent off to demolish the fort of Bangarh. The Rohila artillery too was confiscated, as were their goods, which were promptly sold to the itinerant Banjaras, and the proceeds used to pay off arrears of salary to the Mughal soldiery.[96]

In the closing sections of his account Anand Ram mentions a local festival involving the floating of lamps in the Sot river. This inspires him

---

[95] Ibid., 76–7.

[96] On Mughal dealings with the Banjaras, see Habib, "Merchant Communities", 372–9.

to poetry, but we are soon back to more banal matters, for he recounts the arrival in his camp of Chitra Bhuj, the *dīwān* of the celebrated Raja Jugal Kishor, representative of the Bengal governor in the Mughal court (*wakīl-i nāzim-i Bangāla*) as also a well-known Khatri entrepreneur and revenue-farmer.[97] When he arrived he had an old horse, and everything was in a tattered condition, which was rather surprising since his master was noted for his wealth. On seeing him Anand Ram exclaimed to himself: "What a misfortune! I do not have an army to help Bhaiya Jio [Jugal Kishor] collect his revenue, since he has it on farm (*ijāra*). Nor do I have the money (*zar*) to help the Diwan Jio." He asked Chitra Bhuj the reasons for his arrival and the latter replied that Jugal Kishor, who was in the area to collect money, had been harassed by the *jāgīrdārs* there, and so had gone off to Sambhal. Chitra Bhuj had been left behind as a sort of hostage to satisfy the *jāgīrdārs*. But the menace was such that Chitra Bhuj too had fled and now wanted to pass the night in Anand Ram's camp; he promised to leave the next morning. Anand Ram welcomed him and said he could stay as long as he liked. A separate tent was made ready for him; during his stay Anand Ram pumped him for information. First, he asked, what Raja Jugal Kishor's monthly expenditure was. The reply was Rs 12,000, of which Rs 7000 was for servants, etc., and Rs 5000 for the maintenance of his own household. Anand Ram said: "May God give him more and more (*Allāhumma zid fazid*)." Second, he asked whether this income was less or more than the expenditure. Chitra Bhuj replied that earlier the income had been double of the expenditure. Now it had decreased somewhat in proportion. And as promised he left the next morning.[98]

Soon after his departure there was a major rainstorm – the monsoon had arrived at last. Wading knee-deep, Anand Ram was reduced to spending part of the night seated ruefully on his cot smoking his water-pipe (*huqqā*'), while the tent began to collapse under the weight of water. Of course, his main concern was to ensure against leakages into his pen-and-ink-stand (*qalamdān*), and he instructed his son

[97] Jugal Kishor's grandson, Kunwar Prem Kishor "Firaqi", is the author of the *Waqā'i'-i 'Ālam Shāhī*, ed. Imtiaz 'Ali Khan 'Arshi.

[98] Anand Ram Mukhlis, *Safar Nāma*, 83–4.

(who was meanwhile letting out wails of despair) on how best to take care of it. The next day, when the camp was being cleared up, thousands of snakes were found, which caused a minor panic and a snake-hunt. The rivulet, so recently dubbed a loyal friend, turned out quite a threat. The storm increased the urgency of preparations for the return journey. At first the thought was to take the road via Anupshahr, as it was the shortest and there was no lack of fodder on the way. But on enquiry it was found that the road was not good enough for the royal party, water was scarce, and the road uneven. So they eventually decided to return as they had come.

Anand Ram was initially unhappy with this decision and did not really trust the advice of the advance party (*qarāwalān*). But he eventually accepted it, citing a proverb in Persian: "It is better to tell a lie that placates, than to tell a truth that creates confusion (*fitna*)." So even if what the *qarāwals* had said may have been false, perhaps it was the lesser of two evils as it avoided the likelihood of confusion by regrouping the army. In any event, tempers were running short once more. Near Sambhal one of the men from the army had gone and looted a field of aubergines.[99] The owner was distressed and complained. A Baksariya who was around tried to snatch the goods from the looter and a violent fight broke out. Mir Najm-ud-Din 'Ali then reached the spot, had the two beaten up, and brought an end to the altercation. This ridiculous fight over aubergines, "*bādanjān māro būd*", amused Anand Ram greatly.

The beginnings of the monsoon had brought out the habitual sights and sounds of this season in Hindustan. There was water and greenery all around. Birds, such as the koel, the *papīhā*, and the peacock, began to sing as the returning expedition once more passed by Sambhal. Shaikh Amanullah, a friend of Anand Ram's brother Lala Lajja Ram, who was also a notable and Mughal *mansabdār* of the area, had sent him gifts of mangoes and the local tobacco. Anand Ram praised the mangoes' flavour, and the particular fact that they had no fibres (*bī rīsha*), but noted that it had become increasingly impracticable to continue with all his supplies and cart. So they were left behind with

---

[99] Ibid., 90.

Shaikh Amanullah, while Anand Ram made for Hasanpur. On the way, as the weather turned somewhat hotter, Anand Ram went off to enjoy a smoke in a mango grove and took a nap. But the weather turned hotter still, to the point that two or three men in the emperor's direct entourage died, while many others fell unconscious. One of those who fell sick was Muhammad A'zam, the staff-bearer (*chūbdār*) – water had to be poured down his throat to revive him. But the problem was the general lack of water. Anand Ram too felt a little feverish after his siesta. He thus conceived a great desire to eat watermelon. A passing watermelon-man was accosted; Fateh Singh bought fruit off him at an exorbitant price, the juice of which was extracted and mixed with rose-water, musk, and sugar. The mixture was consumed as an antidote to the heat of the day, and a decision taken to travel henceforth under moonlight to escape the heat. This form of travel suited Anand Ram rather better. "With the telescope of eagerness, in the eye of desire, we looked up to the sky like the Nargis flower," he writes, adding that the moon inspires poetry in him.

Two other acquaintances who were also in Mughal service, Majlis Rai and Lala Nayansukh Rai, arrived to see Anand Ram, and more mangoes were purchased and set aside for ripening. The water level in the rivers having risen, it was now something of a problem to cross the Ganga after Shahbazpur. Boats were few, and everyone was keen to get hold of one: it turned out that the corrupt and incompetent *mīr bahr* had failed in his duty to make a pontoon bridge and had instead monopolised the boats. The camels too were finding it difficult to manage their loads as the earth was wet and slippery. At last Anand Ram managed to get hold of a boat which crossed the river with his goods four times. The fifth time, though, some unruly *qizilbāsh* seized the boat and said they had to make use of it. Anand Ram ironically, and rather appositely, quotes some enigmatic Vaishnava *bhakti* verses of separation in Braj Bhasha to summarise his plight:

Alas, alas, says Uddhau, tears come to my eyes,
as evening approaches, and with it comes my own loneliness.
Having given up Gokul, and renounced Mathura,
with Brindavan in my sights, I'd forgotten my own village.
The poet Debendhara says, it saddens me

to think of the separation from my dwelling.
I boarded the boat of Love, but the boatman let me down.
O lord of Braj! I'm marooned between you and the shore.[100]

However, good news of a sort was on the way. A friend arrived from
Delhi with melons and pineapples, all of which turned out delicious.
The party then reached Gajraula, still on the far side of the Ganga,
where a bridge was being improvised. They were told they would
be allowed to cross, but after waiting the whole day were eventually
forced to make camp without their supplies, which had already gone
across by boat. Quarrels broke out among the returning notables over
who had the right to cross first. Worse still, some of Anand Ram's own
attendants deserted on account of the hardship.[101] He notes that there
were two Kashmiri Pandits in his party who served as cooks (*bar pukht
naukar būdan*). One of them, called Nandu, was particularly treacherous (*namak-harām*); he was a proud sort, with a curled moustache and
beard, who was nevertheless "like a donkey" in his appearance. These
two Pandits had crossed the river on the first day and then temporarily disappeared. Worse, they had kept all the provisions with them.
When Anand Ram crossed over he found and summoned them, his
heart burning like a kebab. He chastised them for their shamelessness
and told them they deserved to be beaten with staves. But finally he
ordered them to get out of his sight and dismissed them from his
service. These little men (*mardak*) were not deserving of employment, he complains. "I have had to face untold hardships on account
of these people, and their irresponsible behaviour," he states, and concludes, "*Wāqa'i' ki safar mihakk-i tajriba-yi ādam ast.* In truth, travel
is a touchstone for Man's experience."

[100] Ibid., 97–8. The editor of the text Sayyid Azhar 'Ali interpreted these verses
with the help of Kailash Chandra Brahaspati, and also produces a version in the
Nagari script. However, this reading appears problematic in parts, and we are grateful to Imre Bangha for a more plausible rendering, on which our own translation
is based. We were initially inclined to identify the author of the poem with the late
seventeenth- and early-eighteenth-century poet Devendra, or Dev, for whom see
McGregor, *Hindi Literature*, 177–9. Specialists of Braj Bhasha like Bangha have
doubted however on stylistic grounds that this verse was in fact from the pen of
the same "Dev".
[101] Anand Ram Mukhlis, *Safar Nāma*, 104.

On the last leg Anand Ram, deprived of food, had consoled himself by constantly drinking coffee. Had this drink, not so long ago an exotic and expensive one in India, already become less so on account of Indonesian production? We have no means of knowing whether what Anand Ram drank was the Mocha or Java variety; we only know that it temporarily dulled his hunger. Finally, on the 19th of the month the famished Anand Ram managed to get across the river as far as Sarai Lal Khan, where he pitched his tent under a mango tree. Then, making his way to Ghazi Nagar, his party crossed the Hindan river and reached Sarai Basant, which was unfortunately in ruins, and had only one grocer's shop (*dukān-i baqqāl*). But by now things had improved, for they had already been able to stock up on provisions in Ghazi Nagar.

That night Anand Ram could not eat and slept early. He then awoke early, bathed, and left camp before dawn, full of eagerness to return home. On the early morning of 23rd Jumada I, Thursday (24th June 1745) he reached Ganj Shahdara, and later the same day managed to cross the Jamuna where the water was not too high, on a 35-boat pontoon bridge (as opposed to the 95-boat bridge across the far wider Ganga). Anand Ram thus at last reached home, where his brother Kashmiri Mal and others awaited him at the gate of the quarter (*dar-i darwāza-yi bāzār-i mohalla*). He notes that now he was able to drink the cool water of his own well, since he had decided not to drink the ice-water on the last leg of his journey:

After freeing myself from the routine auspicious rituals (*rasmiyāt-i shugūn*), I drank the water from the well, which is cool and sweet because of its being blended with the water from the canal. I prostrated myself to thank God. Fourteen *ashrafīs*, and Rs 6249 and 12 annas had been spent in my three-month journey, the details of which expenditure have been entered in my diary (*roznāmcha*). The emperor, on the last day of this month, Thursday, in the morning, in his hunting palankeen entered the palace of Shahjahanabad by the Delhi Gate. The notables congratulated the emperor and, in keeping with their status, offered presents.

Thanks and gratitude to Allah, that today which is the 12th of Ramazan 1158 Hijri (8th October 1745), and the 28th regnal year of Muhammad Shah, on Sunday, these pages which consist of an account of the voyage to Bangarh were completed in the hand of the humble *faqīr* Anand

Ram Mukhlis after four watches of the night had passed, in the days when winter was approaching.[102]

Anand Ram's account was thus of a voyage in his own land, like that of the Portuguese Romantic writer Almeida Garrett a century later, who went down the Tagus from Lisbon to Santarém. But where Garrett blithely mixed factual observation with fiction in his *Viagens na minha terra* (Travels in My Homeland), Anand Ram seems to have been somewhat scrupulous in the matter of generic promiscuity.[103] In its measured pace, and the understated irony of its cadences, it marks a great contrast with other travellers of the early modern period in South Asia with their feverish evocation of an exotic world of *faqīrs* and Sufi madmen, of Liver-Eaters and lusty women of the desert. Women play a very minor role in Anand Ram's account, with the exception of the sati (mentioned in passing), and the charming faces espied while wandering in the by-lanes of Hasanpur. And even the latter may be a genuflection in the direction of the conventions of Indo-Persian poetry rather than an empirical observation. In marked contrast are the travellers from afar, who use the status and situation of women in Hindustan as a crucial barometer for gauging and evaluating the places through which they pass.[104]

Accompanying Anand Ram across the modest terrain of his first travel account has meant that we have roamed a bare few hundred miles in the heartland of Hindustan. Though the reader's patience may at times be tried in the process by this pointillist accumulation of minute details, it is to be hoped that the mining of this relatively little-known text has nevertheless not been devoid of interest. Such texts certainly carry wider implications, of which we may mention a few. In the first place, they can fruitfully be read as part of a body of works of an "empirical" bent that seem to be a growing feature of this period, and which our Ottomanist colleagues have equally remarked.[105] Again, it is

---

[102] Ibid., 107–8.

[103] Almeida Garrett, *Viagens na minha terra*. For a discussion, see Meier, "Almeida Garretts *Viagens na Minha Terra*".

[104] We are grateful to Claudine Salmon for pointing out to us that this feature is a recurring one in travel accounts.

[105] For a comparative perspective, see for example Kafadar, "Self and Others", 121–50.

striking that many such accounts, like those of Nek Rai and Bhimsen (discussed above), as well as Anand Ram are closely linked with the scribal milieu of the court. Any explanation on the emergence of this corpus of works cannot base itself solely on the notion of a shift in the objective conditions of literary production; we need equally to look into a series of issues of a formal nature, having to do with the internal logic (and evolution) of genres in Indo-Persian literature.

Some observations may equally be in order on the tone and content of the text. Anand Ram "Mukhlis" appears in this text as he wishes to be seen, as a sometimes ruefully self-abnegating but always self-indulgent gentleman of leisure caught up on account of the alchemy of politics in a campaign in which he himself is not about to take active part. It is one of the enduring questions of early modern South Asian elite culture how the (at times) conflicting claims of statecraft and merchant activity could be reconciled by groups that sat astride these domains.[106] One of the solutions that exists, theoretically at least, is to deflate the paradox from the very outset, by stating that no such zone of ambiguity existed in terms of social activity, and that the division of labour was clear. But Anand Ram's life (like that of Sabha Chand, Ratan Chand, and so many others) gives the lie to this presumption.[107] Such men were surely aware, as Anand Ram's reflections show, that they were seen by others as ill-suited to the rigours of battle and vulnerable to mockery as mere shopkeepers (*dukāndārs* or *baqqāls*). The travel-text demonstrates that there was no simple solution to this "identity crisis". But the writing of the account, in a cultured and measured Indo-Persian (with its fair share of Indian vernacular words and phrases), was itself a form of response to the crisis, even though Anand Ram obviously strove, as we have noted, to write in as simple and direct a style as possible here. For here was the product of a process of acculturation that gave the mastery of Persian letters not merely to an Indian (rather than a native of Herat, Nishapur, or Isfahan), but to one of the Khatri brethren of the much-maligned Multawi Mal and

---

[106] The question is discussed in the context of southern India in Narayana Rao, Shulman, and Subrahmanyam, *Symbols of Substance*, 44–56, *passim*. A frequently cited work on the subject that differs radically in its interpretation is Pearson, *Merchants and Rulers in Gujarat*.

[107] For an earlier discussion, see Alam, *The Crisis of Empire*, 168–74.

Pakodi Das.[108] If this gives us pause for reflection, it must have done the same to detractors of Anand Ram and his ilk in the eighteenth century as well. Self-mockery and self-promotion could thus be two sides of the same coin, as much for communities as for individuals.

The Further Travels of Anand Ram

Roughly two and a half years after the account discussed above, Anand Ram was once more on the road. This later voyage, even more modest in its extent than the earlier one, yielded a text which sometimes bears the title *Ahwāl-i safar-i sīzdah'rūzah* (An Account of a Thirteen-day Voyage), or *Waqā'i' Sair-i Ganga* (Account of a Trip to the Ganga), and is also a part of Anand Ram's larger *Badā'i' Waqā'i'*.[109] One important manuscript of the work comes from the collection of "Nawwab Mumtaz-ud-Daulah Mufakhkhar-ul-Mulk Husam Jang Mister Richard Johnson Sahib Bahadur", which is to say the celebrated Richard Johnson (d. 1803);[110] earlier it was owned – as indicated by a title page seal from 1188 H. – by a certain 'Ibadullah. The travel was actually done, so it would seem, in the days from 5th Zi al-Qa'da to 17th Zi al-Qa'da 1160 H., but the text was completed and revised on 1 Zi al-Hijja 1160, that is, 3rd December 1747. However, Anand

[108] For a brief discussion of the Khatri role in Persian literary life at Delhi, see Blake, *Shahjahanabad*, 108–12, 130–4.

[109] BL, Oriental and India Office Collections, Ms. IO. 1612 (Cat. 1: cols. 1478–79, no. 2724), fls 1–17. The end of the manuscript contains late-nineteenth-century notations by William Irvine, where he provides an identification of the author as Anand Ram "Mukhlis". He notes that the travel text is an "Account of a thirteen day Journey from Delhi to Garh Muktesar and back". We note a reference to what appears to be an obscurely published English translation of the account, also by Irvine, "Garh Muktesar Fair", 66–71, 102–16, 116–21, 151–6 and 169–72. The same account appears in Anand Ram, *Badā'i' Waqā'i'* (PUL manuscript), "Ahwāl-i sīzdah rūza Safar-i Muktesar", fls 180b–192b.

[110] We may note that the British Library's Oriental and India Office Collections of paintings, drawings, and prints were originally brought together by the East India Company, the library of which was established in 1801. One of the earliest acquisitions in this context was Richard Johnson's collection of Indian miniatures and manuscripts.

Ram himself makes an uncharacteristic slip in the text, dating it to 1156 H., which is impossible from circumstantial evidence (such as the mention in the text of Nadir Shah's death, which only occurred in 1747).

The travel account here begins with very few frills or preliminaries, and after the usual "Bismillah" invocation we enter the text directly.

Having sent out the baggage in advance on 3rd Zi al-Qa'da 1160 [8th November 1747], corresponding to 5th Kartik-i Hindi, I then set out from Shahjahanabad on Thursday, the 5th of the same month, late in morning accompanied by my brother Rai Sukh Ram, and my sons Rai Kripa Ram and Rai Fateh Singh. As several of our relatives were with us, we had acquired several horsemen and foot soldiers from my master [Qamar-ud-Din Khan], and they came along with us as we set out at a gradual pace. At noon, we arrived at the banks of the Jamuna, and from amongst my friends in the town, only my kind brother Lala Bijay Ram, my dear brother Mir Najm-ud-Din 'Ali Khan, my very dear Kashmiri Mal, and the one close to my heart Jaswant Rai, were able to accompany me. On the banks of the river, we spread our carpets, and I instructed my servants to organise the crossing of the river.

But this proved to be a slightly complicated task, setting the tone for a journey that, although simple in appearance, in fact turned out to be full of small annoyances. The party had ten to twelve *chhakrās* (or carts) with goods, besides as many wagons and pack animals, an elephant, horses, and camels, a medicine chest (*dawā'i-khāna*), and palankeens, and all this amounted to quite a lot when crossing a river. It was hence late afternoon by the time they were able to make their way to the other side. At this point in its course the river Jamuna was in three parts. Two sections had to be crossed by a boat for the men and horses, and the third could be forded on foot. But while crossing the last section one of their badly behaved camels managed to get his load soaked, drenching the clothes laden on the camel's back. That day, some of the party wanted to stay put on the riverbank at Ganj Shahdara. But since the advance party had already set up their tents at Ghaziuddin Nagar (Ghaziabad or Ghazi Nagar), the party that brought up the rear had to move ahead quickly. They passed the garden of

Madar-ud-Daula, where unfortunately one of the carts with tents broke down. Some of the soldiers were left behind to take care of the problem. Later, Anand Ram came to hear that these soldiers had had to keep thieves at bay all night long, using arrows and firearms. Clearly, the environs of Delhi were not quite safe; all one had to do was cross the river, and one could find oneself surrounded by bandits. In the middle of the night Anand Ram's party eventually reached Ghaziuddin Nagar. Here, they were able to eat a tasty *khichrī*, reminiscent perhaps of the previous journey, and they all fell fast asleep.

Before leaving Delhi there had been some discussion of the different types of tents that would be carried.[111] A certain type of larger tent was to be shared by the other brothers, a smaller one was set aside especially for Anand Ram, and a very large one (of four units) for the women and children. But since the wind was a bit chilly at that time of year, and one of the tents had been left on the way, some inconvenience was experienced. Anand Ram takes the occasion to cite a metaphorical verse concerning how the eleventh-century conqueror Mahmud of Ghazna had spent a night wrapped up in layers of fur, while a poor traveller had spent a night nearby by the warmth of an oven (*tanūr*). And who could say whose night had been better spent? On Friday, 6th Zi al-Qaʻda, somewhat into the day, the party set out from Ghaziuddin Nagar. Here, introducing a parenthesis in the narrative, Anand Ram reflects on how, when he was young, he had been able to get up early in the morning. But with advancing age and greying hair, he finds this harder to do. And if he wakes up too early now, he has to have a nap in the afternoon.

Since the clothes had been soaked in the river crossing the previous day (and had to be dried), and one of the carts had also broken down, they started late, reached Dasna, and stopped there for coffee and a snack. They then moved on to Dhappa – retracing their earlier journey of 1745 – where they set up camp, and got together with their friends to gossip (*suhbat-i gap*) around a small bucket-fire (*minqal*). Rather than waiting for his coffee-maker (*qahwachī*), Anand Ram decided to prepare the coffee himself in order to be rid of their fatigue.

---

[111] Anand Ram Mukhlis, *Waqāʾiʻ Sair-i Ganga*, fl. 3.

This act brought to his mind a verse of Mirza Sa'ib, on the pleasures of life.

> Hot coffee, a hot bath, some meaty soup,
> and the intoxication of opium,
> a waving peacock's tail in sight,
> and some prepared tobacco.

Such then were the good things of life as seen from the perspective of a Shahjahanabad bourgeois in late Mughal India. Anand Ram notes that he is a great fan of both coffee and the water-pipe (*kudākū*), and why not? For one like him, whose heart had been burnt (*dil sokhta*), could only enjoy other burnt things like roasted coffee and tobacco! He then enters into a brief description of different sorts of tobacco and their use, some of which are genuine and others less so. A certain Mukhlis Khan and Ruhullah Khan, both high nobles from the time of Aurangzeb, had differing views and preferences in the matter. An anecdote completes the digression on tobacco and is followed by remarks and poems on coffee.

The next day he set out after a late morning bath and arrived in Hapur, and after crossing it halted for a time in a mango orchard. Once again coffee was drunk, and, though he had planned to eat as well, the man carrying the food had gone ahead and made him feel rather grumpy at the carelessness of his servants. So they set out and, halting at a few places, reached Mauza Baksar late in the evening.

On the other side of this town was the hospice (*takiya*) of a holy man, a certain Mast Ram Faqir Udasi, a chosen follower of the well-known Baba Dargahi, and the site had a well attached to it.[112] This Mast Ram was still young, but had decided to become a renouncer and devoted himself to the search for God. The signs of divinity were evident on his forehead, writes Anand Ram, and he was in the habit of distributing gifts of watermelon, sugarcane, pumpkin, and a special sweetmeat – all of which they termed *garāhi*. He was also extremely hospitable to all sorts of passing travellers and his kitchen was open to one and all. Anand Ram and his party were able to benefit from his

---

[112] On the Udasis, see Ghurye, *Indian Sadhus*, 141–3.

generosity as the two were already known to each other. Anand Ram promised that he would stop there on his return trip as well.

On Sunday, 8th Zi al-Qaʻda, before sunrise, the party set out once more and managed by late morning to reach their destination at Garh Muktesar. They went through the fair (*mela*) there, and the settlements (*akhāra-hā*) of the *sanyāsī* mendicants, reaching the farther limits of the fair at the village of Pot, some two and a half leagues (*kos*) from Garh Muktesar. A piece of land had been found by the advance party, but Anand Ram did not care for it as it was on low ground. He sent his son Fateh Singh to find an elevated place on the riverbank, but as Fateh Singh failed Anand Ram went out and found such a spot. Except it already had a lean-to (*tambū*) made of thin cloth. Upon enquiring this was found to belong to a certain Bhupat Ram Baqqal who had dealings with the soldiers of the Mughal arsenal (*topkhāna*), and who also had some pretensions to being a warrior. But how could a mere merchant have such pretensions? Just hearing this absurd notion brings out a mocking Hindavi verse from Anand Ram's repertoire:

Mūe makhī ke tangri torūn
aur torūn kachchā sūt.
Mukkae mār pāpar torūn
to sāhī kā pūt.

I can break the legs off a dead fly,
and snap a thread of raw cotton.
With my fist I can crush a papadum,
which shows I'm the son of a merchant.

Anand Ram had his elephant tethered nearby, went up to Bhupat Ram, and asked him courteously to vacate the land so that he could use it. But the merchant was puffed up with pretension, as if he were in the service of the grandees of the empire. He replied rudely and Anand Ram lost his temper. He ordered his men to throw out Bhupat Ram, and despite the fact that a crowd gathered the fellow was expelled summarily. Another tent was still in the vicinity, which inconvenienced them, but it belonged to one of the Barha Sayyids from Miranpur – men who could not be trifled with (unlike the merchant). Anand Ram decided it was best not to tangle with them and instead negotiate. So he sent out one of his servants, Muhammad Fazil, a clever and smooth-tongued man, to deal with the Sayyids. But the Sayyid, whose name was Atal and who was also a *faqīr*, warned them that he was not a mere merchant (*baqqāl*) to be frightened off.

Nevertheless, a diplomatic solution was found. For it turned out that the Sayyid was known to a certain Ujjaini Lal (brother of the *dīwān* of Bareilly), who was known in turn to Anand Ram. This talking point allowed the negotiation to proceed, and after much flattery the Sayyid withdrew his tent, allowing Anand Ram and his party a free space. Their elaborate tents were now set up, with larger and smaller chambers. A small garden was created with the flowering plants that the party had carried along, and a separate bathing area (*hammām*) defined to the left of the main tent. The setting up of these tents was a rather elaborate affair: it all lasted practically the whole day.[113]

Once matters had been settled satisfactorily it was time to think of the Ganga, for the party needed boats for an excursion. It was the custom in the fair, writes Anand Ram, to set up a line of boats like a royal flotilla, with broadcloth tents in the middle. On moonlit nights people sailed out in these boats and it was a wonderful sight to look on to tents pitched on a river where women and young boys all danced colourfully to the sound of drums. But Anand Ram had also seen a number of fights break out on account of the excesses of such occasions. He notes that he had already asked the *faujdār* of Garh Muktesar, who was a *kulāh-posh* (a "hat-wearer", perhaps meaning an Iranian *qizilbāsh* from Nadir Shah's time), and a companion of the great notable Safdar Jang, for some boats that he and his party could use. Despite the fact that this man was unbearably arrogant by nature, he sent a boat to Anand Ram, who went on to arrange two others of his own. These boats were made ready with chintz from faraway Bandar Masulipatnam, and other valuable cloth, to set up a tent in the interior.

On Monday, 9th Zi al-Qa'da, Anand Ram awoke, and following his routine, bathed, then went on to take a dip in the river, which he refers to respectfully as "Ganga-ji". He goes on: "The people of Hind

---

[113] Anand Ram Mukhlis, *Waqā'i' Sair-i Ganga*, fl. 7.

(*ahl-i Hind*) state that one must first bathe outside [the river], and one's body should be cleansed of the pollutants and dirt. After that, one should bathe in the holy water (*dar āb-i tīrath*). This is because one owes this much courtesy as a sign of respect to the holy spot (*tīrath*)."

Anand Ram gave some money to the Brahmins there, and also performed the required rituals. At night he went out on a river expedition with his friends; he and his intimates were in one boat, and the soldiers were asked to follow in others. Since the night was quite advanced, most of the people in the tents on the river were already asleep. After midnight, the party returned home. Next morning it began to blow and rain. An improvised verse is cited: "Clouds appeared like *jogīs* and *sanyāsīs*,/and everyone has become the Ganga and the Jamuna."

On the sixth day of the trip, 10 Zi al-Qa'da, a Tuesday, Anand Ram reports that he awoke, bathed, and went to the tent of his friend Sawai Ram, with whom he chatted and had some coffee. This was a quiet day, mostly spent reading papers relating to his household, signing them, and looking to such matters. In the evening, a set of letters arrived from Shahjahanabad that had been written on the previous day. The news in them was that Amir Beg Khan, resident in Peshawar, had written to the Mughal emperor that Ahmad Khan Afghan Qandahari had become ruler after the killing of Nadir Shah.[114] Nasir Khan, the local governor, had fled. It had hence been decided to send out a Mughal force in the direction of the Punjab. Anand Ram declares that he became quite concerned on hearing this news, foreseeing troubled times once more.

On the seventh day, 11th Zi al-Qa'da, Wednesday, when the sun had risen somewhat, Anand Ram decided to visit the fair. His particular intention was to meet a certain Thakur Sadanand Jio, and making his way through the bazaar, the jewellers' quarter (*darība*), and the settlements of the *sanyāsīs*, he reached the tent of Sadanand. A few days earlier his younger brother Sahajanand – a man of spiritual qualities – had died, and this was a condolence visit to Sadanand.

---

[114] Nadir Shah was killed at Fathabad on the night of 19 June 1747; see Lockhart, *Nadir Shah*, 261–3.

The two men were the sons of a certain Thakur Bakht Mal and considered great renunciants. The brothers both come in for great praise from Anand Ram for all their positive qualities. Their normal residence, it is noted, was in Hardwar, the last resting place (*samādhī*) of their father too; this was an elegant and well-constructed building, generally considered holy. Once a year, out of consideration for his followers, Sadanand himself had the habit of visiting Shahjahanabad after the Kartik Mela, and, after spending the spring festival of Holi there, eventually returned to Hardwar. This Sadanand was always surrounded by fifty to sixty other ascetics, and besides feeding them he was always ready to feed visitors with bread from his *tanūr* (oven), lentils (*mūng dāl*), and spinach. He also wore a special ring with a mirror, the meaning of it being that every man's heart should be as pure and shining as a mirror, so that the rays of God's light could shine through. It turns out from Anand Ram's extended discussion that Sadanand was a Khatri Suri from Jalalpur in the Punjab and belonged to the Udasi sect; Anand Ram himself being a Khatri from the Punjab no doubt felt a particular affinity to him. It was only some hours later that Anand Ram could take his leave.

Since his childhood, he notes, he had the habit of a siesta (*qailūla*); without it the rest of the day was ruined. So, after waking, he went out of the tent and looked at the moon and the boats on the river from the yard. A description of the fair (*kaifiyat-i mela*) follows here, which is curiously ethnographic in nature.[115] Mukhlis notes that the Garh Muktesar *mela* was the most colourful in all of Hindustan. *Sanyāsi faqīrs* gathered there a month before its start and settled there. There were distinct camps (*akhārās*) of various groups

[115] Anand Ram Mukhlis, *Waqā'i' Sair-i Ganga*, fl. 10a. Compare the descriptions of the customs of the Hindus in Mirza Muhammad Hasan "Qatil", *Haft tamāsha*. "Qatil" (1758/59–1817) was in fact a converted Khatri, originally called Diwani Singh, who had been born in Delhi, and who died in Lakhnau. He knew both Arabic and Persian and was a disciple of Mirza Muhammad Baqir Kirmanshah, under whose influence he converted at the age of fourteen to Twelver Shi'ism, though he kept the conversion hidden for two years. The text was written in the late eighteenth century. For a discussion, see Alam and Subrahmanyam, *Writing the Mughal World*, 423–6.

or *firqas*, with thatched roofs, and they competed to innovate in their decoration. There was a raised central part in each *akhārā*, called the *pāduka*, where a flag was flown, with smaller enclosures around. The materials of worship (*adwāt-i parastish*) such as conches were also kept in the centre. The *sanyāsīs* got together every morning and evening and discussed questions regarding notions of renunciation (*ādāb-i sanyās*) as well as other issues, besides carrying out their ceremonies. Anyone who wished to give them a donation dropped it into a circular vessel, of which one *sanyāsī* was in charge, and he then spent all his time counting the money. Mukhlis remarks cynically (perhaps revealing his own Vaishnava hostility to these largely Saiva renouncers) that, rather than hosting any real worship, such places had become mere centres for the collection of money (*chabūtra-i tahsīl*). He also remarks on the fact that Hindu *faqīrs* are of different types. Rather than dilate on these differences, he takes note in particular of the existence of two groups (*firqa*): the *sanyāsīs* and the *bairāgīs*. Quarrels had been going on between them for long years, and the result was that whenever they got together there was always fighting and bloodshed.[116] Of the two, the *bairāgīs* were somewhat better and less quarrelsome, and so they had in the last some years decided not to come to Garh Muktesar any more, whereas the *sanyāsīs* were there in their thousands – some of whom behaved like real kings with flags and armed retainers (*sāhib-i alam-o-hasham*). Others were real merchants (*saudāgar-o-tujjār*) who tried to dominate the fair and its visitors.[117] Within the *sanyāsīs* themselves he notes distinctions. Some went about totally naked save for a grass mat to sleep on and a small piece of sackcloth to cover their heads. Mukhlis is rather dismissive of them: "Having become oblivi-

---

[116] A well-known incident between two ascetic groups, in which the Mughals came to be involved, was at Thanesar in 1567; see the discussion in Bouillier, "La violence", 218–20; the combat is illustrated in Sen, *Paintings from the Akbar Nāma*, 104–9. For a more general discussion, also see Lorenzen, "Warrior Ascetics", 61–75, as well as the classic essay by Farquhar, "Fighting Ascetics of India", 1–17.

[117] See the useful discussion of these varied groups in Pinch, *Peasants and Monks*, 23–47. For the situation of some of these groups in the late eighteenth century, also see Pinch, "Who was Himmat Bahadur?", 293–335.

ous to the real purpose [of such renunciation], they believe that these external things constitute spirituality and asceticism."

He now recalls what he thinks of as an apposite story about Sarmad, the ascetic who was close to Prince Dara Shikoh in the mid seventeenth century. This man too had been in the habit of going about naked. When 'Alamgir-Aurangzeb became the ruler, he sent one of his intimate nobles to make enquiries about Sarmad. This noble returned with the following verse.[118]

Bar Sarmad-i barahna karāmāt muttahamast
Kashf-i ki zāhir ast dar ū kashf-i 'aurat ast

To accuse naked Sarmad of miracles
is itself a form of calumny.
For the only miracle that he reveals
is that of his bare private parts.

Mukhlis notes nevertheless that Sarmad was a good poet, as could be seen from the quatrains he wrote. On the matter of his execution by 'Alamgir he is equivocal, only noting that some people claim he was killed like Mansur because he spoke against the sanctity of the *sharī'a*.

Returning to the fair, Mukhlis notes its extent from Takri village to that of Pot, covering some seven or eight leagues (*kos*). People came from all the nearby cities, such as Muradabad, and congregated on the banks of the river. Even well-born people from Shahjahanabad came there with their tents and establishments, and the shops here were set out with wonderful and diverse goods. Young boys and girls danced to entertain, and there were also acrobats and well-spoken storytellers (*qissa-khwānān-i khwush taqrīr*): even a sad heart was gladdened. After their baths, beautiful fairy-like women sat at the edge of the river and lit lamps; with sandalwood and flowers they worshipped the river goddess Ganga-ji. These women were in general so beautiful that those whose glances met their eyes found the rewards of both the world and the hereafter (*dīn-o-dunyā*). A poet (perhaps Mukhlis himself being coy) had well said:

---

[118] The anecdote is attributed to Khwaja Ahsanullah Zafar Khan in Shahnawaz Khan, *Ma'āsir-ul-Umarā'*, trans. Beveridge and Prashad, vol. 2, 1019. For Sarmad, reputedly a Jew who had converted and become a *majzūb*, also see Bernier, *Travels in the Mogul Empire*, 317; Bernier, *Un Libertin dans l'Inde Moghole*, 318.

O fairy-faced women on the banks of the Ganga,
On the day of your bath, a mere glance towards your admirer
is far better than all your lamp-offerings (*dān*).
O God! Take a message to Shubh Karan
that I'm a *darshanī* Hindu,
and I've come to your shop for *darshan*.[119]

In the time of Jahangir, he now tells us, the emperor went bird-hunting in a boat on the river Jamuna. On his return he saw a beautiful woman who – after a bath – was seated on the banks of the river. It was the day of a solar eclipse and she was offering some coins as alms. When the royal flotilla came near her, the emperor asked for something for himself as well. She took off her gold necklace with a moon pendant and gave it to him. He accepted it with no hesitation and said (in Hindavi), "Be happy (*sukhī raho*)!" and went back to his palace. There he said to the empress Nur Jahan, "My life, a strange thing happened today," and he recounted the details – handing her the necklace at the end. She replied:

> She did her work very well. First, she was on the banks of the Jamuna, a holy spot (*tīrath*). Second, it was the day of a solar eclipse. Third, she gave an offering of gold. Fourth, the person she gave it to was the emperor of Hindustan (*Chhatrapati-i Hindūstān*). And as for Your Honour, don't be oblivious to the fact that you now have a heavy burden on your shoulders. Take care of it as soon as you can.

Then, looking in the mirror, she saw a black spot on her neck. The emperor called for Brahmins versed in the Vedas and other texts and had them perform rituals of expiation until at long last the black spot disappeared. The implication of this somewhat obscure anecdote appears to be that the blemish had appeared because Jahangir had trifled with the virtuous woman on the riverbank and wrongfully accepted the necklace.

We are now on 12th Zi al-Qa'da, the eighth day. At dawn a cold wind was blowing, but Anand Ram still went in a boat some distance along the banks of the river, watching beautiful women bathing and sitting on the banks. On his return he also saw a handsome young boy

---

[119] On the concept of *darshan*, see Eck, *Darśan*.

dancing, whose appearance inspired his poetry. When the sun had risen higher, he returned to his tent, bathed, and – since it was the eve of Purnima (the full moon) – he followed the necessary rituals. After a meal he had his usual siesta; in the afternoon, the *bairāgī* Baba Sarat Ram came to pay him a visit with a small jar of oil and an offering of sugarcane. The Baba, he notes, was of the same community (*ham-qaum*) as himself, that is to say a Khatri. He lived on the other side of the river from Garh Muktesar, where he had his hospice (*takiya*) as an ascetic and renouncer. Through the offices of Bakhtawar Khan, *dārogha* of the vizier Qamar-ud-Din Khan – who was, we have noted more than once, Anand Ram's own master – he had influence over the wife of the latter and had ceased to be that much of an ascetic, and had even deviated from the path of divine trust (*tawakkul*). As an example of this tendency he had made a garden in Garh Muktesar for the vizier's wife. But even so it was thought that he was much better than most of the money-grubbing *faqīrs* around.

After this meeting Anand Ram set out once more in the evening to look out at the lights on the river, for on this night lamps were being lit everywhere, creating a beautiful effect on the water. Beautiful women were placing these lamps in red pieces of paper and floating them out on the river. They also sang songs in praise of Ganga-ji, in a form of worship.[120] At midnight Anand Ram at last returned home where the people in and around his own tent too – such as Muhammad A'zam and Subhani Toshakchi – had arranged for a pretty display of lamps and lights.

Anand Ram clearly enjoys these outings on the water a great deal and says it gave him the feeling of a ruler on a travelling throne (*takht-i rawān*). Indeed, he recalls that the emperor Babur had written of crossing the water in his memoirs, praising boats above all other forms of transport in terms of their comfort – whether for sleeping or for writing.

The next day, Friday 13th Zi al-Qa'da, was at last the full moon day, so that he awoke before dawn and had his bath and also performed the other rituals that were required as best he could. Since it had been

---

120 Anand Ram Mukhlis, *Waqā'i' Sair-i Ganga*, fl. 13a.

decided that they would return on the 14th, it was now time to start
wrapping up the tents, except for three or four of the smaller ones. By
this time more than half of the people of the fair had left for their
homes. On Saturday, 14th Zi al-Qaʿda, the fair finally came to a close,
and the *faqīrs* and ordinary people all dispersed, folding their tents
and burning down all the temporary structures. Nothing was left
now, except the burnt skeletons of buildings. It was a sad sight, as if
a garden with flowers and green plants had been rendered desolate.
In Anand Ram's eyes it was as if a dream had come to an end, as if so
many prized Aleppan mirrors had shattered.

Disturbed and "wonderstruck" (in the formulaic language he is
prone to use from time to time), Anand Ram now set out on his way
back, first reaching Baksar and the establishment of Bhai Mast Ram
Darvesh Udasi, the same ascetic whom he had met on the way to the
river. He sent Anand Ram the usual gifts of watermelon, pumpkins,
sweets, *pān*, and curds. Anand Ram then set out for Dasna. Now, since
the day he had left Shahjahanabad, Anand Ram had not even thought
of eating meat, since that would have been inappropriate in the context of the festival. Now, at last, he asked Bhai Lala Bijay Ram to prepare a mutton *do-pyāza*, which turned out to be quite splendid. On
Sunday, 15th Zi al-Qaʿda, the carts, camels, etc. were sent off towards
Hapur, while the party rested for a time in a garden on the banks
of a stream. From there they made their way to the establishment
of another well-known ascetic, Baba Dargahi Darvesh Udasi, in the
village of Bisri, some three leagues distant from Baksar. The Baba lived
in a small house on an earthen bed with utter simplicity. This was a
man who had undergone much penance and purified himself like the
purest gold. In Anand Ram's view his forehead radiated wisdom and
enlightenment. His daily food was some dry *nān* bread and a bit of
salt. Here then was the opposite of the showy and fraudulent ascetics
who have been commented on in the context of the fair. This dervish
also offered food to travellers and had a great following among the
other Udasi ascetics. He was something of a philanthropist too and
had made small bridges on the Kali Nadi and other rivulets, and dug
wells for the general benefit. Some people believed he was an al-
chemist, for how else could he have got hold of such resources? But

Anand Ram claims all this stemmed purely from the great ascetic's purity and virtue. He showed great affection to Anand Ram and treated him well, offering him and others in his party fruit and other things, including cloves and cardamom. Anand Ram had brought him a message from Qamar-ud-Din Khan, which he then conveyed, and the ascetic then sent back a fitting reply; it turned out that the vizier had asked him to pray for the emperor (who was to die not long after, in 1748), which he agreed to do.

After this brief visit the party made its way to Qasba Hapur through a rather circuitous route, which – even if it had been taken in error – allowed them to look at mustard fields in flower and other pleasing sights. By late afternoon they reached Hapur, somewhat tired. Fortunately, the advance party was already there and had set up a tent where Anand Ram could rest. Then, on Monday 16th Zi al-Qa'da, they reached Dasna and pitched a tent by a well. Here a bonfire was made for the night, and a restful evening was spent with friends, drinking coffee as usual. Anand Ram's brothers, Rai Sukhpat Ram and Rai Basant Ram, had sent him food from the town.

By chance the camp of Kunwar Jivan Mal, son of Raja Bakht Mal, was right next to their tents, and some food was sent to him. At a certain moment in the night when Anand Ram's servant Dondi was distributing the *halwa* that they had received from the saint Baba Dargahi a certain Ganga Das, the son of Madari Lal Kayastha, the chief accountant (*mustaufi*) of Shahjahanabad, whose tent was also nearby, arrived in the camp. His visit was not welcome but had to be borne, and he had to be offered something. These small and unpleasant rivalries from the court cast a slight shadow on what had otherwise been a pleasant evening.

Next day they made their way to the garden of Madar-ud-Daula, where Anand Ram instructed the gardeners to make water flow somewhat better into the flower beds; the party rested and snacked, then moved on. On the road Anand Ram's brother Rai Sukhpat Ram met them – he had come from the city out of eagerness to meet his brother. The brothers embraced, and Anand Ram recited some verses in his honour: "I am so happy to return home,/it's as if I am back in Delhi from the Deccan."

By the time they reached Shahdara on the banks of the Jamuna river, it had become dark. Again the unsafe character of the vicinity of the capital city became clear. Some mounted robbers approached them from the left, but since the party was well protected the villains fled rather than enter into combat. Then, leaving Mir Najm-ud-Din 'Ali Khan and Muhammad Fazil behind, Anand Ram went ahead. At length his party reached the river and crossed it quite easily, as everything had been prepared in advance. But one camel and two horses were left behind for a time. The horses were presently brought across, but the noisy and obstinate camel refused to get on board the boat despite the best efforts of the boatmen. Then on account of the efforts of the servant 'Abdullah and Lala Bijay Ram the camel at last consented to cross at the end of a few hours. By midnight Anand Ram was thus able to return home, though many others of the party only came in later. At home the usual plain rice-and-lentil *khichrī* was made ready. Praises were given by all to God, and verses are set down in his honour. Anand Ram concludes: "Since we were with our relatives, and there were also some problems with the loss of goods, we did experience some inconvenience on this journey, but it passed. But that aside, the days we spent in the fair were full of the pleasure that we had hoped to experience." He then adds a reflective verse, perhaps indirectly stemming from the extended dealing he has had in the previous two weeks with ascetics.

> Worldly goods are the cause of your helplessness;
> they result in harm and humiliation.
> The palace of your comfort
> stands on an unstable base.
> The extent of your desire for worldly things
> creates anxiety in proportion.

Though he has restrained himself in this account (as opposed to the earlier one) in his constant preoccupation with food, as he closes his text Anand Ram cannot quite resist the temptation. He notes that a pickle or preserve made from elephant-foot yam (*zamīn-qand* or *Amorphophallus paeoniifolius*) was a speciality of this fair, and he had brought back twenty loads of it. Five were sent to the Nawwab

Qamar-ud-Din Khan, five to his wives, and some of the others to other friends. The text thus closes on 24th Zi al-Qaʻda, two hours into the morning, written (as he notes) by his own hand, in Anand Ram's old residence in Shahjahanabad.

Closing Reflections

From the outset Anand Ram has announced to his reader that the *Badāʾiʿ Waqāʾiʿ* has the character of a miscellany, a threading together of "stray fragments", as he modestly puts it. It therefore stands somewhat apart in the corpus of early modern South Asian ego-documents that we have dealt with in earlier parts of this book. Though somewhat similar at first glance to the late-sixteenth- and early-seventeenth-century travels of Faizi or Asad Beg, the travel narratives to Bangarh and Garh Muktesar inhabit a somewhat different register and are far more concerned with the interplay between the experience of travel and the subjectivity of the author. Moreover, the different elements in the miscellany adopt distinct tones. At some moments Anand Ram comes rather close to the standard political chronicle, though even here the author's experience and voice emerges quite clearly. Other sections are reflective of his family life and the customs and observances of the Khatri community in Mughal service. The two closing *safar* texts, written after the shock of Nadir Shah's invasion in 1739, clearly show his growing disillusion with the courtly milieu that he has long inhabited. Anand Ram is not afraid to deploy sarcasm, and he also has a constant irony that he turns upon himself and his community in his account of his travels of 1745. This reflexive irony is somewhat less in evidence in the later account.

The milieu under consideration too is different, for we hear far more about ascetics and renouncers in the travel to Garh Muktesar than we have in the previous account. Anand Ram can be unrelenting in his sarcasm here, but the tone is a sadder, less boisterous one, as if he has grown far more world-weary. One is led to understand at the end of the account, after all, that "the palace of your comfort/stands on an unstable base." If the travels in the imperial camp in 1745 have something of an aspect of a *corvée* about them, the later trip to Garh

Muktesar is something else: an excursion where the ostensible religious motive barely conceals a notion that its author is on a sort of brief vacation, a leisurely outing from the depressing humdrum of life in Delhi.

The intended readership for these accounts is a matter of some interest. It is clear that Anand Ram understood that he stood in an interesting situation, where many of his Muslim readers might be mystified by quite a few of the references he made. Thus, Anand Ram sets out to explain small aspects of his Ganga pilgrimage, the organisation of ascetic sects, and other aspects to the reader; earlier Nek Rai had even felt obliged to provide the reader an elementary version of the plot of the *Rāmāyana!* At the same time, Anand Ram seems to assume that his reader is comfortable not only in Persian but in the North Indian vernacular that we have termed Hindavi (as indeed in comprehending poetry in the mixed *rekhta*). This implies that he probably did not expect to be read too widely outside India, and was probably not too concerned about the fact that some parts of his writing might have been opaque to readers in Iran or Central Asia. This is a point of view that differs markedly from that of Faizi or Asad Beg a century and a half earlier, who clearly intended their writings to be accessible as much to readers in Qazwin and Bukhara, as in Delhi and Agra.

With this chapter we have, in a manner of speaking, come full circle, from the times of Babur, and the writers of the generation of his son Humayun. Whereas they spoke of the struggles involved in establishing an empire, and placing it on a firm footing, we are now at a moment when a certain discourse of "decline" has gained ground in many circles. Anand Ram was no grand political theorist in the matter, nor did he offer a dispassionate diagnosis of what had gone wrong — beyond suggesting that internal factional dissensions in the court were a source of may of the troubles. Writing in the 1730s and 1740s, he also had a very limited perception of the threats that the European Companies would soon represent for the Mughals.[121]

---

[121] In contrast, the memoirs from the next generation of Mir Taqi "Mir", do have a number of references to the British and other Europeans; see Mir, *Remembrances*, 207, 219, 221, 249, etc.

Even by the time of his death in 1751 – a few years after his master Qamar-ud-Din Khan and the emperor Muhammad Shah – the shape of things to come was still unclear to those in the Mughal capital. Their preoccupations remained with the north-west when the real threats would come from the east and the south. In this matter, Anand Ram differed markedly in his experience and perceptions from his exact contemporary, the Tamil merchant and go-between Anandaranga Pillai (1709–61), to whom we turn briefly in the conclusion.

6

Conclusion

> Our Oblomov will lack the agent's point of view – let us say
> because he takes himself to be an object. He takes an exclusively
> third-person perspective on himself, and so for him the future is
> just like the past; he has no thought that he can make a
> difference to it.
>
> – Akeel Bilgrami, "Self-Knowledge and Resentment"[1]

THE PRECEDING chapters of this book have taken us over several centuries, as well as over a body of numerous texts from Indo-Islamic history. Our analysis of these materials began – after some larger comparative remarks – with the sixteenth century, at a time when some descendants of Amir Timur returned to Hindustan with a project to reconquer the lands that their ancestor had devastated in a lightning campaign over a century earlier. This period turned out important in terms of ego-documents, showing texts written not only by the ruler Babur himself, but by several others in the next two generations, whether members of the imperial clan or servants at varying levels.

As might have been expected, the half-century-long reign of Babur's grandson Akbar also turned out to be a significant phase in which such materials were produced, both by grand intellectuals like the poet Faizi and by more humble members of the Mughal bureaucracy like Asad Beg Qazwini. In subsequent chapters we moved our

---

[1] Bilgrami, "Self-Knowledge and Resentment", 235. Bilgrami here evokes the figure of Ilya Oblomov, the anti-hero of *Oblomov*, Ivan Goncharov's 1859 Russian novel.

consideration to the seventeenth century, to examine the careers and experiences of individuals such as 'Abdul Latif Gujarati, Mirza Nathan, and Bhimsen Saksena, who often functioned in the frontier regions of the empire. Finally, we devoted an extended analysis to the important eighteenth-century figure of Anand Ram "Mukhlis", located at the Mughal centre, as he recounted what it was like to live through the years after the turbulent 1710s, when the emperor Muhammad Shah was on the throne. The characters who have peopled these chapters have often been socially located not at the most elite levels of Mughal society, but a few notches below, without being countable amongst the "subaltern" classes of peasants or humble artisans.

In a thoughtful survey of the significance of "life histories" in the study of South Asia, two scholars of history and literature have proposed that such narratives can help us "to question the view that Indian society is dominated by collectivities," and instead "demonstrate the significance of individual agency and of notions of self in a region of the world where people have historically been seen to identify themselves in terms primarily of caste, but also kinship and religion."[2] While their focus was chiefly on the colonial and post-colonial periods, they nevertheless acknowledged that such materials could be found in the region "with the arrival of Islam and the subsequent elaboration of life-history forms," pointing in particular to royal memoirs like the *Bābur Nāma*. Of equal significance was their insistence that the appropriate foil for these life histories was not some mythical individual like Burckhardt's Renaissance man "who can do all and dares do all, and who carries his measure in himself." Rather, they argued, "life histories in India are a means for negotiating the irreducible dichotomy of self-in-society; they are a narrative form for expressing and imagining an individual's existence, which includes group identities and relations with others." If these texts can sometimes be quite playful, as we have seen with Anand Ram's, others are insistent that their purpose is to provide lessons (*'ibrat*) for those who follow, presenting themselves above all as witnesses to the truth.

---

[2] Arnold and Blackburn, "Introduction: Life Histories in India", in Arnold and Blackburn, eds, *Telling Lives in India*, 19.

An example of this is the text written in the 1660s entitled *Fathīya 'Ibrīya*, which commences as follows. The author begins by introducing himself to readers as the long-suffering Wali Ahmad ibn Muhammad, whose surname (*laqab*) is Shihab-ud-Din Talish, and who is in fact the smallest and most insignificant of creatures. He continues:

> Those who wish to understand the events of this world, and who wish to explore the truths of the inhabitants of the world, in their service I present the following: regarding the unparalleled Nawwab Mir Muhammad Sa'id Ardistani, an important pillar of the empire which is the refuge of 'Arab and 'Ajam, master of both the pen and the sword, one of the most excellent of the country, who has been honoured by the emperor as a loyal friend, the Khan-i-Khanan and the head of the army, may God keep him from small and great sins and reward him for his good deeds, as mediated by the Prophet and his pious descendants. When he was appointed to the blood-thirsty kingdom of Asham with 12,000 horsemen and numberless footmen, he remained there for six months, troubled by the water and extensive rains and suffering from diverse diseases, betrayed by the untrustworthy Ashamiyan, lacking supplies and food to the point many difficulties had to be confronted, so much so that it is difficult to describe. By the grace of God, they escaped that whirlpool of misfortune, which by itself was a wonderful event that inspires lessons (*'ibrat*). This courageous Nawwab did not abandon his fortitude and kept people informed of what was happening, sending letters to his friends in Hindustan, some of which did not reach their destination.

The text is thus clearly presented as a war narrative on the north-eastern frontier of the Mughals, centring on the campaigns there of the celebrated Mir Muhammad Sa'id, sometimes known as Mir Jumla, an Iranian migrant who had reached Mughal service after years spent in Golkonda. Talish then elaborates on his own role:

> This person participated in this unfortunate expedition from the entry into Asham until the Nawwab met his end, taking part in the meetings and councils day and night. In spite of these misfortunes, our truthful pen has recorded the customs of the evildoing Ashamiyan, avoiding needless metaphors and details, so that the small and great nobles of Hindustan, as well as others in the world, might be informed of all this and draw the proper conclusions. The reader will find evidence of my friendship for the

Mughals and the people of Hindustan, with no trace of enmity. What was lacking in the effort, and what the positive aspects were, are both recounted, with nothing added or subtracted. One of the other purposes of writing this is that when readers peruse it, they may appreciate it, and the *mutasaddīs* of the emperor will bring these affairs to the attention of the court. When someone [in future] is appointed to Bengal, this information will come in useful.[3]

He also requests readers who find errors in the text to take the trouble to correct them and forgive the author, for his intent was not malicious: "since this compilation indicates and enlightens the reader of the avenues of victory (*fath*) and gives lessons (*'ibrat*), I have given it the name *Fathīya 'Ibrīya*." Several distinct features thus become clear from the outset: the author's posture of humility as a form of *captatio benevolentiae*; his insistence on being a foreigner to Hindustan, rather like Mir Jumla himself; the extent of his sufferings in Assam, "the land that drinks blood"; but above all his status as an eyewitness armed with a "truthful pen". Both ethnographer and memoirist, Talish thus follows in the line of 'Abdul Latif, and even more Mirza Nathan.

An important question that arises in this context is the manner in which these authors saw their own role in the events they narrated. Did they see themselves as mere victims of Fate (for which an astonishingly large number of words exist in our texts, such as *nasīb*, *qismat*, and *qazā*), or as active agents, intervening at times decisively in matters? A discussion of the evolution of historiography between the Delhi Sultanate and the Mughals has shed light on the question by opposing those who insisted on the centrality of *taqdīr* (predetermination), and accessorily *karāmāt* (miracles), as distinct from those who argued for the primacy of human judgement or regulation (*tadbīr*). The historian Ali Anooshahr suggests, basing himself on a comparison of classic Sultanate and Afghan historians on the one hand, and the Mughal writers of the late sixteenth century on the other, that the latter had begun to espouse a view where the conception of events as being above all divinely ordained (the outcome of *taqdīr-i ilāhī*) was no

---

[3] Shihab-ud-Din Talish, *Fathīya 'Ibrīya*: BnF, Supplément persan 321, fls 2b–4a. For a partial translation, also see Shihab-ud-Din Talish, *Tarikh-i Asham*.

longer tenable, suggesting instead that they had to do with human actions that could be evaluated dispassionately for their qualities of wisdom or foolishness.[4] Those who succeeded in the political sphere, such as the great rulers of the past, usually showed cunning, judgement, and the ability to deploy ruse, and were not simply individuals who were touched by divine grace. Whereas Central Asian intellectuals of the period might have reacted violently to the claim that "man is the creator of his own actions (*banda khwud khalīq-i afʿāl-i khwud ast*)," such a view was therefore not anathema in Mughal circles by 1600.[5] Furthermore, such opinions may even have percolated into day-to-day affairs of administration, leading to a different view of how "truth-terms" of an empirical nature such as *sihhat* and *sidq* could be deployed while making inquiries into mundane matters such as property and revenue rights.[6]

A brief excursion in a southward direction, beyond the domains where the Mughals ruled, may prove useful to give us some context. In a monograph on "South Indian minds" in the early modern era, David Shulman devotes a chapter to autobiographies and self-portraits, beginning with the twofold proposition that, first, in these works there is an explicit or implicit contract between author and reader "that what the author has to say about his life is factually true"; and second, that these works are also a "conversation, usually cacophonic or polyglossic, between the author and himself or herself."[7] His chief example is an eighteenth-century text in Malayalam by Appattu Atiri, which he qualifies as "unique" in many respects. Atiri's own politico-historical context is provided by the small Kozhikode (Calicut) kingdom in central Kerala, ruled over by the celebrated Samutiri raja.

---

[4] Anooshahr, "Author of One's Fate". Anooshahr contrasts the works of ʿIsami, Rizqullah Mushtaqi, and Nizam-ud-Din Ahmad.

[5] Anooshahr (ibid., 222–3) here quotes the Central Asian author Fazlullah ibn Ruzbihan, who remained wedded to ideas of *taqdīr*.

[6] There is obviously some parallel with contemporary debates opposing the terms *tahqīq* and *taqlīd*; see Kinra, "The Truth is Out There"; and also Pye, "The Sufi Method".

[7] Shulman, *Introspection and Insight*, 118. Here, the author develops arguments that appeared in an earlier work (Shulman, *More than Real*), albeit in a more historical direction.

Here he belonged to an important clan of Nambudiri Brahmins which had long held a position of prestige and importance. However, as the Samutiri began to make aggressive moves in the direction of Kochi, he found it in his interest to support a rival clan of Brahmins. Atiri's family members were arrested and mistreated, and his preferred shrine to the Varaha incarnation of Vishnu was desecrated. Driven to a state of extreme depression, Atiri began to contemplate retirement from active life and a future as a renouncer in the pilgrimage city of Benares. However, he was persuaded against this by his family, in particular his wife (a woman of strong opinions, who plays a significant role in the text). He also feared that conflicts between the Nambudiris and the Samutiri might lead to political anarchy, an acephalous state (*arājakam*) in which social order would dissolve. Therefore, he underwent a long period of arduous penance in his region itself, until finally – eleven years later – the god Shiva visited him and reassured him that his favourite god would be restored, and that he could now return to his normal life as a householder. The god's prediction was progressively fulfilled, and Atiri also installed his nephew Narayanan as his successor, in contradiction to normal Nambudiri conventions.

Shulman finds in this text a strong version of "the autobiographical impulse – factual, first-person narrative, heavily introspective, filled with remembered or reconstructed dialogues, indeed an entire chorus of important voices."[8] He also notices a particular attention to sequence and detail in the telling, as well as to "historical causes" which elucidate what happens in the Nambudiri's microcosm. In comparison to many of the other texts we have surveyed, Atiri's narrative is a simple one, and essentially centres on the resolution of one great life crisis. It also does not involve any great displacement in space, and the action all takes place in and around the Samutiri's modest kingdom. An important place is held in it by predictions and visions, which may not be surprising if (as is suspected) the author was an astrologer himself.

The remarkable and elaborate ego-document, also from South India, of the Tamil merchant and go-between Anandaranga Pillai,

---

[8] Shulman, *Introspection and Insight*, 131.

offers us other insights from the fringes of the Mughal world. Anandaranga was a merchant from an upwardly mobile milieu, since he belonged to the Idaiyar (or Yadava) caste of shepherds, from which certain members had obviously decided to pursue mercantile ventures during the Nayaka period in Tamilnadu. By the early eighteenth century his father Tiruvengadam Pillai had settled in the English Company's centre of Madras, while other members of the family preferred to work with the French Company in Pondicherry. Despite the difficulties that his relatives had had with the French, they seem to have been able to persuade Tiruvengadam to move with his family to Pondicherry and accept a position there, as *courtier*, *dubāsh*, and *chef des marchands*. Anandaranga, who has born in Perambur (near Madras) in 1709, thus shifted to his new home when he was around seven or eight and remained there even after the death of his father in 1726. In time, he grew into the same position as his father, but only after some travails. In 1726 he was left with modest means and acted for a time principally as an areca-nut merchant. The assumption of the governorship of French India in 1734 by Pierre Benoît Dumas saw a significant upturn in his fortunes as he began to play a role not only on behalf of the Company in nearby Porto Novo, but as a private agent of governor Dumas and his brother Gabriel, which included investing in the overseas trade to Mokha and the Mascareigne Islands. Progressively, he diversified his portfolio and extended his reach as far as the textile-producing centres of the interior. His linguistic competence also seems to have expanded from Tamil, Telugu, and Portuguese (a language that Tiruvengadam already used in his correspondence), to French and Persian. Since Dumas was obviously impressed by his intelligence and entrepreneurial skills, he attempted actively to promote Anandaranga in place of the incumbent *courtier* Kanakaraya Mudaliyar. But his position of dominance would only be consolidated with the arrival in January 1742 of Dumas' successor as governor, Joseph-François Dupleix.

It was during the governorship of Dumas, in 1736, that Anandaranga Pillai began the somewhat unprecedented practice of keeping a journal or diary (in Tamil: *tinacharitai*, or *nātkurippu*). He would maintain this diary, written in a relatively colloquial Tamil, intermittently over the next quarter-century, to the eve of his death. The decision to patiently produce this ego-document is never quite explained by him; he opens it with the simple statement: "I proceed to chronicle what I hear with my ears; what I see with my eyes; the arrivals and departures of ships; and whatsoever wonderful or novel takes place."[9] What the reader gets is in fact a far more complex cocktail of materials than this deceptive description would suggest, a mixture of factional intrigue and jockeying within the French colonial establishment, day-to-day social affairs and *faits-divers* in Pondicherry, considerations regarding the wider politics and diplomatic landscape of peninsular India, details of a variety of trading operations, aspects of the festering rivalry with the English Company, and not least of all an account of Anandaranga's own ambitions, frustrations, and resentments. All this is spread over a text which, in its most recent Tamil edition, extends to some twelve volumes and several thousands of pages.[10] It is also significant that once this tradition of diary-making had been inaugurated in Pondicherry, it continued, first with Anandaranga's nephew Tiruvengadam and his descendants, and then with other figures like Vira Nayakkar, through to the times of the French Revolution. Obviously, none of these latter figures had quite the horizons or ambitions of the founder of the tradition.

In the face of such a vast text, the attitudes of historians have varied, even leaving aside those who have simply scoured it for raw "data" on prices, quantities traded, harvests and famines, and so on. It has obviously been tempting to read it as yet another testimony on "eighteenth-century decline", especially in view of the gloomy tone that the diary takes in the later 1750s, as the English emerged in the ascendant, culminating with the French defeat at the end of the Seven Years' War in 1761. But the central paradox that has troubled analysts is the reconciliation of Anandaranga's elevated claims and strident self-assertion with the fact that he was, in the ultimate analysis, dependent

---

[9] Anandaranga Pillai, *The Private Diary*, vol. 1, 1.

[10] See Anandaranga Pillai, *Pirattiyekamāna Ānanta*, 8 vols, followed by Anandaranga Pillai, *Ānantarankappillai nātkurippu*, 4 vols. Additional sections in the text have been edited and published in Anandaranga Pillai, *Ānantarankappillai vi-nātkurippu, 1751–1754*, 3 vols.

for his fortunes on the whims of the French. Kanakalatha Mukund has proposed, for example, that "an important part of Ananda Ranga Pillai's self-perception was his recognition of his own worth and status independent of French influence," pointing to his careful accumulation of ceremonial honours and titles from local rajas, as well as the late Mughal centres of Hyderabad and Arcot and their derivatives.[11] His marriage to the daughter of Seshadri Pillai, *pālaiyakkāran* of Chengalpet, was quite possibly another sign of his anxiety for social status. His exaggerated claims are equally evident in the fact that he sponsored or was presented a number of texts that sang his praises in Tamil, Telugu, and Sanskrit, drawing on tropes of royalty and conquest that were hardly realistic.[12] In the late 1740s, after a successful negotiation with Mahfuz Khan, son of the *nāzim* of Arcot Anwar-ud-Din Khan, here is what he wrote about himself in his diary, referring to "the public talk concerning me".

> The reputation which I had acquired was so great that the Governors of provinces, and all individuals of rank, were unanimous in declaring that there was not, in this world, my equal in diplomatic skill; and all this came to me by the grace of God alone, and not through any talent on my part. As the common talk is of me; of how I spent days and even nights without sleep in the careful conduct of the affairs of the Company; and of how I had been instrumental in extending the glory of the French over the wide world, and in making their name a terror, even to the Emperor of Delhi, and other princes, I am sure that the Europeans and the officers of the Company, who dwell in Pondicherry, will allude to these matters in the letters written by them to those in their native land. I, also, feel convinced that the despatch to the Company will make mention of my strenuous exertions with regard to their affairs. My reputation will then spread throughout France, and all Europe. It is such as could not be purchased by me, even at the cost of 10 lakhs of pagodas. How can I relate the wondrous way in which God, in His exceeding goodness, has made me the possessor of it? I could record, at still greater length, all the credit that I acquired in this business, but as self-laudation is a most unwise thing, I have written as above, giving only hints with regard to it.[13]

[11] Mukund, *The View from Below*, 146.

[12] For a discussion, see Shulman, "Cowherd or King?"

[13] Anandaranga Pillai, *The Private Diary*, vol. 3, 381.

Despite the formulae of self-abnegation, and the attribution of everything to the "grace of God", there can be no doubt that Ananda-ranga had a keen sense of having risen well above the common rung of mortals, and it is interesting that in much the same phase of his life he contrasts himself to his younger brother, also (somewhat confusingly) called Tiruvengadam (like his father). His brother, writes our diarist, "is thirty-four or thirty-five years old, [but] he has no desire to acquire wealth, and no ambition to figure conspicuously in the service of the Company. He is, further, too retiring to hold any discourse with the Europeans." This in contrast to a world where many others from their milieu are eager to push ahead, even in a vulgar and indecent man-ner. For his part, Tiruvengadam, "although naturally possessed of the gifts of high culture, excellent parts, guarded temper, winning manners, handsome presence, and fortunate birth, is not blessed with the courage and spirit of enterprise which is indispensable to raising oneself to distinction. It is this defect that induces him to cast aside all aspirations to greatness, and to prefer to remain at home in obscuri-ty."[14] Anandaranga then makes some reference to the effects of horo-scopes, and the predictions of astrologers, but the contrast between one brother, the achiever, and the other the introverted stay-at-home, is clear enough. Of course, this does not diminish the affection that he clearly feels towards his brother, whose death at the age of forty he marks with a keen sense of loss, far greater than what he expresses for the death of his wife Mangatayi Ammal in April 1756. Of his brother, he writes: "He lived in pleasure like Indra, in giving like Karna, in intellect like Yugi the minister, in courage like the Hima-laya mountain, in grandeur like the ocean; he thus lived forty years, eight months and twenty days, and died in Bhava year on Sunday, the 27th day of Avani between 15 and 16 *nāligais* after nightfall. Then every member of our household felt as if the whole world had come to an end."[15] There was thus a suitably grand cremation, with the corpse carried in an ivory palankeen, and the firing of guns in a salute; as an auspicious sign, two Brahminy kites (*chemparuntu*) even circled over-head during the proceedings.

[14] Ibid., 9–10 (1746).
[15] Ibid., vol. 9, 5–6.

In his analysis of Anandaranga's diary, David Washbrook has stressed its coherence rather than its paradoxical aspects. In his view, "[Anandaranga] never fully identified himself with the French nor saw why borrowing their technology and artefacts necessarily compromised his own identity. Indeed, the entries in his 'diary' are usually multi-dated: referenced also to the Tamil calendar and, at times, to particular constellations of the stars." As a socially conservative figure who broadly defended the values of *varnāshrama-dharma*, he nevertheless emerges in this perspective as a Tamil "patriot" who could still work within the emergent French colonial system. Washbrook therefore concludes:

> Beside the authority of the French king, he also acknowledged that of other "great" kings, of the Mughal Emperor in Delhi and assorted local rulers, such as the Nizam of Hyderabad. He accepted "honours" from them no less than from the French court. If he identified himself clearly with any group, it was "the Tamil people" . . . In several conversations posed in the diary with Dupleix, he staunchly defended the honour of the Tamils against charges of moral cowardice and corruption, especially in relation to the French.[16]

This is perhaps to understate the degree of real tensions that inhabited this life, which are made particularly evident at the moment when Dupleix departed Pondicherry in disgrace, in 1754. Anandaranga had tried desperately to meet the former governor in order to deal with his mounting debts and disastrous financial affairs, only to be rebuffed. He claims to have told him bluntly enough: "From the day when this town became populous and flourishing till now, Europeans have made 40, 50 and 60 lakhs of rupees, have obtained the title of *Nawāb*, and rule the country, using the Fish and other emblems of power. But I who was the root and support of this prosperity have secured nothing but debt." In the end, Dupleix's ship stealthily lifted anchor after he had misled the *dubāsh* about the hour of his departure, a final small betrayal. While Anandaranga conveniently and misogynistically lays much of the blame on his regular scapegoat,

[16] Washbrook, "Envisioning the Social Order", 177.

Madame Jeanne Dupleix, there is no mistaking the bitterness of his tone towards his former patron as well: "He has eaten the fruit of his actions. I need not write it in detail. Twelve years and nine months ago yesterday on the morning of Sunday, January 14, 1742, he landed here from Bengal to become our Governor. In all this time, he has gained lakhs upon lakhs by my efforts, but has never troubled about me." To which he adds: "I dwelt in truth and justice under his government; but from first to last he regarded neither justice nor truth."[17] Even if Fate may ostensibly have predetermined all this, the reality of personal responsibility could not be avoided either.

Looking back at the past four or five generations of historiography on the empire that the Mughals created in South Asia, it is interesting to note how thematic approaches have both shifted, and at times accumulated, in a palimpsest. Works of the late nineteenth century focused above all on the personalities of rulers and dynastic politics; there then emerged an interest in aspects of military and diplomatic history. As the large narrative sources and imperial chronicles were both supplemented by more modest ones, and by archival documents, a strong new tendency made itself felt at the end of the colonial period, namely the investment in agrarian-fiscal history. This was then carried forward into the post-1947 decades, when some of this writing came to bear a distinct Marxist flavour. Within this framework, it was still possible for some historians to delineate elements of a social history that was more than the simple opposition between fiscal oppressors and oppressed, or elites and subalterns. Here then is where matters stood in around 1980.

Since then, it has been possible to discern a further shift in thematic emphasis, which cannot however be termed a changing of paradigms, because so many elements of the older approaches still persist in a productive way. The growing importance of themes of intellectual and cultural history has been of considerable significance, even for those of us who had a firm rooting in social and economic history.[18] Our exploration of ego-documents, whether related to travel

[17] Anandaranga Pillai, *The Private Diary*, vol. 9, 53–4, 56, 58.
[18] For a useful overview of literature, see O'Hanlon, "Cultural Pluralism".

or not, may be seen as a part of this "cultural turn", though it would be presumptuous for us to claim that we have considered more than a modest part of the corpus of relevant materials. Further, our explorations have usually been conducted in conversation with historians of other parts of the world, and above all the Islamic world, from whom we have learnt a great deal. Like the Mughal empire itself, Mughal historiography can only benefit by engaging this dialogue in a balanced and productive way.

Bibliography

'Abdul Baqi Nihawandi, *The Ma'āsir-i-Rahīmī of Mullā 'Abd ul-Bāqī Nahāvandī*, 3 vols, ed. M. Hidayat Husain (Calcutta, 1924–31).

'Abdul Latif Gujarati, *Risāla-i sair-i manāzil wa bilād wa amsār*, National Archives of India, New Delhi, Microfilm: Acc. no. 5915 (of a lost manuscript originally at the Lal Chand Research Library, DAV College, Lahore).

'Abdul Latif Gujarati, *Ruq'āt-i 'Abdul Latīf*, Asiatic Society of Bengal, Kolkata, Ms. F6 (Ivanow 364).

'Abdul Nabi Qazwini, *Tazkira-yi Maikhāna* (1028 H.), ed. Ahmad Gulchin-i Ma'ani (Tehran, 1363 Sh./1984).

'Abdul Qadir Badayuni, *Muntakhab al-Tawārīkh*, 3 vols, ed. W. Nassau Lees and Ahmad Ali (Calcutta, 1865–69).

'Abdul Qadir Badayuni, *Muntakhab al-Tawārīkh*, 3 vols, trans. Vol. 1 by G.S.A. Ranking; vol. 2 by William H. Lowe; and vol. 3 by T. Wolseley Haig (Calcutta, 1884–1922).

'Abdul Wali, Maulavi, "The Antiquities of Burdwan", *Journal of the Asiatic Society of Bengal*, N.S., vol. 13, 1917, 177–89.

'Abdul Wali, Maulavi, "Notes on Archaeological Remains in Bengal", *Journal of the Asiatic Society of Bengal*, N.S., vol. 20, 1924, 489–521.

'Abdullah, Sayyid Muhammad, *Adabiyat-i Fārsī mein Hinduwon kā Hissā* (Lahore, 1967).

'Abdur Rashid, Shaikh, "Muhammad Shah's Letter to Shah Tahmasp II", *Medieval India Quarterly*, vol. 1, no. 2, 1950, 91–110.

'Abdur Razzaq ibn Ishaq Samarqandi, *Matla' us-sa'dain wa majma' ul-bahrain*, Part 1, ed. 'Abdul Husain Nawa'i (Tehran, 1353 Sh.); Part 2, ed. Muhammad Shafi' (Lahore, 1365–8 H./1946–9).

Abbas, Fauzia Zareen, *Abdul Qadir Badauni, as a Man and Historiographer* (Delhi, 1987).

Abu'l Faiz ibn Mubarak (Faizi Fayyazi), *Inshā-i Faizī*, ed. A.D. Arshad (Lahore, 1973).

Abu'l Faiz ibn Mubarak (Faizi Fayyazi), *Kulliyāt-i Faizī*, ed. A.D. Arshad (Lahore, 1967).

Abu'l Faiz ibn Mubarak (Faizi Fayyazi), *Sawāti' al-ilhām* (Kanpur, 1889).

Abu'l Fath, Hakim, *Ruq'āt-i Hakīm Abū'l Fath Gilānī*, ed. Muhammad Bashir Husain (Lahore, 1968).

Abu'l Fazl, Shaikh, *Ā'īn-i Akbarī*, 3 vols, ed. H. Blochmann (Calcutta, 1872–7).

Abu'l Fazl, Shaikh, *Ā'īn-i Akbarī*, 3 vols, 2nd edn, trans. H. Blochmann and H.S. Jarrett, rev. Jadunath Sarkar (Calcutta, 1948).

Abu'l Fazl, Shaikh, *Akbar Nāma*, ed. Agha Ahmad 'Ali and 'Abdur Rahim, 3 vols (Calcutta, 1877–87).

Abu'l Fazl, Shaikh, *Akbar Nāma*, trans. H. Beveridge, 3 vols (Calcutta, 1902–39).

Abu'l Fazl, Shaikh, *Mukātabāt-i 'Allāmī (Inshā'-i Abū'l Fazl)*, ed. Muhammad Hadi 'Ali (Lucknow, 1863).

Abu'l Qasim Namakin, *The Mughal State and Culture, 1556–1598: Selected Letters and Documents from Munshaat-i-Namakin*, ed. Ishtiyaq Ahmad Zilli (New Delhi, 2007).

Ahmad, Nazir, "Adil Shahi Diplomatic Missions to the Court of Shah Abbas", *Islamic Culture*, vol. 43, no. 2, 1969, 143–61.

Ahmad, Nazir, "Letters of the Rulers of the Deccan to Shah Abbas of Iran", in *Medieval India: A Miscellany*, vol. I (Aligarh, 1969), 280–300.

Ahuja, N.D., "'Abd-al-Latif al 'Abbasi and His Account of Punjab", *Islamic Culture*, vol. 41, no. 2, 1967, 93–8.

Ahuja, N.D., "An Indian Memoirist, Traveller, Epistologist and Commentator of Mughal Period (17th Century)", *Punjab University Research Bulletin*, vol. 4, no. 1, 1973, 147–72.

Akyıldız, Olcay, Halim Kara, and Börte Sagaster, eds, *Autobiographical Themes in Turkish Literature: Theoretical and Comparative Perspectives* (Würzburg, 2016).

Alam, Muzaffar, *The Crisis of Empire in Mughal North India: Awadh and the Punjab, 1707–1748* (Delhi, 1986).

Alam, Muzaffar, "Trade, State Policy and Regional Change: Aspects of Mughal–Uzbek Commercial Relations, c. 1550–1750", *Journal of the Economic and Social History of the Orient*, vol. 37, no. 3, 1994, 202–27.

Alam, Muzaffar, "The Pursuit of Persian: Language in Mughal Politics", *Modern Asian Studies*, vol. 32, 1998, 317–49.

Alam, Muzaffar, "The Culture and Politics of Persian in Precolonial Hindustan", in Sheldon Pollock, ed., *Literary Cultures in History: Reconstructions from South Asia* (Berkeley, 2003), 131–98.

Alam, Muzaffar, *The Languages of Political Islam in India, c. 1200–1800* (New Delhi, 2004).

Alam, Muzaffar, "The Mughals, the Sufi Shaikhs and the Formation of the Akbari Dispensation", *Modern Asian Studies*, vol. 43, no. 1, 2009, 135–74.

Alam, Muzaffar, "Introduction to the Second Edition: Revisiting the Mughal Eighteenth Century", in idem, *The Crisis of Empire in Mughal North India: Awadh and the Punjab 1707–1748*, 2nd edition (Delhi, 2013), xiii–lxiv.

Alam, Muzaffar, "Mughal Philology and Rumi's Mathnavī", in Sheldon Pollock, Benjamin A. Elman, and Ku-ming Kevin Chang, eds, *World Philology* (Cambridge, MA, 2015), 178–200.

Alam, Muzaffar, *The Mughals and the Sufis: Islam and Political Imagination in India, 1500–1750* (Ranikhet, 2021).

Alam, Muzaffar, and Sanjay Subrahmanyam, "Discovering the Familiar: Notes on the Travel Account of Anand Ram Mukhlis", *South Asia Research*, vol. 16, no. 2, 1996, 131–54.

Alam, Muzaffar, and Sanjay Subrahmanyam, "From an Ocean of Wonders: Mahmûd bin Amîr Walî Balkhî and His Indian Travels, 1625–1631," in Claudine Salmon, ed., *Récits de voyage des Asiatiques: Genres, mentalités, conception de l'espace* (Paris, 1996), 161–89.

Alam, Muzaffar, and Sanjay Subrahmanyam, "Witnessing Transition: Views on the End of the Akbari Dispensation", in K.N. Panikkar, Terence J. Byres, and Utsa Patnaik, eds, *The Making of History: Essays Presented to Irfan Habib* (New Delhi, 2000), 104–40.

Alam, Muzaffar, and Sanjay Subrahmanyam, "The Making of a Munshi", *Comparative Studies of South Asia, Africa and the Middle East*, vol. 24, no. 2, 2004, 61–72.

Alam, Muzaffar, and Sanjay Subrahmanyam, "The Afterlife of a Mughal *Masnawî*: The Tale of Nal and Daman in Urdu and Persian", in Kathryn Hansen and David Lelyveld, eds, *A Wilderness of Possibilities: Urdu Studies in Transnational Perspective* (Delhi, 2005), 46–73.

Alam, Muzaffar, and Sanjay Subrahmanyam, *Indo-Persian Travels in the Age of Discoveries, 1400–1800* (Cambridge, 2007).

Alam, Muzaffar, and Sanjay Subrahmanyam, *Writing the Mughal World: Studies in Political Culture* (Ranikhet, 2011).

Alam, Muzaffar, Françoise N. Delvoye, and Marc Gaborieau, eds, *The Making of Indo-Persian Culture: Indian and French Studies* (New Delhi, 2000).

Al-Biruni, Abu al-Raihan Muhammad ibn Ahmad, *Kitāb fī Tahqīq ma lil-Hind min maqūlah maqbūlah fī al-'aql aw marzūlah* (Hyderabad, 1958).

Ali, M. Athar, *The Mughal Nobility Under Aurangzeb* (Bombay, 1966).

Ali, M. Athar, "Karnatik at the End of the 17th Century: A Contemporary Account, in Persian", *Proceedings of the Indian History Congress*, vol. 28, 1966, 236–44.

Ali, M. Athar, *The Apparatus of Empire: Awards of Ranks, Offices and Titles to the Mughal Nobility (1574–1658)* (Delhi, 1985).

Ali, M. Athar, "The Use of Sources in Mughal Historiography", *Journal of the Royal Asiatic Society*, 3rd Series, vol. 5, no. 3, 1995, 361–73.

Ali, M. Athar, *Mughal India: Studies in Polity, Ideas, Society, and Culture* (Delhi, 2006).

Almeida Garrett, João Baptista da Silva Leitão de, *Viagens na minha terra*, ed. Maria Ema Tarracha Ferreira (Lisbon, 1994).

Alvi, M.A., and A. Rahman, *Fathullah Shirazi: A Sixteenth Century Indian Scientist* (New Delhi, 1968).

Alvi, Sajida Sultana, ed. and trans. with an Introduction, *Advice on the Art of Governance: Mau'izah-i Jahāngīrī of Muhammad Bāqir Najm-i Sānī, An Indo-Islamic Mirror for Princes* (Albany, 1989).

Amelang, James S., *The Flight of Icarus: Artisan Autobiography in Early Modern Europe* (Stanford, 1998).

Anand Ram Mukhlis, *Badā'i' Waqā'i'-yi Muhammad Shāhī*, Punjab University Library, Lahore, Persian Manuscript Pi XI/89, Accession no. 2140.

Anand Ram Mukhlis, *Chamanistān* (Lakhnau, 1877).

Anand Ram Mukhlis, *Mir'āt ul-Istilāh*, eds Chandar Shekhar, Hamid Raza Qilichkhani, and Human Yusufdihi, 2 vols (Delhi, 2013).

Anand Ram Mukhlis, *Mir'āt ul-Istilāh*, ed. Sharif Husain Qasemi (Delhi, 2016).

Anand Ram Mukhlis, *Muraqqa-e-Mukhlis by Rae Anand Ram Mukhlis*, ed. Ebadat Brelvi (Lahore, 1975).

Anand Ram Mukhlis, "Pari Khāna", ed. 'Arif Naushahi and Mu'in Nizami, *Nāma-yi Bahāristān*, vols. 6–7, nos. 1–2, 2005–6, 197–216.

Anand Ram Mukhlis, *Safar Nāma-yi Mukhlis (The Diary of the Travel of Anand Rām Mukhlis, d. 1164 AH)*, ed. Sayyid Azhar 'Ali (Rampur, 1946).

Anand Ram Mukhlis, *Tazkira-yi shu'arā'*, ed. Saulat 'Ali Khan (Tonk, 2017).

Anand Ram Mukhlis, *Waqā'i' Sair-i Ganga*, British Library, London, India Office Collection, Ms. IO. 1612.

Anandaranga Pillai, *The Private Diary of Ananda Ranga Pillai, Dubash to Joseph François Dupleix, Governor of Pondicherry: A Record of Matters, Political, Historical, Social, and Personal, from 1736–1761*, 12 vols, ed. and trans. J. Frederick Price, K. Rangachari, and H.H. Dodwell (Madras, 1900–28).

Anandaranga Pillai, *Ānantarankappillai nātkurippu*, 4 vols, ed. Ira. Alala-cuntaram (Putuvai, 2005).

Anandaranga Pillai, *Ānantarankappillai vi-nātkurippu, 1751–1754*, 3 vols, ed. Ma. Kopalakirushnan (Chidambaram/Chennai, 2004–8).

Anandaranga Pillai, *Pirattiyekamāna Ānanta Rankappillaiyavarkalin costa likita tinappati ceti kurippu*, 8 vols (reprint, Putuvai, 1998).

Anooshahr, Ali, "Mughal Historians and the Memory of the Islamic Conquest of India", *Indian Economic and Social History Review*, vol. 43, no. 3, 2006, 275–300.

Anooshahr, Ali, "The King Who Would Be Man: The Gender Roles of the Warrior King in Early Mughal History", *Journal of the Royal Asiatic Society*, Series 3, vol. 18, 2008, 327–40.

Anooshahr, Ali, *The Ghazi Sultans and the Frontiers of Islam: A Comparative Study of the Late Medieval and Early Modern Periods* (London, 2009).

Anooshahr, Ali, "Dialogue and Territoriality in a Mughal History of the Millennium", *Journal of the Economic and Social History of the Orient*, vol. 55, nos 2–3, 2012, 220–54.

Anooshahr, Ali, "Author of One's Fate: Fatalism and Agency in Indo-Persian Histories", *Indian Economic and Social History Review*, vol. 49, no. 2, 2012, 197–224.

Anooshahr, Ali, "Mughals, Mongols and Mongrels: The Challenge of Aristocracy and the Rise of the Mughal State in the *Tārīkh-i Rashīdī*", *Journal of Early Modern History*, vol. 18, no. 6, 2014, 559–77.

Anooshahr, Ali, *Turkestan and the Rise of Eurasian Empires: A Study of Politics and Invented Traditions* (New York, 2018).

Anooshahr, Ali, "No Man Can Serve Two Masters: Conflicting Loyalties in Bengal During Shah Jahan's Rebellion of 1624", in Ebba Koch and Ali Anooshahr, eds, *The Mughal Empire from Jahangir to Shahjahan* (Mumbai, 2019), 54–63.

Anooshahr, Ali, "Letter-Writing and Emotional Communities in Early Mughal India: A Note on the Badāyi' al-Inshā", *South Asia: Journal of South Asian Studies*, vol. 44, no. 1, 2021, 1–15.

Anooshahr, Ali, *Slavery in the Early Mughal World: The Life and Thoughts of Jawhar Aftabachi (1520s–1580s)* (New York, 2025).

Ansari, A.S. Bazmee, "Faydī", in *The Encyclopaedia of Islam*, 2nd Edition, ed. Bernard Lewis, *et al.*, (Leiden, 1983), 870–2.

Apte, D.V., D.V. Kale, *et al.*, *English Records on Shivaji, 1659–1682*, 2 vols (Pune, 1931).

Arai, Hakuseki, *Told Round a Brushwood Fire: The Autobiography of Arai Hakuseki*, trans. Janet Ackroyd (Princeton, NJ, 1980).

Arbabzadah, Nushin, "Women and Religious Patronage in the Timurid Empire", in Nile Green, ed., *Afghanistan's Islam: From Conversion to the Taliban* (Berkeley, 2017), 56–70.

Arnold, David, and Stuart Blackburn, eds, *Telling Lives in India: Biography, Autobiography and Life History* (Delhi, 2004).

Asad Beg Qazwini, *Dīwān-i Asad*, British Library, Persian Ms., Or. 5437.

Asad Beg Qazwini, *Nuskha-i Ahwāl-i Asad Beg* (i) Oriental Manuscripts Library and Research Institute, Hyderabad (former Asafiya Collection), Fann-i Sawānih-i 'Umrī 41; (ii) Maulana Azad Library, Aligarh Muslim University, Aligarh, Abdus Salam Collection, No. 270/40 (4); (iii) British Library, London, Or. 1996.

Asad Beg Qazwini, *Risāla-i Tārīkh-i Asad Beg Qazwīnī*, ed. Jamshid Nauruzi (Tehran, 2014).

Asad Beg Qazwini, *Waqā'i'-yi Asad Beg Qazwīnī*, ed. Chander Shekhar (New Delhi, 2017).

Asher, Catherine B., *Architecture of Mughal India, The New Cambridge History of India, I.4* (Cambridge, 1992).

Asher, Catherine B., "Mapping Hindu–Muslim Identities through the Architecture of Shahjahanabad and Jaipur", in David Gilmartin and Bruce B. Lawrence, eds, *Beyond Turk and Hindu: Rethinking Religious Identities in Islamicate South Asia* (Gainesville, FL, 2000), 121–48.

Asif, Manan Ahmed, *The Loss of Hindustan: The Invention of India* (Cambridge, MA, 2020).

Asiye Hatun, *Rüya Mektuplari*, ed. and introd. Cemal Kafadar (Istanbul, 1994).

Askari, Syed Hasan, "The Mausoleum of a Saint of the Madari Order of Sufis at Hilsa, Bihar", *Bengal Past and Present*, vol. 68, 1949, 40–52.

Atçil, Abdurrahman, *Scholars and Sultans in the Early Modern Ottoman Empire* (Cambridge, 2016).

Aubin, Jean, "Comment Tamerlan prenait les villes", *Studia Islamica*, no. 19, 1963, 83–122.

Azfari, Mirza 'Ali Bakht Bahadur Muhammad Zahir-ud-Din, *Wāqi'āt-i Azfarī*, ed. Syed Hamza Hussain Omari, gen. ed. T. Chandrasekharan (Madras, 1957).

Babaie, Sussan, Kathryn Babayan, *et al.*, *Slaves of the Shah: New Elites of Safavid Iran* (London, 2004).

Babayan, Kathryn, *Mystics, Monarchs and Messiahs: Cultural Landscapes of Early Modern Iran* (Cambridge, MA, 2002).

Babayan, Kathryn, *The City as Anthology: Eroticism and Urbanity in Early Modern Isfahan* (Stanford, 2021).

Babur, Zahir-ud-Din Muhammad, *The Bābur-nāma in English*, trans. Annette Susannah Beveridge, 2 vols (London, 1921–2).

Babur, Zahir-ud-Din Muhammad, *Bāburnāma: Chaghatay Turkish Text with Abdul-Rahim Khankhanan's Persian Translation*, ed. Wheeler M. Thackston, 3 vols (Cambridge, MA, 1993).

Babur, Zahir-ud-Din Muhammad, *The Baburnama: Memoirs of Babur, Prince and Emperor*, trans. Wheeler M. Thackston (New York, 2002).

Balabanlilar, Lisa, "The Begims of the Mystic Feast: Turco–Mongol Tradition in the Mughal Harem", *The Journal of Asian Studies*, vol. 69, no. 1, 2010, 123–47.

Balfour, Francis, ed. and trans., *Inshā'-i Harkaran (The Forms of Herkern)* (Calcutta, 1781).

Bashir, Shahzad, *Messianic Hopes and Mystical Visions: The Nūrbakhshīya Between Medieval and Modern Islam* (Columbia, SC, 2003).

Bashir, Shahzad, "India as a Sufi Spacetime in the Work of Jamālī of Delhi", in Jamal J. Elias and Bilal Orfali, eds, *Light Upon Light: Essays in Islamic Thought and History in Honor of Gerhard Bowering* (Leiden, 2019), 316–32.

Bayazid Bayat, *Tazkira-i-Humayun wa Akbar of Bayazid Biyat (A History of the Emperor Humayun from 949 AH [AD 1542] and of His Successor the Emperor Akbar up to 999 AH [AD 1590])*, ed. M. Hidayat Hosain (Calcutta, 1941).

Bayly, C.A., *Empire and Information: Intelligence Gathering and Social Communication in India, 1780–1870* (Cambridge, 1996).

Beelaert, Anna Livia Fermina Alexandra, *A Cure for the Grieving: Studies on the Poetry of the 12th Century Persian Court Poet Khāqānī Širwānī* (Leiden, 1996).

Bergmann, Martin S. "The Legend of Narcissus", *American Imago*, vol. 41, no. 4, 1984, 389–411.

Bernadotte, Oubagarasamy, *Un livre de compte de Ananda Ranga Poullé, courtier de la Compagnie des Indes*, ed. Edmond Gaudart (Pondicherry, 1930).

Bernier, François, *Travels in the Mogul Empire, AD 1656–1668*, trans. Irving Brock and Archibald Constable, rev. Vincent A. Smith (London, 1916).

Bernier, François, *Un Libertin dans l'Inde Moghole: Les voyages de François Bernier (1656–1669)*, ed. Frédéric Tinguely (Paris, 2008).

Beveridge, Annette S., "Further Notes on the Babar-Nama MSS.: The El-

424 BIBLIOGRAPHY

phinstone Codex", *Journal of the Royal Asiatic Society of Great Britain and Ireland*, vol. 39, no. 1, 1907, 131–44.

Bhadra, Gautam, "Two Frontier Uprisings in Mughal India", in Ranajit Guha, ed., *Subaltern Studies, II: Writings on South Asian History and Society* (Delhi, 1983), 43–59.

Bhattacharya, Sudhindra Nath, "Conquest of Islam Khan (1608–1613)", in Jadunath Sarkar, ed., *The History of Bengal, Volume 2: The Muslim Period* (Dhaka, 1948), 247–70.

Bhimsen ibn Raghunandandas, *Nuskhā-i Dilkushā dar ahwāl-i rājahā-i Bundelkhand*, manuscripts British Library, London IO. 94; British Library, London, Or. 23.

Bhimsen ibn Raghunandandas, *Tarikh-i-dilkasha (Memoirs of Bhimsen Relating to Aurangzib's Deccan Campaigns)*, trans. Jadunath Sarkar, rev. V.G. Khobrekar (Bombay, 1972).

Bilgrami, Akeel, "Self-Knowledge and Resentment", in Crispin Wright, Barry C. Smith, and Cynthia Macdonald, eds, *Knowing Our Own Minds* (Oxford, 2000), 207–42.

Binbaş, İlker Evrim, *Intellectual Networks in Timurid Iran: Sharaf al-Dīn ʿAlī Yazdī and the Islamicate Republic of Letters* (Cambridge, 2016).

Biran, Michal, *The Empire of the Qara Khitai in Eurasian History: Between China and the Islamic World* (Cambridge, 2005).

Blake, Stephen P., *Shahjahanabad: The Sovereign City in Mughal India 1639–1739* (Cambridge, 1991).

Bokhari, Afshan, "Masculine Modes of Female Subjectivity: The Case of Jahanara Begam", in Anshu Malhotra and Siobhan Lambert-Hurley, eds, *Speaking of the Self: Gender, Performance, and Autobiography in South Asia* (Durham, NC, 2015), 165–202.

Bouillier, Véronique, "La violence des non-violents, ou les ascètes au combat", in Denis Vidal, Gilles Tarabout, and Éric Meyer, eds, *Violences et Non-Violence en Inde* (Paris, 1994), 213–43.

Brand, Michael, and Glenn D. Lowry, *Fatehpur-Sikri* (Bombay, 1987).

Branfoot, Crispin, "Mangammal of Madurai and South Indian Portraiture", *East and West*, vol. 51, nos 3–4, 2001, 369–77.

Brook, Timothy, *The Confusions of Pleasure: Commerce and Culture in Ming China* (Berkeley, 1999).

Burckhardt, Jacob, *The Civilisation of the Renaissance in Italy*, trans. S.G.C. Middlemore (London, 1898).

Burke, Peter, "Representations of the Self from Petrarch to Descartes", in Roy Porter, ed., *Rewriting the Self: Histories from the Renaissance to the Present* (London, 1997), 17–28.

Busch, Allison, "Portrait of a Raja in a Badshah's World: Amrit Rai's Biography of Man Singh (1585)", *Journal of the Economic and Social History of the Orient*, vol. 55, nos 2–3, 2012, 287–328.

Carrithers, Michael, Steven Collins, and Steven Lukes, eds, *The Category of the Person: Anthropology, Philosophy, History* (Cambridge, 1985).

Chakrabarty, Dipesh, *The Calling of History: Sir Jadunath Sarkar and His Empire of Truth* (Chicago, 2015).

Chandra, Satish, "Cultural and Political Role of Delhi, 1675–1725", in Robert E. Frykenberg, ed., *Delhi Through the Ages: Essays in Urban History, Culture, and Society* (Delhi, 1986), 106–16.

Chandra, Satish, *Parties and Politics at the Mughal Court, 1707–1740*, 4ᵗʰ edn (Delhi, 2002).

Chatterjee, Indrani, "A Slave's Quest for Selfhood in Eighteenth-Century Hindustan", *The Indian Economic and Social History Review*, vol. 37, no. 1, 2000, 53–86.

Chattopadhyaya, Kshatresachandra, "Religious Suicide at Prayag", *Journal of the United Provinces Historical Society*, vol. 10, 1937, 65–79.

Chaudhuri, K.N., "Some Reflections on the Town and Country in Mughal India", *Modern Asian Studies*, vol. 12, no. 1, 1978, 77–96.

Choksy, Jamsheed K., and M. Usman Hasan, "An Emissary from Akbar to 'Abbas I: Inscriptions, Texts and the Career of Amir Muhammad Ma'sum al-Bhakkari", *Journal of the Royal Asiatic Society of Great Britain and Ireland*, Series 3, vol. 1, no. 1, 1991, 19–29.

Coslovi, Franco, "Aspetti 'indiani' della figura di Šāh Madār e della sua *tarīqa*", *Rivista degli studi orientali*, vol. 51, 1978, 187–203.

Crane, Howard, "The Patronage of Zahir-ud-din Babur and the Origins of Mughal Architecture", *Bulletin of the Asia Institute*, vol. 1, 1987, 95–110.

Dadvar, Abolghasem, *Iranians in Mughal Politics and Society, 1606–1658* (New Delhi, 1999).

Dale, Stephen F., "Steppe Humanism: The Autobiographical Writings of Zahir al-Din Muhammad Babur, 1483–1530", *International Journal of Middle Eastern Studies*, vol. 22, no. 1, 1990, 37–58.

Dale, Stephen F., "A Safavid Poet in the Heart of Darkness: The Indian Poems of Ashraf Mazandarani", in Michel Mazzaoui, ed., *Safavid Iran and Her Neighbors* (Salt Lake City, 2003), 63–80 (also in *Iranian Studies*, vol. 36, no. 2, 2003, 197–212).

Dale, Stephen F., *Babur: Timurid Prince and Mughal Emperor, 1483–1530* (Cambridge, 2018).

Dalmia, Vasudha, *Fiction as History: The Novel and the City in Modern North India* (Ranikhet, 2017).

Dankoff, Robert, *An Ottoman Mentality: The World of Evliya Çelebi* (Leiden, 2004).

Dargah Quli Khan, *Muraqqaʻ-i Dihlī: Fārsī Matan aur Tarjuma*, ed. and trans. Khaliq Anjum (New Delhi, 1993).

Davis, Natalie Zemon, *Women on the Margins: Three Seventeenth-century Lives* (Cambridge, MA, 1995).

Dayal, Subah, *Between Household and State: The Mughal Frontier and the Politics of Circulation in Peninsular India* (Berkeley, 2024).

Delvoye, Françoise N., "Les chants dhrupad en langue braj des poètes-musiciens de l'Inde Moghole", in Françoise Mallison, ed., *Littératures médiévales de l'Inde du Nord* (Paris, 1991), 139–85.

Delvoye, Françoise N., "The Image of Akbar as a Patron of Music in Indo-Persian and Vernacular Sources", in Irfan Habib, ed., *Akbar and His India* (Delhi, 1997), 188–214.

Deol, Jeevan, "Eighteenth Century Khalsa Identity: Discourse, Praxis and Narrative", in Christopher Shackle, Gurharpal Singh, and Arvind-pal Singh Mandair, eds, *Sikh Religion, Culture and Ethnicity* (Richmond, 2001), 25–46.

Desai, Madhuri, *Banaras Reconstructed: Architecture and Sacred Space in a Hindu Holy City* (Seattle, 2017).

Desai, Z.A., "Life and Works of Faidi", *Indo-Iranica*, vol. 16, no. 3, 1963, 1–35.

Desai, Z.A., "A Foreign Dignitary's Ceremonial Visit to Akbar's Tomb: A First-hand Account", in Iqtidar Alam Khan, ed., *Akbar and His Age* (New Delhi, 1999), 188–97.

Dickson, Martin B., "Uzbek Dynastic Theory in the Sixteenth Century", in *Trudy XXV-ogo Mezhdunardnogo Kongressa Vosto-kovedov* (Moscow, 1963), 208–16.

Digby, Simon, "Dreams and Reminiscences of Dattu Sarvani, a Sixteenth Century Indo-Afghan Soldier", *The Indian Economic and Social History Review*, vol. 2, no. 1, 1965, 52–80; vol. 2, no. 2, 1965, 178–94 (in two parts).

Digby, Simon, "Some Asian Wanderers in Seventeenth-century India: An Examination of Sources in Persian", *Studies in History*, N.S., vol. 9, no. 2, 1993, 247–64.

Digby, Simon, "The Indo-Persian Historiography of the Lodi Sultans", in François Grimal, ed., *Les Sources et le temps* (Pondicherry, 2001), 243–61.

Digby, Simon, "Bayazid Beg Turkman's Pilgrimage to Makka and Return to Gujarat: A Sixteenth Century Narrative", *Iran*, vol. 42, 2004, 159–77.

Dudney, Arthur, *India in the Persian World of Letters: Khān-i Ārzū among the Eighteenth-Century Philologists* (Oxford, 2022).

Dunbar, Robert W., "Zayn al-Dīn Maḥmūd Vāṣifī and the Transformation of Early Sixteenth Century Islamic Central Asia", Ph.D. dissertation, Central Eurasian Studies, Indiana University, 2015.

Eaton, Richard M., *Sufis of Bijapur, 1300–1700: Social Roles of Sufis in Medieval India* (Princeton, NJ, 1978).

Eaton, Richard M., "Multiple Lenses: Differing Perspectives of Fifteenth-Century Calicut", in Laurie J. Sears, ed., *Autonomous Histories, Particular Truths: Essays in Honor of John Smail* (Madison, WI, 1993), 71–86.

Eaton, Richard M., *The Rise of Islam and the Bengal Frontier, 1204–1760* (Delhi, 1994).

Eck, Diana L., *Darśan: Seeing the Divine Image in India*, 3rd edn (New York, 1998).

Eickelman, Dale F., and James Piscatori, eds, *Muslim Travellers: Pilgrimage, Migration and the Religious Imagination* (Berkeley, 1990).

Elliot, Henry M., and John Dowson, eds, *The History of India as Told by Its Own Historians: The Muhammadan Period*, 8 vols (reprint, Delhi, 1990).

Elman, Benjamin A., *Civil Examinations and Meritocracy in Late Imperial China* (Cambridge, MA, 2013).

El-Moudden, Abderrahmane, "The Ambivalence of *Rihla*: Community Integration and Self-definition in Moroccan Travel Accounts, 1300–1800", in Dale F. Eickelman and James Piscatori, eds, *Muslim Travellers: Pilgrimage, Migration, and the Religious Imagination* (Berkeley, 1990), 69–84.

Elverskoğ, Johan, *Buddhism and Islam on the Silk Road* (Philadelphia, 2010).

Ernst, Carl W., *Eternal Garden: Mysticism, History and Politics at a South Asian Sufi Center* (Albany, NY, 1992).

Ernst, Carl W., "An Indo-Persian Guide to Sufi Shrine Pilgrimage", in Grace Martin Smith and Carl W. Ernst, eds, *Manifestations of Sainthood in Islam* (Istanbul, 1993), 43–67.

Ernst, Carl W., "Admiring the Works of the Ancients: The Ellora Temples as Viewed by Indo-Muslim Authors", in David Gilmartin and Bruce B. Lawrence, eds, *Beyond Turk and Hindu: Rethinking Religious Identities in Islamicate South Asia* (Gainesville, FL, 2000), 98–120.

Ernst, Carl W., "Fayzi's Illuminationist Interpretation of Vedanta: The Shariq al-ma'rifa", *Comparative Studies of South Asia, Africa and the Middle East*, vol. 30, no. 3, 2010, 156–64.

Farid Bhakkari, *Zakhīrat al-Khawānīn*, 3 vols, ed. S. Mu'inul Haqq (Karachi, 1961–74).

Farid Bhakkari, Shaikh, *The Dhakhīratul-Khawānīn of Shaikh Farid Bhakkari: A Biographical Dictionary of Mughal Noblemen*, trans. Ziyauddin A. Desai (Delhi, 1993).

Farooqi, Naimur Rehman, *Mughal–Ottoman Relations: A Study of the Political and Diplomatic Relations Between Mughal India and the Ottoman Empire* (Delhi, 1989).

Faroqhi, Suraiya, *Men of Modest Substance: House Owners and House Property in Seventeenth-century Ankara and Kayseri* (Cambridge, 1987).

Faroqhi, Suraiya, *The Ottoman and Mughal Empires: Social History in the Early Modern World* (London, 2019).

Farquhar, J.N., "Fighting Ascetics of India", *Bulletin of the John Rylands Library*, vol. 9, 1925, 1–17.

Faruqui, Muhammad 'Abdul Hamid, *Chandra Bhan Brahman: Life and Works with a Critical Edition of his Diwan* (Ahmadabad, 1966).

Faruqui, Munis D., *The Princes of the Mughal Empire, 1504–1719* (Cambridge, 2012).

Findly, Ellison Banks, *Nur Jahan: Empress of Mughal India* (New York, 1993).

Fischel, Roy S., *Local States in an Imperial World: Identity, Society and Politics in the Early Modern Deccan* (Edinburgh, 2020).

Fleischer, Cornell H., *Bureaucrat and Intellectual in the Ottoman Empire: The Historian Mustafa Âli (1541–1600)* (Princeton, NJ, 1986).

Fleischer, Cornell H., "Secretaries' Dreams: Augury and Angst in Ottoman Scribal Service", in Ingeborg Baldauf and Suraiya Faroqhi, eds, *Armağan: Festschrift für Andreas Tietze* (Prague, 1994), 77–88.

Fleischer, Cornell H., "Companions to King Errant: Babur and His Lieutenants to the Conquest of Kabul", in İlker Evrim Binbaş and Nurten Kılıç-Schubel, eds, *Horizons of the World: Festschrift for İsenbike Togan* (Istanbul, 2011), 545–56.

Fleischer, Cornell H., "A Mediterranean Apocalypse: Prophecies of Empire in the Fifteenth and Sixteenth Centuries", *Journal of the Economic and Social History of the Orient*, vol. 61, nos 1–2, 2018, 18–90.

Floor, Willem, and Edmund Herzig, eds, *Iran and the World in the Safavid Age* (London, 2012).

Flores, Jorge, *Nas Margens do Hindustão: O Estado da Índia e a expansão mogol, ca. 1570–1640* (Coimbra, 2015).

Flores, Jorge, *The Mughal Padshah: A Jesuit Treatise on Emperor Jahangir's Court and Household* (Leiden, 2016).

Foltz, Richard C., "Two Seventeenth-Century Central Asian Travellers to Mughal India", *Journal of the Royal Asiatic Society of Great Britain and Ireland*, Series 3, vol. 6, no. 3, 1996, 367–77.

Foltz, Richard C., *Conversations with Emperor Jahangir by 'Mutribi' al-Asamm of Samarqand* (Costa Mesa, CA, 1998).

Foster, William, ed., *The Embassy of Sir Thomas Roe to India, 1615–1619* (London, 1926).

Fragner, Bert G., *Persischen Memoirenliteratur als Quelle zu neueren Geschichte Irans* (Wiesbaden, 1979).

Fragner, Bert G., "Farman", in *Encyclopaedia Iranica*, ed. Ehsan Yarshater, vol. 9 (New York 1999), 282–95.

Frykenberg, Robert E., ed., *Delhi Through the Ages: Essays in Urban History, Culture, and Society* (Delhi, 1986).

Gandhi, Mohandas K., *An Autobiography, or the Story of My Experiments with Truth*, trans. Mahadev Desai (Ahmedabad, 1940).

Gandhi, Supriya, "*Dharmaśāstra* in Aurangzeb's India: A Persian Translation of the *Yājñavalkya Smṛti* and *Mitākṣarā*", *The Journal of Hindu Studies*, vol. 16, no. 1, 2023, 33–56.

Gandhi, Supriya, "Fraught Intimacies: Persian and Hindu Publics in Colonial India", *PMLA*, vol. 139, no. 2, 2024, 338–44.

Gandjeï, Tourkhan, "Uno scritto apologetico di Husain Mīrzā, sultano del Khorāsān," *Annali dell'Istituto Universitario Orientale di Napoli*, no. 5, 1953, 157–83.

Ghani, M.A., *A History of Persian Language and Literature at the Mughal Court*, 2 vols (reprint, Westmead, 1972).

Ghosh, Amitav, "The Man Behind the Mosque", *The Little Magazine*, vol. 1, no. 2, 2000; reprinted in idem, *The Imam and the Indian: Prose Pieces* (New Delhi, 2008), 88–105.

Ghurye, G.S., *Indian Sadhus*, 2nd edn (Bombay, 1964).

Goitein, S.D., "Letters and Documents on the India Trade in Medieval Times", *Islamic Culture*, vol. 37, no. 3, 1963, 188–205.

Golchin-i Ma'ani, Ahmad, *Kārwān-i Hind (The Caravan of India: On Life and Works of the Poets of Safavid Era Emigrated to India)*, 2 vols (Mashhad, 1990).

Gommans, Jos, *The Rise of the Indo-Afghan Empire, c. 1710–1780* (Leiden, 1995).

Gommans, Jos, *Mughal Warfare: Indian Frontiers and High Roads to Empire, 1500–1700* (London, 2002).

Gommans, Jos, and Said Reza Huseini, "New Dawn in Mughal India: Longue durée Neoplatonism in the Making of Akbar's Sun Project", *Journal of the Royal Asiatic Society*, 3rd Series, vol. 34, 2024, 455–76.

Gordon, Stewart, "Burhanpur: Entrepot and Hinterland, 1650–1750", *The Indian Economic and Social History Review*, vol. 25, no. 4, 1988, 425–42.

Gordon, Stewart, ed., *Robes of Honour: 'Khil'at' in Pre-Colonial and Colonial India* (Delhi, 2003).

Gould, Rebecca, "How Gulbadan Remembered: The 'Book of Humāyūn' as an Act of Representation", *Early Modern Women*, vol. 6, 2011, 187–93.

Green, Nile, "Auspicious Foundations: The Patronage of Sufi Institutions in the Late Mughal and Early Asaf Jah Deccan", *South Asian Studies*, vol. 20, no. 1, 2004, 71–98.

Grenet, Frantz, "Maracanda/Samarkand, une métropole pré-mongole: Sources écrites et archéologie", *Annales HSS*, vol. 59, nos 5–6, 2004, 1043–67.

Grewal, J.S., *In the By-lanes of History: Some Persian Documents from a Punjab Town* (Shimla, 1975).

Grobbel, Gerald, *Der Dichter Faidī und die Religion Akbars* (Berlin, 2001).

Gross, Jo-Ann, and Asom Urunbaev, *The Letters of Khwājah 'Ubayd Allāh Ahrār and His Associates* (Leiden, 2002).

Gulbadan Begam, *The History of Humāyūn (Humāyūn Nāma)*, ed. and trans. Annette S. Beveridge (London, 1902).

Gulbadan Begam, *Humāyūnnāma*, in Wheeler M. Thackston, ed. and trans., *Three Memoirs of Homayun* (Costa Mesa, CA, 2009).

Gusdorf, Georges, "Conditions et limites de l'autobiographie", in Günter Reichenkron and Erich Haase, eds, *Formen der Selbstdarstellung: Analekten zu einer Geschichte des literarischen Selbstportraits. Festgabe für Fritz Neubert* (Berlin, 1956), 105–23.

Gusdorf, Georges, "Conditions and Limits of Autobiography" (trans. James Olney), in James Olney, ed., *Autobiography: Essays Theoretical and Critical* (Princeton, NJ, 1980), 28–48.

Gyatso, Janet, *Apparitions of the Self: The Secret Autobiographies of a Tibetan Visionary* (Princeton, NJ, 1998).

Habib, Irfan, "Potentialities of Capitalistic Development in the Economy of Mughal India", *Journal of Economic History*, vol. 29, no. 1, 1969, 32–78.

Habib, Irfan, "Merchant Communities in Precolonial India", in James D. Tracy, ed., *The Rise of Merchant Empires: Long-Distance Trade in the Early Modern World, 1350–1750* (New York, 1990), 371–99.

Habib, Irfan, "Timur in the Political Tradition and Historiography of Mughal India", *Cahiers d'Asie centrale*, nos 3–4, 1997, 297–312.

Habib, Irfan, *The Agrarian System of Mughal India, 1556–1707*, 2nd revised edition (Delhi, 1999).

Habib, Irfan, and Tarapada Mukherjee, *Braj Bhūm in Mughal Times: The State, Peasants and Gosʾāins* (Delhi, 2020).

Hadi, Nabi, *Mughalon ke malik-ush-shʿura* (Allahabad, 1978).

Haidar Dughlat, Mirza, *Tārīkh-i Rashīdī: Tārīkh-i Khawānīn-i Mughūlistān (A History of the Khans of Moghulistan)*, ed. and trans. Wheeler Thackston, 2 vols (Cambridge, MA, 1996).

Hakala, Walter N., "A Sultan in the Realm of Passion: Coffee in Eighteenth-Century Delhi", *Eighteenth-Century Studies*, vol. 47, no. 4, 2014, 371–88.

Haneda, Masashi, *Le Chāh et les Qizilbāš: Le système militaire safavide* (Berlin, 1987).

Haneda, Masashi, "La famille Huzânî d'Isfahan (15e–17e siècles)", *Studia Iranica*, vol. 18, 1989, 77–91.

Haneda, Masashi, "Emigration of Iranian Elites to India During the 16th–18th Centuries", in Maria Szuppe, ed., *L'Héritage Timouride: Iran–Asie centrale-Inde, XVe–XVIIIe siècles*, special number of *Cahiers d'Asie Centrale*, nos 3–4, 1997, 129–43.

Hardy, Friedhelm, *Earth as Lamp: The Formation of Śrīvaisnavism and Other Essays*, ed. David Shulman and Aruna Hardy (Delhi, 2021).

Harris, Joseph E., *The African Presence in Asia: Consequences of the East African Slave Trade* (Evanston, 1971).

Harris, Joseph E., "Malik Ambar: African Regent-Minister in India", in Runoko Rashidi and Ivan Van Sertima, eds, *African Presence in Early Asia* (New Brunswick, 1995), 146–52.

Hasan, Farhat, "Mughal Records on the English East India Company: A Calendar to 1740", M.Phil. dissertation, Centre for Advanced Study in History, Aligarh Muslim University, 1987.

Hasan, Zafar, "A Letter from Nadir Shah to Zakariya Khan, the Governor of Lahore and Multan", *Proceedings of the Indian Historical Records Commission*, vol. 4, 1922, 25–9.

Hattox, Ralph S., *Coffee and Coffeehouses: The Origins of a Social Beverage in the Medieval Near East* (Seattle, 1985).

Havlioğlu, Didem, "On the Margins and Between the Lines: Ottoman Women Poets from the Fifteenth to the Twentieth Centuries", *Turkish Historical Review*, vol. 1, 2010, 25–54.

Hodgson, Marshall G.S., *The Venture of Islam: Conscience and History in a World Civilization (vol. 3: The Gunpowder Empires and Modern Times)* (Chicago, 1977).

Horn, Paul, *Die Denkwurdigkeiten schah Tahmasp's des Ersten von Persien* (Strasbourg, 1891).

Hoselitz, Bert F., "Generative and Parasitic Cities", *Economic Development and Cultural Change*, vol. 3, no. 3, 1955, 278–94.

Hulme, Peter, and Tim Youngs, eds, *The Cambridge Companion to Travel Writing* (Cambridge, 2002).

Husain, Afzal, "Growth of Irani Element in Akbar's Nobility", *Proceedings of the Indian History Congress*, vol. 36, 1975, 166–79.

Husain, Afzal, *The Nobility Under Akbar and Jahangir: A Study of Family Groups* (New Delhi, 1999).

Husain, Hidayat, "The Mirza Nama (The Book of the Perfect Gentleman) of Mirza Kamran", *Journal of the Asiatic Society of Bengal*, vol. 9, no. 1, 1913, 1–13.

İnalcık, Halil, "Capital Formation in the Ottoman Empire", *The Journal of Economic History*, vol. 29, no. 1, 1969, 97–140.

Irvine, William, "Garh Muktesar Fair in 1747: Or, a Thirteen Days' Trip", *Indian Magazine and Review*, 1903, 66–71, 102–6, 116–21, 151–6, and 169–72.

Irvine, William, *Later Mughals*, 2 vols, ed. and rev. Jadunath Sarkar (London: Luzac and Co., 1921–2).

'Ishq 'Azimabadi, Husain Quli Khan, *Tazkira-yi Nashtar-i 'ishq*, ed. Sayyid Kamal Hajj Sayyid Javadi, 4 vols (Tehran, 1391 Sh./2013).

Ishwardas Nagar, *Futūhāt-i 'Ālamgīrī: English Translation and Persian Text*, trans. M.F. Lokhandwala and Jadunath Sarkar, ed. Raghubir Sinh and Quazi Karamtullah (Vadodara, 1995).

Iskandar Beg Munshi, *Tārīkh-i 'Alamārā-yi 'Abbāsī*, 2 vols, ed. Iraj Afshar (Tehran, 1957).

Iskandar Beg (Eskandar Beg Monshi), *History of Shah 'Abbas the Great (Tarikh-i 'Alamara-yi 'Abbasi)*, trans. Roger M. Savory, 2 vols (Boulder, 1978).

Islam, Riazul, *A Calendar of Documents on Indo-Persian Relations (1500–1750)*, 2 vols (Karachi, 1979–82).

Iwasaki, Haruko, "Portrait of a Daimyo: Comical Fiction by Matsudaira Sadanobu", *Monumenta Nipponica*, vol. 38, no. 1, 1983, 1–19.

Jackson, Peter, *The Delhi Sultanate: A Political and Military History* (Cambridge, 1999).

Jahangir, Nur-ud-Din, *The Jahangirnama: Memoirs of Jahangir, Emperor of India*, trans. Wheeler M. Thackston (New York, 1999).

Jamal-ud-Din Husain ibn Hasan Inju Shirazi, *Farhang-i Jahāngīrī*, ed. Rahim 'Afifi, 3 vols (Mashhad, 1351–4 Sh./1972–5).

James, George McLeod, *Anand Ram 'Mukhlis': His Life And Works, 1695–1758* (Delhi, *ca.* 2011).

Jauhar Aftabchi, *Tazkirat ul-Wāqi'āt*, trans. into Urdu by S. Moinul Haq (Karachi, 1955).

Jauhar Aftabhchi, *Tazkirat ul-Wāqi'āt*, in Wheeler M. Thackston, ed. and trans., *Three Memoirs of Homayun* (Costa Mesa, CA, 2009).

Joshi, P.M., "Asad Beg's Mission to Bijapur, 1603–1604", in S.N. Sen, ed., *Mahamahopadhyaya Prof. D.V. Potdar Sixty-First Birthday Commemmoration Volume* (Poona, 1950), 184–96.

Joshi, P.M., "Asad Beg's Return From Bijapur and His Second Mission to the Deccan, 1604–1606", in V.D. Rao, ed., *Studies in Indian History: Dr. A.G. Pawar Felicitation Volume* (Bombay, 1968), 136–55.

Joshi, P.M., "Khandesh", in H.K. Sherwani and P.M. Joshi, eds., *History of Medieval Deccan, 1295–1724*, 2 vols (Hyderabad, 1973), vol. 1, 492–516.

Jung, Willi, "Georg Misch's 'Geschichte der Autobiografie'" (trans. Albert Wimmer), *Annali d'Italianistica*, vol. 4, 1986, 30–44.

Justice, Christopher, *Dying the Good Death: The Pilgrimage to Die in India's Holy City* (Albany, NY, 1997).

Kafadar, Cemal, "Self and Others: The Diary of a Dervish in Seventeenth-century Istanbul and First-person Narratives in Ottoman Literature", *Studia Islamica*, vol. 69, 1989, 121–50.

Kafadar, Cemal, *Kim var imiş biz burada yoğ iken: Dört Osmanlı: Yeniçeri, Tüccar, Derviş ve Hatun* (Istanbul, 2009).

Kaicker, Abhishek, *The King and the People: Sovereignty and Popular Politics in Mughal Delhi* (New York, 2020).

Kanalu Ramamurthy, Naveen, "Mirrors and Masks of Sovereignty: Imperial Governance in the Mughal World of Legal Normativism, *c.* 1650s–1720s", PhD, Department of History, UCLA, 2021.

Karaman, K. Kivanç, and Şevket Pamuk, "Ottoman State Finances in European Perspective, 1500–1914", *The Journal of Economic History*, vol. 70, no. 3, 2010, 593–629.

Keshavmurthy, Prashant, *Persian Authorship and Canonicity in Late Mughal Delhi: Building an Ark* (New York, 2016).

Kewal Ram, *Tazkiratul-umara of Kewal Ram: Biographical Account of the*

Mughal Nobility, AD 1556–1707, ed. and trans. S.M. Azizuddin Husain (New Delhi, 1985).

Khan, Iqtidar Alam, *Mirza Kamran: A Biographical Study* (Bombay, 1964).

Khan, Iqtidar Alam, "The Nobility Under Akbar and the Development of His Religious Policy", *Journal of the Royal Asiatic Society of Great Britain and Ireland*, vol. 100, no. 1, 1968, 29–36.

Khan, Iqtidar Alam, *The Political Biography of a Mughal Noble: Mun'im Khan Khan-i Khanan, 1497–1575* (New Delhi, 1973).

Khan, Iqtidar Alam. "The Middle Classes in the Mughal Empire", *Social Scientist*, vol. 5, no. 1, 1976, 28–49.

Khan, Iqtidar Alam, "New Light on the History of Two Early Mughal Monuments of Bayana", *Muqarnas*, vol. 6, 1989, 75–82.

Khan, Iqtidar Alam, "Akbar's Personality Traits and World Outlook: A Critical Reappraisal", *Social Scientist*, vol. 20, nos 9–10, 1992, 16–30.

Khan, Iqtidar Alam, "Akbar's Religious Policy in the Early Phase of His Reign: A Complex Story", *Studies in People's History*, vol. 6, no. 1, 2019, 70–7.

Khan, Majida, "A Kayastha Family of Mughal Officials in the Reign of Aurangzeb", *Proceedings of the Indian History Congress*, vol. 41, 1980, 386–94.

Khan, Mubarak Ali, *The Court of the Great Mughuls (Based on Persian Sources)* (Bochum, 1976).

Khwandamir, *Qanun-i Humayuni, Also Known as Humayun Nama: A Work on the Rules and Ordinances Established by the Emperor Humayun and on Some Buildings Erected by His Orders*, ed. M. Hidayat Hosain (Calcutta, 1940).

Khwurshah ibn Qubad al-Husaini, *Tārīkh-i Qutbī, niz musamma bih Tārīkh-i Ilchī-yi Nizām Shāh: Maqālah-i panjum, tārīkh-i Al-i Timūr az Timūr tā Akbar*, ed. Sayyid Mujahid Zaydi (New Delhi, 1965).

Khwurshah ibn Qubad al-Husaini, *Tārīkh-i ilchī-yi Nizām Shāh: Tārīkh-i Safawīyah az āghāz tā sāl-i 972 Hijrī Qamarī*, eds Muhammad Riza Nasiri and Koichi Haneda (Tehran, 2000).

Kia, Mana, *Persianate Selves: Memories of Place and Origin Before Nationalism* (Stanford, CA, 2020).

Kinra, Rajeev, *Writing Self, Writing Empire: Chandar Bhan Brahman and the Cultural World of the Indo-Persian State Secretary* (Berkeley, CA, 2015).

Kinra, Rajeev, "Handling Diversity with Absolute Civility: The Global Historical Legacy of Mughal *Sulh-i Kull*", *The Medieval History Journal*, vol. 16, no. 2, 2013, 251–95.

Kinra, Rajeev, "The Truth Is Out There (and Also In Here): *Tahqīq* as an

Investigative Modality in Mughal Culture and Scholarship", *Journal of Early Modern History*, vol. 27, no. 4, 2023, 353–67.

Kirmani, Waris, "The Significance of Faidi's Poetry and Its Background", *Indo-Iranica*, vol. 38, nos 3–4, 1985, 26–35.

Koch, Ebba, "The Delhi of the Mughals Prior to Shahjahanabad as Reflected in the Patterns of Imperial Visits", in idem, *Mughal Art and Imperial Ideology: Collected Essays* (Delhi, 2001), 163–82.

Koch, Ebba, *The Planetary King: Humayun Padshah, Inventor and Visionary on the Mughal Throne* (Ahmedabad, 2022).

Koch, Ebba, and Ali Anooshahr, eds, *The Mughal Empire from Jahangir to Shahjahan: Art, Architecture, Politics, Law and Literature* (Mumbai, 2019).

Kolff, Dirk H.A., *Naukar, Rajput and Sepoy: The Ethnohistory of the Military Labour Market in Hindustan, 1450–1850* (Cambridge, 1990).

Kumar, Anil, *Asaf Khan and His Times* (Patna, 1986).

Kumar, Sunil, *The Present in Delhi's Pasts* (New Delhi, 2002).

Kumar, Sunil, "The Delhi Sultanate as Empire", in Peter F. Bang, C.A. Bayly, and Walter Scheidel, eds, *The Oxford World History of Empire, Volume 2: The History of Empires* (Oxford, 2021), 571–96.

Kunt, İ. Metin, *The Sultan's Servants: The Transformation of Ottoman Provincial Government, 1550–1650* (New York, 1983).

Lal, Ruby, "Historicizing the Harem: The Challenge of a Princess's Memoir", *Feminist Studies*, vol. 30, no. 3, 2004, 590–616.

Lal, Ruby, *Domesticity and Power in the Early Mughal World* (Cambridge, 2005).

Lambert-Hurley, Siobhan T., *Elusive Lives: Gender, Autobiography, and the Self in Muslim South Asia* (Stanford, 2018).

Lambourn, Elizabeth, "Of Jewels and Horses: The Career and Patronage of an Iranian Merchant Under Shah Jahan", *Iranian Studies*, vol. 36, no. 2, 2003, 213–58.

Lath, Mukund, *Ardhakathanaka, Half a Tale: A Study in the Interrelationship Between Autobiography and History* (Jaipur, 1981).

Lefèvre, Corinne, *Pouvoir impérial et élites dans l'Inde moghole de Jahāngīr* (Paris, 2017).

Lejeune, Philippe, *Le pacte autobiographique* (Paris, 1975).

Liebrenz, Boris, and Kristina Richardson, eds., *Ayyām Kamāl al-Dīn al-Ḥāʾik: Halab fī awākhir al-qarn al-ʿāshir (The Notebook of Kamāl al-Dīn the Weaver: Aleppine Notes from the End of the 16th Century)* (Beirut, 2021).

Lockhart, Laurence, *Nadir Shah: A Critical Study Based Mainly Upon Contemporary Sources* (London, 1938).

Loiseau, Julien, "De l'Asie centrale à l'Égypte: Le siècle turc", in Patrick Boucheron, *et al.*, *Histoire du Monde au XVe siècle* (Paris, 2009), 33–50.

Lorenzen, David N., "Warrior Ascetics in Indian History", *Journal of the American Oriental Society*, vol. 98, 1978, 61–75.

Lunde, Paul, "The Quest for Arabic Autobiography", *Medieval History Journal*, vol. 18, no. 2, 2015, 430–51.

MacLean, Derryl N., "La sociologie de l'engagement politique: Le Mahdawîya indien et l'État", *Revue des mondes musulmans et de la Méditerranée*, nos 91–4 (2000), 239–56.

Maddison, Angus, *Class Structure and Economic Growth: India and Pakistan Since the Moghuls* (New York, 1971).

Maitra, K.M., *A Persian Embassy to China* (repr. New York, 1970).

Malik, Zahir Uddin, *The Reign of Muhammad Shah, 1719–1748* (Bombay, 1977).

Mano, Eiji, "The Babur-nama and the Tarikh-i Rashidi: Their Mutual Relationship", *Timurid Art and Culture. Iran and Central Asia in the Fifteenth Century*, eds Lisa Golombek and Maria Subtelny (Leiden, 1992).

Mano, Eiji, "Editorial Choices in Preparing the Critical Edition of the Babur-nama", *Theoretical Approaches to the Transmission and Edition of Oriental Manuscripts. Proceedings of a Symposium Held in Istanbul March 28–30, 2001* (Beirut, 2007).

Markiewicz, Christopher, *The Crisis of Kingship in Late Medieval Islam: Persian Emigres and the Making of Ottoman Sovereignty* (Cambridge, 2019).

Marshall, D.N., *Mughals in India: A Bibliographical Survey of Manuscripts* (New York, 1985).

Martinez, Chloe, "Gathering the Threads: Religious Autobiography in Precolonial South Asia", *Medieval History Journal*, vol. 18, no. 2, 2015, 250–77.

Mashita, Hiroyuki, "A Historiographical Study of the So-called Ahwāl-i Asad Bīg", *Zinbun: Annals of the Institute for Research in Humanities, Kyoto University*, vol. 36, no. 1, 2003, 51–103.

Mashita, Hiroyuki, "Asad Beg Qazvīnī", *Encyclopaedia of Islam, III*, eds Kate Fleet, Gudrun Krämer, Denis Matringe, John Nawas, Everett Rowson. Consulted online on 14 June 2021: http://dx.doi.org/10.1163/1573-3912_ei3_COM_27763.

Mauss, Marcel, "Une catégorie de l'esprit humain: La notion de personne celle de 'Moi'", *Journal of the Royal Anthropological Institute of Great Britain and Ireland*, vol. 68, 1938, 263–81.

McChesney, Robert D., "The Conquest of Herat 995–6/1587–8: Sources for the Study of Safavid/Qizilbash–Shibanid/Uzbak Relations", in Jean Calmard, ed., *Études Safavides* (Paris–Tehran, 1993), 69–107.

McChesney, Robert D., "'Barrier of Heterodoxy'? Rethinking the Ties Between Iran and Central Asia in the Seventeenth Century", in Charles Melville, ed., *Safavid Persia: The History and Politics of an Islamic Society* (London, 1996), 231–67.

McGregor, Ronald S., *Hindi Literature From Its Beginnings to the Nineteenth Century* (Wiesbaden, 1984).

Meier, Franziska, "Almeida Garretts *Viagens na Minha Terra*: Zum Verhältnis von Autobiographischem Subjekt und Geschichtserfahrung im Zeitalter der Revolution", *Romanische Forschungen*, vol. 121, no. 3, 2009, 320–42.

Melville, Charles, "From Qars to Qandahar: The Itineraries of Shah 'Abbas I (995–1038/1587–1629)", in Jean Calmard, ed., *Études Safavides* (Paris–Tehran, 1993), 195–224.

Melville, Charles, "Shah 'Abbas and the Pilgrimage to Mashhad", in idem, ed., *Safavid Persia: The History and Politics of an Islamic Society* (London, 1996), 191–229.

Melville, Charles, "Akbar's History of the Timurids", *Iran*, vol. 59, no. 2, 2021, 203–24.

Melvin-Koushki, Matthew, "The Delicate Art of Aggression: Uzun Hasan's Fathnama to Qaytbay of 1469", *Iranian Studies*, vol. 44, no. 2, 2011, 193–214.

Metcalf, Barbara D., ed., *Moral Conduct and Authority: The Place of Adab in South Asian Islam* (Berkeley, 1984).

Metcalf, Barbara D., "Narrating Lives: A Mughal Empress, a French Nabob, a Nationalist Muslim Intellectual", *Journal of Asian Studies*, vol. 54, no. 2, 1995, 474–80.

Mir Taqi Mir, *Remembrances*, ed. and trans. C.M. Naim (Cambridge, MA, 2019).

Misch, Georg, *Geschichte der Autobiografie*, 4 vols (Berlin–Frankfurt, 1907–69).

Moačanin, Nenad, "Some Remarks on the Supposed Muslim Tolerance Towards *Dhimmīs*", *Sudost-Forschungen*, vol. 48, 1989, 209–15.

Monserrate, António [Antoni Montserrat], *The Commentary of Father Monserrate, SJ, on His Journey to the Court of Akbar*, ed. and trans. J.S. Hoyland and S.N. Banerjee (London, 1922).

Moosvi, Shireen, *People, Taxation, and Trade in Mughal India* (Delhi, 2008).

Muhammad Hasan "Qatil", Mirza, *Haft tamāsha*, Urdu translation Muhammad 'Umar (Delhi, 1968).

Mukund, Kanakalatha, *The View from Below: Indigenous Society, Ttemples and the Early Colonial State in Tamilnadu, 1700–1835* (Hyderabad, 2005).

Nagaraju, H.M., *Devaraya II and His Times* (Mysore, 1991).

Nakagawa, Hisayasu, "Naissance au Japon de l'autobiographie moderne : *Oritaku shiba no ki* (Souvenirs de ma vie) d'Araï Hakuseki", *Dix-huitième Siècle*, no. 16, 1984, 387–403.

Narayana Rao, Velcheru, and David Shulman, *A Lover's Guide to Warangal: The "Kridâbhiramamu" by Vinukonda Vallabharaya* (New Delhi, 2002).

Narayana Rao, Velcheru, David Shulman, and Sanjay Subrahmanyam, *Symbols of Substance: Court and State in Nayaka-period Tamilnadu* (Delhi, 1992).

Nathan, Mirza ('Ala-ud-Din Isfahani Shitab Khan), *Bahāristān-i-Ghaybī: A History of the Mughal Wars in Assam, Cooch Behar, Bengal, Bihar and Orissa During the Reigns of Jahangir and Shahjahan*, 2 vols, trans. M.I. Borah (Gauhati, 1936).

Nathan, Mirza ('Ala-ud-Din Isfahani Shitab Khan), *Bahāristān-i Ghaibī*, Bibliothèque nationale de France, Paris, Supplément Persan 252.

Nawa'i, 'Abdul Husain, *Shāh Tahmāsb Safawī: Majmu'ah-i asnad wa mukātabāt-i tarīkhi hamrah ba yāddāsht-hā-yi tafsīlī* (Tehran, 1971).

Nayeem, M.A., *External Relations of the Bijapur Kingdom (AD 1489–1686): A Study in Diplomatic History* (Hyderabad, 1974).

Nayeem, M.A., "Mughal Documents Relating to the Peshkash of the Zamindars of South India, AD 1694–1752", *The Indian Economic and Social History Review*, vol. 12, no. 4, 1975, 425–32.

Necipoğlu, Gülru, Cemal Kafadar, and Cornell H. Fleischer, eds, *Treasures of Knowledge: An Inventory of the Ottoman Palace Library (1502/3–1503/4)*, 2 vols (Leiden, 2019).

Nek Rai, *Tazkirat al-Safar wa Tuhfat al-Zafar*, Salar Jang Museum and Library, Hyderabad, Accession no. 4519, Mss. no. 7.

Nur-ud-Din Muhammad Jahangir, *Tuzuk-i Jahangiri*, ed. Syud Ahmud Khan (Aligarh, 1864).

O'Hanlon, Rosalind, "Manliness and Imperial Service in Mughal North India", *Journal of the Economic and Social History of the Orient*, vol. 42, no. 1, 1999, 47–93.

O'Hanlon, Rosalind, "Cultural Pluralism, Empire and the State in Early Modern South Asia: A Review Essay", *Indian Economic and Social History Review*, vol. 44, no. 3, 2007, 363–81.

O'Hanlon, Rosalind, *At the Edges of Empire: Essays in the Social and Intellectual History of India* (Ranikhet, 2014).

Okada, Amina, and Jean-Louis Nou, *Un joyau de l'Inde moghole: Le mausolée d'I'timad ud-Daulah* (Milan, 2003).

Olney, James, *Metaphors of Self: The Meaning of Autobiography* (Princeton, NJ, 1972).

Olney, James, ed., *Autobiography: Essays Theoretical and Critical* (Princeton, NJ, 1980).

Orsini, Francesca, and Samira Sheikh, eds, *After Timur Left: Culture and Circulation in Fifteenth-century North India* (Delhi, 2014).

Orta, Garcia da, *Colóquios dos Simples e Drogas da Índia*, ed. Conde de Ficalho, 2 vols (Lisbon, 1891).

Orthmann, Eva, *'Abd or-Rahīm Hān-e Hānān (964–1036/1556–1627): Staatsmann und Mäzen* (Berlin, 1996).

Orthmann, Eva, "Sonne, Mond und Sterne: Kosmologie und Astrologie in der Inszenierung von Herrschaft unter Humāyūn", in Lorenz Korn, Florian Schwarz, and Eva Orthmann, eds, *Die Grenzen der Welt: Arabica et Iranica ad honorem Heinz Gaube* (Wiesbaden, 2008), 297–306.

Osman Agha Temeshvarli, *Prisoner of the Infidels: The Memoir of an Ottoman Muslim in Seventeenth-Century Europe*, trans. Giancarlo Casale (Berkeley, 2021).

Overton, Keelan, "Vida de Jacques de Coutre: A Flemish Account of Bijapuri Visual Culture in the Shadow of Mughal Felicity", in Laura Parodi, ed., *The Visual World of Muslim India: The Art, Culture and Society of the Deccan in the Early Modern Era* (London, 2014), 233–64.

Overton, Keelan, "Book Culture, Royal Libraries, and Persianate Painting in Bijapur, Circa 1580–1630", *Muqarnas*, vol. 33, no. 1, 2016, 91–154.

Overton, Keelan, ed., *Iran and the Deccan: Persianate Art, Culture, and Talent in Circulation, 1400–1700* (Bloomington, 2020).

Pascal, Roy, *Design and Truth in Autobiography* (Cambridge, MA, 1960).

Paul, Jürgen, "Forming a Faction: The *Himāyat* of Khwaja Ahrar", *International Journal of Middle Eastern Studies*, vol. 23, no. 4, 1991, 533–48.

Pearson, M.N., *Merchants and Rulers in Gujarat: The Response to the Portuguese in the Sixteenth Century* (Berkeley, 1976).

Phukan, Shantanu, "'Through Throats Where Many Rivers Meet': The Ecology of Hindi in the World of Persian", *The Indian Economic and Social History Review*, vol. 38, no. 1, 2001, 33–58.

Pinch, William, *Peasants and Monks in British India* (Delhi, 1996).

Pinch, William, "Who was Himmat Bahadur?: Gosains, Rajputs and the British in Bundelkhand, *ca.* 1800", *The Indian Economic and Social History Review*, vol. 35, no. 3, 1998, 293–335.

Prem Kishor "Firaqi", Kunwar, *Waqāʾiʿ-i ʿĀlam Shāhī*, ed. Imtiaz ʿAli Khan ʿArshi (Rampur, 1949).

Purnaqcheband, Nader, *Strategien der Kontingenzbewältigung: Der Mogulherrscher Humāyūn (r. 1530–1540 und 1555–1556) dargestellt in der 'Tazkirat al-Waqiʿat' seines Leibdieners Jauhar Aftābči* (Hamburg, 2007).

Pye, Christian Blake, "The Sufi Method Behind the Mughal 'Peace with All' Religions: A Study of Ibn ʿArabi's '*tahqīq*' in Abu al-Fazl's Preface to the *Razmnāma*", *Modern Asian Studies*, vol. 56, no. 3, 2022, 902–23.

Qaisar, Ahsan Jan, "Jahangir's Accession: An Outcome of Orthodox Revivalism?", *Proceedings of the Indian History Congress, 23rd Session* (Aligarh), 1960, 251–2.

Qaisar, Ahsan Jan, *The Indian Response to European Technology and Culture AD 1498–1707* (Delhi, 1982).

Quamruddin, Mohammad, *Life and Times of Prince Murad Bakhsh (1624–1661)* (Calcutta, 1974).

Quinn, Sholeh A., "The Historiography of Safavid Prefaces", in Charles Melville, ed., *Safavid Persia: The History and Politics of an Islamic Society* (London, 1996), 1–26.

Quinn, Sholeh A., *Historical Writing During the Reign of Shah ʿAbbas: Ideology, Imitation, and Legitimacy in Safavid Chronicles* (Salt Lake City, 2000).

Quinn, Sholeh A., *Persian Historiography Across Empires: The Ottomans, Safavids, and Mughals* (Cambridge, 2021).

Rahman, Munibur, "Fayzi, Abu'l-Fayz", in *Encyclopaedia Iranica*, vol. 9, ed. Ehsan Yarshater (New York, 1999), 457–9.

Rana Begum, "A Critical Edition of Diwan-e-Anand Ram Mukhlis with Introduction and Notes", Ph.D. thesis, Department of Persian, Aligarh Muslim University, 2013.

Ray, Sukumar, *Humāyūn in Persia* (Calcutta, 1948).

Raychaudhuri, Tapan, *Bengal Under Akbar and Jahangir*, 2nd edn. (Delhi, 1966).

Raychaudhuri, Tapan, "The State and the Economy: The Mughal Empire", in Tapan Raychaudhuri and Irfan Habib, eds, *The Cambridge Economic History of India, Volume 1 (c. 1200–c.1750)* (Cambridge, 1982), 172–93.

Raymond, André, "Islamic City, Arab City: Orientalist Myths and Recent Views", *British Journal of Middle Eastern Studies*, vol. 21, no. 1, 1994, 3–18.

Raymond, André, *Arab Cities in the Ottoman Period: Cairo, Syria, and the Maghreb* (Aldershot, 2002).

Reynolds, Dwight F., ed., *Interpreting the Self: Autobiography in the Arabic Literary Tradition* (Berkeley, 2001).

Rezavi, Syed Ali Nadeem, "'The Mighty Defensive Fort': Red Fort at Delhi Under Shahjahan: Its Plan and Structures as Described by Muhammad Waris", *Proceedings of the Indian History Congress*, vol. 71, 2010–11, 1108–21.

Rezavi, Syed Ali Nadeem, *Fathpur Sikri Revisited* (Delhi, 2013).

Rezavi, Syed Ali Nadeem, "I'timād 'Ali-Khān: The Career of a Mughal Officer Through His Own Diary", *Studies in People's History*, vol. 7, no. 1, 2020, 79–90.

Richard, Francis, "Jean-Baptiste Gentil, collectionneur de manuscrits persans", *Dix-huitième siècle*, no. 28, 1996, 91–110.

Richard, Yann, "'Abbasi Gojarati, 'Abd-al-Latif bin 'Abdallah Kabir", *Encyclopaedia Iranica*, ed. Ehsan Yarshater, vol. I, pt 1 (New York, 1982), 88–9.

Richards, John F., "Norms of Comportment Among Imperial Mughal Officers", in Barbara D. Metcalf, ed., *Moral Conduct and Authority: The Place of Adab in South Asian Islam* (Berkeley, 1984), 255–89.

Richards, John F., *The Mughal Empire (The New Cambridge History of India, I.5)* (Cambridge, 1993).

Richards, John F., *Power, Administration and Finance in Mughal India* (Abingdon, 1993).

Richards, John F., "The Formulation of Imperial Authority Under Akbar and Jahangir", in J.F. Richards, ed., *Kingship and Authority in South Asia* (reprint, Delhi, 1998), 285–326.

Rizvi, Kishwar, ed., *Affect, Emotion, and Subjectivity in Early Modern Muslim Empires: New Studies in Ottoman, Safavid, and Mughal Art and Culture* (Leiden, 2018).

Rizvi, Saiyid Athar Abbas, *Religious and Intellectual History of the Muslims in Akbar's Reign, With Special Reference to Abu'l Fazl, 1556–1605* (New Delhi, 1975).

Rizvi, Saiyid Athar Abbas, *A History of Sufism in India*, vol. I (New Delhi, 1978).

Rosenthal, Franz, "Die arabische Autobiographie", *Studia Arabica*, vol. 1, 1937, 1–40.

Ross, E. Denison, "A Collection of Poems by the Emperor Babur", *Journal and Proceedings of the Asiatic Society of Bengal*, N.S., vol. 6 (Extra Number) 1910, i–vi, 1–41.

Rötzer, Klaus, "Bījāpūr : Alimentation en eau d'une ville musulmane du Dekkan aux XVIe–XVIIe siècles", *Bulletin de l'Ecole française d'Extrême-Orient*, vol. 73, 1984, 125–96.

Ruggiu, François-Joseph, ed., *The Uses of First Person Writings (Les usages des écrits du for privé): Africa, America, Asia, Europe* (Brussels, 2013).

Sabri, Zahra, "Mir Taqi Mir's Zikr-i Mīr: An Account of the Poet or an Account by the Poet?", *Medieval History Journal*, vol. 18, no. 2, 2015, 214–49.

Saeki, Shōichi, "The Autobiography in Japan", trans. Teruko Craig, *Journal of Japanese Studies*, vol. 11, no. 2, 1985, 357–68.

Saksena, B.P., "A Few Unnoticed Facts About the Early Life of Malik Amber", *Proceedings (Transactions) of the Indian History Congress*, 5th Session, 1941, 601–3.

Salih Kamboh, Muhammad, *'Amal-i Sālih or Shāh Jahān Nāmah*, 3 vols, ed. Ghulam Yazdani (Calcutta, 1923–46).

Sanceau, Elaine, ed., *Colecção de São Lourenço*, vol. 3 (Lisbon, 1983).

Sandilawi, Ahmad 'Ali Khan Hashimi, *Tazkira-yi makhzan al-gharā'ib*, ed. Muhammad Baqir, 2 vols (Lahore, 1968–70).

Saqi Must'ad Khan, *Ma'asir-i 'Alamgiri: A History of the Emperor Aurangzib-'Alamgir (Reign* AD *1658–1707)*, trans. Jadunath Sarkar (Calcutta, 1947).

Sarkar, Jadunath, *Anecdotes of Aurangzeb and Historical Essays* (Calcutta, 1912).

Sarkar, Jadunath, "Travels in Bihar, AD 1608", *The Journal of the Bihar and Orissa Research Society*, vol. 5, pt 4, 1919, 597–603.

Sarkar, Jadunath, *Studies in Mughal India* (Calcutta, 1919).

Sarkar, Jadunath, "A Description of North Bengal in AD 1609", *Bengal Past and Present*, vol. 35, nos. 69–70, 1928, 143–6.

Sarkar, Jadunath, *Studies in Aurangzib's Reign* (Calcutta, 1933).

Sarkar, Jagadish Narayan, *The Life of Mir Jumla, the General of Aurangzeb*, 2nd edn (New Delhi, 1979).

Sartain, E.M., *Jalāl al-Dīn al-Suyūtī: Biography and Background* (Cambridge, 1975).

Scott, Jonathan, *Ferishta's History of Dekkan, from the First Mahummedan Conquests: A Continuation from Other Native Writers, of the Events in That Part of India, to the Reduction of Its Last Monarchs by the Emperor Aulumgeer Aurungzebe*, vol. 2 (London, 1794).

Schulze, Winfried, "Ego-Dokumente: Annäherung an den Menschen in der Geschichte?: Vorüberlegungen für die Tagung 'Ego–Dokumente'", in W. Schulze, ed., *Ego-Dokumente: Annäherung an den Menschen in der Geschichte* (Berlin, 1996), 11–30.

Sela, Ron, *The Legendary Biographies of Tamerlane: Islam and Heroic Apocrypha in Central Asia* (Cambridge, 2011).

Sen, Geeti, *Paintings from the Akbar Nama* (New Delhi, 1984).

Shafi', Muhammad, "Iqtibās az Badā'i' Waqā'i'", *Oriental College Magazine*, vol. 18, no. 1, 1941, 89–124.

Shah Tahmasp Safavi, *Tazkira-i Shah Tahmasp (Memoirs of Shah Tahmasp)*, ed. D.C. Phillott (Calcutta, 1912).

Shahnawaz Khan, Nawwab Samsam-ud-Daula, *Ma'āsir al-Umarā'*, eds Maulavi 'Abdur Rahim and Maulavi Mirza Ashraf 'Ali, vols 1 and 2 (Calcutta, 1888–90).

Shahnawaz Khan, Nawwab Samsam-ud Daula, *Ma'āsir-ul-Umarā', Being Biographies of the Muhammadan and Hindu Officers of the Timurid Sovereigns of India from 1500 to About AD 1780*, trans. H. Beveridge and Baini Prashad, 3 vols (Calcutta, 1911–52).

Sharma, G.D., "Some Aspects of the Mewar Polity at the Time of Maharana Pratap's Accession", *Proceedings of the Indian History Congress*, vol. 38, 1977, 261–5.

Sharma, Mahesh, "Narratives of a Place named Ellora: Myths, Culture and Politics", *The Indian Economic and Social History Review*, vol. 58, no. 1, 2021, 73–111.

Sharma, S.R., *A Bibliography of Mughal India (AD 1526–1707)* (Bombay, 1938).

Sharma, Sunil, *Persian Poetry at the Indian Frontier: Mas'ud Sa'd Salman of Lahore* (New Delhi, 2000).

Sharma, Sunil, *Mughal Arcadia: Persian Literature in an Indian Court* (Cambridge, MA, 2017).

Shaw, Robert B., "A Prince of Kashgar on the Geography of Eastern Turkestan", *Journal of the Royal Geographical Society*, vol. 46, 1876, 277–98.

Sherani, Hafiz Mahmud, "Makhdūm Shaikh Bahā'-ud-Dīn Barnawī", *Oriental College Magazine*, vol. 3, no. 4, 1929, 72–99.

Sherwani, H.K., *Mahmud Gawan, the Great Bahmani Wazir* (Allahabad, 1942).

Sherwani, H.K., *History of the Qutb Shahi Kingdom* (New Delhi, 1974).

Shihab-ud-Din Talish, Ahmad bin Muhammad, *Fathīya 'Ibrīya*, BnF, Supplément persan 321; Bodleian Library, Oxford, Bodl. Or. 589 (Sachau-Ethé 240).

Shihab-ud-Din Talish, Ahmad bin Muhammad, *Tarikh-i Asham, récit de l'expédition de Mir-Djumlah au pays d'Assam,* Translated from the Earlier Hindustani Translation of Mir Bahadur 'Ali Husaini, by Théodore Pavie (Paris, 1845).

Shihab-ud-Din Talish, *Tārīkh-i Asam (Asham),* Urdu trans. Mir Bahadur 'Ali Husaini, ed. Sajid Siddiq Nizami (Lahore, 2015).

Shulman, David, "Cowherd or King?: The Sanskrit Biography of Ananda Ranga Pillai", in David Arnold and Stuart Blackburn, eds, *Telling Lives in India: Biography, Autobiography and Life History* (Delhi, 2004), 175–202.

Shulman, David, *More than Real: A History of the Imagination in South India* (Cambridge, MA, 2012).

Shulman, David, *Introspection and Insight: South Indian Minds in the Early Modern Era* (Delhi, 2023).

Shyam, Radhe, *Life and Times of Malik Ambar* (Delhi, 1968).

Siddiq, Mohammad Yusuf, *Epigraphy and Islamic Culture: Inscriptions of the Early Muslim Rulers of Bengal (1205–1494)* (Abingdon, 2016).

Siddiqui, Iqtidar Husain, *Perso-Arabic Sources of Information on the Life and Conditions in the Sultanate of Delhi* (New Delhi, 1992).

Siddiqui, Iqtidar Husain, "*Inshā'-i Faizī*: A Source of Information on Akbar's Reign", in Iqtidar Alam Khan, ed., *Akbar and His Age* (New Delhi, 1999), 198–208.

Siebertz, Roman, "How to Obtain a *Farmān* from Shah Jahan: The Experience of Joan Tack at Delhi, 1648", in Ebba Koch and Ali Anooshahr, eds, *The Mughal Empire from Jahangir to Shah Jahan: Art, Architecture, Politics, Law and Literature* (Mumbai, 2019), 144–65.

Siebenhüner, Kim, and Sally Church, "Introduction: Autobiographical Writings in Pre-modern Europe and Asia: A Decentred Perspective", *Medieval History Journal*, vol. 18, no. 2, 2015, 193–213.

Silva Rego, António da, ed., *Documentação Ultramarina Portuguesa*, vol. 3 (Lisbon, 1963).

Singh, Abha, "The 'Char Bahar' of Balkrishan Brahman: A Hitherto Unknown Source of the Mid 17th–century", *Proceedings of the Indian History Congress*, vol. 54, 1993, 216–22.

Singh, Chetan, *Region and Empire: Panjab in the Seventeenth Century* (Delhi, 1991).

Snell, Rupert, "Confessions of a 17th-Century Jain Merchant: The Ardhakathānak of Banārasīdās", *South Asia Research*, vol. 25, no. 1, 2006, 79–104.

Sohoni, Pushkar, *The Architecture of a Deccan Sultanate: Courtly Practice and Royal Authority in Late Medieval India* (London, 2018).

Speziale, Fabrizio, and Satoshi Ogura, eds, "Imperial Historiography and the Creation of Persian Scholarship on India: The *Āʾīn-i Akbarī* of Abū al-Fazl (d.1602)", *Journal of Asian and African Studies* (Tokyo), Supplement no. 3, 2024.

Stein, Burton, ed., *South Indian Temples: An Analytical Reconsideration* (New Delhi, 1978).

Stewart, Charles, *The Malfuzat Timury, or Autobiographical Memoirs of the Moghul Emperor Timur* (London, 1830).

Storey, Charles A., *Persian Literature: A Bio-bibliographical Survey* (London, 1927), vol. I: 1.

Subrahmanyam, Sanjay, "A Note on the Kabul Kingdom Under Muhammad Hakim Mirza (1554–1585)", in *La Transmission du savoir dans le monde musulman périphérique, Lettre d'information*, no. 14, 1994, 89–101.

Subrahmanyam, Sanjay, "Palavras do Idalcão: Um encontro curioso em Bijapur no ano de 1561", *Cadernos do Noroeste*, vol. 15, nos 1–2, 2001, 513–24.

Subrahmanyam, Sanjay, "Turning the Stones Over: Sixteenth-Century Millenarianism from the Tagus to the Ganges," *The Indian Economic and Social History Review*, vol. 40, no. 3, 2003, 131–63.

Subrahmanyam, Sanjay, *Explorations in Connected History: Mughals and Franks* (Delhi, 2005).

Subrahmanyam, Sanjay, "Early Modern Circulation Between Central Asia and India and the Question of 'Patriotism'", in Nile Green, ed., *Writing Travel in Central Asian History* (Bloomington, 2014), 43–68.

Subrahmanyam, Sanjay, "Between Eastern Africa and Western India, 1500–1650: Slavery, Commerce and Elite Formation", *Comparative Studies in Society and History*, vol. 61, no. 4, 2019, 805–34.

Subtelny, Maria Eva, "'Alī Shīr Navāʾī: Bakhshī and Beg", *Harvard Ukrainian Studies*, vol. 3–4, no. 2 (1979–80), 797–807.

Subtelny, Maria Eva, "Centralizing Reform and Its Opponents in the Late Timurid Period", *Iranian Studies*, vol. 21, nos 1–2, 1988, 123–51.

Subtelny, Maria Eva, "Babur's Rival Relations: A Study of Kinship and Conflict in 15th–16th Century Central Asia", *Der Islam*, vol. 66, 1989, 102–18.

Sudyka, Lidia, "The Sense of Self in Early Modern South and Southeast India: Overview of the Volume", *Cracow Indological Studies*, vol. 24, no. 1, 2022, 23–8.

Surat Singh, *Tazkira-yi Pīr Hassū Telī*, eds M. Athar Ali and S. Ali Nadeem Rezavi (Aligarh, 2018).

Sviri, Sara, "Dreaming Analyzed and Recorded: Dreams in the World of Medieval Islam", in David Shulman and Guy G. Stroumsa, eds, *Dream Cultures: Explorations in the Comparative History of Dreaming* (New York, 1999), 252–73.

Szuppe, Maria, *Entre Timourides, Uzbeks et Safavides: Questions d'histoire politique et sociale de Hérat dans la première moitié du XVIe siècle* (Paris, 1992).

Szuppe, Maria, "En quête de chevaux turkmènes: Le journal de voyage de Mir 'Izzatullah de Delhi à Boukhara en 1812–1813", in *Inde – Asie Centrale: Routes du commerce et des idées, Cahiers d'Asie Centrale*, nos 1–2, 1996, 91–111.

Szuppe, Maria, "Circulation des lettrés et cercles littéraires: Entre Asie centrale, Iran et Inde du Nord (XVe–XVIIIe siècle)", *Annales HSS*, nos 5–6, 2004, 997–1018.

Tahir Muhammad Sabzwari, *Rauzat al-Tāhirīn*; Bodleian Library, Oxford, Ms. Elliot 314 (Sachau-Ethé no. 100), British Library, London, Ms. Or. 168.

Talbot, Cynthia, "Justifying Defeat: A Rajput Perspective on the Age of Akbar", *Journal of the Economic and Social History of the Orient*, vol. 55, 2012, 329–68.

Tamaskar, B.G., *Life and Work of Malik Ambar* (Delhi, 1978).

Taqi-ud-Din Muhammad Auhadi Daqqaqi Balyani, *Tazkira 'arafāt al-'āshiqīn wa 'arasāt al-'ārifīn*, eds Zabihollah Sahebkary, Amene Fakhr-Ahmad, and Mohammad Ghahreman (Tehran, 2010).

Terreaux-Scotto, Cécile, "Les nouvelles dans la Vita de Benvenuto Cellini", *Cahiers d'études italiennes*, vol. 10, 2010, 129–55.

Tezcan, Baki, "The Politics of Early Modern Ottoman Historiography", in Virginia H. Aksan and Daniel Goffman, eds, *The Early Modern Ottomans: Remapping the Empire* (Cambridge, 2007), 167–98.

Thackston, Wheeler M., *A Century of Princes: Sources on Timurid History and Art* (Cambridge, MA, 1989).

Thackston, Wheeler M., ed. and trans., *Three Memoirs of Homayun: Humayunnama, Tadhkiratu'l-Waqiat, and Tarikh-i Humayun* (Costa Mesa, CA, 2009).

Tirmizi, S.A.I., "Scholar-Diplomatist from Gujarat at the Court of Shah Jahan", in idem, *Some Aspects of Medieval Gujarat* (Delhi, 1968), 85–98.

Travers, Robert, *Empires of Complaints: Mughal Law and the Making of British India, 1765–1793* (Cambridge, 2022).

Trivedi, Kirti K., "The Emergence of Agra as a Capital and a City: A Note on Its Spatial and Historical Background during the Sixteenth and Seventeenth Centuries", *Journal of the Economic and Social History of the Orient*, vol. 37, no. 2, 1994, 147–70.

Tucker, Ernest, "1739: History, Self, and Other in Afsharid Iran and Mughal India", *Iranian Studies*, vol. 31, no. 2, 1998, 207–17.

Tyan, E., "Bayʻa", in *The Encyclopaedia of Islam*, vol. 1 (Leiden, 1960), 1113–14.

Veinstein, Gilles, *Les Ottomans: Variations sur une société d'Empire* (Paris, 2017).

Verma, Som Prakash, *The Illustrated Baburnama* (London: Routledge, 2016).

Von Greyerz, Kaspar, "Ego-Documents: The Last Word?", *German History*, vol. 28, no. 3, 2010, 273–82.

Von Kügelgen, Anke, "Zur Authentizität des 'Ich' in Timuridischen Herrscherautobiographien", *Asiatische Studien/Etudes Asiatiques*, vol. 60, no. 2, 2006, 383–436.

Washbrook, David, "Envisioning the Social Order in a Southern Port City: The Tamil Diary of Ananda Ranga Pillai", *South Asian History and Culture*, vol. 6, no. 1, 2015, 172–85.

Woods, John E., "The Rise of Tīmūrid Historiography", *Journal of Near Eastern Studies*, vol. 46, 1987, 81–108.

Wu, Pei-yi, *The Confucian's Progress: Autobiographical Writings in Traditional China* (Princeton, NJ, 1990).

Yazdani, Ghulam, "Narnaul and Its Buildings" (in 2 parts), *Journal of the Asiatic Society of Bengal*, New Series, vol. 3, 1907, 581–6, 639–44.

Yusuf ʻAli, ʻAbdullah, *The Meaning of the Glorious Qur'an*, text, translation, and commentary, 2 vols (Cairo, 1938).

Zain-ud-Din Khwafi, Shaikh, *Tabaqāt-i Bāburī*, trans. S. Hasan Askari, ed. B.P. Ambastha (Delhi, 1982).

Zain-ud-Din Mahmud Wasifi, *Badāʾiʻ al-Waqāʾiʻ*, ed. Aleksandr N. Boldyrev, 2 vols (Tehran, 1970–1).

Zaman, Taymiya R., "Instructive Memory: An Analysis of Auto/Biographical Writing in Early Mughal India", *Journal of the Economic and Social History of the Orient*, vol. 54, 2011, 677–700.

Zaman, Taymiya R., "Nostalgia, Lahore, and the Ghost of Aurangzeb", *Fragments: Interdisciplinary Approaches to Ancient and Medieval Pasts*, vol. 4, 2015, 1–27.

Zholkovsky, Alexander, "Quote the Poets Ever More: Micro-analyzing Intertextual Gems by Anna Akhmatova, Vladislav Khodasevich and Osip Mandel'shtam", *The Slavic and East European Journal*, vol. 61, no. 1, 2017, 111–28.

Zilfi, Madeline, "The Diary of a Müderris: A New Source for Ottoman Biography", *Journal of Turkish Studies*, vol. 1, 1977, 157–72.

Zilli, Ishtiyaq Ahmad, "Development of *Inshā'* Literature Till the End of Akbar's Reign", in Muzaffar Alam, Françoise N. Delvoye, and Marc Gaborieau, eds, *The Making of Indo-Persian Culture: Indian and French Studies* (New Delhi, 2000), 309–49.

Index